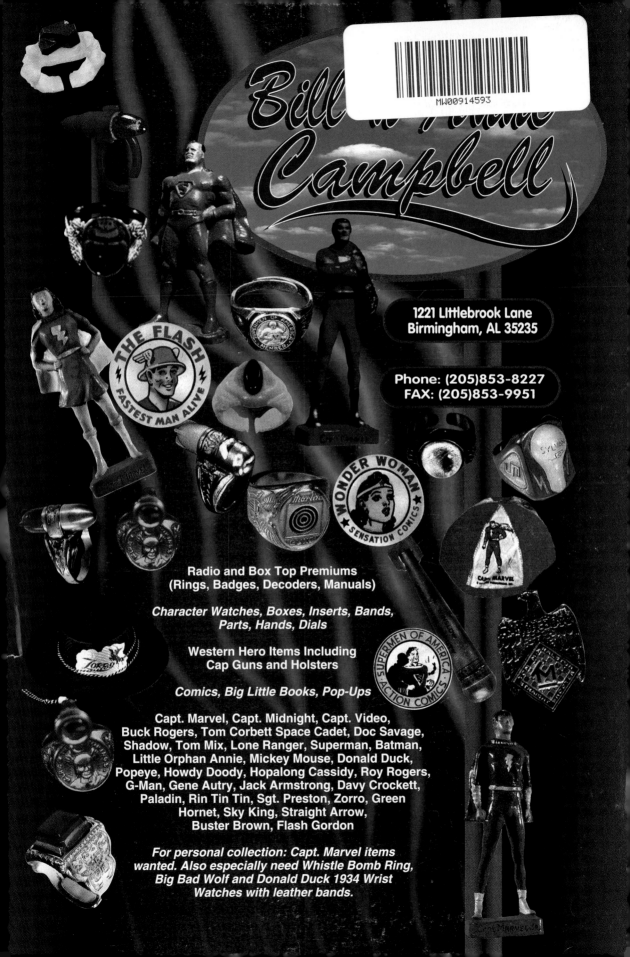

Bill 'n Annie Campbell

1221 Littlebrook Lane
Birmingham, AL 35235

Phone: (205)853-8227
FAX: (205)853-9951

THE FLASH FASTEST MAN ALIVE

WONDER WOMAN ★ SENSATION COMICS ★

Radio and Box Top Premiums
(Rings, Badges, Decoders, Manuals)

Character Watches, Boxes, Inserts, Bands,
Parts, Hands, Dials

Western Hero Items Including
Cap Guns and Holsters

Comics, Big Little Books, Pop-Ups

Capt. Marvel, Capt. Midnight, Capt. Video,
Buck Rogers, Tom Corbett Space Cadet, Doc Savage,
Shadow, Tom Mix, Lone Ranger, Superman, Batman,
Little Orphan Annie, Mickey Mouse, Donald Duck,
Popeye, Howdy Doody, Hopalong Cassidy, Roy Rogers,
G-Man, Gene Autry, Jack Armstrong, Davy Crockett,
Paladin, Rin Tin Tin, Sgt. Preston, Zorro, Green
Hornet, Sky King, Straight Arrow,
Buster Brown, Flash Gordon

For personal collection: Capt. Marvel items
wanted. Also especially need Whistle Bomb Ring,
Big Bad Wolf and Donald Duck 1934 Wrist
Watches with leather bands.

Ted Hake founded Hake's Americana & Collectibles in 1967, the first auction house to specialize in 20th century American popular culture. His early initiatives in hundreds of collecting areas contributed significantly to establishing collectibles as a major pastime for millions of Americans. Over the years, Hake has shared his expertise by writing sixteen reference/price guides covering such subjects as television collectibles, presidential campaigns, advertising, comic characters, and cowboy characters. These books are recognized by collectors and dealers as informative, useful, and accurate. Hake produces his books, sales lists, and auction catalogues from his hometown of York, Pennsylvania. ❖

OTHER BOOKS BY TED HAKE:

THE BUTTON BOOK
(out of print)

BUTTONS IN SETS
with Marshall N. Levin

COLLECTIBLE PIN-BACK BUTTONS 1896-1986: AN ILLUSTRATED PRICE GUIDE
with Russ King

THE ENCYCLOPEDIA OF POLITICAL BUTTONS 1896-1972; POLITICAL BUTTONS BOOK II 1920-1976; POLITICAL BUTTONS BOOK III 1789-1916

THE ENCYCLOPEDIA OF POLITICAL BUTTONS: 1998 REVISED PRICES FOR BOOKS I, II AND III

HAKE'S GUIDE TO ADVERTISING COLLECTIBLES
100 Years of Advertising
from 100 Famous Companies

HAKE'S GUIDE TO COMIC CHARACTER COLLECTIBLES
An Illustrated Price Guide
to 100 Years of Comic Strip Characters

HAKE'S GUIDE TO COWBOY CHARACTER COLLECTIBLES
An Illustrated Price Guide Covering
50 Years of Movie & TV Cowboy Heroes

HAKE'S GUIDE TO PRESIDENTIAL CAMPAIGN COLLECTIBLES
An Illustrated Price Guide to Artifacts
from 1789-1988

HAKE'S GUIDE TO TV COLLECTIBLES: AN ILLUSTRATED PRICE GUIDE

NON-PAPER SPORTS COLLECTIBLES: AN ILLUSTRATED PRICE GUIDE
with Roger Steckler

SIXGUN HEROES: A PRICE GUIDE TO MOVIE COWBOY COLLECTIBLES
with Robert Cauler

A TREASURY OF ADVERTISING COLLECTIBLES
(out of print)

For ordering information write the author at
P.O. Box 1444-PG York, PA 17405

Overstreet Presents:
Hake's Price Guide to
Character Toys

Including Premiums, Comic, Cereal, TV, Movies, Radio & Related Store Bought Items

The CONFIDENT
COLLECTOR™

AVON BOOKS 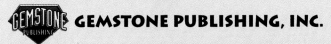 NEW YORK

GEMSTONE GEMSTONE PUBLISHING, INC.
PUBLISHING

Front Cover: Charlie Brown ©1998 United Features Syndicate; Lone Ranger ©1998 Wrather Corp.; Donald Duck ©1998 The Walt Disney Company; Yogi Bear ©1998 Hanna-Barbera Productions; Independence Day (ID4) ©1998 Twentieth Century Fox; Roy Rogers ©1998 Roy Rogers Enterprises; Superman ©1998 DC Comics; Froggy 1998 Buster Brown.
Spine: Quisp ©1998 Quaker Oats.
Back Cover: Wonder Woman and Flash ©1998 DC Comics.
Overstreet ® is a Registered Trademark of Gemstone Publishing, Inc.
Page 40-42, 56: Images provided by & ©1994 PhotoDisk, Inc.

HAKE'S PRICE GUIDE TO CHARACTER TOYS
(2nd Edition) is an original publication by Gemstone Publishing, Inc.

Distributed to the book trade by
Avon Books, Inc.
1350 Avenue of the Americas
New York, New York 10019

Copyright © 1996, 1998 by Ted Hake & Gemstone Publishing, Inc.
Published by arrangement with the author and Gemstone Publishing, Inc.
The Confident Collector and its logo are trademarked properties of Avon Books, Inc.
ISBN: 0-380-80076-4

2nd edition cover design by Arnold T. Blumberg & Brenda Busick

First Avon Books Printing: August 1998
AVON TRADEMARK REG. U.S. PAT. OFF. AND IN OTHER COUNTRIES, MARCA REGISTRADA, HECHO EN U.S.A.

Printed in the United States Of America
10 9 8 7 6 5 4 3 2 1

TABLE OF CONTENTS

PREMIUM CATEGORIES

TABLE OF CONTENTS

ACKNOWLEDGMENTS

My thanks, first of all, to the thousands of collectors who supported the first edition of this book. The time and resources needed to assemble the 5,000 entries of that edition were substantial. The many letters, calls and comments expressing satisfaction with the finished book were deeply appreciated by myself and my associates at Gemstone Publishing. Our second edition adds 48 categories and over 2,000 entries plus newly discovered information, fine tuning of dates and descriptions and a review of all the evaluations. All this occurred with the continuing help of many of our original contributors along with new contributors willing to share special information and additions of new items.

Marshall Levin once again researched and wrote the fascinating histories that precede each subject entry. Gene Seger invites us, through the photography of Tom Kage, into the deepest recesses of the universe known as Buck Rogers in the 25th Century. J. C. Vaughn's "Fakes, Forgeries & Knock-Offs" tells us what we can do to counter crime in the collectibles market. Robert Heide and John Gilman provide a fascinating biography of "Kay Kamen: The Master of Marketing," the genius behind Disney's character merchandising programs. Arnold T. Blumberg authors an outstanding essay on what collecting is all about and issues "A Collective Call to Arms." Benn Ray captures the excitement "Inside the Child's Mind" with a close-up look at "ten cool premiums" and what it took to get them. Jim Ungerman agrees to share his career with us as "The Photographer of Champions" for Wheaties cereal.

Back on the home front, for emotional support and many contributions, I relied on my wife Jonell, my son Ted and my staff at Hake's Americana & Collectibles: Vonnie Burkins, Joan Carbaugh, Russ King, Charlie Roberts, Jeff Robison, Deak Stagemyer and Alex Winter.

Special gratitude is extended to Steve Geppi, President and Chief Executive Officer of Gemstone Publishing, Inc. for making this book possible through his love of our hobby and faith in this project. John K. Snyder, President of Diamond International Galleries, was also instrumental; first, in convincing me to do the original book, and secondly, for so kindly contributing hundreds of rare toys and his pricing expertise to both editions of this guide. My gratitude also goes to Bob Overstreet and his staff at Gemstone Publishing, Inc. Bob prepared our Market Report and allowed this book to reflect values determined by himself and his advisors for his guides on comic books and toy rings. To Bob's staff at Gemstone Publishing fell the immense task of integrating 7,000 photographs and matching descriptions into a finished book. Managing Editor Arnold T. Blumberg approached this Herculean task with his formidable talents and thus predictable success. Pricing Coordinator Mark Huesman's time and energy were also well utilized to assist in the production of this guide. The myriad additional efforts and details required to bring this book into being and distribute it were skillfully handled by Carol Overstreet (Executive Assistant), Benn Ray (Editor), J. C. Vaughn (Marketing Coordinator), Brenda Busick (Art Director), and Karli Sementa (Administrative Assistant). All their contributions are gratefully acknowledged.

Many of our first edition advertisers are included once again in this volume. We take this as a special compliment. A warm welcome to those advertisers joining us for the first time and a special thank you to all for your support.

The final acknowledgment goes to the growing number of individuals contributing photographs and information to make our history of toys more complete and accurate. In addition to hundreds of items from John Snyder's collection, many fascinating toys were provided by Bill Campbell, David J. Howe, Scott Rona, Jim Scancarelli, Gene Seger and Larry Zdeb. These people and all the following contributors (listed on the facing page) adding to the success of our first two editions, either with toys or other forms of assistance, have my sincere thanks. ❖

INTRODUCTION TO THE 2ND EDITION

Nearly two years have passed since the publication of the first edition of this book. Our gratitude is extended to all who supported our original effort to present a comprehensive guide to the fascinating world of collecting toy premiums.

We have not been resting on our laurels. With pride, we present the second edition of **Hake's Price Guide to Character Toys**. This edition adds 48 new categories, over 2,000 toys, a brand new color section and a complete review of prices.

Our new entries come from a multitude of sources. Many collectors provided information on rare items in their collections; John K. Snyder provided hundreds of premiums from his astonishingly broad and in-depth collection, and many new items were offered in the auction catalogues of Hake's Americana & Collectibles, highlighted by rare and previously unknown pieces from the archive of premium creators Sam and Gordon Gold.

Toy collecting is a vibrant, robust and growing segment in the world of popular culture collectibles. More and more collectors are learning of and becoming engrossed in collecting the classic toys of the 1930s-50s. Likewise, the generations that enjoyed the toys of the 1960s-70s era are actively building collections of the more modern, but in many cases remarkably scarce, items and give-aways.

Reflecting the growing strength of our hobby over the past two years are many record prices (see "The Explosion of History: The 1997 Market Report" on page 28), the 1996 premiere of a new collector's magazine, **Toy Ring Journal**, published by Laurie Weinberger (P.O. Box 544, Birmingham, MI 48012-0544), and the 1997 publication of the 3rd edition of **The Overstreet**

Gary Alexander	Robert Hall	M. G. 'Bud' Norris
Andy Anderson	Phil Hecht	Richard Olson
Dave Anderson	S. Leonard Hedeen	Bob Overstreet
Graeme Atkinson	Joe Hehn	Don Phelps
Bob Baker	Robert Heide	Ralph Plumb
Bob Barrett	Bob Hencey	Ed Pragler
Arnold T. Blumberg	Donald Andrew Hershberger, Jr.	Benn Ray
Robert Bruce	John Hintz	Tony Raymond
Scott Bruce	John Hone	Harry Rinker
Joel S. Cadbury	David J. Howe	Scott Rona
Bill Campbell	Bob Hritz	Bruce Rosen
Joe Caro	Steve Ison	Frank Salacuse
Bob Cauler	Tom Kage	Joe Sarno
Ken Chapman	Harvey Kamins	Jim Scancarelli
Mike Cherry	Fred L. King	Jay Scarfone
Tom Claggett	Walter Koenig	Gene Seger
Jerry Cook	Ray La Briola	Joel Siegel
Dan Coviello	Bob Lesser	Jim Silva
Charles Crane	Richard Leibner	Joel Smilgis
Joe Cywinski	Andy Levison	John K. Snyder, Jr.
Jimmy Dempsey	Randy Lieberman	William Stillman
Jerry Doxey	Don Lineberger	John Szuch
Mark Drennen	Larry Lowery	Ernest Trova
Tony Evangelista	Hy Mandelowitz	Tom Tumbusch
Joe Fair	Don Maris	Jim Ungerman
John Fawcett	Harry Matetsky	Jim Wagner
Lee Felbinger	Walter V. Matishak	Howard C. Weinberger
Keif Fromm	Jack Melcher	Mike West
Danny Fuchs	Richard Merkin	Evelyn Wilson
John Gilman	Peter Merolo	Alex Winter
S. Harlan Glassman	Rex Miller	Joe Young
Tony Goodstone	John Mlachnik	Larry Zdeb
Gary Greenberg	Pat Morgan	
Rick Gronquist	DeWayne Nall	

Toy Ring Price Guide (Gemstone Publishing).

Our one concern as we present the second edition is the correct interpretation and utilization of the price evaluations. This applies particularly to rare items greatly in demand. In these cases, there is usually a wide range between the Fine value and the Near Mint value. Each type of item, from paper club manuals to brass rings to celluloid buttons, has its own set of condition standards explained in the Condition Definitions section. Each item must be closely studied and all evidences of wear taken into account to determine the correct condition grade and concurrent value. The select group of collectors who have paid or will pay the Near Mint prices reflected in this guide demand exceptionally high condition standards. A Near Mint item with a significant defect will not command a Near Mint price. Likewise, no amount of optimism or denial can move a Fine item into the select Near Mint category. To expect Near Mint value for an item that fails to meet these rigid and high standards is an ultimately disappointing exercise to both the seller and buyer. Used correctly, we believe both sellers and buyers will find our evaluations an accurate guide to the state of the retail marketplace.

The author and publisher thank all the individuals who contributed to this second edition. We hope it serves you well.

Ted Hake
May, 1998

INTRODUCTION TO THE 1ST EDITION

My world first intersected with the premium concept in 1948, at the age of five. Roy Rogers, aided by Quaker Oats, sent me a postcard featuring a color picture of himself and Trigger. The card thanked me for my contest entry, "being given careful consideration by our judges." Alas, I was not among the 22,501 eventual winners, but I still have and treasure that postcard.

Although a prolific comic book reader, and with more than my share of hours as a 1950s kid spent in front of the radio and television, the rest of my youth was influenced little by premiums. Roy and Quaker Oats did come through once more in 1950 with the Roy Rogers Deputy Star badge. Quaker, Cheerios and Wheaties pocket size premium comic books joined my Dell Comics collection; and somehow, at thirteen, I acquired the Rin-Tin-Tin rifle pen. Most importantly for my future, during this time I became fascinated by the past. My mother's antiques and the local auctions we attended, my father's revelation when I was eight that people collected coins and so could I, and innumerable family visits to museums were all unsuspected precursors to the founding of Hake's Americana & Collectibles.

In 1960, my interest in coin collecting ended when I discovered presidential campaign buttons. As small as coins, but ever more so graphic and colorful, these artifacts of history captured my collecting energies. By 1965, to help with graduate school expenses, I issued my first sales lists devoted to presidential campaign collectibles. Along the way, I also discovered "non-political" buttons,

many with even more graphic appeal than the political issues. Although there was practically no collector interest in non-political buttons, I began including them in my sales catalogues.

My awakening to the world of premiums came in 1967. The sales lists evolved into the nation's first mail and telephone bid auctions focusing on 20th century collectibles. Campaign items had a small but serious base of collectors, while the non-political buttons and related small collectibles often went unsold and seldom drew bids exceeding five dollars.

To my astonishment, a brass badge inscribed "Buck Rogers Solar Scouts" received a bid of twenty dollars from Ernest Trova of St. Louis, who I later discovered was a world famous artist and sculptor. Mr. Trova's interest initiated my quest for more premiums and more collectors.

As the first wave of interest in popular culture collectibles developed around 1967, premiums joined campaign items, advertising, sports, Disneyana, comic characters and movie cowboy heroes in Hake's Americana & Collectibles growing list of specialties.

This book has been in the making ever since. The project almost happened in 1976. I made plans to author a price guide based on premiums appearing in my auction catalogues augmented by examples from several advanced collectors. However, my auction catalogue schedule and two books documenting 8,000 presidential campaign collectibles put the idea on a slow track. The idea de-railed with the 1977 publication of Tom Tumbusch's **Illustrated Radio Premium Catalog and Price Guide**. Twenty-nine years is a long wait, but

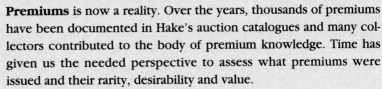

Hake's Price Guide to Character Toy Premiums is now a reality. Over the years, thousands of premiums have been documented in Hake's auction catalogues and many collectors contributed to the body of premium knowledge. Time has given us the needed perspective to assess what premiums were issued and their rarity, desirability and value.

The past several years have seen remarkable changes in the marketplace, particularly for the rarest, most desirable premiums in the top condition grade of Near Mint. Long-time collectors may find some values shockingly high, but these prices reflect actual transactions in the marketplace and the maturation of the hobby. Whatever your collecting interests may be, I hope this book will contribute to your enjoyment of this field of collecting.

Ted Hake
August, 1996

This guide is composed of 350 categories from the collecting areas related to advertising characters, cereal companies, comic books, comic strip and cartoon characters, movies, music, pulps, radio and television. The categories are arranged in alphabetical order by name of the character, company, person, product, program or publication. The most basic name form is used. This applies to character names, in particular, because a given character often appears in several mediums, frequently with a variety of titles.

Each category is introduced by a brief history of the subject. Within each category, each item is illustrated and given a brief descriptive title. Quotation marks in the title denote words actually appearing on the item. Where possible, the exact name assigned by the sponsor to the item is used in the descriptive title, although these are not indicated by quotation marks unless the words actually appear on the item.

All items in a category are arranged in chronological order, with minor exceptions due to photo layout restrictions. The item's title is followed by an exact year of issue, an approximate year of issue, an exact decade of issue or an approximate decade of issue. Accordingly, within each category, items with the earliest specific year of the earliest decade come first. These are followed by items approximated to the earliest specific year. Following all items with an exact or approximate specific year come those items dated exactly or approximately to the earliest decade. The sequence begins anew with items dated to the earliest specific year of the next decade.

Date information is followed by the name of the sponsor or issuer, if known, for the majority of the toys. However, this information is not listed for certain categories where it would merely be redundant. For example, Cracker Jack items are all issued by Cracker Jack and Ovaltine issued all Captain Midnight premiums between 1941-1989, with a few exceptions which are specified. In categories where sponsors are not noted, refer to the historical information introducing that category. Some items saw use both as store items and premiums. Where known, this type of information is included in the description.

Following the date or sponsor information, any descriptive text necessary to explain the item is included. The description ends with three values for the item in Good, Fine and Near Mint condition. **It is most important to read the section defining these condition terms to properly understand and use the values specified for each item.**

TYPES OF ITEMS CATALOGUED

For this guide book, the terms "Comic" and "Premiums" are broadly defined.

"Comic" includes not only characters from newspapers, comic books, animated cartoons but also a gamut of entertainment-related personalities--created or actual—ranging from animated Speedy Alka-Seltzer to live-action Zorro.

"Premiums" includes items by sponsors given away directly—as package insert or loosely—plus items requested and obtained by mail, sometimes requiring small payment and/or purchase proof of the sponsor's product.

Webster's New World Dictionary (3rd College Edition) defines a toy as any article to play with, expecially playthings for children. Since all of the entries in this guide fit this description, whether they are premiums or store-bought toys, it makes sense then to broaden the focus of the book and change the title to **Hake's Price Guide to Character Toys**.

Almost all of the items in this book are of U.S. origin, with some notable exceptions, such as those included in the "Doctor Who" category (most of which originated in Great Britain). There are also foreign items issued under authorized U.S. copyright; prominent examples are the popular 1930s bisque character figures made in Germany or Japan.

This book's listings are comprehensive but not all-inclusive. Omitted items should not be assumed to be either common and inexpensive or rare and costly.

DATING

Toys of each category are listed chronologically. The majority of toys are specifically dated by (a) copyright year on the item, (b) dated source such as a toy catalogue, newspaper or comic book ad, or similar period source. General references of films or broadcast dates were also consulted. In a few instances, an item's patent date (not the copyright date) is used to document its age, when the patent date only is indicated.

Toys offered in overlapping years, for more than one year, or re-issued in later years are dated to the earliest year the item was available. Conversely, a few toys are known to have a copyright year earlier than the actual issue of the item. In these limited examples, the exact or approximate issue date is indicated rather than the copyright year.

If an exact year could not be determined, the item is dated to an approximate year or the known exact decade. When an exact year or decade specification is open to question, the date is denoted by the abbreviation c. for circa to indicate an approximation of issue date.

Using these criteria, the sequence of items within each category is: earliest specific year of the earliest decade followed by earliest approximate year of the earliest decade. After all items with an exact or approximate year are listed, the remaining items dated exactly or approximately to the earliest decade are listed. The sequence begins anew with items dated to the earliest specific year of the next decade.

ABBREVIATIONS

Three abbreviations are used very frequently for recurring descriptive purposes:

c. = circa. An approximate date.

cello. = celluloid. Usually referring to a pinback button or other small collectible having a protective covering of this substance. The term and abbreviation are also used for convenience to indicate similar latter day substances, such as acetate or thin plastic, which gradually replaced the use of flammable celluloid coverings after World War II.

litho. = lithographed process. Usually referring to a pinback button or other small collectible with the design printed directly on metal, usually tin, rather than "cello" version wherein the design is printed on paper with a celluloid protective covering.

Additional abbreviations:
ABC = American Broadcasting Companies, Inc.
BLB = Big Little Book series by Whitman Publishing Co.
BTLB = Better Little Book series by Whitman Publishing Co.
CBS = Columbia Broadcasting System, Inc.
KFS = King Features Syndicate
K.K.Publications = Kay Kamen Publications
MGM = Metro-Goldywn-Mayer Studios, Inc.
NBC = National Broadcasting Co.
NPP = National Periodical Publications, Inc.
RCA = Radio Corporation of America
WDE = Walt Disney Enterprises
WDP = Walt Disney Productions

SIZES

For the majority of items, sizes are not specified with these exceptions. Sizes are specified for pinback buttons measuring two inches in diameter or larger. Sizes are also specified for display signs, maps, posters, standees, items produced in more than one size, and items where size was deemed an important distinguishing factor.

DEFINITIONS

Physical condition and appearance of a toy are primary factors in determining its value, along with rarity, demand and packaging (see next two sections). Condition judgments are certain to have some subjective nuances between individuals. Still, general criteria exist in the collecting community.

Only a small fraction of items, unless recently produced or stored away at time of issue, can properly be termed Mint, i.e. in original new condition with absolutely no flaws. Items evaluated in this guide will very seldom be encountered in Mint condition. Therefore, the highest grade evaluated for each item is Near

Mint, i.e. nearly perfect like new condition with only the slightest detectable wear on close inspection. Additional values are provided for each item in the grades of Fine and Good.

Condition concerns vary according to an item's basic material, and the items in this guide fall into four basic categories. **Accurately determining an item's condition is the crucial step in arriving at a price equitable to both the seller and buyer. Because of the wide value gap, particularly for rarer items, between Near Mint condition and the lower grades, it's essential for the proper use of this book to understand and apply the following condition definitions, in the complete absence of wishful thinking.**

PAPER AND CARDBOARD

Near Mint: Fresh, bright, original crisply-inked appearance with only the slightest perceptible evidence of wear, soil, fade or creases. The item should lay flat, corners must be close to perfectly square and any staples must be rust free.

Fine: An above average example with attractive appearance but moderately noticeable aging or wear including: small creases and a few small edge tears; lightly worn corners; minimal browning, yellowing, dust or soiling; light staple rust but no stain on surrounding areas, no more than a few tiny paper flakes missing, small tears repaired on blank reverse side are generally acceptable if the front image is not badly affected.

Good: A complete item with no more than a few small pieces missing. Although showing obvious aging, accumulated flaws such as: creases, tears, dust and other soiling, repairs, insect damage, mildew, and brittleness must not combine to render the item unsound and too unattractive for display.

METAL: (primarily club badges and rings)

Near Mint: Item retains 90% or more of its original bright finish metallic luster as well as any accent coloring on the lettering or design. Badges must have the original pin intact and rings must have near perfect circular bands. Any small areas missing original luster must be free of rust, corrosion, dark tarnish or any other defect that stands out enough to render the naked eye appearance of the piece less than almost perfect.

Fine: An above average item with moderate wear to original luster but should retain at least 50%. There may be small, isolated areas with pinpoint corrosion spotting, tarnish or similar evidences of aging. Badges must have the original pin, although perhaps slightly bent, and rings must have bands with no worse than minor bends. Although general wear does show, the item retains an overall attractive appearance with noticeable luster.

Good: An average well-used or aged item missing nearly all luster and color accents. Badges may have a replaced pin and ring bands may be distorted or obviously reshaped. There may be moderate, not totally defacing, evidence of bends, dents, scratches, corrosion, etc. Aside from a replaced pin, completeness is still essential.

CELLULOID OR LITHOGRAPHED TIN PINBACK BUTTONS

Near Mint: Both celluloid and lithographed tin pinbacks retain the original, bright appearance without visual defect. For celluloid, this means the total absence of stain (known as foxing to button collectors). There can be no apparent surface scratches when the button is viewed directly; although when viewed at an angle in reflected light, there may be a few very shallow and small hairline marks on the celluloid surface. The celluloid covering must be totally intact with no splits, even on the reverse where the button paper and celluloid covering are folded under the collet. Lithographed tin buttons may have no more than two or three missing pinpoint-size dots of color and no visible scratches. Even in Near Mint condition, a button image noticeably off-center, as made, reduces desirability and therefore value to some price below Near Mint depending on the severity of the off-centering.

Fine: Both styles of buttons may have a few apparent scattered small scratches. Some minor flattening or a tiny dent noticeable to the touch, but not visually, is also acceptable. Celluloids may have a very minimal amount of age spotting or moisture stain, largely confined to the rim area, not distracting from the graphics and not dark in color. There may be a small celluloid split on the reverse by the collet, but the celluloid covering must still lay flat enough not to cause a noticeable bump on the side edge. Lithographed tin buttons may have only the slightest traces of paint roughness, or actual rust, visible on the front.

A variation of the celluloid pinback is the celluloid covered pocket mirror which holds a glass mirror on the reverse rather than a fastener pin. Condition definitions for pocket mirrors match those for celluloid buttons except a fine condition item may have a clouded or smoked mirror and some streaks on the silvering. A cracked mirror typically reduces desireability to the level of Good condition.

Good: Celluloid pinbacks may have moderately dark spotting or moisture stain not exceeding 25% of the surface area. There could be some slight evidence of color fade, a small nick on the front celluloid, or a small celluloid split by the reverse collet causing a small edge bump. Dark extensive stain, deep or numerous scratches and extensive crazing of the celluloid covering each render the button to a condition status of less than good and essentially unsalable. Lithographed tin buttons must retain strong color and be at least 75% free of noticeable surface wear or they too fall into the likely unsalable range.

OTHER MATERIALS: Ceramic, Glass, Wood, Fabric, Composition, Rubber, Plastic, Vinyl, Etc.

Near Mint: Regardless of the substance, the item retains its fresh, original appearance and condition without defect. Only the slightest traces of visually non-distracting wear are acceptable.

Fine: Each material has its inherent weakness in withstanding age, typical use or actual abuse.

Ceramic, porcelain, china, bisque and other similar clay-based objects are susceptible to edge chips. These are acceptable if minimal. Glazed items very typically develop hairline crazing not considered a flaw unless hairlines have also darkened.

Glass is fragile and obviously susceptible to missing chips, flakes or hairline fractures but acceptable in modest quantity.

Wood items, as well as the faithful likeness composition wood, generally withstand aging and use well. Small stress fractures or a few small missing flakes are acceptable if the overall integrity of the item is not affected.

Fabric easily suffers from weave splits or snags plus stain spots are frequently indelible. Weaving breaks are generally acceptable in limited numbers but fabric holes are not. Stains may not exceed a small area and only a blush of color change.

Composition items, typically dolls or figurines, tend to acquire hairline cracks of the thin surface coating. This is commonly expected and normally acceptable to the point of obvious severity. Color loss should not exceed 20% and not involve critical facial details.

Rubber items, either of solid or hollow variety, tend to lose original pliability and evolve into a rigid hardness that frequently results in a warped or deformed appearance. Some degree of original flexibility is preferred or, at least, minimal distortion.

Plastic and vinyl items have a tendency to split at areas of high stress or frequent use. This is frequently expected and excused by collectors up to the point of distracting from overall appearance or function.

Good: Items of any material are expected to be complete and/or functional. Obvious wear is noticeable, but the item retains its structural soundness. Wear or damage must not exceed the lower limits of being reasonably attractive for display purposes.

RARITY & DEMAND DETERMINE VALUE

A toy's value rests largely on its degree of rarity plus collector demand. Rarity is a constant--either few examples of a given object were produced originally or few are known to remain.

Demand, however, is influenced by a number of variables. An item must have popular appeal, otherwise rarity is not a salient consideration. Appeal is typically based on the subject matter of the item or the type of item. Superman appeals to more collectors than Rocky Jones, Space Ranger and more collectors specialize in rings than pedometers.

Following popular appeal, with rarity being equal, the condition of an item is the primary factor in determining value. Whatever the rarity factor may be, only a very small percentage of known specimens of any item will still exist in high grade condition. The desire to own items in close-to-new condition is a commonly-shared trait among collectors. The resulting competition accounts for the wide gap in value between an example in fine condition and one in Near Mint condition. The rarer the item, the greater this value differential is likely to be. Collectors willing to forego top condition examples and the inherent competition-driven high prices may add much purchasing power to available funds if lesser grade examples are acceptable.

Among the remaining factors that create value are cross-over interest, emotional factors and geographic variation.

Cross-over interest occurs when a toy has the same appeal but for a different reason to various collectors. A Lone Ranger Frontier Town cereal box may appeal to a cereal box collector, a generalist premium collector, a Lone Ranger collector and a collector specializing in cut-out toys. Cross-over interest frequently increases demand and therefore prices for those kinds of items.

Emotional factors include the determination to acquire a toy once owned and lost, the desire to finally own an item never acquired during childhood or the desire to "complete" a particular collection. For others, collecting premiums may spring from aesthetic considerations or perceived investment potential. Emotions play the role of a wild card in the factors establishing value. (For more on this theme, see "A Collective Call to Arms" on page 50).

Geographical factors also play some role in determining values. Radio premiums of the 1930s were likely offered and distributed in larger numbers in the most populous areas, frequently in the Eastern United States. Even today, premiums may be offered on a regional or local basis generating a sense of scarcity and increased value among those outside the distribution area. Ultimately, geographic differences diminish as old and new premiums are distributed among collectors by sales and auction catalogues, publications with buy and sell advertising, and collectibles shows attended by collectors and dealers from all points.

VALUATIONS IN THIS BOOK

Values in this guide are based on the author's 31 years experience in auctioning toys. Also considered were results of other auctions, sales lists, show prices, known transactions between individuals and advice from collectors with various specialties. (Also see "The Principles of Pricing" on page 109). The values listed are for retail sales, not prices paid by dealers (See "Selling Your Items" on page 26).

The Good, Fine, and Near Mint condition grades used in this book cover the vast majority of toys. The value for an item can be determined only in conjunction with the standards for each grade outlined in the section on Condition Definitions.

For items falling between the three grades, i.e. Very Fine or Very Good, an approximate value is the mid-point value between the two grades closest to the condition of the item under consideration.

Truly Mint items, like new and with absolutely no wear or defect, could command a price 10% or even greater than the Near Mint listed value. Conversely, an item with severe damage or missing parts may lose 50% or more of the Good listed value.

The final consideration in establishing valuations is packaging. Most collectors highly value items complete with original packaging, box or carton, when applicable.

Earlier toys of the 1930s to mid-1950s–before the collectibles era we know now–were generally saved by the recipient without regard to packaging or other contents. This is particularly true of mail order premiums. Mailing boxes and envelopes from this era were seldom graphic but frequently held instruction sheets, other paper inserts such as a premium catalogue, or an order form for re-ordering another of the premium at hand. A "complete" premium package—assuming acceptable condition—can command up to 25% more value than the actual premium item alone. Many of the most desirable instruction sheets, or similar papers, are included and priced in this guide. Many items are also assigned a separate value for an example boxed and complete with papers, all in Near Mint condition.

Needless to say, toys of the mid-50s and after are also enhanced approximately 25% in value if all original packaging is present.

The range of items covered by this guide is vast and assigned values are as low as a few dollars to as high as many thousands. Within this collecting universe are subjects and areas of specialization to match any collecting budget.

RESTORED ITEMS

Original toys damaged and restored are marketable, particularly scarcer examples, due to continuing demand as available examples leave the marketplace and enter private collections.

Restoration takes many forms depending on the material substance of the toy. Examples range from simply cleaning an item to completely refinishing one. In between, typical restorations include book rebinding, refilling minor chips or flakes, color or scratch retouching, replacement of missing part(s).

Responsible dealers and collectors volunteer full disclosure on restorations at the time offered for sale. Even an expertly restored item will seldom exceed the value of another example in unrestored Fine condition.

Proper restoration is a delicate process often overlooked by the well-meaning but inexperi-

enced restorer. Countless items drop dramatically in value by a devout scrubbing that removes not only soiling but character as well. Paint restorations may be neatly done but in a color hue so unfaithful to the original that distracting appearance results. Repairs using improper tapes or glues usually turn brown, radically diminishing the appearance and value of the "restored" toy.

Wisdom will leave repairs and restorations to proven professionals unless an individual is confident of his or her restoration skills and willing to accept the marketplace judgment of these skills.

REPRODUCTIONS AND FANTASIES

Every hobby with valuable items attracts thieves who operate by deception. Toys and popular culture collectibles in general are not exempt from this immoral practice. A collector may avoid being deceived by acquiring some basic knowledge about the chosen specialty, by exercising reasoned judgment when faced with an apparent bargain and by patronizing dealers who unconditionally guarantee their merchandise as authentic.

Deceptive items usually take the form of reproductions and fantasies. The fantasy item is an object, never licensed by the copyright owner, that did not even exist during the time period that produced original and authorized collectibles. Fantasy collectibles are produced after the fact, typically when a person, character, movie, etc. is the subject of collector interest. The people making fantasy items intend them to appeal to, or intentionally defraud, collectors unaware of the item's unauthorized status and relative newness. Frequently such items bear illegitimate copyright notices and spurious dates. The best defenses are familiarity with authentic items issued in a particular category or a guarantee from a reputable dealer.

Reproductions, undated and unmarked as such, will undoubtedly be encountered by active collectors. Unlike a fantasy item, the reproduction has its original, authentic counterpart. In some circumstances, a questionable item may be compared directly to a known original to determine any difference. Producing reproductions doesn't require ethics, but it does require some care and skill to produce a copy with most, if not all, the distinguishing features of the original. Careful observation of originals, some appreciation of the materials and manufacturing techniques in use when the original was produced and a healthy degree of skepticism are potent weapons against reproductions. Copied items very seldom match all the characteristics of the original. If any doubts surface, postpone the purchase and get a second opinion, or at least obtain a written receipt with the seller's money-back guarantee of authenticity.

Here are a few basic warnings and tips to keep in mind regarding reproductions:

Tin Signs--many authentic signs have been reproduced and many fantasy signs created. The reproductions are frequently executed in a size different than the originals. Buyers need personal expertise or the guarantee of a reputable dealer knowledgeable in this area.

Framed Items--covering an item with glass, or even shrink wrap, may hide a multitude of problems. A generous layer of grime or highly reflective glare may obscure the image enough to hide what proves to be a photocopy, color laser copy or printed reproduction.

Printed Items--small single sheet paper items and cards are easy to reproduce. Color laser copies are particularly deceptive, but detectable on close inspection. Sometimes this technology is put to use to reproduce wrist or pocket watch dials as well as other deceptions. Both color and black/white reproductions of paper items sometimes reproduce small tears, creases or other flaws on the paper of the original item being copied. These defects may show on the copy while the paper used to pro-

duce the copy is actually not torn, not creased or otherwise flawed.

Pinback Buttons--very few buttons were made in both celluloid and lithographed tin varieties. However, a small number of lithographed tin buttons have been reproduced as celluloids. Nearly all buttons described in this guide as lithographed tin (litho.) should be regarded with much suspicion if encountered as a celluloid version. Most button reproductions are celluloid copies made by photographing celluloid originals. This sometimes results in a slightly blurred appearance, sometimes the dot screen fills in on the reproduction and sometimes the covering of plastic is noticeably different than the celluloid of the 1950s and earlier. A shiny metal back doesn't prove much. The metal used now may quickly oxidize while the metal used in the 1960s and earlier may retain its shine.

Metal Badges--these are more costly to copy than paper items or buttons but a limited number have been subject to reproduction. These are typically very exact copies of the front image. However, most originals had a soldered bar pin on the reverse. Most reproductions feature a small oval metal plate with two small raised areas used to anchor the bottom bar of the pin.

Reproductions and fantasies are an annoying aspect of nearly all hobbies, but not cause for despair. In the normal course of enjoying and learning about a particular specialization, the ability to discern the small number of deceptive items is acquired almost automatically. Just proceed with a bit of caution at the outset and rely on fellow collectors for advice concerning reputable dealers. (For more information, see "Fakes, Forgeries & Knock-Offs" on page 40). ❖

The only constant is
CHANGE!

JLA Cover

Quality Heroes Cover

Don't be left behind!

You know the market has been through a lot of changes the past few years, but you won't have a true picture of just how drastic the changes have been unless you pick up **The Overstreet Comic Book Price Guide #28**. From Bob Overstreet's Market Report to the most thoroughly researched and documented prices in the the industry, this is one book you can't afford to miss!

888-COMIC-BOOK
888-266-4226

Gemstone Publishing products are available through your local comic shop. Can't find a comic shop? Try the Toll Free **Comic Shop Locator Service** *at (888)COMIC BOOK!*

When we introduced **The Guide #1**, we rocked the collecting world. There are even more changes in **The Overstreet Comic Book Price Guide #28**. Don't miss history in the making!

Did you miss the BIG changes?

The first premium?--truly a trivia question without answer. The word in the context of this guide means something offered free or at a reduced price as an inducement to buy. The concept of a premium is ancient and certainly dates to the days of barter when some clever trader offered an extra "free" item to clinch a deal.

For much of history and in America's earliest years, premiums were not needed. Merchants offered only very basic necessities that could not be home-grown or home-made. The premium came to America with the industrial revolution when towns formed, work became more specialized and competition arose among merchants offering virtually the same products at the same prices. The premium became the means to gain an edge over the competition.

Paper was somewhat a luxury commodity in the infancy of America. Paper production—still from rag content rather than wood pulp—became less scarce in the early 1800s, common by the 1850s, abundant following the Civil War. The use of illustrated advertisements increased after the War although still by primitive printing or engraving processes enabling only black on white reproduction.

The effectiveness of supplemental color also was limited only to printers with proper lithographing equipment and skilled craftsmen. Mass-produced color was still distant as was the ability to color-print in large sizes. These factors contributed to the immense popularity of give-away advertising trade cards of the 1870s-1890s, the first mass-produced premiums. Card inserts in product packaging began in the late years of the century.

The development of celluloid for commercial use in the mid-1890s opened the way for an entirely new, cost effective, and well-received way of advertising, particularly suited for premiums.

Paper and celluloid, along with brass for metal items, became the mainstays of comic premiums until World War II. However, celluloid buttons lost ground in the 1930s Depression era to the even less expensive lithographed tin button.

Certainly the most notable early combination of comic character and premiums rests on the scrawny shoulders of a homely and bald street waif attired only in a nightshirt, The Yellow Kid. He appeared on buttons, gum cards and postcards by various sponsors in ubiquitous fashion. The Yellow Kid was followed closely by another popular comic character—also created by R.F. Outcault—namely Buster Brown and his faithful sidekick dog Tige. Buster was traditionally associated with the shoe line bearing his name, although lending his endorsement popularity to tonics and several other products.

In 1904, the Brown Shoe Company issued what is considered the first comic book premium--**Brown's Blue Ribbon Book of Jokes and Jingles**. This first of four 5"x7" books featuring Outcault art, issued in a Jokes and Jingles series between 1904 and 1910, was printed in two versions. The earliest version includes Pore Li'l Mose with Buster Brown and other characters while the second version replaces Mose with the Yellow Kid.

Kellogg's, another prolific premium sponsor, issued their apparent first premium in 1909. The 3-1/2"x4-3/4" two-fold booklet carries a 1907 patent date and a 1909 W.K. Kellogg copyright date. The color booklet features three interior pages picturing costumed animals in various activities. Two additional pages, with similar pictures printed on each side, are each cut horizontally into five strips allowing the user to create numerous pictorial variations of the animals by alternating the strips depicting heads, mid-sections and legs. Kellogg must have been very satisfied with this premium as the company soon produced a new edition in a 6"x8" size and offered the booklet well into the 1930s.

The early characters from comic strip land were followed by live entertainment stars: silent movie serial buttons emerged c. 1916;

the first radio premiums directed to adult listeners began in the early 1920s and the early 1930s began the Golden Age of radio and related premiums dominated by Little Orphan Annie (Ovaltine) and Tom Mix (Ralston). Premiums had become a widespread marketing tool by both radio and print mediums aimed at youngsters, who in turn, beseeched parents to buy the sponsoring product.

World War II curtailed the quantity and quality of premiums although not eliminating them. Following the war, a new mass entertainment medium—television—quickly grew from infancy to a giant, overpowering radio and newspapers.

1948 marks the first use of a television premium associated with a character destined to become a popular culture icon. Howdy Doody began his television career in 1947. Shortly into the presidential election year of 1948, the show's producers decided to conduct their own Howdy Doody for President campaign. On March 23rd, Buffalo Bob Smith offered his audience an "I'm For Howdy Doody" 1-1/4" celluloid pinback button (picturing Howdy as he first appeared, not as we know him today). Only five stations carried the show at the time and the offer was announced only seven times. An astonishing 60,000 requests poured into the NBC mail room. The power of TV advertising aimed at the juvenile market was proven and Colgate, Continental Baking, Ovaltine and Mars candy quickly signed as long-term Howdy Doody sponsors.

The premium tradition continued briefly in the early TV years—principally Howdy Doody, Cisco Kid, Hopalong Cassidy and Roy Rogers—but by the mid-1950s, the mail premium heyday dissipated due to media costs (limiting advertisers from sponsoring entire programs) coupled with escalated premium manufacturing costs.

Premiums for youngsters continue, of course, from the mid-1950s to the present, although almost universally made of plastic or paper. More elaborate premiums for adults include radios, watches and figural objects.

Throughout the years, cereals have been the most prominent and faithful sponsor of youth premiums, followed by a host of other food products. Since the 1960s, fast food franchises have joined the ranks. From the thousands of premium creations over the last century, the ring is the most popular with collectors today. The 1990s saw the revival of rings used as premiums and several firms currently issue limited edition rings as collectibles.

Over the decades, premiums have changed their forms but lost none of their appeal. They certainly still exist in profusion and will continue to do so as long as sponsors seek to find that certain incentive to gain an edge on the competition.

HISTORY OF PREMIUM COLLECTING

Premiums of all types have been consciously preserved in collections, or at least saved due to benign neglect by original owners and their descendants since the 1870s. At various times, these objects were appreciated for their beauty, novelty or association with a favorite character. Adults and children accumulated premiums as they were encountered on a daily basis. There existed virtually no marketplace wherein collectors bought, sold and traded premiums.

The marketplace for premiums first began in the mid-1960s with the advent of nostalgia memorabilia collecting. Why this occurred at this time is open to interpretation and speculation. Disposable income is certainly one of the factors. Rational people don't buy Radio Orphan Annie decoder badges unless the bills are paid. The age range of these new collectors is another key factor.

The mid to late 1960s was a prosperous time for many Americans. The vanguard of collectors motivated by nostalgia was largely between the ages of 30 and 45. These people had many of life's crucial decisions–marriage, family, home buying, behind them. They were in control of their lives with established jobs and professions. Disposable income was available. They also had memories: memories of childhood, memories of the time they were not in control, memories of hard times and sacrifice.

Being 30 to 45 years old, this group spent

part or all of their childhood under the cloud of the Depression and World War II. One might well assume these stressful years be best forgotten, and millions tried. However, for the new collectors still in touch with their child-hoods, these very years became the focus of their collecting interests.

Many of today's most established collectible hobbies trace their roots to nostalgia memora-bilia collecting begun in the mid-1960s.

The passions of these people while approxi-mately ten to twelve years old in the 1930s and 1940s form the original foundation for collect-ing premiums, Disneyana, comic books, comic strip characters, science fiction, cowboys, space and superheroes, movie posters, sport and non-sport cards, many toy categories and more.

Although the objects collected in the mid-1960s, and now, have no inherent value, the memories associated with them are invaluable. Most frequently, the collector of 1930s-1940s items was attempting to acquire a beloved item once owned and lost or an item much desired in childhood but never acquired. The motivations remain much the same for later generations.

Ted Hake's specialty was sales lists of presi-dential campaign items in the mid-1960s when nostalgia memorabilia collecting first devel-oped. In 1967, Hake's Americana & Collectibles began, with an auction format, adding premiums and similar non-political items to the catalogue. Hake's became the first collectibles business in the United States spe-cializing in the sale of 20th century popular culture collectibles through a mail and tele-phone bid auction.

About the same time, comic book conven-tions were established--small and isolated by current standards. For roughly six years, the premium marketplace was limited to Hake's, the occasional comic book convention, pot-luck at local antiques shops or shows, and clas-sifieds in the few national hobby-oriented pub-lications such as **The Antique Trader** and **Collectors News**.

The first attempt to bring premium collectors together was Jack Melcher's **Radio Premium**
Collectors Newsletter, published in January, 1973 and continued approximately two years. Additional efforts in the 1970s included: Tom Claggett's **The Premium Exchange**, 1976; Hy Mandelowitz's **The Premium Guide**, 1977; Ted Hake's **Collectibles Monthly**, 1977; Joe Sarno's **Space Academy Newsletter**, 1978.

The biggest event of the 1970s was the publi-cation of the first radio premium price guide by Tom Tumbusch in 1977 titled **Illustrated Radio Premium Catalog and Price Guide**. This book, and later editions, gave collectors and dealers an organized survey of available radio premiums and brought many new collec-tors into the hobby.

Another 1970s event was the 1974 discovery of old stocks from the Brownie Manufacturing Company and the Robbins Company. The Brownie find involved c. 1950 plastic premi-ums while the Robbins find consisted of c. 1936-1941 metal premiums, a few dies and a small number of unique prototype premiums. While both finds were reputedly "large," from that time until now there has been no percep-tible impact on prices. Whatever was found seemed to be immediately absorbed by collec-tors of that era and further dissipated in the ensuing years. The minor exception is an abundant supply of the 1950 Straight Arrow cave ring missing the photo inserts.

The premium hobby continued to grow in the 1980s. Joel Smilgis began publishing **Box Top Bonanza** in 1983 and continued until 1991. The first convention devoted to premi-ums was organized by Jimmy Dempsey and held in Evansville, Indiana July, 1984. To the joy of some and sorrow of others, this proved to be the exact weekend selected by General Mills in Minneapolis to auction off their premi-um archive as a benefit for the city's Como Zoo. The decade was capped by the 1987 inau-gural of a regularly scheduled specialty show for premium collectors. Organized by Don Maris and now known as the Dallas Big D Show, this event occurs each July and November.

1990 brought a new specialty publication. Scott Bruce's **Flake The Breakfast Nostalgia**

Magazine was devoted to cereal box collecting and related premiums. Bruce ceased publication in 1996 in favor of a web site titled "Flake World" at **www.flake.com**. The site addresses many aspects of cereal-related collecting and is a source for Bruce's books: **Cerealizing America: The Unsweetened Story of American Breakfast Cereal** (Faber & Faber, 1995), **Cereal Box Bonanza: The 1950s** (Collector Books, 1996) and his newest title published in 1998, **Cereal Boxes & Prizes: 1960s.**

In 1992, Hake's Americana & Collectibles auctioned Jimmy Dempsey's premium ring collection and received then-record prices. In 1993, the Supermen of America contest prize ring in Near Mint condition established a record of $125,000 as the most expensive comic premium sold to date. These events heralded the 1994 publication of the **Overstreet Premium Ring Price Guide** which joined the **Overstreet Comic Book Price Guide** as the accepted references for these collecting fields. The third edition of the **Overstreet Toy Ring Price Guide** was published in 1997.

Most significantly, the 1990s saw increasing recognition of the rarity of many premiums, particularly in high grade condition. This is especially true regarding the historical importance of premiums associated with certain comic book titles. This book recognizes the price increases of the 1990s and the growing appeal of premiums to collectors across the fields of radio, television, comic books, pulps, cereal boxes, movies, music and advertising.

BUILDING A COLLECTION

Any dedicated collector will attest to the joys and satisfaction of being one. Even the most experienced were newcomers at the outset and most will admit to mistakes and judgment errors along the way. Most are still driven by the exciting possibility of a "new find" regardless of the years and depth of their collection.

Beginning collectors often explore various fields of interest, casually or intensely, before generally settling into a specific choice of collectible within financial means. This guide

book will hopefully demonstrate to beginning premium collectors the wide range of specialization options to fit any budget.

Needless to say, unseasoned collectors can benefit by purchasing from dealers who guarantee their collectibles as authentic and have a clear return policy in the event of an error in representation.

The first step in collection building is to acquire the appropriate reference books. References show at least a segment of the universe of collectibles in a given area and often provide the author's opinion regarding value.

Armed with some basic knowledge, the next step is to see, handle and price the collectibles of interest. Typically, this occurs at a local flea market or perhaps a more specialized collectibles show. This participation in the marketplace, whether as a buyer or merely as an observer, brings the new collector in contact with the collecting fraternity. Meeting collectors and dealers with a shared interest, learning about collector clubs and discovering any relevant specialized publications will provide the information necessary to focus collecting interests. This focus must be acquired to minimize the number of errors that occur in every learning process.

When collection building begins in earnest there are many sources. Locally, successful finds can occur at estate auctions, garage sales, flea markets, general line antiques shops and collectibles co-operative stores. An advertisement in the local newspaper could yield a bonanza–or nothing.

Regional sources likely include larger flea markets and general line antiques shows. Hopefully, for a greater concentration of interesting items, there may be some shows of a specialized nature such as paper Americana, sport and non-sport cards, comic books, toys and advertising memorabilia.

National sources for premium collectibles include many magazines and newspaper format publications that carry display and classified advertising. There are also mail and telephone bid auctions such as we offer at Hake's Americana & Collectibles, specialists in comic artifacts and premiums such as Diamond International Galleries, and any of the dealers advertising in this book.

SELLING A COLLECTION

The collectibles marketplace necessarily relies on sellers as well as buyers. **The prices in this book are retail values.** Dealers will pay a percentage of these prices based on their own business practices, operational costs and assessment of value.

Sellers with a collection, as opposed to a few random items, must decide whether to wholesale to a dealer in a single transaction or whether to invest the time, energy and financial costs inherent in retailing the collection piece by piece to collectors. Each approach has advantages and disadvantages. Prospective sellers can well use the resources described in the section Building A Collection for the opposite purpose of selling a collection.

If selling to a dealer, the sale price will likely be maximized by selling all the items–the good with the bad–all at once, all for one price. The dealer's offer, or reaction to a price asked by the seller, will be based on quantity, quality, condition and the dealer's instincts as to how easily and quickly the items may be marketed to his clientele.

An in-person transaction is ideal–it becomes the dealer's responsibility to evaluate exactly what he is buying. Conversely, a transaction by mail will require the seller to list, photograph, photocopy and/or video tape the items as well as to evaluate and make representations regarding condition. The dealer cannot react to a price or make an offer without this essential information. A tentative price agreement still leaves the seller the chore of packing and shipping. The dealer will want to see what he is buying before accepting the transaction as complete and making payment.

Should a seller aspire to full retail prices, the role of "dealer" is assumed by necessity. The choices become in-person sales or mail order sales.

A seller may elect to become a vendor at local, regional or national shows. Assuming the size of the collection warrants this option, the seller must balance hopes of obtaining retail prices against the costs of personal time, transportation expense, booth rental fee, lodging and food; all the while assuming adequate show publicity or tradition and acceptable weather, when a factor, for crowd turn-out. In addition are sales tax and income tax reporting requirements.

If a seller chooses the mail order option, travel and booth expenses trade place with advertising costs. Personal time costs likely increase and certainly extend into weeks and months as the process unfolds: advertising copy preparation with descriptions and perhaps photos, mail and telephone orders with attendant correspondence, packing, shipping and fielding complaints from some percentage of customers dissatisfied with a purchase. Taxes remain a constant.

The novice seller, aiming for retail prices, faces a final hurdle. Whether selling in-person or via mail, don't count on a sell-out. The highest quality items and obviously under-priced items will sell quickly. The seller will soon be left with an inventory, probably the bulk of the collection, comprised of average, damaged and low grade items. To move this material will require repeated show participation or advertising. Offering a dealer what remains of the "collection" at this point will probably be met with a polite "I'll pass" response.

In summation, selling an intact collection to a dealer offers immediate cash in a single payment and elimination of time and expenses required for retailing. A higher profit could be realized by retailing to collectors, if the time and expenses required are accurately calculated with regard to the collection's realistic retail value. ❖

THE EXPLOSION OF HISTORY:
THE 1997 MARKET REPORT

BY BOB OVERSTREET

DRIVING THE MARKET

The market for comic character toys is at an all-time high. One of the main reasons for the surge in interest is the constant entry of new collectors or players into the marketplace. There are no artificial limits which can be placed on the type of person who experiences the nostalgic impulse. Anyone can decide to collect, and many people are deciding to do precisely that. In a sense, they want to buy back their childhood memories (and in some cases their fathers' and grandfathers' as well!) by connecting with toys from their past. (For more on this theme, see "A Collective Call to Arms" on page 50).

Another important aspect driving the market is the increase in the available information about the comic characters' past through new books, TV shows, movies and the Internet. The explosion of historical information on cable and broadcast television (on the History Channel, A&E, The Learning Channel, Discovery, and PBS, among others) has by its nature also included the importance of popular culture. Radio and TV shows focusing on collectors have been popping up across the country. New adaptations of classic characters have also revitalized interest in some properties. Characters like Tarzan, Casper, the Shadow, Phantom, the Marvel Family, Dick Tracy, Zorro, Mr. Magoo, Felix the Cat, Betty Boop, Popeye, Bozo and a host of others have all made a comeback in the 1990s. We have also seen a fresh new interest in old time radio shows. A number of companies have been releasing tapes of shows from the '30s and '40s. Now anyone can buy just about any of the popular shows, allowing many potential fans to hear these programs for the first time.

This Superman Circular Patch sells for $10,000 in NM!

It might seem like stating the obvious, but there are uncounted toys coming out these days from movies, supermarkets, gas stations and fast food chains. This is a great driving force for the hobby both now and in the future because it involves more and more young people in collecting each day. Even the ones who aren't collectors to start with will one day graduate from school, start earning a living, and become subject to the same nostalgic impulses as the rest of us. They'll think back to some of these recent items and seek to crystallize those fond memories by purchasing the items they remember.

As far as store-bought items are concerned, 1997 proved to be a record year with a reported $23 billion in sales.

AUCTION REPORT

Availability of scarcer toy items has always been terribly important in maintaining the interest of serious collectors. Good fortune for collectors came in the form of an auction featuring some of Gordon Gold's collection through Christie's in November 1996 (See **Hake's Price Guide To Character Toy Premiums**, 1st Edition, or our website, **www.gemstonepub.com**, for background information on premium creators Sam and Gordon Gold). Here is a sampling of some of the cash sales from his auction:

Three Stooges Moving Pictures Machine promotion 1937, 6 pieces—$13,800; Superman

Pep poster and cereal box advertising movie stars with display poster—$2,530; Two Hopalong Cassidy posters and shelf display with cereal box promoting trading cards—$1,840; 1950s Buck Rogers Space Ranger Promotion Kit (8 pieces)—$1,840; Kellogg's Pep Cereal Box, 2 display posters and average set of Pep buttons—$3,450; Kellogg's Cloth Dolls (8)—$1,725; Orphan Annie and Captain Sparks ad items (3)—$1,725; Popeye display posters (3)—$2,300; Superman poster, 1946—$4,025; Superman art for Pep Pin and Pep Pin die-cut display—$5,175. Gordon Gold's archive file copy items sold by Christie's, and more recently by Hake's Americana, created much interest and excitement among collectors, along with numerous record prices.

THE SALES FORCE

Another important aspect of the market is the sales force. Today there are more dealers in toys than any other area of comic character memorabilia. In one publication alone we have documented over 2,000 different individuals who are selling comic character toys. We have also noted that the hobby now boasts more than 100 price guides. Many of these price guides are excellent references for characters like Howdy Doody, Hopalong Cassidy, Pez, Cap Guns, Sheet Music, Comic Books, Hot Wheels, Character Cereal Boxes, Disney and Warner Brothers characters, Dolls, Teddy Bears, and of course Beanie Babies, just to name a few. One magazine on toy figures now prints more than 200,000 copies per month, so the interest shows no signs of flagging.

Almost all of the premiums and store bought toys produced prior to 1960 are legitimately scarce in high grade. In fact, we would almost venture to guess that if we attached all the Near Mint-Mint product left over from 1900-1959, we would probably be hard pressed to fill a good-sized barn in Indiana. Remember, they're not making these items any more, but money will probably be printed seven days a week for as long as we live.

Photo Doody sold at auction for a record $113,431!

COWBOY CHARACTERS

Another area of strength in the market is cowboy characters. Nickelodeon's *Nick At Nite* and *TV Land* have helped fuel an amazing amount of interest in the Old West, including this year's 65th anniversary of the Lone Ranger. While interest may dim in westerns from time to time, it always seems to come back.

SALES REPORT

Because of the large number of bonafide auction houses, toy shows around the world numbering in the thousands each year, and ads placed in numerous weekly and monthly publications (as well as on the Internet), the trading market has become substantially a cash market. Listed below is a small selection of the tens of thousands of sales that took place in the last year for a diverse array of toys. Conditions of sold items are listed where available.

ARCHIE

Post Alpha-Bits Archie Car Cereal Box Flat, $252.

BATMAN

"Batman's Last Chance" One-Sheet, (1949) $2,300; Bond Bread Small Sign Showing Robin, $420; Paper Mask, Philadelphia Newspaper (1943) $1,984.

THE BEATLES

Vinyl Brunch Bag, $547.

BIG BOY

Composition Bobbing Head, $825.

BLACK FLAME OF THE AMAZON

Black Flame Map, VG $450.

BLONDIE

Dagwood Philadelphia Inquirer Rotocomic Button, $123.

BOBBY BENSON

"H-Bar-O" Cast Iron Cap Gun, $404; "H-Bar-O Ranger" Enameled Brass Star Badge, $420.

BUCK ROGERS IN THE 25TH CENTURY

"25th Century Acousticon Jr." 2-1/4" Cello. Button, $2,000; "Buck Rogers and His Amazing Adventures 2430 A.D." Blotter, $450; Boxed Card Game by All-Fair, $1,713; Combat Game Assembled, $1,323; Repeller Ray Brass Ring with Green Stone, $2,700; Repeller Ray Brass Ring with Green Stone, VF $2,000; Solar Scouts Radio Club Manual, $616.

The Hoppy Bunny Statuette (in box) fetches $4,400 in NM!

The Batman Cardboard Mask in VF brings $1,984!

BUSTER BROWN

"Buster Brown Shoes" Boxed Pocket Watch, (1912) $1,569.

CAPTAIN AMERICA

Membership Card, (1941) $1,000; Membership Card and Mailer, VG/FN $3,100.

CAPTAIN MARVEL

Compass Ring, $1,860; Compass Ring, NM $1,600; Captain Marvel Jr. Statue, VF $2,300; "Magic Lightning Box" Punch Out Premium, $75; Captain Marvel Photo (Signed by CC Beck), $200; Mary Marvel Statuette in Box (Fawcett Premium), VF $2,550. Hoppy Bunny Statuette in Box, $4,400.

CAPTAIN MIDNIGHT

Mirro-Flash Code-O-Graph Brass Decoder, (1946) $85; Flight Commander Ring, $500; Flight Commander Signet Ring, (1957) $923; Flight Commander Signet Ring, Instructions, Mailer, $1,900; Initial Printing Ring, $400; "Secret Squadron" Membership Card, (1957) $125; Mystic Sun God Ring, NM $1,300; Mystic Sun God Ring, Instructions and Mailer, NM $2,550; Ovaltine Cup, boxed $150; Secret Compartment Ring, $250; "Secret Squadron" Manual with Mailer, $220; Flight Commander Signet Ring, VG $500; Mystic Sun God Ring, $1,150; Whirlwind Whistling Brass Ring, $425; Sliding Secret Compartment Ring (Pilots) with Instructions and Box, $375.

CAPTAIN VIDEO

"CV" Secret Seal Brass Ring; $500.

CISCO KID

"Wrigley's Cisco Kid Signal Arrowhead," $385.

COMIC MISC.

Funny Family Comic Character Calendar, $427; "New Funnies" Andy Panda Pinback, $350; Raggedy Ann Dairy Premium Storybook, $288; Sears Funny Paper Puppets Punch-outs, $455.

This Captain America Card (with envelope) brings $3,100 in VF!

CRACKER JACK

Cracker Jack Boy Tin Litho. Figural Tab, $265.

DAVY CROCKETT

"Walt Disney's Davy Crockett" Metal Compass Ring, NM $325; Disney/Gimbel's Club Button, $264; Patches Store Display Sign, $420; "Walt Disney's Davy Crockett" Metal Compass Ring, $250.

DELL COMICS

"Dell Comics Are Good Comics" Tin Rack Sign, $504; Dell Comics Club Early 1950s Member Certificate, $170.

DICK TRACY

Belt with Badge, $250; Blue Ribbon Pop-Up Book, $500; Belt Attachment with Link Chain and Loop, $200; "Inspector General" 2-1/2" Brass Badge, $863; Rubber Band Machine Gun Punch-Out, $690.

DISNEY CHARACTERS MISC.

Jungle Book Sign with Set of Bowl Hanger Figures, $452.

The Green Hornet Seal (Secret Compartment) Ring fetches $1,508!

DIZZY DEAN

"Win with Dizzy Dean" Brass Ring, VF $200; Post's "Dizzy Dean Winners" Brass Ring, $200.

DOC SAVAGE

Pulp Club Lapel Stud, $300.

DONALD DUCK

"Wanna Fight" Cello. Button, $656; "Donald Duck Jackets" Cello. Button, $789; Donald Duck Living Toy Ring with Kellogg's Pep Magnet, $434.

DR. SEUSS

Dr. Seuss Early Flit Insect Spray Cartoon Booklet, $483; Squander Bug World War II Bond Poster, $465.

ELVIS PRESLEY

Boxed Guitar, $1,356.

FELIX THE CAT

"Evening Ledger Comics" Cello. Button, $433.

FRANK BUCK

"Bring 'Em Back Alive Ivory Initial Ring" $250.

FRANK MERRIWELL

"Club Member/Follow the Adventures of Frank Merriwell" Cello. Button, FN $150.

GABBY HAYES

Quaker Cannon Ring (Brass Barrel Version), $175.

GENE AUTRY

Bandit Trail Game (Store Item), $914.

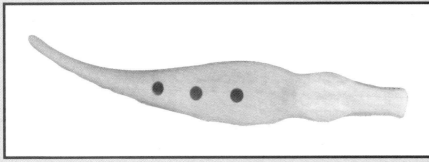

The Jack Armstrong Crocodile Ivory Whistle in VF sells for $4,410!

JIMMIE ALLEN

Commander Rank Brass Badge, $862; Commander Certificate, $202; Pouch, $250.

JOHN WAYNE

Dixie Premium Color Picture, $175.

GREEN HORNET

Black Beauty Boxed Corgi Car, $501; Seal (Secret Compartment) Ring $1,508.

HOPALONG CASSIDY

Australian Candy Tin, $404; Boxed Wallet with Special Agent Pass and Lucky Coin, $762; Compass/Hat Ring, $200; Cookie Set of 12 Tin Tabs, $1,428; English Timex Watch Button, $404; Greeting Cards Die-Cut Large Store Display Sign, $1,852; Wristwatch on Saddle Display Box, $550; Savings Bank Membership Kit $500; Unused Cookie Box Flat, $1,751;

HOP HARRIGAN

Superfortress Complete Punch-Out, $528.

HOWDY DOODY

"I'm For Howdy Doody" Pin on Card, $496; Floater Pencil $118; Jack-in-the-Box Plastic Ring, $2,500; Magic Kit, $216; Merchandising Catalogue, (1955) $575; "Howdy Doody Original Marionette" ("Photo Doody"), $113,431; Poll Parrot Tuk-A-Tab Masks and Disguise Kit, (in Original Envelope) $1,042; Royal Pudding Display Sign, $612; Poll Parrot Magic Eye Picture, $229; Luden's Premium 3-D Comic Strips, $403.

HOWIE WING

Weather Forecast Ring, NM $400.

JACK ARMSTRONG

Baseball Centennial Ring, FN $702; Baseball Centennial Ring, VG $950; Crocodile Glow in the Dark Plastic Whistle, $4,410; Cub Pilot Kit, Complete $641.

JUNIOR JUSTICE SOCIETY OF AMERICA

Silver Finish Club Badge, VG $750.

KELLOGG'S CEREAL MISC.

Pep Military Insignia Litho. Buttons (Set of 36), VG $459; Pep Comic Character Litho. Button Set (Set of 86 Characters), VF $1,295.

KISS

Guitar Boxed (Store Item), $625.

LASSIE

Lassie Friendship Silvered Brass Ring, VG $150.

LITTLE NEMO

Flip of Little Nemo Mechanical Valentine by Tuck, $365; Store Display (Winchester Ad), $3,000.

LITTLE ORPHAN ANNIE

Birthday Ring, $400; "Little Orphan Annie's

The Superman Contest Prize Ring from 1940 sells for $29,000 in F+!

Song" Sheet Music (with Letter and Mailer), (Ovaltine) $110; Orphan Annie Voter's Button, (Ovaltine) VF $589; "Snow White and the Seven Dwarfs Cut-Out Book," $638; Secret Guard Nurse Uniform, $567; Silver Star Member Secret Message Ring, $275; Silver Star Triple Mystery Secret Compartment Ring, $1,162; Secret Guard Magnifying Ring, VF $2,800; "SG" Secret Guard Brass Ring, $2,800; "SG" Secret Guard Brass Ring, GD $800.

THE LONE RANGER

Lone Ranger and Tonto Full Store Card of Plastic Rings, $731; Atomic Bomb Ring, NM $300; Cobakco Membership Card, $350; Filmstrip Ring (with Film), $175; Flashlight Ring (with Instructions and Mailer), $165; Gold Ore Ring, VF $1,700; Iron Mold for Ice Cream Cones, $688; Paper Movie Pop Gun, $350; Saddle Ring (with Film), $150; Six Shooter Ring, FN $125; Weather Forecasting Ring, $250.

LONE WOLF TRIBE

Chief Wolf Paw Metal Bracelet, $252.

MAD COMICS

"What Me Worry?" Doll by Baby Barry, VG $1,494.

MELVIN PURVIS

Secret Operator/Law & Order Patrol Brass Ring, $175.

MICKEY MOUSE

Christmas Comic Giveaway for Shoes "Merry Christmas From Mickey Mouse," (1939) F+ $1,553; Mickey & Donald with Sword and Rifle Sunoco Blotter, $288; "Chief" Club Rank Button, $2,434; "Mickey Mouse as Santa" Plaza Theatre Button, $1,751; Emerson Radio (Brown Wood Version), $1,840; Globe Trotters Bread Sign, $602; "Mickey Mouse Good Teeth" Cello. Button, $211; Newspaper Strip 1st Premium Postcard, VF $405; Volume 2 Gum Card Album (complete), $2,543; Mickey Mouse Waddle Book (Unpunched Tanglefoot Waddle Only), $690.

MISTER SOFTEE

"Mr. Softee" Plastic Ring, $40.

MOVIE MISC.

"Freaks' M-G-M's Amazing Picture" Cello. Button, FN $766; Judy Garland Ideal Toy Co Novelty Doll Button, $366; Martin/Lewis Double Head Hand Puppet, $402; Range Busters Movie Serial Club Button, $183.

MR. PEANUT

Wood Jointed Figure (with Cane), VF $350.

NABISCO

Munchy the Spoonman Fabric Pillow, $815.

THE PHANTOM

Phantom Ring, Silver $300; Three-Sheet, FN $5,460; Syroco Figure (purple outfit), VF $960; Phantom's Mark Australian Comic Club Stick-pin, $259.

PILLSBURY

Funny Face Goofy Grape Contest Prize Wristwatch, $748; Funny Face Paper Face Masks, (Lot of Seven) $2,175; Funny Face Unused Drink Stand, $4,975.

The Phantom Three-Sheet fetches $5,460!

PINOCCHIO

Jiminy Cricket Cardboard Cut-Out Set with Membership Card, $100; "Tell the Truth" Ring, VF $596.

POGO

Walt Kelly "Little Fir Tree" Comic, FN $325.

The Superman Bowman Gum Box fetches $7,500 in VF!

POPEYE

"Popeye in Technicolor!" One-Sheet Poster $714; Puppet Show Punch-Out Book, 1936 $1,045; Jeep Enamel and Silvered Brass Pin, $240.

POST

Honeycomb Gold Ore Ring, $150

QUISP AND QUAKE

Quake World Plastic Ring, MINT $2,000; Quake Volcano Plastic Ring, MINT $600; Quisp Friendship Figural Plastic Ring, MINT $1,500; Quaker Fun Bowl, $350.

RADIO MISC.

"Whistler" Radio Program Ink Blotter, $173.

REDDY KILOWATT

Earliest Hard Rubber Figure on Base, VF $1,470; Figure Inside Light Bulb, $460.

RINGS MISC.

"Andy Pafko" Baseball Scorer Brass Ring, $175; Baseball Game Mechanical Ring, (Canadian) MIB $400; Fireball Twigg Explorer Ring, $125; Football Ring, (1948) $400; Joe DiMaggio Club Ring, VF $1,100; Joe DiMaggio Club Ring, VG

$500; Joe Louis Face Ring with Promo Ad, $2,700; Joe Penner Face Puzzle Ring with Top, FN $500; Olympic Ring, (1936 Berlin) $1,190; Peter Paul Weather Ring, $200; Roger Wilco Magni-Ray Brass Ring, $75; "Ted Williams" Mechanical Ring, FN $750;

RIN-TIN-TIN

Color Litho. Button Nabisco Premium With Mailer, $75.

ROY ROGERS

"Dale Evans" Post's Raisin Bran Tin Ring, $125; "Roy Rogers Sears Corral" Sales Manual, $966; Branding Iron/Initial Brass Ring, $175; Roy Rogers Hat Ring, $600; Post's 3-D Picture Cereal Box Wrapper, $572; Post Cereal Promo Folder with Record, FN $403; Post's Puzzle Offer Cereal Box Wrapper, $308; Rodeo Program, (1944) $200; Roy Rogers Saddle Ring, $400; Roy Sign for Quaker Premium Ring, $483; Sheriff Post's Tin Ring (Roy Rogers series), $75.

SERGEANT PRESTON OF THE YUKON

Electronic Ore Detector with Box, $200; "Distance Finder" with Box, $100; "Official Seal" Litho. Button, $3,850.

The Tom Mix Spinner Ring in FN brings $3,500!

THE SHADOW

"On the Air"" Blue Coal Sign, VF $1,200; "Blue Coal" Ring, $580; "The Shadow" Glow-in-the-Dark Cello. Magic Button, VF $962; "The Shadow Club" Silvered Brass Lapel Em-blem, $350; "Blue Coal" Ring, MINT, $600; "Blue Coal" Ring (Mailer and Instructions ONLY), $1,200; Limited Edition Shadow Secret Agent Ring, MIB $125; 10K Limited Edition Shadow Secret Agent Ring, MIB $400.

SHIELD G-MAN CLUB

"Shield G-Man Club" Cello. Button (Blue Border, 1-3/4" size), $1,052.

SHIRLEY TEMPLE

1 1/4" "Theater Club" Button, $183.

SHOES MISC.

"PF Flyers" Decoder Ring, $100.

THE SKY BLAZERS

Wonder Bread Badge, FN $105.

SKY KING

Magni-Glo Writing Ring $85; Navajo Treasure Ring, $125; Tele-Blinker Ring, $150.

SPEEDY ALKA-SELTZER

"Pron-Tito" Flicker Key Fob, $144.

STAR TREK

Replica of Enterprise Cereal Prize, $250.

STRAIGHT ARROW

Two Red-Feathered Headband with Mailer with Feather, $175.

SUPER CIRCUS

"Super Circus Side Show" Punch-Out Kit, (Unpunched) $155.

SUPERMAN

Limited Edition 10K Club Ring in Tin Box, GARC $450; Airplane Ring F-87, $175; "Superman Candy & Toys" Empty Box by Novel Package Corp., $825; Superman Candy Secret Compartment Initial Brass Ring, VG

**The Captain Midnight Mystic Sun God Ring
(with instructions and mailer)
sells for $2,550 in NM!**

$5,000; Superman Contest Prize Ring, (1940) F+ $29,000; Gum Box, (1940) $7,500; Muscle Building Club Button, $232; Nestles Ring, $150; Pep Calendar, $1,200; Radio Quiz Master Premium, $220; Set of Four Letters/Christmas Adventure Promotion, (1940) $1,200; Superman-Tim Ring, VG $1,720; "Superman's Christmas Play Book" Premium Comic, (1945) FN $548; "Supermen of America" Circular Emblem, NM $10,000.

TARZAN

Ape Ring, $400; Jungle Map (Canadian Version), VF $414; "Tarzan Tablets" Store Sign, $272.

TELEVISION MISC.

Groucho Marx Doll with "DeSoto/Plymouth Service" Ad, $2,237.

TERRY AND THE PIRATES

Premium Libby Comic Book, FN $1,296.

THREE LITTLE PIGS

Ring, MIB $300.

TOM MIX

Spinner Ring ,– FN $3,500; Revival Wristwatch

(50th Anniversary, Ralston), (1982-83) $252; Boxed Compass Gun, $400; Circus Felt Pennant, (1937) $603; "Good Luck" Silver Charm, $418; Look Around Ring, $175; "Captain" Silvered Brass Spur Badge, $350; "Ranch Boss" Brass Rank Badge, $500; "Ranch Boss" Commission Certificate, $300; Ribbon Pin, $200; Magic-Light Tiger-Eye Ring (with Instructions), MIB $350; Toy TV Set (with 2 Disks, Box and Instructions), $200; Siren Ring, $150; "Wrangler" Brass Badge, VF $160.

UNDERDOG
Yellow Plastic Vending Ring, $304.

THE WIZARD OF OZ
Bolger 1-1/4" Button, $317; Swift's Peanut Butter Mobile (Cut), $1,079.

WONDER WOMAN
"Sensation Comics" Litho. Button, F+ $2,850.

THE YELLOW KID
Tin Sand Pail, $1,800; "Sunday World Newspaper" Poster with Outcault Art, $777. ❖

TOP VALUED ITEMS

TOP TWENTY SUPER RARE CHARACTER ITEMS

Item	Item ID	Year	Price
1) **Howdy Doody** Photo Doody Ad Doll	HOW-1	1940s	$113,431
2) **Superman** Leader Patch	SUP-8	1940	$15,000
3) **Superman** Action Comics Patch	SUP-7	1940	$10,000
4) **Captain Marvel** Syroco Statuette	CMR-44	1943	$8,100
5) **Captain Marvel** Kerr Co. Statuette	CMR-45	1946	$8,100
6) **Superman** Bowman Bubble Gum Box	SUP-23	1940	$7,500
7) **Buck Rogers** Solar Scouts Sweater Patch	BRG-70	1946	$5,500
8) **Sky King** Secret Compartment Belt Buckle	SKY-3	1948	$5,500
9) **Superman** Rectangular Patch	SUP-17	1940	$5,500
10) **Superman** Enameled Brass Shield	SUP-76	1949	$5,000
11) **Tom Mix** Bisque 5" Figurine	TMX-26	1933	$5,000
12) **Jack Armstrong** Crocodile Glow in the Dark Whistle	JAC-50	1940	$4,500
13) **Tom Mix** Ranch Boss Badge Prototype	TMX-86	1937	$4,000
14) **Tom Mix** Ralston Straight Shooters Badge Prototype	TMX-87	1937	$4,000
15) **Doc Savage** Bronze Medallion	DOC-10	1930S	$3,500
16) **Don Winslow** Golden Torpedo Decoder	DON-20	1942	$3,500
17) **Alley Oop** Statuette with Hunting Club	COM-43	1946	$3,050
18) **Tarzan** "Drink More Milk" Bracelet	TRZ-22	1934	$3,000
19) **Junior Justice Society** Brass Badge	JUN-1	1942	$2,500
20) **Batman** Batplane Movie Promo	BAT-2	1943	$2,000

TOP TEN MOST VALUABLE STANDEES/SERIAL POSTERS

Item	Item ID	Year	Price
1) **Superman** Fleischer Cartoon Standee	SUP-34	1941	$27,000
2) **New Adventures of Batman & Robin** Three-sheet	BAT-5	1949	$8,000
3) **Adventures of Captain Marvel** Six-sheet	CMR-2	1941	$7,500
4) **Atom Man Vs. Superman** 6' Standee	SUP-97	1950	$7,500
5) **Captain America** Three-sheet	CAP-8	1944	$6,000
6) **Adventures of Captain Marvel** One-sheet	CMR-3	1941	$6,000
7) **Captain Midnight** Three-sheet	CMD-75	1940s	$6,000
8) **Phantom** Three-sheet	PHN-8	1940s	$6,000
9) **Spy Smasher** Three-sheet	SPY-5	1942	$6,000
10) **"The Day The Earth Stood Still"** 5' Standee	MOV-44	1951	$5,500

TOP TEN MOST VALUABLE ADVERTISING SIGNS

Item	Item ID	Year	Price
1) **Superman** War Savings Bond Poster	SUP-82	1940s	$10,000
2) **Kellogg's Pep** for Pep Buttons	KEL-43	1945	$5,000
3) **Captain Marvel** Statuettes Store Sign	CMR-61	1946	$4,200
4) **Yellow Kid** Announcement Poster for the N.Y. Journal	YLW-1	1896	$3,500
5) **Captain Midnight** Skelly Oil	CMD-2	1939	$3,000
6) **Lone Ranger** Kix Contest	LON-120	1941	$3,000
7) **Buck Rogers** Sylvania Sign	BRG-135	1952	$2,300
8) **Hopalong Cassidy** "Buzza Cardozo" Greeting Cards	HOP-48	1950	$1,800
9) **Donald Duck** Sylvania Radio Bulbs	DNL-31	1940s	$1,600
10) **Tom Mix** Ralston	TMX-109	1930s	$1,600

TOP TEN MOST VALUABLE PAPER ITEMS

Item	Item ID	Year	Price
1) **Buck Rogers** Cut-Out Book and Stage	BRG-17	1933	$5,000
2) **Red Ryder** Victory Patrol Membership Kit	RYD-7	1943	$3,600
3) **Red Ryder** Victory Patrol Comic Book Kit	RYD-11	1944	$3,200
4) **Lone Ranger** with Guns Cereal Standee	LON-220	1957	$3,100
5) **Mickey Mouse** Post Toasties Box	MCK-25	1934	$2,550
6) **Superman** Cut-Out Book	SUP-13	1940	$2,500
7) **Lone Ranger** Frontier Town	LON-170	1948	$2,400
8) **Captain America** Membership Club Kit	CAP-4,5,6	1941	$2,250
9) **Mickey Mouse** Post Toasties Box	MCK-26	1935	$2,100
10) **Batman** Paper Mask	BAT-1	1943	$2,000

TOP TEN MOST VALUABLE PREMIUM COMICS

Item	Item ID	Year	Price
1) Century of Comics (100 pages)	COM-14	1933	$17,500
2) Funnies on Parade	COM-13	1933	$11,000
3) Lone Ranger Ice Cream	LON-80	1939	$4,000
4) Superman's Christmas Adventure	SUP-15	1940	$4,000
5) Buster Brown Blue Ribbon Book of Jokes	BWN-3	1904	$3,400
6) Tom Mix Comics #1 (Ralston)	TMX-127	1940	$2,700
7) Joe Penner (Cocomalt)	JOP-3	1938	$1,700
8) Merry Christmas for Mickey Mouse	MCK-48	1939	$1,600
9) Terry and the Pirates Ruby Of Genghis Khan	TER-5	1941	$1,500
10) Captain Marvel and the Lieutenants of Safety	CMR-111	1950	$850

TOP TEN MOST VALUABLE PIN-BACK BUTTONS

Item	Item ID	Year	Price
1) Sergeant Preston of the Yukon red/black on yellow	SGT-9	1949	$5,000
2) U. S. Jones Cadets Comic Book Club	USJ-4	1941	$4,500
3) Wonder Woman Sensation Comics	WON-1	1942	$3,500
4) The Flash Flash Comics	FLA-1	1942	$3,200
5) Chief Mickey Mouse	MCK-1	1928	$2,500
6) The Scarecrow of Oz for Baum book	WIZ-5	1915	$2,500
7) Buck Rogers 25th Century Acousticon Dictagraph	BRG-80	1936	$2,000
8) Sincerely Yours, Mickey Mouse 3-1/2"	MCK-21	1933	$2,000
9) Sergeant Preston of the Yukon full-color	SGT-44	1956	$2,000
10) Captain Battle Boys' Brigade Silver Streak Comics	CBT-1	1941	$1,750

TOP TEN MOST VALUABLE RINGS

Item	Item ID	Year	Price
1) Superman Prize	SUP-5	1940	$100,000
2) Superman Secret Compartment (Gum)	SUP-28	1940	$50,000
3) Operator 5	OPR-1	1934	$22,500
4) Superman Secret Compartment (Candy)	SUP-27	1940	$22,000
5) Little Orphan Annie Altascope	LAN-127	1942	$21,250
6) Sky King Kaleidoscope	SKY-15	1940s	$11,000
7) Cisco Kid Secret Compartment	CIS-12	1950	$9,200
8) Spider	SPD-2	1939	$9,200
9) Superman/Tim	SUP-86	1949	$9,000
10) Valric of the Vikings Magnifying	RGS-11	1940s	$7,500

FAK FORGER & KNOCK

A Unique Opportunity to M

The good news is the professionals still aren't fooled. Despite the challenges posed by today's knock-off artists and their technology, seasoned dealers and collectors alike can still easily spot a fake.

The bad news is we're not taking full advantage of the re-

sources at our disposal. We've got the means to deal with our criminal element, but we've got to exercise the *will* to do so.

If you're knowledgeable and can spot a phony a mile away, you might think this doesn't concern you. If you think that way, you're wrong.

How would you feel if you knew someone was deliberately lowering the value of your collection? What would you think if you found out someone was stealing from you? Who would you talk to if you saw someone ripping off a fellow collector?

Each of these questions is much more than a "what if...?" scenario. Every day, some unsuspecting collector is duped into purchasing an item that isn't what it pretends to be, and for too long many other collectors have simply looked the other way.

Forgery is one of the--if not the--biggest problems faced by collectors today, but it's not only collectors who are cast under the

by
J. C. Vaughn

...ke a Difference

shadowy specter of doubt. It's everywhere in modern society. Compact discs, famous paintings, stocks, bonds and hard currency have been the targets of high-tech mimicry.

Much of this stems from the rapid growth in graphics technology. Color reproduction is an arena where "state-of-the-art" is yesterday's news. There are now continual upgrades in computer software and hardware, and these advancements are creating a progression of opportunities for those who would rather steal than create.

Despite the best efforts of insurance companies, we've all heard the stories of paintings which have turned out to be fakes. Wall Street has tried to keep it hushed, but stocks and bonds have been illegally reproduced like never before. On the macroeconomic level, Federal authorities have uncovered attempts by other nations to erode our currency with massive counterfeiting operations (hence the new $100.00 bill).

If a country is willing to potentially take on the entire United States, it should be no surprise then that some jerk from Podunk is willing to scam us or our fellow collectors.

This is a problem, potentially a serious one, but it is a problem we can deal with.

In fact, we already have the means to

stop this sort of thing. There is a relationship between publishers, producers and fans unlike any other area of society. The many magazines, newspapers, other publications and conventions which thrive in our fields are fueled by the desires of collectors...and more importantly, by regular interaction with them.

There isn't a comic book show, antique show, or toy show that goes on in any portion of the country where there isn't an expert nearby who would be willing to donate his or her time to stopping the spread unauthorized replicas. This is a challenge across the industry, and it should cut straight across the boundaries of rival publishers, dealers and collectors.

Imagine it this way: a young collector, someone new to the hobby but really excited about it, plunks down $30.00 for **Cerebus** #1. He may be new, but he's seen the book in **Comics Buyer's Guide** or **The Overstreet Comic Book Price Guide** for much more than that and he knows a good buy when sees one.

When the young collector finds out later from a veteran collector that it's an imitation, he is only out $30.00, but the hobby loses at least a degree of his enthusiasm. The next time he sees a great deal, even a perfectly legitimate one, he will hesitate.

Perhaps he will pass it up entirely. And then an honest dealer will lose out on that collector's money. Not only does the young collector get swindled, but so does the next dealer he deals with. So does that dealer's family. So, in turn, do the businesses where they spend their money.

Further, the copyright owners get ripped off because they are not paid their royalties. The employees of the copyright owners lose because their company missed out on money it was due. Their families miss out on money the wage earner would have brought home. The retailers who their families patronize lose out, too.

Don't fall into the trap of imagining some faceless corporation. These are real people who are being affected.

Perhaps it's time for a uniform standard, a code of ethics or some similar statement which publishers and dealers alike can propose together and sign. The first step, though, is don't panic. We *can* deal with this.

Deal with collectors and dealers who have earned your trust. Look for unconditional guarantees of authenticity. Find out what a potential trading partner's reputation is *from more than one source*, and support the folks you know stick to the high road.

Editor's note: Copyright infringement is a second degree felony and many (if not most) copyright holders have legal representatives who are actively seeking out those who abuse their property through unauthorized duplication. Those legal representatives are generally very happy to work with anyone who reports such abuse. For those who undertake the reproduction of an item, it's definitely wise to play it "better safe than sorry" and thoroughly investigate the ownership of the character in question. ❖

*J.C. Vaughn is marketing coordinator for Gemstone Publishing. His column, **Vaughn On Comics**, appears in the **Overstreet's FAN Universe** section of the Gemstone website at **www.gemstonepub.com/fan/jcv** every week. He is the author of many articles, short stories, and screenplays. He is also a regular pitching writer for UPN's **Star Trek: Voyager**.*

the Master of MARKETING

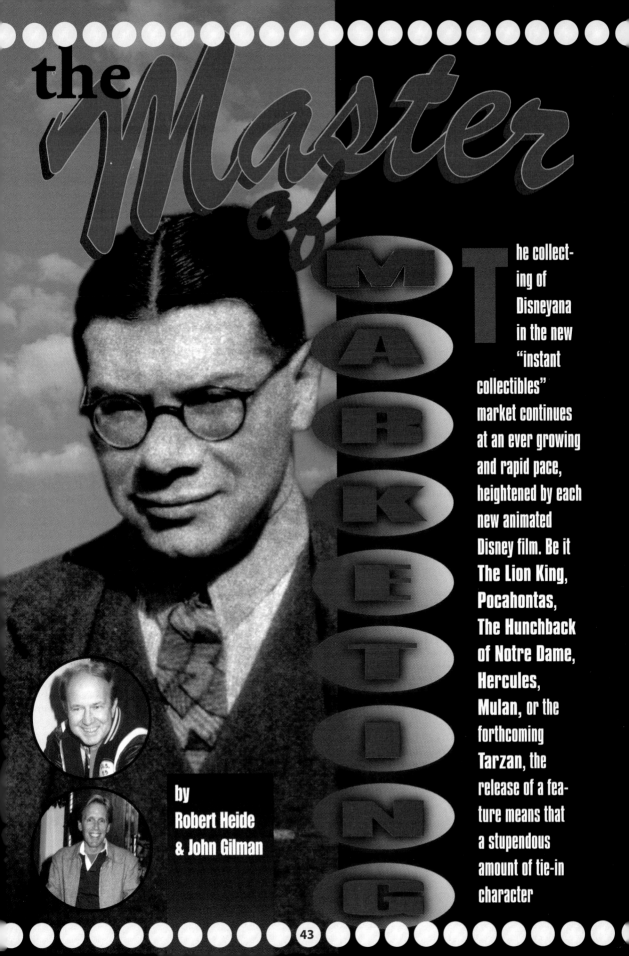

by
Robert Heide
& John Gilman

The collecting of Disneyana in the new "instant collectibles" market continues at an ever growing and rapid pace, heightened by each new animated Disney film. Be it **The Lion King, Pocahontas, The Hunchback of Notre Dame, Hercules, Mulan,** or the forthcoming **Tarzan,** the release of a feature means that a stupendous amount of tie-in character

Kay Kamen poses with *Our Gang* in 1931.

thing concerning the art of animated film during the vintage years, the man behind the proliferation of Disney merchandise during that era, from 1933 to 1949, was primarily a salesman named Herman "Kay" Kamen. In 1932, Kamen was personally selected by Walt Disney to become the sole and exclusive representative of the character merchandising division of Walt Disney Enterprises. Walt Disney and his brother Roy had heard of this super-salesman via Kamen's national reputation. Kamen had a remarkable ability to aggressively promote and sell retail dry goods, including children's toys, games, and roller skates, as well as necessities. To market products, Kamen used all of the sales techniques available at the time, including print media and radio.

EARNING HIS REPUTATION

Kay Kamen, as he was best known, was born Herman Samuel Kamen in Baltimore, Maryland on January 27, 1892. Kamen's first advertising accounts in the '20s were manufacturers of products featuring characters from Hal Roach's **Our Gang**. Farina, Buckwheat, Pete the Pit Bull, and the rest of the Gang could be seen on playroom furniture sets, on dishware, as toys, in storybooks, in **Big Little Books**, and on back-to-school pencil boxes. Products even included Spanky Candy and **Our Gang** Chewing Gum.

merchandise from dozens of manufacturers are shipped to stores everywhere. Consumers buy and use home products, such as **Lion King** Band-Aids, crayon sets or toothpaste. Collectors purchase these same objects as "future investibles," or simply for the sheer fun and enjoyment of collecting. Limited-edition artwork, such as prepared animation cels, appeal to more sophisticated collectors who prefer authenticated items over mass-produced products. In the world of Disneyana, however, it is still those standard Golden Age Mickey, Minnie, Pluto, Horace, Clarabelle and Goofy items that are of most interest to the advanced collector.

Although Walter Elias Disney was at the helm of every-

Originally based in Omaha and later in Kansas City, Kamen's advertising and public relations/promotions company, in partnership with Streeter Blair, went on to develop a huge overall sales campaign for retail stores nationwide. The partners' venture, called "The Boys Outfitter," used an extremely effective sales technique involving both the retailer and the consumer. In a national campaign, a comic character named Tim, who represented the all-American boy, and his sidekick dog, Pup, helped sell knickers, suspenders, caps, sweaters, shirts, socks, jackets, shoes and other haberdashery items.

During the promo-

If your radio sounds like Uncle Donald... IT'S TIME TO GET NEW TUBES !

DO IT TODAY FOR GOOD LISTENING TOMORROW!

SYLVANIA *Set Tested* **RADIO TUBES**

Top, early pinback premium, 1938. Bottom, 1940s die-cut sign.

tion, kids could sign up and get an **Official Tim's Handbook**, which included secret codes and moral pointers for "good boys and pie-eaters," with instructions on how boys could establish pie-eaters clubs in their own neighborhoods. The clubs also involved Mom, who baked the pies and also went shopping with her son for his fall, winter, spring and summer outfits—after receiving reminders in the mail from "The Boys Outfitter." All of this activity was developed and masterminded by Kay Kamen, who never let a sales opportunity pass him by.

A BIG BEGINNING AT DISNEY

The "Tim" campaign ceased when Kamen was exclusively contracted with Walt Disney Enterprises. Disney and Kamen drew up an unusual contract in 1933, in what was regarded as the worst year of the Great Depression. The deal provided that, up to the first $100,000 in profit, 60 percent went to Disney, with Kamen receiving 40 percent. After the initial $100,000, the split was 50/50.

One of the first things Kamen executed after signing the original contract was to cancel the

Tim, as shown on this enameled and silvered brass badge, was reincarnated as Superman's pal in the 1940s.

George Borgfeldt Corporation's exclusive licensing agreement to produce and distribute Disney character merchandise. He also replaced Disney's British licensing representative, William Banks Levy, with his nephew George Kamen, who headed the British and foreign offices of Kay Kamen Ltd. Both Levy and Borgfeldt Corporation continued to produce selectively as Disney licensees. Kay Kamen Ltd. forged ahead with new, higher standards of artwork and design applied to Disney licensed products.

Kamen's modest headquarters in New York, at 729 Seventh Avenue, was soon exchanged for posh Art-Deco style office suites at 1270 Sixth Avenue in Rockefeller Center. In Chicago, Kamen was at 1171 Merchandise Mart, while the West Coast offices were in the Disney Studios, at 2719 Hyperion Boulevard in Hollywood. The Kamen organization included network sales offices to assist licensed manufacturers and distributors. The company also had a special department for retail store exploitation and a production department to handle art, advertising, packaging and promotion. The arms of the

Poolside (left to right): Walt Disney, banker Gunther Lessing, Kay Kamen, and Roy Disney. Hollywood 1933.

Walt Disney and Kay Kamen.

Kamen-Disney partnership soon extended to Paris, Milan, Lisbon, Toronto, and as far away as Australia and South America.

The financial arrangement struck between Disney and Kamen (cohorts called them the "Dime-Store Kids") turned Kamen into a millionaire and allowed him a private rail car for cross-country business forays. For Disney, licensing profits soon exceeded the income from the **Silly Symphony** and **Mickey Mouse** cartoons. Walt Disney's share of the profits were fed back into the making of animated shorts, which became more artful, winning Disney and Mickey further accolades and fans throughout the world.

Top and bottom, early promo bread signs. Center, "Wanna Fight" cello. button features an image of a long-billed Donald, 1930s.

SELLING MICKEY AND HIS PALS

All the practical sales experience Kamen acquired with "Tim" and Our Gang paid off when he turned to selling Mickey Mouse and his original barnyard pals—Minnie, Pluto, Horace, Clarabelle and Goofy. Kamen, labeled "The King of Character Merchandise" by the toy industry, fiercely promoted the Mickey Mouse image in 1933 through 1934.

Specific sales campaigns he then developed centered on Donald Duck, the Big Bad Wolf and the Three Little Pigs, all of whom competed with Mickey for cartoon stardom during the Depression. In the late '30s, vast character merchandise campaigns were also initiated in advance of the release of **Snow White and the Seven Dwarfs** to sell products featuring Snow White, Doc, Bashful,

Sneezy, Happy, Sleepy, Grumpy and Dopey. The **Silly Symphony** characters favored by merchandisers and seen on various products of this era included Elmer the Elephant, Ferdinand the Bull, Funny Little Bunnies, Toby Tortoise and more. In the 1940s, Disney merchandise featured Pinocchio, the **Fantasia** parade of characters, Dumbo, Bambi, Bongo, Jose Carioca, Panchito the Bantam Chicken and Brer Rabbit.

Kamen produced his first catalog of Disney merchandise in 1934. Seven other catalogs were issued in 1935, 1936-37, 1938-39, 1940-41, 1947-48 and 1949-50. When

Top, Globe Trotters door hanger, 1930s. Center, U.S. Treasury War Bond Certificate, 1944. Bottom: Post Toasties cereal box from 1934.

Walt Disney signs an exclusive contract with Kay Kamen.

copies of these can be found, they are valuable source books for Disneyana collectors. In fact, scholars and collectors of Disney merchandise from the 1930s and '40s have copied some of these catalogs to use in their research.

FAMOUS KAMEN DEALS

One of the most lucrative deals Kamen made was with the Ingersoll-Waterbury Clock Company of Waterbury, Connecticut. This company was the first to put Mickey Mouse on a watch and clocks, which were introduced and featured at the Chicago "Century of Progress" 1933 World's Fair. These watches and clocks are among the most sought-after Disney collectibles.

Another major contract with the toy train manufacturer, Lionel Corporation of Irvington, New Jersey, produced the famous Mickey

Mouse wind-up handcar. It sold for $1 during the Christmas selling season in 1934. Both the Ingersoll and Lionel companies were saved from bankruptcy in the Depression by these Disney products.

Advertising Age, the trade magazine for the ad business, heralded Kamen's bread and dairy product promotional campaigns for reviving the toy industry. Mickey Mouse was the first to sell loaves of various packaged breads. He was soon followed by characters from the feature films **Snow White and the Seven Dwarfs** and **Pinocchio**, and by Donald Duck, who would also sell Florida orange and grapefruit juices.

THE WAR YEARS

Patriotism on the home front during World War II meant the consumer industry had to yield to "win-the-war" munitions production. Kamen, however, always kept busy with those licensees who had something they could produce and sell in a wartime economy. He also helped to develop and promote the use of Disney character insignias for various branches of the armed services and as airplane nose art.

In addition to Mickey Mouse, Donald Duck, **Fantasia** characters and other standards from the Disney menagerie—including many new characters never before seen—marched in to find a place in the war effort. These included insects (the Seabees), dogs and other variations of Disney comic images. Like Disney, Kamen also kept a sharp focus on the south-of-the-border "good neighbor policy" during the war.

THE KAMEN ERA ENDS IN TRAGEDY

Unfortunately, the last great merchandise campaign Kamen instituted was for **Cinderella**, released in 1950. Ruth Ivener, vice-president of Kay Kamen Ltd., received Kamen's last letter in the New York office. Postmarked October 26, 1949, and mailed

from Paris, it contained a flurry of business details and jokes about Kamen's fear of flying, but the tone was upbeat, and generally, Kamen was looking forward to the future. Tragically, at age 56, Kay Kamen and his beloved wife, Katie, died in an Air-France crash over the Azores.

The fabulous Kay Kamen era (1933-49) in Disney merchandising could easily be described as one of the great success stories of the century. Most of the early merchandise currently collected as Disneyana is directly linked to the genius of Kay Kamen's vision, and of course, that of Walt Disney. Today, the Disney name is known around the world; the name of Kay Kamen should also be remembered because of his contribution to the world of Disneyana. The Kamen-Disney liaison was the very stuff of dreams. ❖

*Robert Heide and John Gilman are the authors of 12 books on American popular culture including: **The Mickey Mouse Watch** and **Disneyana** (both from Hyperion Books); **Home Front America: Popular Culture of the World War II Era** (Chronicle); **Box-Office Buckaroos** and **Popular Art Deco** (Abbeville Press); **Cartoon Collectibles** and **Starstruck** (Double-day); and **Dime-Store Dream Parade**.*

Heide is also a playwright who wrote film scenarios for Andy Warhol.

*The co-authors both live in New York City; their guidebooks **Greenwich Village** and **O' New Jersey** are available from St. Martin's Press, New York.*

Top, Miller's Mickey Mouse Magazine, #1, 1933. Bottom, War Bond poster, 1944. At Right, a Mickey Mouse volume authored by Robert Heide and John Gilman.

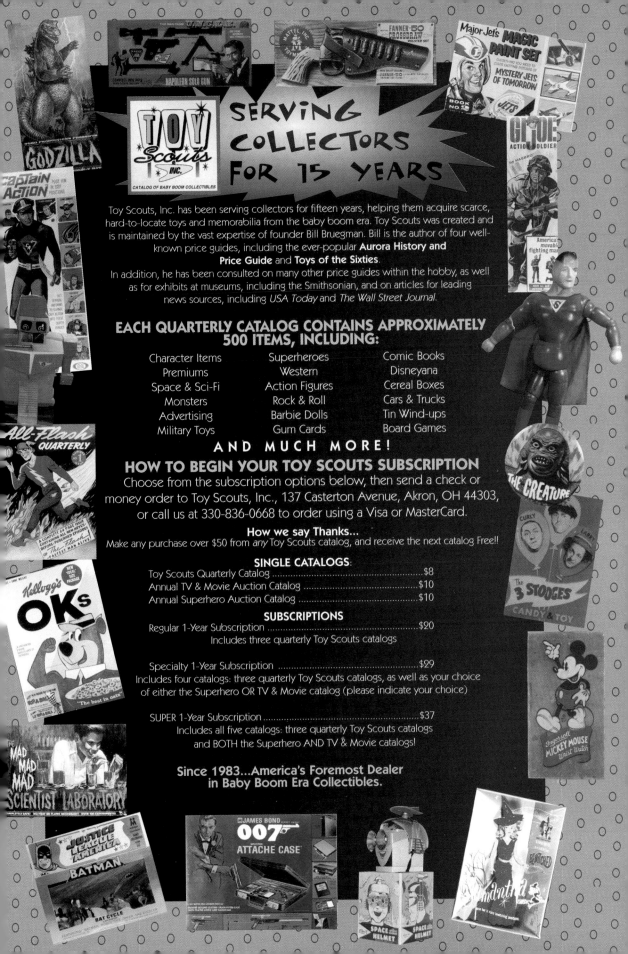

by
Arnold T.
Blumberg

A Colle

If
you've
read this
far into the book,
you're probably a collector,
but have you ever wondered why
that is? Are collectors born or bred? And are we just
pursuing a leisure-time hobby, or are we doing
something much more, acting as pre-
servers of the past,
as caretakers of other eras?
Let's look for some answers together...

Convention
photos by Donald
Andrew Hershberger, Jr.
All other images are
©1998 their respective
copyright holders.

PART ONE: THE POWER OF NOSTALGIA

It's a daunting task to take on such a grand theme, but we should ask the question: What makes us collectors, and what is it that draws us all to a book like **Hake's Price Guide?** Very often in our industry, business concerns overshadow the real reasons why we're all here. There are always investors and speculators in the collectible market, sometimes doing more harm than good, and it's easy to lose focus and get caught up in the financial maelstrom. But when the storm has passed, the true collectors remain, searching and accumulating as the hobby goes on. So what is it that differentiates us from the others? What makes us true collectors?

The answer is deceptively simple. While the process of collecting is often intellectually stimulating, the real motivation lies in the heart. It is pure emotion that drives collectors; we all seek fulfillment in collecting, whether it's comic books or toys or even original art. We're searching for things that make us feel whole, and very often they're the things we left behind as we grew older.

The power of nostalgia draws us back to artifacts from our childhood, and we have to possess

them and file them away, capturing those moments in time so that no one will ever forget them. It's our most practical bid for immortality—a chance not only to reclaim youth or an innocence lost, but to insure a seamless continuity from one generation to the next...assuming of course that our children will embrace our past as willingly as they build their own.

Nostalgia, however, is powerful enough to insure that. Collecting represents the desire to recapture the past, and that often includes a past we never actually experienced. A true collector is capable of appreciating and even loving the artifacts of an era beyond their actual lifetime as if they were a part of them. A child of the 1970s and '80s like myself may be drawn to collect memorabilia from the '60s or even the '30s—Star Trek collectibles, Marx Brothers memorabilia—and feel the same way as he would twenty years later, when the remnants of his own childhood beckon him to dealers' tables at some future convention.

1935 sheet music from the Marx Brothers' Night at the Opera.

The Star Trek V Communicator from Proctor and Gamble.

Collecting isn't about age, or even the actual time in which you grew up. Collecting is about a feeling, a passion for the icons of the past—a driving force that requires all collectors to gather the relics of other eras so that their uniqueness and meaning will never be lost even when the people who made and enjoyed them are long gone. At its best, nostalgia not only keeps us connected to our own past, but weaves us into history, bridging the gap between generations and uniting all collectors in a single purpose.

What that purpose may be, and the responsibility it entails, will be dealt with later.

PART TWO:
THE TOYMAKERS

Other factors are crucial in determining why we choose to collect the things we do. All collectors are compulsive, and mated with the desire to accumulate is the desire to know—the need to learn about the things we love. The hunger for knowledge is part of the quest; we are only now beginning to appreciate the big picture, and all the people and events that shaped a century of comic character memorabilia. We are all intrigued by what drives us, and that story is starting to unfold in books like this one. We eagerly seek out that world and willingly immerse ourselves in it, sometimes to the detriment of our concentration on other matters. To people who are not collectors, this obsession may seem a bit odd, but it is that willingness to be a part of something fanciful that also defines us.

The web-slinger's credo can teach collectors something abut responsibility.

Possibly the most potent power a collector possesses is the ability to retain a youthful attitude; the same power also drives the toymakers who create the collectibles in the first place. Comic characters and entertainment personalities can't become collectible icons without a carefully planned marketing strategy that directs the development of these characters, making them available in a wide range of media and shaping them into a success (See John K. Snyder's "The Principles of Pricing" on page 109 for a specific example of this process—the development of the Superman collectible market). There are just as many who are lost to the mists of time due to a failure of proper promotion, but these too are collectible and sought-after for their obscurity and historical value; in the mind of a collector, there is a reason for anything to be worth holding onto.

We basically gravitate to one kind of collectible or another due to shrewd planning as much as the whim of our heart. These collectibles were, after all, designed by adults, particularly in the early days of the hobby—the newspaper and radio era of the 1920s and '30s—and they were deliberately created to entice adults, drawing them and their children into various promotions. These designers were not only creating the collectibles, but the need and desire for them, and children were quick to respond when exposed to the message through common consumer goods like bread and milk, especially when those were part of that "nutritious meal" endorsed by their parents. Brand loyalty was filtered down to the next generation thanks to the efforts of Superman, the Lone Ranger, Mickey Mouse, and hundreds of others, who extolled the virtues of eating and drinking the right kinds of foods. Interestingly, such a product endorsement is seen today by some as a "sell-out"—the very characters and personalities created to sell products inspired such emotional devotion that the adults who grew up with them cringe to see them reduced to simple hawksmen. Even the familiar strains of a Beatles song in a Nike commercial provokes more acrimony than brand loyalty.

Nevertheless, back then kids enjoyed simply wearing a ring ornamented by their favorite character, or playing with a toy ray-gun from some

Any kid could be the "Boss" of the house with this Tom Mix badge.

galactic radio adventure. A child might even feel more confident and superior when wearing, say, a Tom Mix "Ranch Boss" badge, and that too was a well-planned psychological tactic on the part of the designers. Children were cultivated as future consumers, but as a by-product of this process, the comic character market was invented and nurtured, helped along by the men and women who mapped out its path, and by the children who embraced it and took it to their hearts.

By extension, this century of invention and creativity has actually created the modern collector as well. Take a look at the past hundred years, and the attitudes of the adult generations that have lived in each successive decade. As the years go by, and the comic character market builds and becomes an intrinsic part of American pop-culture, the adults of this country slowly change, becoming more prone to nostalgia and sentiment, and more likely to retain their youth well into the later years of their life. By the time we reach the Baby Boom generation, which is only now facing the turmoil of middle age, we see for the first time a segment of the population that, while mature, has remained young in spirit and unwilling to relinquish their hold on the past.

This phenomenon has affected the next generation as well. As mentioned earlier, collectors of today have the ability to react passionately to artifacts from eras they did not experience first-hand. "Generation X," the twenty-somethings of the 1990s (of which I am a member), were more often than not raised by parents who cherished their childhood and treasured their youthful outlook. As a result, we have been infused with a built-in nostalgia for their past as well as ours. Naturally, this influences our choice of collectibles as well, and explains why we are all drawn to the same characters and categories. New collectors are as likely to seek out items from many decades past, and this draws the world of collecting closer together.

PART THREE: THE VALUE OF HISTORY

There is at least one issue that often polarizes collectors and threatens this burgeoning unity—why make a price guide? For many, price guides are detrimental to the health of the hobby, unnecessarily naming values and setting standards for collectibles with no chance for whole-hearted agreement on everyone's part. To some, they are mildly interesting, and to others they are blatantly manipulative. Still others regard price guides as useful, even essential tools, providing the hobby with a concrete system for evaluating condition and determining values for items they regularly buy and sell. Even young children who eagerly collect comic books like to look up a favorite in a price guide and see how much their issues are worth.

So although some like price guides and some hate them, why do we bother, particularly with one as huge and complicated as **Hake's Price Guide**? There's a simple answer to that too. If this volume you hold in your hands were merely a price guide—a checklist of existing collectibles and how much they are currently worth—it would be useful and informative, but only to the few people actively involved in buying and selling collectibles. Frankly, anyone who collects can find a practical use for a price guide, as it represents the ultimate "want list" for whatever category they collect (and with **Hake's Price Guide**, we hope one day to have an exhaustive list of all existing collectibles in these categories).

This book and others like it, however, is much more than that. It is a reference for the future—a permanent record documenting a century of imagination and ingenuity. The series of events and achievements that created the fantasy world and entertainment culture we cherish are part of a history that up until now has been given far less significance than it deserves. Thousands of creative individuals dreamed of realities beyond our own and brought them home to us in exciting forms, enthralling us with wonders and adventures we

The Man of Steel was one of the first characters shaped by marketing into a latter-day legend.

would never otherwise experience. As an ongoing project to provide leisure activities and entertainment for the human mind, all of these accomplishments should be properly recognized, and books like these are at the vanguard of that effort.

Seen in this light, the pricing data reflected in this book is almost incidental. After all, whether you agree with a price or not, that number has only been attributed to an item because of our desire for that collectible in the first place; *we* determine value. And let's face it, for those of us driven to reassemble our childhood, having reference material on what we should be hunting for is essential. There is also an undeniable potency in picking up a book, thumbing through its pages, and finding things you once owned— "Hey, I had that!"—a sort of instant nostalgic gratification. Ultimately, however, compiling a reference work on the scale of this guide is not really about the money; it's about the collectibles and what they mean to us. We already hold them in our hearts and minds, and to see them recorded in this book demonstrates that we haven't let them fade into obscurity. To hold a reference guide that catalogs all the collectibles we know and love from our youth is a powerful feeling—an affirmation of *our* worth and importance as much as that of the items listed. *That's* where the value is.

Collectors mingle in the nostalgic atmosphere of a collectible convention, one of hundreds held across the country every year.

PART FOUR: THE NEW CARETAKERS

So where do we go from here? Well, Spider-Man's credo has always been "with great power comes great responsibility," and if collectors hold the power to shape and direct the future of the hobby in their hands, then the power we wield collectively must be treated responsibly as well. This is about much more than acquiring material possessions, investing in lucrative collectibles, or even the power of nostalgia itself—

it's about the whole history of pop culture, and preserving the past for the benefit of the future.

Picture a typical collectors' convention, where an elderly woman is rocking in a chair and keeping an eye out for prospective customers. She has a table filled with rare, intricately designed toys. They represent exquisite workmanship; clearly crafted to look beautiful and last, they were also made to delight children and adults long after the designers were gone. Now they are all in the possession of this old woman, and she has been their caretaker, preserving the work of the toymakers whose names have long since receded into memory. She may be the only person left alive who even knows that such toys exist, and now she is ready to pass them on, even though they might be scattered and sold into the hands of several different collectors, never to be complete again. Maybe she needs the money, or maybe her apartment complex has added a "no exquisite toys" clause to her rental agreement, but that doesn't matter; her time as caretaker is ending.

Now a man several decades younger than the old woman happens by the table and is instantly struck by the style and quality of the toys. He feels a connection to them and to the old woman as well, and he knows that he has to buy all of them and keep the set complete. This compulsion is not merely a desire to acquire, but a need to know and understand the story behind the collectibles. In the end, the old woman leaves the convention with some money and an empty table, and the man has carried away a prize of considerable worth. He not only bought something that makes him happy, but he felt a bond with a kindred spirit, and silently accepted the responsibility of carrying on where the old woman left off. He is now the protector of those fragile moments in history—the new caretaker. He not only carries away items with great collectible value, but he becomes the steward of their story, and if he doesn't know it himself, he might turn to a book like this one to find out.

We are all caretakers with a responsibility to preserve the past we love. But this task never ends, and there is still a great deal to do. Imagine how much easier it would have been if a book like **Hake's Price Guide** were published decades ago, as the items in question were being made and distributed. Instead of guessing at some things and grasping at crumbling papers for others, we would have first-hand knowledge of the people, places, and things we so cherish today. We would have reference works that provide a clear guide for what exists and what remains to be collected, and that would be of incalculable value to enthusiastic collectors, much more so than knowing how much money they're worth.

Nostalgia is a powerful current, not only washing over us and enveloping us in its power but moving us along in time as well. By the year 2000, the waves of nostalgia will have continued to wash forward, and the 1980s will be the decade of choice, the "hot" era for those of us who regularly mine the past. It is inevitable that the tide will always turn again, and as responsible historians, we too must move with the times and record what has been to have a clearer understanding of what will be (it's a responsibility we take seriously here; as you will note, this year's edition boasts a number of category additions like Doctor Who, Kiss, and The Simpsons, to demonstrate that we are moving forward as well as looking back). Preserving the past is vital, but the diligent historian also records events as they occur, before they too recede into the mists of time and are difficult to accurately recover. If we are so concerned with preserving the past, then the time for recognizing the importance and value of the last twenty or thirty years of collectibles is now.

The care and respect we must give to the whole history of this hobby extends to collectors themselves. This serves as a call to arms—a declaration of our desire to protect and preserve the history of our hobby, past, present, and future—but that can't be accomplished without cooperation from all collectors. As we have already discussed, there is an unfortunate tendency in this hobby to polarize in opinion and attitude, and nowhere more strongly and less reasonably than on the issue of age. Collectors of past generations must realize that a clear understanding of the terminology, characters, and world they know cannot be achieved by the new collectors without time. The desire is already there in the heart of every collector, but it must be properly cultivated. The old must respect and welcome the new, teaching them the value of the history they're taking on and encouraging them to delve farther into the past before it vanishes forever.

The young collectors of tomorrow will eventually learn how important it is to cherish the past, but they must also be able to enjoy the present and their own interests, and that in turn is something the previous generation must learn and accept. The collectibles of new collectors have as much validity as those of previous generations, and after all, we are all part of the same noble effort. Although some might characterize ours as a disposable "junk" society, we should know better. Collectors are the only people who can appreciate and preserve American cultural heritage through toys and collectibles. We are *all* caretakers, and as the self-appointed guardians of a world of imagination that too few people see in its entirety, we would be foolish not to acknowledge that *every* era has a value, and one not always quantifiable in dollars and cents. It's a value that can't be estimated with calculators and market reports...but only with the human heart. ❖

A metal lunchbox recalls peanut butter sandwiches and favorite TV shows, one of hundreds of items sold at "cons."

*Arnold T. Blumberg is Managing Editor of Gemstone Publishing. He writes two columns for the Gemstone website at www.gemstonepub.com/fan; **Ground Control**, covering science fiction entertainment news; and **Waxing Nostalgic**, on collecting in general. He has been published in **Comic Book Marketplace**, **Collectors' Showcase.**, and his own small-press publication, **LLYR: The Magazine of the Celtic Arts**. He is also a regular pitching writer to UPN's **Star Trek: Voyager**.*

Chil

These days, picking up a premium isn't such a hard job--just walk into a fast-food joint and ask for the toy of the week. Sure, they'll charge you, and they might even embarrass you by making you order one of those kid's meals, but basically it's that simple. Of course, traditional premiums still exist in cereal boxes, but even more toys are currently available from collector magazines in the form of mail-in coupons; from fan clubs in the form of

exclusive action figures; as promotional movie items; and I even walked into a 7-11 one day craving nothing more than a refreshing diet beverage and left with a neon Mountain Dew sign as a prize giveaway. With most collectors, it's not about the fast food they eat, the articles in the magazines they read, the inside information about their favorite films, characters or stars, or even about which convenience store to shop in--it's about the premiums. Everywhere you turn, there's always someone trying to push some promotional item off on you or sell you some bauble; premiums today are more abundant than ever.

But how have we gotten to this stage of premium development? Over the years, premiums have become a fascinating area to collect, because you're not just collecting items, but ideas. For example, just as I've struggled in researching this article to make the marketing connections behind these premiums, the adults who created them struggled to get into the minds of children in order to create toys that appealed to them. The following list of ten clever items (in chronological order) illustrates the growth of premiums and reflects important periods in their

10 COOL PREMIUMS

development while showcasing some break-throughs in the field. These items also reveal aspects of society at the time, and as such, they are elevated to a historical rather than trivial status.

THE d's

by
Benn Ray

FRANK MERRIWELL TIP TOP LEAGUE MEMBERS BADGE

In the 1880s, "dime novels," the predecessors to pulp magazines, were all the rage. In 1886, writer Gilbert Patten (under the pseudonym Burt L. Standish) created Frank Merriwell, a role model and inspiration to boys and girls everywhere, and an imaginary friend for kids unable to make real ones (remember, this was the turn of the century, so many kids grew up in isolation, lacking cable TV and e-mail pen pals).

This badge represents *the* first premium character badge ever manufactured. In the early 1900s, ad campaigns were a new concept, and the designers of *The Frank Merriwell Badge* were taking a risk by diving into uncharted marketing waters. This item was offered in *Tip Top Weekly*, the self-proclaimed "Ideal Publi-cation for the American Youth."

Solidly and substantially made, finished in gilt and beautifully embossed (and as we all know, embossing is the sign of true quality), the badge signified membership in the Tip Top League. The concept was that other kids would look at this badge with envy and want one for themselves, and as a result, would become members of the Tip Top League. That membership could be proudly displayed for the humble sum of twenty cents–ten cents in cash or stamps, and ten cents in coupons (offered in *Tip Top Weekly*). Without coupons, the badge would run you 50 cents (a small fortune in those days). Since the coupons were free to *Tip Top* readers, the badge was half-price to them.

1900

COCOMALT "BUCK ROGERS CUT-OUT ADVENTURE BOOK"

In 1929, Buck Rogers became the first American comic strip to explore science fiction. This Cocomalt premium offered in 1933 is rare, despite the success of Buck Rogers. The *Buck Rogers Cut-Out Book* offered fans the opportunity to live out the adventures being broadcast on the radio show. Although the book featured a stage (a separate cardboard sheet for use as the theatre stage), scenes (The Attack Upon Niagara, The Court Of Venus, Dr. Huer's Laboratory, and The Metal Cities Of Venus) and characters (Buck, Wilma, Dr. Huer, Black Barney, Little Willie, Killer Kane, Ardala, the Queen of Venus), it was the 25th Century inventions (disintegrator ray machine, rocket planes, radio-telescope) that captured the imaginations of fans.

All that was required from the person seeking this premium was four easy tasks: drink Cocomalt regularly–at least once a day (insuring that Buck Rogers fans would be the most hyperactive kids on the block); note your weight and general improvement on the chart on the back page of the pamphlet offering the book; have your mother, father or legal guardian sign the chart; and send in the completed chart with about two inches of the strip of tin that comes off the Cocomalt can. To assure honesty, parents also had to answer six questions about Coco-malt's effect on the child: did the child appear to display an improved physical condition, was he or she more alert, did he or she sleep better, did he or she eat better, was the child doing better in school, and was the parent impressed with the results the malt had on their children? Details are still a little unclear as to whether or not you'd get the book if Cocomalt had no effect on you.

1933

"DOC SAVAGE AWARD" BRONZE MEDALLION

Doc Savage was the superhero of pulp magazines in the 1930s-1940s, and the medallion which bore his name/likeness was awarded (as explained in the application) to honor those who performed an outstanding task, not necessarily heroic in size and nature, but for those who did their best in making the most of their opportunities.

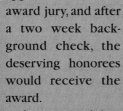

If you knew someone like that, you requested an application for the award which you would then fill out. You had to write the reasons why you believed your candidate should be considered, and collect six signatures and addresses of people who vouched for the candidate, with the signature of a civic, religious, or business leader in the applicant's community. Finally, you had to return the application to the award jury, and after a two week background check, the deserving honorees would receive the award.

If your candidate checked out, they would be awarded the Doc Savage medallion by *Doc Savage Magazine* for service, loyalty and integrity. With all you had to go through to get someone else the award, it's no wonder this item is so scarce (the person who actually took the time to fill all this out deserved an award of their own). That, or there weren't many people in the 1930s who could match up to the award jury's high standards.

LONE RANGER ICE CREAM CONES ENAMELED/SILVERED METAL PICTURE BRACELET

The Lone Ranger was born in 1933 at a Detroit radio station. This western "White Knight," who wanted no thanks or recognition for his good deeds, became a popular mode of escape via radio for the average citizen struggling to survive The Great Depression. By 1937, the call of "Hi-Yo Silver!" was echoing around the nation, and The Lone Ranger was used to hawk just about any form of food imaginable (in fact, many people who grew up listening to this radio show even now still exhibit a type of Pavlovian response whenever they hear the *William Tell Overture*—the Lone Ranger's theme song). This 1938 premium, released by the Lone Ranger Inc., was available from ice cream vendors that used Hav-a-wrap cones (the paper wrapper that offers sanitary protection for your ice cream sugar cone). My question is, were people prissier back then, or were their hands dirtier?

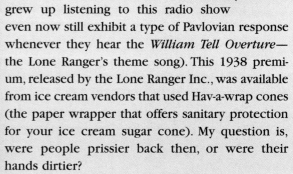

In order to get his real Indian bracelet with genuine simulated silver, embossed with a picture of the Lone Ranger and a lovely desert scene, you'd have to collect twenty-five Hav-a-wrap coupons from the back of the sanitary paper on the Lone Ranger cones, or six Hav-a-wrap coupons and a three cent stamp. The bracelet was only available through *The Lone Ranger* premium comic book, however, which would cost an additional fifteen Hav-a-wrap coupons. So, all in all, this complicated premium would ultimately cost the eager Lone Ranger fan a total of forty Hav-a-wrap coupons. That's a lot of ice cream there, buddy.

"SUPERMAN'S CHRISTMAS ADVENTURE" COMIC BOOK

1940

Jerry Siegel and Joe Shuster created Superman in the early 1930s, but it wasn't until 1938 and *Action Comics* #1 that people were finally given the opportunity to believe a man could fly. By 1940, the massive marketing campaign that would insure the Man of Steel's status as an American icon was already well underway, with Macy's taking the lead at their annual Thanksgiving Day Parade, in which the Superman figure balloon was the largest participant. *The Journal American*, WOR Radio, Superman Inc., and Leader Novelty, all co-sponsors with Macy's, mailed out tickets for a Superman play held at the Macy's Herald Square store in New York shortly after Thanksgiving, the height of the Christmas shopping season. After children marveled at the Man of Tomorrow's feats of strength and heroism, they were given this book. The story involved Superman saving Santa (and invariably Christmas itself) and featured a line of Superman Christmas toys at the end of the book which were conveniently on sale at the store. Not only did this mark the first time Superman toys were given as Christmas presents, but they were also the first-ever group of superhero toys (a staple—now called action figures—on many kids' Christmas lists), and this book would go down in history as the first-ever superhero premium comic giveaway.

Proving that the commercialization of the holiday season has existed for years, this was the kick-off that led to the organized marketing of Superman toys during the Christmas season in every toy store. Other stores also used the book during the holidays, stamping their company name/logo in a white block created for promotional purposes, reminding child and parent alike where these Superman toys could be bought.

U.S. JONES CADETS MEMBERSHIP KIT

1941

At the outset of World War II, U.S. Jones, defender of democracy and the all-American way, had a brief comic book life. The thing about democracy, it seems, is that it must always be defended. However, the character of Jones (derivative of Captain America and The Shield) and the lousy comic art insured that after his appearance in *Wonderworld Comics* #28, he would only last for two issues in his own title even though the books were heavily steeped in patriotism.

Despite the fact that these comics are neither ultra-rare or comparatively valuable, the *U.S. Jones Cadets Membership Kit* is considered by many collectors to be the *Action Comics* #1 of club kits, with less than five known examples in complete condition—an example of the tried and true formula of rarity+demand=#1 hit collectible (and the eye-appeal and quality of this item only serves to make it even more desirable).

Ten cents plus a three cent stamp with a coupon found in *U.S. Jones* #1 would entitle Cadets to a special National Emergency Kit, consisting of a membership card, book of instructions on how to organize an air raid courier service, a secret decoder book (what self-respecting child of the WWII era would be caught without secret codes), and a membership badge. After you became a member and pledged to defend democracy (although exactly how is still somewhat vague), you would receive coded instructions on how to proceed with the fight. The only other stipulation was that Cadets needed to believe in the Constitution and the Ten Commandments, suggesting that separation of Church and State was not a particularly important issue with U.S. Jones.

WONDER WOMAN SENSATION COMICS LITHO. BUTTON

In December 1941, Wonder Woman, comics' first major female superhero, debuted in *All Star Comics* #8. Unfortunately, it hasn't always been easy for women to attain recognized equality, and even a Wonder Woman was not exempt. In *All-Star Comics* #11 (June/July 1942) a question was posed to boys and girls everywhere: Do you believe that a woman should be permitted to become a member of the Justice Society of America, and that if Wonder Woman holds the lead in the final count, she should become a member? A follow-up question asked, "Would you like us to form a Junior Justice Society which all of you can join?"

Of course nothing could be more democratic, allowing the readers to vote new members into the society. However, the reason the vote was necessary was due to the hero's gender, something that would inspire outrage today. As a special incentive, one thousand readers who sent in this coupon would receive a free copy of *All-Star Comics* #12. The same offer was posed in *Sensation Comics*, where Wonder Woman was the feature story. In an ad in *Sensation Comics* #5, ten thousand Wonder Woman buttons (in five brilliant colors) were also supposedly sent out, although due to the rarity of this item, that figure is questionable.

In her quest to attain Justice Society membership, Wonder Woman received celebrity endorsements from World Heavyweight Champions Jack Dempsey and Gene Tunney, and Miss Alice Marble, the former World's Amateur Tennis Champion. Finally, after a smartly conceived marketing campaign, she was allowed to join the ranks of The Justice Society of America, filling the slot of...secretary. Wonder Woman might have been a little over-qualified for the job (an Amazon Princess as a secretary?), but as she proved, taking dictation and fetching coffee was only a starting point for a character who was to later become a core member of the Justice League of America, where she would end up sharpening her fighting skills instead of pencils. So in a way, Wonder Woman took an entry-level position and climbed the superhero equivalent of the corporate ladder to become, at the very least, a senior partner in the firm.

NABISCO TOYTOWN CUT-OUTS

Assuming that given the opportunity, almost every child would want to build his own town, Nabisco offered kids the chance to do just that. Randomly inserted into boxes of Shredded Wheat were three of thirty-six different *ToyTown Cut-Outs*. The most avid town builders not only would have to buy numerous boxes of Shredded Wheat in order to complete the set but would also be, as a result of eating all that shredded wheat, the most regular kids in the neighborhood. The good thing about getting duplicate cards, however, was that it would only make your town bigger. At its most minimal, the town stood with houses, garages, barns, ice cream parlors, a fire house, a post office, a bank, a library, an antique store (prophecy?), a town hall interestingly enough (which today would be a shopping mall), and, surprisingly, no Walmart whatsoever. Aside from the lack of shopping malls and Walmarts, this item would be virtually outdated for children today, since the town did not include the now-familiar great American wasteland known as the suburbs.

Upon getting your cut-outs, you would color each town piece (buildings, trees, etc.), and Nabisco even included a color guide for the slower and unoriginal kids. Once you finished coloring, you'd play a little "insert tab A into slot B" type action. When finished assembling the buildings, you could then lay out your town any way you desired, or you could follow the suggested town layout. After a quick bathroom stop, it would be on to another box of Shredded Wheat to continue your empire building.

SPACE PATROL "TERRA V" ROCKET FILM PROJECTOR (ALSO KNOWN AS THE PROJECT-O-SCOPE)

In his quest for interplanetary justice, Commander Buzz Corey and the crew of the spaceship Terra policed the planets of the 30th Century for ABC television/radio networks beginning in 1950. This 1953 Space Patrol item was much more than just a simple ready to use toy; it was a delicate and important instrument to be handled carefully. The Project-O-Scope was comprised of two scientifically designed lenses, a flashlight bulb, a flashlight battery (AA—back then batteries were included), and genuine microfilm just like spies use. The unit was designed for exciting play as both a film projector and a handy flashlight to help you do things like blind the hell out of the neighborhood cat, and it came in the form of an authentic reproduction of the famous Space Patrol "Terra V" Rocket Ship.

Unfortunately, this item did require its owner to handle it carefully, as dropping the Project-O-Scope resulted in breaking the bulb. Also included were four series of film strip adventures, with six pictures to each series (conveniently numbered for easy referencing). So, once you received your Project-O-Scope, you could turn out the lights and impress your li'l honey with the adventures of Buzz Corey and Space Patrol. A dark room and the li'l honey were not included in the offer.

OFFICIAL RIN-TIN-TIN CAVALRY GUN & HOLSTER

Introduced in 1923, this wonder dog would go on to become Warner Brothers' first major film star. Years later, when Rin-Tin-Tin entered into the medium of television, he would join up with Corporal Rusty and the troopers of the 101st Cavalry, the Fighting Blue Devils, to help bring order to the lawless West of the 1880s. Since the show was sponsored by the National Biscuit Company (that's Nabisco to you and me), a wide variety of Rin-Tin-Tin premiums were offered.

In 1956, in conjunction with Screen Gems, Inc., Rin-Tin-Tin and Nabisco offered something every little boy loves—a gun. And not just any gun, but one so lifelike that if you were to wield it playfully in the streets nowadays, your local city police department would respond with a hail of real bullets.

The Official Rin-Tin-Tin Cavalry Gun and Holster was an authentic reproduction of the very same shootin' irons used by the Fighting Blue Devils on ABC's *The Adventures of Rin-Tin-Tin*. This pistol boasted real trigger action, a smoking barrel when fired, bronzed antique finish, break action, plastic grips, a holster of genuine black leather, a handsome Rin-Tin-Tin trophy belt also genuine leather with buckle and a bullet clip with three metalized plastic bullets. All it took for a young Rin-Tin-Tin enthusiast to arm himself and help keep law and order in his own neighborhood just like his favorite TV dog was one boxtop from Nabisco Shredded Wheat and $2.00.

The 10 premiums listed above are rare and much sought after by many collectors. As I researched the items in this article, I came to a historical understanding: some of the characters may have faded in time, only to be replaced by newer ones (most just as transient), but how they were marketed has not significantly changed. Although attitudes towards marketing have become more cynical over the generations as the populace becomes more media savvy, the marketing of characters (early examples of product endorsements) has remained consistent.

The premiums in this article were all designed by adults, and every adult at some point in their life is a child; so while working with these toys I managed to transcend the nostalgia of my childhood and view the childhoods of my father and grandfather through the toys they played with and the characters they followed. In a way, it's almost as much fun being an adult researching and writing about toys manufactured for children as it is collecting them and even designing them—it's as close as one can get to regaining lost youth. ❖

Benn Ray is Editor of Gemstone Publishing. He regularly writes several columns for the Gemstone website at www.gemstonepub.com/fan; *Top o' the Stack*, covering current issues in comics and featuring reviews; *Benn's Geek Corner*, a showcase of odd character related collectibles he's been able to sneak out of friends' attics; and *Psychotic Reactions*, reviewing current record albums in release. He has also been published in *Comic Book Marketplace*, *The Baltimore City Paper*, and *The Overstreet Toy Ring Price Guide* as well as on various web magazines such as *The Daily Review*, *Mania.com*, and *The Bucket*.

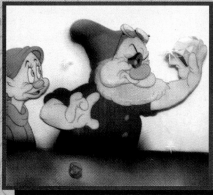

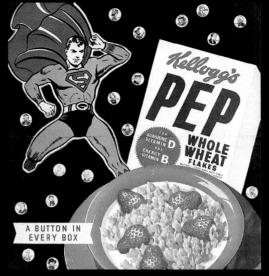

Superman Full Color Display, 1946.
Sold in New York for $4,025 at Christie's East.

© Walt Disney Studios

Walt Disney Studios, *circa* 1930s.
Sold in New York for $4,025 at Christie's East.

Animation Art • Film Memorabilia • Hollywood Movie Posters • Pop Memorabilia

Sports Memorabilia • Television Memorabilia • Toys • Western Memorabilia

For further information on buying or selling,

please contact the Popular Arts Department at 212 606 0543.

CHRISTIE'S*east*

219 East 67th Street, New York, New York 10021

CARL BARKS & ANOTHER RAINBOW

Expect the highest quality fine arts collectibles from the winning team that has offered signed lithographs, figurines, coffee-table books, and other memorabilia for the past 17 years. Pictured at the right is **Pick and Shovel Laborer**, a magnificent oil painting of Uncle Scrooge McDuck, completed by Barks in the 1970s, that has been released and sold out as a limited edition signed and numbered 13½" x 11" lithograph. The bone china figurine of **Pick and Shovel Laborer** is now in very limited supply. Inquire! Copies of sold out items are usually available through our location service. Call or write for details, or send $1.00 for our latest catalog, to Another Rainbow at the address below.

GLADSTONE COMICS

Gladstone Publishing, an imprint of the Bruce Hamilton Company, produces comic books and comic albums featuring the Disney Ducks for distribution in the United States and Canada.

Representative covers of our current titles, **Walt Disney's Comics and Stories**; **Uncle Scrooge**; and **Uncle Scrooge Adventures in Color** featuring Carl Barks, Don Rosa, and William Van Horn, are shown at right. These titles, which retail for $6.95 to $10.95 each, are available primarily through comic book specialty stores or directly by subscription. Look for them at your local comic shop or write to us.

VINTAGE COLLECTIBLES

ORIGINAL ART:

- Oil Paintings
- Comic Book Pages
- Newspaper Strips
- Pencil Sketches

RARE OLD COMIC BOOKS:

- Uncle Scrooge
- Donald Duck
- WDC&S & others

Vintage collector/dealer (and publisher) Bruce Hamilton has been a specialist in the field for 30 years. Want lists, and inquiries, are welcome. Hamilton may be contacted at the address below.

Character images © Disney Enterprises, Inc.

THE BRUCE HAMILTON COMPANY ANOTHER RAINBOW • GLADSTONE PUBLISHING

PO Box 2079 • Prescott, AZ 86302 • (520) 776-1300 • FAX: (520) 445-7536

Questions? E-mail us at: bhc@primenet.com

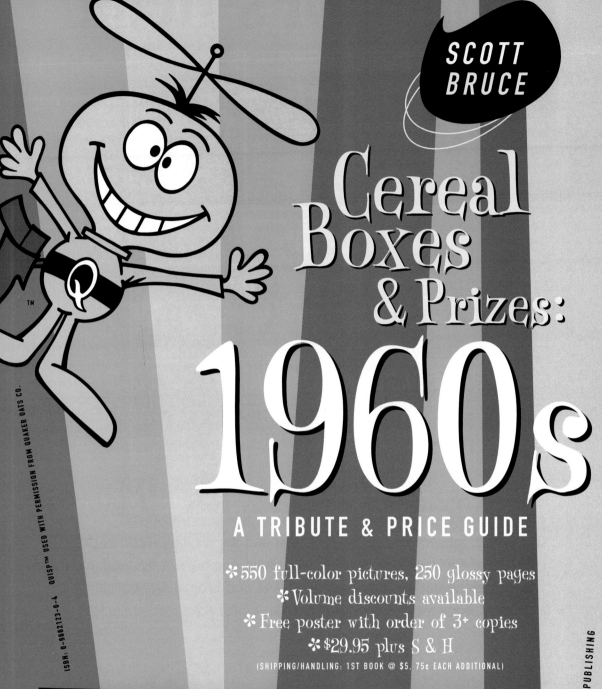
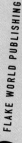

Collector's Item!

CBM is your gateway to the nostalgic past and the exciting world of popular collectibles! Get the inside story on the rarest, the highest-demand and the most undervalued **Golden Age, Silver Age** and **Bronze Age** collectibles. **Comic Book Marketplace**… the magazine for advanced collectors!

A GEMSTONE PUBLICATION

Comic Book Marketplace • PO Box 180700 • Coronado • CA • 92178 • (619) 437-1996

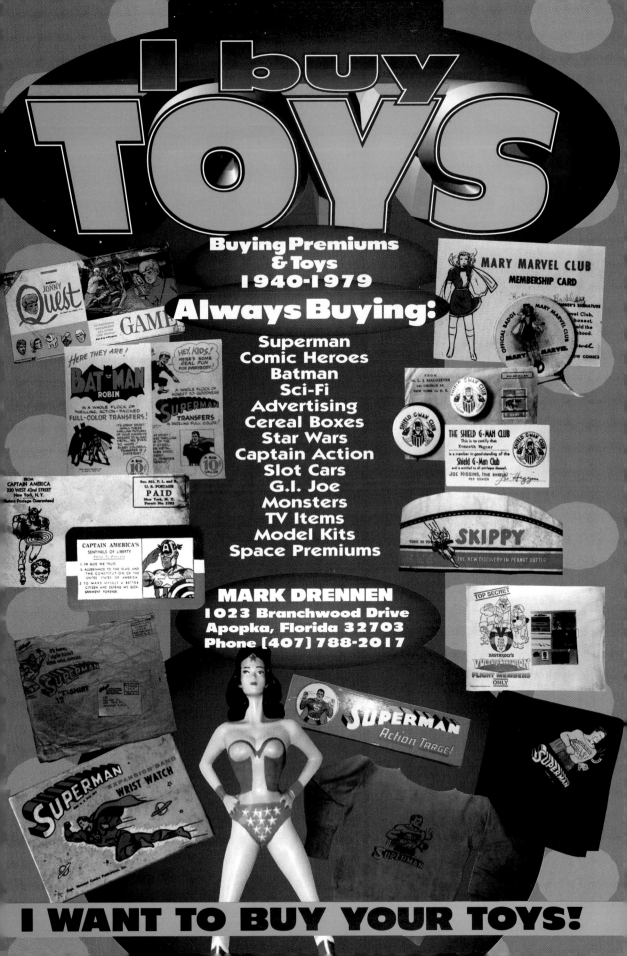

Walt Disney Classics Collection
Gold Circle Dealer

Looney Tunes
Spotlight Collection

SUNDAY FUNNIES

16833 SouthCenter Pkwy
Tukwila, WA 98188
1-800-664-4891
www.sundayfunnies.com

Walt Disney Art Classics
Preferred Gallery

Disney's
Halcyon Days
Enameled Collectibles

Call for a
complimentary
copy of our
newsletter

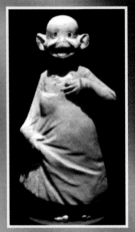

James Ungerman, "Wheaties Photographer."

In 1937-38, over 60 years ago, a young man was contacted by General Mills to travel around the country—from Florida to Ohio, from Louisiana to Texas—to photograph American heroes of the day, baseball players, while they indulged in a great American activity—eating breakfast. After over 1,000 photographs, a choice few were selected to become a part of the collective American psyche. However, these heroes did not eat just any breakfast; these Gods of the Diamond ate something special that helped make them the great players of their time—Wheaties, the Breakfast of Champions. This is that young man's story.

THE PHOTOGRAPH

AN INTERVIEW WITH WHEATIES

How did you get started in photography?

I'd just finished high school. The owner of the original Radisson Hotel in Minnesota had a nephew in Chicago who had an appendicitis operation and missed some school. He wanted to know if I would take this boy, spend a summer with him, and teach him English and Physics, and I agreed to do it. We lived at the Radisson Farm where they had a cottage, and I took pictures all the time we were together. The man's wife was so impressed with my pictures she said, "you know, James," she called me James, "you should be a photographer." It stimu-lated me to the point where I thought maybe I should go into photography. I was interested in art anyway. To be a really great photographer, you have to understand lighting and artwork. So that's how I got started.

What did you do after you decided to be a photographer?

I went to work in Minneapolis as a commercial photographer for a company called The Bureau of Engraving. It was the largest engraving, printing, photography and art company west of Chicago. I worked there for ten years (1931-41).

We did commercial photography, and a lot of food photography for two of our biggest accounts, Pillsbury and General Mills. I also got to be a real pal of Betty Crocker's because they would cook stuff in their kitchen and bring it over to our kitchen in my studio.

You were well-fed at work?

I got a lot of good eating, but I got fooled once. They came over with a cake that had a lot of beautiful frosting on it. So I brought it home one night for my wife who had her bridge club over. We were a little disappointed when we discovered it was fake. It had a cardboard center.

How did you go from shooting pictures of food to shooting pictures of baseball players eating food?

I was shooting mostly food ads for Betty Crocker, Wheaties, etc. I was known basically for my food photography, but I did everything in commercial photography. They decided they wanted to do the sports program for Wheaties and shoot ads of the ballplayers and use their pictures on the boxes as well as in national advertising. That's when they contacted our

Press. They called me "The Wheaties Photographer" because I was the only guy there who took pictures for General Mills and the Wheaties ads. So I was a different type of photographer than you would see working the baseball fields.

What was the process and how were the photos set up?

It was all location shooting. I had to carry my equipment with me. If I was going to shoot a scene at a table where they were eating Wheaties, either by themselves, with another player, or their families, I would make arrangements with the hotels where we were staying. One year I was sent right to their homes. We shot once in The Chase Hotel in St. Louis, where the Cardinals stayed. The dining room maitre d' was so impressed that they had the Wheaties photographer there that they set up a big table in the main dining room stacked high with Wheaties boxes and flowers. He let me take pictures of their storage rooms, and he had it all lined up with Wheaties boxes, trying to impress me [laughing].

ER *of* CHAMPIONS
by Benn Ray
IOTOGRAPHER JAMES UNGERMAN

company. I even had several of my pictures on the back cover of *Saturday Evening Post*, *Ladies Home Journal*, all those places.

What circumstances led to your becoming known as "The Wheaties Photographer?"

Most of the photographers involved were all sports/news photographers who worked for either local newspapers or United Press International or the Associated

Bob Feller
of the
Cleveland Indians

So some of the photos of the players sitting at their dining room tables eating Wheaties were actually at their dining room table eating Wheaties?

Yeah, absolutely. That was true with Jimmy Foxx. There were many that were shot that way.

What types of shots were you most interested in?

I wasn't too interested in action shots, just mostly eating shots.

Did your equipment ever pose any special problems?

Yeah, it did. When you travel on location, there's only so much equipment you can carry, so it has to be pretty portable. I had the regular equipment you would use to photograph action shots. I only carried three lights, the tripod, a lot of wires and two large handheld cameras. I used the tripod for the stuff I shot at the tables. I used Kodak film of course. The big problem with indoor photography is trying to find an outlet to plug in the lights without blowing the fuses at somebody's house.

How did you get to meet all the players?

We traveled by train and then we'd have to rent a car and go to their homes. I always traveled with advertising men from one of the ad agencies that General Mills used. They would sign up the players for the testimonials, do the written work, and I did the picture work. On one trip, Bill Slocum (a retired sports writer for New York newspapers) agreed to go with us to Florida, Texas, and Louisiana. He knew all the players, and that was a big help to get into the stadiums and meet them.

Were any players particularly bad subjects?

I had a few bad ones. Lefty Grove always had a reputation for being a nasty fellow to get along with. He was a hell of a pitcher. At that time, he

Dizzy Dean at his Chicago apartment feeding his dog.

Lefty Grove is attentive to a model at the Benjamin Franklin hotel, Philadelphia. PA.

was living in Philadelphia, so we arranged with the dining room captain of our hotel to shoot pictures of Lefty Grove eating Wheaties in the main dining room during the middle of the morning when there weren't any people around. I hired a model to serve the food and stand by him while he's at the table eating Wheaties, and she was late. He became very irritable, saying he couldn't wait around, and he was getting madder by the minute. The model had to go out and rent a waitress costume, so she was maybe two or three minutes late. Finally, as he's getting ready to leave, she walks in. She was beautiful--blonde, young, about twenty years old--and he just became all smiles. He stayed there for half-an-hour while I got some good pictures of him. He was so impressed with this gal and the pictures that he invited me over to a health club he belonged to and I got a picture of him sitting in a sweat box with just his head sticking out.

Who was one of your favorite subjects to work with?

Dizzy Dean was great. I photographed him both at Wrigley Field and at his apartment in Chicago. I went to the apartment one day and got a picture of him standing in front of the refrigerator, kneeling down with a big box of Wheaties under his arm and grabbing for a bottle of milk. He had a little dog, and he was fixing a bowl of milk to put some Wheaties in for the dog. He was always very accommodating, but most of them were pretty good guys.

Who were some of the biggest names you shot?

I photographed about thirty-five guys who are all in the Hall of Fame right now: Carl Hubble,

Stan Musial, Dizzy Dean, Bobby Feller (I photographed him when he was only about nineteen years old, playing for the Indians). You name the great ones, I photographed them.

Who were your favorite players?

My favorite baseball player was Ted Williams, and in my opinion he was the best hitter in major league baseball. I also thought Charlie Gehringer was the best second baseman in the major leagues.

Did you ever photograph a player you were in awe of?

Yeah, I met a few like that. Carl Hubble would be one of them. He was very reserved and a great, great pitcher. He wasn't the kind of guy who was very chummy, but he was always very nice.

Did any of the players hate or not eat Wheaties that you know of?

No.

All of them loved Wheaties?

As far as I know they did.

What's "The Breakfast of Champions?"

It's a breakfast food.

Wheaties?

Yeah.

I always thought it was Little Chocolate Donuts.

Wheaties give Jimmy Foxx that homerun swing.

Why did you leave the Wheaties gig?

After ten years with the Engraving Bureau, I got a telegram from the War Department and spent four years as a chief photographer illustrating all the books for the technical manuals. Have you ever photographed inside a tank? It's not too easy. It's all white to begin with, and you don't have room to move around in the damned thing. It's difficult to get into, let alone bringing in lights and cameras inside one of those things; it's a hell of a problem.

Watch Jimmy Foxx blast that ball!

Wheaties give Jimmy extra nourishment to help build extra drive and stamina —what every athlete needs!

What did you do after the war?

I worked for ten years in New York City in a big studio as general manager and art director. Then I spent twenty-one years with Kodak in sales and marketing, and then I retired.

Are you still taking pictures now?

No, not anymore. For a number of years, I took family pictures and that sort of thing, but nothing for money, just things I wanted to do. I've always been a gardener and I've taken a lot of pictures of trees, flowers and landscapes and things like that.

On a personal level, what was your favorite subject matter to shoot?

Food, because there was always something to eat afterwards. I never gained an ounce though.

Well, with all that equipment you had to carry...

Yeah, that tired a man out. My real desire, after spending twenty-one years with Kodak as a sales manager who cracked the whip on about forty-five guys, dealing with the deadlines all the time and all the rushing in New York City, was just to take peaceful pictures—to go out in the country and take pictures of cows in the pasture, mountains or flowers—nothing that talks back or tells you what to do, not working with art directors that want it a certain way while you think it would be better another way.

How would you summarize your career?

I enjoyed it. I spent my whole career in photography and I met a lot of interesting people. The highlight would be the baseball stuff because that was so unusual. ❖

In Tribute and Memory to Samuel H. Gold

The Man who started Children's Premiums in the USA and Europe

From Gordon K. Gold, his Son and Partner for over 20 years

I miss my Father and the excitement of the Premium business very much.

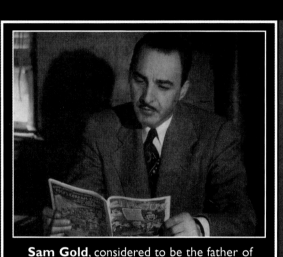

Sam Gold, considered to be the father of children's premiums in the United States. Gold was called the "Premium King" by large national advertisers and ad agencies and named the top idea man in the premium industry by *Life Magazine* (April 19, 1949).

A few of the Children's Premiums produced by Sam and Gordon K. Gold for Food & Cereal Companies --

- ◆ **General Mills Lucky Charms Kite**
- ◆ **Nabisco Walt Disney's Love Bug Auto.**
- ◆ **Quaker Cap'n Crunch Wiggle Figures**
- ◆ **Best Foods Bosco Bear Rocket Chute**
- ◆ **General Foods Archie's Car**

Gordon K. Gold was licensed to use some of the most famous names in the world, just to name a few, The Walt Disney Characters, Range Rider, Gene Autry, King Comics, Flintstones, Quaker Oats, General Mills Monster Characters.

Gordon K. Gold gave one of the largest antique toy collections in the country, more than 2,500 toys, to the **Museum of The City of New York** in honor of his father, Samuel H. Gold. Over 500,000 people paid to see this collection.

Christie's East held an auction of Gordon K. Gold's Premiums and Displays in **November 1996**, and 60 lots brought prices from $1,100 for one lot to $13,225 for the **Three Stooges Moving Picture Machine** poster and premium.

Hake's Americana & Collectibles has recently featured and sold some of Gordon K. Gold's Premium items in their catalog. These items were from Mr. Gold's personal collection.

Gordon K. Gold, considered "a premium legend in his own time," has created and produced over 3,000 children's premiums.

For more information, write
Gordon K. Gold, P.O. Box 2734,
Chapel Hill, N.C. 27515.

PRESERVE YOUR COLLECTION WITH TRUE R-KIVAL™ PROTECTION

PRESERVE LIKE THE PROS

Both the U.S. Library of Congress and the National Archives buy preservation supplies from Bill Cole Enterprises —
If you're not currently buying from BCE, here's why you should:

 We manufacture Mylar® Sleeves in more sizes and styles! Custom sizes are no problem!

 You can protect your collection with state-of-the-art technology!

 Protect puzzles, posters, blotters, membership cards, membership certificates, ring papers, post cards, ad signs, newsletters, books, premium comic books, comic strips, original art, photographs, catalogs, patches, records, newspaper premium ads and more!

 We have over 20 years of experience as preservation professionals!

 We also offer acid-free backing boards!

Call or write for our complete catalog today — And get a $5 coupon good towards your first order.

Visit our web site at:
http://www.neponset.com/bcemylar
E-mail: bcemylar@internetmci.com

 Bill Cole Enterpriſeſ, Inc.

P.O. Box 60, Dept. HPG2, Randolph, MA 02368-0060 (781) 986-2653   FAX (781) 986-2656

Comic-Gards™, Arklites™, Thin-X-Tenders™, Time-X- Tenders™, Life-X-Tenders™, and R-Kival™ are trademarks of Bill Cole Enterprises, Inc. All references to Mylar® refer to archival quality polyester film such as Mylar® type D by Dupont Co., or equivalent material such as Melinex® 516 by ICI Corp.

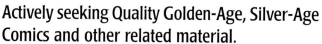

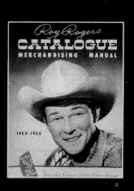

AVALON
COMICS & COLLECTIBLES

In our nine years we have gained one of the best reputations in the business, for:

Grading
Plain Dealing
Fairness to beginners
Choice selection
Super service

And we have consistently issued one of the best catalogs in the business!

68 jam-packed pages
150 photographs

Featuring over 15,000 comic books from 1933-1975, and choice memorabilia from 1880-1980.

Character & personality items
Vintage Superman collectibles
Disneyana
Cowboy & Western items
Movie posters
Antique advertising
Premiums, Pulps, Big Little books
Cardboard & Hardcover books & much, much more!

Please sign up to receive our catalogs!

Send your name, address and $2 (in the U.S. and Canada, $3 foreign) to get our current and next catalog, or send $5 to receive our current and next three catalogs ($7 foreign).

Avalon Comics
P.O. Box 234
Boston, MA 02123

PHONE: (617) 262-5544
FAX: (617) 948-2300

Larry Curcio, proprietor
Overstreet® Senior Advisor 1994-1998
Comic Buyers Guide Customer Service Award
Winner 1990-1998

Collector Seeks
Krazy Kat Original Art

*F*ollow the Leader in Golden and Silver Age Comics with

BEDROCK CITY

COMIC COMPANY ™

6517 Westheimer
(at Hillcroft)
Houston, Texas 77057
(713) 780-0675

2204-D FM 1960 W.
(at Kuykendahl)
Houston, Texas 77090
(281) 444-9763

fax (713) 780-2366

www.bedrockcity.com

Shazam © 1997 D.C. Comics

SHOWCASE NEW ENGLAND

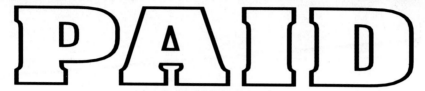

PAID

$400,000
PAID
in Canada, 1997

$460,000
PAID
in California, 1998

$110,000
PAID
in Louisiana, 1996

$274,000
PAID
in New York, 1995

$225,000
PAID
in Illinois, 1996

We pay amounts from

$1,000 to $50,000

EVERY WEEK

for books we need.

102

DIRECTORY OF COMIC AND NOSTALGIA SHOPS FOR
HAKE'S PRICE GUIDE TO CHARACTER TOYS SECOND EDITION
(PAID ADVERTISING - STORE LISTINGS)

ALABAMA

Wizard's Comics
324 North Ct.
Florence, AL 35630
PH: (205) 766-6821

ARIZONA

Greg's Comics
2722 South Alma
School Rd. #8
Mesa, AZ 85210
PH: (602) 752-1881

CALIFORNIA

Treasures Of Youth
1201 C St.
Hayward, CA 94541
PH: (510) 888-9675

Golden Apple Comics
7711 Melrose Ave.
Los Angeles, CA 90046
PH: (213) 658-6047
WEB: www.goldenapple
comics.com

Golden Apple Comics
8962 Reseda Blvd.
Northridge, CA 91324
PH: (818) 993-7804
WEB: www.goldenapple
comics.com

COLORADO

All C's Collectibles, Inc.
1113 So. Abilene St. #104
Aurora, CO 80012
PH: (303) 751-6882

CONNECTICUT

D-J's Comics & Cards
166 Washington Ave.
North Haven, CT 06473
PH: (203) 234-2989

FLORIDA

Whiz Bang! Collectibles
952 E. Semoran Blvd.
Casselberry, FL 32707
PH: (407) 260-8869
FX: (407) 260-2289
WEB: www.whizbangtoys.com

Tropic Comics South, Inc.
1870 N.E. 163 St.
N. Miami Beach, FL 33162
PH: (305) 940-8700
FX: (305) 940-1551
E-MAIL: abcsales@a-bomb
comics.com
WEB: www.a-bombcomics.com

Tropic Comics, Inc.
313 S. State Rd. #7
Plantation, FL 33317
PH: (954) 587-8878
FX: (954) 587-0409
E-MAIL: trcsales@tropic
comics.com
Web: www.tropiccomics.com

GEORGIA

Oxford Comics Inc.
2855 Piedmont Rd. NE
Atlanta, GA 30305
PH: (404) 233-8682

Odin's Cosmic Bookshelf
Killian Hill Crossing
4760 Hwy. 29, Ste.A-1
Lilburn, GA 30047
PH: (770) 923-0123

ILLINOIS

Yesterday
1143 W. Addison St.
Chicago, IL 60613
PH: (773) 248-8087

The Paper Escape
205 West First St.
Dixon, IL 61021
PH: (815) 284-7567

June Moon Collectibles
245 N. Northwest Hwy.
Park Ridge, IL 60068
PH: (847) 825-1411

Tomorrow Is Yesterday, Inc.
5600 N. 2nd St.
Rockford, IL 61111
PH: (815) 633-0330

Keith's Komix, Inc.
528 S. Roselle Rd.
Schaumburg, IL 60193
PH: (847) 534-9436

Jack Melcher, Buy Where The
Dealers Buy
P.O. Box 14
Waukegan, IL 60079-0014
PH: (847) 249-5626

KENTUCKY

Red Rock Collectables
929 Liberty Rd.
Lexington, KY 40505
PH: (606) 225-5452
E-MAIL:
redrock@mindspring.com
Web: www.2redrock.com

MARYLAND

Geppi's Comic World
1722 N. Rolling Rd.
Baltimore, MD 21244
PH: (410) 298-1758
FX: (410) 298-1727

Diamond International
Galleries
1966 Greenspring Drive, Ste
401
Timonium, MD 21093
PH: (888) 355-9800
FX: (410) 560-7143
E-MAIL: questions@diamondgal-
leries.com
WEB:
www.diamondgalleries.com

MASSACHUSETTS

New England Comics
(Eight Boston Area Stores)
P.O. Box 310
Quincy, MA 02269
PH: (617) 774-0140

MISSOURI

Decades of Toyys
3315 Woodson Rd.
Breckenridge Hills, MO
63114-4718
PH: (314) 427-8693
E-MAIL:
DECADES@FASTRANS.NET
WEB:
Users.FastRans.Net/DECADES/
DeFault.ASP

NEW YORK

Wow Comics
2084 White Plains Rd.
Bronx, NY 10462
PH: (718) 829-0461
FX: (718) 828-1700
E-MAIL: wowcomics@aol.com
WEB:
www.pelhamparkway.com/wo
w/wow.htm

Gotham City Comics
800 Lexington Ave.
New York, NY 10021
PH: (212) 980-0009
E-MAIL: gothamct@aol.com

Village Comics
214 Sullivan St.
New York, NY 10012
PH: (212) 777-2770
E-MAIL: Infosales/village
comics.com
WEB: www.villagecomics.com

Dragon's Den
Poughkeepsie Plaza
Poughkeepsie, NY 12601
PH: (914) 471-1401
WEB: www.dragons-den.com

OKLAHOMA

Starbase 21
2130 S. Sheridan Rd.
Tulsa, OK 74129
PH: (918) 838-3388

TENNESSEE

Reward Investments, LLC
745 W. Elk Ave.
Elizabethton, TN 37643
PH: (423) 547-3655

TEXAS

Bedrock City Comic Co.
6517 Westheimer
Houston, TX 77057
PH: (713) 780-0675

VIRGINIA

Geppi's Comic World
Crystal City
1606 Crystal Square Arcade
Arlington, VA 22202
PH: (703) 413-0618

WASHINGTON

O'Leary's Books
3828 100th St. S.W.
Tacoma, WA 98499
PH: (253) 588-2503
PH: (800) 542-1791
FX: (253) 589-9115

WISCONSIN

Westfield's Comics, Etc.
676 S. Whitney Way
(next to Marshall's)
Madison, WI 53711
PH: (608) 277-1280
WEB: www.westfield.com

Westfield Comics
8608 University Green
P.O. Box 620470
Middleton, WI 53562-0470
PH: (608) 836-1945
FX: (608) 836-6950
E-MAIL:
westfield@westfield.com
WEB: www.westfield.com

CLASSIFIED ADS

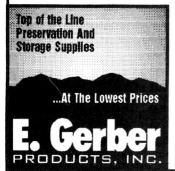

Overstreet Presents:

Hake's Price Guide to

Character Toys

Including Premiums, Comic, Cereal, TV, Movies, Radio & Related Store Bought Items

PRICING SECTION

THE PRINCIPLES OF PRICING:
AN INTRODUCTION TO THE PRICING SECTION

BY JOHN K. SNYDER, JR.

SELECTION OF MATERIAL

This edition of **Hake's Price Guide To Character Toys** is the result of more than 30 years of collecting, trading, buying, selling, and research in the field of character collectibles. The 350 characters and shows included in this volume are widely agreed to be the most sought-after in terms of both importance and collectibility. The 102 types of collectible categories represent the most highly defined breakdown ever documented of items featuring those characters.

This edition is also an expansion on what we learned by publishing the first edition. There are approximately 2,000 new items listed in this volume. There are 48 new character categories; the listings for many characters have been revised, some of them extensively, and a brand new selection of interesting items are presented in the color section.

Documenting this rich avenue of American pop-culture history is clearly an organic, on-going process with many vital components. Just as we strive to record everything from major and minor trends to individual items, so do our readers. Serious collectors are the driving force behind the growth of this book. Whether supplying photos of rare toys or simply asking the question that gets us looking in the right direction, it is our fellow collectors who are our primary inspiration.

No one book could hope to include every character, but if you have information about an important character we haven't included yet, or if you know of items for any of these which should be listed, please don't hesitate to contact the author by mail, fax or e-mail. Creating a historical archive like this book is a process which only works at its best when everyone participates! Send your information to: **Ted Hake**
Hake's Price Guide To Character Toys
P.O. Box 1444
York, PA 17405
Fax: (717) 852-0344
E-mail: hake@hakes.com

PUTTING A PREMIUM ON COLLECTIBLES

The first time we set out to do this book, many people thought it would be impossible. When you consider the amount of information presented, you'll see why. Any serious history of character toys would be severely flawed without the inclusion of premiums.

Premiums have a long but mostly undocumented history in the United States. Like any other collectible, their values are governed chiefly by supply and demand, but unlike store-bought toys, premiums were created with more than one objective in mind.

Whereas regular toys are created to make money for their manufacturer by entertaining children, premiums are created to advertise another product, to boost sales and awareness of that product, and generally to create some sort of identification with that product. Premiums are often money-makers for the companies which offer them, but sometimes they are the exact opposite. It depends on how one measures success. In the present era of mass marketing, when demographics, mailing lists and even e-mail mailing lists can be generated from responses to a premium offer, the revenue from the premium itself is not the only benchmark a firm has for success. With a premium, the company not only generates money, information and product identification, but it also frequently creates a collectible. Such collectibles carry with them the potential to be put on display, perhaps prominently, garnering prestige and further recognition for the company and its product.

ABOUT PRICING

The prices in this guide represent an honest and responsible evaluation of current market values. The prices are a moving average of auction results, dealer retail prices and market prices compiled from data supplied by advisors since the completion of the last edition of this book. As with most other types of collectibles, prices often vary widely from region to region according to supply and demand. With that in mind, every buyer and seller should determine pricing based on both the prices listed in this book and the factors specific to their region. The final judgement of what the price should be is that of the author, Ted Hake, and should be considered an informed opinion.

While finding an item for sale priced well under market value is a thrill for any collector, it is in everyone's interest that the true market value be reflected in any serious price guide. Imagine trying to replace your favorite pinback, poster or whistle ring for what it cost when issued rather than for the current going price. In most cases, you couldn't find anyone to take you seriously. At best, dealers would think you were joking. That's where a price guide such as this can be of immediate service. As indicated above, though, the prices in this book reflect a starting point from which collectors and dealers alike may choose to begin.

20TH CENTURY COLLECTIBLES

As we stand on the edge of a new millennium, we also stand on the threshold of a new era in collecting. This age will be remembered as a pivotal period in the history of pop-culture Americana since in less than two years the 20th Century will for the first time be seen as a complete unit. This event is significant not just as the turn of the century and the beginning of a new millennium, but because it represents a fundamental change in how we think about the things we collect.

A collector, for instance, might maintain an impressive collection of pre-World War II toys, comic books from 1956 to 1969, movie posters from the disaster films of the 1970s, or any other niche that collecting might offer. Seen from the other side of January 1, 2001, though, such collections will still be interesting and they will still be valuable, but they will also seem strangely incomplete. Sooner or later, someone will ask that collector, "Why did you stop there?"

For most, the nature of the stopping point will seem odd or obscure. Why would someone who collects Superman collect Superman comics up to 1974? Why would they collect all the comics, but not the toys? Why the movie posters, but not the other types of movie memorabilia? On the other side of the century, these questions will be harder to answer than they are within the boundaries of the present century.

Phrases like "Golden Age" and "Silver Age" may give way in common usage to broader, more inclusive, less arbitrary terms. "Twentieth Century Collectibles" is a phrase which is entering the collector's vernacular with both force and authority because it is simply the one phrase that covers the spectrum. And why not? It makes sense to collectors and to those who document sociological phenomena. It not only means exactly what it says, but it explains itself to potential new collectors. Thousands of people may know what the "Bronze Age" of American comic books is, but most people in the country should understand the phrase "Twentieth Century Collectibles."

SUCCESS: A COMMON THREAD

The characters we love and collect have diverse origins, but there's a common thread that runs through the ones who become the most successful in the long run. It has almost nothing to do with artistic direction, the quality of the material, special effects, or the rate of inflation.

A character may be introduced on a TV show, a cartoon, a newspaper comic strip, in a comic book, video game or a feature film. From any one of these venues a fad, flash-in-the-pan, or short-lived hit may be created, but these things are almost never sustained by one medium.

Characters like Mickey Mouse and Superman may have broken in through film and comic books, respectively, but each was the beneficiary of well-planned marketing and development programs which took those characters through just about every other available medium. The marketing of either Mickey or Superman makes an excellent case study in the development of a character.

As an example, **Action Comics** #1 (June 1938) launched Superman in comic books. At its peak, though, its circulation was approximately 1.5 million copies per month. The daily newspaper strip (January 1939) first introduced The Man of Steel to adults. A companion comic published in the summer of 1939,

John K. Snyder, Jr. holding a bound volume of **Superman** #1-12 from the Geppi library. **Superman** #1 featured the debut of "The Supermen of America," the fan club that led to many of the most sought-after Superman collectibles.

Superman #1, followed, and included the first mention of The Supermen of America, the official Superman fan club. The club's first contest began December 1, 1939 and ended January 28, 1940, with the Supermen of America member ring offered as a prize (now one of the most highly collectible Superman premiums). The audience, though now including adults and children, wasn't anywhere near its high point. On February 12, 1940, the Superman radio show took to the airwaves for the first time, and entire families–estimated at over 20 million listeners an episode–began tuning in three times a week.

Terms like "multimedia campaign" might not have been used then, but that's exactly what took place. In short order, Superman was in the movies and advertised on bread, milk and other food products; soon there were also toys and items of clothing sold in abundance. With expansion to television, the audience grew further, and there was, in fact, a mini-industry of just Superman items. The 1978 release of *Superman* with Christopher Reeve revitalized the Superman market.

Today, Superman polls as one of the most highly recognized characters around the world. A thoroughly orchestrated campaign put him in that position, and the same is true for many other characters.

Editor's note: For further insight into this area, turn to "The Master of Marketing" (page 43) and "A Collective Call to Arms" (page 50). Also, refer to the photo-listings in the Superman section to see how the marketing plan was carried out.

As publishers of the most respected price guide for comic books, **The Overstreet Comic Book Price Guide** (now in its 28th edition), we've seen this process played out in microcosm hundreds--perhaps thousands--of times. Great characters are launched; they become a hit within that particular niche, but eventually they slow down and then drop out all together. The same, obviously, can be said about characters created for TV, film or any other medium.

This in no way diminishes the thrill of collecting a character which is considered dormant. The successful character will have many toys or premiums while others will have fewer, but sometimes those few items make for the most rewarding finds. Nostalgia is a powerful driving force, and much of the joy it creates is personal. Each collector creates his own definition of what is highly desirable, and a price guide can only serve as a reflection of market activities and the value others place on items. ❖

OTHER REFERENCES

The Overstreet Comic Book Grading Guide (1st Edition)
by Robert M. Overstreet & Gary M. Carter
$12.00 Soft Cover
100-point grading system
for comic book condition

The Overstreet Comic Book Price Guide (28th Edition)
by Robert M. Overstreet
$18.00 Soft Cover $24.00 Hard Cover
Comic Books from 1897 to Present

The Overstreet Toy Ring Price Guide (3rd Edition)
by Robert M. Overstreet
$20.00 Soft Cover
Toy Rings from 1893 to Present

John K. Snyder, Jr. is President of Diamond International Galleries, and is a leading expert on comic character collectibles. He has served as a pricing advisor to The Overstreet Comic Book Price Guide, The Overstreet Toy Ring Price Guide, Hake's Price Guide To Character Toys, Collecting Figures magazine, Tomart's Radio Premiums Price Guide, Krause's Radio Premiums Price Guide and Toys & Prices, and the Original Comic Art Price Guide. His articles can also be found on the web at www.gemstonepub.com and www.diamondgalleries.com.

NOTE: Prices listed for all items represent GOOD, FINE, and NEAR MINT conditions.

ACE DRUMMOND

World War I air ace Eddie Rickenbacker created the story line for this aviation strip, with illustrations by Clayton Knight, for King Features in 1934. The strip was not a major success and was dropped in the late 1930s. A 13-episode adventure serial based on the strip was produced by Universal Pictures in 1936, with John King as Drummond and Noah Beery, Jr., as Jerry, his mechanic. The serial was released to TV in 1949.

ACE-1

ACE-1. "Ace Drummond" Cello. Button,
1936. Universal Pictures. For 13-chapter movie serial "Ace Drummond" with added inscription "Capt. Eddie Rickenbacker's Junior Pilot's Club". - **$75 $200 $325**

ADMIRAL BYRD

Richard E. Byrd (1888-1957), American aviator and pre-eminent polar explorer, flew to the North Pole and back in 1926, made a spectacular transatlantic flight in 1927, and starting in 1928, led several important expeditions to Antarctica. The second such expedition featured weekly on-site short wave broadcasts--*The Adventures of Admiral Byrd*--over the CBS network from November 1933 to January 1935. The program was sponsored by Grape-Nuts Flakes.

ADM-1   ADM-2   ADM-3

ADM-1. Commander Byrd Cello. Button,
c. 1928. Identified "Commander Richard E. Byrd". - **$10 $20 $30**

ADM-2. Admiral Byrd Cello. Button,
c. 1930. Profile picture inscribed "Rear Admiral Richard Evelyn Byrd, U.S.N." - **$8 $15 $25**

ADM-3. "Authorized Map Of The Second Byrd Antarctic Expedition",
c. 1933. General Foods. 18x24" opened. - **$25 $50 $80**

(FRONT)   ADM-4   (BACK)

ADM-4. Byrd Map Hard Cardboard Version,
c. 1933. Thick cardboard back with two hangers. - **$40 $85 $130**

ADM-6

ADM-5

ADM-5. "South Pole Radio News" Photo Newspaper,
c. 1933. Grape-Nuts, "The Cereal Byrd Took To Little America". Issue #3 shown. At least three issues known. Each - **$15 $30 $50**

ADM-6. "To The South Pole With Byrd" Booklet,
1933. Ralston Purina Co. - **$10 $15 $20**

ADM-7   ADM-8

ADM-7. Map Flyer,
1933. Grape Nuts Cereal premium. Talks about receiving and using the map. - **$5 $15 $25**

ADM-8. South Pole Radio News #2,
1933. Grape Nuts Cereal premium. - **$15 $30 $50**

      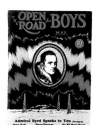

ADM-9

ADM-10

ADM-9. "Trail Blazers" Watch,
c. 1933. - **$200 $400 $500**

ADM-10. Magazine Cover Article,
1936. May issue of "The Open Road For Boys" with article and photos from his 1929 expedition to Little America of South Pole. - **$10 $15 $25**

ADM-11

ADM-12

ADM-11. Blotter,
1930s. Golden Guernsey Milk premium. - **$20 $40 $60**

ADM-12. Admiral Byrd Grape Nuts Booklet,
1930s. - **$15 $30 $45**

ADVENTURE COMICS

Major Malcolm Wheeler-Nicholson got into the comic book publishing business in early 1935 with *New Fun*. Although sales weren't very good, he decided to try a second title. *New Comics* #1 appeared in late 1935 with paper covers and 80 pages of color and black and white stories and art. Siegel and Shuster did Federal Men and Sheldon Mayer and Walt Kelly also contributed. Starting with issue #12, the title became *New Adventure* and finally *Adventure Comics* with issue #32. Like *New Fun*, *Adventure Comics* was part of the foundation of DC Comics. DC cancelled the title in 1983.

ADC-1

ADC-2

ADC-3

ADC-1. "Special Operator" Cello. Button,
c. 1937. New Adventure Comics magazine. -
$60 $150 $250

ADC-2. Club Member Cello. Button,
c. 1937. Inscribed "Special Operator/Junior Federal Men Club/New Adventure Comics Magazine." - **$60 $150 $250**

ADC-3. "Special Operator" Cello. Button,
c. 1939. Adventure Comics magazine. - **$75 $175 $275**

ADC-4

ADC-4. "Junior Federal Men Club" Member Card,
c. 1939. Adventure Comics magazine. Ink stamped Chief Operator's name "Steve Carson". - **$60 $100 $160**

ADVERTISING MISC.

Literally thousands of product makers in the past century have offered premiums in token or sporadic fashion. An absolute listing of all known advertising premiums would necessitate a massive set of volumes in book form while still leaving gaps of information lost in time. This section offers an overview of advertising premiums and similar items of established appeal to collectors. Represented are some of the most famous trademark characters of our popular culture. A more comprehensive listing is contained in *Hake's Guide To Advertising Collectibles/100 Years of Advertising From 100 Famous Companies* published in 1992.

ADV-1

ADV-2

ADV-1. Friends Oats Promo Booklet,
1800s. Uses children to promote cereal products. -
$20 $40 $60

ADV-2. J & P Coats Promo Calendar,
1888. Thread ad shows dogs reading paper. Classic example of animals being used to promote products. -
$8 $15 $25

ADV-3

ADV-4

ADV-3. J & P Coats Promo Card,
1880s. Thread ad shows captured lion. Early use of animals, later used cartoon characters. - **$8 $15 $25**

ADV-4. J & P Coats Promo Card,
1880s. Thread ad shows mice dressed up on front. Calendar on back. - **$8 $15 $25**

ADV-5   ADV-6   ADV-7

ADV-5. Quaker Oats Card,
1890. - **$10 $30 $50**

ADV-6. Roasted Oats Promo Card,
1899. - **$10 $30 $50**

ADV-7. Friends Oats Promo Booklet,
1890s. Front and back shown. - **$20 $40 $60**

(FRONT)   ADV-8   (BACK)

ADV-8. Frogs Thread J & P Coats Trade Card,
1890s. - **$15 $30 $60**

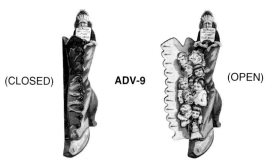

(CLOSED)   ADV-9   (OPEN)

ADV-9. Mother Goose Series - Mother in Shoes Trade Card,
1890s. Nestle's Chocolate. - **$30 $60 $90**

(FRONT)   ADV-10   (BACK)

ADV-10. Spider's Spool Cotton Trade Card,
1890s. - **$20 $40 $60**

ADV-11   ADV-12

ADV-11. Promo Card,
1900. Domestic sewing machine ad card shows elves climbing trees. - **$15 $25 $40**

ADV-12. Wheatlet Cereal Standee,
1900. Cereal and Flour Premium. 6" standee of girl in a long pink dress. - **$25 $50 $75**

ADV-13   ADV-14   ADV-15

ADV-13. Star Nursery Rhymes Book,
1901. Star Soap premium. Twenty page book in color with beautiful art. - **$25 $50 $75**

ADV-14. Mapl-Flake Promo,
1902. - **$15 $30 $50**

ADV-15. Mother Goose Series - Mother in Shoes Trade Card,
1900s. Nestle's Food. - **$10 $30 $45**

ADV-16   ADV-17

ADV-16. Ceresota Mill Worker Cloth Doll,
1912. 12" premium for Ceresota flour. - **$35 $75 $110**

ADV-17. The Ad-ven-tur-ous Billy And Betty,
1923. VanCamp Products. Fairy tales, 30 pages. Beautifully illustrated stories of Billy and Betty VanCamp. - **$30 $60 $100**

ADV-18

ADV-19

ADV-18. Red Goose Pocket Watch & Fob,
1927. Watch - **$200 $450 $650**
Fob - **$50 $120 $160**

ADV-19. Red Goose Alarm Clock,
1920s. - **$200 $400 $650**

ADV-20

ADV-21

ADV-20. "Red Goose Shoes" Card Toy,
1920s. "Mov-I-Graff." 3-1/2x6-1/2" card featuring fine chain mounted on character face to form various facial images when card is jiggled or tapped. - **$10 $18 $30**

ADV-21. Buffalo Bill Photo,
1920s. Circus premium of famous star. - **$20 $35 $50**

ADV-22

ADV-23

ADV-22. Lone Eagles Club Card
1934. Lone Eagles Magazine. See PUL-4. - **$20 $60 $85**

ADV-23. Lone Eagles Of America Club Letter
1934. National Lone Eagle Magazine. - **$5 $15 $25**

ADV-24

ADV-25

ADV-24. H. C. B. (Hot Cereal Breakfast) Club Grand Award Certificate,
1935. Cream-of-Wheat premium. - **$20 $40 $60**

ADV-25. H. C. B. (Hot Cereal Breakfast) Club Letter/Poster-on-Back,
1935. Cream-of-Wheat premium. - **$20 $40 $60**

ADV-26

ADV-27

ADV-26. Kool-Aid Membership Card,
1938. Kool-Aid Drink. Club card for Junior Aviation Corps. - **$15 $25 $40**

ADV-27. Behind The Eight Ball Club Kit,
1938. National Salesman Club. Has rules, membership card, small plastic eight ball, and box.
Complete - **$30 $65 $125**

ADV-28

ADV-29

ADV-28. Miller Wheat Flakes Cereal Sign 13x16 1/2"
1930s. Wheat Flakes promotional for free punch-out rubberband gun. - **$50 $100 $150**

ADV-29. Butter-Nut Bread Beanie,
1930s. Beanie type hat given away by bakeries. - **$10 $25 $40**

ADV-30

ADV-31

ADV-30. Richfield Puzzle,
1930s. Richfield Oil. India golf puzzle with mailer. -
$25 $50 $75

ADV-31. Richfield Puzzle,
1930s. Richfield Oil. Chinese golf puzzle with mailer. -
$25 $50 $75

ADV-32

ADV-33

ADV-34

ADV-32. Airplane Model League Of America Coupon,
1930s.American Boys Magazine. Coupon for joining club. -
$5 $10 $15

ADV-33. Airplane Model League Of America Membership Card,
1930s.American Boys Magazine. Club card. -
$10 $25 $35

ADV-34. Rippled Wheat - Jack Dempsey 6" Standee,
1930s. - **$50 $175 $275**

ADV-35

ADV-36

ADV-37

ADV-35. "Light Up A Kool" Willie Penguin Iron Cigarette Lighter,
1930s. - **$100 $200 $300**

ADV-36. "RCA" Cardboard Fan,
1930s. Radio Corp. of America. - **$35 $60 $100**

ADV-37. RCA Nipper Salt & Pepper Shaker Set,
1930s. By Lenox, 3" tall white china. - **$25 $50 $85**

ADV-38

ADV-39

ADV-38. G-Men Fingerprint System (Red Heart),
1930s. Instruction book. G-Man records and mailer. Gives children instructions on how to obtain fingerprints. Talks about capture of John Dillinger and gives advice from #1 G-Man J. Edgar Hoover. - **$30 $75 $100**

ADV-39 "Knot Hole League Of America" Patch,
1930s. Goudey Gum fabric patch plus member card for "Lou Gehrig" baseball club. Patch - **$50 $125 $250**
Card (Not Shown) - **$35 $75 $125**

ADV-40

ADV-41

ADV-42

ADV-40. "Michelin" Plastic Ashtray,
1930s. Likely produced into 1950s. - **$35 $70 $100**

ADV-41. Nipper Papier Mache Store Display,
1930s. Victor Talking Machine Co. - **$150 $225 $350**

ADV-42. Aristocrat Tomato Composition Figure,
1930s. White base or black base. - **$125 $200 $350**

ADV-43

ADV-44

ADV-45

ADV-43. Kool-Aid 10x12" Sign,
1930s. Has attached membership certificate for Junior Aviation Corps. - **$50 $100 $200**

ADV-44. T.W.A. Kool-Aid Club Instruction Form,
1930s. - **$20 $40 $60**

ADV-45. Kool-Aid Aviation Club Cap,
1930s. - **$30 $75 $90**

ADV-52

ADV-53

ADV-54

ADV-46

ADV-47

ADV-48

ADV-46. Sunny Jim Cloth Doll,
1930s. Force Cereal premium. - **$50 $75 $150**

ADV-47. ESKO-GRAM Sign,
1930s. With promo list that promotes premiums. - **$30 $80 $125**

ADV-48. Stamp Album For 48 Stamps,
1940. Tydol Oil. - **$10 $20 $30**

ADV-52. "RCA Victor Little Nipper" Cello. Button,
c. 1948. "Club Member" designation for children's records series. - **$25 $40 $75**

ADV-53. Fearless Fosdick Matches,
1949. Unused - **$8 $15 $25**

ADV-54. Dorothy Dix Food Advisor Booklet,
1949. Sealtest. Four page radio premium. - **$15 $25 $35**

ADV-55

ADV-56

ADV-49

ADV-49. Stamps For Album,
1940. Tydol Oil. Each Loose or Mounted - **$1 $2 $3**

ADV-55. Tums Broadcasting Equipment,
1940s. Radio premium with mailer. - **$25 $50 $75**

ADV-56. Macy's Red Star Club Badge,
1940s. Scarce. - **$20 $50 $70**

ADV-57

ADV-58

ADV-59

ADV-51

ADV-50

ADV-57. Red Goose Tin Whistle,
1940s. Shoe premium. - **$10 $30 $45**

ADV-58. War Bond Matchbook Promo,
1940s. Striking surface on Hitler's rear end. - **$30 $75 $125**

ADV-59. Rocket Gyro X-3 with Mailer,
1940s. Sponsor Hometown Grocers. - **$20 $60 $75**

ADV-50. Flibbity Jibbit Book Premium,
1943. Junkets Dessert premium. 32 pages. Vernon Grant art. - **$25 $50 $75**

ADV-51. Chiquita Banana Fabric Doll Pattern With Envelope,
c. 1944. Kellogg's Corn Flakes. First version offered.
Near Mint Packaged - **$100**
Loose Uncut - **$20 $40 $60**

ADV-60

ADV-61

ADV-60. Zoom Bullet Pen And Mailer,
1940s. Premium bullet yellow pen from Zoom Cereal for Future Flyers. - **$10 $35 $50**

ADV-61. Tip-Top Bread Dial,
1940s. Select Presidents of U.S. - **$10 $20 $35**

ADV-62

ADV-63

ADV-64

ADV-62. Philip Morris 1' Tall Standee,
1940s. 4" wide. Classic picture of Johnny , who always called out, "Call for Philip Morris." - **$50 $100 $150**

ADV-63. "Dr. Kool" Plaster Figure Paperweight,
1940s. - **$75 $150 $225**

ADV-64. Kool Plastic Salt & Pepper Set,
1951. Boxed - **$20 $50 $80**
Loose - **$15 $25 $35**

ADV-65

ADV-66

ADV-67

ADV-65. "Fearless Fosdick" Product Sticker,
1954. Wildroot Cream-Oil Hair Dressing. 3x7" probable design for store window display. - **$20 $40 $75**

ADV-66. 7up "Fresh Up Freddie" Litho. Button,
c. 1959. - **$10 $20 $30**

ADV-67. 7up "Fresh-Up Freddie" Soft Rubber Doll,
c. 1959. - **$50 $125 $250**

ADV-68

ADV-69

ADV-68. "Oscar Mayer" Plastic Weinermobile,
1950s. "Little Oscar" figure rises and lowers. - **$75 $175 $250**

ADV-69. Missile Game Set,
1950s. Consists of map, punch-outs, manual, instructions, game board, and mailer. Hi-C Minute Maid premium. - **$35 $75 $100**

ADV-70

ADV-71

ADV-70. "RCA" Victor Plastic Salt & Pepper Set,
1950s. RCA Victor Corp - **$30 $45 $60**

ADV-71. Bardahl Detective Club 10x15" Sign,
1950s. Rare. Shows all the villains. - **$100 $250 $450**

ADV-72

ADV-73

ADV-72. Fireball Twigg Midget Kite Kit with Mailer,
1950s. 6 Kites. - **$20 $40 $65**

ADV-73. Grape-Nuts Flakes Fireball Twigg Kite Premium Sign,
1950s. - **$20 $50 $90**

ADV-74

ADV-75

ADV-74. Red Goose Shoe,
1950s. St. Louis Zoo punch-outs. - **$30 $75 $100**

ADV-75. Flap Happy Bird with Mailer,
1950s. Post Toasties premium. - **$20 $40 $60**

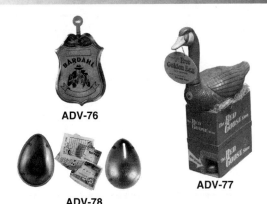

ADV-76

ADV-78

ADV-77

ADV-76. Bardahl Club Shield Litho. Tab,
1950s. - **$5 $10 $20**

ADV-77. Red Goose Display Goose,
1950s. Scarce. Goose lays plastic golden eggs. -
$400 $750 $950

ADV-78. Red Goose Gold Plastic Egg-Bank,
1950s. Bank contained prize, connected to previous item. -
$10 $25 $35

ADV-79

ADV-79. Esso Space Captain Sign (Silver Wings),
1950s. Canada. - **$30 $60 $100**

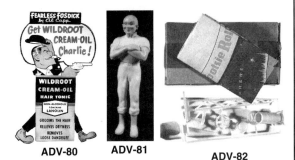

ADV-80   ADV-81

ADV-82

ADV-80. Fearless Fosdick 15x36" Standee,
1950s. Scarce. Wildroot Hair Tonic. Five pieces attached
to box. - **$400 $850 $1250**

ADV-81. Mr. Clean Vinyl Doll,
c. 1961. Procter & Gamble. - **$30 $50 $80**

ADV-82. Astronaut -Orbit - Target Game,
1962. Tootsie Roll premium. Plastic rocket with man and
paper targets. Shows statistics of seven U.S. and Russian
men who have been in space. Instruction and mailer
enclosed. Near Mint Boxed Unassembled - **$100**
Assembled With Target - **$20 $40 $60**

ADV-83

ADV-83. Esso "Happy Motoring" Coloring Book,
1963. Esso/Humble Oil. 24 pages picturing national land-
marks described by "Happy" Oil Drop character. -
$10 $20 $30

ADV-85

ADV-84   ADV-86

ADV-84. Robin Hood Decoder and Mailer,
1963. ARO Milk premium. - **$30 $80 $125**

ADV-85. "Bud Man" Ceramic Stein,
c. 1969. Re-issued in 1990s. Original marked under base.
Ceramarte made in Brazil. - **$125 $175 $300**

ADV-86. Football Movie Viewer And Slides,
1969. Chiquita. 26 slides of photos of All Star football players like Bubba Smith, Mercury Morris, Joe Greene, Bob
Lilly, and others. Also includes mailer and yellow plastic
viewer. - **$50 $100 $175**

ADV-87

ADV-87. P.F. Branding Iron Kit With Whistle On Card,
1960s. Scarce. B.F. Goodrich premium. Plastic kit with
membership card on back. - **$75 $150 $200**

ADV-88

ADV-89

ADV-88. Marky Maypo Vinyl Figure,
1960s. Maypo Cereal. - **$25 $50 $75**

ADV-89. Wheat Chex Magic Kit,
1960s. 24 trick instruction book, includes items: 7 paper, 1 ring, 8 plastic, 3 wood, 3 metal. - **$25 $50 $75**

ADV-90

ADV-91

ADV-92

ADV-93

ADV-90. SpaghettiOs Spoon Premium,
1960s. - **$10 $20 $30**

ADV-91. Colonel Sanders Composition Bobbing Head,
1960s. - **$50 $110 $175**

ADV-92. Bud Man Foam Rubber Doll,
c. 1970. - **$75 $125 $160**

ADV-93. "Chicken Hungry" Flexible Plastic Ring,
1972. Red Barn System. - **$10 $20 $35**

ADV-94

ADV-95

ADV-96

ADV-94. Indian Sticker Badges,
1972. Ovaltine premium. 6 different. Each - **$4 $8 $12**

ADV-95. "Bazooka Joe" Cloth Doll,
c. 1973. Bazooka Gum. 19" tall. - **$12 $25 $40**

ADV-96. Colonel Sanders 100 Club Award,
1970s. Quality Service Club Award, approx. 4" in diameter. - **$20 $40 $50**

ADV-97

ADV-98

ADV-99

ADV-100

ADV-97. Eskimo Pie Cloth Doll,
1970s. 12" premium. - **$20 $40 $60**

ADV-98. Ben Franklin Stuffed Doll,
1960s. Franklin Life Insurance Premium. - **$20 $40 $60**

ADV-99. "Burger Chef" Hand Puppet,
1970s. Soft vinyl head with fabric chef hat and body. - **$50 $125 $200**

ADV-100. Tastykake Cloth Doll,
1970s. Scarce. Tastykake Bakery. - **$25 $50 $80**

ADV-102

ADV-101

ADV-103

ADV-101. "Heinz" Talking Plastic Alarm Clock,
1980s. Battery operated. - **$50 $100 $150**

ADV-102. Raid Bug Plastic Wind-Up,
1980s. - **$35 $75 $125**

ADV-103. Raid Battery Operated Plastic Robot With Remote Control,
1980s. - **$125 $250 $300**

ADV-104

ADV-105

ADV-106

ADV-104. Hershey "Messy Marvin Magic Decoder",
1980s. Hershey's Chocolate Syrup. Mechanical cardboard with two diecut letter openings. - **$5 $12 $20**

ADV-105. Twinkie the Kid 4' Anniversary Standee,
1990. - **$30 $85 $125**

ADV-106. "Oscar Mayer" Weinermobile,
c. 1991. Re-issue without Little Oscar figure. -
$10 $15 $20

AIR JUNIORS

One of the earliest radio clubs designed to encourage happy boys and girls to learn about flying airplanes and aspire to become pilots when they grew up, the *Air Juniors* club was formed in 1929. It was sponsored by the Commonwealth Edison Electric Shops. The project was promoted on the WENR Radio station broadcasting out of Chicago. The idea for the club piggybacked on the popularity of Charles Lindbergh's flight from New York to Paris in May of 1927.

AIR-1

AIR-2

AIR-3

AIR-1. Member's Card,
1929. - **$20 $60 $85**

AIR-2. Club Letter,
1929. - **$10 $15 $30**

AIR-3. Club Member Pin,
1929. Scarce. - **$75 $125 $200**

ALPHONSE & GASTON

"You first, my dear Gaston!" "After you, my dear Alphonse!" Frederick Opper's pair of acutely polite Frenchmen and their friend Leon first appeared in the Hearst Syndicate Sunday pages in 1902. The strip was a hit with readers, but after 1904 the characters appeared only occasionally in Opper's other strips, particularly *Happy Hooligan* and *And Her Name Was Maud*. An early collection of color reprints was published by the *N.Y. American & Journal*.

ALP-1

ALP-2

ALP-1. "Alfonse & Gaston" Cut-Out Supplement,
1902. New York American & Journal newspaper.
Uncut - **$25 $50 $75**

ALP-2. Cello. Button,
c. 1903. Advertises South Dakota State Fair. - **$8 $15 $30**

ALP-3

ALP-4

ALP-3. Handkerchief,
c. 1903. Probable store item. - **$15 $30 $45**

ALP-4. Cello. Button,
1903. Advertises Omaha Grocers and Butchers picnic. -
$10 $20 $35

ALP-5

ALP-6

ALP-7

ALP-5. Cello. Button Without Imprint,
c. 1903. - **$15 $30 $50**

ALP-6. Alfonse Tinted White Metal Charm,
c. 1904. There is a matching Gaston. Each - **$5 $12 $20**

ALP-7. Aluminum Cartoon Card,
c. 1904. Store item set of 10 aluminum cards, only one featuring Alphonse & Gaston. Card pictures lady waiting at her bed as they deliberate who should go first. -
$15 $25 $40

ALP-8

ALP-8. Postcard,
1906. American Journal Newspapers. - **$8 $15 $25**

AMERICAN BANDSTAND

It started in 1952 on WFIL, a Philadelphia ABC affiliate, and went on to become one of television's longest-running and most successful shows. Dick Clark brought *American Bandstand* to prime-time ABC in 1957, where it ran for 13 weeks from October through December. Since then, under various names and in different formats and time slots, Clark's program has showcased thousands of contemporary bands, singers and dancers. Currently, Dick Clark hosts reruns of *American Bandstand* on the VH-1 cable network. Promotional items associated with the show typically carry an American Broadcasting Co. copyright.

AME-1

AME-2

AME-8

AME-9

AME-10

AME-1. Bandstand Yearbook,
1955. WFIL-TV Philadelphia. Local program hosted by Bob Horn, pre-dating Dick Clark era. - **$15 $25 $40**

AME-2. "Dick Clark Yearbook",
1957. - **$10 $30 $40**
Mailer - **$5 $10 $20**

AME-8. "Platterpuss" Cat Cloth Doll With Tag,
1950s. Store item. 14" tall with tag inscription "Official Autograph Mascot/Dick Clark American Bandstand". - **$40 $75 $125**

AME-9. "Secret Diary",
1950s. Store item. - **$20 $35 $50**

AME-10. American Bandstand Patch of Dick Clark,
1950s. - **$10 $20 $35**

AME-3

AME-4

AME-5

AME-11

AME-12

AME-3. "This Week Magazine" Cover Article,
November 16, 1958. Sunday supplement magazine of various newspapers. - **$5 $8 $12**

AME-4. "Dick Clark Yearbook",
c. 1959. - **$10 $20 $30**

AME-5. Store Display With Jewelry,
1950s. Scarce. Displays 17 pieces including necklace, cuff links and tie clasps. Complete - **$200 $400 $650**

AME-11. American Bandstand Ad Promo Display,
1950s. Promotes Vicks Cough Drops. - **$25 $50 $90**

AME-12. Cello. Button,
1950s. WFIL-TV (Philadelphia). - **$10 $20 $35**

AME-6

AME-7

AME-13

AME-14

AME-15

AME-6. "Dick Clark"/"IFIC" 3" Litho. Buttons,
1950s. Beech-Nut Gum, TV show sponsor. "Ific" is from slogan "Beech-Nut Gum Is Flavor-Ific."
Picture Version - **$10 $15 $20**
Initials Version - **$5 $8 $12**

AME-7. Dick Clark Doll,
1950s. Store item by Juro. - **$150 $300 $400**

AME-13. Cardboard Record Case,
1950s. Store item. - **$25 $60 $90**

AME-14. "Caravan Of Stars" Program,
c. 1964. - **$15 $20 $30**

AME-15. "Where The Action Is" TV Show Program,
c. 1966. - **$12 $20 $30**

AME-16

AME-17

AME-16. "Caravan Of Stars" Concert Program,
1967. - **$15 $25 $35**

AME-17. "20 Years Of Rock And Roll Yearbook",
1973. - **$12 $20 $30**

AMOS 'N' ANDY

Amos Jones and Andrew H. Brown, rustic blacks striving to succeed in the big city, were born in the imaginations of Freeman Gosden and Charles Correll, two white show business producers. Amos and Andy ran the Fresh Air Taxicab Co. and--together with George Stevens, the Kingfish of the Mystic Knights of the Sea Lodge--enchanted and entranced a huge radio audience in the 1930s. The program, probably the most successful radio series ever, was aired locally in Chicago beginning in March 1928 and went to the NBC network in August 1929. Sponsors included Pepsodent toothpaste until 1937, Campbell's soup until 1943, and Rinso soap, Rexall drugs and Chrysler automobiles. *The Amos and Andy Music Hall* ran on CBS radio from 1954 to 1960, and a prime-time television series with a black cast appeared on CBS from 1951 to 1953. A feature film about the show and its place in history is in development.

AMO-1

AMO-2

AMO-1. Cast Photo & Mailer,
1929. Pepsodent Co. Photo Only - **$5 $15 $30**
With Mailer And Letter - **$30 $75 $105**

AMO-2. Fan Postcard,
1929. Surebest Bread. Photo pictures actual portrayers of radio broadcast Amos and Andy. - **$10 $20 $30**

AMO-3

AMO-4

AMO-3. Gosden & Correll Biography Folder,
1930. Accompanied Pepsodent cardboard standup figure set of two. - **$5 $15 $25**

AMO-4. Pepsodent Cardboard Standup Figure Set,
1930. Each - **$20 $40 $75**

AMO-5

AMO-5. "Amos 'N' Andy On The Screen" Movie Herald,
1930. R-K-O Radio Pictures. Double-fold leaflet, photos show front cover and both sides opened. - **$20 $40 $75**

AMO-6

AMO-7

AMO-6. Cardboard Candy Box,
1930. Williamson Candy Co. - **$75 $150 $225**

AMO-7. Photo Card,
1930s. Exhibit card from numbered set of about 20.
Each - **$5 $12 $20**

AMO-8

AMO-8. Cardboard Standup Figures With Letters And Envelope,
1931. Set of six figures with two letters promoting Pepsodent toothpaste and urging dental visit.
Near Mint In Envelope - **$250**
Each Standup - **$10 $20 $30**

AMO 9

AMO-10

AMO-9. Song Book,
1931. Check and Double Check movie theme. - **$20 $35 $50**

AMO-10. Ford Automobile Promotion Letter,
1931. Ford Motor Co. local dealers. Promotion letter for Ford products in dialect text on Fresh Air Taxi Cab Co. letterhead. - **$40 $85 $150**

AMO-11

AMO-12

AMO-11. Candy Display Box,
1931. Williamson Candy Company. Candy bars held in box on Amos' back. - **$150 $300 $500**

AMO-12. Puzzle,
1932. Pepsodent Co. - **$25 $75 $100**

AMO-13

AMO-14

AMO-13. Radio Episode Script,
December 25, 1935. Pepsodent. For episode "Amos' Wedding". - **$10 $20 $30**

AMO-14. Radio Theme Song Sheet Music,
1935. Pepsodent Toothpaste, also store item. Pepsodent Imprint - **$10 $20 $40**
Store Item - **$10 $20 $35**

AMO-15

AMO-15. "Eagle's-Eye View Of Weber City (Inc.)" Map,
1935. Pepsodent Co. Prize to each entrant of "Why I Like Pepsodent Toothpaste" contest.
Near Mint In Envelope - **$100**
Map Only - **$15 $30 $60**

AMO-16

AMO-17

AMO-16. Pepsodent Contest Winner Check,
1936. Rare. - **$400 $750 $925**

AMO-17. "Campbell's Soup" 13x20" Paper Poster,
c. 1938. - **$20 $50 $100**

AMO-18

AMO-19

AMO-20

AMO-18. "Amos" Wood Jointed Doll,
1930s. Store item. - **$150 $300 $500**

AMO-19. "Andy" Wood Jointed Doll,
1930s. Store item. - **$75 $125 $200**

AMO-20. Bisque Figurines,
1930s. Store item. Pair - **$100 $225 $350**

AMO-21

AMO-22

AMO-21. Detroit Sunday Times Supplement Photo,
1930s. - **$15 $25 $40**

AMO-22. "Fresh Air Taxicab Company" Stock Certificate,
1930s. - **$100 $180 $250**

AMO-23

AINTIT A DANDY
CANDY NOVELTY

AMO-24

AMO-23. "Fresh Air Taxicab Company" Stock Certificate,
1930s. Seen with advertising on bottom margin for "Ford Furniture Stores In Northwestern New Jersey." - **$100 $180 $250**

AMO-24. Glass Candy Container,
1930s. Store item usually identified as Amos 'n' Andy is actually an unlicensed candy novelty called "Aintit A Dandy." Painted with Amos in blue suit, brown hair; Andy in red suit, brown derby. Value for example with tin cover on underside. - **$150 $300 $600**

AMO-25

AMO-26

AMO-25. Amos 'N' Andy Candy Wrapper,
1930s. Store item. Williamson Candy Co. "An Oh Henry Product." - **$40 $85 $150**

AMO-26. Lead Ashtray,
1930s. Store item. - **$100 $225 $400**

AMO-27

AMO-28

AMO-27. "Free Ride In Fresh Air Taxi" Litho. Button,
1930s. Amos 'N Andy Fresh Air Candy. From known series of 19 with different slogan on each including one example picturing the taxi. Each - **$10 $20 $40**

AMO-28. Amos and Andy Broadcast Sign,
1940s. - **$50 $125 $225**

AMO-29

AMO-29. Amos and Andy Plenamins Promo Band,
1940s. - **$20 $40 $65**

ANNIE OAKLEY

Born in a log cabin in Ohio, Annie Oakley (1860-1926) was a skilled marksman even as a child. Nicknamed "Little Sure Shot," she joined the Buffalo Bill Wild West Show in 1885 and toured the world for 17 years. Her trick shooting was a consistent sensation and she continued setting and breaking records as late as 1920.

Hollywood began producing romanticized versions of the Annie Oakley legend as early as 1935. On the big screen she has been portrayed by--among others-- Barbara Stanwyck, Betty Hutton, Gail Davis, and Geraldine Chaplin; on Broadway by Ethel Merman; on television by Jamie Lee Curtis in a made-for-TV movie; and, memorably, by Gail Davis. Produced by Gene Autry Flying A Productions, the *Annie Oakley* television series with Gail Davis aired originally on ABC from 1954 to 1956, sponsored by Canada Dry, TV Time popcorn and Wonder bread. There was a brief revival in 1964-1965. *Annie Oakley* comic books appeared in the 1940s and 1950s.

ANN-1

ANN-2

(ENLARGED VIEW)

ANN-1. Movie Version "Annie Oakley" Dixie Ice Cream Picture, 1935. Pictures Barbara Stanwyck in title role from RKO Radio Pictures release. - **$10 $20 $40**

ANN-2. Movie "Annie Oakley" Lobby Hanger, 1935. RKO Radio Pictures. 17" tall diecut stiff paper string hanger assembled into rectangle bottom. Pictured is title star Barbara Stanwyck. - **$50 $100 $150**

ANN-3

ANN-4

ANN-5

ANN-3. Canada Dry Ginger Ale "Free Carton" Coupon,
1954. Carton insert paper offering free carton for six bottle caps mailed to bottlers with offer expiring June 30. - **$5 $10 $15**

ANN-4. "Annie Oakley And Tagg" Cello. Button,
c. 1955. Club issue by unknown sponsor. Also inscribed "Gail Davis/Member/Sharpshooter." - **$50 $100 $150**

ANN-5. Annie Oakley Litho. Button,
c. 1955. - **$10 $20 $30**

ANN-6   ANN-7

ANN-6. Annie Oakley Cello. Button,
c. 1955. Pictures Gail Davis. Australian issue. - **$30 $60 $90**

ANN-7. Annie Oakley Cello. Button,
c. 1955. Pictures Gail Davis. - **$20 $40 $75**

ANN-8

ANN-8. "Hostess Surprise Party" Puzzle Folder,
c. 1955 Hostess Cupcakes. Leaflet with diecut strip panels to be arranged properly to reveal her as surprise hostess and her Hostess products. - **$15 $30 $50**

ANN-9   ANN-10

ANN-9. Wonder Bread Flipper Badge,
c. 1955. Two-sided cardboard with pin fastener plus pull string for completion of front and back message "Annie Oakley Says Eat Wonder Bread." - **$10 $25 $40**

ANN-10. Wonder Bread Cardboard Badge,
c. 1955. 4" cardboard urging TV viewership. Back is blank with fastener pin at top margin, probable design for store clerk. - **$15 $30 $50**

ANN-11

ANN-12

ANN-11. Wonder Bread Coloring Contest Store Sign,
c. 1955. 6-1/2x12" cardboard placard for contest offering prize of tickets to live rodeo performance. - **$25 $50 $75**

ANN-12. Wonder Bread Rodeo Announcement,
c. 1955. Waxed paper bread loaf insert strip for live performance in "Days Of '47 Rodeo" believed titled by commemorative nature year. - **$5 $10 $15**

ANN-13

ANN-13. Annie Oakley Hat,
1950s. Store bought. - **$20 $50 $90**

THE ARCHIES

Archie Andrews, typical American teen, first appeared in December 1941 in *Pep Comics* and in more than 50 years has not yet aged a day. Artist Bob Montana created Archie, his girlfriends Betty and Veronica, his pal Jughead, his rival Reggie, and dozens of other students at Riverdale High. They have appeared in comic books, a syndicated newspaper strip, paperback books, 15-and 30-minute radio shows (from 1943 to 1953 on the Mutual and NBC networks), and, starting in 1968, a continuing succession of TV cartoons on CBS or NBC. Archie became a merchandising success as well as a cartoon phenomenon: his bubble gum rock band even produced three hit songs.

ARC-1

ARC-1. Final July Issue Of "Hi" Magazine Before Becoming Archie Magazine,
1948. Diamond Sales Corporation. Clothing store promotion announcing forthcoming title change plus picturing cast members of radio show. - **$20 $40 $60**

ARC-2   ARC-3

ARC-2. Magazines,
1948. Archie Comics Publications Inc.
Each - **$15 $25 $40**

ARC-3. "Archie Pin-Up Calendar,"
1952. 6x9" calendar sheet obtained by mail coupon in back of Archie comic books. - **$15 $30 $60**

ARC-4

ARC-5

ARC-4. Club Member Cello. Button,
1950s. Version without accent border. - **$5 $10 $15**

ARC-5. Archie Spring-Loaded Plastic Head,
1969. Post Cereals. - **$5 $10 $20**

ARC-6

ARC-6. "Post Super Sugar Crisp" Box With "The Archies Record",
1969. Example from set of 4 boxes. Each - **$20 $50 $80**

ARC-7

ARC-7. Comic Book Club Kit,
1960s. Includes envelope, letter, card, cello. button.
Set - **$20 $50 $70**

ARC-8   ARC-9   ARC-10

ARC-8. "Official Member Archie Club" Cello. Button,
c. 1960s. For comic book club. - **$3 $8 $12**

ARC-9. Club Member Cello. Button,
c. 1960s. One of at least two versions accented by rim color. - **$5 $10 $15**

ARC-10. Archie Club Felt Beanie,
1960s. - **$25 $60 $100**

ARC-11   ARC-13

ARC-12

ARC-11. "Archies Gang!" Vending Machine Paper,
1970. Archie Comic Publications Inc. Advertises vending items including 16 buttons and five booklets. - **$5 $10 $15**

ARC-12. Picture Or Slogan Litho. Buttons,
1970. Store item vending machine set of sixteen.
Each Picture - **$2 $4 $8**
Each Slogan - **$1 $3 $5**

ARC-13. Welch's Jelly Glasses,
1971. Set of eight. Each - **$3 $5 $10**

AUNT JEMIMA

Aunt Jemima Pancake Flour was formulated in 1889 in St. Joseph Missouri, but it was the 1892 Columbian Exposition in Chicago that made Jemima a national figure. The R.T. Davis Mill & Manufacturing Co. hired Nancy Green, a black cook from Kentucky to stand outside its exposition booth and cook pancakes--more than a million, it is claimed--during the course of the fair. Ms. Green traveled the country making personal appearances as Aunt Jemima for the next 30 years until her death in 1923. Quaker Oats bought the product and name in 1924, and today there are over three dozen Aunt Jemima breakfast products. Various Aunt Jemima variety programs ran on CBS between 1929 and 1953 in either 5-minute or 15-minute versions. The trademark face has been re-drawn a number of times, most recently in 1989.

AUN-1

AUN-2

AUN-1. Cello. Button,
c. 1896. First issue is not inscribed "Pancake Flour."
Without Inscription - **$35 $100 $150**
With Inscription - **$25 $75 $100**

AUN-2. Needle Book With Doll Offer,
c. 1910. Davis Milling Co. Diecut paper folder holding
sewing needles and related plus panel ad for "Aunt
Jemima Rag Doll Family." - **$30 $75 $125**

AUN-3

**AUN-3. Aunt Jemima, Uncle Mose Doll Fabrics With
Envelope,**
c. 1915. Scarce. Aunt Jemima Mills Co.
Near Mint Uncut In Mailer - **$900**
Each Cut Or Assembled - **$100 $225 $300**

AUN-4

AUN-5

AUN-6

AUN-4. Cloth Doll,
1929. Scarce. Near Mint Uncut - **$600**
Assembled - **$75 $175 $350**

AUN-5. Hard Plastic Salt & Pepper Set,
c. 1949. - **$15 $25 $40**

AUN-6. Premium Doll (unstuffed) and Instructions,
1948. - **$30 $90 $150**

AUN-7

AUN-8

AUN-7. Plastic Syrup Pitcher With Box,
c. 1949. Boxed - **$30 $75 $100**
Loose - **$15 $50 $75**

AUN-8. Plastic Cookie Jar,
1950s. - **$100 $300 $400**

AUN-9

AUN-9. Vinyl Stuffed Doll Set,
1950s. Set of four - **$75 $175 $300**

AUN-10

AUN-10. "Pastry Mix Set",
1950s. Store item by Junior Chef. Complete -
$35 $60 $125

AUN-11

AUN-12

AUN-13

AUN-11. Chrome Metal Cigarette Lighter,
1960s. - **$25 $50 $75**

AUN-12. "Breakfast Club" 4" Litho Button,
1960s. - **$12 $25 $35**

AUN-13. Litho. Tab With Color Portrait,
1960s. - **$8 $12 $18**

AUNT JENNY

Known under a number of names--*Aunt Jenny, Aunt
Jenny's Real Life Stories, Aunt Jenny's Thrilling Real
Life Stories, Aunt Jenny's True-Life Stories*, and in
Canada as *Aunt Lucy*--this 15-minute serial drama ran
five times a week on CBS radio for almost 20 years,
from 1937 to 1956. Jenny, played by Edith Spencer and
Agnes Young, was assisted by her announcer Danny,
played by Dan Seymour, in relating the troubles of her
friends and neighbors, providing a golden thought of

the day, and offering cooking tips, invariably involving Spry, her longtime sponsor.

AJR-1

AJR-2

AJR-1. Cast Member Photo With Mailer Envelope,
c. 1937. Lever Brothers. Facsimile signature "Best Wishes/Dan Seymour-Sincerely Jennifer F. Wheeler (Aunt Jenny)". Mailer - **$3 $5 $10**
Photo - **$8 $12 $20**

AJR-2. Fan Photo With Mailer,
c. 1937. Lever Bros. 8x10" black and white with facsimile signature "Jennifer F. Wheeler (Aunt Jenny)".
Mailer - **$3 $5 $10**
Photo - **$8 $12 $20**

AJR-3

AJR-4

AJR-5

AJR-3. Cook Book,
1942. Spry Cooking Oil. Fifty pages of recipes. -
$10 $20 $35

AJR-4. Recipe,
1940s. Spry Cooking Oil. Green premium cardboard disc - Coconut cake. - **$10 $20 $30**

AJR-5. "Complete Birthday Kit" With Mailer Box,
1940s. Spry Cooking Oil. Contents include small candles, candle holders, cake frosting tints, cake recipe leaflet, birthday scroll piece for cake. - **$8 $12 $20**

AJR-6

AJR-7

AJR-6. Cake Knife With Advertising On Cardboard Cover,
c. 1940s. Scarce. - **$30 $90 $125**

AJR-7. "Aunt Jenny's Recipe Book-12 Pies Husbands Like Best",
1952. Lever Brothers. - **$5 $12 $25**

AJR-8

AJR-9

AJR-10

AJR-8. Recipe,
1950s. Spry Cooking Oil. Yellow premium cardboard disc - Cherry rolls. - **$10 $20 $30**

AJR-9. "Old Home Recipes" Folder,
1940s. Spry cooking oil. Unfolds to 3-1/2x13" sheet printed on both sides. - **$3 $6 $10**

AJR-10. "Favorite Recipes" Booklet,
1940s. Spry cooking oil. 6x7" with 52 pages. - **$5 $12 $20**

BABE RUTH

George Herman "Babe" Ruth (1895-1948), baseball legend and American national hero, began playing professionally in 1914 for the old Baltimore Orioles before being purchased by the Boston Red Sox. He was a formidable pitcher, but it was his bat that propelled him to greatness. He led the major leagues in home runs in 10 of the 12 years between 1919 and 1930, and in 1927 he hit a record 60. He played in the outfield for the New York Yankees from 1920 to 1935 and Yankee Stadium became known as "The House That Ruth Built." The Babe appeared on several network radio shows: *Play Ball* and *The Adventures of Babe Ruth* sponsored by Quaker cereals in 1934, the *Sinclair Babe Ruth Program* in 1937, *Here's Babe Ruth* in 1943 and *Baseball Quiz* in 1943 and 1944. Eleven issues of *Babe Ruth Sports Comics* were published by Harvey Publications from 1949 to 1951. Ruth was the subject of two feature films, *The Babe Ruth Story* (1948) and *The Babe* (1992). The Babe Ruth Birthplace & Official Orioles Museum in Baltimore, Maryland showcases his early years, playing career, and great moments in baseball history.

BAB-1

BAB-2

BAB-1. "Babe Ruth Song" Litho. Button,
1928. Promotes sheet music for song following his 1927 record-breaking year of 60 home runs in season. -
$15 $30 $60

BAB-2. "Babe's Musical Bat",
c. 1930. German made store item. 4" long wood replica bat with insert harmonica reeds. - **$50 $85 $150**

BAB-3   BAB-4

BAB-3. "Babe Ruth's Baseball Club" Contest Prize,
1934. Quaker Puffed Wheat. Second prize in weekly contests of Babe Ruth model Spalding fielder glove with facsimile Ruth signature. - **$150 $300 $500**

BAB-4. "Babe Ruth's Baseball Club" Contest Prize,
1934. Quaker Puffed Wheat, also store item. Weekly contest third prize boxed Spalding "Babe Ruth Home Run Special" baseball. Box - **$150 $300 $400**
Baseball - **$100 $250 $400**

BAB-5

BAB-5. Baseball Scorer,
c. 1934. Quaker Cereals. Cardboard mechanical disk card.
- **$25 $60 $100**

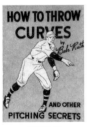

BAB-6   BAB-7   BAB-8

BAB-6. Quaker Cereal "How To Throw Curves" Booklet,
1934. - **$15 $30 $75**

BAB-7. Quaker Cereal "How To Knock Home Runs" Booklet,
1934. Two additional "How To" booklets (not shown) are "Play The Infield" and "Play The Outfield". Each - **$15 $30 $75**

BAB-8. Quaker Oats "Babe Ruth Hitting A Homer" Flip Booklet,
1934. Pages flip for batting sequence. - **$30 $65 $125**

BAB-9   BAB-10   BAB-11

BAB-9. Cello. Baseball Scorer Fob,
1934. Quaker Cereals. Pictures him in Boston cap, back has scoring wheel. - **$50 $150 $300**

BAB-10. Quaker Cello. Club Button,
1934. - **$25 $50 $85**

BAB-11. Quaker Cereal Patch,
1934. - **$20 $75 $100**

BAB-12   BAB-13   BAB-14

BAB-12. "Babe Ruth Club" Litho. Button,
c. 1934. - **$40 $75 $125**

BAB-13. Cello. Baseball Scorer Fob,
1934. Quaker Cereals. Pictures him in New York cap, back has scorer wheel. - **$50 $100 $250**

BAB-14. "Ask Me" 3" Cello. Button,
c. 1934. Store employee button promoting Quaker premium card game "Ask Me-The Game Of Baseball Facts". - **$100 $250 $350**

BAB-15

BAB-15. Ask Me Game,
c. 1934. Scarce. Quaker Cereals. Includes mailer, cards and instructions. Complete - **$75 $250 $350**

BAB-16   BAB-17   BAB-18

BAB-16. Babe Ruth Brass Ring,
1935. Quaker Cereals. No inscriptions but Babe Ruth Club premium picturing baseball symbols. - **$50 $100 $150**

BAB-17. Quaker "Babe Ruth Champions" Brass Club Badge,
1935. - **$25 $50 $85**

BAB-18. Quaker "Babe Ruth Champions" Cello. Club Button,
1935. Pictures him in Boston cap. - **$25 $50 $85**

BAB-19

BAB-20

BAB-19. Babe Ruth Brass Baseball Charms Bracelet,
1935. Quaker Cereals. - **$50 $100 $150**

BAB-20. "Babe Ruth" Brass Belt Buckle,
1930s. Store item by "Harris Belts" marked on reverse. - **$40 $75 $150**

BAB-21

BAB-22

BAB-23

BAB-21. "Esso Boys Club" Silvered Metal Badge,
1930s. Figural baseball accented in red/blue with inscription "Charter Member". - **$25 $50 $85**

BAB-22. "Play Ball With Babe Ruth" Cello. Button,
1930s. Universal Pictures. Promotion for "Christy Walsh All America Sports Reels" movie feature. - **$50 $85 $175**

BAB-23. "Babe Ruth" Cello./Steel Bat Replica Pocketknife,
1930s. Name inscribed on one side plus tiny baseball depiction. - **$40 $75 $125**

BAB-24

BAB-25

BAB-26

BAB-24. Esso Gasoline "Babe Ruth Boys Club" Contest Coupon,
1930s. Offers premium for acquiring new members. See BAB-21. - **$15 $25 $40**

BAB-25. Club 3" Fabric Patch,
1930s. Possibly Quaker Cereals. - **$15 $30 $50**

BAB-26. "Bambino/The Real Ball Game" 4" Cello. Button,
1930s. For mechanical batting practice game based on Babe Ruth popular nickname by unidentified maker. - **$75 $175 $300**

BAB-28

BAB-27

BAB-27. "Official Babe Ruth Wrist Watch" With Display Case,
1949. Store item by Exacta Time. Plastic display case is replica baseball.
Near Mint In Case With Coupons And Box - **$1750**
Watch Only - **$150 $400 $750**

BAB-28. "Babe Ruth" Plastic Ring,
c. 1949. Inset picture of him swinging bat. From Kellogg's set of sixteen picturing sports and movie stars, airplanes and 19th century western personalities. - **$25 $40 $60**

BABY SNOOKS

Baby Snooks was a 7-year-old brat and America's radio listeners loved her. Born in the imagination of Ziegfeld Follies star Fanny Brice, the irrepressible imp was introduced to the world on February 29, 1936, in *The Ziegfeld Follies of the Air,* a lavish 60-minute extravaganza on CBS. The program had a brief life, but Baby Snooks was to appear continuously on one network program or another for the next 15 years until Fanny Brice's death in 1951. Sponsors included Maxwell House coffee, Post Toasties cereal, Sanka, Jell-O and Tums.

BSN-1

BSN-2

BSN-1. "Fanny Brice's Baby Snooks Pops" Lollipop Pail,
c. 1938. Store item by E. Rosen Co. 3" tall by 3-1/4" diameter litho. tin featuring three different images around perimeter. - **$40 $75 $125**

BSN-2. "Radio Guide" Magazine With Fannie Brice Cover,
1938.- **$5 $10 $20**

BSN-3

BSN-4

BSN-5

BSN-3. Composition/Wood/Wire "Flexy" Doll With Outfit And Tag,
1939. Store item by Ideal Toy & Novelty Co. -
$100 $200 $300

BSN-4. Whitman Cut-Out Doll Book,
1940. Store item. Designs by Queen Holden. -
$100 $200 $300

BSN-5. "My Second Childhood" Cover Article,
1944. May issue of "Tune In" national radio magazine including three-page article about "Baby Snooks" radio portrayal by Fannie Brice. - **$10 $15 $20**

BSN-6

BSN-7

BSN-6. Plastic Figure On Metal Bar Pin,
c. 1940s. Figure finished in gold color. - **$10 $30 $50**

BSN-7. Cardboard Dancing Puppet,
1950. Tums. Flexible diecut paper mid-section. -
$30 $75 $150

BACHELOR'S CHILDREN

Radio's beloved serial, *Bachelor's Children* tells the story of Dr. Bob Graham and the twin teenage girls he promised to raise. In true soap opera form, he eventually marries one of them. The popular series, which won awards for "realism," aired on CBS from 1936 to 1946, sponsored by Old Dutch cleanser, Wonder bread, and Colgate.

BCH-1

BCH-1. "Bachelor's Children" Story Synopsis Book With Mailer,
1939. Old Dutch Cleanser. 25-page hardcover including cast member photo plates. Near Mint With Mailer - **$35** No Mailer - **$5 $12 $20**

BCH-2

BCH-2. Wonder Bread Fan Newsletter,
c. 1945. - **$10 $20 $35**

BAMBI

One of Disney's most endearing creatures, *Bambi* debuted as a Technicolor feature cartoon at New York City's Radio City Music Hall on August 21, 1942. Since then, Bambi the deer, Thumper the rabbit, Flower the skunk and the Wise Old Owl have continued to enchant young and old audiences alike. Based on the Felix Salten story, Disney's Bambi was also published as a Better Little Book in 1942 and in comic book form several times in the early 1940s and as recently as 1984.

BAM-1

BAM-2

BAM-1. "Thumper" Glass Tumbler,
c. 1942. Probably a dairy product container. Reverse has descriptive verse. - **$75 $150 $200**

BAM-2 "Prevent Forest Fires" 14x20" Poster,
1943. U.S. Forest Service. - **$100 $225 $400**

BAM-3 **BAM-4** **BAM-5**

BAM-3. Paper Bookmark,
c. 1943. U.S. Department of Agriculture-Forest Service.-
$8 $15 $25

BAM-4. Wristwatch,
1949. Store item by US Time. - **$50 $125 $200**

BAM-5. Signed Studio Fan Card,
1940s. Signed by Disney staff artist. - **$50 $75 $125**

THE BANANA SPLITS

This imaginative live-action show consisted of four people wardrobed in outfits of Fleegle the dog, Bingo the gorilla, Drooper the lion and Snorky the baby elephant. The group was musically inclined in addition to adventuresome and appeared in 60-minute shows produced by Hanna-Barbera on NBC, sponsored by Kellogg's, from 1968 to 1970. The show's official title was a lengthy *Kellogg's of Battle Creek Presents The Banana Splits Adventure Hour.* Characters were voiced by Paul Winchell (Fleegle), Daws Butler (Bingo), Allan Melvin (Drooper) and Don Messick (Snorky).

BSP-1

BSP-1. Club Kit,
1968. Mailing envelope plus pennant, membership book, code machine, certificate, group portrait, membership card, sticker. Complete - **$100 $300 $450**

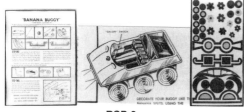

BSP-2

BSP-2. "Banana Buggy" Model Kit,
c. 1968. Kellogg's. Yellow vinyl with motor and sticker sheet.
Mint Boxed - **$750**
Assembled - **$100 $200 $400**

BSP-3

BSP-3. Record In Sleeve,
1969. Kellogg's. Includes song "Doin' The Banana Split" and three others. With Mailer - **$25 $50 $75**
No Mailer - **$15 $40 $65**

BSP-4 **BSP-5**

BSP-4. Fleer Gum "Tattoo" Vending Machine Card,
1969.- **$5 $10 $15**

BSP-5. Record With Sleeve,
1969. Kellogg's. Song "Tra-La-La Song" and three others. With Mailer - **$25 $50 $75**
No Mailer - **$15 $40 $65**

BSP-6

BSP-7 **BSP-8**

BSP-6. Banana Splits Character Stamp Pad Set,
c. 1970. Kellogg's. Plastic case holding six character image ink stamp blocks plus instruction slip. -
$75 $150 $275

BSP-7. Drooper Vinyl Figure,
1971. Store item by Sutton. Bagged - **$40 $60 $100**
Loose - **$15 $35 $70**

BSP-8. Fleegle Vinyl Figure,
1971. Store item by Sutton. Bagged - **$40 $60 $100**
Loose - **$15 $35 $70**

BSP-9 **BSP-10**

BSP-9. "Fleegle" Cello. Button,
1972. Hanna-Barbera copyright. From Banana Splits character series which includes Bingo, Snooper and Snorky.
Each - **$5 $10 $15**

BSP-10. 7-Eleven Plastic Cups,
1976. Each - **$15 $25 $35**

BARBIE

Until 1959, when Barbie first appeared, dolls were pretty much the same for hundreds of years. They were baby dolls to be mothered and nurtured by their youthful owners who would probably be mothers with their own real babies someday. Dolls came on the market with eyes that opened, movable arms and legs and finally dolls that wet and needed to be fed and changed--not too exciting. Barbie started a revolutionary trend; she wasn't a baby doll, but a young lady out in the world with fashionable clothes, cars, and boyfriends...and she had a bosom! Ruth Handler, Barbie's creator, has been quoted as saying "Barbie was originally created to project every little girl's dream of the future."

Barbie's boyfriend Ken came along in 1961; her best friend Midge arrived in 1963. Little sister Skipper was introduced in 1964 as were her male friend Ricky and girlfriend Skooter. After recent debate about the "politically incorrect" nature of the messages some of the Barbie products have carried to young girls, Barbie is getting a substantial physical "make-over" to bring her more in line with a realistic body type. As the times change, so does Barbie. The Barbie product line by Mattel continues to rank among the most successful offerings of the toy industry.

BAR-1

BAR-1. "Mattel Dolls For Fall '64" Retailer's Catalogue,
1964. - **$40 $75 $125**

BAR-2   **BAR-3**   **BAR-4**

BAR-2. Fan Club Membership Card,
1964.- **$10 $20 $35**

BAR-3. Wristwatch,
1964. Store item. - **$35 $65 $100**

BAR-4. "Barbie" Magazine,
March-April, 1965. One of a series by Mattel.
Each - **$5 $10 $20**

BAR-5

BAR-5. Club Kit,
1965. Mailing envelope holding cover letter, Barbie Magazine subscription coupon, club chapter application form, membership card, fabric peel-off sticker.
Near Mint Complete - **$100**

BAR-6

BAR-7   **BAR-8**

BAR-6. Barbie & Friends 6x10x30" Glass And Metal Mattel Electrical Display Sign,
1960s. Florescent lighted. - **$100 $200 $300**

BAR-7. Silvered Metal Adjustable Ring,
1960s. Rhinestones around Barbie's profile in brass.
$35 $60 $100

BAR-8. Necklace With Metal Pendant,
1974. - **$10 $20 $35**

BARNEY GOOGLE

"Barney Google, with his Goo-Goo-Googly Eyes," the 1923 hit song by Billy Rose and Con Conrad, was about a feisty little sport in a top hat, the cartoon creation of Billy De Beck that has been called one of the 10 greatest American comic strips of all time. The daily Barney strip first appeared in 1919 on the sports page of the Chicago Herald-Examiner, where he was soon joined by his pitiful racehorse Spark Plug. Readers loved them. Snuffy Smith, a Kentucky hillbilly, was introduced to the strip in 1934; his name was added to the title a few years later and by the mid-1940s he had taken full title. Fred Lasswell continued the strip after De Beck's death in 1942. A series of movie shorts was produced in the 1920s and a few animated TV cartoons were produced in the 1960s.

BNG-1

BNG-2

BNG-1. Fabric Doll,
1922. Store item. - **$50 $75 $150**

BNG-2. "Spark Plug" Glass Candy Container,
1923. Store item. Saddle blanket area originally had orange paint. - **$75 $150 $300**

BNG-3

BNG-4

BNG-5

BNG-3. "Official Song Of The Secret And Mysterious Order Of Billygoats" Sheet Music,
1928. - **$20 $40 $60**

BNG-4. Brotherhood Of Bulls Membership Card,
1920s. Scarce. Chicago Herald and Examiner. - **$30 $60 $120**

BNG-5. Brotherhood Of Billy Goats Membership Card,
1920s. Scarce. Chicago Herald and Examiner. - **$30 $60 $120**

BNG-6

BNG-7

BNG-8

BNG-9

BNG-6. "The Atlanta Georgian's Silver Anniversary" Litho. Button,
1937. Named newspaper. From set of various characters. - **$25 $75 $150**

BNG-7. "Sunday Herald And Examiner" Litho. Button,
1930s. Chicago newspaper. From "30 Comics" set of various characters. - **$15 $25 $40**

BNG-8. Enamel On Silvered Brass Pin,
c. 1930s.- **$ 50 $75 $150**

BNG-9. "Barney Google/Detroit Times" Cello. Button,
1930s. Newspaper contest serial number issue from comic character series. - **$10 $20 $30**

BNG-10

BNG-11

BNG-10. Boston Sunday Advertiser 11x17" Cardboard Display Sign,
1930s. - **$75 $150 $250**

BNG-11. "Buy War Stamps" 14x18" Poster,
c. 1944. U.S. Government. - **$40 $75 $125**

BATMAN

The legendary Batman--and the huge Bat-industry he was to spawn--was introduced in *Detective Comics* #27 of May 1939. Since then, the Caped Crusader and his sidekick, Robin the Boy Wonder, have battled crime and the forces of evil in comic strips, in live-action and animated cartoon TV series, on the radio, on prime-time network television, in comic books, movie serials, feature films and in the hearts of millions of fans, young and old. Artists Bob Kane and Jerry Robinson, and writer Bill Finger also produced an array of notable knaves, among them the Riddler, Penguin, the Joker and Catwoman. Batman's two greatest successes were the 1966-1968 ABC television series with Adam West and Burt Ward as the Dynamic Duo and a string of famous actors as the various villains (which also spawned its own feature film--and the famous line "Some days you just can't get rid of a bomb."--starring the same regular cast of heroes and villains); and the 1989 blockbuster film starring Michael Keaton, Jack Nicholson, and Kim Basinger. This hit movie, directed by Tim Burton, was followed by three sequels: *Batman Returns* (1992), *Batman Forever* (1995), which handed the Bat-cowl from Keaton to Val Kilmer and featured Jim Carrey as the Riddler, and the lackluster *Batman and Robin*, starring George Clooney as the latest Batman, with Alicia Silverstone as Batgirl. These productions generated hundreds of toys, premiums, posters, games, models, dolls, etc. Holy Merchandise, Batman!

Batman presently stars in four monthly titles, *Batman*, *Detective Comics*, *Batman: Shadow of the Bat*, and *Batman: Legends of the Dark Knight*, as well as a quarterly title, *The Batman Chronicles*, and numerous specials. He is currently also featured with Superman and other Justice League of America characters in *JLA*.

An additional monthly Bat-title, *Batman Adventures*, is tied into the cartoon incarnation of the Caped

Crusader, which has enjoyed a strong showing. Debuting on Fox in 1992, *Batman-The Animated Series* featured a "Dark Deco" design style and superb voice cast lead by Kevin Conroy as Bruce Wayne/Batman, Mark Hamill as the Joker, and Efrem Zimbalist, Jr. as Alfred. Other notable voices included Michael Ansara (Mr. Freeze), Adrienne Barbeau (Catwoman), Melissa Gilbert (Barbara Gordon/Batgirl), and Richard Moll (Two Face). Former TV Batman Adam West also lent his voice to one episode of the production. The series was well received by fans and critics alike and lasted for an 85-episode run (the final season as *The Adventures of Batman & Robin*). In addition to a number of toys and other licensed products, the series launched two spin-offs, *Batman: Mask of the Phantasm*, a theatrically released feature (1993) and *Batman: Sub-Zero*, a direct-to-home video feature (1998), a succession of comic books rendered in the visual and story-telling style of the series, and a new, ongoing cartoon on the WB Network, *The New Batman/Superman Adventures* (1997).

BAT-1

BAT-1. Paper Mask,
c. 1943. Scarce. Philadelphia Record newspaper, probably others. Back announces new daily and Sunday comic strips. - **$300 $1200 $2000**

BAT-2

BAT-2. Batplane Movie Promo,
1943. Various sponsors. - **$750 $1500 $2000**

BAT-3

BAT-3. "Full Color Transfers",
1944. Rare. Not a premium but earliest known merchandise (10 cents) item for Batman. Back of sheet has ad for Detective Comics. - **$300 $650 $1250**

BAT-4   BAT-5

BAT-4. "Batman's Last Chance" One-Sheet,
1949. Columbia Pictures serial. - **$700 $1400 $2800**

BAT-5. "New Adventures of Batman & Robin Three-Sheet,
1949. Columbia Pictures serial. - **$1500 $5000 $8000**

(1943 FRONT)   (1947 FRONT)   (BACK)

BAT-6

BAT-6. Batman Infantile Paralysis Card,
1940s. Scarce. March of Dimes premium. Small version offered in 1943, large version in 1947.
1943 version - **$100 $200 $500**
1947 version - **$30 $90 $180**

BAT-7   BAT-8

BAT-7. Batman/Superman Christmas Card,
1940s. Rare. - **$500 $1000 $1500**

BAT-8. DC Comics Fan Card,
1960. - **$30 $50 $90**

BAT-9

BAT-10

BAT-9. Batman Beanie,
1966. - **$10 $20 $30**

BAT-10. Batman Periscope,
1966. Kellogg's OKs cereal premium. - **$30 $60 $90**

(FRONT)   **BAT-11**   (BACK)

BAT-11. Batman Kellogg's Frosted Flakes Box (Flat),
1966. Promotes Batman printing set premium. -
$300 $800 $1200

(FRONT)   **BAT-12**   (BACK)

BAT-12. Batman Kellogg's OKs Cereal Box (Flat),
1966. Features Yogi Bear on front, Batman on back.
Promotes Batman periscope premium. -
$400 $950 $1700

BAT-13

BAT-13. "My Batman Collection" Metal Coin Set With Plastic Holders,
1966. Set of 20 coins.
Set In Holders - **$100 $200 $325**
Each Coin - **$3 $7 $12**

BAT-14   **BAT-15**   **BAT-16**

BAT-14. "Crimefighter" 1-3/8" Litho. Button,
1966.- **$5 $10 $15**

BAT-15. "Batman And Robin Deputy Crimefighter,
1966. Cello. button 3-1/2", store item. - **$10 $20 $30**

BAT-16. "Batman Golden Records" Boxed Set,
1966. N.P.P. Inc. Includes comic book, LP record, Batman Crimefighters litho. button, flicker ring and club membership card with secret code. Complete - **$20 $40 $75**

BAT-17   **BAT-18**

BAT-17. "Batman" Litho. Button,
1966. From red, white and blue set of 14 in 7/8" size, also issued in similar set colored red, green, yellow, black. Each - **$3 $8 $12**

BAT-18. Cardboard Mask,
1966. General Electric television. One mask on front, other on reverse. - **$5 $10 $15**

BAT-19   **BAT-20**

BAT-19. "Batman And Robin Buttons" Vending Machine Display Paper,
1966. - **$5 $8 $15**

BAT-20. Batman 1" Size Litho. Button Set,
1966. Vending machines but scarcer than 7/8" size. 14 different. Red/White/Blue Style Each - **$12 $20 $45**
Red/Green/Yellow Style Each - **$12 $25 $50**

BAT-21

BAT-21. Contest Card With Three Picture Playing Pieces,
1966. Safeway Or Merit Gasoline. Shows both TV and comic book characters. - **$60 $125 $250**

BAT-22

BAT-23

BAT-24

BAT-22. "Batman Coins" On Card,
1966. Store item by Transogram.
Complete On Card - **$20 $40 $75**
Loose Coin - **$1 $2 $3**

BAT-23. Fan Photo,
1966. Adam West and Burt Ward with facsimile
signatures. - **$25 $40 $65**

BAT-24. All Star Dairies 24x44" Cardboard Sign,
1966.- **$150 $300 $500**

BAT-25

BAT-26

BAT-25. Metal License Plate,
1966. Store item by Groff Signs. - **$10 $20 $35**

BAT-26. Metal License Plate,
1966. Store item by Groff Signs. - **$10 $20 $35**

BAT-27

**BAT-27. "Batman Ring Club" 4x5" Flicker Display
Card,**
1966. Showing both images. - **$75 $100 $125**

BAT-28

BAT-29

BAT-28. Metal License Plate,
1966. Store item. - **$10 $20 $35**

**BAT-29. "Flicker Pictures" Vending Machine Display
Paper,**
1966. - **$10 $20 $35**

BAT-30   BAT-31

BAT-30. Batman Poster 27x40",
1966. Toothpaste premium for TV show. - **$50 $100 $150**

BAT-31. Robin Poster 27x40",
1966. Toothpaste premium for TV show. - **$50 $100 $150**

BAT-32

BAT-33

BAT-32. Robin Flexible Rubber Ring,
1966. Vending machine issue. - **$35 $55 $75**

BAT-33. "Batman Fudge Crusader-Sundae" Wrapper,
1966. Parallelogram waxed paper. - **$5 $10 $15**

BAT-35

BAT-34

BAT-34. "Batman Print Set,"
1966. Kellogg's Sugar Frosted Flakes. Plastic case holding
six different plastic stamps and ink pad. Stamps picture
Batman, Robin, Joker, Penguin, Riddler, Batmobile. Near
Mint Boxed - **$100**
Unboxed - **$20 $40 $60**

BAT-35. "Batman & Robin Mask" Appliance Store Kit,
1966. Issued to promote General Electric television.
Envelope originally held 50 thin cardboard flip masks print-
ed on both sides plus pictured example 33x40" wall poster.
Envelope - **$5 $10 $20**
Poster - **$75 $175 $300**

BAT-36

BAT-37

BAT-38

BAT-36. Batman/Magazine Promotion 3-1/2" Cello. Button,
1966. Authorized issue for Electronic Industries magazine. Probably a trade show item. - **$50 $125 $200**

BAT-37. Batman/Robin Clock Face Flicker Ring,
c. 1966. Vending machine issue. - **$20 $30 $40**

BAT-38. "Batman's Buddy" Cello. Button,
c. 1966. Hy Vee grocery chain. - **$5 $12 $20**

BAT-39

BAT-40

BAT-39. Club Card,
1966. Membership card for TV show. - **$10 $20 $30**

BAT-40. Flicker Miniature Pictures,
1966. Vending machine set of six. Each- **$5 $12 $18**

BAT-41

BAT-41. Plastic Flicker Rings,
1966. Set of 12 in either silver or blue base.
Silver Base Each - **$8 $15 $25**
Blue Base Each - **$5 $15 $20**

BAT-42

BAT-42. "Batman Candy & Toy" Boxes,
1966. Store item by Phoenix Candy Co. Set of eight with front and back numbered pictures (1-16).
Each Box - **$10 $20 $30**

BAT-43

BAT-44

BAT-43. Holloway Candies 17x22" Cardboard Store Sign,
1966. Milk Duds, Black Cow, Slo-Poke candies. Offered three different coloring books with six-pack candy purchase.- **$100 $175 $250**

BAT-44. "Batman" English Cello. Button,
1966. A&BC Chewing Gum Ltd. - **$10 $20 $35**

BAT-45

BAT-46

BAT-45. Pop Tarts Comic Booklet,
1966. "The Mad Hatter's Hat Crimes" from set of four. - **$3 $8 $25**

BAT-46. Pop Tarts Comic Booklet,
1966. "The Penguin's Fowl Play" from set of four. - **$3 $8 $25**

BAT-47

BAT-48

BAT-47. Pop Tarts Comic Booklet,
1966. "The Catwoman's Catnapping Caper" from set of four.- **$3 $8 $25**

BAT-48. Pop Tarts Comic Booklet,
1966. "The Man In The Iron Mask" from set of four. - **$3 $8 $25**

BAT-49

BAT-50

BAT-51

BAT-49. Composition Bobbing Head Figure,
c. 1966. Store item. - **$100 $350 $600**

BAT-50. "Robin" English Cello. Button,
1966. A&BC Chewing Gum Ltd. - **$10 $20 $35**

BAT-51. Batman Glass Tumbler,
1966. - **$8** **$12** **$20**

BAT-52   BAT-53

BAT-52. Robin Glass Tumbler,
1966. - **$8** **$12** **$20**

BAT-53. "Curly Wurly/Blam" Litho. Button,
c. 1966. English product. - **$8** **$12** **$20**

(STICKER, CARD, BUTTON SHOWN)
BAT-54

BATMAN
BAT-55

BAT-54. "Batman Club" Items,
c. 1966. Ron Riley's Batman Club of WLS/WBKB-TV,
Chicago. Includes 2" litho. button, 3-1/2" sticker plus card.
Button - **$3** **$6** **$10**
Sticker - **$5** **$10** **$15**
Card - **$8** **$12** **$20**

BAT-55. Batman 6' Standee,
1966.- **$125** **$275** **$375**

BAT-56

BAT-57

BAT-56. High Relief Plastic 33x48" Store Display Sign,
1969. Issued to promote Aurora Batmobile kit offered as
premium by Burry's cookies. - **$250** **$600** **$900**

BAT-57. Photo And Record,
1960s. DC Comics. Photo reads "To All My Batman Fans-
'Bats' Wishes Bob Kane." Record co-written by Kane titled
"Have Faith In Me". Pair - **$50** **$85** **$150**

BAT-59

BAT-58

**BAT-58. "Batman And, Of Course, Robin" Movie Serial
Re-Release 27x41 " Poster,**
1960s. Columbia Pictures. For reissue of original 1943 serial. - **$50** **$125** **$250**

BAT-59. Batman Record,
1975. Power Records, a division of Peter Pan Industries.
Features "4 Exciting All-New Adventure Stories!" -
$3 **$5** **$8**

BAT-62

BAT-60   BAT-61

BAT-60. Batman Enameled Brass Ring,
1976. Store item made by Aviva. - **$5** **$12** **$20**

BAT-61. Batman Enameled Brass Ring,
1976. Store item made by Aviva. - **$5** **$12** **$20**

BAT-62. Batman Diecut Enameled Brass Ring,
1976. Store item made by Aviva. - **$5** **$12** **$20**

BAT-63

BAT-64

BAT-63. "Super Heroes Magnetic Dart Game",
1977. Cheerios. - **$10** **$25** **$50**

**BAT-64. "The Dark Knight" Plastic Display Sign With
Press Release,**
1986. Press release on mini-series by Frank Miller.
Display - **$20** **$35** **$60**
Press Release - **$3** **$5** **$10**

BAT-65

BAT-66

BAT-65. McDonald's Happy Meals 14x14" Plastic Translight Panel,
1992. Depicts eight figures and vehicles. - **$25 $60 $100**

BAT-66. McDonald's Happy Meals 14x14" Plastic Translight Panel,
1992. Depicts six cups. - **$10 $20 $30**

BAT-67

BAT-68

BAT-67. McDonald's Happy Meals 14x14" Plastic Translight Panel,
1992. Depicts four vehicles. - **$10 $20 $30**

BAT-68. Batman Standee With Cups,
1990s. - **$100 $200 $300**

THE BEATLES

The Beatles were Paul McCartney, John Lennon, George Harrison, and Ringo Starr (Richard Starkey), four lads from Liverpool, England, who became the dominant musical force of the turbulent 1960s and have remained cultural icons to this day. The Fab Four burst onto the American scene in an explosive live appearance on the Ed Sullivan Show on CBS-TV in February 1964, and though their last public concert was less than three years later, Beatles records and tapes still sell in the millions. Their movies--*A Hard Day's Night* (1964), *Help!* (1965) and the psychedelic animated feature *Yellow Submarine* (1968)--an animated Saturday morning series produced by King Features (1965-1969) and sponsored primarily by the A. C. Gilbert toy company, and comic books all added to the luster; but it was the brilliance and charm of the music that revolutionized rock and roll.

John Lennon was killed on December 8, 1980. In terms of lasting influence, The Beatles continue to sway not only music but pop culture in general. *A Hard Day's Night* is commonly considered to be one of the best rock and roll films ever made, while *Help!* is widely thought of as a precursor to the modern music video and a direct inspiration for the Monkees (see their category elsewhere in this book). With the release of *The Beatles Anthology I-III* (three 2-CD sets) and the companion video tape set, the surviving Beatles again set sales records around the world. These releases were accompanied by a large amount of Beatles merchandise, as well as the first new Beatles songs in years, mixing recently discovered Lennon vocals with new backing tracks by the surviving band members. Beatles memorabilia of all sorts, both original issues and later reproductions, are usually copyrighted NEMS Enterprises or SELTAEB.

BEA-1

BEA-2

BEA-1. "The Cavern" Ashtray,
c. 1963. Souvenir item. From Liverpool club where Beatles made January 1961 debut. - **$75 $125 $200**

BEA-2. Vinyl Doll Set,
1964. Store item by Remco Plastics. Each has life-like hair. Each - **$40 $70 $100**

BEA-3

BEA-3. "Beatle Dolls" 7x18" Paper Store Poster,
1964. Remco Industries. - **$100 $200 $300**

BEA-4

BEA-4. "The Bobb'n Head Beatles" Boxed Set,
1964. Store item. Composition figures by Car Mascots Inc. Boxed Set - **$400 $600 $1000**
Each Loose - **$75 $125 $200**

BEA-5

BEA-5. Cincinnati Concert Program,
1964. - **$15 $30 $60**

BEA-6

BEA-6. Calendar Cards,
1964. Various advertisers.
Each - **$8 $12 $20**

BEA-7

BEA-7. "Color Oil Portraits" Set Of 4,
1964. Store item. Cut-out "Buddies Club" card on header.
Packaged With Uncut Card - **$50 $75 $100**

BEA-8

BEA-9

BEA-8. "I'm A Official Beatles Fan" Button,
1964. Authorized issue in several variations all marked on
rim curl "Copyright NEMS Ent. Ltd. 64" and Green Duck
Co., Chicago-Made In U.S.A."
Litho. 4" Size - **$10 $20 $40**
Cello. 3-1/2" Size - **$10 $20 $35**
Litho. 1-3/8" Size - **$20 $40 $65**

BEA-9. "Free/One Beatle Button" Ad Paper,
c. 1964. 5x7" glossy paper pennant printed on both sides
including back offer for Beatles billfold. - **$50 $125 $200**

BEA-10   **BEA-11**   **BEA-12**

BEA-10. Vending Machine Litho. Button,
1964. Set of nine (four pictures/five slogans) either in
black/white/red, blue/orange, red/white/blue, or
black/white/blue. Pictures - **$3 $8 $15**
Slogans- **$3 $6 $10**

BEA-11. "Life Member" Fan Club Patch,
c. 1964. - **$15 $30 $60**

BEA-12. "I Love" 3-1/2" Cello. Buttons,
c. 1964. Each - **$8 $15 $25**

BEA-13

BEA-13. "Official Fan Club News Bulletin",
c. 1964. Includes six stapled photo pages. - **$25 $40 $75**

BEA-14   **BEA-15**   **BEA-16**

BEA-14. Flicker Ring Set,
c. 1964. Set of four.
Silver Base Each - **$8 $12 $15**
Blue Base Each - **$5 $7 $10**

BEA-15. "Ringo Starr" Soaky Bottle,
1965. Colgate-Palmolive. Only Ringo and Paul were produced. - **$40 $75 $125**

BEA-16. "Paul McCartney" Soaky,
1965. Colgate-Palmolive. Only Paul and Ringo were produced. - **$40 $75 $125**

BEA-17

BEA-18

BEA-17. "Help" Packaged Bandage,
c. 1965. Movie promotion on Curad bandage. -
$10 $20 $35

BEA-18. Nestle's Quik Container,
1966. Has offer for inflatable doll set. - **$150 $300 $600**

BEA-19

BEA-19. Beatles Inflatable Vinyl Dolls Set,
1966. Store item, also Nestle's Quik and Lux Soap.
Each - **$15 $25 $45**

BEA-20

BEA-21

BEA-20. "Sgt. Pepper's Lonely Hearts Club Band" 2-1/8" Litho. Button,
c. 1967. Great Britain issue for original record release although no copyright or company name. - **$10 $25 $50**

BEA-21. "Yellow Submarine Magazine",
1968. Store item published jointly by Pyramid Publications and King Features. - **$20 $40 $75**

BEA-22

BEA-22. Yellow Submarine European Movie Theater Mobile,
c. 1968. Two diecut thick cardboard pieces 17x25" and 6x10" for forming ceiling dangle mobile. Each piece is printed identically both sides with tiny inscriptions for French theater and possibly disco entertainment spot. - **$150 $250 $500**

BEA-23

BEA-23. Corgi "Yellow Submarine" Replica,
1968.
Near Mint Boxed - **$600**
Loose - **$150 $300 $450**

BEA-24

BEA-24. Yellow Submarine Rub-Ons,
1969. Nabisco Wheat (Or Rice) Honeys. Set of eight.
Each - **$15 $25 $40**

BEA-25

BEA-26

BEA-25. Australian Fan Club Cello. Button,
1960s. -
$25 $50 $85

BEA-26. Rubber Figure Charms,
1960s. Believed vending machine issue. Set of four, each 2-1/2" tall. Each - **$5 $10 $15**

BETTY BOOP

Max Fleischer created the Boop-Oop-a-Doop girl as an animated cartoon in 1931. The sexy little flirt, modeled on singer Helen Kane and actress Mae West, was an immediate success and became Paramount's leading cartoon feature. Along with her dog Bimbo and her pal Koko the clown, Betty vamped and sang her way through comedies and adventures throughout the 1930s. Several actresses provided Betty's voice but Mae Questel is most closely identified with the character. A Sunday comic strip was distributed by King Features (1935-1938) and published as an Avon paperback in 1975. A children's show, *Betty Boop Fables*, had a brief run on NBC radio in 1932-1933, and the cartoons were packaged for TV in 1956 and re-released in color in 1971. Many merchandised items appeared in the 1930s at the height of Betty's popularity. Her continuing appeal produced an even wider range of licensed items in the 1980s-1990s.

BTY-1

BTY-2

BTY-1. Betty Boop/Gus Gorilla Fan Card,
1933. Fleischer Studios. Text refers to Paramount Pictures and NBC. - **$35 $75 $150**

BTY-2. Fleischer Studios Fan Card,
c. 1933. Personalized by first name of recipient. Text refers to Paramount, not NBC. - **$35 $75 $150**

BTY-3

BTY-3. "Betty Boop's Movie Cartoon Lessons By Max Fleischer" Book,
c. 1935. Store item. Softcover 32-page illustrated guide "How To Make Movie Cartoons." - **$200 $400 $600**

BTY-4

BTY-4. Mask,
1930s. "Bob-O-Link Shoes" ad on reverse.
$30 $60 $125

BTY-5

BTY-6

BTY-7

BTY-5. Composition/Wood Jointed Doll,
1930s. Scarce in high grade. Store item by Cameo Products. 12-1/2" tall. - **$250 $600 $1200**

BTY-6. Wood Jointed Doll,
1930s. Store item, 4-1/2" tall.- **$5 $10 $175**

BTY-7. China Wall Pocket,
1930s. Store item. - **$75 $150 $200**

BTY-8

BTY-9

BTY-8. Bisque Figure,
1930s. Store item. 3" size. - **$50 $100 $150**

BTY-9. China Ashtray,
1930s. Store item. - **$50 $75 $150**

BTY-10

BTY-11

BTY-12

BTY-10. Spanish Envelope,
1930s. Held transfer.
Envelope Only - **$10 $20 $35**
Complete - **$15 $30 $60**

BTY-11. "Bimbo" Cello. Button,
1930s. Inscribed "A Paramount Star Created By Fleischer Studios". - **$25 $40 $75**

BTY-12. Cello. Button,
1930s. Rim inscription "A Paramount Star Created By Fleischer Studios".- **$40 $85 $175**

BTY-13

BTY-13. "Socks Appeal By Bimbo" Booklet,
1930s. Given with pair of Bimbo socks. - **$50 $90 $135**

BTY-14

BTY-15

BTY-16

BTY-14. "Saturday Chicago American" Litho. Button,
1930s. From set of 10 various characters. - **$20 $45 $75**

BTY-15. "Ko-Ko/Max Fleischer's Talkatoons" Litho. Button #25,
1930s. Western Theater Premium Co. From numbered set of 50 either black, white, red or with additional yellow accent. - **$10 $20 $35**

BTY-16. Betty Boop Postcard with Mickey Rooney,
1930s. - **$30 $60 $120**

BIG BOY

In 1936 Bob Wian, running a little diner called Bob's Pantry in Glendale, California, added a double-decker cheeseburger to his menu. A few weeks later, according to legend, a chubby little boy wearing oversize pants and suspenders walked in. Wian was enchanted, dubbed him Big Boy, changed the name of the diner and began using an image of the boy as his advertising logo. Wian sold his first franchise to the Elias Brothers in Michigan in 1952, and other franchises quickly followed. The Marriott Corp. bought the business in 1967, and there are now more than 300 Big Boy restaurants in North America and Japan. A giveaway comic book was started in 1956 and continued to 1996.

BIG-1

BIG-2

BIG-3

BIG-1. Big Boy Die-Cut Menu,
1949. - **$20 $40 $80**

BIG-2. Big Boy Ad Card,
1956. For Free comic. - **$10 $20 $40**

BIG-3. "Adventures Of The Big Boy" Comic Book #1,
1956. Art by Bill Everett. - **$50 $150 $600**

BIG-4

BIG-5

BIG-4. Early Litho. Button,
1950s. Light green rim. - **$15 $35 $60**

BIG-5. "Nat'l Big Boy Club" Litho. Member Button,
c. 1960. - **$10 $20 $35**

BIG-6

BIG-7

BIG-6. Bobbing Head Figure,
1960s. Painted composition figure with spring-mounted head. - **$250 $500 $800**

BIG-7. Ceramic Salt & Pepper Set,
1960s. - **$60 $150 $250**

BIG-8

BIG-9

BIG-10

BIG-8. Club Member Litho. Button,
c. 1960s. - **$5 $10 $20**

BIG-9. Silvered Metal Tie Bar,
c. 1960s. "Big Boy" name on miniature figure. - **$10 $20 $35**

BIG-10. Vinyl Figure By Dakin,
1970. - **$60 $120 $175**

BIG-11

BIG-12

BIG-11. Cloth Dolls,
c. 1978. Dolls are Big Boy, Dolly and Nugget. Each - **$5 $10 $15**

BIG-12. "Adventures Of The Big Boy" Comic Book,
1978. See The Overstreet Comic Book Price Guide for values of Issues #2 through #466.

BIG-13

BIG-14

BIG-15

BIG-13. Watch,
c. 1970s. - **$35 $60 $100**

BIG-14. Vinyl Figure Night Light,
1970s. Electrical. - **$35 $60 $125**

BIG-15. Limited Edition 5" Metal Figure,
1980s. - **$20 $40 $80**

BILL BARNES

Street and Smith began publication of its pulp *Bill Barnes Air Trails* in the early 1930s and shortened the name of the magazine to *Air Trails* around 1937. Issues contained Bill Barnes air adventure stories, aviation news and features, and information on model planes. Barnes made his comic book debut in issue #1 of *Shadow Comics* in 1940 and had his own book from 1940 to 1943 under various titles: *Bill Barnes Comics, America's Air Ace Comics* and *Air Ace.*

BBR-1   BBR-2   BBR-3

BBR-1. "Bill Barnes Air Adventurer" Pulp Magazine,
September 1935. Published by Street & Smith. -
$15 $25 $50

BBR-2. "Bill Barnes/Air Adventurer" Gummed Paper Envelope Sticker,
1930s. Street & Smith Co., publisher of Bill Barnes pulp magazine. - **$20 $40 $65**

BBR-3. "Bill Barnes/Air Adventurer" 11x14" Window Card,
1930s. Street & Smith Publications. Pictures example pulp magazine cover. - **$50 $100 $150**

BBR-4

BBR-4. "Air Warden Cadets" Club Kit,
c. 1943. Cello. Button - **$25 $50 $80**
Airplane Spotting Booklet - **$8 $15 $30**
Group Of Six Related Sheets - **$15 $20 $30**

BILLY AND RUTH

Billed as America's Famous Toy Children, Billy and Ruth and their dog Terry were the fictional stars of annual pre-Christmas toy catalogues published for the toy industry as early as 1936. Created by Philadelphia-based L.A. Hoeflich, the catalogues promoted the toys of different participating manufacturers. Retailers who subscribed to the service printed their own store information on the front cover and thus had a ready-made catalogue for their customers. In the late 1950s, as independent toy retailers went out of business, Billy and Ruth became casualties of the new marketplace.

BLR-1

BLR-1. "In Toy World With Billy And Ruth" Catalogue,
1936. 32 pages of illustrated and priced period toys. -
$50 $100 $150

BLR-2   BLR-3

BLR-2. Promotional Cello. Button,
c. 1936. - **$15 $30 $60**

BLR-3. Club Member Button,
1940s. - **$15 $30 $45**

BLR-4

BLR-4. Christmas Toy Catalogue,
1951. - **$20 $35 $60**

BLR-5

BLR-5. Christmas Toy Catalogue,
1952. - **$20 $35 $60**

BLR-6   BLR-7

BLR-6. Christmas Toy Catalogue,
1954. - **$15 $25 $50**

BLR-7. Christmas Toy Catalogue,
1955. - **$12 $25 $50**

BLR-8

BLR-8. "Around The World With Billy And Ruth" Game Kit,
1955. Billy And Ruth Promotion, Inc., Philadelphia. Mail envelope holding cover letter, instruction sheet, playing piece sheets to be scissored, paper playing board map opens to 13-1/2x17". Near Mint In Mailer - **$70**
Game - **$15 $25 $40**
Letter - **$5 $10 $15**

BILLY BOUNCE

Little is known of this comic strip rotund youngster other than he briefly had his own strip in 1905 based on various youthful characters created by C. W. Kahles. Apparently Billy Bounce earned some syndication beyond home base of the *New York World*, as known premiums are mostly a few newspaper advertising pin-back buttons. A *Billy Bounce* hardcover book exists crediting W.W. Denslow, noted for his *Wizard of Oz* illustrations, as both author and illustrator.

BYB-1   BYB-2

BYB-1. "Compliments Of Billy Bounce" Cello. Button,
1904. Pictured is W. W. Denslow character with copyright by T. C. McClure. - **$100 $300 $600**

BYB-2. "Philadelphia Press" Cello. Button,
c. 1905. - **$70 $140 $200**

BYB-3   BYB-4

BYB-3. "Billy Bounce In The Sunday Sentinel" Cello. Button,
c. 1905. Also comes with "Washington Times" imprint. - **$75 $150 $250**

BYB-4. "Billy Bounce" Hardcover Book,
1906. Store item published by Donohue Co. Story by Denslow & Bragdon with pictures by Denslow (noted "Oz" artist). - **$60 $125 $200**

BLACK FLAME OF THE AMAZON

This radio adventure series was produced in California but apparently found air time only in the Midwest on the Mutual network. The syndicated program dramatized the adventures of explorer Harold Noice in the jungles of South America. Accompanied by his young friends Jim and Jean Brady, his aid Pedro, and the native guide Keyto, Noice did battle with lawless types and dealt with wild animals and strange savage customs. Sponsors included Mayrose processed meats and Hi-Speed Gasoline. In Detroit the series aired on station WXYZ from February to May 1938, sponsored by Hi-Speed Gasoline.

(ENLARGED VIEW)

BLF-1

BLF-1. Map 21 1/2 x 17",
1930s. Rare. Radio show sign sponsored by Hi-Speed Gas. - **$150 $300 $450**

BLF-2

BLF-3   BLF-4

BLF-2. Cardboard Ruler,
1930s. Rare. Mayrose Meats. - **$40 $100 $150**

BLF-3. Stamp,
1930s. Rare. Shows picture of Amazon warriors. One of 24 in set. Each - **$10 $20 $30**

BLF-4. Paper Mask,
1930s. Hi-Speed Gasoline. - **$20 $60 $90**

BLF-5   BLF-6   BLF-7

BLF-5. "Hi-Speed Explorer" Litho. Button,
1930s. Hi-Speed gasoline. - **$10 $15 $25**

BLF-6. "Hi-Speed Explorer" Brass Compass Ring,
1930s. - **$125 $235 $375**

BLF-7. "Paco Explorer" Litho. Club Button,
1930s. - **$12 $25 $40**

BLONDIE

One of the world's most popular comic strips, Blondie was created by Chic Young for King Features in 1930. This family comedy centers on the hectic misadventures of the Bumsteads--Blondie and Dagwood, their children Cookie and Alexander (originally Baby Dumpling), their dog Daisy and her pups, the neighbors Herb and Tootsie Woodley, Dagwood's boss Mr. Dithers and his wife Cora and the indestructible mailman Mr. Beasley. Hollywood turned out more than two dozen Blondie films with Penny Singleton and Arthur Lake in the lead roles and a half-hour radio program ran from 1939 to 1950, sponsored by Camel cigarettes, Super Suds and Colgate. Two TV series, in 1957 and again in 1968, failed to match the success of the strip or the movies.

BLD-1

BLD-2

BLD-1. "Sunday Examiner" Newspaper Contest Litho. Button,
1930s. Part of a set. - **$10 $20 $30**

BLD-2. Esso Ad Folder,
1940. - **$15 $30 $50**

BLD-3

BLD-3. Comic Strip Gasoline Promo Folder,
1940. Esso Oil. Closed 5x7-1/2" sheet with full color cover and inner comic story that opens to final 10x15" with photo ad for lubrication services on reverse. - **$20 $40 $60**

BLD-4

BLD-5

BLD-4. "Blondie Goes To Leisureland" Paper Game,
1940. Westinghouse Co. - **$15 $25 $35**

BLD-5. "Blondie 100 Selected Top-Laughs" Book,
1944. Store item published by David McKay Co. Reprint of 100 daily strips from late 1930s through early 1940s. - **$20 $35 $50**

BLD-6

BLD-7

BLD-6. "Comic Togs" Litho. Button,
1947. From clothing maker series of various characters. -
$25 $40 $75

BLD-7. "Penny Singleton" Photo,
1940s. Radio and films Blondie portrayer. - **$5 $20 $25**

BOB HOPE

From a small-time vaudeville comic, Bob Hope went on to become one of the world's most beloved performers. His *Pepsodent Show*, which premiered on NBC in 1938, was one of radio's biggest hits for a dozen years. He made a series of successful "Road" movies with Bing Crosby and Dorothy Lamour from 1940 to 1962 and has made countless TV appearances since 1950. He has also devoted much time and energy entertaining American troops all over the world. Hope is to be knighted in 1998 by Britain's Queen Elizabeth II. Thanks for the memories, Bob.

BOB-1

BOB-2

BOB-1. Post Card,
1930s. NBC Radio. - **$20 $40 $75**

BOB-2. "They Got Me Covered" Book,
1941. Pepsodent toothpaste. - **$5 $15 $30**

BOB-3   BOB-4

BOB-3. Hair Pin Card,
1940s. Store item. - **$8 $12 $18**

BOB-4. Hope-Lamour Birthday Card,
1940s. Store item. - **$8 $15 $30**

BOB-5

BOB-6

BOB-5. Biography Booklet,
c. 1960. NBC/Chrysler Corp. For Chrysler Theater series on NBC-TV. - **$8 $15 $25**

BOB-6. "Popsicle" 8x20" Contest Poster,
1961. Joe Lowe Corp. Pictures water recreation prizes including grand prize of a swimming pool. - **$25 $40 $70**

BOB-7

BOB-8

BOB-7. Bob Hope Veterans' Cause Photo,
c. 1970. 3-1/2x3-1/2" card picturing him autographing veteran's leg cast with reverse inscription about craft kits given to hospitalized Vietnam veterans. - **$5 $10 $15**

BOB-8. "Vote Bob Hope" 3" Cello. Button,
c. 1975. NBC-TV. - **$5 $10 $15**

BOBBY BENSON

Bobby was the 12-year-old owner of a ranch in south Texas. With his cowgirl pal Polly and a cast of regulars, *Bobby Benson's Adventures* started riding the airwaves on CBS in 1932. As long as the show was sponsored by H-O (Hecker's Oats) cereal, the ranch was called the H-Bar-O. When H-O dropped out as sponsor in 1936, the ranch became the B-Bar-B and the show continued briefly. It was revived as *Bobby Benson and the B-Bar-B Riders* on the Mutual network from 1949 to 1955. Among the early cast members were Dead-End Kid Billy Halop as Bobby and Tex

Ritter, Don Knotts and Al Hodge. A series of comic books was published by Magazine Enterprises from 1950 to 1953.

BNS-2

BNS-1

BNS-1. Fan Club Photo,
c. 1932. - **$10** **$20** **$35**

DNS-2. "H-Bar O Transfer Book",
1933. Paper cover holding strip of 12 sheets of transfer pictures to be cut apart and applied by water. - **$15** **$60** **$100**

BNS-3

BNS-3. H-Bar-O Ranger Belt,
1933. H-O Cereals. Cowhide leather companion belt to BNS-7, unmarked and offered separately. - **$10** **$20** **$30**

BNS-4

BNS-4. H-Bar-O News,
1933. Hecker H-O Co. 11x15" color print 16-page club newsletter edition including two center pages picturing 15 premiums. Pictured example is Vol. 1 #2. - **$15** **$25** **$40**

BNS-5

BNS-6

BNS-5. "H-Bar-O Ranger" Enameled Brass Star Badge,
1933. Scarce. - **$100** **$200** **$400**

BNS-6. "H-Bar-O Herald" Vol. 1 #1 Newspaper,
September 1933. Contents mention Benson radio broadcasts to begin September 18. - **$15** **$30** **$50**

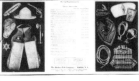

BNS-7

BNS-8

BNS-7. "H-Bar-O Ranger" Holster,
1933. H-O Cereals. 7-1/2" long cowhide leather with wool cover panel, rear leather belt loop. See separately offered belt BNS-3. - **$30** **$60** **$90**

BNS-8. "H-Bar-O Rangers/Bobby Benson" Premium Offer Folder,
1934. - **$25** **$50** **$75**

BNS-9

BNS-10

BNS-9. Certificate,
1934. Hecker H-O Cereal. - **$15** **$30** **$45**

BNS-10. H-Bar-O Newspaper Vol. 1 #3,
1934. Hecker Oats cereal. - **$10** **$20** **$35**

BNS-11

BNS-12

BNS-11. "H-O" Cast Iron Cap Gun,
c. 1934. 7" long with cereal initials inscription on one side, offered in Bobby Benson premium folder of that year. - **$50** **$85** **$150**

BNS-12. Catalog,
1934. Hecker Oats Cereals. Six page color catalog. - **$30** **$70** **$100**

BNS-13

BNS-13. Code Rule,
1935. - **$20 $35 $60**

BNS-14

BNS-14. Code Book,
1935. - **$15 $30 $50**

BNS-15   **BNS-16**   **BNS-17**

**BNS-15. "Bobby Benson In The Tunnel Of Gold"
Booklet,**
1936. Hecker Cereals. - **$9 $27 $55**

BNS-16. "Bobby Benson And The Lost Herd" Book,
1936. Hecker Cereals. - **$9 $27 $55**

BNS-17. Glass Bowl,
1930s. Comes in green, yellow or red.
Each - **$10 $20 $30**

BNS-18

BNS-18. Photos With Envelope,
1930s. Ten different known. Photo not shown depicts Bart.
Envelope Or Each Photo - **$5 $8 $12**

BNS-19   **BNS-20**

**BNS-19. "Bobby Benson And The H-O Rangers In
Africa" 19x25" Map,**
1930s. Map - **$100 $175 $300**
Envelope - **$30 $60 $120**

**BNS-20. "Bobby Benson Ranger/H-Bar-O" Foil On
Metal Badge,**
1930s. - **$20 $40 $75**

BNS-21

BNS-21. Store Display Box With Glass Tumblers,
1930s. Tumblers were obtained with two boxes of Force
Toasted Wheat Flakes, six different characters.
Boxed Display - **$100 $150 $300**
Each - **$5 $8 $12**

BNS-22   **BNS-24**

BNS-23

BNS-22. "H-Bar-O Rangers Club" Cello. Button,
1930s. - **$10 $15 $20**

BNS-23. Star Junior Police Badge,
1930s. Scarce. Gold badge with #808 which is number
used on Bobby Benson premiums. - **$50 $125 $175**

BNS-24. "Special Captain" Cello. Club Rank Button,
1930s. - **$25 $50 $75**

BNS-25   **BNS-26**

BNS-25. "H-Bar-O Ranger" Enameled Brass Bracelet,
1930s. - **$75 $125 $250**

BNS-26. "H-Bar-O Ranger/808" 2" Long Enamel Brass Tie Clip,
1930s. Near Mint On Card With Mailer - **$300**
Tie Clip Only - **$50 $100 $200**

BNS-27

BNS-27. "H-Bar-O" Card Game,
1930s. Deck of 32 playing cards and instruction leaflet for 18 games.- **$20 $35 $50**

BNS-28

BNS-28. B-Bar-B Riders Club Kit With Mailer Envelope,
c. 1948. Contents of Bobby Benson humming lariat, photo, membership certificate. Each Item - **$20 $35 $75**

BONANZA

The story of the Cartwright family, set on their Ponderosa Ranch in Nevada in the 1860s, premiered on NBC in September 1959 and aired weekly until 1973-- the second-longest Western series on television. One of the nation's most popular shows during most of the 1960s, it was also the first Western to be televised in color. The Ponderosa was a man's world, with Lorne Greene as the widowed father Ben and Pernell Roberts, Dan Blocker and Michael Landon as his sons Adam, Hoss and Little Joe. The program often focused on the relationships between the characters rather than on typical Western violence. It can still be seen in re-runs.

BON-1   BON-2   BON-3

BON-1. "Bonanza Booster" 2-1/4" Cello. Button,
c. 1960. - **$60 $125 $200**

BON-2. Fort Madison Iowa 2-1/4" Rodeo Button,
1964. From series of event buttons beginning in 1957. - **$40 $75 $125**

BON-3. "Bonanza Days" 3" Cello. Button,
1964. For celebration in site city of series, picturing all four original cast members. - **$20 $40 $65**

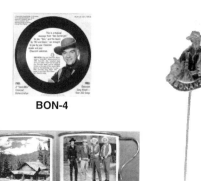
BON-4   BON-6

BON-5

BON-4. 33 RPM Record,
1964. Chevrolet. - **$5 $10 $20**

BON-5. "Ponderosa Ranch" Tin Cup,
c. 1965. Store item. Pictures all four original stars. - **$8 $15 $30**

BON-6. "Bonanza" Enamel Diecut Brass Stickpin,
c. 1965. European made, depicts Ben Cartwright on horseback. - **$25 $50 $75**

BON-7

BON-7. "Adam" And "Joe" European Litho. 2-1/2" Stickpin Buttons,
c. 1965. Each - **$15 $25 $50**

BON-8

BON-8. "The Ponderosa Ranch Story" Booklet,
1969. Ranch souvenir. - **$15 $25 $40**

BON-9   BON-10

BON-9. Badge,
1960s. Premium for TV series. Red stone in middle. -
$25 $50 $75

BON-10. "Michael Landon/Little Joe" Fan Photo,
1960s. - **$15 $25 $40**

BON-11

BOZ-3

BOZ-4

BON-12

BON-11. "Bonanza" Cello. Button,
c. 1960s. Australian issue picturing Lorne Greene. -
$20 $40 $60

BON-12. "I Met Hoss Cartwright" Litho. Tin Tab,
c. 1970s. Nickey Chevrolet, as spelled. - **$8 $15 $30**

BOZO THE CLOWN

Bozo, a children's popular favorite since 1950 through
Dell comic books and endorsement of Capitol Records
for youngsters, added television prominence by the
syndicated series developed and marketed beginning
in 1959 by Larry Harmon. The TV series combined an
extensive library of cartoon films and/or a live segment, also franchised by Harmon, featuring a local
host portraying the likeable circus clown.

BOZ-3. Glass With Lid,
1965. Held peanut butter. Set of five.
Each - **$5 $10 $15**
Lid - **$2 $5 $10**

BOZ-4. Mirror,
1966. TV promo for "Bozo Show." - **$10 $25 $40**

BOZ-6

BOZ-5

BOZ-5. Patch And Membership Card,
1960s. TV promo for "Bozo Show." Store bought. -
$10 $20 $30

BOZ-6. Plastic Push Puppet,
c. 1960s. Store item by Kohner. - **$10 $15 $30**

BOZ-1

BOZ-2

BOZ-7

BOZ-8

BOZ-1. "I Am A Bozo Pal" Cello. Button,
c. 1950s. Serial number club button sponsored by WDSM-
TV, Superior, Wisconsin. - **$5 $10 $15**

BOZ-2. Bread Wrapper,
c. 1950s. Colorful wrapper. - **$25 $50 $75**

BOZ-7. Plastic Portrait Ring,
1960s. - **$20 $50 $80**

BOZ-8. "I Visited Bozo's Circus" Litho. Button,
c. 1970s. WGN-TV (Chicago). - **$3 $6 $10**

BOZ-9   BOZ-10

BOZ-9. Illuminated Plastic Snow Dome,
c. 1970s. Store item, battery operated. - **$40 $75 $150**

BOZ-10. "Bozo Is Love" 3" Cello. Button,
c. 1970s. Various TV stations. Pictured example from
Grand Rapids, Michigan station. - **$3 $8 $12**

THE BREAKFAST CLUB

Don McNeill's *Breakfast Club*, a happy blend of
Midwestern corn and audience participation, ruled
morning radio for most of its 24 years on the air (1933
to 1968)--one of the longest-running network radio
shows ever. The program, broadcast from Chicago,
was essentially spontaneous and unrehearsed, combining contributions sent in by listeners, songs,
prayers, marches around the breakfast table, poetry,
anecdotes and occasional interviews with guest stars.
There were many sponsors over the years. McNeill's
familiar closing line--"Be good to yourself"--typified
the warmth and charm of this popular and successful
program. A TV simulcast in 1954 did not catch on.

BRK-1

BRK-1. Club Member Folder Kit,
c. 1944. Folder has contest and new member forms,
comes with "Victory Garden" card.
Folder - **$15 $25 $40**
Card - **$5 $12 $20**

BRK-2   BRK-3

BRK-2. Don McNeill Club Book,
1944. Says "Good Morning Breakfast Clubber & Good
Morning to Ya" on cover. Contest rules & large photo of
radio show cast & band. - **$15 $35 $50**

**BRK-3. Don McNeill Featured In Radio Mirror
Magazine,**
1948. July, 1948 issue features Don McNeill and family on
cover with photos and major story about him on the inside.
The Radio Mirror Magazine was to radio as TV Guide is to
television. This issue is also important because it was one
of the transition mags to also include television material.
On the cover, note the small words after "Radio." Inside
are the first photos of Buffalo Bob and Howdy Doody with a
picture of the 1st 20-seat Peanut Gallery. The Howdy
Doody marionette is the same as the one pictured on the
pinback when Howdy was running for President and the
Howdy photo is totally different than the one we are used
to seeing. - **$25 $50 $75**

BRK-4   BRK-5

BRK-6

BRK-4. "Don McNeill For President" Litho. Button,
c. 1948. ABC Breakfast Clubs. - **$3 $5 $10**

BRK-5. Club Charter Member Card,
1940s.- **$5 $20 $30**

BRK-6. Fan Club Folder,
1940s. - **$5 $20 $30**

BRK-7

BRK-7. Don McNeill Club Card,
1940s. Postcard premium from the radio show. -
$15 $30 $45

BRK-8   BRK-9

BRK-8. Don McNeill's Breakfast Club Sign 12x36",
1940s. Promotes radio show and victory bond drive in drug
stores. - **$50 $100 $150**

BRK-9. "Don McNeill Sent Me" Litho. Button,
c. 1950. Apparently to be worn to grocery or other retail
store. - **$3 $6 $10**

BRK-11

BRK-10

BRK-10. Don McNeill's Breakfast Club Book,
1953. Radio premium. "Twenty Years of Memory Time." -
$25 $50 $75

BRK-11. "20 Years Of Corn" Booklet,
c. 1953. - **$10 $20 $35**

BRK-12

BRK-13

BRK-12. "Kiddie Party Ideas" Booklet,
c. 1950s. Fritos. - **$20 $75 $100**

**BRK-13. "Don McNeill/Himself Hide-Away" 2-1/4" Cello.
Button,**
1950s. - **$4 $8 $12**

BRK-14

BRK-14. Various Yearbooks,
1940s-1950s. Issued annually.
1942 - **$10 $20 $40**
1947 - **$8 $15 $30**
1948 - **$8 $15 $30**
1949 - **$8 $15 $30**
1950 - **$7 $15 $30**
1954 - **$7 $12 $25**

BREAKFAST IN HOLLYWOOD

Radio veteran Tom Breneman was the host of
Breakfast at Sardi's on the Blue network until he
bought his own restaurant in 1943 and started broadcasting *Breakfast with Breneman*. The program, a variety show with audience participation, soon changed
its name to *Breakfast in Hollywood* and aired on the
ABC network with Breneman as host until his untimely
death in 1948. Kellogg's cereals sponsored the show
from 1945 to 1948. A United Artists film version was

released in 1946 featuring Breneman, Bonita Granville,
Beulah Bondi, Spike Jones, the King Cole Trio, and
other Hollywood notables.

BHL-1

BHL-2

BHL-1. Tom Breneman's Book,
1943. Fifty page premium for breakfast. Pictures Orson
Welles, Jimmy Durante, Lum & Abner, Xavier Cugat and
others. - **$20 $35 $50**

BHL-2. Tom Breneman's Booklet,
1945. Ivory Flakes. Eight page premium features Hedda
Hopper, Lum & Abner and others. Has "Breakfast in
Hollywood" song on back. Has 25¢ cover. - **$15 $25 $45**

BHL-3

BHL-3. Tom Breneman's Ticket Postcard,
1945. Premium ticket that can be used as postcard after
attendance at show. - **$10 $20 $30**

BHL-4

BHL-5

BHL-4. Tom Breneman's Peeks Book Mailer,
1940s. Kellogg's Cereal. - **$5 $10 $15**

BHL-5. Tom Breneman's Peeks Book,
1940s. Kellogg's Cereal. Photos of famous stars and a
behind the scenes look at a movie breakfast in Hollywood -
$15 $35 $50

THE BROWNIES

Palmer Cox (1840-1924) tried cartooning in San Francisco in the 1860s and early 1870s then set up a studio in 1875 in New York City. He had some success being published in early *Life* humor magazines but his main claim to fame grew out of cartoons of Brownieland beginning in the *St. Nicholas* monthly children's magazine. Cox had been inspired by Scottish immigrant folk tales he heard as a boy in Granby, Canada. The frontispiece in the first book *The Brownies: Their Book* from 1887 reads: "Brownies, like fairies and goblins, are imaginary little sprites who are supposed to delight in harmless pranks and helpful deeds. They work and sport while weary households sleep and never allow themselves to be seen by mortal eyes." The Brownies world was a microcosm of society at its best and worst, all portrayed most skillfully through the mind and pen of Palmer Cox and his intricate work throughout the Victorian era and into the early 20th century. Brownieland complemented the times and most probably influenced the creation of *Little Nemo, Kewpies, Teenie-Weenies, Bucky Bug, Raggedy Ann* and other characters set in the world of fantasy.

BRW-1

BRW-1. Estey Organs and Pianos Trade Card,
1890. - **$12 $20 $35**

BRW-2

BRW-2. "Palmer Cox's Brownie Paper Dolls",
1892. Brownies Chocolate Cream Drops.
Each - **$15 $25 $40**

BRW-3

BRW-3. World's Fair Trade Card - Chairs,
1892. - **$15 $30 $50**

BRW-4

BRW-4. World's Fair Pin, Needle & Thread Booklet,
1892. - **$15 $30 $50**

BRW-5

BRW-5. World's Fair Trade Card - Stoves/Furnaces,
1893. Scarce. - **$25 $60 $100**

BRW-6

BRW-6. "Palmer Cox Primers" Booklets,
1897. Jersey Coffee and others. Set of 12.
Each - **$15 $25 $40**

BRW-7

BRW-7. "See-Saw" Dexterity Puzzle,
1890s. Imprinted for Parkhurst-Duker Co. clothing, Quincy, Illinois . 1/2x1-1/2x3-1/2" cardboard frame holding glass over cardboard playing surface picturing three Brownies. Inner surface tilts adding to difficulty of placing three balls in holes. - **$50 $100 $150**

BRW-8

BRW-8. Luden's Cough Drop 6x9" Sign,
1890s. Rare. Earliest known character die-cut sign ad. -
$250 $750 $1050

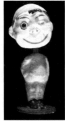 

BRW-9

BRW-10

BRW-9. Brownie Type Bobbing Head with Glass Eye,
1890s. Made in Germany. - **$125 $250 $600**

BRW-10. Candy Fig Box,
1890s. - **$40 $120 $200**

BRW-11

BRW-12

BRW-11. Brownies Song Book,
1890s. - **$25 $60 $100**

BRW-12. Lion's Coffee Cut-Outs,
1890s. Each - **$10 $20 $40**

BRW-13

BRW-13. Advertising Cards,
1890s. Buttermilk Toilet Soap. Each - **$10 $20 $40**

BRW-14

BRW-14. Advertising Trade Card,
1890s. Snag-Proof Boots. Card opens to Brownies as
sportsmen using boots. - **$15 $30 $60**

BRW-15

BRW-16

**BRW-15. "Merry Christmas From The Brownies"
Cardboard Box,**
1890s. Probably held candy or dates. - **$25 $50 $75**

BRW-16. Metal Figure Stickpin,
1890s. Tinted luster. - **$10 $15 $25**

BRW-18

BRW-17

BRW-17. "Libretto Of Palmer Cox's Brownies" Booklet,
c. 1904. 16-page song folio from stage production. -
$20 $40 $60

BRW-18. Brownie Ruler,
1900s. Mrs. Winslow Syrup premium. 8" long. -
$75 $100 $150

BUCK JONES

Movie serials, known then as chapter plays, blossomed in the 1930s, drawing countless thousands of
youngsters to local movie palaces every Saturday to
find out how their hero would save himself from the
perilous predicament at the end of the previous
episode. Buck Jones was king of the Western serials.
Charles Gebhart (1889-1942) was a cowpuncher, a
mechanic, a soldier and a trick rider. Around 1917 he
found work as a Hollywood stuntman. Three years
later, as Buck Jones, he had his first starring role. In
all, Buck Jones was to make more than 125 movies,
but it was as the hero of six chapter plays released
between 1933 and 1941 that he was to find his greatest
success. Kids everywhere waited breathlessly for the
next Buck Jones serial. A radio series, *Hoofbeats*,
sponsored by Grape-Nuts Flakes, ran for 39 episodes
in 1937-1938. In the early 1940s Buck Jones starred
with Tim McCoy and Raymond Hatton in Monogram
Pictures' *Rough Riders* movies.

BKJ-1

BKJ-2

BKJ-1. Rangers' Club Newsletter,
c. 1931. Columbia Pictures. - **$25 $60 $100**

BKJ-2. "Rangers' Club Of America" Cello. Button,
c. 1931. - **$20 $35 $60**

BKJ-3

BKJ-3. "Buck Jones' Ranger Club" Movie Cards,
c. 1931. Columbia Pictures Corp. Black and white photo cards, each with club membership coupon on reverse. Each - **$10 $20 $30**

BKJ-4

BKJ-4. Ranger Club Card With Fabric Patch,
c. 1931. Card - **$10 $20 $30**
Patch - **$20 $40 $80**

BKJ-5

BKJ-6

BKJ-5. Ranger's Club Member Application Card,
c. 1931. - **$10 $15 $30**

BKJ-6. "Buck Jones Rangers' Club Of America" Cello. Button,
c. 1931. Version of blue photo with red rim. - **$15 $25 $50**

BKJ-7

BKJ-7. "Rangers Club Of America" Cowboy Outfit,
c. 1931. Hat - **$20 $35 $60**
Bandanna. - **$25 $40 $75**
Chaps, Includes Metal Rivet Accents And Club Logo - **$75 $150 $300**

BKJ-8

BKJ-9

BKJ-8. "Buck Jones Ranger" Enameled Brass Badge,
c. 1931. Scarce. - **$50 $125 $200**

BKJ-9. "Buck Jones Rangers Club Of America" Leather Holster With Belt,
c. 1931. Photo pictures embossed club symbol on holster cover panel. - **$75 $125 $200**

BKJ-10

BKJ-10. Song Folio/Club Manual,
1932. Published by Bibo-Lang. Copyright "Book No. 1" with club ranks, pledge, etc. - **$20 $60 $120**

BKJ-11

BKJ-12

BKJ-11. "The Red Rider" Cello. Button,
1934. Universal Pictures. For 15-chapter movie serial "The Red Rider". - **$60 $125 $200**

BKJ-12. "The Phantom Rider Club" Cello. Button,
1936. Scarce. Universal Pictures. For 15-chapter movie serial "The Phantom Rider". - **$75 $175 $300**

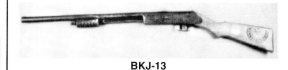

BKJ-13

BKJ-13. "No. 107 Daisy Buck Jones Special" Air Rifle,
c. 1936. Store item by Daisy Mfg. Co., also used as premium. Compass and sundial on stock, sundial pointer often missing. - **$100 $200 $300**

BKJ-14

BKJ-15

BKJ-16

BKJ-14. Horseshoe Brass Badge,
1937. Grape-Nuts Flakes. - **$15 $25 $40**

BKJ-15. Grape-Nuts Flakes Premium Catalogue Folder Sheet,
1937. Offers about 40 premiums with expiration date December 31. - **$15 $35 $60**

BKJ-16. "Buck Jones Club" Brass Ring,
1937. Grape-Nuts Flakes. - **$80 $127 $175**

BKJ-17

BKJ-17. Cello. Over Brass 3-1/4" Bullet Holder For Pencil,
c. 1937. Grape-Nuts Flakes. Inscription "From Buck Jones To His Pal" followed by personalized name designated by orderer. - **$60 $120 $175**

BKJ-18

BKJ-19

BKJ-18. Prize Folder,
1937. Four page Grape-Nuts Flakes premium prize list - **$22 $52 $84**

BKJ-19. Club Membership Offer "Grape-Nuts Flakes" Sample Box,
1937. 4" tall "New Package Adopted In 1936" with back panel ad expiring December 31, 1937. - **$50 $125 $200**

BKJ-21

BKJ-20

BKJ-20. "Buck Jones In The Cowboy Masquerade" Booklet,
1938. Ice cream cone premium, Buddy Book #8. - **$10 $20 $35**

BKJ-21. "Buck Jones Movie Book",
1938. Daisy Mfg. Co. - **$20 $30 $60**

BKJ-22

BKJ-22. "UCA Salve" Premium Catalogue Folder Sheet,
c. 1938. Has endorsement of Buck Jones and opens to 9x20" with air rifle only related premium to him. - **$20 $50 $75**

 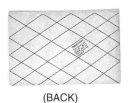

(BACK)

(FRONT)   **BKJ-23**

BKJ-23. Photo Puzzle Card,
1930s. Scarce. Movie premium. Very odd photo of Buck in deep thought, his cigarette smoke forming into the shape of his horse. Also note that his gun is pointed up towards him. Card is meant to be cut apart at lines on back and used as a puzzle. - **$20 $50 $85**

BKJ-24

BKJ-25

BKJ-24. Photo,
1930s. Sepia of him and horse Silver with facsimile autograph. - **$10 $20 $30**

BKJ-25. "Ranger's Club" Movie Serial Ticket,
1930s. Front is designed for punching admittance to 15-chapter serial, back has Buck Jones Rangers Pledge and song lyrics. - **$15 $25 $40**

BKJ-26

BKJ-27

BKJ-28

BKJ-26. Fan Photo,
1930s. - **$8 $15 $25**

BKJ-27. Portrait Photo,
1930s. Probably a premium photo. - **$10 $25 $35**

BKJ-28. "Chicago Stadium Rodeo" Cello. Button,
1930s. Single event issue. - **$20 $50 $75**

BKJ-29

BKJ-30

BKJ-31

BKJ-29. "For U.S. Marshal/Buck Jones" Cello. Button,
1930s. - **$40 $80 $150**

BKJ-30. "Buck Jones Club" Cello. Button,
1930s. Probably movie serial club. - **$40 $80 $150**

BKJ-31. "Riders Of Death Valley Club" Cello. Button,
1941. Universal Pictures. For 15-chapter movie serial
"Riders Of Death Valley". - **$50 $80 $150**

BUCK ROGERS IN THE 25TH CENTURY

Buck Rogers was the first American comic strip to
plunge into science fiction and it enjoyed great success after it was introduced in January 1929. The story
was adapted by Phil Nowlan from his futuristic novel,
illustrated by Dick Calkins and syndicated by the John
F. Dille Co. Buck wakes after 500 years of suspended
animation and, along with young Wilma Deering and
the old scientist Dr. Huer, battles to save America and
the earth from various enemies, in particular Killer
Kane and Ardala Valmar, who want to conquer the
world. The strip ran until 1967 (a companion Sunday
strip appeared from 1930 to 1965) and both were
revived in 1979 to 1983. A successful radio adaptation
was broadcast from 1932 to 1947, sponsored first by

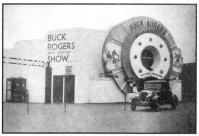

The Buck Rogers exhibit building at the 1934
Chicago World's Fair in the Enchanted Island area.

Kellogg, then Cocomalt, Cream of Wheat, Popsicle and
General Foods. A TV version had a brief run in 1950-
1951 and a revised series, produced by Glen Larson
and starring Gil Gerard and Erin Gray, debuted in 1979
and lasted two seasons. Movie adaptations appeared
in 1939, with Buster Crabbe, and 1979 (released theatrically but also serving as the pilot for the Larson
series). Crabbe had a memorable cameo in one
episode of the '80s series. There have also been a variety of Big Little Books and comic books over the years.

BRG-1

BRG-2

**BRG-1. "Amazing Stories" Pulp Magazine With First
Buck Rogers Story ,**
1928. Vol. 3 #5, August issue with story "Armaggedon-
2419 A.D." (Sequel "Airlords of Han" appeared here May,
1929.) - **$500 $1000 $1500**

BRG-2. "With My Very Best Regards" Fan Picture,
1929. Newspaper premium, black on green paper 6x9".
Large 11-1/2x17-1/2" black on orange paper version
appeared 1932. Each - **$150 $250 $400**

BRG-3

BRG-4

BRG-3. "The Planet Venus" Coloring Sheet,
1931. Newspaper offer in black and white with art by
Russell Keaton.
Uncolored - **$250 $500 $800**
Colored - **$150 $350 $600**

BRG-4. Newspaper Comic Strip Portraits Premiums,
1932. Black and white, each about 8x10-1/2". Each -
$75 $150 $300

BRG-5

BRG-6

BRG-5. "Pep" Leaflet With Radio Show Ad,
1932. Kellogg's. - **$20 $40 $60**

BRG-6. Radio Broadcast Publicity Leaflet,
1932. Kellogg's Corn Flakes. Sponsorship indicated for Buck Rogers and Singing Lady programs. - **$12 $25 $40**

BRG-7

BRG-8

BRG-7. "Mystery Color Puzzle" Paper Sheet,
1932. Newspaper offer in black and white 8-1/4x10-3/4".
Uncolored - **$150 $300 $500**
Colored - **$100 $250 $400**

BRG-8. "Bucktoy" Set Of Six Cut Out Cards,
1932. Newspaper offer of set of six issued from 1932 to 1934. Stiff paper 2-3/8x5-5/8" in black and white (except Dr. Huer in green) to cut and color.
Each Uncut And Uncolored - **$100 $200 $300**
Each Uncut And Colored - **$75 $150 $200**
Each Cut And Colored - **$50 $75 $125**

BRG-9

BRG-9. Origin Storybook,
1933. Kellogg's. Reprinted in 1994 but no Kellogg's ad on back cover. Near Mint With Envelope - **$475**
Loose - **$60 $250 $425**
White Paper Letter (2 Versions) Each - **$40 $80 $125**

BRG-11

BRG-10

BRG-10. "Buck Rogers 25th Century A.D." BLB,
1933. Softcover with Cocomalt ad on back cover. Sent boxed. See next item. - **$20 $60 $150**

BRG-11. Mailer And Letter For Cocomalt BLB,
1933. Accompanied previous item. Mailer - **$20 $50 $75**
Yellow Paper Letter - **$40 $80 $125**

BRG-12

(ENLARGED VIEW)
BRG-13

BRG-12. "Solar System Map" Letter,
1933. Cocomalt. Orange paper. - **$35 $75 $125**

BRG-13. Solar System Map 18x25",
1933. Cocomalt. Sent rolled in a tube. Beware of 1970s color reproductions on glossy paper or color photocopies. - **$250 $500 $800**

BRG-14   BRG-15

BRG-14. Buck And Wilma Cocomalt Browntone Picture,
1933. - **$50 $100 $150**
Blue Paper Letter **$35 $75 $125**

BRG-15. Buck and Wilma Paper Masks,
1933. Cocomalt. Made by Einson-Freeman. Note curly hair design on Wilma. An unlicensed store item marked "Made in Japan" without curly hair and on less slick paper was also issued. See BRG-95. Each - **$100 $200 $300**

BRG-16

BRG-16. Cocomalt "Buck Rogers Cut-Out Adventure Book" Order Folder,
1933. Full color 9x13" Sent with BRG-10 and BRG-13. - **$75 $150 $300**

BRG-17

BRG-17. Cocomalt "Buck Rogers Cut-Out Adventure Book",
1933. Rare. Came with letter and separate cardboard sheet for theater stage. Has 20 stand-ups.
Complete Uncut - **$1500 $3500 $5000**
Complete, Figures Cut - **$300 $600 $1200**

BRG-18

BRG-18. "The Rocket Flash" Contest Prize Picture,
1933. Newspaper giveaway reading "Congratulations to YOU as one of the Buck Rogers fans who picked the winning ship in the race to Mars." 6x9" black and white with art by Russell Keaton. - **$250 $600 $1200**

BRG-19

BRG-20

BRG-19. "Woofian Dictionary" Folder,
1933. Newspaper offer containing words used by "Woofs," amazing animals living on the plateaus of Jupiter. Shown open. Beige paper. - **$100 $200 $400**

BRG-20. "Buck Rogers In The 25th Century" Cello. Button,
1935. Cream of Wheat. Full color on dark blue 1" with Whitehead & Hoag Co. back paper. - **$30 $60 $100**

BRG-21

BRG-22

BRG-21. "Buck Rogers On The Air" Radio Station Listing Sheet,
c. 1933. Cocomalt. Three versions or more on blue or white paper, sizes vary. Each - **$25 $60 $100**

BRG-22. "Buck Rogers" Cardboard Helmet,
1934. Cocomalt. Helmet - **$75 $125 $200**
Mailer - **$25 $50 $100**
Blue Paper Letter **$35 $75 $125**

BRG-23

BRG-24

BRG-23. "Wilma Deering" Cardboard Helmet,
1934. Cocomalt. Helmet - **$75 $125 $200**
Mailer - **$25 $50 $100**
Blue Paper Letter **$35 $75 $125**

BRG-24. Cardboard Pop Gun,
1934. Cocomalt. Came with Buck or Wilma paper helmet.
Gun - **$75 $125 $200**
Mailer (Two styles) - **$25 $50 $100**

BRG-25

BRG-25. Buck Rogers Painted Lead Figure,
1934. Cocomalt. Wilma and Killer Kane also issued. Each in full color packaged individually with leaflet in a cellophane bag. Each With Leaflet - **$40 $75 $125**
Each Figure Only - **$20 $40 $75**

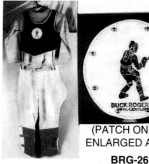

BRG-27

(PATCH ON VEST
ENLARGED ABOVE)

BRG-26

BRG-26. Child's Playsuit,
1934. Scarce. Store item and Cream of Wheat. Came with
suede cloth helmet XZ-42. Jersey is orange. Sizes 4 to 14
made. Playsuit also made for girls with khaki skirt.
Uniform, Complete Except Helmet - **$250 $700 $1300**
Vest Only With Patch - **$100 $250 $350**

BRG-27. "Buck Rogers 25th Century" Navigation Helmet by Daisy,
1934. Store item (brown suede cloth version) and Cream
of Wheat (leather version). Suede version XZ-42 was
included with previous item and came unboxed in three
sizes. Leather version XZ-34 issued in 1935 came boxed
in three sizes. Suede version has white cloth or metal visor
frame. Leather version came only with metal visor frame. -
$150 $300 $750

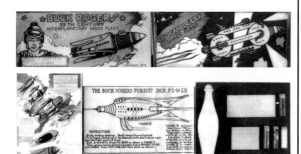

BRG-28

BRG-28. Rocketship Balsa Wood Model,
1934. Six in set (#6 shown), each boxed ready-made or
unfinished with color/bw instruction sheet. Sold in stores
(Sears offered #1,3,and 4) or as newspaper premium. Only
#4 "Super Dreadnought" was available (unfinished) as
Cream of Wheat premium. The full set of models was completed by late 1935. Instruction sheets 11x17" were available as late as 1939. Each Boxed - **$200 $350 $600**
Instruction Sheet - **$50 $80 $150**

BRG-29

BRG-29. "Buck Rogers Thwarting Ancient Demons" Booklet,
1934. Big Thrill Chewing Gum. Booklet #1 of six Buck
Rogers titles in set of 24. 2-3/8x3" with eight pages. Buck
is shown on one corner of the Goudey Co. wrapper.
Booklets are usually brittle from age. Each - **$25 $50 $75**

(HANDLE ENLARGED)

BRG-30

BRG-30. Rocket Pistol XZ-31 and Holster XZ-33 by Daisy,
1934. Store item. Gun is 9-1/2" long with black finish and
cocking handle. The three-color suede cloth holster and
belt came unboxed or boxed with the gun, sold as "25th
Century Combat Set." This box pictures Buck firing his
pistol. Gun - **$60 $150 $300**
Holster - **$50 $150 $250**
Gun Box - **$100 $250 $500**
Combat Set XZ-32 Box (Not Shown) - **$200 $400 $600**

BRG-31

BRG-31. Scientific Laboratory,
1934. Store item by Porter Chemical Co. Pictured are box,
envelope that holds instruction manuals (three) and envelope for slide covers. Many other items came in boxed set.
No complete sets known. Empty Box - **$350 $750 $1500**
Other Items Shown - **$100 $200 $300**

(ENLARGED VIEW OF LABEL ABOVE)

BRG-32

BRG-32. "Buck Rogers Telescope",
1934. Store item, part of Scientific Laboratory set. 14" long, not the later Cream of Wheat or Popsicle versions. - **$100 $250 $400**

BRG-33   BRG-34   BRG-35

BRG-33. "A Century Of Progress" Chicago World's Fair Litho. Button,
1934. Blue, orange and white 1-1/8" by Greenduck Co. - **$75 $150 $350**

BRG-34. Birthstone Initial Ring,
1934. Cocomalt. Unmarked brass Buck Rogers tie-in issue and other non-Buck offers, top has personalized single initial designated by orderer. Also offered by Popsicle, 1939. - **$150 $325 $475**

BRG-35. Saturday Chicago American Litho. Button,
c. 1934. Multicolor on white 1-1/8" by Greenduck Co. - **$40 $75 $150**

BRG-36

BRG-36. "Caster" Booklet,
1934. Boxed Caster sets were store item by Rapaport Brothers. Three booklet versions. Booklet includes eight daily strips and photos of caster and mold sets. Sets also made in 1935 for total of 5 different.
Each Booklet - **$75 $150 $250**

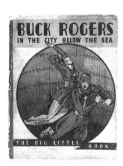 

BRG-37   BRG-38

BRG-37. "Buck Rogers In The City Below The Sea" BLB,
1934. Cocomalt. Softcover premium version but has no Cocomalt advertising. - **$50 $100 $200**

BRG-38. "Buck Rogers On THe Moons Of Saturn" BLB,
1934. Cocomalt. Softcover premium version but has no Cocomalt advertising. - **$50 $100 $200**

BRG-39

BRG-39. "A Century Of Progress-I Was There" Brass Key Fob,
1934. From Buck Rogers exhibit at the fair during 1934 season. 1" holed as made. Giveaways included a pad and pencil set and a generic jigsaw puzzle. - **$200 $400 $800**

 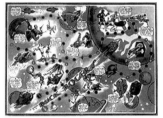

BRG-40

BRG-40. "Buck Rogers Game Of The 25th Century A.D.",
1934. Store item by Lutz and Sheinkman, Inc. with Stephen Slesinger copyright. Box holds 13x18" board with cardboard spinner, four cardboard markers in a punch-out frame, two wood bowling pin-like markers and instruction sheet. Complete - **$200 $350 $750**
Board Only - **$100 $200 $300**

BRG-41

BRG-41. Set of Three Board Games,
1934. Store item and Cream of Wheat premium. Came with 40 cards and 12 miniature bowling pin-shaped wood markers. Made by Lutz & Sheinkman.
Complete Boxed Set - **$300 $600 $1000**
Each Board - **$75 $150 $250**

BRG-42   BRG-43

BRG-42. "Rocket Ship Knife" Box,
1935. Scarce. Cream of Wheat and store item.
Box Only - **$150 $250 $400**

BRG-43. "Buck Rogers" Steel/Cello. Pocketknife,
1935. Scarce. Store item produced by Adolph Kastor with manufacturer's name, Camillus Cutlery Co., on one of the two blades. Also a premium from Cream of Wheat. Same image on both grips in red, green or blue styles. Color easily worn off. - **$300 $750 $1500**

BRG-44

BRG-44. Rocket Pistol XZ-35 and Holster XZ-36 by Daisy,
1935. Store item. Gun is 7-1/2" long with black finish and cocking handle. Leather holster with round hole on holster front straps. Holster came with 30" leather belt. No box for holster. Gun - **$75 $175 $350**
Holster - **$35 $75 $150**
Gun Box - **$100 $200 $300**
Combat Set XZ-37 Box (Not Shown) - **$200 $400 $600**

BRG-45

BRG-45. Disintegrator Pistol XZ-38 and Holster XZ-39 by Daisy,
1935. Store item and Cream of Wheat. Used in 1939 as Popsicle premium. Copper finish. Flint produces spark. Leather holster with diamond-shaped hole on front straps. Holster came with 30" leather belt. No box for holster.
Gun - **$125 $250 $500**
Holster - **$75 $150 $300**
Gun Box - **$200 $350 $500**
Combat Set XZ-40 Box (Not Shown) - **$250 $450 $700**

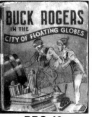  

BRG-46   BRG-47   BRG-48

BRG-46. "Buck Rogers In The City Of Floating Globes" BLB,
1935. Cocomalt. Issued only as softcover with Cocomalt ad on back. - **$75 $200 $400**

BRG-47. "Tarzan Cups" Premium Booklet Featuring Buck Rogers,
1935. Tarzan Ice Cream Cups or Lily Tulip brand. In the Big Little Book style, 1/2" thick. From Whitman set of six different characters, each obtained for 12 cup lids. - **$75 $150 $300**

BRG-48. "Punch-O-Bag",
1935. Morton's Salt premium by Lou Fox, Chicago. Came in 3"x5" envelope. Various colors each showing a different character. Balloon typically missing or disintegrated.
Envelope Only - **$25 $50 $75**

BRG-49   BRG-50

BRG-49. "Buck Rogers 25th Century Adventures" Printing Set,
1935. Store item and Cream of Wheat. Set No. 4080 by StamperKraft Co. Includes 14 character stamps. - **$150 $400 $750**

BRG-50. "Cosmic Conquests" Boxed Printing Set,
1935. Store item by StamperKraft Co. Set #4090 with 22 character stamps. A set with 15 character stamps and alphabet was issued as #4090-S.
Each Set - **$150 $300 $500**

BRG-51

BRG-51. Pocketwatch,

1935. Store item by Ingraham Co. Lightning bolt hands in copper color and case back pictures Comet Man. A 1971 version has black hands and a blank case back.
Boxed With Golden Cardboard Insert - **$500 $1600 $2600**
Watch Only - **$300 $800 $1350**

BRG-52

BRG-54

BRG-53

BRG-52. "Buck Rogers On The Air For Cream Of Wheat" Gummed Back Paper Sticker,

c. 1935. Dark blue and yellow. - **$50 $100 $150**

BRG-53. "Buck Rogers 25th Century Catalog,"

1935. John Dille folder catalog of items available from company by mail order. Some items shown were also used as premiums. Black and white folder opens to 9x12". - **$100 $200 $400**

BRG-54. School Bag With Strap,

1935. Store item and Cream of Wheat premium made of suede cloth. - **$300 $800 $1500**

BRG-55

BRG-56

BRG-55. Dixie-Style Ice Cream Cup Lid,

c. 1935. C.B.S. Radio. Red lettering on tan cardboard. Reads "Listen To Buck Rogers In The 25th Century On CBS!" - **$75 $150 $250**

BRG-56. Pencil Box No. 35228,

1935. Store item and Cream of Wheat premium. Red and blue, issued with contents. Between 1934 and 1938 at least 40 different boxes were made in various sizes and colors. - **$75 $150 $250**

BRG-57

BRG-58

BRG-57. "Astral Heroes" Printing Set,

1935. Store item by StamperKraft Co. Set number 4070 with seven character stamps. Complete Boxed -
$175 $325 $600

BRG-58. "Ardala" Metal Alloy Figure By Britains,

1936. Cream of Wheat. Full color paint. Each with moveable arm. Set (with name under base) of Buck, Wilma, Killer Kane, Ardala, Dr. Huer, Robot. Reproductions in metal made by DP Miniatures in 1989 do not have name under base.
Robot - **$250 $500 $750**
Others, Each - **$150 $300 $450**

BRG-59

BRG-59. Cartoon Adventures Perforated Strip Cards,

1936. Store item. Set of 24 (#425-448) from a larger set of 48 that includes other newspaper comic characters. Cards are 2-1/4x2-3/4".
Each In Buck Rogers Set - **$35 $75 $125**

BRG-60

BRG-61

BRG-60. Buck Rogers Standing On North America Picture,

1936. Newspaper premium offered as "Dandy Picture Of Buck Rogers." Black and white 5-1/2x8-1/2" stiff paper. Example shown was later signed by the artist Dick Calkins. Scarce. Unsigned - **$200 $350 $600**

BRG-61. "Chief Explorer" Leaflet and "Star Explorer" Dial Device,
1936. Cream of Wheat. Offers Chief Explorer badge, Star Explorer (star finder device), Four-Power Telescope (smaller than one with Scientific Laboratory and not Popsicle version), Dr. Huer's Invisible Ink Crystals and Balloon Globe of the World. Leaflet - **$100 $250 $400** Dial - **$100 $200 $300**

BRG-62   **BRG-64**

BRG-63

BRG-62. Dixie Ice Cream Lid,
1936. Browntone photo. Inscribed for Cream of Wheat radio series. Lid also issued with Breyers Ice Cream imprint. A generic three-fold album with slots to hold the lids was available. - **$25 $40 $60**

BRG-63. "Lite-Blaster" Flashlight,
1936. Cream of Wheat. Design in four colors. - **$200 $400 $800**

BRG-64. Dixie Ice Cream Picture,
1936. Photo of Matthew Crowley, radio portrayer. Full color, 8"x10", obtained by redeeming lids. - **$40 $75 $150**

BRG-65

BRG-65. "Irwin Projector" With Comic Character Films,
1936. Unmarked but offered as premium with six Buck Rogers film loops of 16mm black and white cartoon art (from group of 13 titles) in Cream of Wheat Buck Rogers Solar Scouts Club Manual. Films also issued on reels of four different lengths in 2-1/2" or 4" boxes.
Boxed Projector - **$50 $80 $150**
Each Boxed Film - **$5 $10 $15**

BRG-66

BRG-66. Liquid Helium Water Pistol XZ-44 And Box By Daisy,
1936. Store item. Used in 1939 as Popsicle premium. No holster made. Gun examples are now non-functional due to aging of bladder. A red, yellow and black promotional flier was issued.
Red and Yellow Version - **$200 $400 $800**
Copper Colored Version - **$250 $500 $1000**
Box Only - **$300 $600 $1200**

BRG-67

BRG-67. Boxed Card Game,
1936. Store item by All-Fair. Box comes in two sizes, larger one shown. 35 full-color cards plus instruction card. Cards are in pairs except for Killer Kane. - **$150 $300 $500**

BRG-68

BRG-68. "Solar Scouts" Radio Club Manual,
1936. Cream Of Wheat. Offers 18 premiums. Color cover with black and white contents. - **$100 $250 $500**

BRG-69   **BRG-70**

BRG-71

BRG-69. Repeller Ray Brass Ring With Green Stone,
1936. Scarce. Cream Of Wheat and newspaper premium offer. Original stone is faceted. Beware of replacements. Within Buck Rogers Solar Scouts club, also known as "Supreme Inner Circle" ring. Offered again in 1939. - **$300 $1000 $3000**

BRG-70. "Solar Scouts" Sweater Patch,
1936. Cream of Wheat. Rare. Less than 10 known. 3-1/2" red and blue on yellow felt. - **$1500 $4250 $5500**

BRG-71. Solar Scouts Member Brass Badge,
1936. Cream of Wheat and newspaper premium offer. Facsimile Buck Rogers signature on reverse. Offered again in 1939. - **$25 $60 $100**

BRG-72

BRG-72. "Spaceship Commander" Leaflet,
1936. Cream of Wheat. Offers badge, banner, magnetic compass, stationery, Wilma handkerchief. -
$75 $150 $250

BRG-73   **BRG-74**   **BRG-75**   **BRG-76**

BRG-73. "Spaceship Commander/Buck Rogers Solar Scouts" Silvered Brass Badge,
1936. Cream of Wheat and newspaper premium offer. Metallic blue accent paint, holed at bottom to serve as whistle. Offered again in 1939. - **$85 $175 $300**

BRG-74. "Chief Explorer/Buck Rogers Solar Scouts" Brass Badge,
1936. Cream of Wheat and newspaper premium offer. Red enamel paint background. Badge inscribed on back "Awarded For Distinguished Achievement" with facsimile Buck Rogers signature. Offered again in 1939. -
$100 $200 $350

BRG-75. "Chief Explorer" Brass Badge,
1936. Scarce. Cream of Wheat and newspaper premium offer. Variety with gold luster and no red enamel paint. -
$150 $350 $525

BRG-76. Wilma Deering Brass Pendant With Chain,
1936. Rare. Cream of Wheat and newspaper premium offer. Back inscription "To My Pal In The Solar Scouts". Offered again in 1939. - **$300 $1000 $1500**

BRG-77

BRG-78

BRG-77. "Buck Rogers Rocketship" Balsa Flying Toy With Mailer Envelope,
1936. Rare. Mrs. Karl's Bread by Spotswood Specialty Co., also Cream of Wheat premium. Envelope is plain, comes with wood stick and rubber band launcher. -
$100 $250 $500

BRG-78. Letter - Chief Explorer,
1936. Cream of Wheat Premium. Talks about badge and Solar Scouts club information. - **$50 $100 $150**

BRG-80

BRG-79

BRG-79. "Daisy Comics",
1936. Daisy Mfg. Co. Contents include Buck Rogers comic story and shows guns for him plus features on cowboys Buck Jones and Tim McCoy. Thinner and smaller format than a standard comic book. - **$50 $100 $220**

BRG-80. "25th Century Acousticon Jr." 2-1/4" Cello. Button,
1936. Rare. Hearing aid device by Dictograph Products Co. Black, blue, red and fleshtone on white background. -
$300 $1000 $2000

(SMALL SET)

(LARGE SET BOX LID)

BRG-81

BRG-81. Chemical Laboratory Boxed Set,
1937. Store item with instruction sheet in two sizes by Gropper Toy Co. Small Set - **$350 $750 $1250**
Large Set - **$500 $1000 $1500**

BRG-82   **BRG-83**   **BRG-84**

BRG-82. Tootsietoy #1031 "Battle Cruiser",
1937. Metal "Buck Rogers Battle Cruiser TSDDM3030." Used as Popsicle premium in 1939. Came in several color variations over the years. Reissued in early 1950s by Dowst in silver color with U.S. Air Force insignia but without Buck Rogers name. The reissue is scarce.
Near Mint Boxed - **$350**
Loose - **$75 $150 $225**
Reissue Loose - **$125 $200 $350**
Reissue NM on Blister Card - **$400**

BRG-83. Tootsietoy #1032 "Destroyer" With Box,
1937. Metal "Buck Rogers Venus Duo-Destroyer MK 24 L". Used as Popsicle premium in 1939. Came in several color variations over the years. Reissued in early 1950s by Dowst in silver color with U.S. Air Force insignia but without Buck Rogers name. The reissue is scarce.
Near Mint Boxed - **$350**
Loose - **$75 $150 $225**
Reissue NM on Blister Card - **$400**
Reissue Loose - **$125 $200 $350**

BRG-84. Tootsietoy #1033 "Attack Ship",
1937. Metal "Buck Rogers Flash Blast Attack Ship TS 310 Z". Used as Popsicle premium in 1939. Came in several color variations over the years. Reissued in early 1950s by Dowst in silver color with U.S. Air Force insignia but without Buck Rogers name. The reissue is scarce.
Near Mint Boxed - **$350**
Loose - **$75 $150 $225**
Reissue NM on Blister Card - **$400**
Reissue Loose - **$125 $200 $350**

BRG-85

BRG-85 "Combat Game!",
1937. Store item by Warren Paper Products Co. Set No. 110. Many full color pre-cut stiff thin cardboard pieces to form Rocket Ship Control Base with accessories of spaceships, guns and 11 standup characters. Total of 65 pieces plus instructions. Boxed Complete - **$500 $1200 $1750**
Complete No Box - **$300 $650 $1200**

BRG-86   BRG-87

BRG-88

BRG-86. "Earth Jupiter Transport NNS36" Metal Spaceship,
1937. Tootsietoy, perhaps intended as fourth rocketship in their series but may exist as prototype only. Also slides on string. - **$500 $1000 $1500**

BRG-87. Canadian Club Member Cello. Button,
1937. Issuer unknown but 1" in blue/white/orange. Curl reads "Shaw Mfg. Toronto." - **$250 $600 $1200**

BRG-88. Buck Rogers Metal Figure 1-3/4" Tall,
1937. Packaged with Tootsietoy rocketships. Sold with boxed set #5450 only. Buck (Silver Color) Or Wilma (Gold Color) Each - **$60 $125 $175**

BRG-89

BRG-89. Vicks And Other Premium Comic Books,
c. 1938. Vicks Chemical Co. shown with their logo and same comic with local store imprint. These thin books reprinted stories from earlier Famous Funnies comic books. Three additional similar thin versions were produced: two by Pure Oil and one by Salerno.
Each - **$50 $125 $275**

BRG-91

BRG-90

BRG-90. "Vicks Comics" Comic Book,
1938. Vicks Chemical Co. published by Eastern Color Printing Co. 64 pages of stories printed earlier in Famous Funnies. Five pages relate to Buck Rogers, the others feature various characters. - **$75 $200 $550**

BRG-91. "Rocket Rangers" Club Member Card,
1939. Pictures "Inter-Planetary Battle Cruiser" on yellow card. Each card acquired by sending offer coupon clipped from newspaper comic strip. Five later versions were on blue or white cards, the last issued in 1980.
First Version - **$75 $150 $275**
Later Versions - **$20 $50 $100**

BRG-92

BRG-92. "Strange World Adventures Club" Serial Club Cello. Button,
1939. Universal. Made by Philadelphia Badge Co. in blue and silver 1-1/4" design. Offered with a membership card by various theaters. One of the rarest and most desirable movie serial club buttons.
Button - **$300 $750 $1500**
Card - **$150 $250 $500**

BRG-93

BRG-94

BRG-97. Newspaper Contest 1-1/4" Cello. Buttons,
1930s. "Buffalo Evening News" example pictures aviator character from early Buck Rogers daily newspaper strip. "Pittsburgh-Post Gazette" example pictures Buck Rogers.
Buffalo - **$50 $100 $150**
Pittsburgh - **$60 $125 $200**

BRG-98. "Buck Rogers Gang" Club Member Cello. Button,
1930s. Issuer unknown. 1-1/2" red on cream. -
$200 $400 $600

BRG-93. "Whistling Rocketship" Cardboard Punch-Out Assembly Kit With Envelope,
1939. Scarce. Muffets cereal. Example photo shows portrait details from tail fins.
Unused With Envelope - **$250 $500 $750**
Assembled - **$200 $400 $600**

BRG-94. "Gift List Radio News" Catalog,
1939. Popsicle. Full color 7-1/2x10" with four pages. A different version was issued in 1940. Each - **$75 $150 $300**

BRG-99

BRG-100

BRG-99. Buck Rogers Style Rocketship,
1930s. Store item by Barclay in red, blue and yellow similar to Tootsietoy rockets. - **$100 $175 $300**

BRG-100. "Lucky Coin",
1930s. Issuer unknown. 1-1/2" in the style of a "wooden nickel." - **$100 $250 $400**

BRG-95

BRG-96

BRG-101

BRG-102

BRG-95. Wilma Unlicensed Mask,
1930s. Store item, marked "Made In Japan". Unlike 1933 Cocomalt premium, hair is not curly and less slick paper stock resulted in duller color. See item BRG-15. -
$40 $80 $150

BRG-96. School Map,
1930s. Rare. Probable Dixon Pencil Co. Yellow-tone, 8-1/2"x11" paper sheet came folded with Buck Rogers art in red border scenes on map of North America.-
$200 $400 $600

BRG-101. "Follow Buck Rogers" Cello. Button,
1930s. Washington Herald newspaper. Red type and blue image on white 1-1/4" from a set that includes other comic character strips appearing in the newspaper. -
$350 $750 $1200

BRG-102. "Punch-O-Bag,"
1940. Store item from late 1940s by Lee-Tex Rubber Products Corp. Glassine bag 5x7" in red and blue held balloon usually missing or disintegrated.
Bag Only - **$60 $125 $250**

BRG-97

BRG-98

BRG-103

BRG-104

BRG-103. Matchbook,
1940. Popsicle/Creamsicle. May 4th version for new radio sponsorship. Also issued with April 6th date for southern states. Empty or Incomplete - **$10 $20 $40**
Complete With All Matches - **$20 $40 $80**

BRG-104. Matchbook,
1940. Popsicle. May 4th version for new radio sponsorship. Also issued with April 6th date for southern states. -
Empty or Incomplete - **$10 $20 $40**
Complete With All Matches - **$20 $40 $80**

BRG-105

BRG-106

BRG-105. "Onward School Supplies" 18x24" Paper Hanger Sign,
1940. Printed on both sides. A larger 18"x50" version came rolled on a wood dowel. Small Version - **$150 $250 $400**
Large Version - **$250 $500 $800**

BRG-106. School Supplies 11x16" Paper Store Poster,
1940. Onward School Supplies. Announces rubber band gun free with school supply purchase. - **$150 $350 $750**

BRG-107

BRG-108

BRG-107. Cardboard Punch-Out Rubber Band Gun,
1940. Onward School Supplies. Punch-out sheet includes standup targets of Sea Monster, Wing Bat Wu, Spaceship. 5"x10", red and black art. Unpunched - **$75 $200 $300**

BRG-108. "School Sale" Newspaper-Size Circular,
1940. Photo examples show top half of front cover plus two illustration details. - **$35 $60 $100**

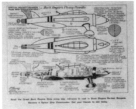

BRG-109

BRG-109. "Flying Needle" Airship Diagram Sheet,
1941. Various daily newspapers. For "Buck Rogers Rocket Rangers" club of aspiring "Spaceship Commander" readers. 8-1/2"x11", red on white, not a punch-out. -
$100 $200 $350

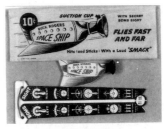

BRG-110

BRG-110. Cardboard Spaceship With Envelope,
1942. Morton's Salt. Includes cardboard "Secret Bomb Sight". Suction cup nose stiffens with age.
Complete With Envelope - **$50 $100 $250**

BRG-111

BRG-111. "Buck Rogers Ranger" Aluminum Dog Tag With Chain,
c. 1942. Rare. Item has 1935 copyright but probably issued a few years later. Black details wear off easily. -
$350 $850 $1200

BRG-112

BRG-112. Rocket Rangers Iron-On Transfers,
1944. Newspaper premium. Set of three sent individually for Buck, Wilma and Rocketship. Photos show offer and two transfers. Transfers are red and blue on 3x6" tissue paper. Last photo is example of two older tranfers with outlined image of Buck.
Each Ranger Transfer - **$50 $85 $125**
Each Older Transfer - **$10 $25 $40**

BRG-113

BRG-113. "Atomic Bomber" Jigsaw Puzzle Boxed Set,
1945. Store item by Puzzle Craft Industries, Chicago. Each puzzle is 8-1/2x11" with art by Dick Calkins. Two versions of box lid. Exceptionally colorful.
Each Puzzle Or Box - **$100 $200 $300**

BRG-114

BRG-114. Atomic Pistol U-235 By Daisy,
1945. Store item. Silver or black color finish. No holster made. A red, black and yellow promotional flyer was issued. Gun - **$75 $200 $350**
Box - **$75 $200 $350**
3-Page Story Folder - **$40 $75 $150**

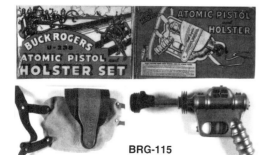

BRG-115

BRG-115. Atomic Pistol U-238 By Daisy,
1946. Store item. Gold color finish. Gun - **$100 $250 $400**
Leather Holster - **$100 $250 $400**
Box - **$75 $200 $350**
3-Page Story Folder **$40 $75 $150**

BRG-116

BRG-117

BRG-116. Glow-In-Dark Ring Of Saturn,
1946. Post's Corn Toasties radio premium. White plastic topped by red plastic stone. - **$100 $200 $500**

BRG-117. "Ring Of Saturn" Instruction Folder,
1946. Post's Corn Toasties radio premium. -
$125 $150 $175

BRG-118

BRG-118. "Adventure Book,"
1946. Daisy three-section folder issued with boxed guns Atomic Pistol U-235 and Atomic Pistol U-238. Folder in black and white reprints six daily newspaper comic strips. -
$40 $75 $150

BRG-119

BRG-120

BRG-119. Full Color Blotter,
c. 1946. Chicago Herald-American. 3-1/2x8-1/2" newspaper promotional. - **$75 $175 $300**

BRG-120. Post's Corn Toasties Cereal Box,
1946. Rare. Post Cereal. Advertises radio program on The Mutual Network. Complete Box - **$300 $600 $1000**
Back Panel Only - **$200 $300 $500**

BRG-121

BRG-122

BRG-121. "Daisy Handbook,"
1946. Daisy Mfg. Co. The first of several booklets promoting Daisy products. Contents include 10 Buck Rogers daily newspaper strip reprints. - **$35 $100 $275**

BRG-122. Drawing Of Pluton,
1948. Newspaper premium with Rick Yager art in dark red on tan paper 8-1/2x11". Sent to readers who mailed in their own conception drawing. - **$100 $250 $500**

BRG-124

BRG-123

BRG-123. Pittsburgh "Post-Gazette Sunday Funnies" Comic Book,
1949. Newspaper insert 16 page comic including Buck Rogers and other characters. - **$300 $550 $800**

BRG-124. Buck Rogers And Flame D'Amour Trading Cards,
1949. Store item by Comic Stars, Inc. Full color 2-1/4x3-1/2" part of a set including other characters. Art by Murphy Anderson. Buck - **$10 $25 $50**
Flame - **$8 $20 $40**

BRG-125

BRG-126

BRG-125. Cardboard "Flying Saucer",
c. 1940s. Store item by unknown maker marked S. P. Co. Has metal rim. - **$35 $75 $150**

BRG-126. Amoco Gasoline Penny Cards,
1940s. Black on cream thin cardboard 3x3". Many in series that include non-Buck Rogers characters. Images are pages out of Big Little Books.
Each Buck Rogers - **$50 $100 $150**

BRG-127

BRG-128

BRG-127. Letter - How To Get Rocket Ranger Insignia,
1940s. Newspaper Premium. Have to hold up to mirror to read message. This letter, the following three items, and many others not shown, were issued in series by newspapers running the Buck Rogers daily strip and its associated club, the Rocket Rangers. These letters were offered to young readers in 1939 through 1942, 1944, 1946, 1948 through 1950, and 1952. - **$30 $40 $50**

BRG-128. Letter - How To Get Secret Signals,
1940s. Newspaper Premium. Came with membership card. - **$30 $40 $50**

BRG-129

BRG-130

BRG-129. Letter - Special Order #1,
1940s. Newspaper Premium. Mars fighting globes described. - **$30 $40 $50**

BRG-130. Letter - Special Orders #2,
1940s. Newspaper Premium. Shows secret visible code system. - **$40 $80 $90**

BRG-131

BRG-131. Space Ranger Kit,
1952. Sylvania Electric Products Inc. Six full color punch-out sheets, each 10-1/2x14-1/2". Kit includes string. One punch-out is a membership card. See BRG-134 & 135.
Unpunched In Envelope - **$50 $100 $150**

BRG-132

BRG-133

BRG-132. "Rocket Rangers" Member Litho. Tin Tab,
1952. Newspaper premium made by L.J. Imber, Chicago. -
$25 $75 $150

BRG-133. Octopus Space Station Tray Puzzle,
1952. Store item by Milton Bradley. 10x14" originally sold with paper sleeve. Sleeve - **$25 $50 $75**
Puzzle - **$35 $60 $100**

BRG-134

BRG-134. Large Display Poster,
1952. Promotes Space Ranger Kit premium from Sylvania. See BRG-131. - **$300 $600 $800**

BRG-135

BRG-136

BRG-135. Large Die-Cut Sign,
1952. Promotes Sylvania and shows Space Ranger Kit pieces. See BRG-131. - **$750 $1500 $2300**

BRG-136. "Buck Rogers/Satellite Pioneers" Litho. Tin 2" Tab,
1957. Red and black on white made by Greenduck Co. -
$20 $40 $65

BRG-137

BRG-137. "Satellite Pioneers Cadet Commission" Bulletin Folder,
1958. Various newspapes. Sent folded. -
$30 $60 $100

BRG-138

BRG-138. Starfinder,
1958. Newspaper premium. Satellite Pioneers Club. Guide to major constellations. See BRG-139. - **$25 $60 $75**

BRG-139

BRG-139. "Satellite Pioneers" Bulletin,
1958. Newspaper premium. Secret Order No. 1 on pink paper mailed with Star Finder folder. See BRG-138. -
$25 $50 $85

BRG-140

BRG-141

BRG-140. Satellite Pioneers Club Bulletin,
c. 1958. Various newspapers. Cover portrait faces right.
Includes "Map of the Solar System." - **$20 $30 $50**

BRG-141. "Satellite Pioneers" Picture Card,
1960. Offered by various newspapers. - **$15 $25 $40**

BRG-142

BRG-142. Captain Action & Action Boy Comic,
1967. Ideal Toy & Novelty Co. Features Buck Rogers and
other character accessory sets for use with Captain Action
12" figure. - **$10 $25 $75**

BRG-143

BRG-144

BRG-143. Captain Action Card Game,
1967. Kool-Pops/Kool-Aid. Buck Rogers and other characters on 36 card game. Came in separate mailing box.
Complete - **$35 $75 $125**

BRG-144. Captain Action/Buck Rogers Flicker Ring,
1967. Ideal Toys. Silver base marked "Hong Kong" came
with boxed figure.
Silver "Hong Kong" Base - **$30 $45 $60**
Blue Base - **$10 $20 $30**
Silver "China" Modern Base - **$5 $10 $15**

BRG-145

BRG-146

BRG-145. Buck Rogers Profile Ring,
1960s. Issuer unknown. Brass base with black and white
paper image under beveled edge plastic top. First example
surfaced in late 1960s. No documentation known and possibly a fantasy creation but uncommon. -
$150 $325 $500

BRG-146. Warren Paper Co. Promotional Items,
c. 1971. Color poster, stiff paper zap pistol and postcard
(not shown). Poster - **$20 $40 $75**
Pistol - **$20 $40 $75**
Postcard - **$10 $20 $30**

BRG-147

BRG-148

BRG-147. Television Series Promotional Poster,
1979. Burger King. 17x22" color paper giveaway poster. -
$15 $30 $50

**BRG-148. Television Series Plastic Cup Promotional
Poster,**
1979. Burger King issue advertising Coca-Cola. 13x19"
color paper poster advertising set of eight tumblers. -
$25 $50 $75

BRG-149

BRG-150

BRG-149. Coca-Cola Plastic Tumblers,
1979. Distributed in theaters playing Buck Rogers movie. Eight different smaller size and five different larger size, each showing one character from the movie.
Small - **$5 $10 $15**
Large - **$15 $30 $50**

BRG-150. Coca-Cola Glass Tumblers,
1979. Two sizes for four different characters. These may exist as test or prototypes only. Near Mint Each - **$200**

BRG-152

BRG-151

BRG-151. "Adventures Of Big Boy" Comic Book,
1979. Restaurant giveaway issue No. 270 with Buck Rogers movie skit. - **$5 $10 $15**

BRG-152. "Star Of The '80s" 3" Metal Button,
1979. Gottlieb pinball game advertising button, probably distributed at industry trade show. White and blue on black background. - **$10 $25 $40**

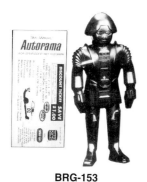

BRG-153

BRG-154

BRG-153. Twiki Photo,
1981. Detroit 29th Annual Autorama show giveaway 8x10" black and white photograph. Shown with admission discount ticket. - **$10 $20 $30**

BRG-154. Color Postcard,
1981. Quick Fox 5x8" promo for Gray Morrow Buck Rogers book. - **$10 $20 $35**

BRG-155

BRG-156

BRG-155. Buck Rogers Slurpee Video Game Plastic Tumbler,
1982. Southland Corporation. 1982 version has blue scene while 1983 version has red scene.
1982 Issue - **$10 $20 $30**
1983 Issue (Shown) - **$5 $10 $15**

BRG-156. TV Show Shoulder Patch,
1980s. Issuer unknown. Blue on white cloth insignia. Same design as patch worn on character's uniform, left shoulder, during 1979-81 TV series. - **$5 $12 $20**

BUGS BUNNY

Probably the world's best-known rabbit, Bugs Bunny evolved into the brash character we know in the late 1930s in the Leon Schlesinger cartoon studios at Warner Brothers, dubbed "Termite Terrace" by its employees. He first uttered his memorable "Eh, what's up, Doc?" to Elmer Fudd in *The Wild Hare* in 1940, and the mischievous wabbit has been asking it ever since in the voice made famous by Mel Blanc. (Following Blanc's death, Jeff Bergman has occasionally voiced the wise-cwacking wabbit).

Until 1969 the cartoons were released or produced by Warner Brothers. Bugs' first comic book appearance was in 1941 in the first issue of *Looney Tunes and Merrie Melodies* and a Sunday newspaper strip started in 1943. Many cartoons, comic books and animated TV specials in the years since have been accompanied by a seemingly endless parade of merchandise, usually copyrighted by Warner Brothers.

BUG-1

BUG-1. Animator Bob Clampett Personal Christmas Card,
c. 1942. Inner design includes art of Clampett boiled in kettle stirred by Bugs. - **$60 $150 $225**

BUG-2

BUG-3

BUG-2. Color 8"x10" Picture,
1940s. Comic book premium from Dell. - **$30 $60 $90**

BUG-3. Mailer,
1940s. Subscription mailer for Looney Tunes comic. -
$15 $30 $50

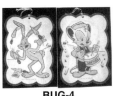

BUG-4

BUG-5

BUG-6

BUG-4. Bugs, Sniffles Cardboard Plaques,
1940s. Store items. Glows in the dark.
Each - **$15 $25 $40**

BUG-5. Rubber Squeaker Figure,
1940s. Store item by Oak Rubber Co. - **$25 $50 $90**

BUG-6. Dell Comics Picture,
1940s. - **$15 $30 $50**

BUG-7

BUG-7. Dell Comics Christmas Card,
1940s. - **$20 $50 $70**

BUG-8

BUG-8. Dell Looney Tunes Comic Book Character Picture Strip,
1951. Dell Publishing Co. with Warner Bros. Cartoon Inc. copyright . Folder strip of five pictures, each about 6x8". -
$25 $50 $75

BUG-9

BUG-10

BUG-11

BUG-9. "What's Up Doc?" Litho. Button,
1959. Came on doll. - **$25 $50 $80**

BUG-10. "Help Crippled Children" Litho. Tin Tab,
c. 1950s. - **$3 $8 $12**

BUG-11. Bugs Bunny Beanie,
1950s. - **$40 $100 $150**

BUG-12

BUG-13

BUG-12. "Magic Paint Book",
1961. Kool-Aid. Includes offer for "Smiling Pitcher".-
$8 $15 $35

BUG-13. "March Of Comics" #273,
1965. Various sponsers. - **$3 $8 $16**

BULLWINKLE AND ROCKY

Rocky the flying squirrel and his pal Bullwinkle the moose were created by Jay Ward in one of television's successful early animated cartoons. From 1959 to 1963 they battled the evil little Mr. Big and his cohorts Boris and Natasha in *Rocky and His Friends* on ABC, in *The Bullwinkle Show* from 1961 to 1964 on NBC and then back to ABC until 1973. Other regulars included Mr. Peabody the time-traveling beagle, his human friend Sherman, the inept Mountie Dudley Do-Right and his criminal foe Snidely Whiplash. *Fractured Fairy-Tales*, offering skewed send-ups of classic folk and fairy-tales, was another regular feature of the show. Comic books started appearing in the early 1960s. Toys, games and other merchandise usually carry the copyright of P.A.T. Ward Productions.

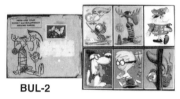

BUL-2

BUL-1

BUL-1. "P-F Flyers" Bullwinkle & Rocky 12x21" Cardboard Store Sign,
c. 1959. B. F. Goodrich Co. Also promotes Rin-Tin-Tin, The Lone Ranger, Captain Gallant. - **$50 $100 $150**

BUL-2. "Sewing Cards" Kit With Envelope,
1961. Set of six cards for yarn threading.
Near Mint In Mailer - **$150**
Each Card- **$5 $10 $15**

BUL-4

BUL-3

BUL-3. "March Of Comics" Booklet,
1962. Child Life Shoes. Comic #233. - **$11 $32 $75**

BUL-4. Bullwinkle's Safety Coloring Book,
1963. General Mills. - **$10 $25 $50**

BUL-5

BUL-5. "Electric Quiz Fun Game",
1963. General Mills. Battery operated. - **$25 $40 $75**

BUL-6   (CLOSE-UP)

BUL-6. Cheerios 21x28" Double-Sided Paper Sign,
c. 1963. - **$40 $75 $125**

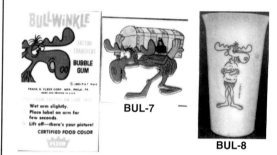

BUL-7   BUL-8

BUL-7. "Tattoo" Fleer Gum Wrapper,
1965. Example from set with different tattoo images. -
$8 $15 $25

BUL-8. Plastic Tumbler,
1960s. Issuer unknown. - **$15 $25 $40**

BUL-9   BUL-10

BUL-9. Bullwinkle Trading Coin,
1960s. Old London Dipsy Doodles and Corn Doodles. Numbered set of 60 plastic coins with paper inserts picturing Bullwinkle and other Jay Ward characters.
Each - **$5 $10 $15**

BUL-10. Fan Club Membership Card,
1970. Charlton Comics. Part of fan club kit. - **$5 $10 $15**

(BOTH PICTURED IN ADS)

BUL-11   **BUL-12**

BUL-11. T-Shirt,
1970. Charlton Comics. - **$35 $75 $125**

BUL-12. Sweatshirt,
1970. Charlton Comics. - **$50 $100 $150**

BUL-13   **BUL-14**   **BUL-15**

BUL-13. Pepsi Collector Series Glasses,
1970s. Each - **$8 $12 $18**

BUL-14. Bullwinkle Pez Dispenser,
1970s. Issued with yellow or brown antlers. -
$40 $125 $175

BUL-15. TV Ad 2-1/2" Cello. Button,
c. 1990s. Channel 5, unidentified location. By Reno,
Nevada maker without copyright. - **$5 $10 $15**

BURNS AND ALLEN

Longtime vaudeville stars, George Burns and Gracie
Allen made a successful transition to radio in 1932 and
broadcast continuously on CBS or NBC until Gracie
decided to retire in 1958. George was the straight man,
Gracie the scatterbrain and the show ranged from
standup gags to situation comedy. The program also
introduced Mel Blanc's Happy Postman character.
Sponsors over the years included Robert Burns and
White Owl cigars, Campbell's soup, Grape-Nuts
Flakes, Chesterfield cigarettes, Hinds lotion, Hormel
Packing Co., Swan soap, Maxwell House coffee and
Block Drugs. A popular half-hour TV show aired from
1950 to 1958 on CBS. "Say goodnight, Gracie."

BUR-1   **BUR-2**   **BUR-3**

**BUR-1. "Gracie Allen's Anniversary Gift To Guy
Lombardo" Booklet,**
1933. General Cigar Co., maker of Robert Burns cigars.
Humor dialogue between Gracie and George Burns on
what to buy orchestra leader Lombardo for his fourth
anniversary of radio broadcasts.- **$10 $18 $25**

BUR-2. Photo,
1937. Philadelphia Record newspaper premium. -
$10 $25 $45

BUR-3. Grape-Nuts 12x18" Sign,
1930s. Scarce. Printed on both sides and with hanging
cord. - **$300 $600 $1200**

BUR-4   **BUR-5**   **BUR-6**

BUR-4. Fan Photo,
1930s. Campbell's Soups. - **$15 $25 $40**

BUR-5. Fan Photo,
1930s. Columbia Broadcasting System. - **$10 $20 $30**

BUR-6. Radio Broadcast Listing Folder,
1930s. Grape-Nuts. - **$15 $30 $45**

BUR-7   **BUR-8**

**BUR-7. "Gracie Allen's Missing Brother" Boxed Jigsaw
Puzzle,**
1930s. Store item by Commanday-Roth Co. Comes with
leaflet describing the search for him in pictured crowd
scene. Boxed - **$15 $25 $40**
Loose - **$8 $15 $25**

BUR-8. Gracie Allen "How To Become President" Cello. Button,
c. 1940s. - **$35 $75 $125**

BUR-9

BUR-9. "Motorola TV Coffee Servers" Boxed Set,
1950s. Motorola, maker of TV sets. Offered at 99 cents per set, glass items by Pyrex. Boxed - **$25 $40 $50**

BUSTER BROWN

Buster Brown was the creation of R. F. Outcault. The color strip first appeared in the Sunday New York Herald of May 4, 1902, a half-dozen years after Outcault's first great strip, *The Yellow Kid.* Buster was a pint-size prankster, constantly bedeviling those around him, then apologizing. His ever-present companion was Tige, a Boston terrier with an evil toothy grin. The strip was a huge success and ran until 1920. A number of newspaper strip reprint books and advertising booklets featuring cartoon panels appeared in the early part of the century. Outcault sold merchandising rights to the Buster Brown character to more than 50 manufacturers of everything from bread to soap to harmonicas; today we can still buy Buster Brown shoes and children's clothes. A weekly drama based on the strip ran on CBS in 1929 and was revived as *Smilin' Ed McConnell's Buster Brown Gang* for NBC. It aired from 1943 to 1953, when it transferred to television, retaining Buster Brown Shoes as sponsor. On McConnell's death in 1954, Andy Devine took his place and the show was re-named *Andy's Gang.* The star of the show was Froggy the Gremlin. Buster Brown has been a rich source of toys, comic books and premiums for 90 years. "Plunk your magic twanger, Froggy!"

BWN-1

BWN-2

BWN-1. "New York Herald/Young Folks" Cello. Button,
c. 1902. Early newspaper issue. - **$75 $150 $275**

BWN-2. "Buster Brown And His Bubble" Postcard,
1903. From numbered set of 10, each including The Yellow Kid. Each - **$25 $50 $75**

BWN-3

BWN-3. "Brown's Blue Ribbon Book Of Jokes And Jingles",
1904. Scarce. Brown Shoe Co. Considered the first comic book premium. First of four in 5x7" format. Two versions of Book #1: Early version includes Pore Li'l Mose, second version replaces Mose with the Yellow Kid. - **$485 $1940 $3400**

BWN-4

BWN-4. Bloomingdale's Christmas Postcard,
1904. One of the most sought-after of all Buster Brown cards. - **$50 $75 $150**

BWN-6   BWN-7

BWN-5

BWN-5. "Buster Brown's Experiences With Pond's Extract" Booklet,
1904. - **$120 $480 $850**

BWN-6. "Buster Brown Bread" Cello. Button,
c. 1905. Issued in both yellow and gray rim variations. - **$10 $20 $35**

BWN-7. "Buster Brown Shoes" Cello. Pocket Mirror,
c. 1905. - **$75 $175 $300**

BWN-8

BWN-9

BWN-8. Enamel And Brass Stickpin,
c. 1905. Initials on bottom edge stand for 'Buster Brown Blue Ribbon Shoes'. - **$60 $150 $225**

BWN-9. "Quick Meal Steel Ranges" Booklet,
c. 1905. - **$57 $228 $400**

BWN-10

BWN-10. "Buster Brown's Blue Ribbon Book Of Jokes & Jingles No. 2",
1905. One of earliest premium comic books. - **$200 $800 $1400**

BWN-11

BWN-11. Paper Mask,
c. 1905. - **$40 $75 $125**

BWN-12

BWN-13

BWN-12. "Buster Brown Stocking Magazine",
1906. - **$25 $50 $85**

BWN-13. Buster Brown Mirror,
1900s. Shoe Premium. - **$40 $80 $160**

BWN-14

BWN-14. Assortment of Postcards from several series,
1900s. Buster Brown and his dog Tige.- **$15 $30 $40**

BWN-15

BWN-15. "Buster's Book Of Jokes And Jingles No. 3",
1900s. Third of four in series. - **$200 $800 $1400**

BWN-16   BWN-17

BWN-18

BWN-16. "Buster Brown Shoes" Cello. Button,
c. 1910. Red background. - **$60 $125 $200**

BWN-17. Black Background Version Cello. Button,
c. 1910. - **$60 $125 $200**

BWN-18. "Buster Brown Shoes" Store Ad Fan,
c. 1910. Diecut cardboard with wooden rod. Imprinted for various stores. - **$75 $150 $250**

BWN-19   BWN-20   BWN-21

BWN-19. Cigar Tin,
c. 1910 Store item. Price includes lid. - **$400 $1000 $1600**

BWN-20. Entry Card For Pocketwatch Premium,
c. 1912. - **$20 $40 $80**

BWN-21. Buster And Tige Pocketwatch,
c. 1912. - **$250 $500 $750**

BWN-22

BWN-22. "Buster Brown's Book Of Travels",
1912. Brown Shoe Co. 12 pages 3-1/2x5". - **$85 $340 $600**

BWN-23

BWN-23. Wood Whistle,
1910s. Shoe Premium - **$25 $50 $75**

BWN-24

BWN-25

**BWN-24. "Buster Brown Walking Club" Oval Cello.
Button,**
c. 1920s. Includes "Tread Straight" trademark arrow
symbol. - **$20 $40 $65**

BWN-25. Magic Kit,
1934. Includes "Magic Ball, My Magic Ink, My Secret Ink,
Trick Hospital Bandage". In Mailer - **$15 $25 $50**

BWN-26

BWN-27

BWN-26. Cello. Fob,
1930s. - **$25 $60 $125**

BWN-27. Litho. Tin Clicker,
1930s. - **$15 $25 $40**

BWN-28

BWN-29

BWN-28. Felt Patch,
1930s. - **$10 $20 $35**

BWN-29. Buster Brown Blotter,
1930s. - **$20 $40 $60**

BWN-30

BWN-31

BWN-32

BWN-30. Tin Whistle,
1930s. Shoe Premium - **$30 $70 $100**

BWN-31. Tin Whistle,
1930s. - **$20 $40 $60**

BWN-32. Buster Brown Comics #1,
1945. Scarce. Brown Shoe Co. No number and no date,
covers refer to various shoe stores. - **$60 $175 $500**

BWN-34

BWN-33

BWN-33. Toy Currency,
c. 1940s. Various denominations collected for prizes.
Each - **$2 $4 $6**

BWN-34. Buster Brown Knife,
1940s. Shoe premium, rare. - **$30 $60 $120**

BWN-35

BWN-36

BWN-37

BWN-35. Slide,
1940s. Premium slide for neckerchief. - **$30 $60 $90**

BWN-36. Card,
1940s. Buster Brown Shoes premium. When folded, eyes
and mouth move when pulled. - **$20 $40 $50**

BWN-37. Punch-Out Gun Sheet,
1940s. Unpunched - **$15 $25 $40**

BWN-38

BWN-39

BWN-38. 50th Anniversary Commemorative Coin,
1954. Gold plastic medalet inscribed on both sides by text for 50 years of children's shoes. - **$5 $10 $15**

BWN-39. "Captain Kangaroo's Grandfather Clock" Punch-Out Sheet,
1956. Buster Brown Shoes, copyright Keeshan-Miller Enterprises. Unpunched - **$10 $20 $30**

BWN-40

BWN-41

BWN-40. Buster Brown Beanie,
1950s. - **$15 $25 $40**

BWN-41. Buster Brown Secret Agent Periscope,
1960s. - **$20 $40 $60**

BWN-42

BWN-42. Buster Brown/Capt. Kangaroo Hat Punch-out,
1960s. - **$20 $30 $40**

BWN-43

BWN-44

BWN-45

BWN-43. Palm Puzzle,
1960s. - **$5 $12 $20**

BWN-44. Plastic Flicker Ring,
1960s. Image changes from Buster and Tige to "Stop" and "Go" signs. - **$30 $45 $60**

BWN-45. "Buster Brown Big Foot" Plastic Whistle Ring,
c. 1960s. Blowing into big toe creates whistling sound. - **$10 $15 $20**

CALIFORNIA RAISINS

In the mid-1980s much of America was captivated by a bunch of cool raisins with an irresistable beat--the California Raisins had arrived. Created in clay by Will Vinton for the California Raisin Advisory Board (CALRAB) and animated for musical television commercials by the Claymation process, these diminutive sports were anything but dry. The commercials began in 1986, featuring the raisins' signature song *I Heard It Through The Grapevine*. Small vinyl figures of the raisins were widely promoted as premiums or giveaways by CALRAB.

CAL-1

CAL-1. Musical Sandwich Toy,
1987. Del Monte Fruit Snacks. Figural plastic with push button to play "Grapevine" song. Boxed - **$15 $30 $50** Unboxed - **$10 $20 $30**

CAL-2

CAL-3

CAL-2. Vinyl Bank,
1987. - **$5 $12 $25**

CAL-3. Store Display,
1988. Hardee's Food Systems. Came with six vinyl figures. Complete - **$40 $75 $125**

CAL-4

CAL-5

CAL-4. Vinyl Tote Bag,
1988. - **$5 $10 $15**

CAL-5. Plastic Radio,
1988. Flexible rubber arms and legs, microphone in hand. - **$15 $25 $35**

CAMPBELL KIDS

Philadelphia artist Grace Drayton created the Campbell Kids to promote the company's canned soup in 1904. She called them Roly-Polys, and after initial use in cards on Philadelphia streetcars the kids greeted the world at large in advertising in the *Ladies' Home Journal* in 1905. Since then the kids have had a long and distinguished promotional career in various forms, such as dolls, salt & pepper shakers, lunch boxes, etc., and in print advertising. In 1976 the kids were dressed in colonial costumes to mark the nation's bicentennial. Today's kids are a bit taller and thinner than the originals, but they're still easily recognized and still selling soup.

CAM-1

CAM-2

CAM-1. "Campbell's Menu Book,"
1910. Softcover 48-page booklet of recipes for 30 days of the month based on 21 varieties of soups. Campbell Kids are pictured on cover and title page. - **$10 $20 $30**

CAM-2. "Campbell's Kid Club" Cello. Button,
c. 1930s. 1-1/2" "Official Badge". - **$35 $75 $125**

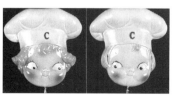

CAM-3

CAM-4

CAM-3. Hot Pad Holders,
c. 1940s. Set of 5x5" painted plaster wall plaques with embedded wire hook hanger.
Each - **$10 $25 $40**

CAM-4. Campbell Kid Plaster Wall Plaque With Thermometer,
c. 1940s. - **$60 $100 $150**

CAM-5

CAM-6

CAM-7

CAM-5. "I'm A Campbell Kid" Cello. Button,
c. 1950s. Variation of girl kid in western outfit from series including next two examples. - **$8 $15 $25**

CAM-6. "I'm A Campbell Kid" Cello. Button,
c. 1950s. Version of girl kid as milkmaid. - **$8 $15 $25**

CAM-7. "I'm A Campbell Kid" Cello. Button,
c. 1950s. Version of boy kid as chef. - **$8 $15 $25**

CAM-8

CAM-9

CAM-8. Squeaker Doll,
1950s. 7" tall painted soft hollow rubber chef doll. - **$75 $150 $250**

CAM-9. Tomato Soup And Fruit 17x22" Paper Store Sign,
c. 1950s. Design includes chalkboard motif held by Campbell Kids. - **$20 $40 $60**

CAM-10

CAM-11

CAM-12

CAM-10. Campbell Kids Silver Plate Spoons,
1950s. Each - **$8 $12 $15**

CAM-11. Campbell Kid Plastic Salt & Pepper Set,
1960s. - **$15 $25 $45**

CAM-12. "A Story Of Soup" Coloring Book,
1976. 11x14" official publication with 24 pages featuring Campbell Kids illustrating soup use from prehistoric times through present. - **$10 $20 $30**

CAM-13

CAM-13. Bicentennial Doll Set,
1976. Pair of 10" vinyl dolls in fabric outfits offered as mail premium. Each - **$15 $30 $50**

CAM-14

CAM-14. Boxed Dolls,
c. 1970s. Made by Product People. 7" tall painted soft vinyl boy and girl dolls in identical display carton.
Each Near Mint Boxed - **$75**
Each Loose - **$15 $30 $50**

CAP'N CRUNCH

Cap'n Crunch, a sweetened breakfast cereal that is supposed to stay crunchy down to the bottom of the bowl, was introduced in 1963 by Quaker Oats. In an unusual twist, the name of the cereal was also the name of the cartoon character created to promote it. The Cap'n was created in-house by Quaker and the TV ad campaign was designed by Jay Ward Productions, best known for Bullwinkle and Rocky animated cartoons. Other characters include Seadog, Jean LaFoote, Wilma the White Whale, Harry S. Hippo and Soggie. There have been many premium offers and giveaways. A Saturday morning animated cartoon was still running well into the 1990s.

CRN-1

CRN-1. "I'm Dreaming Of A Wide Isthmus" Comic Booklet,
1963. From set of three. Each - **$5 $10 $15**

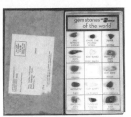 

CRN-2   CRN-3

CRN-2. "Treasure Kit",
c. 1965. Contains 14 "Gemstones Of The World." - **$5 $15 $35**

CRN-3. "Cap'n Crunch Coloring Book",
1968. - **$8 $15 $25**

CRN-5

CRN-4

CRN-4. Cap'n Crunch Daily Log,
1969. A combo desk calendar, engagement diary, and reference book. 120 pages. Quaker Oats gift to those who promoted cereal during 1968.- **$25 $75 $100**

CRN-5. "Sticky Wicket" Target Game,
1970. - **$10 $20 $35**

CRN-6   CRN-7

CRN-6. "Jean LaFoote" Vinyl Bank,
1972. - **$30 $50 $100**

CRN-7. Vinyl Bank,
1972. - **$25 $50 $75**

CRN-8

CRN-8. Seadog Spy Kit,
1974. Kit - **$10 $20 $35**
Instructions - **$5 $10 $15**

CRN-9   CRN-10

CRN-9. Fabric Doll,
1976. - **$15 $30 $40**

CRN-10. Figural Plastic Ring,
c. 1970s. - **$150 $250 $350**

CRN-12

CRN-11

CRN-13

CRN-11. Cannon Plastic Ring,
c. 1970s. - **$30 $50 $75**

CRN-12. Whistle Plastic Ring,
c. 1970s - **$30 $45 $60**

CRN-13. Ship In Bottle Plastic Ring,
c. 1970s. - **$30 $45 $60**

CRN-14   CRN-15

CRN-14. Plastic Treasure Chest Bank,
1970s. - **$10 $20 $35**

CRN-15. Plastic Sea Cycle Model,
1970s. Near Mint Boxed - **$35**
Assembled - **$10 $20 $30**

 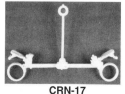

CRN-16   CRN-17

CRN-16. "Detective Crunch Squad" Paper Wallet,
1970s. - **$8 $12 $25**

CRN-17. Finger Tennis Game,
1970s. Plastic agility toy for two players. - **$5 $10 $15**

 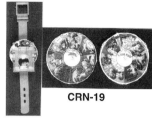

CRN-18   CRN-19

CRN-18. "La Foote" Miniature Plastic Vehicles,
1970s. Balloon operated for movement.
Each - **$5 $10 $15**

CRN-19. Story Scope With Disks,
1970s. At least three disks cut from box backs.
Scope Unit - **$8 $15 $30**
Each Disk - **$2 $5 $10**

CRN-20

CRN-20. Cap'n Crunch Wiggle Figure,
1970s. Cap'n Crunch Berries. Six in set: Cap'n Crunch, Seadog, Jean LaFoote (pirate), Alfie (big boy with glasses), Little Boy (no glasses), Brunhilde (girl). Cap'n Crunch, Seadog Near Mint Unassembled Each - **$60**
Others Near Mint Unassembled Each - **$40**
Cap'n Crunch, Seadog Assembled Each - **$15 $25 $40**
Others Assembled Each - **$10 $15 $25**

CRN-21

CRN-21. Cap'n Crunch Box Inserts,
c. 1981. Plastic mechanical toys of flying saucer and tennis game plus booklet "Crunch Berry Beast's Farm Animals Stamp Album." Saucer Toy Near Mint Packaged - **$20**
Loose - **$5 $10 $15**
Tennis Game Toy Near Mint Packaged - **$20**
Loose - **$3 $8 $12**
Stamp Album - **$5 $10 $15**

CRN-22   CRN-23

CRN-22. "Cap'n Crunch" 15x17x21" Treasure Chest Toy Box,
1987. Believed to be contest prize. - **$25** **$50** **$75**

CRN-23. Frame Tray Puzzle,
1987. - **$3** **$5** **$8**

CRN-25

CRN-24

CRN-24. Crunch The Soggie Target Game,
1987. Came with three balls covered with velcro strips. - **$5** **$8** **$12**

CRN-25. Flicker Button 2-1/4",
1980s. - **$8** **$12** **$18**

CAPTAIN ACTION

The Ideal Toy Company produced a series of jointed, posable dolls of Captain Action, his protégé Action Boy, and the villainous Dr. Evil in 1966-1968. The dolls were outfitted with costumes, boots, and assorted weaponry. Also offered were boxed character costumes and accessories, including flicker rings of Captain Action and his alter-ego superheroes Aquaman, Batman, Buck Rogers, Captain America, Flash Gordon, the Green Hornet, the Lone Ranger, the Phantom, Sgt. Fury, Spider-Man, Steve Canyon, Superman or Tonto. Kool-Pops offered a deck of Captain Action playing cards as a mail-order premium, and National Periodical published five *Captain Action* comic books in 1968-1969.

CAC-1

CAC-1. Catalogue Folder,
1966. Ideal Toy Corp. Opens to 9x12" picturing Captain Action nine different outfit sets. - **$20** **$40** **$60**

CAC-2   CAC-3

CAC-2. Captain Action Doll,
1966. Ideal Toys. Store bought.
Boxed With Accessories - **$950**
Loose Figure - **$275**

CAC-3. Dr. Evil Doll,
1967. Ideal Toys. Store bought. Arch-enemy of Capt. Action. Boxed With Accessories - **$1400**
Loose Figure - **$450**

CAC-4

CAC-4. Kool-Pops "Captain Action" Card Game With Mailer Box,
1967. - **$35** **$75** **$125**

CAC-5   CAC-6   CAC-7   CAC-8

CAC-5. Captain Action/The Lone Ranger Flicker Ring,
1967. Ideal Toys. Silver base marked "Hong Kong" came with boxed figure. Silver "Hong Kong" Base - **$30** **$45** **$60**
Blue Base - **$10** **$20** **$30**
Silver "China" Modern Base - **$5** **$10** **$15**

CAC-6. Captain Action/Tonto Flicker Ring,
1967. Ideal Toys. Silver base marked "Hong Kong" came with boxed figure. Silver "Hong Kong" Base - **$30** **$45** **$60**
Blue Base - **$10** **$20** **$30**
Silver "China" Modern Base - **$5** **$10** **$15**

CAC-7. Captain Action/The Phantom Flicker Ring,
1967. Ideal Toys. Silver base marked "Hong Kong" came with boxed figure. Silver "Hong Kong" Base - **$20** **$35** **$50**
Blue Base - **$10** **$20** **$30**
Silver "China" Modern Base - **$5** **$10** **$15**

CAC-8. Captain Action/Batman Flicker Ring,
1967. Ideal Toys. Silver base marked "Hong Kong" came with boxed figure. Silver "Hong Kong" Base - **$20** **$35** **$50**
Blue Base - **$10** **$20** **$30**
Silver "China" Modern Base - **$5** **$10** **$15**

CAC-9

CAC-9. Uncut Flicker Ring Strip,
1967. Vari-Vue Co. Strip of 16 flicker images alternating between Captain Action and other different action character outfits made for his use. - **$15 $25 $40**

CAP-10

CAC-10. "Captain Action" First Issue Comic Book,
1968. Issue #1 for October-November by National Periodical Publications featuring his origin plus appearance by Superman. - **$10 $25 $60**

CAPTAIN AMERICA

World War II had begun but direct U.S. involvement was still nine months away when Captain America debuted in *Captain America Comics* in March 1941. Steve Rogers, a 4-F desperate to serve his country in the conflict looming on the horizon, volunteered to take the "Super Soldier Formula" which turned him into the one-man army known as Captain America. With his teenage sidekick, Bucky, he battled the Nazi hordes (usually commanded by the nefarious Red Skull) and numerous other villains until January 1950, when his title was canceled. The comic was revived for a brief, three-issue run in 1954, then went dormant until Marvel Comics' Stan Lee brought Cap into the modern era in *The Avengers* #4 (1964), and launched a string of solo stories in *Tales of Suspense* #59 which culminated in the title switching its name to *Captain America* with issue #100. That series ended with #454 and was followed immediately by a 13-issue mini-series. Currently a new, ongoing *Captain America* comic is published monthly and is scheduled to be joined by a second ongoing monthly shortly after this guide is published. Cap's partners have included Bucky (WWII era) and the Falcon ('70s & '80s), as well as many other Marvel characters for shorter periods. *The Overstreet Comic Book Price Guide* carries a list of Captain America's other appearances. While the character is an integral part of Marvel's continuity, he has not enjoyed nearly the mainstream success of Spider-Man, the Hulk or The X-Men.

A 15-episode Republic Pictures serial starring Dick Purcell appeared in 1944 (and was re-released in 1953), followed by two TV movies starring Reb Brown (1979). In 1989, a would-be feature film starring Matt Salinger (son of author J.D. Salinger) went straight to home video. None of these productions had any lasting impact, nor did the original 13-episode animated series (1966). Fox Television is scheduled to debut a new *Captain America* cartoon in the Fall of 1998. Their success with *The X-Men* and the recently ended *Spider-Man* indicates that this patriotic character could finally break out of comic books and into wider pop culture.

CAP-1

CAP-1. Mailing Envelope Version One,
1941. "A" on helmet is below "G" of Guaranteed. - **$150 $350 $550**

CAP-2

CAP-2. Membership Card Version One,
1941. "A" on helmet is pointed. Blue color much lighter than version two, plus other differences in size and placement of type and words as well as amount of white shading on helmet. Design changed sometime between issuance of membership numbers 50,105 and 56,623. - **$250 $650 $850**

CAP-3   CAP-4

CAP-3. "Captain America/Sentinels of Liberty" Enameled Brass Badge (Version One),
1941. - **$200 $400 $800**

CAP-4. Mailing Envelope Version Two,
1941. "A" on helmet is below "g" of postage. - **$150 $350 $550**

CAP-5

CAP-6

CAP-5. Membership Card Version Two,
1941. "A" on helmet is squared off at the top. Blue color much darker than version one and other small differences. (See CAP-2). - **$250 $650 $850**

CAP-6. Enameled Copper Member's Badge (Version Two),
1941. Same size and inscription as CAP-3, but in copper rather than brass luster. - **$250 $450 $850**

CAP-7

CAP-7. Mailing Envelope Version Three,
1941. "A" on helmet is below the spacing between the words "Postage Guaranteed." Also, in the address the "W" of "west" is formed by two "V"s that overlap and form a tiny "V" at the center. At this time, it is not clear if this envelope was used with the Version One or the Version Two membership card and badge. - **$150 $350 $550**

CAP-8

CAP-9

CAP-8. Three-Sheet,
1944. Scarce. Republic Pictures serial. 41" by 81". - **$2000 $4000 $6000**

CAP-9. "Return Of Captain America" 27x41" Movie Poster,
1953. Republic Pictures. Example is 1953 re-issue of 1944 serial. - **$150 $300 $500**

CAP-10

CAP-11

CAP-12

CAP-10. "Captain America" 3-1/2" Cello. Button,
1966. Store item. #3 from numbered series. Near Mint Bagged - **$35**
Loose - **$10 $15 $25**

CAP-11. Litho. Metal Bicycle Attachment Plate,
1967. Store item by Marx Toys. - **$12 $25 $50**

CAP-12. "Keep Saving Energy" 2-1/2" Cello. Button,
1980. Marvel Comics. - **$10 $20 $30**

CAP-13

CAP-14

CAP-15

CAP-13. "Captain America And The Campbell Kids" Comic Book,
1980. Copyright by Marvel Comics and Campbell Soup Co. - **$3 $8 $12**

CAP-14. Limited Edition Of Badge In Holder,
1990. Marked repro on back. Mint - **$35**

CAP-15. 50th Anniversary Pin Set,
1990. 1500 produced. Three in a holder. Mint - **$80**

CAPTAIN BATTLE

Captain Battle had a brief run as a superpatriot comic book hero in the early 1940s. He made his first appearance in *Silver Streak Comics* #10 in May 1941, then in Captain Battle Comics from 1941 to 1943. Readers who promised to uphold the principles of Americanism and the Constitution could join the Captain Battle Boys' Brigade. Two issues of *Captain Battle Jr.* were published in 1943-1944.

CBT-1

CBT-1. "Captain Battle Boys' Brigade" Cello. Button,
1941. Scarce. Silver Streak Comics. - **$400 $1000 $1750**

CBT-2

CBT-2. Membership Kit Mailer, Letter and Card,
1941. The 1-3/4" cello. club button came as part of this kit. The membership card has a list of 5 "Aims" printed on the reverse.
Mailer - **$50 $150 $200**
Letter - **$150 $300 $500**
Membership Card - **$150 $300 $500**

CAPTAIN 11

Following the success of Captain Video and Space Patrol, the Rocket Ranger Club was formed in 1955. This club was designed to encourage children to watch Channel 11, a Midwestern station. Premiums issued for the club were only produced and distributed on a regional basis and are quite rare. The creed of the club focused on telling children to obey the laws and their parents at all times. The kit included a variety of decoders and planet credits, which enabled the young listeners to receive special messages and follow the exploits of the Rocket Ranger.

CVN-1

CVN-2

CVN-1. Membership Card,
1955. - **$15 $30 $50**

CVN-2. Mailer,
1955. - **$10 $20 $30**

CVN-3

CVN-3. Membership Certificate And Creed,
1955. - **$20 $40 $60**

CVN-4

CVN-5

CVN-4. Super Zoom Decoder,
1955. Rare. - **$75 $200 $300**

CVN-5. Zoom Code Card,
1955. - **$40 $80 $120**

CVN-6

CVN-6. Venus Credits Play Money,
1955. Six different. Each - **$3 $10 $15**

CVN-7

CVN-7. Martian Credits Play Money,
1955. Seven different. Each - **$3 $10 $15**

CAPTAIN EZRA DIAMOND

Captain Diamond's Adventures aired on the NBC Blue radio network from 1932 to 1937, offering weekly tales of sea adventures as related by Captain Diamond in his lighthouse. Al Swenson played the Captain, and his young visitor each week was Tiny Ruffner. Diamond Salt was the sponsor.

CEZ-1

CEZ-2

CEZ-1. "Adventure Map Of Captain Ezra Diamond" 17x22",
1932. - **$15 $25 $50**

CEZ-2. "Adventure Map Of Captain Ezra Diamond" 16x22",
1933. - **$15 $25 $50**

CEZ-3

CEZ-5

CEZ-4

CEZ-3. Cast Member Fan Photo,
c. 1933. White background version. - **$5 $10 $15**

CEZ-4. Fan Photo Of Cast,
c. 1933. Black background version. - **$5 $10 $15**

CEZ-5. Weather Forecast Card,
c. 1933. Lighthouse window area holds litmus paper. -
$20 $40 $60

CAPTAIN FRANK HAWKS

Frank Hawks (1897-1938) was a skilled pilot and an air instructor for the army during World War I. He set a number of speed records, including two in nonstop flights from Los Angeles to New York in 1929 and 1933. As a spokesman for Post cereals in the 1930s he made guest appearances on the radio and was always available to speak to the press. Boys and girls were urged to join Capt. Hawks' Sky Patrol to win free prizes. Ironically, Hawks was killed in an airplane crash.

CFH-1

CFH-2

CFH-3

CFH-1. Photo With Achievement Inscription,
c. 1935. Facsimile signature includes "Snapped Over The Andes At 19,000 Feet Altitude On May 4 1935". -
$10 $25 $40

CFH-2. Club Manual,
1935. Post's 40% Bran Flakes. - **$15 $30 $60**

CFH-3. Sky Patrol Propeller Badge,
1935. Three ranks. Member - **$10 $15 $30**
Flight Lieutenant - **$15 $25 $60**
Flight Captain - **$20 $35 $80**

CFH-4

CFH-5

CFH-6

CFH-4. "Capt. Hawks Sky Patrol" Brass Ring,
1936. Depicts portrait, cloud and propeller design. -
$75 $190 $300

CFH-5. "Air Hawks" Club Folder,
1936. Post's 40% Bran Flakes. Eight pages of contents include illustrated premium offers, contest information on how to get 28 prizes. - **$15 $25 $50**

CFH-6. "Capt. Frank's Air Hawks" Brass Ring,
1936. - **$50 $100 $150**

CFH-7

CFH-8

CFH-9

CFH-7. Fan Photo,
c. 1936. - **$10 $20 $30**

CFH-8. Air Hawks Wings Badge,
1936. Three ranks. Silver - "Member" - **$10 $15 $30**
Brass - "Squadron Leader" - **$15 $25 $60**
Bronze - "Flight Commander" - **$20 $35 $80**

CFH-9. Goggles,
1936. Rare. Circular goggles. Premium obtained with 4 Post Bran Flakes box tops. - **$50 $75 $100**

CFH-10

CFH-11

CFH-10. Sacred Scarab Ring,
1937. Post's Bran Flakes. Scarab in green. Also issued for Melvin Purvis. - **$250 $500 $1200**

CFH-11. Sky Patrol Premium Booklet,
1937. Post's 40% Bran Flakes. Offers eight premiums including club badge, manual, ring, ID bracelet.-
$15 $25 $50

CFH-12

CFH-12. "Sacred Scarab Ring" Newspaper Ad,
1937. Post's Bran Flakes. Ring offer expiration date December 31. Scarab in green, also issued for Melvin Purvis. Newspaper Ad - **$8 $12 $20**

CFH-13

CFH-14

CFH-13. Bracelet With Photo Picture,
1930s. Rare. Assumed to be related to Capt. Hawks cereal campaign. - **$100 $200 $400**

CFH-14. Brass Paperweight and Perpetual Calendar,
1940. - **$100 $200 $300**

CAPTAIN GALLANT

Two-fisted Captain Gallant, played by Olympic gold medalist and seasoned actor Buster Crabbe, premiered in a black-and-white series on NBC-TV in February 1955. Filmed originally in Morocco and later in Libya and Italy, the show was essentially a Western in Arab garb, with the Captain chasing camel thieves rather than cattle rustlers. Crabbe's son Cullen was featured as Cuffy Sanders, his ward. The show was sponsored by Heinz Foods until 1957, then by General Mills in repeats from 1960 to 1963. The following year the show was syndicated to local stations as *Foreign Legionnaire*. Items are usually copyrighted by Frantel Inc.

CGL-1

CGL-1. Captain Gallant #1 Comic Book,
1955. Heinz Foods. Membership certificate on back cover. - **$5 $10 $15**
See the Overstreet Comic Book Price Guide for values of other issues.

CGL-2

CGL-2. "Captain Gallant Hat" With Mailer,
c. 1955. H. J. Heinz Co. Fabric hat with cover letter, instructions and order coupon. Near Mint In Mailer - **$300**
Mailer Or Letter Only Each - **$15 $25 $50**
Hat Only - **$50 $100 $200**

CGL-3

CGL-4

CGL-3. "Tim Magazine For Boys" Cover Article,
June 1957. - **$15 $25 $40**

CGL-4. Captain Gallant And Cuffy Photos,
1950s. Each - **$10 $25 $40**

CGL-5

CGL-5. "Junior Legionnaires" Club Card,
1950s. - **$20 $40 $60**

CGL-6   CGL-7   CGL-8

CGL-6. "Junior Legionnaire" Litho. Tab,
1950s. - **$12 $25 $50**

CGL-7. TV Sponsor Paper Store Pennant,
1950s. P.F. footwear of B.F. Goodrich. - **$20 $40 $60**

CGL-8. "Captain Gallant" Cuffy Cello. Button,
1950s. Holsum Bread. - **$20 $50 $75**

CGL-9   CGL-10   CGL-11   CGL-12   CGL-13

CGL-9. "Captain Gallant Junior Legionnaire" Silvered Metal Badge,
1950s. Cardboard insert photo. Probably came with store bought gun set. - **$40 $80 $125**

CGL-10. Heinz Diecut Embossed Metal Member Badge,
1950s. "57" numeral under flame image. For mounting on Heinz premium Legionnaire's hat. Scarce. -
$50 $100 $250

CGL-11. "The Italy Star" Metal And Fabric Award Medal,
1950s. Back has Captain Gallant logo and name. -
$10 $20 $50

CGL-12. Foreign Legion Replica Award Medal,
1950s. Fabric ribbon holding gold luster metal pendant with military motifs and "GRI" inscription. - **$15 $25 $50**

CGL-13. Foreign Legion Replica Award Medal,
1950s. Fabric ribbon suspending silver luster metal pendant depicting cat-like animal killing dragon-like creature with commemorative date 1939-1945. - **$15 $25 $75**

CAPTAIN MARVEL

Young Billy Batson, a homeless orphan, only had to utter the name of the wizard Shazam to be transformed into Captain Marvel, the World's Mightiest Mortal. Created by artist C. C. Beck and writer Bill Parker, Captain Marvel was introduced in *Whiz Comics* #2 in February 1940. It was a huge success, outselling all its competition and generating a Mary Marvel, Captain Marvel Jr., Uncle Marvel, several Lt. Marvels and Hoppy the Marvel Bunny. The Captain Marvel club was announced in *Whiz Comics* #23, on October 31st, 1941.

The Captain subdued criminals and mad scientists for 13 years until a costly lawsuit for copyright infringement of the Superman character ended his run in 1954, but not before dozens of toys, novelties and premiums had been issued. Several comic book revivals and spinoffs have been published over the years. *The Adventures of Captain Marvel*, a 12-episode chapter play starring Tom Tyler as the Captain and Frank Coghlan Jr. as Billy was released by Republic Pictures in 1941. In 1974 a television series with Michael Gray as Billy was produced by Filmation Studios.

Ironically, Captain Marvel is now owned by DC Comics, publishers of *Superman*, and has enjoyed a recent resurgence. *The Power of Shazam!*, a 1994 hard cover graphic novel and 1995 monthly series of the same name, relaunched the character. Mary Marvel has appeared with Supergirl and in a solo story in *Showcase '96*. Captain Marvel, Jr. joined the Teen Titans, a group of other young heroes, marking his first regular incorporation into the mainstream of DC's continuity in *Teen Titans* #17 (1998).

CMR-1

CMR-1. Advs. of Captain Marvel Title & Scene Cards
1941. Each chapter has 8 cards--one title card and seven scene cards (portraying action images from the film). The cards for Chapter 1 were in full color, while Chapters 2-12 were in duotone. Three of the seven scene cards for each chapter featured Captain Marvel and are considered more desirable. All 96 are rare.
Captain Marvel Title Card Chapter 1 - Color
Scarce. Less than 10 known. - **$600 $900 $1500**

Captain Marvel Title Cards Chapters 2-12 - Duotone
Scarce. - **$100 $250 $400**

Captain Marvel Scene Cards Chapter 1 - Color
With Captain Marvel - **$100 $250 $400**
Without Captain Marvel - **$50 $100 $150**

Captain Marvel Scene Cards (Chapters 2-12) - Duotone
With Captain Marvel - **$50 $100 $150**
Without Captain Marvel - **$25 $50 $75**

CMR-2

CMR-3

CMR-2. Adventures of Captain Marvel Six-Sheet Movie Poster,
1941. Six-sheet and three-sheet posters were commonly created to span the entire run of a serial. Whereas a theater might have displayed a one-sheet for only the week that particular chapter was playing, the six-sheet would be displayed for the length of the serial. The Adventures of Captain Marvel Six-Sheet is rare, with less than 10 known. Full color. - **$2500 $5500 $7500**

CMR-3. Adventures of Captain Marvel One-Sheet Movie Posters
1941. Like most serials, the Captain Marvel one-sheets were created to promote the individual chapters of the serial.
Chapter 1
Rare. Full color. Less than 10 known. Chapter 1 one-sheet does not have insert box as do Chapters 2-12; one, full poster image. - **$2000 $4500 $6000**

Chapters 2-12
Scarce. Full color. One-sheets for Chapters 2-12 have insert boxes. Those with inserts featuring Captain Marvel are considered more desirable.
With Capt. Marvel Insert - **$1000 $2000 $3000**
Without Capt. Marvel Insert - **$500 $1000 $1500**

CMR-4

CMR-5

CMR-6

CMR-4. "Captain Marvel Club/Shazam" Club Litho. Button,
1941. - **$20 $35 $50**

CMR-5. Yellow Rectangular Patch,
c. 1941. Rare. Fawcett premium. - **$75 $200 $300**

CMR-6. Blue Rectangular Patch,
c. 1941. Fawcett premium. - **$25 $50 $100**

CMR-7

CMR-7. Blotter 6",
1941. Rare. Promotes "The Adventures of Captain Marvel" 12 chapter serial. - **$250 $500 $750**

CMR-9

CMR-8

CMR-8. "Captain Marvel Comic Hero Punch-Outs Book",
1942. Store item by Samuel Lowe Co. - **$50 $125 $200**

CMR-9. "Flying Captain Marvel" Punch-Out With Envelope,
c. 1942. Store item and club premium.
Unused - **$10 $15 $20**

CMR-10

CMR-10. Captain Marvel Jr. #1 Promotional Kit,
1942. Rare. Elaborate kit of 12 separate pieces plus mailing envelope. Includes full-color picture of front cover of **Capt. Marvel Jr.** #1. Complete - **$300 $800 $1000**
Capt. Marvel Jr. Cover Promo Only - **$150 $300 $600**

CMR-11

CMR-11. Membership Kit With Spy Smasher Tie-In,
1942. Kit includes envelope with "Remember Pearl Harbor" imprint, club member's cello. button, Whiz Comics subscription form, insert promoting Spy Smasher movie, membership card with secret code on reverse, insert with Captain Marvel's Secret Message which decodes as "Read all about Capt. Marvel Jr. in Master Comics. Gee Fellers it's great. On sale everywhere."
Near Mint Complete - **$500**
Button - **$20 $40 $65**
Subscription Form - **$20 $35 $50**
Membership Card - **$25 $50 $100**
Spy Smasher Insert - **$50 $75 $150**
Secret Message - **$20 $40 $60**

CMR-12

CMR-13

CMR-12. "Captain Marvel Club/Shazam" Cello. Club Button,
1942. - **$20 $40 $65**

CMR-13. "The Three Famous Flying Marvels" Punch-Outs,
c. 1943. Store item and club premium.
Unused - **$8 $12 $20**

CMR-14

CMR-15

CMR-14. "Secret Message Postcard",
1943. Scarce. - **$75 $150 $250**

CMR-15. "E.-Z. Code Finder",
c. 1943. Scarce. - **$150 $400 $500**

CMR-16

CMR-17

CMR-16. "Captain Marvel Comic Story Paint Book",
c. 1943. Store item by Samuel Lowe Co. - **$60 $180 $600**

CMR-17. "Magic Lightning Box" Punch-Out Paper Toy In Envelope,
c. 1943. Store item and club premium. Captain Marvel figure moves up and down inside box, scarcest item in punch-out series. - **$40 $75 $125**

CMR-18

CMR-18. Club Mailing February,
1943. Included Spy Smasher litho. button to make recipient an honorary member of Spy Smasher Victory Batallion, cover letter, sheet with new items including figure by Multi-Products, subscription offer coupon, Captain Marvel tie coupon, envelope.
Five Paper Items - **$100 $200 $300**
Spy Smasher Button **$15 $25 $50**

CMR-19   CMR-20   CMR-21

CMR-19. "Captain Marvel's Fun Book",
1944. Store item and also available from Fawcett for 25¢. - **$28 $84 $225**

CMR-20. "Captain Marvel Well Known Comics" Booklet,
1944. Bestmaid give-away published by Samuel Lowe Co. - **$15 $45 $120**

CMR-21. "Captain Marvel's Rocket Raider" Paper Toy Kit,
c. 1944. Store item and club premium.
Unused - **$10 $15 $20**

CMR-22   CMR-23

CMR-22. "Fawcett's Comic Stars",
c. 1944. Store item with three metal stars depicting Captain Marvel, Hoppy The Marvel Bunny, Sherlock Monk.
Near Mint With Envelope - **$250**
Each Star - **$20 $40 $60**

CMR-23. "Captain Marvel Painting Book",
c. 1944. Store item by L. Miller & Sons, London, England. - **$50 $75 $125**

CMR-24

CMR-24. Christmas Letter To Members,
1944. Cover letter plus sheet showing official items for 1945. Letter - **$25 $50 $75**
Premium Sheet - **$15 $35 $60**

CMR-25

CMR-25. Magic Picture,
1944. Billy Batson's broadcast on front, says "Can you help Billy Batson". - **$50 $85 $120**

CMR-26

CMR-27

CMR-28

CMR-26. "Captain Marvel Club/Shazam" Litho. Button,
1944. - **$20 $50 $85**

CMR-27. Punch-Out "Magic Eyes" Picture With Envelope,
c. 1944. Store item and club premium.
Unused - **$10 $15 $20**

CMR-28. "Captain Marvel Club/Shazam" Cello. Button,
1944.- **$20 $40 $60**

CMR-29

CMR-29. "One Against Many" Picture Puzzle,
c. 1944. Store item and club premium. - **$10 $25 $40**

CMR-30

CMR-31

CMR-30. "Hoppy And Millie In Musical Evening" Cardboard Toy,
c. 1944. Store item and club premium.
Unused - **$8 $12 $20**

CMR-31. "Buzz Bomb" Punch-Out Toy,
c. 1944. Store item and club premium.
Unused - **$10 $20 $35**

CMR-32

CMR-32. "Shazam" Punch-Out Game With Envelope,
c. 1944. Store item and club premium.
Unused - **$10 $20 $30**

CMR-33

CMR-33. "Magic Picture" Cardboard Toy,
c. 1944. Store item and club premium. Scarcer than others in series. Unused - **$25 $40 $100**

CMR-34

CMR-35

CMR-36

CMR-34. "Captain Marvel, Jr. Ski Jump" Paper Assembly Toy In Envelope,
c. 1944. Store item and club premium. - **$10 $15 $20**

CMR-35. "Captain Marvel" Canadian Comic Book Glow-In-Dark Patch,
c. 1945. Anglo-American Publishing Co. Set of ten "Glo-Crests." Captain Marvel - **$200 $600 $800**
Others: Commander Steel, Crusaders, Dr. Destine, Freelance, Hurri-Kane, Kip Keene, Purple Rider, Red Rover, Terry Kane. Each - **$35 $75 $150**

CMR-36. Toss Bag,
1945. Five varieties: Captain Marvel or Mary Marvel either flying or standing plus Hoppy. Each - **$15 $35 $75**

CMR-37

CMR-38

CMR-39

CMR-37. Skull Cap,
1945. Scarce. Fawcett Premium. No brim. -
$75 $150 $300

CMR-38. Girl's Pink Felt Beanie,
1945. Rare. Marked Capt. Marvel with figure on front and back. Fawcett premium. - **$150 $400 $425**

CMR-39. Boy's Blue Felt Beanie,
1945. Fawcett premium. - **$75 $150 $300**

CMR-40

CMR-41

CMR-40. Whiz Wheaties Comic,
1946. Thirty-two pages. Captain Marvel premium. Issued taped to Wheaties box. -
$75 $300 $ - (not found in Mint condition)

CMR-41. Flute With Balloon,
1946. - **$30 $60 $90**

CMR-42

CMR-43

CMR-42. Magic Flute With Whistle on Card,
1946. End piece in green or grey plastic.
Near Mint On Card - **$150**
Loose - **$25 $50 $75**

CMR-43. "Shazam" Paper Pop-Up String Toy,
1946. Fawcett Publications. - **$40 $75 $125**

CMR-44   CMR-45   CMR-46   CMR-47

CMR-44. Captain Marvel Syroco-Style 5" Figure,
1943. Rare. Fawcett premium by Multi Products, Chicago. "Captain" spelled out on base. No box produced. Less than 10 known. - **$2700 $5400 $8100**

CMR-45. Captain Marvel 5" Figure,
1946. Rare. Fawcett premium by Kerr Co. of unknown blend of resin-like materials. "Capt." on base. No box produced. Less than 10 known. - **$2700 $5400 $8100**

CMR-46. Captain Marvel Jr. 5" Figure,
1946. Fawcett premium by Kerr Co. of unknown blend of resin-like materials. No box produced. - **$850 $1700 $2550**

CMR-47. Mary Marvel 5" Figure,
1946. Fawcett premium by Kerr Co. of unknown blend of resin-like materials. Light color hair. No box produced. - **$775 $1550 $2350**

CMR-48   CMR-49   CMR-50   CMR-51

CMR-48. Mary Marvel 5" Figure,
1946. Rare. Similar to previous item. Hair may be light or dark. Wearing red dress with red belt and red lightning bolt. - **$1200 $2400 $3550**

CMR-49. Captain Marvel 6-1/2" Figure,
1946. Scarce. Fawcett premium by Kerr Co. of plastic. For C.C. Beck designed box in Near Mint add $750. -
$1700 $3400 $5100

CMR-50. Captain Marvel Jr. 6-1/2" Figure,
1946. Scarce. Fawcett premium by Kerr Co. of plastic. For C.C. Beck designed box in Near Mint add $750. -
$1100 $2200 $3250

CMR-51. Mary Marvel 6-1/2" Figure,
1946. Scarce. Fawcett premium by Kerr Co. of plastic. For C.C. Beck designed box in Near Mint add $750. -
$1000 $2400 $3400

CMR-52

CMR-53

CMR-52. Marvel Bunny 6" Figure,
1946. Rare. Fawcett premium by Kerr Co. of plastic. Most examples have damaged or repaired ears. For C.C. Beck designed box in Near Mint add $750. -
$1000 $3000 $4400

CMR-53. "Mary Marvel" Diecut Fiberboard Figure Badge,
1946. Full color litho. paper front. - **$100 $200 $350**

CMR-54

CMR-55

CMR-54. Mary Marvel Promo Card,
1946. Rare. - **$30 $70 $100**

CMR-55. Tie-Clip,
1946. On Card - **$25 $50 $75**
Clip Only - **$15 $25 $40**

CMR-56

CMR-56. "Captain Marvel Adventures" Vol. 10 #55,
1946. Scarce. Atlas Theater, Detroit. Theater replaced original cover of issue #55 with their own cover picturing generic heroes. - **$100 $300 $450**

CMR-57   CMR-58   CMR-59

CMR-57. Captain Marvel Glow-In-The-Dark Picture,
1946. - **$75 $150 $300**

CMR-58. Captain Marvel Jr. Glow-In-The-Dark Picture,
1946. - **$75 $150 $250**

CMR-59. Mary Marvel Glow-In-The-Dark Picture,
1946.- **$75 $150 $250**

CMR-60

CMR-61

CMR-60. Hoppy Glow-In-The-Dark Picture,
1946. Came unframed. - **$50 $75 $150**

CMR-61. Statuettes Store Sign,
1946. Rare. R. W. Kerr Co. Art by C. C. Beck. 6 known. -
$1200 $2700 $4200

CMR-62   CMR-63

CMR-62. "Captain Marvel Adventures" Wheaties Comic Book,
1946. Copies were taped to box. Good - **$50**
About Fine - **$150**

CMR-63. "Note Paper" Boxed Set,
1946. Held 18 sheets and envelopes.
Near Mint Boxed - **$400**
Each Sheet - **$5 $10 $15**

CMR-64   CMR-65   CMR-66   CMR-67

CMR-64. "Captain Marvel" Litho. Button,
1946. From set of 10 picturing Fawcett characters. -
$40 $75 $125

CMR-65. "Mary Marvel" Litho. Button,
1946. From set of 10 picturing Fawcett characters. -
$40 $75 $125

CMR-66. "Captain Marvel Jr." Litho. Button,
1946. From set of 10 picturing Fawcett characters. -
$30 $75 $100

CMR-67. "Billy Batson" Litho. Button,
1946. From set of 10 picturing Fawcett characters. -
$30 $50 $90

CMR-68   CMR-69   CMR-70   CMR-71

CMR-68. "Hoppy The Marvel Bunny" Litho. Button,
1946. From set of 10 picturing Fawcett characters. -
$30 $50 $80

CMR-69. "Bulletman" Litho. Button,
1946. From set of 10 picturing Fawcett characters. -
$20 $50 $80

CMR-70. "Golden Arrow" Litho. Button,
1946. From set of 10 picturing Fawcett characters. -
$20 $50 $80

CMR-71. "Ibis" Litho. Button,
1946. From set of 10 picturing Fawcett characters. -
$20 $50 $80

CMR-72   CMR-73   CMR-74   CMR-75

CMR-72. "Nyoka" Litho. Button,
1946. From set of 10 picturing Fawcett characters. -
$20 $50 $80

CMR-73. "Radar" Litho. Button,
1946. From set of 10 picturing Fawcett characters. -
$20 $50 $80

CMR-74. Captain Marvel Felt Club Patch,
1946. - **$30 $60 $100**

CMR-75. Captain Marvel Jr. Felt Patch,
1946. Blue - **$25 $50 $100**
Dark Green (Scarce) - **$50 $150 $250**

CMR-76   CMR-77

CMR-76. "Mary Marvel" Felt Patch,
1946. Scarce. Fawcett Publications. - **$75 $200 $300**

CMR-77. Felt Pennant,
1946. Blue - **$40 $80 $150**
Yellow - **$50 $100 $200**

CMR-79

CMR-78

CMR-80

CMR-78. Plastic Keychain Fob,
1946. Back inscription "This Certifies That The Holder Of
This Key Ring Is A Bonafied Member Of The Captain
Marvel Club". - **$30 $75 $150**

CMR-79. Rocket Raider Compass Ring,
c. 1946. Red and black enamel paint on brass, unmarked
but attributed to Captain Marvel. - **$400 $800 $2000**

CMR-80. Captain Marvel Club Premiums Ad,
1946. Fawcett Publications. Comic book page offering six
premiums including set of 10 character litho. buttons picturing Marvels and other Fawcett adventure characters. -
$1 $3 $5

CMR-81

CMR-83

CMR-82

CMR-81. Sweater,
1947. Store item by Somerset Knitting Mills, Philadelphia. -
$100 $300 $400

CMR-82. Tin Wind-Up Race Car #2,
1947. Store item by Automatic Toy Co. Numbered set of
four. Boxed With Keys - **$250 $600 $1200**
Each Car Loose, No Keys - **$60 $125 $225**

CMR-83. Capt. Marvel Jr. Die Cast Figure,
1947. Unauthorized 3-1/8" tall white metal figure by H & B
Toys of New Jersey. Known as "Robe Boy" and only two
examples known. A matching Captain Marvel is unknown. -
$1500 $2500 $5000

CMR-84

CMR-85

CMR-86

CMR-84. "Captain Marvel" Watch,
1948. Store item and probable premium. Made in two sizes. Boxed - **$200 $500 $800**
Watch Only - **$100 $200 $425**

CMR-85. "Capt. Marvel Jr." Wristwatch,
1948. Scarce. Offered by the Fawcett Club and not known with a box. Luminous hands and blue plastic strap. - **$300 $600 $1250**

CMR-86. "Mary Marvel" Wristwatch,
1948. Fawcett Publications copyright.
Boxed - **$150 $300 $650**
Watch Only - **$75 $150 $275**

CMR-87

CMR-88

CMR-87. "Shazam-Captain Marvel Club" Litho. Button,
1948. Fawcett Publications. - **$40 $75 $110**

CMR-88. Captain Marvel & Others Blotter Pad,
1948. Imprinted for J. T. Flagg Knitting Co. by publisher Brown & Bigelow Co. Cello. cover also pictures Red Ryder, Little Beaver, Gene Autry. - **$75 $150 $250**

CMR-89

CMR-90

CMR-89. "All Hero Comic" Tattoo Transfers Pack,
c. 1948. Fawcett Publications. Retail packet of 23 with envelope sample images of Captain Marvel, Bulletgirl and Bulletman, Mary Marvel, Radar. - **$75 $150 $250**

CMR-90. Portrait Picture,
1940s. Comes with blank bottom margin or with "Capt. Marvel Appears Monthly In Whiz Comics."
Blank - **$40 $75 $125**
Text - **$50 $100 $150**

CMR-91

...

CMR-92

CMR-91. Merchandise Sheet,
1940s. Regularly issued by Captain Marvel Club. - **$10 $20 $30**

CMR-92. Captain Marvel Club Membership Ad,
1940s. Fawcett Publications. Comic book page ad offering Secret Code Finder, Magic Membership Card, Official Club Button. - **$1 $3 $5**

CMR-93

CMR-94

CMR-93. "Mechanix Illustrated" Subscription Offer,
1940s. Fawcett Publications. Comic book page ad utilizing Captain Marvel as promoter for sister publication by Fawcett. - **$1 $3 $5**

CMR-94. "Captain Marvel's Radar Racer" Punch-Out In Envelope,
1940s. From series by Reed & Associates copyright by Fawcett Public ations. Assembly parts are for race car pictured on envelope.
Unpunched - **$50 $125 $200**

CMR-95

CMR-95. Club Letter,
1940s. Example of many sent to club members. -
$15 $30 $60

CMR-97

CMR-96

CMR-96. Club Letter With Envelope,
1940s. Text for Jack Armstrong contest by Wheaties offering actual Piper Cub airplane as grand prize.
Envelope - **$10 $30 $50**
Letter- **$20 $40 $75**

CMR-97. Pencil,
1940s. Scarce. - **$35 $125 $225**

CMR-98

CMR-98. "Magic Membership Card",
1940s. - **$40 $100 $175**

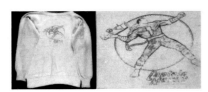

CMR-99

CMR-99. Child's Sweatshirt,
1940s. Scarce. - **$50 $100 $200**

CMR-100

CMR-100. "Jig-Saw" Puzzle #1,
1940s. Store item by L. Miller & Son Ltd., England.
Boxed - **$35 $75 $150**

CMR-101

CMR-102

CMR-101. "Comic Heroes Iron-Ons" Packet,
1940s. Envelope held 24 transfers.
Complete In Envelope - **$100 $150 $200**

CMR-102. "War Stamps Savings Book" Envelope,
1940s. Held World War II savings stamp booklet. -
$40 $100 $200

CMR-104

CMR-103

**CMR-103. "Mechanix Illustrated" Magazine
Subscription Handbill,**
1940s. Captain Marvel pictorial endorsement for magazine subscription. - **$20 $40 $75**

CMR-104. "Magic Whistle" Diecut Cardboard,
1940s. American Seed Co., Lancaster, Pennsylvania.
Working whistle that opens to show premiums earned by selling seed products. - **$25 $60 $100**
Envelope - **$30 $60 $90**

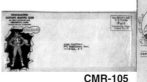

CMR-105

CMR-105. Club Christmas Kit In Mailer Envelope,
1940s. Came with cover letter and sheet of 20 Fawcett character gummed stamps.
Near Mint In Mailer - **$150**
Letter - 15 **$35 $60**
Stamp Sheet - **$15 $35 $60**

CMR-107

CMR-106

CMR-108

CMR-106. "Captain Marvel/Shazam" Cello. On Silvered Brass Pencil Clip ,
1940s.- **$30 $50 $75**

CMR-107. "Captain Marvel" Power Siren,
1940s. Store item. Red plastic siren whistle with metal loop ring. - **$85 $175 $350**

CMR-108. "Captain Marvel And The Good Humor Man" Movie Comic,
1950. Jack Carson on cover. - **$40 $110 $330**

CMR-109

CMR-109. "The Boy Who Never Heard Of Captain Marvel" Comic Booklet,
1950. Bond Bread. Pocket size comic with 24 pages. Two other titles in series are "Captain Marvel And The Stolen City" and "Captain Marvel Meets The Weatherman." Each - **$30 $75 $185**

CMR-110   CMR-111   CMR-112

CMR-110. "Captain Marvel And The Lieutenants Of Safety" Comic Book #1 ,
1950. Rare. Fawcett Publications/Ebasco Services. - **$110 $325 $850**

CMR-111. "Captain Marvel And The Lieutenants Of Safety" Comic Book #2 ,
1950. Rare. Fawcett Publications/Ebasco Services. - **$110 $325 $850**

CMR-112. "Captain Marvel And The Lieutenants Of Safety" Comic Book #3 ,
1951. Rare. Fawcett Publications/Ebasco Services. - **$110 $325 $850**

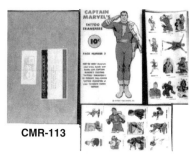

CMR-113

CMR-113. Coco-Wheats "Tattoo Transfers" Kit With Maller Envelope,
1956. Mailer - **$10 $20 $30**
Illustrated Inner Envelope With Two Sheets - **$25 $55 $80**

CMR-114

CMR-115

CMR-114. "Shazam Is Coming" 4" Cello. Button,
1972. N.P.P. Inc. - **$10 $25 $50**

CMR-115. "Power of Shazam" Sign,
1994. 19x35" sign promoting the return of Captain Marvel to comics. - **$20 $35 $50**

CAPTAIN MIDNIGHT

A shadowy plane and a mysterious pilot...diving furiously from the night sky...Captain Midnight and his Secret Squadron battled the sinister forces of evil on radio during most of the 1940s. The program originated in 1939 over WGN in Chicago, sponsored by the Skelly Oil Co. and broadcast in the Midwest. The following year it went national on the Mutual network sponsored by Ovaltine, which had just dropped Little Orphan Annie. Captain Midnight's Secret Squadron was one of radio's major producers of premiums. For an Ovaltine seal and a dime kids became Secret Squadron members. Decoder badges, pins, patches, mugs, maps, booklets, wings and rings followed in great profusion until the show closed in 1949.

The Captain made his first comic book appearance in *The Funnies* #57 in July 1941, moved to *Popular Comics* a year later and had his own book from

September 1942 to September 1948. A 15-episode chapter play was released by Columbia Pictures in 1942. The *Captain Midnight* TV series premiered in 1953, starring Richard Webb as the American super-hero and aired for four years on ABC and CBS, still sponsored by Ovaltine, still offering Secret Squadron mugs and decoder badges. The Secret Squadron logo, SS, was changed to SQ.

In the late 1950s, after Ovaltine declined to give up the copyrighted Captain Midnight name, the show was syndicated in reruns as *Jet Jackson, Flying Commando*. In 1988 Ovaltine offered a Captain Midnight SQ Secret Squadron watch in exchange for a proof-of-purchase seal.

CMD-1   **CMD-2**

CMD-1. Radio Portrayer Photo In "The Guiding Light" Booklet,
1938. Guiding Light Publishing Co./Ovaltine. Radio program synopsis booklet picturing Ed Prentiss, the radio voice of Captain Midnight on Mutual Network although identified by "Ned Holden" name of Guiding Light character. - **$35 $75 $150**

CMD-2. Skelly Large 36x84" Cardboard Display Sign,
1939. Rare. Has three brass grommet holes to aid in displaying. - **$800 $1500 $3000**

CMD-4

CMD-5

CMD-3

CMD-3. "Trick And Riddle Book",
1939. Skelly Oil Co. - **$10 $40 $60**

CMD-4. Skelly Oil "Flight Patrol Reporter" Vol. 1 #1 Newspaper,
Spring 1939. Six issues between Spring 1939 and March 1940. First Issue - **$40 $100 $175**
Other 5 Issues - **$25 $75 $125**

CMD-5. Skelly Oil "Flight Patrol Reporter" Vol. 1 #2 Newspaper,
June 15, 1939.- **$25 $75 $125**

CMD-6   **CMD-7**

CMD-6. Flight Patrol Badge Application,
1939. Skelly Oil Co. - **$30 $75 $150**

CMD-7. Treasure Hunt Rules,
1939. Skelly Oil Co. - **$20 $30 $40**

CMD-8

CMD-8. Membership Card,
1939. Skelly Oil Co. - **$20 $60 $100**

CMD-9

CMD-9. "Air Heroes" Stamp Album,
1939. Skelly Oil. Holds 16 stamps. Empty - **$10 $20 $35**
Complete - **$25 $65 $85**

CMD-11

CMD-10

CMD-12

CMD-10. Portrait Photo,
1939. Skelly Oil Co. - **$25 $50 $85**

CMD-11. "Happy Landings" Photo,
1939. Skelly Oil Co. Captain Midnight with Patsy and Chuck. - **$20 $40 $75**

CMD-12. "Chuck Ramsey" Portrait Photo,
1939. Skelly Oil Co. - **$20** **$40** **$65**

CMD-13

CMD-14

CMD-13. Portrait Photo With Treasure Hunt Back,
1939. Skelly Oil Co. - **$60** **$110** **$160**

CMD-14. Unmarked Known As 'Chuck's Treasure Map'
9x11".
1939. Skelly Oil Co. - **$50** **$150** **$225**

CMD-15

CMD-16

CMD-15. Mysto-Magic Weather Forecasting Flight
Wings Badge,
1939. Skelly Oil Co. With litmus paper - **$15** **$30** **$50**
Without litmus paper - **$10** **$20** **$30**

CMD-16. "Flight Patrol Commander" Brass Badge,
1939. Rare. Skelly Oil Co. One of the rarest Captain
Midnight badges. - **$400** **$1200** **$1700**

CMD-18

CMD-17

CMD-17. Skelly Oil "Fly With Captain Midnight" Radio
Sponsorship Announcement Brochure,
1940. Pictures Captain Midnight, Chuck, Patsy, Steve, Ivan
Shark. Skelly president announces show with list of midwest stations. - **$100** **$250** **$400**

CMD-18. Skelly Flight Patrol Member Card,
1940. - **$35** **$75** **$125**

CMD-19

CMD-20

CMD-19. Membership Card,
1940. Skelly Oil Co. - **$20** **$60** **$100**

CMD-20. Skelly Flight Patrol Brass Spinner Medal,
1940. Spinner disk pictures Captain Midnight, Patsy
Donovan, Chuck Ramsey, propeller design. -
$10 **$15** **$30**

CMD-23

CMD-21

CMD-22

CMD-21. "Mexican Jumping Beans" Paper Bag,
1940. Skelly Oil Co. For premium game utilizing jumping
beans. - **$75** **$175** **$225**

CMD-22. "Mexican Ringo-Jumpo" Game Sheet,
1940. Skelly Oil Co. For jumping bean game. -
$100 **$175** **$300**

CMD-23. "Captain Midnight's Flight Patrol Reporter"
Vol. 1 #6 Newspaper,
1940. Skelly Oil Co. Last issue. - **$25** **$75** **$125**

CMD-24

CMD-24. Skelly Oil "Flight Patrol" Airline Map,
1940. Scarce. 11x17" opened. - **$150** **$400** **$650**

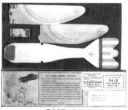 

CMD-25

CMD-26

CMD-25. "Wright Airplane" Balsa/Paper Assembly Kit
With Box ,
1940. Scarce. Wings inscribed "Captain Midnight SS-1"
and "Wright Aerial Torpedo". Near Mint Boxed - **$300**
Assembled - **$50** **$150** **$225**

CMD-26. Mystery Dial Code-O-Graph Brass Decoder,
1941. First Captain Midnight decoder. - **$35** **$60** **$90**

CMD-27

CMD-27. "Detect-O-Scope",
1941. Cardboard tube holds metal piece to judge altitudes.
Also see item CMD-31. - **$35 $75 $125**

CMD-28

CMD-28. Club Manual With Member Papers,
1941. With card and parents letter.
Complete Near Mint - **$275**
Manual Only - **$70 $140 $225**

CMD-29

CMD-29. American Flag Loyalty Pin With Paper,
1941. Patriotic text paper held in tube on pin reverse.
Badge - **$40 $100 $150**
Paper - **25 $50 $75**

CMD-30

CMD-30. "Flight Commander" Handbook,
1941. - **$75 $150 $250**

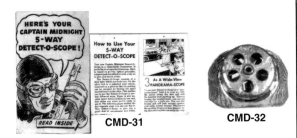

CMD-31 **CMD-32**

CMD-31. "Detect-O-Scope" Instruction Leaflet,
1941. - **$35 $75 $125**

CMD-32. Whirlwind Whistling Brass Ring,
1941. No Captain Midnight markings. - **$150 $340 $525**

CMD-33

CMD-33. "Whirlwind Whistling Ring" Instruction Sheet,
1941. - **$100 $110 $125**

CMD-34

CMD-35 **CMD-36**

CMD-34. Flight Commander Brass Decoder Ring,
1941. Inner side has "Captain Midnight Super Code 3". -
$150 $350 $550

CMD-35. "Super Book Of Comics" Comic Book #3,
1941. Various sponsors. - **$15 $45 $120**

CMD-36. Club Manual,
1942. - **$60 $125 $200**

CMD-37

CMD-37. "Flight Commander" Club Manual,
1942. Leaflet including "Official Commission" certification
panel. - **$75 $150 $250**

CMD-40

CMD-38 **CMD-39**

CMD-38. Photomatic Decoder Brass Badge,
1942. Original glossy black and white photo usually missing or replaced as club manual instructed owner to insert a
photo of themselves.
With Original Photo - **$75 $150 $250**
Without Original Photo - **$35 $65 $100**

CMD-39. Flight Commander Flying Cross Brass Badge,
1942. - **$50 $125 $225**

CMD-40. Mystic Eye Detector Look-In Brass Ring,
1942. Brass eagle cover over viewer mirror, issued by
Captain Midnight, Radio Orphan Annie, The Lone
Ranger. - **$75 $115 $150**

CMD-41   CMD-42

CMD-41. Sliding Secret Compartment Brass Ring,
1942. Also offered as Klx Pilot's Ring in 1945. -
$75 $115 $200

CMD-42. Marine Corps Insignia Brass Ring,
1942. - **$150 $325 $500**

CMD-43

CMD-43. "Magic Blackout Lite-Ups" Kit With Envelope,
1942. Near Mint In Mailer - **$500**
Illustrated Folder Only - **$75 $150 $250**

CMD-44

CMD-44. MJC-10 Plane-Detector Set,
1942. Rare. Tube with seven disk inserts and 12 airplane
silhouettes. Complete - **$200 $500 $850**
Tube Only - **$50 $100 $225**

CMD-45

CMD-46

CMD-45. Newspaper Comic Strip Introduction Page,
1942. Full page ad from Chicago Sun edition of Sunday,
July 5. - **$25 $60 $100**

CMD-46. Shoulder Insignia 3-1/2" Wide Fabric Patch,
1943. - **$60 $125 $175**

CMD-47

CMD-48

CMD-47. Army "Sleeve Insignia" Folder With Envelope,
1943. Came with Captain Midnight insignia.
Folder - **$60 $125 $175**
Envelope - **$10 $30 $40**

CMD-48. "Pilot's Badge" With Order Sheet,
c. 1943. Brass wings badge. Badge - **$50 $125 $200**
Coupon - **$25 $50 $75**

CMD-50

CMD-49

CMD-49. Pilot's Badge "Award Of Merit" Certificate,
c. 1943. - **$75 $150 $200**

CMD-50. Distinguished Service Ribbon,
1944. - **$75 $175 $250**

(BOOKLET
INTERIOR)

CMD-51

CMD-51. Service Ribbon Booklet,
1944. Radio premium. Booklet - **$50 $100 $150**
Mailer - **$15 $30 $45**
Mother's Letter - **$15 $30 $40**

CMD-52

CMD-53

CMD-52. "Invention Patent" Acknowledgement Postcard,
1944. Fawcett comic book premium. Assigns registration number for unknown invention by youthful fan. - **$50 $100 $150**

CMD-53. Club Manual,
1945. - **$40 $100 $175**

CMD-54

CMD-55

CMD-56

CMD-54. Magni-Matic Decoder Metal Badge,
1945. - **$40 $75 $200**

CMD-55. Mirro-Flash Code-O-Graph Brass Decoder,
1946. - **$40 $75 $150**

CMD-56. Mystic Sun God Ring,
1946. - **$250 $500 $1200**

CMD-57

CMD-58

CMD-57. Mystic Sun-God Ring Leaflet,
1946. - **$100 $112 $125**

CMD-58. Club Manual,
1946. - **$50 $90 $160**

CMD-59

CMD-60

CMD-59. Contest Entry Acknowledgement,
1947. Thank you card to entrant of contest closing March 31 with winners to be announced on radio program on or about April 14. - **$25 $60 $100**

CMD-60. "Quick Giggles" Contest Winner Notification,
1947. Winner's notice including prize "Secret Aztec Ring" (Mystic Sun God Ring). - **$20 $50 $85**

CMD-62

CMD-61

CMD-63

CMD-61. Shake-Up Mug,
1947. Portrait on orange plastic with blue lid. - **$40 $85 $175**

CMD-62. Whistling Code-O-Graph Plastic Decoder,
1947. Whistle with movable code wheel. - **$40 $75 $125**

CMD-63. Manual,
1947. First of smaller format. - **$35 $75 $125**

CMD-64

CMD-65

CMD-64. "Spy-Scope" With Instructions,
1947. Plastic small telescope in two varieties of plastic rims. Rare Blue Rims - **$40 $75 $150**
Orange Rims - **$30 $60 $110**
Instructions - **$15 $25 $40**

CMD-65. Manual,
1948 - **$40 $85 $140**

CMD-66

CMD-67

CMD-66. Mirro-Magic Brass/Plastic Decoder,
1948. Red plastic reverse usually warped and often
missing. - **$125 $200 $325**

CMD-67. Initial Printing Ring,
1948. Brass ring with personalized single initial designated
by orderer. - **$150 $325 $500**

CMD-68

CMD-69

CMD-68. Iron-On Transfer With Mailer Envelope,
1948. Scarce. Cellophane transfer on tissue sheet with
reverse lettering for application to fabric.
Envelope - **$15 $25 $40**
Transfer - **$35 $75 $125**

CMD-69. "Tattoo Transfers" Kit,
c. 1948. "Pack No. 8" with both Fawcett and Wander Co.
(Ovaltine) copyright. Two sheets with 22 transfers. -
$20 $50 $100

CMD-70

CMD-70. Club Manual,
1949. - **$50 $100 $200**

CMD-72

CMD-73

CMD-71

CMD-74

CMD-71. Key-O-Matic Code-O-Graph Brass Decoder,
1949. Without key. - **$40 $85 $150**

CMD-72. Key-O-Matic Code-O-Graph Brass Key,
1949. Used with decoder to set letter and number combinations. - **$75 $100 $150**

CMD-73. "Captain Midnight" Litho. Button,
1940s. Scarce. Issuer unknown. Pictures him at radio
microphone, no identification other than his name. -
$200 $450 $700

CMD-74. Plaster Figure,
1940s. Store item from series of characters (76 known).
Issued between 1941-1947 in white plaster to be painted.
Captain Midnight - **$50 $100 $150**
Most Others- **$5 $10 $15**

CMD-76

CMD-75

SECRET SQUADRON 1955-56 MANUAL AND CODE BOOK

CMD-77

CMD-75. Three-Sheet,
1940s. Scarce. Columbia Pictures serial. 41" by 81". -
$2000 $4500 $6000

CMD-76. Plastic Mug With Decal,
1953. - **$15 $25 $50**

CMD-77. Manual,
1955-56. Scarce. - **$60 $200 $350**

CMD-78

CMD-81

CMD-79

CMD-80

CMD-78. Membership Card,
1955-56. - **$40 $75 $125**

CMD-79. "SQ" Plane Puzzle Decoder Plastic Badge,
1955-56. Near Mint Decoder With Mailer And Cardboard
Holder- **$550**
Decoder Only - **$100 $300 $450**

CMD-80. "SQ" Cloth Peel-Off Patch,
1955-56. Unused - **$10 $30 $60**

CMD-81. Flight Commander Handbook,
1955-56. - **$80 $225 $450**

CMD-83

CMD-82

CMD-82. Mailer and Letter,
1955. Mailer and cardboard insert for 1955 decoder. Letter descibes the rocket power of Ovaltine and its benefits.
Letter - **$10** **$20** **$40**
Mailer - **$20** **$40** **$60**

CMD-83. Photo,
1955. Scarce. TV promotion premium. - **$75** **$150** **$200**

CMD-84

CMD-84. Postcard Notice,
1957. Rare. Notice that Ovaltine ran out of shakers and will send when new shipments arrive. - **$50** **$100** **$150**

CMD-85

CMD-85. "Secret Squadron" Membership Kit,
1957. Complete With Envelope - **$175** **$475** **$800**
Club Manual - **$60** **$200** **$325**
Member Card - **$30** **$60** **$100**
Silver Dart Decoder - **$50** **$175** **$350**

CMD-86   **CMD-87**   **CMD-88**

CMD-86. Silver Dart "SQ" Jet Plane Decoder Plastic Badge,
1957. - **$50** **$175** **$350**

CMD-87. Peel-Off Cloth Patch,
1957. Unused - **$10** **$20** **$40**

CMD-88. Flight Commander Signet Ring,
1957. Silvered plastic depicting jet plane inscribed "SQFC". - **$400** **$800** **$1200**

CMD-90

CMD-89

CMD-89. Plastic Shake-Up Mug,
1957. - **$25** **$45** **$75**

CMD-90. "Flight Commander's Handbook",
1957. - **$100** **$200** **$300**

CMD-92

CMD-91

CMD-93

CMD-91. Flexible Record With Sleeve,
c. 1970. Longines Symphonette Society. Set of eight radio show program recordings. Each - **$3** **$5** **$8**

CMD-92. Flight Commander Commission Reproduction Certificate,
c. 1970. Longines Symphonette Society. Accompanied vinyl records re-issue of radio programs. - **$10** **$18** **$30**

CMD-93. Punch-Out Decoder,
c. 1970. Longines Symphonette Society. Unpunched - **$8** **$12** **$20**

CMD-95

CMD-94

CMD-94. Record,
1972. Ovaltine premium with sleeve. - **$15** **$25** **$50**

CMD-95. Cover Letter And Watch,
1987. Offered for Ovaltine 30th anniversary year of 1988.
Letter - **$10** **$12** **$25**
Watch- **$20** **$50** **$125**

CMD-96

CMD-97

CMD-96. Cover Letter And T-Shirt,
1988. Ovaltine 30th Anniversary Premium.
Letter - **$3** **$6** **$12**
T-Shirt- **$5** **$20** **$35**

CMD-97. Cover Letter And Patch,
1989. Ovaltine offer from preceding 30th anniversary year
of 1988. Letter - **$3** **$5** **$8**
Patch - **$5** **$15** **$25**

CAPTAIN TIM HEALY

Kids interested in collecting postage stamps in the
1930s and 1940s could tune in their radios to the Tim
Healy programs. From 1934 to 1945 under a variety of
names--*Stamp Club, Ivory Stamp Club, Captain Tim's
Adventures, Calling All Stamp Collectors* and *Captain
Tim Healy's Adventure Stories*--and sponsored by
Ivory soap or Kellogg's Pep cereal, Tim Healy
described the romance of stamps and encouraged
kids to become collectors. The few premiums offered
were, naturally, stamp-related.

CTH-1

CTH-2

**CTH-1. Ivory Soap Stamp Club Album With Letter And
Envelope,**
1934. Cover Letter - **$3** **$5** **$10**
Album - **$5** **$20** **$25**

CTH-2. Member's Stamp-Shaped Brass Pin,
1934. Ivory Soap. Red Background - **$10** **$20** **$35**
Black Background - **$10** **$30** **$50**

CTH-3

CTH-3. "Ivory Stamp Club" Folder,
1934. Ivory Soap. Closed 4x6" sheet that opens to four
panels printed in color on both sides to illustrate 68-page
stamp album offered by Captain Tim Healy. - **$8** **$15** **$25**

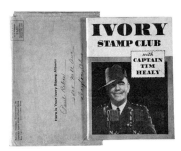
CTH-4

CTH-4. Stamp Club Book,
1934. Ivory Soap. Features pictures of Stamps of the
World.- **$15** **$30** **$45**
Mailer - **$5** **$10** **$15**

CTH-5

CTH-6

CTH-7

CTH-5. Ivory Stamp Club Album With Envelope,
c. 1935. Ivory Soap. - **$5** **$20** **$25**

CTH-6. "Spies I Have Known" Booklet,
1936. Ivory Soap. Photo-illustrated stories about famous
spies known by Captain Tim Healy. - **$10** **$20** **$35**

CTH-7. Autographed Captain Tim Healy Photo,
c. 1938. Ivory Soap. - **$10** **$20** **$35**

CTH-8

CTH-9

CTH-8. "Capt. Tim Healy" Dixie Ice Cream Picture,
c. 1939. Reverse has biography and radio broadcast
scenes. - **$8 $15 $25**

CTH-9. Dixie Ice Cream Picture,
c. 1940. - **$8 $15 $25**

CAPTAIN VIDEO

Captain Video was television's first venture into the
solar system, beating Buck Rogers by a year. The
show premiered on the Dumont network in June 1949
with Richard Coogan as the super cop, a role taken
over in 1951 by Al Hodge. The series, one of the most
popular children's shows of its time, was notoriously
low-budget, with props made of cardboard or household items, but it featured such futuristic devices as an
Opticon Scillometer, a Radio Scillograph, an Atomic
Rifle, a Discatron and a Cosmic Ray Vibrator.
Sponsors such as Post cereals and Power House
candy bars offered many premiums--rings, a plastic
ray gun, a Captain Video helmet, a Rite-O-Lite flashlight and Luma-Glo card for writing secret messages.
The series ended its network run in 1955, went local in
New York City in 1956 and finally dissolved in 1957.
The Captain appeared in comic books in 1949-1951
and a 15-episode chapter play with Judd Holdren in
the title role was released by Columbia Pictures in 1951.

CVD-1

CVD-3

CVD-2

CVD-1. Picture Ring,
c. 1950. Power House candy bars. Brass holding plastic
dome over black/white photo of Richard Coogan holding
ray gun. - **$100 $225 $350**

CVD-2. "Picture Ring" Instruction Leaflet,
c. 1950. Power House candy bars. - **$25 $50 $75**

CVD-3. "CV" Secret Seal Brass Ring,
1951. Two-piece top is designed to emboss in paper "CV"
initials, but top cover frequently snapped off. Rim pictures
tiny rocketship and four stars. - **$200 $425 $750**

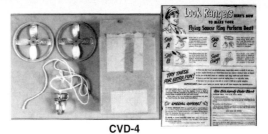

CVD-4

CVD-4. Post Toasties "Flying Saucer Ring" Set,
1951. Saucers of metal or plastic, non-glow or glow-in-
dark. Near Mint Boxed - **$1500**
Ring And Two Saucers - **$400 $800 $1200**

CVD-5

CVD-6

CVD-5. "Flying Saucer Ring" Instruction Sheet,
1951. Post Toasties. Includes order coupon for additional
rings with expiration date March 31, 1952.-
$120 $135 $150

CVD-6. "Secret Seal Ring" Leaflet And Card,
1951. Power House candy bar. Instructions plus identification card. - **$300 $450 $600**

CVD-7

CVD-7. "Flying Saucer Ring" Instruction Sheet,
1951. Power House Candy Bar. Different design than Post
Toasties version. - **$40 $75 $125**

CVD-9

CVD-8

CVD-10

CVD-8. Cast Photo,
c. 1951. Facsimile signatures of Al Hodge and Don Hastings. - **$15 $25 $60**

CVD-9. Radio Scillograph Set,
1952. TV premium advertised in comics. - **$75 $180 $360**

CVD-10. Captain Video Space Man,
1953. Post's Raisin Bran. Hard plastic set of 12.
Each - **$5 $12 $20**

CVD-11

CVD-11. "Secret Ray Gun",
1950s. Power House candy bars. Includes instruction sheet and "Luma-Glo" card. Complete - **$40 $75 $120**
Gun Only - **$15 $25 $40**

CVD-13

CVD-12

CVD-12. "Electronic Video Goggles" With Envelope,
1950s. Power House candy bars.
In Envelope - **$100 $150 $300**
Loose - **$75 $150 $250**

CVD-13. "Video Ranger" Club Member Card,
1950s. Scarce. Probable Post's Cereals. - **$35 $85 $140**

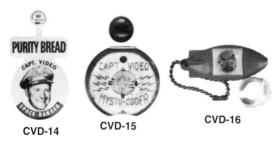

CVD-16

CVD-14   CVD-15

CVD-14. Purity Bread Litho. Tin Tab,
1950s. - **$15 $35 $65**

CVD-15. Mysto-Coder Brass Decoder With Clip Fastener,
1950s. Front has red plastic removable dome over Captain Video photo, back has two plastic code wheels. - **$75 $175 $300**

CVD-16. Plastic Rocket Ring/Pendant With Keychain,
1950s. Rocketship includes glow portrait of Captain Video, magnifying glass and whistle. - **$250 $400 $800**

CVD-17

CVD-17. "Rocket Ring" Instruction Sheet,
1950s. Scarce. Power House candy bars. - **$175 $200 $225**

CASEY, CRIME PHOTOGRAPHER

Flashgun Casey, Press Photographer, Crime Photographer--under whatever name, "the ace cameraman who covers the crime news of a great city" for the Morning Express was first broadcast on CBS in 1943. With Staats Cotsworth as the crusading crime fighter, the program ran until 1950, then was revived from 1953 to 1955. Sponsors included the Anchor Hocking Glass Co., Toni Home Permanents and Philip Morris cigarettes. A television adaptation for CBS (1951-1952) featured Richard Carlyle, then Darren McGavin, in the title role. A brief run of comic books appeared in 1949-1950.

CCP-1

CCP-1. Photo Of Cast,
1940s. - **$25 $50 $75**

CASPER THE FRIENDLY GHOST

Casper, The Friendly Ghost, created by Joe Oriolo, made his debut in animated cartoons in 1945 and has grown over the years into a merchandising giant through films, comic books, and television series. Between 1950 and 1959 Paramount/Famous Studios produced 62 *Casper* cartoons telling the simple story of the ghost who just wanted to make friends, not scare people. ("A g-g-ghost!") Casper made his first television appearance in 1959 on ABC in *Matty's Funday Funnies*, sponsored by Mattel toys. Other series followed in 1963, 1969, and *1979 (Casper and the Angels*, NBC). Two NBC specials, *Casper's Halloween* and *Casper's First Christmas*, also aired in 1979. The cartoons have been in syndication since 1963. A $50 million *Casper* film produced by Steven

Speilberg was released in the summer of 1995, with a direct-to-video sequel that recently followed.

Casper made his first comic book appearance in 1949, then started again in 1950, and again in 1953, this time from Harvey Comics, which has also produced a wide variety of spin-off comic books and magazines. Harvey also acquired the television rights from Famous/Paramount in 1958. The merchandising of Casper has been extensive, including everything from costumes to candy dispensers to jewelry, records, toys, etc. Casper has also been an official recruiter for the Boy Scouts of America, and in 1972 he flew to the moon (painted on the side of Apollo 16).

CSP-1

CSP-2   CSP-3

CSP-1. Sliding Tile Puzzle On Card,
c. 1961. Store item by Roalex Co. Plastic puzzle for forming images of Casper, Katnip, Baby Huey, Little Audrey. On Card - **$25 $60 $85** Loose - **$10 $20 $40**

CSP-2. "Casper" Soaky Bottle,
1960s. Colgate-Palmolive Co. store item. Hard plastic container for liquid soap. -
$10 $20 $35

CSP-3. "Wendy" Soaky Bottle,
1960s. Colgate-Palmolive Co. store item. Hard plastic container for liquid soap. -
$10 $25 $35

CSP-4

CSP-5

CSP-4. "Casper's Ghostland Trick Or Treat" 12x12" Store Sign,
1960s. Thin plastic with Harvey Famous Cartoons copyright. - **$15 $30 $50**

CSP-5. Vending Machine Display Paper,
1960s. Depicts Casper and shows three monsters appearing on flicker rings. - **$30 $45 $60**

CSP-6

CSP-6. Mugs
1971. In blue, red, yellow, and green colors.
Each - **$5 $10 $20**

CSP-7   CSP-8

CSP-7. "Casper Day BSA Cub Scouts Equipment Center" 3" Cello. Button,
1975. - **$8 $15 $25**

CSP-8. Cub Scouts Recruitment Litho. Button,
1976. Boy Scouts of America (BSA). Harvey Comics copyright. - **$5 $10 $15**

(OPEN)

(CLOSED)

CSP-9

CSP-9. Plastic Decoder (Blue),
1997. Boston Chicken premium. - **$5 $10 $15**

CEREAL BOXES

See entries by name of company, program and character.

CHANDU, THE MAGICIAN

Chandu was actually Frank Chandler, an American secret agent who used ancient occult powers he learned from a Hindu yogi to combat evil. The 15-minute program originated on Los Angeles radio station KHJ in 1932 and ran on Mutual until 1936, sponsored in the west by White King soap and in the east by Beech-Nut products. The series was revived in 1948, based on the original scripts, with White King again as sponsor. It had a final run as a half-hour weekly show on the ABC network in 1949-1950.

CHA-1

CHA-1. "Chandu Book Of Magic,"
1932. Rio Grande Oil Co. Twelve-page booklet of illustrated tricks plus sponsor ad on back cover. - **$35 $75 $125**

CHA-2

CHA-3

CHA-2. "The Return Of Chandu" Movie Serial Pressbook,
1934. Principal Distributing Corp. - **$100 $250 $400**

CHA-3. "The Return Of Chandu" 27x41" Movie Serial Poster,
1934. Principal Distributing Corp. - **$150 $300 $600**

CHA-4

CHA-5

CHA-6

CHA-4. Fan Photo,
1930s. Pictures four unidentified cast members. - **$60 $125 $200**

CHA-5. Radio Listing Folder,
1930s. White King Soap. Contents include listing of stations in Central and Western United States carrying Chandu broadcasts. - **$75 $140 $200**

CHA-6. Paper Mask,
1930s. Possible Beech-Nut Gum. Probable give-away. - **$35 $60 $125**

CHA-7

CHA-8

CHA-9

CHA-7. Chandu Club Cello Button,
1930s. - **$75 $150 $300**

CHA-8. "Chandu Magicians Club" Cello. Member Button,
1930s. - **$75 $150 $250**

CHA-9. "Beech-Nut's King Of Magic" Leaflet,
1930s. Contents include radio cast photo, magic trick offer. - **$20 $40 $60**

CHA-10

CHA-11

CHA-12

CHA-10. Magic Slate,
1930s. Ernst Kerr Co., Detroit department store radio sponsor on WJR. Comes with wood stylus marker. - **$50 $125 $200**

CHA-11. "Beech-Nut Holiday Trick" Greeting Postcard,
1930s. Back lists radio cast members with holiday message. - **$25 $50 $75**

CHA-12. Beech-Nut Galloping Coin Trick,
1930s. Boxed Set - **$25 $60 $100**

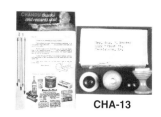

CHA-13

CHA-14

CHA-13. "Chandu Ball And Base" Boxed Trick,
1930s. Beech-Nut Gum. With letter and instruction leaflet. - **$25 $50 $90**

CHA-14. "Chinese Coin On String" Trick With Mailer Envelope,
1930s. Beech-Nut Gum. - **$25 $50 $75**

CHA-15

CHA-16

CHA-15. Photo - Gayne Whitman in Costume,
1930s. Beech-Nut Gum. - **$25 $60 $100**

CHA-16. Photo - Gayne Whitman in Business Suit,
1930s. Beech-Nut Gum. - **$35 $75 $125**

CHA-17   CHA-18

CHA-17. "Betty Lou Regent" Portrait Print,
1930s. Probably Beech-Nut Gum. 8-1/2x11" textured paper black and white photo also identifying Betty Webb as the portrayer. - **$15 $30 $50**

CHA-18. "Bob Regent" Portrait Print,
1930s. Probably Beech-Nut Gum. 8-1/2x11" textured paper black and white photo also identifying Bob T. Bixby as the portrayer. - **$15 $30 $50**

CHA-19   CHA-20

CHA-19. Letter,
1930s. For costume photo. With color photos of products on back. - **$10 $20 $40**

CHA-20. Letter,
1930s. For Bobby Regent photo. With color photos of products on back. - **$10 $20 $40**

CHA-22

CHA-21

CHA-21. Letter,
1930s. For Mrs.Bobby Regent photo. With color photos of products on back. - **$10 $20 $40**

CHA-22. Radio Broadcasts Guide 11x21" Cardboard Sign,
1930s. Beech-Nut Gum. - **$125 $275 $400**

CHA-23

CHA-23. "Svengali Mind Reading Trick",
1930s. Beech-Nut Gum. Boxed - **$25 $50 $100**

CHA-24   CHA-25

CHA-24. "The Great Beech-Nut Buddha Money Mystery" Packet,
1930s. Magic trick based on Chandu radio series. - **$20 $40 $60**

CHA-25. "Hypnotized Silver Sphere" Trick With Box And Order Sheet,
1930s. Beech-Nut Gum. - **$25 $50 $75**

CHA-26

CHA-26. "Chandu White King Of Magic" Boxed Trick Set,
1930s. White King Soap. Complete - **$100 $150 $250**

CHA-27

CHA-27. "Card Miracles" Boxed Set,
1930s. White King Soap. - **$25 $50 $75**

CHA-28   CHA-29

CHA-28. "Assyrian Money Changer" Trick With Mailer Envelope,
1930s. White King Soap. With instruction card, wooden block, two metal bands for holding penny. - **$25 $50 $75**

CHA-29. "Brazilian Beads" Trick With Mailer Envelope,
1930s. White King Soap. Comes with instructions, glass vial containing beads and cork. - **$25 $50 $75**

CHARLES LINDBERGH

Charles Augustus Lindbergh (1902-1974), Midwestern farm boy, barnstorming stunt flier and airmail pilot, flew into history on May 22, 1927, when he completed the first nonstop solo flight across the Atlantic in his monoplane Spirit of St. Louis. America's Lone Eagle--Lucky, Plucky Lindy--became an instant international hero, with banner headlines, medals, awards, receptions, banquets, and a ticker tape parade up Broadway in New York City. Souvenirs and commemorative memorabilia followed in great profusion. James Stewart starred in the 1957 biographical movie *The Spirit of St. Louis*.

CLD-1

CLD-2

CLD-3

CLD-1. "Welcome Lindy" Cello. Button,
1927. Depicts and names his aircraft "Spirit Of St. Louis." - **$30 $60 $100**

CLD-2. Transatlantic Flight Commemorative Plate,
1927. Store item. 8-1/2x8-1/2" limoges china plate by "Golden Glow" process of somewhat irridescent quality on outer margin around full color Lindbergh portrait. Pictured example has imprint for local sponsor. - **$10 $20 $30**

CLD-3. Spirit Of St. Louis Pin,
1927. Brass pin on card - **$50 $75 $100**

CLD-4

CLD-5

CLD-4. Flight School 13x15" Poster,
1927. U.S. Army Flying Schools. Recruiting poster with Lindbergh tributes concluding "The Army Trained Him." - **$30 $60 $100**

CLD-5. Flight Celebration Cap,
1927. Fabric over cardboard headband holding fabric crown. Pictured example has stamped name of local sponsor on headband rear. - **$25 $50 $75**

CLD-6

CLD-7

CLD-6. "Welcome Home" Felt Pennant,
1927. 8x26". - **$40 $80 $150**

CLD-7. "The Lone Eagle" Lindbergh/Bulova Endorsement Plaque,
c. 1927. Bulova watches. 9x12" walnut wood plaque with mounted metal photo portrait plate including endorsement statement for sponsor plus facsimile Lindbergh signature. - **$50 $100 $150**

CLD-8

CLD-9

CLD-8. "Our National Hero Col. Lindbergh" China Ashtray,
c. 1927. Full color portrait on glazed pastel yellow. - **$10 $20 $35**

CLD-9. "Mystery Picture" Card,
c. 1927. Majestic Radio, "Mighty Monarch Of The Air." 3-1/2x5-1/2" black and white optical illusion card with instructions for causing Lindbergh image to enlarge, disappear, re-appear. - **$8 $15 $25**

CLD-10

CLD-11

CLD-10. Lindbergh High School Tribute Album,
1928. Little Falls High School, Little Falls, Minnesota. Tribute photo folio by his high school alma mater with 24 pages including numerous youth photos in addition to those from his adult flying career. - **$150 $300 $500**

CLD-11. "Two Great Flyers" Cello. Button,
c. 1928. Flexible Flyer Sleds. - **$12 $20 $30**

CLD-12

CLD-13

CLD-12. Parachute Product Endorsement Photo,
c. 1928. Irvin Air Chutes. 8x10" black and white with product inscription on margin "He has saved his life on four different occasions by using Irvin Air Chutes." - **$10 $20 $40**

CLD-13. "Lindy Bread" Wrapper,
c. 1928. Cottage Bakery, Springfield, Ohio. 10-1/2x15" waxed glassine loaf wrapper. Photo shows entire wrapper and detail from it. -
$25 $60 $100

CLD-14

CLD-15

CLD-14. Hauptmann Trial Official Pass,
1935. Single day authorization pass for January 14 day of trial for accused Lindbergh baby kidnapper and slayer Richard Bruno Hauptmann. - **$150 $250 $500**

CLD-15. Premium Map 31-1/2"x 42",
1935. Heinz 57. Map of famous aviator flights. Shows 25 famous pilots and 25 different planes. Photos could be cut out and used as cards. - **$75 $150 $200**

CLD-16

CLD-16. Lindbergh Infant Kidnapping Murder Trial Summary,
c. 1936. Tastyeast, Inc. Cover letter and 24-page photo and text booklet summarizing evidence and trial of accused kidnapper and slayer. Contents include editorial by newscaster Gabriel Heatter.
Near Mint Complete - **$85**
Booklet Only - **$15 $40 $60**
Letter Only - **$5 $10 $15**

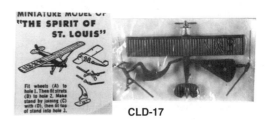

CLD-17

CLD-17. "The Spirit Of St. Louis" Miniature Model,
c. 1956. Kellogg's. Cellophane pack holding assembly parts for 2x3" replica aircraft.
Cereal Box With Offer - **$25 $50 $75**
Model Kit - **$25 $50 $75**

CHARLIE CHAPLIN

Charles Spencer Chaplin (1889-1977) was born in London and spent most of his early years in homes and institutions. By 1898 he was working on stage, and in 1913 he signed a contract to make comic movies with Mack Sennett's Keystone Studios. The next year, in *Kid Auto Races at Venice*, Chaplin unveiled his screen persona as "The Little Tramp" in baggy pants, floppy shoes, bowler hat and bamboo cane--a role he was to play in more than 70 films and one that brought him international acclaim as a true comic genius. Chaplin took The Tramp from Keystone to Essanay in 1915, to Mutual in 1916, and to First National in 1917. In 1919 he helped form United Artists so he could produce and distribute his films independently. From *The Tramp* in 1915 to *Limelight* in 1952, Chaplin's fame and box-office appeal continued to grow.

The Tramp was adapted in a newspaper comic strip, *Charlie Chaplin's Comic Capers*, for the *Chicago Record-Herald* and national syndication in 1915-1917, and *Baggy Pants*, an animated cartoon, aired on NBC in 1977-1978, but the humor and pathos of Chaplin's character proved impossible to capture in either medium.

In the late 1940s and 1950s Chaplin was wrongfully accused of "Communist leanings" by the American Legion and other right-wing organizations. He moved to Switzerland, returning only in 1972 to receive a special Academy Award. He was knighted in 1975, and his Little Tramp remains to this day the universal embodiment of the eventual triumph of the individual.

CPN-1 CPN-2 CPN-3

CPN-1. "Chas. Chaplin" Statuette,
1915. Includes wire cane. Store item. - **$50 $75 $125**

CPN-2. Charlie Chaplin Composition/Cloth Doll,
c. 1915. Scarce. Store item by Louis Amberg & Son. -
$100 $250 $500

CPN-3. "Chas. Chaplin" Statuette,
1915. 9" tall painted plaster figurine with underside token insert "Sold By Mark Hampton Co. Inc." with New York City address and copyright year. - **$35 $75 $100**

CPN-4

CPN-4. Movie Promo,
1916. National Theatre Premium. 16 pages, shows coming attraction. - **$10 $25 $35**

CPN-5

CPN-5. "Charlie Chaplin's Comic Capers" Book,
1917. Store item published by M. A. Donohue & Co. Softcover 9-1/2x16" with 16 black and white pages reprinting daily comic strips. - **$100 $200 $400**

CPN-6

CPN-6. "Charlie Chaplin in The Movies" Book,
1917. Store item published by M. A. Donohue & Co. Softcover 9-1/2x16" with 16 black and white pages reprinting daily comic strips. - **$100 $200 $400**

CPN-8

CPN-7

CPN-7. "The Kid" Handbill,
1920. Paper sheet for silent film starring Chaplin and "The Wonder Boy" Jackie Coogan in his first role. -
$10 $20 $30

CPN-8. "The Gold Rush" Movie Promotion Mask,
1924. Diecut stiff paper for silent film release. -
$25 $60 $100

CPN-9

CPN-11

CPN-10

CPN-9. "The Gold Rush" Movie Program,
1925. From world premiere at Grauman's Egyptian Theater, Hollywood for dramatic comedy written, directed and starring Chaplin. - **$35 $75 $125**

CPN-10. Chaplin Image Party Favor,
c. 1920s. Store item. 7-1/2" crepe paper and confetti table marker with 3" figure of him formed by glossy paper and fabric. - **$10 $20 $30**

CPN-11. Charlie Chaplin Candy Container Bank,
1920s. Store item. Glass plus metal lid. - **$75 $150 $250**

CPN-12

CPN-13

CPN-12. Charlie Chaplin Cello. Button,
1920s. Sampeck Suits. - **$15 $30 $50**

CPN-13. Mask,
1920s. Made in England. Possible premium. - **$20 $40 $80**

CPN-14

CPN-14. Cardboard 9" Puppet With Mailer and Instructions,
1920s. Made in England. Possible premium.
Puppet - **$25 $50 $75**
Mailer - **$10 $20 $30**
Instructions - **$5 $10 $15**

CHARLIE McCARTHY

Edgar Bergen and Charlie McCarthy accomplished the seemingly impossible--a successful ventriloquist act on radio. After years of knocking around vaudeville, Bergen and Charlie broke into radio with a guest appearance on Rudy Vallee's show in 1936. They were an instant hit and five months later they were stars on the Chase & Sanborn Hour. Week after week Charlie feuded with W. C. Fields and flirted with Dorothy Lamour and America loved him. Another dummy, Mortimer Snerd, was added in 1939 and Effie Klinker joined the crew in 1944 but Charlie ruled supreme. Chase & Sanborn's sponsorship ended in 1948 and other sponsors (Coca-Cola, Hudnut, Kraft cheese) carried the show until it ended in 1956. Charlie made an early TV appearance on the *Hour Glass* variety show in 1946 and, along with Bergen, hosted *Do You Trust Your Wife?* in 1956-1957 and *Who Do You Trust?* on

daytime TV from 1957-1963. A comic strip had a brief run in the late 1930s and comic books were published in the late 1940s and early 1950s.

CHE-1

CHE-2

CHE-1. "Chase & Sanborn Radio News" Newsletter,
c. 1937. - **$25 $50 $75**

CHE-2. "Adventure Pops" Cardboard Folder,
1938. Held six lollipops by E. Rosen Co. From a set of five. Each - **$25 $60 $100**

CHE-3

CHE-3. "Radio Party" Game,
1938. Chase & Sanborn Coffee. Includes spinner and 21 figures. Complete - **$20 $40 $65**

CHE-4

CHE-5

CHE-6

CHE-4. Animated Alarm Clock,
1938. Store item by Gilbert. - **$300 $600 $1200**

CHE-5. Cardboard Figure,
c. 1938. Chase & Sanborn Coffee. - **$25 $50 $125**

CHE-6. Mortimer Snerd Cardboard Figure,
c. 1938. Chase & Sanborn Coffee. - **$40 $100 $200**

CHE-7

CHE-8

CHE-7. Effanbee Doll "Edgar Bergen's Charlie McCarthy" Cello. Button,
c. 1938. For "An Effanbee Play-Product". - **$30 $60 $100**

CHE-8. Photo,
1938. Philadelphia Record newspaper premium - $15 $30 $50

CHE-9   CHE-10

CHE-9. Ventriloquist Doll Detective Outfit,
c. 1938. Store item believed to be Effanbee. - $200 $400 $700

CHE-10. Ventriloquist Doll In Tuxedo,
c. 1938. Store item believed to be Effanbee. - $200 $400 $700

CHE-12

CHE-11

CHE-11. "Radio Guide" Magazines With McCarthy Covers,
1938-1939. Issues for July 9, 1938 and February 25, 1939. Each - $10 $15 $20

CHE-12. "Speaking For Myself On Life And Love" Book,
1939. Chase & Sanborn Coffee. - $10 $20 $35

CHE-13

CHE-14

CHE-13. Silver Plate Spoon With Mailer,
c. 1939. Mailer Only - $10 $15 $25
Standard Tuxedo Design Spoon - $5 $10 $15

CHE-14. Detective Outfit Design Spoon,
c. 1939. - $20 $40 $75

CHE-15   CHE-16   CHE-17

CHE-15. Painted Plastic Portrait Pin,
c. 1939. - $15 $30 $60

CHE-16. "Goldwyn Follies Club" Cello. Button,
1930s. Metro-Goldwyn-Mayer. - $15 $30 $50

CHE-17. Bust Portrait Brass Ring,
1940. Chase and Sanborn coffee. - $150 $240 $350

CHE-18

CHE-19   CHE-20

CHE-18. "Gold-Plated Ring" Coupon Sheet,
1940. Scarce. Clipping from can wrapper of Chase & Sanborn Coffee offering ring for 10 cents plus the clipping. - $10 $20 $30

CHE-19. Composition Bank,
c. 1940. Store item. - $40 $75 $150

CHE-20. Bergen/McCarthy Glass,
c. 1940. - $25 $60 $100

CHE-21

CHE-21. Contest Card,
1944. - $12 $25 $50

CHARLIE THE TUNA

Charlie is the out-of-luck character created for Star-Kist Foods in the 1960s. Charlie's ambition was to impress Star-Kist (and viewers) with his demonstrations of esthetic "good taste," inevitably rejected by "Sorry, Charlie. Star-Kist doesn't want tuna with good taste. Star-Kist wants tuna that tastes good." Despite-- or because of--his loser image, Charlie became a winner in premium popularity.

CTU-1
CTU-2
CTU-3
CTU-4

CTU-1. Talking Cloth Doll,
1969. - **$35 $60 $100**

CTU-2. Metal Alarm Clock,
1969. - **$20 $50 $100**

CTU-3. "Charlie For President" Litho. Button,
1960s. - **$8 $15 $25**

CTU-4. Plastic Radio,
1970. Battery operated, base often missing.
Complete - **$40 $60 $90**
No Base - **$15 $25 $40**

CTU-5
CTU-6
CTU-7

CTU-5. Plastic Figural Camera,
1971. - **$20 $20 $75**

CTU-6. Oval Bathroom Scale,
1972. - **$20 $40 $75**

CTU-7. Metal Wristwatch,
1973. - **$25 $40 $65**

CTU-8
CTU-9

CTU-8. Mug,
1977. - **$5 $15 $25**

CTU-9. "25th Anniversary" Wristwatch,
1986. Authorized Star-Kist limited edition metal case watch accompanied by paper slips for Charlie the Tuna history and other mail premiums. Near Mint Boxed - **$65**
Watch Only - **$20 $35 $50**

CTU-10
CTU-11

CTU-10. Plastic Telephone,
1987. - **$10 $20 $35**

CTU-11. Ceramic Bank,
1988. - **$25 $50 $75**

CHEERIOS MISC.

Cheerios ready-to-eat oat cereal was introduced by General Mills as Cheerioats in 1941 and has remained a perennial favorite with kids and adults ever since. Over the years the Cheerios box has carried cutout toys and promotions for a wide variety of merchandisers, notably the Lone Ranger, Wyatt Earp, Superman, the Muppets, Bugs Bunny, Snoopy and Peanuts, Star Trek, Star Wars and Mickey Mouse. Disney comic books and 3-D glasses were featured giveaways in the 1940s and 1950s. The items in this section are primarily a selection of Cheerios non-character premiums.

CEE-1
CEE-2

CEE-1. "Hall Of Fun/Groucho Marx" 3-D Picture,
c. 1942. Assembled from box back. Set of eight.
Box Panel Or Assembled - **$25 $40 $60**

CEE-2. "Hall Of Fun/Joe E. Brown" 3-D Picture,
c. 1942. Assembled from box back. Set of eight.
Box Panel Or Assembled - **$10 $15 $25**

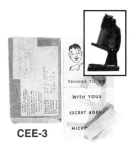

CEE-3

CEE-3. Secret Agent Microscope,
1950. Secret Agent black microscope with six slides. Eight page instruction booklet and mailer. - **$30 $60 $100**

CEE-4

CEE-4. "Confederate Currency" Album With Envelope,
1954. Reproductions of Confederate money. -
$40 $80 $150

CEE-5

CEE-6

CEE-5. "Confederate Money" Box,
1954. Front panel pictures one of nine different designs of
replica currency bills of Confederate States of America
issued individually as box insert.
Complete Box - **$25 $50 $90**

CEE-6. 3D Wiggle Picture Display,
1950s. Cheerios Cereal. Features Cheerio Kid and
Donald Duck. - **$20 $40 $65**
Each of 4 Extra Pictures - **$3 $6 $9**

CEE-7

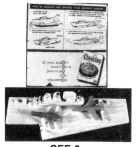

CEE-8

CEE-7. Cheerios Kid Statue,
1950s. Scarce. - **$40 $100 $175**

**CEE-8. Aircraft Carrier And Planes Plastic Toy With
Instructions And Box,**
1960s. Planes are launched by rubber band. Near Mint In
Mailer - **$75**

CEE-9

CEE-9. "Cape Cheerios Rocket Base" Box Panel Set,
1960s. Completed by parts from five box backs.
Uncut Backs Each - **$15 $30 $50**

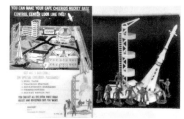

CEE-10

CEE-10. "Cape Cheerios Rocket Base",
c. 1960s. Premium by Marx.
Complete Boxed - **$30 $50 $75**

CHICK CARTER

Like father, like son, for detective work done. Nick
Carter, a sleuth of considerable prominence to readers
of pulp magazines and hardbound novels of the 1930s,
fathered a son in his image--at least for purposes of
radio and movie serial producers. The elder Carter, by
name, was avoided for reasons unknown in broadcast
and screen versions. *Chick Carter, Boy Detective*
began as a radio drama on the Mutual network July 5,
1943 and ran until July 6, 1945. *Chick Carter, Detective*,
a 1946 Columbia Pictures 15-episode serial, dropped
all pretense that Chick was a youngster. Chick was an
instant adult, portrayed by Lyle Talbot, a veteran actor
of gangster and crime movie roles.

CCK-1

CCK-1. Chick Carter Club Card,
1944. - **$15 $30 $60**

CCK-2

CCK-2. Radio Club Promo Booklet,
1945. - **$20 $50 $85**

CCK-3

CCK-3. Club Kit Folder,
1945. - **$30 $80 $150**

CHICK CARTER INNER CIRCLE

This is to certify that
is a Charter Member of the CHICK CARTER INNER
CIRCLE, and a regular listener to the CHICK CARTER
radio program. The bearer may participate in all
INNER CIRCLE activities and is entitled to use the
INNER CIRCLE INSIGNIA.
1945
BOY DETECTIVE

CCK-4

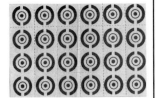

CCK-5

CCK-4. Club Kit Card,
1945. Rare. - **$15 $55 $80**

CCK-5. Set of 24 Inner Circle Logo Stickers,
1945. - **$10 $20 $48**
Each - **$2**

CHINA CLIPPER

In spite of the early 1930s Depression years, air travel demand continued almost unabated. The enterprising Pan American Airways offered a challenge based on need: a transport aircraft capable of 2,500 mile non-stop flight to span the Pacific. Aircraft makers responded quickly. On November 22, 1935 the first of the romantically-named "China Clipper" flights began to the Orient. The selected aircraft, one by Martin and one by Boeing, were masterpieces of huge payload capacity, incredible size and magnificent interior elegance for crew and passengers. So remarkable was this advance in aviation technology, a 1936 movie starring Pat O'Brien detailed the account of the initial flight that compared in public stature to Lindbergh's earlier solo flight of the Atlantic. The "China Clipper" mystique and adulation resulted in several tribute premiums issued by Quaker Oats.

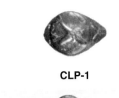

CLP-1

CLP-3

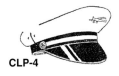

CLP-2

CLP-1. China Clipper Brass Ring,
1935. Quaker Puffed Wheat and Rice. - **$40 $80 $120**

CLP-2. China Clipper 2" Brass Bar Badge,
1935. Quaker Puffed Wheat and Rice. - **$20 $40 $75**

CLP-3. Quaker "China Clipper" Balsa Model,
1935. Quaker Puffed Wheat and Rice. 12" wing span.
Assembled - **$25 $75 $100**

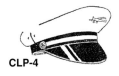

CLP-4

CLP-5

CLP-4. Pilot's Cap,
1936. Quaker Puffed Wheat/Puffed Rice. White twill with gilt braid, brass buttons, black bill, metal airplane ornament. - **$50 $100 $200**

CLP-5. Girl's Bracelet,
1936. Quaker Puffed Wheat/Puffed Rice. Gold luster metal with personalized single initial on wing design. -
$25 $50 $75

CLP-6

CLP-7

CLP-6. Boys Life Magazine - Feature And Picture On Cover,
1936. China Clipper pictures on cover with story about the Pan-American Clippers. - **$15 $25 $40**

CLP-7. Standee 10x14",
1939. Rare. Kraft Malted Milk. Promo for China Clipper model plane - **$100 $250 $350**

CLP-8

CLP-9

CLP-8. Poster,
1939. Rare. 32x44". Beautiful colorful poster for grocery stores which shows how to get free photos and models of the China Clipper.- **$100 $225 $350**

CLP-9. Model Mailer,
1939. Kraft Malted Milk. - **$30 $60 $90**

CLP-10

CLP-10. "Giant Model Of The Famous China Clipper" Cardboard Punch-Out Folder,
1939. Pan-American Airways. Folder opens to 11x30". -
$40 $100 $200

THE CINNAMON BEAR

First aired in 1937, *The Cinnamon Bear* was a syndicated children's Christmas tale broadcast five times a week between Thanksgiving and Christmas. In 26 chapters it followed the adventures of Judy and Jimmy Barton and Paddy O'Cinnamon as they travel through Maybe Land in search of their stolen Silver Star-- across the Root Beer Ocean, face-to-face with the Wintergreen Witch and Captain Taffy the Pirate. The show was sponsored by department stores, principally Wieboldt's of Chicago, and ran annually for many years.

CIN-1

CIN-2

CIN-3

CIN-1. Wieboldt's Litho. Tin Tab,
1940s. Rare. - $75 $250 $450

CIN-2. Foil Silver Star Picturing Paddy,
c. 1940s. - $50 $100 $175

CIN-3. "TV Club" Litho. Button With Cardboard Bear Attachment,
1950s. Wieboldt's department store. - $40 $100 $150

THE CISCO KID

The beloved bandito and his sidekick Pancho were created by O. Henry in a short story, *The Caballero's Way*, in the early 1900s and have lived a long entertainment life. They appeared in several silent movies and in 23 sound features between 1929 and 1950, starring either Warner Baxter (who won an Oscar for *In Old Arizona* in 1929), Cesar Romero, Duncan Renaldo or Gilbert Roland. A radio series aired on Mutual from 1942 to 1956 and a popular television version with Renaldo and Leo Carrillo was syndicated between 1950 and 1956. Over 150 half-hour episodes were filmed by ZIV Television--in color, though at the time TV could broadcast only in black and white. Comic books appeared in the 1940s and 1950s and a daily comic strip ran from 1951 to 1968. Most premiums date from the successful broadcast period of the 1950s. A 1994 telefilm brought Cisco and Pancho back to TV audiences in the forms of Jimmy Smits and Cheech Marin, respectively. "Oh Pancho! Ooooh Ceesco!"

CIS-1

CIS-2

CIS-1. "Safety Club Member" Cello. Button,
c. 1948. - $25 $50 $75

CIS-2. Cisco Kid Paper Mask,
1949. Various sponsors. Pictured example for Cisco Kid cookies, Cisco Kid sweet buns by Schofer's Bakery. -
$10 $20 $35

CIS-3

CIS-4

CIS-5

CIS-3. "I'm A Cisco Kid Fan!" Cello. Button,
1949. ZIV Co. Radio Productions. Issued to show sponsors for promotional purposes. - $10 $20 $30

CIS-4. "Wrigley's Cisco Kid Club" Cello. Button,
c. 1949. Wrigley's Gum. - $25 $50 $75

CIS-5. Pancho Paper Mask,
1949. Various bakeries. - $10 $20 $35

CIS-6

CIS-6. Merchandising Portfolio,
1949. ZIV Co. Radio Productions . Contains over 25 promotional items such as bw photos, sample ads, source list for premiums. Complete - $100 $300 $500

CIS-7

CIS-7. Range War Game With Punch-Outs,
1949. Rare. - **$250 $750 $1000**

CIS-8
CIS-9
CIS-10

CIS-8. "Wrigley's Cisco Kid Signal Arrowhead",
c. 1949. - **$125 $250 $400**

CIS-9. "Cisco Kid" Ring,
c. 1940s. Name appears on each side. - **$75 $150 $250**

CIS-10. "Cisco Kid" Aluminum Saddle Ring,
1950. Name in raised letters on saddle seat. -
$200 $425 $650

CIS-11
CIS-12

CIS-11. Cisco Kid Humming Lariat,
1950. Eddy's Bread. Cardboard rectangle with string and
streamer roll of crepe paper to "Execute The Thrilling Rope
Tricks Done By The Famous Cisco Kid". - **$30 $75 $120**

CIS-12. Secret Compartment Photo Ring,
c. 1950. Rare. Brass bands holding plastic compartment
with brass lid over bw picture. - **$1500 $5000 $9200**

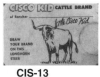

CIS-13

CIS-13. "Cisco Kid Ranchers Club" Kit,
c. 1950. Dan-Dee Pretzel And Potato Chip Co.
Certificate - **$15 $40 $75**
Card - **$10 $20 $30**
Button - **$10 $25 $50**
Letter - **$15 $40 $75**

CIS-14
CIS-15

CIS-14. Freihofer's Bread Labels,
c. 1950. From a set. Each - **$10 $15 $20**

CIS-15. "Ranchers Club" Card,
c. 1950. Pro-tek-tive Shoes. - **$10 $20 $35**

CIS-16

CIS-16. Mylar Reflective Mask With Envelope,
c. 1950. Scarce. Dolly Madison Ice Cream.
In Envelope - **$75 $160 $250**
Loose - **$25 $60 $100**

CIS-17
CIS-18
CIS-19

CIS-17. Glass,
c. 1950. Probably held diary product. Seen in lime
green/black or yellow/brown. Each - **$25 $60 $100**

CIS-18. Cello. Button,
c. 1950. Possibly for rodeo appearance. - **$20 $40 $75**

CIS-19. "Cisco Kid On TV-Radio" Litho. Tin Tab,
c. 1950. Various sponsors. Various hat colors. -
$10 $25 $40

CIS-20
CIS-21
CIS-22

CIS-20. TV-Radio Pancho Litho. Tab,
c. 1950. Various sponsors. Various hat colors. -
$10 $25 $40

CIS-21. Kern's Bread Postcard,
1951. - **$12 $20 $35**

CIS-22. Triple "S" Club Litho. Button,
c. 1951. - **$15 $25 $50**

CIS-23

CIS-23. "Triple 'S' Club" Papers With Envelope,
1951. Imprinted for Nolde Bros. Bakery and WTAR Radio,
Norfolk, Virginia. Contents are replica "Western Union"
transmittal telegram plus Code Book leaflet.
Near Mint In Envelope - **$100**
Folder - **$15 $25 $40**
Telegram - **$10 $20 $30**

CIS-24

CIS-25

CIS-26

**CIS-24. Kern's Bread "Triple S Club" Clothing
Transfer,**
c. 1951. Tissue paper with reverse image to be applied by
warm iron on fabric. - **$15 $40 $50**

CIS-25. Portrait Photo,
1952. Butter-Nut Bread. - **$10 $20 $30**

CIS-26. Bread Label Folder,
1952. Freihofer's Bread. Holds 36 different bread labels. -
$50 $75 $150

CIS-27

CIS-28

CIS-27. Cisco Photo,
1952. Butter-Nut Bread. Shows Cisco riding Diablo.
Promotes radio and TV show. - **$10 $20 $30**

CIS-28. Pancho Photo,
1952. Butter-Nut Bread. Shows Pancho and horse Loco.
Promotes radio and TV show. - **$10 $20 $30**

CIS-29

CIS-29. Paper Masks Set,
1953. Tip-Top Bread. Each - **$10 $20 $30**

CIS-30

CIS-30. Tip-Top Bread Puzzle,
1953. With Envelope - **$20 $50 $75**
Puzzle Only - **$8 $15 $35**

CIS-32

CIS-31

CIS-33

CIS-31. Photo,
1950s. Farm Crest Bakery. - **$15 $30 $75**

CIS-32. Plastic Tumbler,
1950s. Leatherwood Dairy. - **$15 $30 $75**

CIS-33. Glass Bowl,
1950s. Dairy product container. - **$10 $15 $25**

CIS-34

CIS-34. Tip-Top Bread Labels,
1950s. At least 28 in set. Each - **$5 $10 $15**

CIS-35

CIS-36

CIS-41. "Cisco Kid Ranchers Club" Member Kit,
1950s. Probable various breads. Includes two certificates, manual, application, "Cattle Brand" card.
Complete - **$75 $200 $350**

CIS-35. Tip-Top Bread Folder,
1950s.Tip-Top Bread. Eight pages. Holds 16 star bread labels. Large photo inside of Cisco holding gun. Bread labels tell story of Bolders & Bullet when completed. -
$50 $75 $150

CIS-36. Tip-Top Labels,
1950s. Tip-Top Bread. Bread labels were cut in shape of star to fit folder. Each - **$6 $10 $15**

CIS-42

CIS-43

CIS-42. TV "Sponsor's Name" 10x18" Cardboard Sample Store Sign,
1950s. - **$40 $75 $125**

CIS-43. "Cisco Kid" Silvered Brass Hat Ring,
1950s. Name on brim. - **$200 $425 $650**
Without Name - **$10 $20 $30**

CIS-37

CIS-38

CIS-44

CIS-45

CIS-44. "TV Channel 10" Member Cello. Button,
1950s. Dolly Madison and Aristocrat. Comes with beige or green background. Green - **$25 $50 $75**
Beige - **$40 $90 $140**

CIS-45. "Cisco Kid" Silvered Brass Keychain Fob,
1950s. Store item stamped "Japan". - **$15 $25 $40**

CIS-37. Photo Cards,
1950s. Tip-Top Bread but various sponsors.
Each - **$5 $15 $25**

CIS-38. Cardboard Clicker Gun,
1950s. Dr. Swetts beverages but various sponsors. -
$20 $35 $60

CLARA, LU 'N' EM

This low-key comedy about three gossipy housewives was created by three Northwestern University coeds to amuse their sorority sisters. After graduation they took it to Chicago radio station WGN, which ran it locally in 1930-1931 and then as an evening program on NBC until 1932 when it became the nation's first daytime soap opera. The sponsor was Colgate. The program ran until 1936 and was revived for a short run on CBS in 1942 for Pillsbury flour.

CIS-39

CIS-40

CIS-39. Cardboard Clicker Gun,
1950s. Tip-Top Bread. - **$15 $30 $60**

CIS-40. Shopping Mall Photo,
1950s. Printed for "Thruway Plaza," likely various mall sponsors. - **$12 $20 $35**

CLN-1

CIS-41

CLN-1. Cast Member Photo,
c. 1932. Fan photo 5x7" black and white with facsimile first name signature of each. - **$15 $25 $40**

CLN-2

CLN-2. Certificate and Mailer,
1932. Radio premium. Beautiful cardboard membership certificate for Ladies Liberty Order. - **$25 $50 $100** Mailer - **$10 $20 $30**

CLN-3

CLN-3. Newspaper,
1932. Radio premium. The Ladies Clarion Blast - Vol. #1. - **$20 $50 $75**

CLN-4

CLN-4. "Clara, Lu' n' Em" Puzzle,
c. 1933. Colgate. Envelope - **$5 $10 $25** Puzzle - **$20 $50 $75**

CLYDE BEATTY

Clyde Beatty (1903-1965), world-famous wild animal trapper and trainer, played himself in two chapter plays: *The Lost Jungle* for Mascot in 1934 and *Darkest Africa* for Republic in 1936. In both he defeats hostile forces, human and animal, and wins the girl. His *Clyde Beatty Show* on radio, on the other hand, was said to dramatize actual incidents from his life in the wild and at his circus. The program was syndicated in the late 1940s and ran on the Mutual network from 1950 to 1952, sponsored by Kellogg's cereal. Scattered comic book appearances included a 1937 giveaway by Malto-Meal and a 1956 giveaway by Richfield Oil.

CLY-1

CLY-2

CLY-1. Lion Head Brass Ring,
1935. Quaker Wheat Crackels. Unmarked Clyde Beatty premium. - **$200 $350 $500**

CLY-2. Jungle Animal Brass Link Charm Bracelet,
1935. Scarce. Quaker Wheat Crackels. Unmarked Clyde Beatty premium. - **$75 $200 $350**

CLY-3

CLY-3. "Clyde Beatty & His Wild Animal Act" Punch-Out Album,
1935. Scarce. Quaker Wheat Crackels. Made by Fold-A-Way Toys. Unpunched - **$100 $250 $400**

CLY-4

CLY-5

CLY-4. Quaker Oats Circus Book,
1935. Inside front offers punch-out animal act, lion head ring, jungle bracelet, bullwhip. - **$20 $50 $75**

CLY-5. "Cole Bros. Circus" Cello. Button,
1930s. - **$8 $12 $25**

CLY-6

CLY-7

CLY-6. Circus Souvenir Cello. Button,
1930s. - **$10 $20 $30**

CLY-7. "Hingees" Punch-Out Kit In Envelope,
1945. Store item. Unused - **$25 $40 $75**

COCA-COLA

Since the mid-1890s, Coca-Cola has distributed premiums in staggering numbers and almost every conceivable material and variety. What started as a patent medicine tonic soon evolved into a soda fountain or bottled drink sold in more than 160 countries globally. Coca-Cola premiums never lack for distinct self-advertising but over the years have frequently been related to war, entertainment and comic characters, sports, toy trucks, educational materials and much more. Hundreds of items intended originally as only convenience items to stores and customers now swell the ranks of advertising collectibles. The quantity of Coca-Cola premiums issued in the past century have resulted in several reference books devoted solely to this output.

COC-1

COC-1. Cello. Note Pad,
1902. Front cover has full color portrait, back has art illustrating sales growth 1886-1901. - **$150 $300 $500**

COC-2. Cardboard Baseball Score Counter,
c. 1907. - **$20 $40 $60**

COC-3   COC-4

COC-3. Cello. Pocket Mirror,
1909. Illustration by Hamilton King. - **$150 $250 $500**

COC-4. Cello. Pocket Mirror,
1917. Pictures World War I era girl. - **$150 $250 $500**

COC-5   COC-6

COC-5. "Toonerville Refreshment Palace" Leaflet,
1931. From a series for distribution by salesman. - **$15 $30 $45**

COC-6. Cleveland Press "Big Wheels Club" Cello. Button,
1930s. - **$15 $25 $40**

COC-7   COC-8

COC-7. "Bottlers Club" Cello. Button,
1930s. - **$40 $85 $150**

COC-8. Warplane 13x15" Cardboard Sign,
1943. From series bordered in white and gold. Each - **$20 $40 $60**

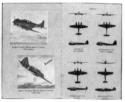

COC-9

COC-9. "Know Your War Planes" Booklet,
c. 1943. Coca-Cola. - **$20 $50 $75**

COC-10

COC-10. Warplane Cards,
1943. Set of 20. Set - **$40 $80 $125**

COC-11   COC-12   COC-13

COC-11. Warplane 13x15" Cardboard Sign,
1943. From series bordered in simulated wood. Each - **$20 $40 $60**

COC-12. Felt Fabric Beanie,
1940s. - **$20 $50 $75**

COC-13. "Kit Carson" Tie With Clasp,
c. 1951. 15" bolo tie with 1" brass slide clasp with TV portrayer Bill Williams portrait flanked by image of single Coca-Cola bottle. - **$40 $80 $125**

COC-14

COC-15

COC-16

COC 14. "Kit Carson Kerchief" 16x24" Cardboard Store Poster,
1953. Coca-Cola. - **$25 $75 $150**

COC-15. "Kit Carson" Fabric Kerchief,
1953. Picturing Bill Williams, TV series star. -
$15 $25 $50

COC-16. TV Promo,
1953. Four page Coca Cola premium. Tells about Old West and Kit Carson background. Talks about design of Kit Carson Kerchief premium. Promotes TV show "Adventures of Kit Carson." - **$15 $40 $75**

COC-17

COC-17. Stagecoach,
1953. Coca Cola TV premium. In mailer w/ complete instructions. - **$50 $100 $150**

COC-18

COC-19

COC-20

COC-18. "hi fi Club" Member Litho. Button,
c. 1959. - **$12 $18 $30**

COC-19. Celluloid 9" Wall Sign,
1950s. - **$40 $65 $125**

COC-20. Plastic Cooler Replica,
c. 1950s. 4x4x5" wide. - **$35 $75 $110**

COC-21

COC-22

COC-23

COC-21. Diecut 5' Standee,
1960s. - **$75 $200 $400**

COC-22. Christmas Elf Cloth Doll,
1980s. - **$15 $25 $35**

COC-23. Canadian 3" Cello. Endorsement Button,
1980s. By Coca-Cola Ltd. of Canada picturing Bill Cosby. -
$5 $10 $15

COMIC CHARACTER MISC.

Comic strip characters, particularly prior to World War II and the following early years of television, could almost be considered "family" to readers. No surprise, then, that advertisers sensed that premiums based on such familiar and well-loved characters would boost sales. Historically, the Yellow Kid and Buster Brown led the way. These and 73 others of intense popularity are listed in *Hake's Guide To Comic Character Collectibles* published in 1993, as well as other pages of this book. This section is devoted to comic characters that may have a large number of associated collectibles but relatively few offered as actual premiums.

COM-1

COM-1. "Little Sammy Sneeze" Book,
1905. Rare. By Winsor McCay. Rarely found better than very good. - **$500 $1800 $3300**

COM-2

COM-3

COM-2. Tad Dorgan "Tad's Joke Book",
1911. New York Sunday American. 10x12" Sunday supplement with 16 pages. - **$10 $30 $50**

COM-3. T. E. Powers "The Little Hatchet Joke Book",
c. 1911. New York Sunday American. 10x12" Sunday supplement with 16 pages. - **$10 $30 $50**

COM-4   COM-5

COM-4. T. E. Powers "Joy & Gloom Joke Book",
c. 1911. New York Sunday American. 10x12" Sunday supplement with 16 pages. - **$10 $30 $50**

COM-5. Gus Mager "The Monkey Joke Book",
1912. New York Sunday American. 10x12" Sunday supplement with 16 pages. - **$10 $30 $50**

COM-6   COM-7

COM-6. Jimmy Swinnerton "Swinnerton's Joke Book",
1912. New York Sunday American. 10x12" Sunday supplement with 16 pages. - **$10 $30 $50**

COM-7. T. E. Powers "Married Life Joke-Book",
1912. New York Sunday American. 10x12" Sunday supplement with 16 pages. - **$10 $30 $50**

(FRONT)   (BACK)

COM-8

COM-8. Pamphlet,
1922. Philadelphia Bulletin. 12 page premium."Jerry Muskrat Wins Respect." Harrison Cady art. - **$25 $50 $75**

COM-10   COM-11

COM-9

COM-9. Little Jimmy Writing Tablet,
1920s. Scarce. - **$20 $40 $80**

COM-10. Sunday Comic Section 7x11" Cardboard Sign With Jiggs,
c. 1920s. Boston Sunday Advertiser. - **$35 $65 $100**

COM-11. "Reg'lar Fellers" BLB,
1933. - **$10 $25 $50**

COM-12

COM-13   COM-14

COM-12. "Tillie The Toiler" Jigsaw Puzzle,
1933. Various newspapers supplement. - **$8 $12 $20**

COM-13. "Funnies on Parade" #1,
1933. Scarce. Probably the 1st regular format comic book. Proctor & Gamble giveaway. - **$1100 $3300 $11000**

COM-14. "Century of Comics" #1,
1933. Scarce. 100 pages. Probably the third comic book. Wheatena/Malt-O-Milk giveaway. - **$3400 $10200 $17500**

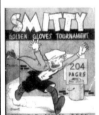

COM-15   COM-16

COM-15. "Smitty Golden Gloves Tournament" BLB,
1934. Cocomalt. - **$10 $25 $50**

COM-16. Sears, Roebuck "Funny Paper Puppets" Punch-Out Sheet,
1935. Unpunched - **$75 $200 $350**

COM-17

COM-18

COM-19

COM-17. "Tailspin Tommy In The Great Air Mystery/A Universal Picture " Cello. Button,
1935. For movie serial picturing cast members Clark Williams, Noah Beery, Jr., Jean Rogers. - **$30 $60 $100**

COM-18. "Tailspin Tommy Club" Cello. Button,
c. 1935. Evening Sun newspaper. - **$20 $40 $75**

COM-19. "Tailspin Tommy" Cello. Button,
c. 1935. Newark Star-Eagle. From series of newspaper contest buttons, match number to win prize. - **$5 $10 $15**

COM-20

COM-20. "Scrappy's Animated Puppet Theater" Punch-Out Kit,
1936. Pillsbury's Farina cereal.
Unpunched - **$30 $75 $125**

COM-21

COM-21. Red Falcon Adventures,
1937. Rare. 8 page comic premium, Seal Right Ice Cream.
Issue #1 - **$110 $265 $375**
Issues #2-#5 - **$65 $155 $265**
Issues #6-#10 - **$55 $135 $185**
Issues #11-#50 - **$30 $90 $130**

COM-22

COM-23

COM-24

COM-22. Federal Agent Fingerprint Outfit,
1938. Gold Medal toy. - **$30 $60 $120**

COM-23. Harold Teen Dummy Punchout 11x20",
1938. Rare. Malt-O-Meal Cereal premium. - **$150 $300 $500**

COM-24. Moon Mullins Dummy Punchout 11x20",
1938. Pure Oil premium. - **$75 $150 $250**

COM-25

COM-26

COM-27

COM-25. Harold Teen Bat-O-Ball,
1938. Morton Salt premium. - **$20 $40 $80**

COM-26. Lillums Bat-O-Ball,
1938. Morton Salt premium. - **$20 $40 $80**

COM-27. Shadow Bat-O-Ball,
1938. Morton Salt premium. - **$20 $40 $80**

COM-28

COM-28. "Sears Toyland" Christmas Comic Book,
1939. Scarce. Features Chicago Tribune Syndicate characters. - **$100 $250 $600**

COM-30

COM-29

COM-29. Junior G-Man Badge,
1930s. Large bronze color shield premium. - **$25 $50 $75**

COM-30. "Ella Cinders Spinner",
1930s. United Features Syndicate. Cello. over metal disk
that has underside center bump for spinning. -
$50 $100 $150

COM-31

COM-32

COM-31. "Moon Mullins" Pocketknife,
1930s. Imprinted for local sponsor. Cello. grip also pictures
comic strip sidebar characters Little Egypt and
Mushmouth. - **$35 $75 $150**

**COM-32. "Read America's Greatest Comics" Newsboy
Apron With Jiggs,**
1930s. Philadelphia Sunday Ledger. 13-1/2x18" canvas
fabric with neck strap and tie strings. - **$50 $150 $300**

COM-33

COM-34   COM-35

COM-33. Sky Pilot Pin Brass Wings,
1930s. - **$15 $40 $60**

**COM-34. Aviation Department Boy Flight Commander
Brass Badge,**
1930s. - **$20 $50 $75**

COM-35. Boy Chief of Police Brass Badge,
1930s. - **$20 $50 $75**

COM-36   COM-37

COM-38

COM-36. Fire Department Boy Chief Brass Badge,
1930s. - **$20 $50 $75**

COM-37. Junior Sheriff Brass Badge,
1930s. - **$15 $25 $50**

COM-38. Herby Cloth Doll,
1930s. Back view showing artist's facsimile signature on
leg area. - **$40 $80 $125**

COM-39

COM-39. World War II Promotion Civil Defense Book,
1942. Features Flash Gordon, Phantom, Blondie & others.
"Eat Right To WorkAnd Win." - **$30 $90 $240**

COM-40

**COM-40. "Smilin' Jack's Victory Bombers"
Assembly/Play Game,**
c. 1943. Store item by Plane Facts, Inc. - **$75 $250 $400**

COM-41

**COM-41. "Santa's Christmas Comic Variety Show"
Book,**
1943. Sears, Roebuck & Co. Features Dick Tracy, Orphan
Annie, Terry and the Pirates, many others. -
$50 $100 $250

COM-42

COM-43

COM-42. Kings Features Stationary Sheet,
1944. - **$10 $25 $50**

COM-43. Alley Oop (Test) Product Statuette,
1945. Rare. - **$750 $1500 $2750**
With club/handle that fits inside arm add **$100 $200 $300**

COM-44

COM-45

COM-44. Joe Palooka Matchbook,
1948. - **$10 $20 $40**

COM-45. "Black Cat" Comic Book Ad Matchbook,
1940s. Harvey Comics. - **$10 $20 $40**

COM-46

COM-47

COM-48

COM-49

COM-46. Royal Northwest Mounted Police Brass Badge,
1940s. Scarce. - **$30 $60 $120**

COM-47. Moon Mullins Cloth Doll,
1940s. - **$40 $80 $125**

COM-48. Smitty Cloth Doll,
1940s. - **$40 $80 $125**

COM-49. "New Funnies/Andy Panda" Cello. Button,
c. 1940s. New Funnies Comics. - **$50 $75 $150**

COM-50

COM-51

COM-50. C99 Ranch Gang Code Book,
1940s. Eight pages with decoder. Sponsor unknown. -
$15 $25 $35

COM-51. Billy West Promo Card,
1950. Scarce. - **$20 $50 $75**

(MAILER FOR #4)

COM-52

(MAILER FOR #5)

COM-52. Katy Keene Paper Dolls & Mailer,
1951. Comic premiums for Katy Keene #4 & #5. -
Each - **$50 $75 $125**

COM-53

COM-53. Metro Sunday Promo,
1951. Rare. Features 29 comic characters from Metro
Sunday newspapers. - **$200 $500 $850**

COM-54

COM-54. Funny Paper Hour Card,
1954. Denver Post. Birthday card premium. - **$10 $25 $35**

COM-55

COM-56

COM-55. Sparky's Fire Dept. Inspector Silvered Brass Badge,
1950s. - **$20 $40 $60**

COM-56. Jon Hall Ramar Of Jungle Membership Card,
1950s. Rare. Membership card for Safari Scouts. 2 cards attached with code and order form for badge and tattoos. - **$25 $50 $75**

COUNTERSPY

Washington calling David Harding, Counterspy! In 1942, with the nation at war, the call was answered. One of radio's long-running adventure series, *Counterspy* aired on ABC, NBC or Mutual from 1942 to 1957. With Don MacLaughlin as the ace agent, Counterspy fought Axis enemies during the war and other security threats once the war was won. Sponsors over the years included Mail Pouch chewing tobacco, Schutter Candies, Pepsi-Cola and Gulf Oil.

COU-1

COU-1. Pepsi-Cola 8x19" Paper Store Sign,
1949. - **$50 $100 $150**

COU-2

COU-3

COU-4

COU-2. Club Member Certificate,
1949. Scarce. Pepsi-Cola. For "Counter-Spy Junior Agents Club". - **$15 $50 $75**

COU-3. Junior Agent Glow-In-Dark Brass Badge,
1949. Pepsi-Cola. Centered by plastic lens over bw glow portrait. - **$25 $45 $75**

COU-4. Matchbook,
1940s. Old Nick candy bars. - **$10 $30 $60**

COU-5

COU-5. "Junior Counterspy" Activity Booklet,
1951. Gulf Oil. Story pages feature David Harding, Counterspy. - **$10 $25 $40**

CRACKER JACK

This blend of popcorn, peanuts and molasses candy has been a best-selling snack food for about 100 years. F. W. Rueckheim, a German immigrant, had opened a small popcorn stand in Chicago in 1872. He sold the first version of his candy combination at the 1893 Columbian Exposition; the product proved to be popular, but the kernels stuck together. By 1896 the company had found not only a process to keep the kernels separate, but also a name--cracker jack was a new slang term for excellent or superior, and F. W. promptly trademarked it for his sweet.

By 1899 Cracker Jack was being packaged in a waxed-sealed box to keep it fresh, by 1902 it was listed in the Sears catalogue and in 1908 it became part of sports Americana in the song *Take Me Out to the Ball Game*. A happy customer is said to have contributed the company slogan, The More You Eat, The More You Want. In 1910 the company started inserting coupons in the packages to be traded in for prizes and two years later the coupons were replaced by the prizes themselves.

Since 1912 every package has contained a toy surprise inside. Sailor Jack, modeled after F. W.'s grandson, appeared in advertisements in 1916 with his dog Bingo and made it onto the box in 1919. The company was sold to Borden in 1972 and today Cracker Jack, still with a toy in every box, is marketed worldwide.

CRJ-1

CRJ-2

CRJ-1. Early Sample Box,
c. 1896. 1x1-3/4x2-3/4" long sample container for "Reliable Confections" by "F. W. Rueckheim & Bro.," Chicago. Trademark registration date is March 24, 1896 and precedes the added "Eckstein" partnership designation of 1902. - **$125 $250 $500**

CRJ-2. "The Cracker Jack Bears" Postcard,
1907. Example from set of 16. - **$12 $20 $30**

CRJ-3

CRJ-4

CRJ-3. Portrait Cello. Button,
c. 1908. With "Cracker Jack" back paper. One of a series also issued by tobacco companies. - **$20 $40 $60**

CRJ-4. "Cracker Jack" Wagon In White Metal,
c. 1910. Scarce. Metal has gold luster and wagon interior has cardboard insert floor. Horse's legs are usually broken. - **$75 $150 $250**

CRJ-5

CRJ-5. "Cracker Jack Riddles" Booklet,
c. 1920s. - **$15 $30 $60**

CRJ-6

CRJ-7

CRJ-6. "Cracker Jack Drawing Book",
c. 1920s. - **$20 $30 $60**

CRJ-7. Miniature Litho. Tin Wagon,
c. 1920s. - **$25 $65 $110**

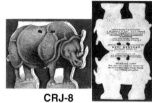

CRJ-8

CRJ-9

CRJ-8. Rhinoceros Paper Prize,
c. 1920s. From set of 16 "Jumping Animals" to fold. Each - **$35 $75 $125**

CRJ-9. "Cracker Jack/The Famous Confection" Top,
c. 1920s. Silver finish with incised lettering and slightly thicker metal than later versions. - **$40 $75 $125**

CRJ-10

CRJ-10. Cardboard String Toy,
c. 1920s. - **$25 $60 $90**

CRJ-11

CRJ-11. Chicago World's Fair Miniature Booklet,
1933. Ten pictures. - **$40 $80 $175**

CRJ-12

CRJ-13   CRJ-14

CRJ-12. "Magnetic Fortune Teller" With Envelope,
c. 1930s. Gold printing on thin cellophane of various solid colors. - **$15 $25 $50**

CRJ-13. Litho. Tin Spinner Top,
c. 1930s. - **$15 $25 $40**

CRJ-14. Litho. Tin Top,
c. 1930s. - **$10 $20 $35**

CRJ-15

CRJ-16

CRJ-15. Toy Cart,
c. 1930s. Litho. tin with wood shaft. - **$10 $20 $30**

CRJ-16. Beanie,
1930s. Rare. Wool Beanie with bell on spring. -
$50 $100 $175

CRJ-17

CRJ-18

CRJ-19

CRJ-17. Tin Litho. Pocketwatch Replica,
c. 1930s. - **$20 $40 $75**

CRJ-18. Aluminum Snapper,
1930s. - **$10 $25 $35**

CRJ-19. Tin Litho. Standup,
1930s. From a set of 10: Chester, Harold Teen, Herby,
Kayo, Moon Mullins, Orphan Annie, Perry, Skeezix,
Smitty, Uncle Walt. Each - **$35 $65 $100**

CRJ-20

CRJ-21

**CRJ-20. "The Cracker Jack Line" Litho. Tin Train
Engine,**
1930s. - **$40 $75 $125**

CRJ-21. Litho. Tin Delivery Truck,
1930s. - **$40 $75 $125**

CRJ-22

**CRJ-22. "Tune In With Cracker Jack" Litho. Tin
Miniature Desk Radio Replica,**
1930s. Scarce. - **$65 $140 $200**

CRJ-23

**CRJ-23. "Free Comic Valentine" 9x26" Paper Store
Sign,**
Late 1930s. Pictures examples from believed set of 25
given individually by purchase of individual boxes. -
$75 $150 $300

CRJ-24

CRJ-25

CRJ-24. "Cracker Jack Shows" Tin Circus Wagon,
c. 1930s. Depicts caged lion on each side. -
$30 $60 $100

CRJ-25. Diecut Paper Frog,
1930s. - **$20 $40 $75**

CRJ-26

CRJ-27

CRJ-28

CRJ-26. Tin Miniature Book Bank,
1930s. - **$50 $80 $150**

CRJ-27. Tin Bank,
c. 1930s. Brass luster. - **$25 $50 $75**

CRJ-28. Litho. Tin Diecut Bookmark,
1930s. One of scarcer in series. - **$15 $30 $60**

CRJ-29

CRJ-30

CRJ-31

CRJ-29. Litho. Tin Fortune Wheel,
1930s. Reveals fortune words by revolving upper disk to
spell name of fortune-seeker. - **$15 $25 $40**

CRJ-30. Paper Fortune Wheel,
c. 1930s. Similar design and function to litho. tin version. -
$10 $20 $35

CRJ-31. "Cracker Jack Air Corps" Dark Metal Wings,
1930s. Lapel stud reverse. - **$ 15 $30 $50**

CRJ-32

CRJ-32. "Cracker Jack" Transfer Sheet Set,
1940s. 25 in set. - **$50 $125 $200**

CRJ-33

CRJ-34

CRJ-33. "Midget Auto Race" Paper Prize,
1940s. - **$15 $25 $40**

CRJ-34. Baseball Card Sheet 8x11".
1991. Uncut 36 card sheet with miniature replicas of Topps
Gum "40 Years Of Baseball" cards. Uncut - **$25 $50 $75**

DAN DUNN

Detective Dan began in 1933, and after the first issue
sold poorly, the title was changed. Norman Marsh created this popular comic strip, now called *Dan Dunn,
Secret Operative 48*, for the Publishers' Syndicate.
Offered as a low-cost alternative to *Dick Tracy*, the
strip ran daily and Sunday for 10 years, appearing in
as many as 135 newspapers. The hard-boiled Dunn,
along with his sidekick Irwin Higgs, his dog Wolf, and
an orphan girl named Babs, fought urban crime and
such arch-fiends as Wu Fang and Eviloff. At the height
of its popularity in the 1930s the strip was reprinted in
Big Little Books and in several comic books. Two
issues of *Dan Dunn*, a dime novel pulp, were published
in 1936, and a radio version of *Dan Dunn, Secret
Operative 48* was syndicated in 1944.

DUN-1

DUN-2

DUN-1. Detective Dan Button,
1933. Rare. First comic book character club premium. The
club was canceled after the first issue of *Detective Dan*
failed. - **$600 $750 $1000**

DUN-2. "Dan Dunn Detective Magazine" First Issue,
1936. Vol. 1 #1 monthly issue for September. -
$50 $100 $150

DUN-3

DUN-4

**DUN-3. "Dan Dunn/Secret Operative 48 And The
Counterfeiter Ring" Booklet,**
1938. From "Buddy Book" ice cream cone series printed by
Whitman. 126 pages in Big Little Book format with page art
reprinted from comic strips. - **$20 $50 $80**

**DUN-4. "Dan Dunn Plays A Lone Hand" Whitman
Penny Book,**
1938. - **$8 $15 $25**

DUN-5

DUN-6

DUN-7

DUN-5. "Dan Dunn Junior Operative" Cello. Button,
1930s. - **$75 $125 $200**

**DUN-6. "Dan Dunn Detective Corps/Secret Operative
48" Badge,**
1930s. Probably a newspaper promotion item. Silvered tin
shield with embossed lettering. - **$20 $40 $60**

DUN-7. Dan Dunn "I'm Operative 48" Cello. Button,
1930s. Philadelphia Evening Ledger Comics. From colorful
series depicting Ledger comic strip characters. -
$50 $75 $125

DANIEL BOONE

Dan'l Boone (1734-1820), legendary Kentucky frontiersman, hunter, farmer and wilderness scout, was
brought to life by 20th Century-Fox in a successful
adventure series on CBS-TV from 1964 to 1970. The
show starred Fess Parker, who a decade earlier had
found fame playing Davy Crockett on the *Disneyland*
series. The stories were centered on Boone's
Kentucky settlement days, his expeditions and his
struggles with the Indians. Other featured actors
included Patricia Blair, Ed Ames, Albert Salmi and
Roosevelt Grier. Merchandised items are usually copy-

righted by 20th Century-Fox TV. An hour-long animated TV special sponsored by Kenner toys premiered on CBS in 1981 with Richard Crenna as the voice of Boone.

DNL-1

DNL-2

DNL-1. Picture,
1963. Cut-out premium found on back of Frosted Flakes box. - **$10 $25 $35**

DNL-2. Fess Parker As Daniel Boone 5" Hard Plastic Doll,
1964. American Tradition Co. Store item. Accessories of fur hat, plastic rifle and strap with bag and powder horn. - **$35 $60 $125**

DNL-3

DNL-3. Trail Blazers Game,
1964. N.B.C. tie-in with Milton Bradley. Includes Trail Blazers Club application. - **$20 $40 $75**

DNL-4

DNL-4. Vinyl Zippered Pencil Case,
1964. Fess Parker/Daniel Boone Trail Blazers Club. Includes NBC premium leaflet offering wallet, ring binder, kaboodle kit, etc. - **$10 $20 $35**

DNL-5

DNL-6

DNL-5. "Fess Parker As Daniel Boone" Vinyl Wallet,
1964. N.B.C. Holds miniature magic slate and four photos from TV series. - **$15 $30 $50**

DNL-6. "Official Daniel Boone Fess Parker Woodland Whistle",
c. 1964. Autolite. - **$20 $40 $60**

DNL-7

DNL-7. "TV Channels" Cover Article,
1969. Weekly issue for July 6 of schedule guide supplement to Baltimore News American. - **$5 $10 $15**

DAVEY ADAMS, SON OF THE SEA

Details on this pre-World War II radio drama starring Franklin Adams are scarce but the program offered listeners membership in the DASC, the Davey Adams Shipmates Club, along with such premiums as a siren ring, a secret compartment members badge and a manual showing sailor knots and marine codes. Lava soap was the sponsor of this short-lived 1939 series.

DVM-1

DVM-2

DVM-1. Club Charter Member Certificate,
1939. Scarce. Lava soap. - **$25 $50 $75**

DVM-2. Club Letter,
1939. Lava soap. Offers Secret Compartment Shipmate's Badge. - **$5 $12 $20**

DVM-3

DVM-4

DVM-3. "D.A.S.C." Siren Ring,
1939. Scarce. Initials for "Davey Adams Shipmates Club." - **$200 $375 $600**

DVM-4. Shipmates Club Brass Decoder Badge,
1939. Lava Soap. Decoder wheel front, back has secret
compartment. - **$60 $125 $250**

DVM-5

**DVM-5. "Davey Adams Shipmates" Club Kit With
Pencil,**
c. 1939. Pan American Airways. Mailing envelope containing Radiogram bulletin, Secret Flying Orders booklet,
mechanical pencil with secret compartment, all identified
by sponsor name. Near Mint Complete - **$550**
Pencil - **$50 $100 $150**
Each Paper Item - **$25 $50 $75**

DAVY CROCKETT

Frontier scout, Indian fighter, bear killer, congress-
man, statesman, martyred at the Alamo--Davy Crockett
(1786-1836) was a natural for television. Five fictionalized episodes from his life were broadcast on the
Disneyland series on ABC in 1954 and 1955, starring
Fess Parker in a coonskin cap and carrying his trusty
rifle Old Betsy. Parker became an instant star, Crockett
became an idol to an estimated 40 million viewers, *The
Ballad Of Davy Crockett* landed on the *Hit Parade* and
a merchandising mania swept the country. Some 500
products were licensed by Disney--toys, games, rifles,
books, lunch boxes, costumes, coonskin caps--and
unlicensed merchandise capitalizing on the craze followed in great profusion. Disney re-edited the films
and released them to theaters as *Davy Crockett, King
of the Wild Frontier* in 1955 and *Davy Crockett and the
River Pirates* in 1956 and the original episodes were
rebroadcast a half-dozen times over the next 20 years.
An animated TV special sponsored by Kenner toys
aired on CBS in 1976.

DVY-1

DVY-1. Gimbel's Club Kit In Mailer Envelope,
1955. Gimbel's department store. Disney authorized con-
tents include photo and member card.
Near Mint In Mailer - **$90**
Photo - **$15 $25 $40**
Card - **$8 $15 $25**

DVY-2

**DVY-2. "Davy Crockett In The Raid At Piney Creek"
Comic,**
1955. American Motors give-away. - **$10 $20 $45**

(ENLARGED VIEW)

DVY-3

DVY-3. "Frontier Action Ring" On Card,
1955. Karo Syrup. Plastic ring holds flicker portrait.
On Card - **$160 $300 $450**
Loose - **$150 $225 $300**

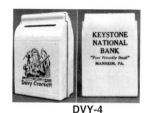 

DVY-4

DVY-5

DVY-4. Plastic Bank,
c. 1955. Various local sponsors. - **$10 $20 $35**

DVY-5. Ceramic Cookie Jar,
c. 1955. Store item. - **$150 $250 $400**

DVY-6

DVY-6. Frosted Glass,
c. 1955. Farmers Dairy Milk Ice Cream. - **$8 $15 $25**

DVY-8

DVY-7

DVY-7. "Candies And Toy" Box,
c. 1955. Super Novelty Candy Co. with Disney copyright.
Cut-out cards on box back. Uncut Box - **$10 $40 $80**

DVY-8. "Davy Crockett Cookies" Box,
1950s. Federal Sweets & Biscuit Co. - **$25 $60 $125**

DVY-9   DVY-10

DVY-9. "Frontier Bread" Waxed Paper Bread Wrapper,
1950s. - **$15 $30 $50**

DVY-10. Coonskin Cap Punch-Out Sheet,
1950s. Nabisco. With simulated fur design.
Unused With Tail - **$15 $30 $60**

DVY-11

DVY-11. Cardboard Money Saver,
1950s. Various sponsors. - **$12 $20 $35**

DVY-12   DVY-13   DVY-14

DVY-12. Deed of Land,
1950s. Scarce. - **$30 $75 $100**

DVY-13. "Jackson Daily News Fan Club" 2-1/4" Cello. Button,
1950s. - **$35 $75 $125**

DVY-14. "Davy Crockett Frontier Club" Cello. Button,
1950s. - **$20 $35 $ 60**

DVY-15   DVY-16   DVY-17

DVY-15. "Big Yank Frontiersman" Litho. Button,
1950s. Clothing company. - **$10 $20 $30**

DVY-16. "Pfeifers Davy Crockett Fan Club" Litho. Button,
1950s. - **$20 $40 $80**

DVY-17. "King Of The Wild Frontier" Cello. Button,
1950s. Disney authorized. - **$10 $20 $40**

DVY-18   DVY-19   DVY-20   DVY-21

DVY-18. "Frontiersman" Litho. Button,
1950s. Disney authorized. - **$15 $30 $50**

DVY-19. "Walt Disney's Davy Crockett" Metal Compass Ring,
1950s. Peter Pan Peanut Butter. - **$150 $275 $400**

DVY-20. "Frontier Club" Litho. Tab,
1950s. - **$15 $30 $45**

DVY-21. Fess Parker/Crockett English Metal Badge,
1950s. Store item by "DCMT Ltd." of England. Silver finish,
red lettering, black/white insert photo. - **$20 $50 $80**

DVY-22   DVY-23

DVY-22. Leatherette Jacket,
1950s. Store bought. TV merchandise - **$50 $100 $225**

DVY-23. Composition Bobbing Head,
1950s. Store item. - **$75 $125 $200**

DC COMICS

Former pulp magazine writer and army cavalry officer Major Malcolm Wheeler Nicholson published the first issue of *New Fun* (subsequent issues became *More Fun*) in 1935. Tabloid size with a full color cover and 32 black and white pages, it was the first comic book with original material in a Sunday comic page format. Although he wasn't making any money, the Major added *New Comics* (later to become *Adventure Comics* late in 1935). Most notable is that these two titles featured art by Walt Kelly as well as stories by Jerry Siegel and Joe Shuster in their pre-Superman days.

Next came *Detective Comics* in early 1937. The Major was so broke by now he was forced to take a partner, his printer. The new company was called Detective Comics, Inc. or DC Comics. Nicholson left soon afterwards. The new owners decided to add another title, *Action Comics*. Editor Vincent Sullivan was looking for new material when he saw samples of Superman by co-workers Siegel and Shuster. He decided to use the character. *Action* #1 debuted in June 1938 and the comic book world was changed forever.

Sullivan also edited *Detective Comics* and after he suggested artist Bob Kane come up with something, Batman came out in issue #27 in 1939. Within one year editor Vincent Sullivan oversaw the beginnings of the two greatest comic book characters to ever see print. These characters are covered in their own sections while this section touches on additional DC characters.

DCM-1

DCM-1. "Boy Commandos" Transfers Pack,
1948. DC Comics copyright. Store packet of transfer pictures based on comic book military cartoon characters. - **$50 $125 $200**

DCM-2   DCM-3   DCM-4

DCM-2. "Green Lantern" 3-1/2" Cello. Button,
1966. #13 from series. Near Mint Bagged - **$35**
Loose - **$10 $15 $25**

DCM-3. "Aquaman" 3-1/2" Cello. Button,
1966. #15 from series. Near Mint Bagged - **$35**
Loose - **$10 $15 $25**

DCM-4. "Hawkman" 3-1/2" Cello. Button,
1966. #16 from series. Near Mint Bagged - **$35**
Loose - **$10 $15 $25**

DCM-5

DCM-5. Super Powers Metal Lunch Box,
1983. Aladdin Industries, Inc. Features Superman, Batman and Wonder Woman. - **$20**

DCM-6

DCM-6. "DC/Keebler President's Drug Awareness Campaign" Kit,
1983. Various paper items including those with facsimile endorsement signature of Nancy Reagan.
Complete - **$5 $10 $15**

DCM-7   DCM-8

DCM-7. Green Lantern Glow-In-Dark Plastic Ring,
1992. DC Comics re-introduction of the character. - **$1 $2 $4**

DCM-8. Justice League Of America Litho. Button,
1997. - **$1 $2 $3**

DCM-9   DCM-10

DCM-9. Zero Hour Litho. Tin Tab,
1994. From mini series.
Unbent - **$1 $2 $3**

DCM-10. "U.S." (Uncle Sam) Comics Cello. Promo Button,
1997. DC/Vertigo mini series. - **$1 $2 $3**

DEATH VALLEY DAYS

One of the earliest radio dramas, *Death Valley Days* premiered on NBC in 1930. The stories of miners and homesteaders in the California desert, told by a character called the Old Ranger, were based on actual happenings and the show earned a reputation for historical accuracy. The program moved to CBS in 1941 and evolved into *Death Valley Sheriff* and then *The Sheriff* in 1945 when it aired on ABC. It ended its long radio life in 1951, sponsored from the beginning by 20 Mule Team Borax and Boraxo soap products. A syndicated television adaptation ran for 558 episodes, from 1952 to 1975, with Ronald Reagan, Robert Taylor, Dale Robertson or Merle Haggard playing the Old Ranger. The series has been rerun under a variety of titles.

DTH-1   DTH-2

DTH-1. "Radio Stars" Leaflet,
1930. Pictures John White, Old Ranger, Virginia Gardiner. - **$8 $15 $25**

DTH-2. "Death Valley Days" Storybook,
1931. - **$5 $15 $25**

DTH-4

DTH-3

DTH-3. "Old Ranger's Yarns Of Death Valley" Magazine,
1933. - **$5 $15 $25**

DTH-4. "Hauling 20 Mule Team Borax Out Of Death Valley" Puzzle,
1933. - **$15 $30 $60**

DTH-5

DTH-6

DTH-5. "Picture Sheet" Newspaper Style Folder Promoting Radio Show,
1933. - **$8 $20 $25**

DTH-6. "Death Valley Days" Charles Marshall Song Book,
1934. - **$5 $15 $25**

DTH-7   DTH-8

DTH-7. "Cowboy Songs As Sung By John White...",
1934. - **$5 $15 $25**

DTH-8. "Death Valley Tales" Storybook,
1934. - **$5 $15 $25**

DTH-9   DTH-10

DTH-9. "The World's Biggest Job" Radio Broadcast Script With Cover Folder And Envelope,
1935. For April 11 episode about construction of Boulder Dam. - **$10 $20 $40**

DTH-10. "High Spots Of Death Valley Days" Vol. 1 #1 Booklet With Envelope,
1939. Includes six previous broadcast stories plus radio script for May 19, 1939 episode.
Booklet - **$10 $20 $40**
Envelope - **$3 $10 $15**

DTH-11

DTH-11. Old Ranger Seed Packets With Mailer,
1939. Pacific Coast Borax Co.
Each - **$20 $40 $65**
Mailer - **$25 $50 $75**

DTH-12

DTH-13

DTH-12. "Old Ranger" Fan Postcard,
1930s. Pacific Coast Borax Co. Text for weekly broadcasts on NBC Blue Network in East and Red Network in West with back text for "Death Valley Days" program title. - **$5 $10 $15**

DTH-13. "20 Mule Team" Model Kit,
1950s. Borax. Issued for many years from the 1950s through 1970s. Packaged in one or two boxes. Near Mint In Box - **$35**

DELL COMICS

Dell Publishing Company founder George Delacorte started in the comic book business in 1929 with *The Funnies,* a 24-page weekly tabloid with eight pages in color, all original features and a ten cent price. 36 issues appeared, then Delacorte tried a few black and white titles in the early 1930s. Late in 1935 he introduced *Popular Comics,* the first Sunday comic page reprint title to compete with *Famous Funnies.* This proved successful enough for Delacorte to begin *The Funnies,* using the title a second time, the summer of 1936. Both titles used original material in conjunction with reprints. Next came *The Comics* in March 1937. The Four Color series began in 1939. Delacorte really began rolling in 1940 as Dell published *Walt Disney's Comics and Stories,* followed by *Looney Tunes and Merrie Melodies* in 1941 and original stories featuring Captain Midnight and Andy Panda in *The Funnies* of 1942. *Four Color* #9 (the first Donald Duck comic with original story and art) appeared in 1942. Carl Barks, Walt Kelly, *Marge's Little Lulu, The Lone Ranger, Roy Rogers, Gene Autry, Tarzan* and a host of others appeared in comics with the Dell logo. Many paper premiums to promote comic book subscriptions are listed in this book under sections for specific characters.

DEL-1

DEL-2

DEL-1. Dell Characters 8x10" Color Print,
1950. - **$50 $125 $225**

DEL-2. "KE" Plastic Puzzle Game,
1952. Played by pegs with "Secret Formula" instruction sheet. Complete Puzzle Only - **$10 $40 $60**

DEL-3

DEL-3. Comic Book Rack 6x15" Litho. Tin Sign,
c. 1950. Display attachment picturing 13 Dell Comics characters. - **$100 $250 $500**

DEL-4

DEL-4. Club Membership Card,
1952. - **$8 $15 $30**

DEL-5

DEL-5. Dell Comic Club Promo & Club Card,
1953. Scarce. Barks cover. Folder - **$25 $75 $125**
Card - **$10 $30 $50**

DEL-6

DEL-7

DEL-6. "Walt Disney Comics And Stories" Christmas Gift Subscription Certificate,
c. 1950s. - **$20 $60 $100**

DEL-7. "Official Dell Comics Club/Member" Aluminum Cased Lincoln Penny,
1950s. Pictured example has 1953 penny, rim inscription "Keep Me And You Will Have Good Luck". - **$8 $12 $20**

DENNIS THE MENACE

Mischief-maker supreme, Dennis the Menace made his first appearance as a daily cartoon panel in 1951 and as a Sunday page the following year. Based on cartoonist Hank Ketcham's own son, Dennis, trailed by his dog Ruff, has been harassing his suburban neighborhood ever since. Frequent victims include his parents, Henry and Alice Mitchell and their neighbor, cantankerous George Wilson. The strip has been a consistent winner, so much so that the title itself has entered the language. Many paperback and hardcover reprints have been published and the first of many Dennis comic books appeared in 1953. A prime-time television series starring Jay North as Dennis ran on CBS from 1959 to 1963 and was rerun on NBC from 1963 to 1965. Most merchandised items are related to the comic strip; those based on the TV series are usually copyrighted by Screen Gems Inc.

DNS-1

DNS-2

DNS-1. "Dennis The Menace On Safety" Booklet,
1956. National Safety Council. - **$5 $10 $25**

DNS-2. Spoon Offer Kellogg's Sugar Pops Cereal Box,
1961. - **$40 $100 $180**

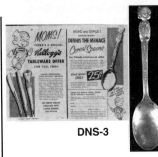

DNS-3

DNS-4

DNS-3. Spoon Ad Paper With Silver Plate Spoon,
1961. Kellogg's Rice Krispies. Ad - **$3 $5 $8**
Spoon - **$5 $10 $20**

DNS-4. "Dennis The Menace Takes A Poke At Poison",
1961. Food and Drug Administration.
Original 1961 Edition - **$1 $3 $6**
Later Reprints - **$1 $2 $4**

DNS-5

DNS-6

DNS-5. "Cast Your Ballot" Litho. Button,
1968. Sears. - **$8 $12 $20**

DNS-6. Fan Photo,
1960s. - **$5 $10 $15**

DNS-7

DNS-8

DNS-7. "..And Away We Go!" Comic Book,
1970. Caladryl medication. - **$1 $3 $6**

DNS-8. Joey From Dennis The Menace 2-1/4" Cello. Ad Button,
1972. Dairy Queen. - **$5 $10 $15**

DNS-9

DNS-10

DNS-9. Dennis The Menace Plastic Assembly Ring,
1970s. Dairy Queen. From same series as next three items picturing characters from "Ketcham" copyright comic strip. Parts separate for ring assembly.
Near Mint Unfolded On Tree - **$100**
Assembled - **$40 $60 $80**

DNS-10. Joey From Dennis The Menace Plastic Assembly Ring,
1970s. Dairy Queen. Near Mint Unfolded On Tree - **$100**
Assembled - **$40 $60 $80**

DNS-11   DNS-12

DNS-11. Margaret From Dennis The Menace Plastic Assembly Ring,
1970s. Dairy Queen.
Near Mint Unfolded On Tree - **$100**
Assembled - **$40 $60 $80**

DNS-12. Ruff From Dennis The Menace Plastic Assembly Ring,
1970s. Dairy Queen. Near Mint Unfolded On Tree - **$100**
Assembled - **$40 $60 $80**

DETECTIVES BLACK AND BLUE

Adventures of Detectives Black and Blue, an early syndicated comedy crime show from Los Angeles radio station KHJ, aired from 1932 to 1934. The series followed the adventures of a pair of shipping clerks/amateur sleuths in their bumbling attempts at criminology. "Detec-a-tives Black and Blue, good men tried and true."

DTC-1   DTC-2   DTC-3

DTC-1. Fabric Double-Billed Detective Cap,
c. 1932. Iodent toothpaste. Front bill names radio show and sponsor. - **$20 $40 $65**

DTC-2. "Detectives Black & Blue/Iodent Toothpaste" Brass Badge,
c. 1932. - **$20 $50 $85**

DTC-3. "Detectives Black & Blue/Folger's Coffee" Brass Badge,
c. 1932. - **$20 $50 $85**

DEVIL DOGS OF THE AIR

The combination early in 1935 of a Warner Brothers real life U.S. Marine Flying Corps action adventure movie *Devil Dogs of the Air* and James Cagney in the starring role was quickly seized by Quaker Oats as a likely basis for premiums. A March 3, 1935 Sunday newspaper ad by Quaker offered Devil Dog ring, emblem badge and model airplane kit premiums based specifically on the movie plus closely related premiums of aviator goggles and leatherette flying helmet. Quaker Oats was thoroughly identified as Cagney's favorite cereal and the premium offer expiration date was May 15, 1935.

DVL-1   DVL-2

DVL-1. Quaker Oats Cardboard Sign,
1935. Rare. Displays the premiums and pictures James Cagney. - **$1000 $1850 $2500**

DVL-2. Ad Sign for Premiums,
1935. Scarce. Regular paper, color. - **$50 $125 $225**

DVL-3   DVL-4

DVL-3. Quaker Cereals "Man's Wings/How To Fly" Booklet,
1935. Scarce. Includes photo strip with James Cagney plus flight instruction pages. Has a 1931 copyright by Reilly & Lee Co. - **$30 $100 $150**

DVL-4. Quaker Oats Premium Order Blank,
1935. - **$10 $25 $50**

DVL-5   DVL-6   DVL-7

DVL-5. "Devil Dogs" Brass Badge,
1935. Quaker Cereals premium. - **$20 $40 $75**

DVL-6. "Military Order Of Devil Dogs" Brass Identification Tag,
c. 1935. Probably Quaker Cereals premium. - **$30 $75 $100**

DVL-7. Brass Ring,
1935. Quaker Cereals premium. Gold-plated with initial. -
$50 $125 $200

DVL-9

DVL-8

DVL-8. Plane With Mailer and Instructions,
1935. Quaker Oats premium. - **$25 $50 $100**
Mailer - **$20 $40 $60**
Instructions - **$20 $40 $60**

DVL-9. Plane Goggles,
1935. Quaker Oats premium. Rare. - **$30 $75 $150**

DICK DARING'S ADVENTURES

Merrill Fugit played Dick Daring and Donald Briggs
was Coach Greatguy in this 15-minute afternoon
adventure series that had a brief run in 1933 on the
NBC Blue network. Quaker Oats sponsored the show
and offered merchandised and generic premiums in
exchange for boxtops.

DDA-1

DDA-2

DDA-1. "Bag Of Tricks" Book,
1933. Quaker Oats. - **$5 $20 $50**

**DDA-2. Quaker Underground Cavern Headquarters
Map, Matching Puzzle,**
c. 1933. Paper map and cardboard puzzle with identical
design. Each - **$20 $100 $150**

DDA-3

DDA-3. "Coach" Rogers Card "To Mother",
c. 1933. Promotes "Dick Daring Radio Programs" starring
him and his friend Toby. - **$5 $10 $15**

DDA-4

DDA-5

DDA-4. Quaker Jigsaw Puzzle,
c. 1933. Puzzle scene of headquarters beneath city. -
$20 $100 $150

DDA-5. "New Bag Of Tricks" Book,
1934. Quaker Oats. - **$8 $25 $50**

DICK STEEL, BOY REPORTER

Fresh from his role as Dick Daring, Merrill Fugit moved
on to portray boy reporter Dick Steel in another 15-
minute adventure series aired on NBC in 1934. The
Educator Biscuit company was the sponsor and premiums included membership badges, booklets revealing
secrets of police reporting and how to start a newspaper and such detective paraphernalia as a false mustache, invisible ink and handcuffs.

DST-1

DST-2

DST-1. "Secrets Of Police Reporting" Manual,
1934. Scarce. Educator Hammered Wheat Thinsies. -
$30 $150 $250

DST-2. "Neighborhood News" Vol. 1 #1 Newspaper,
February 15, 1934. Envelope Mailer - **$5 $10 $15**
Newspaper - **$50 $125 $175**

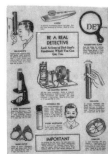

DST-3

DST-4

DST-3. Radio Cast Photo,
c. 1934. Shown entering United Airlines airplane. -
$20 $40 $75

DST-4. Premium Order Sheet,
c. 1934. Hammered Wheat Thinsies and Toasted Cheese
Thins. Ten premiums offered. - $15 $35 $60

DST-5	DST-6	DST-7

DST-5. "Chief Editor" Silvered Metal Badge,
c. 1934. Rare. Awarded to "Reporter" advancing in rank. -
$50 $150 $275

DST-6. "Reporter" Badge only,
c. 1934. - $10 $20 $40

**DST-7. "Dick Steel News Service/Special Police
Reporter" Brass Badge,**
c. 1934. Design includes radio front, lightning bolts, portrait, eagle. - $30 $60 $100

DST-8

DST-9

DST-8. "Detective Bureau" Curved Brass Badge,
c. 1934. Rare. Awarded to "Special Police Reporter" as
advancement in rank. Ownership of original badge was
required. Kids collected three Wheat Thinsies labels and
three names from friends, and sent them in with a form to
receive this badge. - $15 $50 $75

DST-9. Dick Steel Whistle,
1934. Scarce. - $20 $75 $90

DST-10

DST-11

DST-10. News Service Pamphlet,
1934. Hammered Wheat Thinsies. Four page premium
"How to publish your own newspaper." - $25 $60 $75

DST-11. Press Card,
1934. Rare. Membership card for Radio Reporters Club. -
$50 $100 $150

DICK TRACY

October 4, 1931 saw the birth of *Dick Tracy* in the
Sunday Chicago Tribune. Eight days later the first
daily strip appeared. So began Chester Gould's continuing saga of crime and violence that has produced a
collection of appropriately named rogues and villains
from Boris Arson to the Brow, Pruneface to Littleface,
Flattop to the Mole, Gravel Gertie and B.O. Plenty and
many others. Teamed with Tracy were his sidekicks
Pat Patton and Sam Catchem and his enduring fiancee
Tess Trueheart.

Despite the fanciful characters, the strip has been recognized for its realism and attention to details of
police procedure and crime prevention. Tracy's popularity spread out into other media as well. Radio series
ran on the CBS, Mutual and NBC networks from 1935
to 1939 sponsored by Sterling Products and Quaker
cereals. The majority of early premiums came from
Quaker in 1938-39. The show was revived on ABC from
1943 to 1948 sponsored by Tootsie Rolls candy.

Four 15-episode chapter plays with Ralph Byrd as
Tracy were released between 1937 and 1941, followed
by four full-length films between 1945 and 1947, and
ultimately the 1990 Disney blockbuster with Warren
Beatty, Madonna as Breathless Mahoney and Al
Pacino as Big Boy Caprice. A live-action television
series with Ralph Byrd again in the title role ran for a
season (1950-1951) on ABC and was syndicated
throughout the 1950s, and 130 five-minute animated
comic cartoons were released in the 1960s. Tracy cartoons were also reprised as segments of *Archie's TV
Funnies* (1971-1973) on CBS.

The fearless crimefighter's first comic book appearance of many was in 1936 in *Popular Comics #1*. *The
Celebrated Cases of Dick Tracy*, a hardbound anthology, was published in 1970. There have been countless
Dick Tracy premiums over the years.

DCY-1

DCY-2

DCY-1. Paper Mask,
1933. Text on back tab reads "Free with one package of
Handi-Tape." Published by Einson-Freeman Co. -
$75 $150 $300

DCY-2. "Dick Tracy And Dick Tracy, Jr." Book,
1933. Perkins Products Co. - $15 $30 $60

DCY-3

DCY-4

DCY-3. "Dick Tracy/Junior" Cello. Button,
c. 1933. Unknown sponsor but made by Parisian Novelty
Co. - **$100 $200 $350**

DCY-4. Belt Attachment With Link Chain And Loop,
1934. Scarce. Dated and inscribed "Dick Tracy Detective
Agency." - **$100 $250 $350**

DCY-5   DCY-6   DCY-7

DCY-5. "Big Thrill" Chewing Gum Booklets,
1934. Goudey Gum Co. Set Of Six, Each - **$10 $20 $40**

**DCY-6. "Dick Tracy Detective Club" Brass Shield
Badge,**
c. 1937. Reverse has leather cover slotted to wear on
belt. - **$40 $75 $150**

**DCY-7. "Dick Tracy Detective Club" Brass Shield
Badge,**
c. 1937. Reverse has leather coin pouch with snap shut
flap.- **$30 $65 $125**

DCY-8

DCY-9

**DCY-8. "Diamond Theatre Dick Tracy Club" Cello.
Badge,**
c. 1937. - **$50 $80 $150**

DCY-9. Club Manual,
1938. - **$60 $100 $150**

DCY-11

DCY-10

DCY-10. Quaker Two-Sided Sign,
1938. Rare. Shows the 1938 premiums. -
$250 $450 $650

DCY-11. Quaker Silvered Brass Initial Ring,
1938. No Tracy inscriptions, personalized initials designated by orderer. Sent in Tracy mailer. - **$200 $400 $1000**

DCY-12

(ENLARGED VIEW)

DCY-12. Newspaper Premium Ad,
1938. Quaker Cereals. - **$5 $10 $20**

DCY-13   DCY-14

DCY-13. "Secret Service Patrol" Litho. Club Button,
1938. Quaker Cereals. - **$15 $30 $50**

DCY-14. "Secret Service Patrol" Cello. Button,
1938. Rare celluloid version, probably for Canadian membership. - **$80 $175 $350**

DCY-15

DCY-16

DCY-15. "Secret Service Patrol Promotion Certificate",
1938. Quaker Cereals. Add $20 for each applied promotion
foil sticker. Without Stickers - **$15 $30 $50**

DCY-16. Sergeant 2-3/4" Tall Brass Badge,
1938. - **$40 $75 $150**

DCY-17

DCY-18

DCY-19

DCY-17. Sergeant Promotion Letter,
1938. Congratulatory letter also listing qualification for next rank of Lieutenant. - **$15 $35 $75**

DCY-18. Lieutenant Silvered Brass Badge,
1938. - **$50 $125 $225**

DCY-19. "Captain" 2-1/2" Brass Rank Badge,
1938. - **$75 $150 $300**

| DCY-20 | DCY-21 |

DCY-20. "Inspector General" 2-1/2" Brass Badge,
1938. Scarce. - **$250 $450 $900**

DCY-21. Secret Service Secret Compartment Brass Ring,
1938. -**$75 $200 $350**

| DCY-22 | DCY-23 |

DCY-22. Patrol Leader Brass Bar,
1938. Rare. Awarded after "Inspector General" rank. - **$200 $450 $650**

DCY-23. Lucky Bangle Brass Bracelet,
1938. Scarce. Charms of Tracy, Junior and four-leaf clover. - **$60 $125 $200**

| DCY-24 | DCY-25 |

DCY-24. "Dick Tracy Air Detective" Brass Wings Badge,
1938. - **$25 $50 $85**

DCY-25. "Dick Tracy Air Detective" Brass Wing Bracelet,
1938. Scarce. Top of bracelet opens to place on wrist. - **$125 $325 $625**

DCY-26

DCY-26. Rocket Gyro X-3 with Mailer,
1938. Rare. - **$100 $250 $450**

DCY-27

DCY-27. Official Detecto Kit,
1938. Scarce. Quaker Cereals. Includes mailer, bottle of "Q-11 Secret Formula", four negative-like black photos and instructions. Complete - **$100 $300 $425**

| DCY-28 | DCY-29 |

DCY-28. Secret Service Cardboard And Metal Phones,
1938. Scarce. Quaker Cereals. Pair - **$75 $200 $350**

DCY-29. Dick Tracy Flagship Balsa Wood Plane,
1938. Scarce. - **$100 $300 $450**

| DCY-30 | DCY-31 | DCY-32 |

DCY-30. "Dick Tracy Returns" Movie Serial Handbill,
1938. Republic Pictures. - **$20 $45 $75**

DCY-31. "Secret Code Book Revised Edition",
1939. Quaker Puffed Wheat & Puffed Rice. - **$30 $60 $100**

DCY-32. Quaker Radio Play Script,
1939. "Dick Tracy And The Invisible Man" first of two booklets. - **$20 $50 $100**

DCY-33

DCY-34

DCY-33. Quaker "Dick Tracy's Ghost Ship" Booklet,
1939. By Whitman with actual radio broadcast script. -
$30 $75 $125

DCY-34. Quaker Fold-Out Premium Sheet,
1939. Pictures 11 premiums including Tracy Flag Ship
Rocket Plane, Pocket Flashlight, Radio Adventures
Booklet, Siren Code Pencil. - **$30 $60 $100**

DCY-35

DCY-36

**DCY-35. Quaker "Secret Detective Methods And Magic
Tricks" Booklet,**
1939. Picture example shows both covers. -
$30 $60 $100

DCY-36. "Dick Tracy Secret Service" 3" Pen Light,
1939. Metal tube and plastic end cap. Seen with green or
red tube - **$25 $60 $100**

DCY-37

DCY-38

DCY-39

**DCY-37. "Dick Tracy Junior Secret Service" Brass
Attachment,**
1939. Originally attached by cord to Dick Tracy pen light. -
$15 $30 $65

DCY-38. "Member" Brass Badge,
1939. - **$15 $30 $60**

DCY-39. "Second Year Member" Brass Badge,
1939. - **$20 $40 $75**

DCY-40

DCY-41

**DCY-40. "Dick Tracy Secret Service Patrol/Girls
Division" Brass Badge,**
1939. - **$25 $60 $100**

DCY-41. Signal Code Siren Cap Pencil With Envelope,
1939. Near Mint In Mailer - **$175**
Pencil Only - **$50 $100 $150**

DCY-42

DCY-43

**DCY-42. "Girls Dick Tracy Club" Silvered Brass Chain
Link Bracelet,**
c. 1939. Shield charm has red enamel accents (shown
without chain). - **$40 $75 $150**

DCY-43. Wood Pencil And Wood Pen,
c. 1939. Each - **$20 $40 $75**

DCY-44

DCY-44. Chinese Checkers Game,
1939. No Dick Tracy or Quaker identification on game but
comes in envelope with Tracy pictured on mailing label.
13x13" cardboard playing board plus paper marker pieces.
Complete In Envelope - **$50 $100 $150**
Game Only - **$25 $50 $75**

DCY-45

DCY-46

DCY-47

DCY-45. "Dick Tracy/Detective" Metal Lapel Stud,
1930s. Unknown sponsor. Brass finish over white metal
version. - **$15 $25 $40**

DCY-46. Picture Card,
1930s. Retailer incentive candy premium. Retailers
received a few of these cards at the bottom of display
boxes containing smaller individually wrapped cards with
caramel candies. The larger premium cards could be distributed to favorite customers. 6x8" full color. -
$50 $125 $200

DCY-47. Diecut Paper Mask,
1930s. Imprinted for Philadelphia Inquirer. Published by
Einson-Freeman Co. - **$60 $110 $160**

DCY-48

DCY-48. Detective Set,
1930s. Store item. Includes tin badge. **$75 $125 $200**

DCY-49   DCY-50   DCY-51

DCY-49. "Detective" Cello. Button Facing Left, No Gun,
1930s. Back paper advertises comic strip in "The Chicago Tribune" or sometimes with name of New York City newspaper. - **$20 $35 $75**

DCY-50. "Detective" Cello. Button Facing Left With Gun,
1930s. Promoted newspaper comic strip with various newspapers indicated on back paper. - **$15 $30 $60**

DCY-51. "Detective" Cello. Button Facing Forward,
1930s. Chicago Tribune back paper. Promotes comic strip appearing in that newspaper. - **$20 $35 $60**

 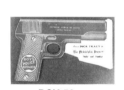 

DCY-52   DCY-53

DCY-54

DCY-52. Foil Paper Shield Card,
1930s. Depicts badge inscribed "Dick Tracy Badge" and "Junior Detective First Grade". - **$40 $90 $150**

DCY-53. "Boy's Police Automatic" Cardboard Noisemaker Gun,
1930s. Philadelphia Inquirer. - **$20 $40 $60**

DCY-54. Pocketknife,
1930s. Celluloid grips on steel made by Imperial Co. - **$50 $100 $175**

DCY-55   DCY-56   DCY-57   DCY-58

DCY-55. Genung's Store Advertising Cello. Button With Dick Tracy/Little Orphan Annie,
Early 1930s. Rare. Considered one of the rarest and most desirable comic character buttons. - **$400 $900 $1500**

DCY-56. "Dick Tracy/A Republic Picture" Enameled Brass Shield Badge,
1930s. - **$25 $60 $90**

DCY-57. "Detective/Dick Tracy Club/Sun Papers" Silvered Embossed Tin Badge,
1930s. Probably Baltimore newspaper. - **$25 $60 $100**

DCY-58. "Cleveland News Dick Tracy Club" Brass Badge,
1930s. - **$25 $50 $80**

DCY-59

DCY-60

DCY-61

DCY-59. "Dick Tracy" Enameled Brass Hat Ring,
1930s. - **$75 $150 $250**

DCY-60. "Family Fun Book",
1940. Tip-Top Bread radio premium. 14 pages with no super-heroes inside. - **$50 $150 $450**

DCY-61. "Dick Tracy Detective Club" Enameled Brass Diecut Tab,
1942. - **$25 $60 $100**

DCY-62

DCY-62. "Junior Dick Tracy Crime Detection Folio",
c. 1942. Includes detective's notebook, jigsaw puzzle, cardboard code finder, etc. Near Mint Set - **$275**

DCY-63

DCY-63. Junior Detective Kit Newspaper Advertisement,
1944. Tootsie V-M Chocolate Drink Mix. - **$8 $12 $20**

DCY-64

DCY-64. Junior Detective Kit,
1944. Tootsie V-M Chocolate Drink Mix. Includes manual, decoder, membership card, suspect sheets, ruler, line-up chart, badge. Two manual varieties: Type 1 includes anti-Japanese propaganda, Type 2 eliminates this and has different mailer. See color section for other differences.
Type 1 Near Mint Complete - **$550**
Type 2 Near Mint Complete - **$400**

DCY-65
DCY-66

DCY-65. Tip-Top Bread Cardboard Noisemaker Gun,
1944. Urges radio broadcast listenership. - **$20 $45 $85**

DCY-66. "Dick Tracy's G Men" Cardboard Blotter/Ruler Card,
1945. Local theaters for 15-week movie serial. - **$35 $75 $125**

DCY-67

DCY-68

DCY-67. Cardboard Rubber Band Pistol,
1949. Dick Tracy Hat premium.
Unpunched - **$50 $100 $150**

DCY-68. Cardboard Tommy Gun,
1949. Rare. Dick Tracy Hat premium.
Unpunched - **$200 $400 $800**

DCY-69

DCY-69. "Straight From The Shoulder" Anti-Crime Booklet,
c. 1949. Crime Prevention Council of Illinois. Chester Gould art, printed in Illinois Penitentiary. - **$25 $50 $75**

DCY-71

DCY-70

DCY-72

DCY-70. Kit Die-Cut Sign,
1952. Dick Tracy Hat promo shows pieces of Junior Detective kit. - **$100 $200 $400**

DCY-71 "Hatfull Of Fun!" Game Book,
1940s. Miller Brothers Hats. - **$20 $60 $125**

DCY-72. "Dick Tracy Jr./Detective Agency" Silvered Brass Tie Clip,
1940s. Store item. - **$40 $65 $100**

DCY-73

DCY-73. Sparkle Plenty Plaster Bank,
1940s. Store item by Jayess Co. - **$150** **$300** **$600**

DCY-74   **DCY-75**

DCY-74. "Sunday Post-Gazette" 3" Cello. Button,
c. 1950. - **$50** **$100** **$150**

DCY-75. Dick Tracy And B.O. Plenty Knife,
c. 1950. Store item includes whistle, magnifier and grips
that glow in the dark. Grips usually cracked by rivet. -
$20 **$40** **$75**

DCY-77

DCY-76   **DCY-78**

DCY-76. Chester Gould Personal Christmas Card,
c. 1950. 6x9-1/2" stiff paper picturing and naming 10 characters. - **$30** **$60** **$100**

DCY-77. "Dick Tracy Crimestopper" Tin Shield Badge,
c. 1950. Lettering in black and red. - **$35** **$70** **$125**

**DCY-78. "Dick Tracy TV Detective Club" Member
Certificate,**
1952. Copyright Chicago Tribune. - **$20** **$30** **$40**

DCY-79

DCY-79. Cardboard Flip Badge,
1952. Ward's Tip-Top Bread. - **$20** **$40** **$90**

DCY-80

**DCY-80 Coco-Wheats Iron-On Transfers Set With
Mailer Envelope,**
1956. Inner envelope holding two transfer sheets picturing
Tracy friends and villains. Mailer - **$10** **$15** **$25**
Illustrated Envelope With Two Sheets - **$25** **$50** **$75**

DCY-81   **DCY-82**

DCY-81. Post's Cereals "Red" Decoder Card,
1957. To decode answers to red "Crimestopper" messages
on cereal box. - **$15** **$25** **$40**

DCY-82. Post's Cereals "Green" Decoder Card,
1957. To decode answers to green "Crimstopper" messages on cereal box. - **$15** **$25** **$40**

DCY-83   **DCY-84**

DCY-83. "Dick Tracy Crime Stoppers" Litho. Tin Tab,
1950s. Sponsored by Mercury Records. - **$75** **$150** **$250**

DCY-84. "Dick Tracy Detective Club" Brass Clip Shield,
1950s. Slotted gripper from set of store bought elastic
suspenders. - **$15** **$25** **$40**

DCY-85   **DCY-86**   **DCY-87**

**DCY-85. Detective Club 2-1/4" Tall Fabric Sticker
Patch,**
c. 1950s. - **$40** **$85** **$150**

DCY-86. Enameled Brass Suspender Gripper,
c. 1950s. From set of elastic fabric suspenders, store
item. - **$10** **$20** **$35**

**DCY-87. "Dick Tracy/Crimestopper" Silvered Metal
Badge,**
1961. Came with next item. - **$5** **$12** **$20**

DCY-88. Crimestopper Club Kit,
1961. Sponsor unknown. Many contents including badge (see previous item). Fairly common due to warehouse find in the 1980s. Near Mint Boxed - **$50**

DCY-89. Sweepstakes Contest Packet,
1962. Procter & Gamble. Includes leaflet, instruction sheet, store purchase coupons. - **$30 $60 $90**

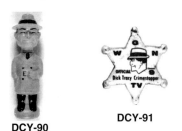

DCY-90 Soaky Bottle,
1965. Colgate-Palmolive. - **$10 $20 $35**

DCY-91. "WGN-TV" Crimestopper Litho. Tin Tab,
1960s. Chicago TV station. - **$15 $30 $60**

DCY-92. Tracy Villains Stationery Sample Kit,
c. 1971. Boise Cascade Paper Group. Six 11x14" posters, stationery sheets and envelope. - **$20 $35 $50**

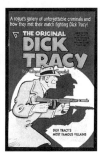

DCY-93. Dick Tracy/Detective Badge On Card,
1990. Store item. Carded - **$10**
Loose - **$1 $2 $4**

DCY-94. "Dick Tracy Party Rings" On Card,
1990. Total of eight. Store Item.
Carded Set - **$20**
Each Ring - **$1 $2 $3**

DCY-95. Comic Book Giveaway,
1990. Gladstone published Dick Tracy Rogues Gallery book made for bakeries. Sixteen pages, featuring Blank, Flattop, Brow, Pruneface and other villains. - **$3 $8 $20**

DIONNE QUINTUPLETS

Their names were Annette, Cecile, Emilie, Marie and Yvonne and their combined weight at birth was less than 10 pounds. They were born on May 28, 1934, in Callander, Ontario. They were the Dionne quintuplets and they created an international sensation. Tourists and entrepreneurs flocked to see them, they were made wards of the government to protect them from exploitation, it was said, and a promotional and merchandising bonanza was born. The Quints appeared in three films between 1936 and 1938 with Jean Hersholt as Dr. Allan Roy Dafoe, the country doctor who delivered and cared for them and they earned fees in exchange for lending their names and images to promote a wide range of products, from soup to margarine to Karo syrup. Marketers took full advantage of the age of these charming little girls. Palmolive beauty soap, for example, offered adult purchasers a Dionne quintuplets cutout book--especially for the children.

DIO-1. Quaker 15x32" Paper Store Poster,
1935. Offered photo portrait set. - **$40 $75 $125**

DIO-2. Ink Blotter,
1935. Various sponsors. - **$3 $20 $30**

DIO-3. Cardboard Fan,
1935. Various advertisers. - **$8 $20 $30**

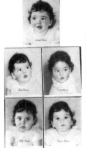

DIO-5

DIO-6

DIO-4

DIO-4. Quaker Cereals Color Photo Portrait Set,
1935. - **$15 $30 $60**

DIO-5. China Mug,
c. 1935. Probable store item. - **$20 $40 $60**

DIO-6. Chrome Finish Metal Cereal Bowl,
1935. Quaker Oats. - **$10 $30 $50**

DIO-7

DIO-7. "Quintland",
c. 1935. Canadian published visit souvenir in mailer cover. - **$10 $35 $50**

DIO-9

DIO-8

DIO-8. Silver Plate Spoons,
c. 1935. Probably Quaker Cereals. Set of five.
Each - **$5 $10 $15**

DIO-9. "Dionne Pops" Display Box,
1936. Vitamin Candy Co. - **$40 $100 $200**

DIO-10

DIO-11

DIO-10. Portrait Fan,
1936. Various advertisers. - **$10 $25 $40**

DIO-11. Cardboard Fan,
1936. Various advertisers. - **$8 $20 $30**

DIO-12

DIO-13

DIO-12. Ink Blotter Pad,
c. 1936. Various advertisers. Clear plastic cover. -
$12 $20 $35

DIO-13. Dionne Quintuplet Bread 3-1/2" Cello. Button,
c. 1936. - **$15 $35 $60**

DIO-14

DIO-15

DIO-14. "Quintuplet Bread" Paper Hanger,
c. 1936. Schulz Baking Co. Went on door knob. -
$10 $20 $35

DIO-15. Shirley Temple/Dionnes 9x12" Store Card,
1937. Modern Screen magazine. - **$50 $125 $225**

DIO-16

DIO-16. "Dionne Quin Cutout Book",
1937. Palmolive Soap. With Mailer - **$25 $75 $150**
No Mailer - **$20 $60 $100**

DIO-18

DIO-17

DIO-17. The Country Doctor Booklet,
1937. Lysol. Radio premium. 32 page story about the
Dionne Quintuplets. - **$25 $50 $75**

DIO-18. Cardboard Wall Calendar,
1938. Published by Brown & Bigelow with local imprints. -
$10 $20 $35

DIO-19

DIO-20

DIO-19. "Souvenir Of Callander" China Tray,
c. 1938. Birthplace souvenir. - **$25 $75 $100**

DIO-20. "Lysol Vs. Germs" Booklet,
1938. Lehn & Fink Products. - **$12 $25 $40**

DIO-21

DIO-21. Dionne Quintuplets Wood Pin,
c. 1938. Birthplace souvenir. - **$25 $50 $90**

DISNEY CHARACTERS MISC.

Walter Elias Disney (1901-1966) and his talented skills dominated the animation field throughout his working career and established the monumental success of the current Disney international empire. Entering animation shortly after World War I, Disney and his associates created dozens of household name animated characters headed, of course, by Mickey Mouse, but including Oswald The Rabbit, Donald Duck, Goofy, Pluto, Snow White and The Seven Dwarfs, Dumbo, Bambi, Cinderella, Alice In Wonderland, Peter Pan and Sleeping Beauty to name only the most obvious. Disney was the leader in creating full-length animated films--*Snow White* (1937), *Pinocchio* and *Fantasia* (1940)--and joined these successes with live-action films starting in the late 1940s including classics *Treasure Island, 20,000 Leagues Under The Sea, Davy Crockett* and *Mary Poppins*. Children's TV entertainment during the 1950s-1960s was dominated by *Disney's Mickey Mouse Club* and *Zorro* in addition to the popular family series beginning under the *Disneyland* title. Over the years, the quantity and beloved quality of Disney characters have prompted more premiums than any other single source.

DIS-1

DIS-2

DIS-1. "Silly Symphony" Cardboard Fan,
c. 1935. Various sponsors. - **$60 $150 $250**

DIS-2. Department Store 18x25" Christmas Hanger Sign,
c. 1935. Various stores for toy departments. Paper printed identically both sides. - **$150 $400 $750**

DIS-4

DIS-3

DIS-3. Walt Disney Cigarette Card,
1935. Imperial Tobacco Premium from England. Tells on back that in 1920 Disney was a hack artist making only 5 pounds a week, then says today he is making 80,000 pounds a year. - **$35 $75 $100**

DIS-4. Goofy Ink Blotter,
1939. Sunoco. Igloo and polar bear. - **$15 $35 $60**

DIS-5

DIS-5. Morrell Hams "Walt Disney Calendar",
1942. 12 Disney character scenes. - **$100 $250 $400**

DIS-6

DIS-6. War Bond Certificate,
1944. United States Treasury Finance Committee. Also see Donald Duck items DNL-20 & 21. - **$40 $75 $150**

DIS-7

DIS-7. "Winter Draws On" Safety Booklet,
c. 1944. Safety Education Division Flight Control
Command. - **$25 $50 $80**

DIS-8

DIS-9

DIS-8. "Cinderella" Movie Promotion 6" Cello. Button,
1950. RKO movie theaters. - **$25 $50 $75**

DIS-9. "Wheaties" Box With "Walt Disney Comic Books" Ad,
1950. 32 comics offered 1950-1951.
Complete Box - **$85 $150 $250**

DIS-10

DIS-10. Wheaties Comic Set A,
1950. Set of eight. #8 not shown. Each - **$4 $12 $25**

DIS-11

DIS-11. Wheaties Comic Set B,
1950. Set of eight. Each - **$4 $12 $25**

DIS-12

DIS-12. Wheaties Comic Set C,
1951. Set of eight. Each - **$4 $12 $25**
(Set D, Not Shown, Same Values)

DIS-13

DIS-14

DIS-13. "Walt Disney's Comics And Stories" Gift Subscription Christmas Card,
c. 1951. Dell Publishing Co. - **$35 $60 $100**

DIS-14. Cheerios 3-D Comics,
1954. 24 in set. Each - **$8 $25 $50**

DIS-15

DIS-16

DIS-15. Brer Rabbit "Ice Cream For The Party As Told By Uncle Remus" Comic Booklet,
1955. American Dairy Association. - **$35 $105 $280**

DIS-16. Lady And The Tramp "Butter Late Than Never" Comic Booklet,
1955. American Dairy Association. - **$10 $30 $75**

DIS-17

DIS-17. Plastic Dogs Newspaper Advertisement,
1955. Scotch Tape. Set of seven. Each - **$3 $5 $10**

DIS-18

DIS-18. Hardy Boys Secret Compartment Doubloon Ring,
1956. Weather-Bird Shoes. Holds pop-out plastic coin picturing them on one side and 1808 Spanish coin on other side. Second content is cardboard disk printed by treasure map directions on one side and sponsor logo on other. - **$75 $125 $175**

DIS-19

DIS-20

DIS-19. "Walt Disney's Magazine" Vol. 4 #1,
1958. Example issue. Published 6/57 - 10/59. Continuation of Walt Disney's Mickey Mouse Club Magazine.
Each - **$10 $20 $40**

DIS-20. Sleeping Beauty Prince Philip Ring,
1959. Plastic topped by sword on shield inscribed "Truth/Virtue". - **$20 $40 $60**

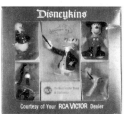

DIS-21

DIS-22

DIS-23

DIS-21. Disneykins Boxed Set,
c. 1961. RCA Victor. - **$35 $60 $100**

DIS-22. Sword In The Stone Character Plastic Ring,
1963. Depicts Sir Ector. Eight in set. Each - **$10 $15 $20**

DIS-23. Sword In The Stone Character Plastic Ring,
1963. Depicts Wart as "Fish". Eight in set.
Each - **$10 $15 $20**

DIS-24

DIS-25

DIS-24. Sword In The Stone Character Plastic Ring,
1963. Depicts Wart as "Squirrel". Eight in set.
Each - **$10 $15 $20**

DIS-25. Sword In The Stone Mechanical Plastic Ring,
1963. Miniature sword withdraws from holder. -
$10 $15 $20

DIS-27

DIS-26

DIS-26. "Mary Poppins Pop-Up" Cereal Box,
1964. Nabisco Rice Honeys. Back panel pictures and describes box insert plastic toy. - **$50 $125 $200**

DIS-27. Jungle Book Swingers Plastic Figures,
1966. Nabisco Wheat and Rice Honeys. Set of six: Mowgli, Baloo, King Louie, Buzzy, Bagheera, Kaa.
Each - **$3 $8 $12**

DIS-28

DIS-28. "Jungle Book Swap Cards",
1967. Nabisco. Australian numbered set of 24.
Set - **$15 $30 $50**

DIS-29

DIS-29. "The Love Bug Coloring Book",
1969. Hunt's Ketchup. - **$5 $8 $15**

DIS-30

DIS-30. "Crazy College Pennant Collector's" 17x22" Poster With Pennants,
1975. Wonder Bread. Poster Only - **$5 $8 $15**
Complete - **$20 $40 $60**

DIS-31

DIY-4

DIS-31. "Crazy License Plates Collectors'" 22x26" Poster With Stickers,
c. 1975. Wonder Bread. Poster Only - **$5 $8 $15**
Complete - **$20 $40 $60**

DIY-4. Disney Studio Christmas Card,
1955. Features illustrated aerial view of Disneyland with 1956 calendar. - **$75 $125 $250**

DIS-32   DIS-33

DIY-5

DIS-32. "NSDA Convention/Anaheim, California" Glass Soda Bottle,
1977. National Soft Drink Association. - **$8 $15 $35**

DIS-33. "The Jungle Book Fun Book",
1978. Baskin-Robbins Ice Cream. - **$5 $8 $12**

DIY-5. Guide Book,
1956. Second annual issue. - **$40 $75 $125**

DISNEYLAND

Sunday, July 17, 1955 began a new concept in Disney entertainment. The day officially opened Disneyland, a 230-acre complex in Anaheim, California on ground that was flat orange groves only a year before. The park's major components--Main Street U.S.A., Fantasyland, Frontierland, Adventureland, Tomorrowland--have been continuously refined and expanded annually to assure fresh entertainment year by year. Disneyland shops, of course, retail a virtually endless array of souvenir items with ceramics and jewelry quite popular. Giveaway premiums of paper items, buttons and the like, are quite frequent.

DIY-6   DIY-7

DIY-6. "Sleeping Beauty Castle" Souvenir Book,
1957. Sold at Disneyland. - **$15 $30 $60**

DIY-7. Flicker Picture Card,
c. 1958. 2x2-1/2" "Souvenir From The Art Corner At Disneyland" picturing Tinkerbell at castle. - **$15 $25 $40**

DIY-1   DIY-2   DIY-3

DIY-8   DIY-9

DIY-1. "The Story Of Disneyland" Guide Book,
1955. The first guide book. - **$50 $80 $150**

DIY-2. "The Disneyland News" Vol. 1 #1,
1955. - **$50 $100 $175**

DIY-3. "Fly TWA To Disneyland" Schedule Book,
1955. Effective July 1 for July 17 opening day. - **$35 $75 $150**

DIY-8. "Disneyland And Santa Fe" Brochure,
1950s. Park brochure with Santa Fe advertising. - **$10 $20 $40**

DIY-9. "Chesterfriend Chocolate Cigarettes" Plastic Pack,
1950s. Disneyland Candy Palace. Park souvenir. - **$15 $30 $50**

DIY-10

DIY-11

DIY-10. "Butter Mints" Tin Container,
1950s. Disneyland Candy Palace. Park souvenir. -
$20 $40 $60

DIY-11. "Walt Disney's Guide To Disneyland" Book,
1960. Sold at Disneyland. - **$15 $35 $75**

DIY-12

DIY-13

**DIY-12. "Win A Trip To Disneyland" Donald Duck
Contest Form,**
1960. - **$5 $10 $18**

DIY-13. Souvenir Guide,
1968. Park souvenir. - **$10 $25 $40**

DIY-14

DIY-14. "Pirate Party Kit",
1960s. Chicken of the Sea. Based on Pirate Ship
Restaurant in Disneyland. Many pieces including eight
place mats, paper game, hats, eye patches, etc.
Complete In Envelope - **$25 $50 $75**

DIY-15

DIY-16

**DIY-15. Pepsi "I've Been To The Golden Horseshoe" 2"
Litho. Button,**
1960s. - **$15 $25 $50**

DIY-16. "Club 55" Employee 10K Gold Award Ring,
1975. Awarded to 92 employees of continuous service
since Disneyland opening in 1955. Images on band include
Disneyland castle, inner band has award date and initials
of recipient. - **$250 $500 $1000**

DIY-17

DIY-18

**DIY-17. "Disneyland 25th Birthday Party" 2-1/4" Cello.
Button,**
1980. - **$5 $12 $20**

DIY-18. 40th Anniversary Cookie Jar,
1995. Nestle Products. 11" tall large three-dimensional
ceramic limited edition replica of Sleeping Beauty castle. -
$25 $50 $75

DIXIE ICE CREAM

The disposable paper drinking cup, called the Health
Cup, had been around for 15 years when the Individual
Drinking Cup Company changed its name to the Dixie
Cup and began offering ice cream franchises in
Cleveland in 1923. Dixie Cup has since become part of
the language. Lithographed photographs printed on
the underside of the cup lids helped sell the five-cent
ice cream. The first were a set of 24 animals featured
on the *Dixie Circus* radio program (Blue network, 1929-
1930, and CBS, 1930-1931 and 1934). In the early 1930s
a set of 24 MGM movie stars followed, with an offer of
enlarged photographs in exchange for a number of
lids. A "Defend America" lid series in the early 1940s
featured pictures of tanks and battleships, also available as enlarged full color pictures in exchange for
lids. The company continued offering lids and picture
sets into the early 1950s.

DIX-1

DIX-1. Early Waxed Cardboard Lid,
c. 1920. Scarce. Patent date of 1918. Lid reads "This
Lunch Box Dixie Made By The Individual Drinking Cup Co.,
Inc." - **$10 $25 $50**

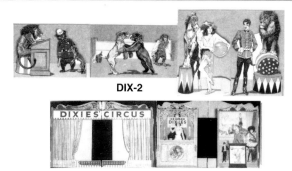

DIX-2

DIX-8

DIX-9

DIX-2. Circus Punch-Out Set,
1929. Stage and cut-outs in Series A-F and possibly more.
Stage - **$25 $60 $100**
Each Cut-Out - **$3 $5 $10**

DIX-8. "United Nations At War" Lid Set,
c. 1944. Set of 24. Each - **$3 $5 $10**

DIX-9. Al "Lash" LaRue Dixie Picture,
1947. - **$8 $12 $20**

DIZZY DEAN

Baseball's Jerome Herman Dean or Jay Hanna Dean (1911-1974), known to all as "Dizzy," was an outstanding pitcher for the St. Louis Cardinals from 1932 to 1938 and then for the Chicago Cubs (1938-1940). He was named the National League's Most Valuable Player in 1934, when his win-loss record of 30-7 helped carry the Cardinals to the World Championship. In 1952 his life story was the basis of the movie *Pride of St. Louis* and he was elected to the Baseball Hall of Fame in 1953. Dean did the radio broadcasts of St. Louis games from 1941 to 1949, where his grammar proved to be as challenging as his pitching--"he slud into third!" In 1948 Dean did a dozen weekly shows on NBC radio for Johnson Wax. His *Dizzy Dean Winners*, sponsored by Post cereals in the 1930s and promoted in Sunday comic sections, offered pins, rings and other premiums to young fans.

DIX-3

DIX-4

DZY-1

DZY-2

DIX-5

DIX-3. "Animal Heroes Of Dixie's Circus Radio Stories" Lids, c. 1930. Waxed cardboard set of 24 numbered cup lids, each 2-1/4" diameter. Each - **$1 $3 $5**

DIX-4. "Portraits" 12x17" Cardboard Store Sign,
c. 1935. Easel sign picturing example of Barbara Stanwyck from "Annie Oakley" 1935 movie. - **$75 $175 $300**

DIX-5. "Movie Stars Ice Cream Dixie Lids" 6x18" Paper Sign,
c. 1930s. - **$50 $100 $150**

DZY-1. Sepiatone Facsimile Autographed Portrait,
1935. - **$20 $50 $75**

DZY-2. Grape-Nuts Booklet,
1935. - **$25 $50 $75**

DIX-6

DIX-6. "America's Fighting Forces" Dixie Pictures,
c. 1942. Four examples from set. Each - **$5 $10 $18**

DZY-3

DZY-4

DIX-7

DIX-7. "United Nations At War" Dixie Pictures,
c. 1944. Four examples from set. Each - **$5 $10 $18**

DZY-3. "Dizzy Dean Winners" Club Brass Badge And Certificate,
1935. Post Cereals. Example picture shows badge on certificate. Badge - **$10 $20 $35**
Certificate - **$15 $30 $50**

DZY-4. Post's "Dizzy Dean Winners" Brass Club Badge,
1935. Figural baseball with profile portrait. - **$10 $20 $35**

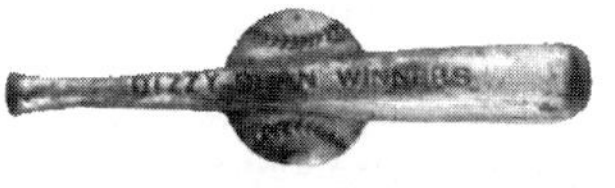

DZY-5

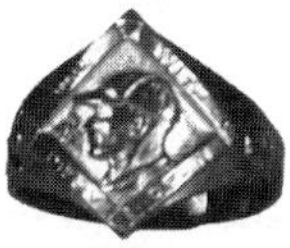

DZY-6

DZY-5. Post's "Dizzy Dean Winners" Brass Bat Figural Pin,
1935. - **$15 $40 $75**

DZY-6. "Win With Dizzy Dean" Brass Ring,
1935. Raised portrait and other baseball symbols. - **$75 $160 $275**

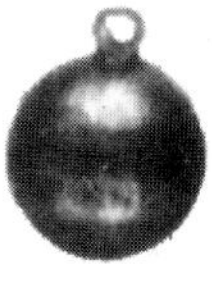

DZY-7

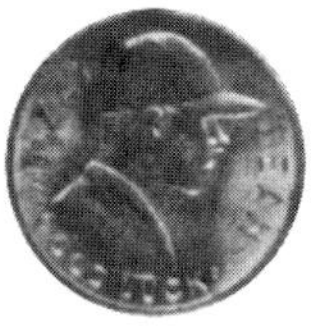

DZY-8

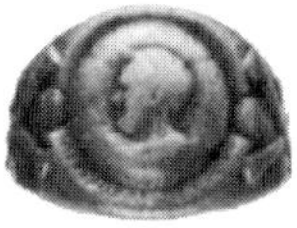

DZY-9

DZY-7. "Dizzy Dean Winners" Brass Baseball Charm,
1935. - **$15 $25 $40**

DZY-8. "Dizzy Dean-Good Luck" Brass Token,
1935. Portrait in horseshoe, back has short inspirational sports text. - **$10 $20 $40**

DZY-9. Post's "Dizzy Dean Winners" Brass Ring,
1936. - **$75 $160 $275**

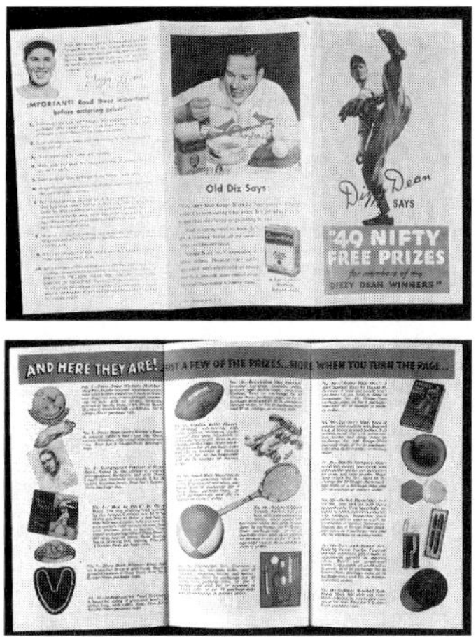

DZY-10

DZY-10. "Dizzy Dean Winners" Premium Leaflet,
1936. Grape-Nuts. Pictures "49 nifty free prizes." - **$20 $45 $75**

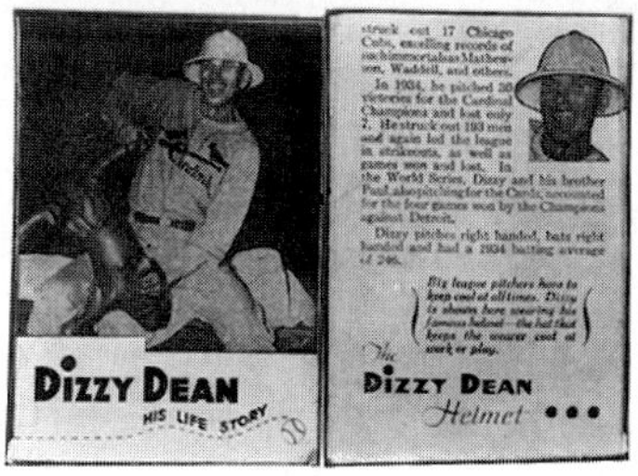

DZY-11

DZY-11. "Dizzy Dean Helmet" Leaflet,
1930s. Store item. Folder including "His Life Story" as supplement to safari-like pith helmet purchase. - **$10 $20 $30**

DOC SAVAGE

Doc Savage was the superhero of popular pulp magazine stories by Lester Dent and others, published by Street & Smith starting in March 1933. He made his first comic appearance in *Shadow Comics* #1 of March 1940. Two months later he had his own comic book, which lasted only until October 1943, but he continued to show up occasionally in *Shadow Comics* until 1949. There were brief excursions into radio in 1934-1935 and 1942-1943, Warner Brothers made a film--*Doc Savage, Man of Bronze*--starring Ron Ely in 1975 and there have been comic book revivals into the 1990s, but nothing equaled the success of the original pulps. Fans who joined the Doc Savage Club and followed the membership code could obtain badges and other premiums.

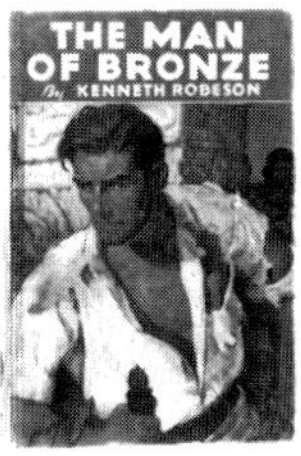

DOC-1

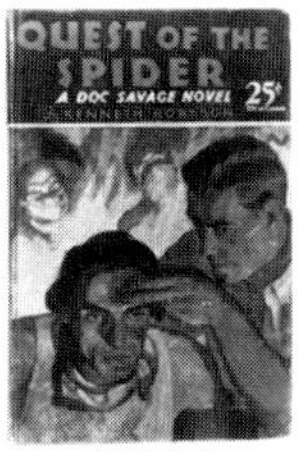

DOC-2

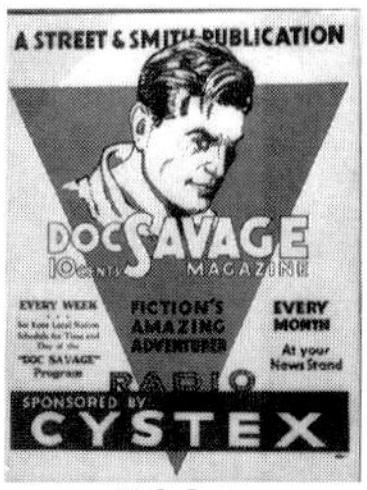

DOC-3

DOC-1. "The Man Of Bronze" Hardcover Book,
1933. Store item from Street & Smith Co. Ideal Library Series. - **$40 $80 $125**

DOC-2. "Quest Of The Spider" Hardcover Book,
1933. Store item from Street & Smith Co. Ideal Library Series. - **$40 $80 $125**

DOC-3. "Doc Savage Magazine" 11x14" Cardboard Window Poster,
1930s. Scarce. Promotes "Doc Savage Radio Program Sponsored By Cystex". - **$125 $250 $500**

DOC-5

DOC-6

DOC-4

DOC-10

DOC-11

DOC-4. Pulp Magazine Ad Sticker,
1930s. Example shown has trimmed margins. -
$40 $75 $150

DOC-5. Pulp Subscriber Portrait,
1930s, Doc Savage Magazine. Color print of painting by
Walter M. Baumhofer especially for magazine. -
$125 $150 $350

DOC-6. Pulp Subscriber Portrait,
1930s. Scarce. Doc Savage Magazine. Print of painting
believed by Walter M. Baumhofer especially for
magazine. - **$75 $140 $200**

DOC-10. "Doc Savage Award" Bronze Medallion,
1930s. Rare. Less than 10 known. Doc Savage pulp magazine. Inscribed "Service-Loyalty-Integrity" below portrait. -
$500 $2500 $3500

DOC-11. Application For Doc Savage Award,
1930s. Scarce. - **$75 $200 $300**

DOC-7

DOC-12

DOC-13

DOC-7. "The Code Of Doc Savage" Wallet Card,
1930s. Street & Smith Publishing Co. - **$40 $85 $135**

**DOC-12. "Doc Savage Club/Member" Rubber On Wood
Stamp Block,**
1930s. Photo example includes image of ink stamped picture. - **$85 $175 $275**

DOC-13. Movie Card,
1975. Warner Bros. - **$5 $10 $20**

DOC-8

DOC-9

DOC-14

DOC-14. Commemorative Certificate,
1975. Warner Bros. From "The Man Of Bronze" film kit. -
$10 $25 $40

**DOC-8. "Doc Savage Club" Member's Bronze Lapel
Stud,**
1930s. - **$75 $150 $300**

DOC-9. Lapel Stud Card With Envelope,
1930s. Pair - **$75 $250 $350**

DOC-15

DOC-15. "Doc Savage/Brotherhood Of Bronze" Fan Club Kit,
1975. Issued by comic artist Jim Steranko. Contents consist of Bulletin #1 (#2 and #3 followed), membership card, button. Near Mint Complete - **$60**
Each Piece - **$5 $10 $15**

DOCTOR WHO

Doctor Who was the longest-running science-fiction television series in history, airing on the BBC from 1963 to 1989. The show chronicled the adventures of an eccentric Time Lord from the planet Gallifrey who stole a time machine called a TARDIS (Time And Relative Dimension In Space) and left to explore the universe. Accompanied by dozens of traveling companions over the next twenty-six seasons, the Doctor himself was capable of "regenerating" when near death, allowing the production to replace the lead actor when necessary. By the end of the series, seven actors had played the Doctor regularly: William Hartnell, Patrick Troughton, Jon Pertwee, Tom Baker, Peter Davison, Colin Baker, and Sylvester McCoy.

Stories were aired in serialized form, with several half-hour episodes comprising a complete adventure. The first to air, "An Unearthly Child," introduced the Doctor, his granddaughter Susan, and the two human teachers who would accompany them for several years. It was the second story however, titled "The Daleks," that introduced the Doctor's most popular alien adversaries and made the series an instant hit. *Doctor Who* quickly became a British pop-culture phenomenon and a childhood mainstay, with a wide variety of premiums and other merchandise available. Two feature films starring Peter Cushing as the Doctor were released in the mid-'60s, and several stage plays were also produced over the years. In the mid-'70s, syndication of the series in America via PBS and Lionheart resulted in a massive following in the States, and the series continues to air on PBS stations across the country.

By 1989, failing ratings and changes in the BBC resulted in the show's cancellation. A 1996 revival TV-movie co-produced by the BBC and Universal aired on the Fox network, starring Paul McGann as the new Doctor, and Eric Roberts as the latest incarnation of the evil Master, the Doctor's arch-nemesis.

Over the past thirty-five years, *Doctor Who* has become a beloved science fiction and television icon, with a worldwide following that continues to flourish despite the lack of an ongoing series. The Doctor's adventures continue in a series of novels published first by Virgin and now by the BBC, and in a comic strip featured in Marvel UK's *Doctor Who Magazine*. Most items are copyright BBC Enterprises. "There's no point in being grown-up if you can't be childish sometimes!"

DWH-1

DWH-1. Kellogg's Sugar Smacks Badges,
1971. Cereal offered 6 different celluloid badges. Sample box with promotional artwork (which continued to run after the end of the offer) and advertisement also shown. Boxes came in 'standard' and 'mini' sizes.
Each Badge - **$7 $10 $15**
Complete Set - **$150 $225 $300**
Unopened Small Box - **$75 $90 $150**
Unopened Large Box - **$105 $135 $225**

DWH-2

DWH-3

DWH-2. Radio Times 10th Anniversary Special,
1973. Features photos, interviews, and story synopses. -
$35 $75 $150

DWH-3. Weetabix Cards,
1975. Cereal offered 6 different sets of 2 cards each for use as playing pieces with board game on back of box. There were two Weetabix sets offered in 1975 and 1977.
SET 1 (1975)
Each Unpressed Figure - **$15**
Complete Figures - **$30**
Complete Set - **$105 $200 $300**
Each Box-Back - **$10**
Unopened Box - **$60**

SET 2 (1977)
Each Unpressed Figure - **$10**
Complete Figures - **$22**
Complete Set - **$75 $120 $225**
Each Box-Back - **$7**
Unopened Box - **$45**

DWH-4

DWH-5

DWH-4. Ty-Phoo Tea Cards,
1976. Offered with tea bags, accompanied by poster and
book of comic book reprints. 12 cards in set.
Each Card - **$1 $2 $3**
Complete Set - **$105**
Book - **$15 $22 $45**
Poster - **$35 $60 $105**
Opened Box - **$22**
Unopened Box - **$75**
Complete Set of All Items - **$450**

DWH-5. Promotional Poster,
1977. Produced for Crosse & Blackwell baked beans. -
$45 $75 $105

DWH-6

DWH-7

DWH-6. Doctor Who Weekly #1,
October 17, 1979. Marvel Comics. Newsprint magazine
featured articles, interviews, and an ongoing comic strip
starring the current Doctor and a variety of companions,
many of whom were original to the strip. The magazine has
undergone substantial design improvements, and is still
published continuously under the title **Doctor Who
Magazine**. With Free Gift - **$11**
Without Free Gift - **$7**

DWH-7. Radio Times 20th Anniversary Special,
1983. Features photos, an original story, and a pull-out
poster. Also available in a United States edition from
Starlog. - **$7 $15 $35**

DWH-8

DWH-9

DWH-8. Dalek Model Kit,
1984. Sevans Models.
Complete and Unassembled in Box - **$75**

DWH-9. Doctor Who Gloves,
1985. PeshawearUK Ltd. Available in a variety of sizes in
black and silver with the neon logo on the back of the
hand. - **$7 $18 $30**

DWH-10

DWH-11

**DWH-10. Golden Wonder Snacks Comic Book
Giveaway,**
1986. Snack packages offered reprint comic books and
also advertised 1987 Doctor Who calendar. Sample pack-
ages and comic shown. Unopened Packets - **$7**
Opened Packets - **$4**
Each Comic - **$1**
Complete Set - **$15**

DWH-11. Doctor Who Slippers,
1989. Mothercare. A matching pair of pajamas were also
produced. - **$15 $35 $60**

DONALD DUCK

Donald Duck was born in 1934 as a minor character in
The Wise Little Hen, a Disney animated short and
comic strip. By his second cartoon appearance he was
a star. Clarence Nash, a milk salesman, was the voice
of Donald and Dick Lundy did the animation. The iras-
cible duck's first solo performance in the comics was
in a Sunday feature in August 1936, drawn by Al
Taliaferro and written by Bob Karp and a daily strip
started in 1938. Nephews Huey, Louie and Dewey were
introduced in 1937. Comic books, reprints of the strip,
64-page comic magazines as well as three decades of
animated films and cartoons in theaters and on television have kept Donald a major Disney star. *Donald
Duck's 50th Birthday*, a 60-minute spectacular on CBS-
TV in 1984, reviewed his illustrious career.

DNL-1

DNL-2

DNL-1. "Donald Duck Jackets" Cello. Button,
c. 1935. Scarce. Norwich Knitting Co. - **$200 $450 $900**

DNL-2. Butter Creams 11x14" Cardboard Advertising Sign,
1937. - **$100 $200 $350**

DNL-3

DNL-3. "Blue Sunoco" Cardboard Ink Blotter,
1938. - **$25 $60 $100**

DNL-4

DNL-5

DNL-4. "Walt Disney's 1939 All Star Parade" Announcement Folder,
1939. Sheffield Cottage Cheese. Pictures 10 glass tumblers distributed over 10 weeks picturing total of 45 Disney characters. - **$40 $75 $125**

DNL-5. Pint Milk Bottle,
c. 1939. Various milk companies. - **$75 $150 $250**

DNL-6

DNL-7

DNL-6. Plastic Bowl,
1930s. Post Grape Nuts Flakes. Beetleware bowl in various colors with alphabet and numbers around bowl. Donald Duck pictured in center. - **$25 $50 $75**

DNL-7. Long-Billed Donald Bisque Toothbrush Holder,
1930s. Store item. - **$80 $250 $500**

DNL-8

DNL-9

DNL-8. Long-Billed Double Figure Toothbrush Holder,
1930s. Store item. - **$125 $400 $600**

DNL-9. Mickey And Minnie With Donald Toothbrush Holder,
1930s. Store item. - **$100 $250 $400**

DNL-10

DNL-11

DNL-10. "Wanna Fight" Cello. Button,
1930s. Scarce. Image of irate long-billed Donald. - **$200 $400 $750**

DNL-11. Dell Comic Book Promo,
1940. - **$30 $60 $90**

DNL-12

DNL-13

DNL-12. Sunoco Ink Blotter,
1942. Donald with adding machine. - **$15 $25 $60**

DNL-13. Sunoco Ink Blotter,
1942. Donald driving from garage. - **$15 $25 $60**

DNL-14

DNL-15

DNL-14. "This Is A Victory Garden" 12x18" Sign,
c. 1942. Printed masonite board with wood rod pole for insertion in World War II home produce garden. - **$200 $400 $600**

DNL-15. "The Spirit Of '43" 27x41" Government Movie Poster,
1943. Donald war-time patriotic cartoon used as added attraction to featured films. - **$200 $500 $750**

DNL-16   DNL-17

DNL-16. "USCG Patrol" Booklet,
1943. U.S. Coast Guard. - **$25 $50 $75**

DNL-17. Goodyear "Donald Duck Says:" Booklet,
c. 1943. Donald demonstrates how to make synthetic rubber. - **$25 $40 $75**

DNL-18   DNL-19

DNL-18. "Saludos" Studio Fan Card,
c. 1943. - **$30 $50 $70**

DNL-19. War Bond Poster,
1944. Scarce. - **$100 $200 $400**

DNL-21
(FRONT)

DNL-20

DNL-21
(BACK)

DNL-20. War Bond Certificate with Paper Frame,
1944. United States Treasury War Bond Committee. Also see Disney Miscellaneous item DIS-6. - **$60 $100 $200** Certificate Only - **$40 $75 $150**

DNL-21. War Bond with Cardboard Stand-Up Frame,
1944. Scarce. - **$40 $80 $160**

DNL-22

DNL-22. Three Caballeros Studio Fan Card,
c. 1945. - **$15 $35 $75**

DNL-23

DNL-23. "Walt Disney's Comics And Stories" Comic Book Gift Subscription Postcard,
1946. - **$20 $50 $75**

DNL-24

DNL-25

DNL-24. Dell Comics Christmas Mailer,
1947. Inner panels picture comic book cover faced by subscription offer. - **$11 $33 $115**

DNL-25. "Donald Duck In Bringing Up The Boys" Book,
1948. Store item and K.K. Publications premium.
With Mailer - **$18 $72 $125**
Book Only - **$14 $43 $100**

DNL-26

DNL-27

DNL-26. Donald Duck "Living Toy" Ring,
1949. Donald's head and miniature cereal box both have magnets for moving his head.
Complete - **$250 $325 $400**
Ring Only - **$150 $200 $250**

DNL-27. "Living Toy Ring" Newspaper Advertisement,
1949. Kellogg's Pep. - **$10 $20 $35**

DNL-28

DNL-29

DNL-28. "Living Toy Ring" Instruction Sheet,
1949. Kellogg's Pep. - **$125 $150 $175**

DNL-29. Mustard Product Glass Jar/Bank,
1940s. Nash Mustard.
With Label And Lid - **$50 $100 $150**
With Lid, No Label - **$20 $35 $60**

DNL-30

DNL-31

DNL-30. "Nu-Blue Sunoco" Cardboard Blotter,
1940s. Donald with smiling gasoline pump. - **$15 $25 $60**

DNL-31. Sylvania Radio Bulbs 18x28" Sign,
1940s. Rare. This Version - **$400 $800 $1600**
Smaller Version (scarce) - **$100 $200 $400**

DNL-32

DNL-32. Figural Glass Jar With Metal Bank Lid,
1940s. Donald Duck Peanut Butter - **$30 $60 $90**

DNL-33

DNL-34

DNL-33. Sunoco Ink Blotter,
1940s. Donald being hit by punching bag. - **$15 $25 $50**

DNL-34. "Walt Disney's Comics And Stories" Gift Subscription Card,
1940s. - **$40 $80 $125**

DNL-35

DNL-35. Sunoco "How's Your I.Q." Booklet,
1940s. Automotive quiz. - **$30 $60 $100**

DNL-36

DNL-36. Dell Comics/K.K. Publications Pictures With Envelope,
1940s. Set of 10. Near Mint In Mailer - **$600**
Each - **$15 $30 $50**

DNL-39

DNL-37

DNL-38

DNL-37. "Donald Duck Peanut Butter" Litho. Button,
1940s. Sponsor inscription on reverse, probable set of eight also including Mickey Mouse, Minnie Mouse, Joe Carioca, Pinocchio, Snow White, Bambi, Dumbo.
Each - **$10 $20 $40**

DNL-38. "Ducky Dubble Club Of America/Member" Cello. Button,
1950. Scarce. Depicts Donald eating Twin popsicle. - **$100 $175 $300**

DNL-39. Decal Window Sign,
1950. Ice Cream Novelties, Inc. - **$20 $50 $75**

DNL-40

DNL-40. Premium Catalogue,
1950. Ice Cream Novelties, Inc. - **$10 $20 $35**

DNL-41

DNL-42

DNL-41. Icy-Frost Beanie,
1950. Rare. - **$100 $200 $400**

DNL-42. Icy-Frost Twins Cardboard Sign,
1950. - **$50 $100 $200**

DNL-43

DNL-44

DNL-43. "Walt Disney's Comics And Stories" Comic Book Subscription Folder,
1953. - **$12 $30 $70**

DNL-44. "Donald Duck Bread" 30x38" Cardboard Standee Sign,
1950s. - **$125 $200 $350**

DNL-45

DNL-46

DNL-45. Donald Duck Bread Cardboard Bank,
1950s. - **$25 $50 $75**

DNL-46. Bread Labels,
1950s. Examples shown from state and country sets. Each - **$3 $5 $10**

DNL-47

DNL-49

DNL-48

DNL-47. Donald Duck Beverages Cola Glass,
1950s. - **$10 $20 $50**

DNL-48. "Donald Duck Cola" Cardboard 9x10-1/2" Store Counter Sign,
1950s. Printed in Canada. This Example - **$30 $50 $100**
Larger Version - **$50 $100 $175**

DNL-49. Beverages Trade Show 2-1/2" Cello. Button,
1950s. Canadian issue. Matte finish with center strip blank to write name. - **$200 $400 $600**

DNL-51

DNL-50

DNL-50. Orange Juice 6x13" Cardboard Display Sign,
1950s. - **$40 $90 $175**

DNL-51. Donald & Ludwig Ceramic Mug Set,
1961. RCA Victor. Each - **$10 $20 $30**

DNL-52

DNL-53

DNL-52. Place Mats & Offer,
1964. RCA. Set - **$20 $40 $60**

DNL-53. Donald Duck Puppets Wheat Puffs Cereal Container/Bank,
1966. Vinyl with metal lid by Nabisco. - **$8 $15 $30**

(CLOSED)

(OPEN)

DNL-54

DNL-54. 60th Anniversary Watch,
1994. Boxed - **$30 $60 $90**

DNL-55

DNL-55. Donald Duck with Gong,
1995. Disneyana convention premium. - **$75 $100 $200**

DON WINSLOW OF THE NAVY

Don Winslow was conceived by Lt. Commander Frank V. Martinek in the early 1930s as the hero of a series of novels written to promote Navy recruiting. A Bell Syndicate comic strip, also originally written by Martinek and drawn by Leon Beroth and Carl Hammond, premiered in March 1934 and ran until July 1955. Winslow made his comic book debut in *Popular Comics* #1 of February 1936 and appeared in various Dell and Fawcett comics, among others, into the 1950s. Don Terry starred in two chapter plays, *Don Winslow of the Navy* in 1942 and *Don Winslow of the Coast Guard* in 1943, both of which were released to television in 1949. Winslow, along with his pal Lt. Red Pennington and his girlfriend Mercedes Colby, also fought the forces of evil on the radio from 1937 to 1943. His Squadron of Peace first did battle with the international Scorpia spy network, then turned its attention to the Axis menace of World War II. The series originated on WMAQ in Chicago and was aired on the NBC Blue network from 1937 to 1939 sponsored by Kellogg's cereals and Iodent toothpaste, and on ABC in 1942-1943 sponsored by Post cereals and Red Goose shoes.

DON-1

DON-2

DON-1. Secret Code Book,
1935. 20 page premium from Metropolitan newspaper. - **$75 $150 $225**

DON-2. "Squadron Of Peace" Brass Ring,
1938. Kellogg's. Each ring serially numbered. See DON-5. - **$300 $750 $1500**

DON-3

DON-4

DON-3. "Don Winslow Periscope" Countertop Display,
c. 1939. Kellogg's Wheat Krispies. Diecut cardboard 5x13x17" tall holding example periscope plus order coupons tablet. With Periscope - **$200 $400 $600** Without Periscope - **$100 $200 $300**

DON-4. Periscope Order Coupon,
1939. Kellogg's Wheat Krispies. - **$15 $25 $50**

DON-5

DON-6

DON-5. Guide Book,
1939. Iodent Toothpaste. This booklet (folded) and the serially-numbered membership ring came in the mailer which has typed notation "Ring" on the label.
Mailer - **$25 $50 $100**
Booklet - **$60 $125 $200**

DON-6. "The Don Winslow Creed" Certificate,
c. 1939. Iodent toothpaste and tooth powder. 9x12" parchment-like paper. - **$50 $125 $200**

DON-7

DON-8

DON-7. Club Manual And Creed,
1939. Kellogg's. Near Mint In Mailer - **$200**
Manual - **$25 $60 $100**
Creed - **$10 $20 $35**

DON-8. "Squadron Of Peace" Member Card,
1939. Kellogg's Wheat Krispies. - **$20 $50 $75**

DON-9   DON-10   DON-11

DON-9. "Ensign/Squadron Of Peace" Silvered Brass Badge,
1939. Kellogg's. - **$10 $20 $35**

DON-10. "Lt. Commander/Squadron Of Peace" Silvered Brass Badge,
1939. Kellogg's. Scarce. Highest rank of series. -
$250 $750 $1000

DON-11. Honor Coin,
c. 1939. Kellogg's. Center has spinner disk, back inscription is "Take Me For Luck". - **$50 $100 $150**

DON-12

DON-13

DON-12. Kellogg's Cardboard Periscope,
1939. Scarce. Slanted mirrors in each end. -
$50 $150 $300

DON-13. "Guardians Of Peace" Cereal Box Backs,
c. 1939. Kellogg's Wheat Krispies.
Each Back - **$8 $12 $20**

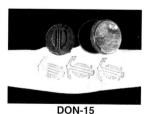

DON-14   DON-15

DON-14. "Don Winslow's Secret And Private Code" Paper Sheet,
c. 1939. Includes Creed and decipher instructions. -
$20 $40 $60

DON-15. Identification Stamp Miniature Kit,
c. 1940. 1" tin container holding ink pad and rubber stamp personalized by initials designated by orderer with anchor design. - **$50 $100 $150**

DON-16

DON-17

DON-16. "League For Defense" Kit,
1940. Fleer's Dubble Bubble Gum. Includes pencil autograph of "Don And Red" on card with Navy text plus member card. Each - **$20 $50 $75**

DON-17. "Group Leader" Cello. Button,
1940. Scarce. Fleer's Dubble Bubble Gum. Radio club premium for League For Defense. - **$125 $300 $400**

DON-18

DON-19

DON-18. "Scorpia's Scrambled Code" Cardboard Sheet and Photo With Mailer Envelope,
1940. Scarce. Fleer's Dubble Bubble Gum. Explains code system with secret message to be deciphered.
Mailer - **$15 $40 $75**
Code Sheet - **$20 $65 $100**
Winslow and Red Pennington Photo - **$30 $75 $100**

DON-19. Catapult Bomber,
1942. Scarce. Post Toasties. - **$150 $350 $450**

DON-20

DON-20. Golden Torpedo Decoder,
1942. Rare. Post Toasties. Came in two pieces, with wood top, cardboard side and metal fin. One of the toughest premiums to find. - **$800 $2500 $3500**

(FRONT)

DON-21

(BACK)

DON-21. Undercover Deputy Certificate With Instructions,
1942. Scarce. Post Toasties. Goes with Golden Torpedo Decoder. - **$100 $250 $350**

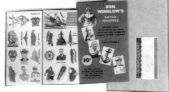

DON-22   **DON-23**

DON-22. Don Winslow & Red Pennington Plaster Salt & Pepper Set,
1940s. Store item. From series of character sets. -
$25 $50 $90

DON-23. Coco-Wheats "Tattoo Transfers" With Mailer Envelope,
1956. Transfer sheets picture 22 characters.
Mailer - **$10 $15 $25**
Illustrated Inner Envelope With Two Sheets - **$25 $50 $75**

DON-24

DON-24. Secret Code Booklet with Shirt/Box,
1950s. Set - **$50 $100 $150**

DOROTHY HART, SUNBRITE JR. NURSE CORPS

Junior Nurse Corps was broadcast on CBS radio in 1936-1937 and on the Blue network in 1937-1938. The series, sponsored by Sunbrite cleanser and Quick Arrow soap flakes, both products of Swift and Company, centered on the activities of teen nursing student Dorothy Hart and her Aunt Jane. The program was aimed at an audience of teenage girls, focusing on the nurse's life and the importance of knowing first aid, as well as on historical events. There were many premiums offered in exchange for Sunbrite and Quick Arrow labels; most of the premiums were nursing-oriented.

DOR-1   **DOR-2**

DOR-1. Nurse Pin Back,
1937. Radio premium. Different photo in center. This photo variety is scarcer than next example. - **$20 $40 $60**

DOR-2. Cello. Club Button,
1937. - **$10 $20 $30**

DOR-3

DOR-3. Club Premium Catalogue Fold-Out Sheet,
1937. For 1937-1938 season. - **$35 $100 $150**

DOR-4   **DOR-5**

DOR-4. Club Newspaper,
September 1937. - **$15 $30 $50**

DOR-5. Indian Princess Sa-ca-ja-wea Photo,
1937. Radio cast member. - **$10 $25 $35**

DOR-6   **DOR-7**

DOR-6. Cast Member Photo,
1937. - **$10 $25 $35**

DOR-7. Sunbrite Junior Nurse Corps Card,
1937. Rare. Membership card for radio show. -
$30 $75 $100

DOR-8   **DOR-9**   **DOR-10**

DOR-8. "Sunbrite Junior Nurse Corps" Brass Ring,
1937. - **$75 $125 $250**

DOR-9. "Sunbrite Junior Nurse Corps" Brass Badge,
1937. - **$25 $40 $60**

DOR-10. "Graduate" Rank Brass Badge,
1937. - **$25 $65 $100**

DOR-11

DOR-12

DOR-11. Radio Program/Premiums Promo Card,
1937. Cardboard ink blotter including imprint for radio stations WHK, Cleveland and WLW, Cincinnati. - **$8 $15 $25**

DOR-12. "Supervisor" Highest Rank Brass Badge,
1937. - **$35 $75 $125**

DOR-13

DOR-13. "Sunbrite Junior Nurse Corps" Silvered Brass Bracelet,
1937. - **$30 $85 $120**

DR. SEUSS

Theodor Seuss Geisel (1904-1991), creator of verbally complex fantasies that have enchanted millions of children throughout the world for over 50 years, was born and raised in Springfield, Massachusetts, graduated from Dartmouth in 1925, and was soon contributing humor to magazines such as *Liberty* and *Judge*. After some success illustrating the "Quick Henry, the Flit!" insecticide ads, Geisel published the first of his nearly 50 books in 1937. Among the best-known: *Horton Hatches the Egg* (1940), *How the Grinch Stole Christmas* (1957), *The Cat in the Hat* (1957), *Yertle the Turtle* (1958), *Green Eggs and Ham* (1960) and *The Lorax* (1971). Television cartoon adaptations of some of the titles premiered on CBS or ABC between 1966 and 1994, winning Peabody and Emmy awards. Geisel also won Academy Awards for two documentary films (*Hitler Lives* in 1946 and *Design for Death* in 1947) and for his animated short *Gerald McBoing Boing* in 1951. Gerald also had a brief run in a series of comic books published by Dell in 1952-1953.

DSU-1

DSU-1. "Flit Cartoons" Booklet,
1929. Stanco Inc. 24-page booklet of Seuss art single cartoon panels illustrating use of "Flit" insecticide spray. - **$100 $200 $300**

DSU-2

DSU-2. "Secrets Of The Deep Or The Perfect Yachtsman" Booklet,
1935. Essomarine Oils & Greases. 36 pages including 18 character cartoons by Dr. Seuss. - **$35 $70 $125**

DSU-3

DSU-3. "Moto Monster" Puzzle With Envelope,
1930s. Essolube motor oil. 11-1/2x17" envelope and assembled 150-piece jigsaw puzzle picturing various named motoring villain monsters "Foiled By Essolube" use.
Near Mint With Envelope - **$125**
Puzzle Only - **$25 $50 $75**

DSU-4

DSU-4. "Seuss Navy" Glass Tumbler,
1940. Drinking glass designed for naval event gauged for minimum beverage consumption of Lubber to maximum consumption of Admiral. - **$25 $50 $75**

DSU-5

DSU-5. World War II Paper Poster,
1943. U.S. Government Printing Office. Unsigned but Dr. Seuss art 8x32" anti-patriotic "Squander Bug" character for promotion of more War Bond purchases. - **$100 $250 $400**

DSU-6

DSU-7

DSU-6. Esso "Meet Gus!" Cello. Button,
1940s. Esso/Standard Oil. Back paper has "Happy Motoring!" slogan plus logo.
With Back Paper - **$30 $50 $100**
Without Back Paper - **$20 $35 $75**

DSU-7. "Seuss Navy" Glass Tumbler,
1940s. Esso products. Beverage glass with consumption gauge markings monitored by "Official When-Hen." - **$35 $75 $125**

DSU-8

DSU-9

DSU-10

DSU-8. "The 5000 Fingers Of Dr. T" Hair Barrettes On Card,
1953. Store item based on characters created by Dr. Seuss for Columbia Pictures Wonderama movie of same title. Near Mint On Card - **$75**
Loose - **$15 $30 $40**

DSU-9. "The 5000 Fingers Of Dr. T" Hair Barrettes On Card,
1953. Similar to preceding item except barrettes are in silver luster rather than gold. Near Mint On Card - **$75**
Loose - **$15 $30 $40**

DSU-10. "The 5000 Fingers Of Dr. T" Pins On Card,
1953. Figural miniature pins of horn, harp and trombone based on Dr. Seuss creations from Columbia Pictures Wonderama movie of same title.
Near Mint On Card - **$75**
Loose - **$15 $30 $40**

DSU-11

DSU-11. "Chief Gansett" Beer Coaster,
c. 1950s. Narragansett Lager & Ale, Rhode Island. 4-1/4" diameter cardboard disk featuring sponsor character art by Seuss. - **$5 $12 $20**

DSU-12

DSU-13

DSU-12. Puzzle,
1964. Premium with 18 characters pictured. - **$20 $30 $40**

DSU-13. Book,
1968. Crest Toothpaste premium. 56 page story of "Horton Hatches the Egg". - **$20 $40 $60**

DSU-14

DSU-14. "The World Of Dr. Seuss" Lunch Box With Bottle,
1970. Store item by Aladdin Industries. Steel box and plastic bottle. Box - **$35** **$75** **$125**
Bottle - **$10** **$20** **$30**

DSU-15

DSU-16

DSU-15. Cat In The Hat Alarm Clock,
1978. Store item. Metal case and alarm bells, wind-up. -
$50 **$75** **$150**

DSU-16. Seuss Character Litho. Button,
c. 1970s. Probable various stores for Christmas promotion of Dr. Seuss copyright items. - **$15** **$30** **$50**

DSU-17

DSU-18

DSU-17. Cat In The Hat 30th Birthday 2-1/2" Cello. Button,
1987. - **$10** **$18** **$25**

DSU-18. "Cat In The Hat" 2-1/2x2-1/2" Cello. Button,
1995. Macy's department store. For promotional use by store employee. - **$10** **$25** **$40**

DUDLEY DO-RIGHT

The misadventures of the noble Mountie Dudley Do-Right began life as a segment of *The Bullwinkle Show* in 1961. The dedicated lawman appeared on his own in *The Dudley Do-Right Show*, which premiered on ABC in 1969 and started in syndication the following year. *Dudley Do-Right* comic books were published in 1970-1971. Square-jawed and bone-headed, the ever-chivalrous Dudley pursued his arch-enemy, Snidely K. Whiplash (voiced by Hans Conreid), in one melodramatic tale after another. His romantic interest in Nell, his boss's daughter, was not returned; she preferred his horse, Horse. Items are usually copyrighted P.A.T.-Ward Productions.

DUD-1   DUD-2   DUD-3

DUD-1. Dudley Do-Right Figural Rubber Magnet,
1960s. By "Magnetic Novelties" with "Ward" copyright. -
$3 **$6** **$10**

DUD-2. "Dudley Do-Right" Stuffed Fabric Pillow,
1960s. - **$15** **$25** **$40**

DUD-3. Dudley Do-Right Plastic Ring,
1970. Charlton Comics. From membership kit. -
$25 **$60** **$100**

DUD-4   DUD-5   DUD-6

DUD-4. T-Shirt,
1970. Charlton Comics. - **$35** **$75** **$125**

DUD-5. Sweatshirt,
1970. Charlton Comics. - **$50** **$100** **$150**

DUD-6. Portrait Wristwatch,
c. 1971. Battery watch inscribed "Buren 17 Jewels" with Jay Ward Productions copyright. - **$75** **$150** **$200**

DUD-7

DUD-7. "Dudley Do-Right Emporium Catalogue,"
1972. Jay Ward Productions. 24-page illustrated and priced listing of dozens of Ward character items including the Dudley Do-Right Mountie Stetson hat. - **$35** **$75** **$125**

DUD-8   DUD-9   DUD-10

DUD-8. Vinyl Lunch Box,
1972. Store item by Ardee Industries. - **$250 $600 $900**

DUD-9. "Snidely Whiplash" Cello. Button,
c. 1972. P.A.T.-Ward copyright. - **$8 $15 $25**

DUD-10. "Nell" Cello. Button,
c. 1972. P.A.T.-Ward copyright. - **$8 $15 $25**

DUD-11
DUD-12

DUD-11. "Pepsi Collector Series" Glass Tumblers,
1973. Pepsi-Cola. Each - **$5 $10 $15**

DUD-12. Patch On Card,
1970s. - **$10 $20 $30**

DUD-13

DUD-13. "Bendee" Figure On Card,
1985. Store item. Flexible figure on blister card by Jesco Products. Carded - **$10 $25 $35**
Loose - **$5 $12 $20**

DUFFY'S TAVERN

"Where the elite meet to eat," *Duffy's Tavern* was the radio creation of actor/director Ed Gardner in 1940. Gardner played Archie, the manager and with Abe Burrows did most of the writing. Shirley Booth originated the role of Miss Duffy, daughter of the never-present proprietor. The program was a 30-minute comedy variety with show-business guests dropping by each week for banter with Archie. It premiered on CBS in March 1941, went to the Blue network in 1942, to NBC in 1944 and was last heard in 1951. Sponsors included Schick, Sanka, Ipana toothpaste and Blatz beer. A 1945 Paramount film was essentially a reprise of the radio show.

DUF-1
DUF-2

DUF-1. "Duffy's First Reader By Archie" Booklet,
1943. Bristol-Myers Co. - **$15 $25 $40**

DUF-2. Song Book,
1944. Possible premium. Six pages. - **$20 $60 $80**

DUF-4

DUF-3

DUF-3. "Etiket By Archie" Cover Article,
1944. June issue of "Tune In" national radio magazine including three-page photo article by Ed Gardner, Archie of Duffy's Tavern. - **$10 $20 $30**

DUF-4. "Ed (Archie) Gardner" Record Album,
1947. Monitor, an appliance maker. Set of four 78 rpm records of actual broadcasts. - **$10 $25 $50**

DUF-7

DUF-5
DUF-6

DUF-5. Ceramic Mug,
1948. Probably a cast member item. - **$50 $100 $150**

DUF-6. Ed Gardner As Archie Fan Photo,
1940s. - **$5 $15 $25**

DUF-7. "Meet 'Archie' Thursday Night" Cello. Button,
1940s. Promotion for Duffy's Tavern radio show. - **$10 $20 $35**

DUMBO

The enchanting cartoon feature film of a baby circus elephant with big ears, Walt Disney's Dumbo was released in 1941 to great popular acclaim. Critics praised it and the public flocked to see the delightful tale of a flying elephant and his pal Timothy the Mouse. The musical score won Oscars for Frank Churchill and Oliver Wallace--most notable were the *Pink Elephants on Parade* dream sequence, the crows' song, and *When I See An Elephant Fly*. There have been a number of Dumbo comic-book presentations, including early giveaways by Weatherbird shoes (1941) and multiple issues of the *Dumbo Weekly* by Diamond D-X gas stations (1942). Other premiums and merchandised items followed.

DMB-1

DMB-2

DMB-1. Song Book,
1941. Various sponsors. - **$10 $25 $40**

DMB-2. "The Gossipy Elephants" Glass Tumbler,
1941. Probably held dairy product. Set of six.
Each - **$35 $65 $100**

DMB-3

DMB-4

DMB-3. Dumbo Cloth Beanie,
1941. Probable premium. - **$100 $200 $300**

DMB-4. "Dumbo Song Book" 2-1/4" Litho. Button,
1941. Various sponsors. - **$40 $80 $125**

DMB-5

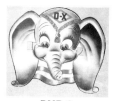

DMB-6

DMB-5. "The Adventures Of Walt Disney's Dumbo" Binder Folder With Issues,
1942. Diamond D-X Gasoline. Folder for 16 "Dumbo Weekly" four-page color comics. Folder - **$35 $100 $360**
First Issue - **$40 $120 $280**
Other Issues - **$14 $41 $110**

DMB-6. D-X Gasoline Mask,
1942. Rare. - **$30 $60 $120**

DMB-7

DMB-8

DMB-7. "D-X" Gasoline Station Cello. Button,
1942. - **$20 $30 $60**

DMB-8. "D-X Dumbo Club" Member Card,
1942. Diamond D-X Gasoline. Card includes chart to mark off first 16 copies of "Dumbo Weekly" obtained plus signature line for adult sponsor pledging a trial purchase of D-X products. - **$15 $40 $75**

DMB-9

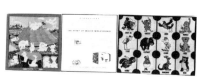

DMB-10

DMB-9. Cardboard Bookmark,
1940s. Heath Publishing Co. - **$20 $40 $60**

DMB-10. Bread Label Picture Set,
1950s. Donald Duck Bread. 11x11" mounting sheet for 12 Dumbo character bread loaf labels.
Label Sheet - **$15 $30 $50**
Each Label - **$2 $4 $6**

THE EAGLE

The first appearance of this patriotic hero was in issue #1 of *Science Comics* in February 1940. He then showed up in issue #8 of *Weird Comics*; in four issues of his own book, *The Eagle*, in 1941-1942; and in a second *Eagle* series of two issues in early 1945. The 1941-1942 membership club for fans was known as American Eagle Defenders.

EAG-1

EAG-1. Member's Cello. Button,
1942. Scarce. - **$200 $750 $1500**

EDDIE CANTOR

Over a span of more than 50 years in show business, Eddie Cantor (1892-1964) went from singing waiter to radio superstar. Cantor juggled, sang, played in blackface in vaudeville and on the stage, made movies, hosted television series and toured Europe, but it was on the radio in the 1930s that the banjo-eyed comic achieved his greatest success. He premiered on the comedy-variety *Chase & Sanborn Hour* on NBC in September 1931 and during the next 20 years in various shows, mainly on NBC, he had a succession of major sponsors: Pebeco toothpaste (1935-1936), Texaco gasoline (1936-1938), Camel cigarettes (1938-1939), Sal Hepatica laxative (1940-1946), Pabst beer (1946-1949) and Philip Morris cigarettes (1951-1952). The manic comic often joked about his wife, Ida, and their five daughters, introduced many young performers and featured such accented characters as the Mad Russian and Parkyakarkas. On television he hosted *The Colgate Comedy Hour* (NBC, 1950-1954) and the *Eddie Cantor Comedy Theatre* (syndicated, 1954-1955).

EDD-1

EDD-2

EDD-1. "Eddie Cantor's Picture Book",
1933. Chase & Sanborn Coffee. - **$5 $20 $30**

EDD-2. Folder,
1934. Chase and Sanborn radio premium. Includes 8 page foldout- **$15 $35 $50**

EDD-3

EDD-4

EDD-3. Ink Blotter,
1934. Various advertisers. - **$5 $15 $20**

EDD-4. Calendar Postcard,
1934. Various advertisers. - **$5 $15 $25**

EDD-5

EDD-6

EDD-5. Magic Club Book And Trick,
1935. Pebeco Milk of Magnesia. Trick includes 12 cards and two instruction sheets. Book - **$15 $35 $50**
Trick Packet - **$5 $20 $30**

EDD-6. "Eddie Cantor Magic Club" Enameled Brass Club Badge,
1935. Pebeco toothpaste. - **$15 $40 $65**

EDD-7

EDD-8

EDD-9

EDD-7. Jokes Booklet,
1936. Pebeco Toothpaste. - **$15 $35 $50**

EDD-8. Pebeco Toothpaste 12x19" Paper Store Sign,
c. 1936. - **$50 $100 $150**

EDD-9. "Tune In" Magazine With Cover Article, 1944. Monthly issue for August of "National Radio Magazine" including three-page article written by him and accompanied by photos. - **$5 $10 $15**

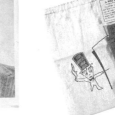

EDD-10

EDD-11

EDD-10. Photo,
1937. Philadelphia Record newspaper premium. - **$5 $12 $20**

EDD-11. Magic Trick With Bag,
1930s. Pebeco Toothpaste Club premium. Includes 13 cardboard pieces- **$25 $50 $75**

EDD-12

EDD-13

EDD-12. Calendar Card,
1946. Pabst Blue Ribbon Beer. -
$10 $20 $30

EDD-13. "Eddie Cantor For President" Litho. Button,
1948. - $10 $18 $35

EDW-4

EDW-5

EDW-4. "The Grab Bag" Movie Promotion,
1930s. Cloth bag holding 10 paper figures based on movie
"The Perfect Fool". - $40 $75 $125

EDW-5. "All Star Radio Show-Plymouth Radio
Broadcast" Folder,
1930s. Plymouth Motors. - $12 $20 $30

ED WYNN

Ed Wynn (1886-1966) came to radio after a long career
as a headliner in vaudeville and on Broadway. He was
reluctant to try radio but he successfully made the
transition from the visual comedy of his stage character, *The Perfect Fool*, to his radio persona, *The Fire
Chief*, sponsored by Texaco "Fire Chief" gasoline, on
NBC from 1932 to 1935. Wynn had several other radio
shows in the 1930s and a brief run on *Happy Island* in
1944-1945 for Borden's milk, did comedy variety
shows on television in 1949-1950 and 1958-1959 and
appeared in a number of dramatic roles on television
in the 1950s and 1960s.

ELLERY QUEEN

Sophisticated detective and mystery writer Ellery
Queen was the hero of a number of popular novels
written by Frederic Dannay and Manfred Lee. He had
several incarnations on radio, beginning with Hugh
Marlowe in *The Adventures of Ellery Queen* on CBS in
1939 and ending on ABC in 1948. Sponsors included
Gulf Oil, Bromo-Seltzer and Anacin. Live-action TV
series appeared on DuMont and ABC from 1950 to
1952 and on NBC 1958-1959 and 1975-1976. Queen's
first comic book appearance was in *Crackajack
Funnies* #23 in May 1940 and he had his own book in
the late 1940s and early 1950s. A number of second-
feature Ellery Queen films were released between 1935
and 1952, most starring Ralph Bellamy or William
Gargan as the gentleman detective.

EDW-1

EDW-3

EDW-2

ELL-1

ELL-2

ELL-1. "Ellery Queen Club Member" Cello. Button,
c. 1939. - $50 $120 $200

ELL-2. "The Adventure Of The Last Man Club" BTLB,
1940. Store item. Whitman #1406. - $15 $30 $50

ELSIE THE COW

In the late 1930s the Borden Company ran a series of
advertisements for its milk featuring a herd of cartoon
cows. One, dubbed Elsie, became a star at the 1939
New York World's Fair when visitors to the Borden
exhibit insisted on knowing which of the cows there
was Elsie. Borden put Elsie to work during World War
II touring the country to sell war bonds and promote
its milk. Contests to name Elsie's calf in 1947 and
twins in 1957 brought overwhelming public responses.

EDW-1. Texaco Fire Chief Cardboard Mask,
c. 1933. - $40 $90 $150

EDW-2. "The Chief" Movie Cello. Button,
1933. Metro-Goldwyn-Mayer Pictures. - $15 $35 $85

EDW-3. Wood Jointed Figure,
c. 1935. Store item. - $40 $75 $125

Elsie is still appearing in Borden advertising and in bovine appearances around the country. Merchandising has included giveaway comic books, fun activity books and a wide variety of glass and ceramic items related to food and drink such as bowls, glasses and mugs.

ELS-8

ELS-8. "Borden's Cheese Comic Picture Book," 1940s. Sixteen-page booklet of single page Elsie cartoons related to use of various Borden cheese products. - **$15 $45 $120**

ELS-1

ELS-2

ELS-9

ELS-9. "Elmer" Boxed China Mug, 1950. Box Only - **$30 $50 $80** Mug Only - **$10 $20 $30**

ELS-1. Brass 2-1/4" Badge, c. 1939. Likely issued during 1939 New York World's Fair. - **$15 $30 $65**

ELS-2. Wood Pull Toy, 1944. Store item by Wood Commodities Corp. Boxed - **$100 $200 $350** Loose - **$50 $100 $200**

ELS-3

ELS-4

ELS-10

ELS-11

ELS-10. Activity Booklet, 1957. 100th birthday fun book, 20 pages. - **$20 $50 $100**

ELS-3. Store Display Poster, 1945. 30x45". - **$20 $40 $75**

ELS-4. Elsie And Baby China Lamp, c. 1947. Store item. - **$75 $150 $250**

ELS-11. Elsie Ceramic Mug, 1950s. - **$10 $20 $35**

ELS-5

ELS-6

ELS-7

ELS-12

ELS-13

ELS-12. Elsie Diecut Sign, 1950s. - **$50 $100 $200**

ELS-5. "Elsie" Ceramic Mug, 1940s. - **$15 $30 $50**

ELS-6. "Beulah" Ceramic Mug, 1940s. - **$10 $20 $30**

ELS-13. Plush Doll With Rubber Head, 1950s. 15" tall. - **$25 $50 $100**

ELS-7. "Borden's" Glass Tumbler, 1940s. - **$15 $25 $40**

ELS-15

ELS-16

ELS-14

ELS-14. "Elsie's Fun Book",
1950s. - **$12 $35 $85**

ELS-15. Plastic Ring,
1950s. - **$15 $20 $30**

ELS-16. "A Trip Through Space" Booklet,
1950s. - **$10 $30 $60**

ELS-17

ELS-17. Ceramic Cookie Jar,
c. 1950s. - **$100 $150 $250**

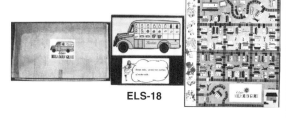

ELS-18

ELS-18. "Elsie's Milkman Game",
1963. - **$25 $40 $70**

ELS-19

ELS-19. "Elsie The Borden Cow" Litho. Button,
1960s. - **$5 $10 $18**

Elvis Presley was born in a two-room house in Tupelo, Mississippi, in 1935. He died in his Memphis, Tennessee mansion in 1977 with an estate valued at more than $30 million. In his lifetime--and since his death--the rock 'n' roll legend spawned a merchandising cornucopia that has yet to subside. The national mania exploded in 1956 when Presley appeared on *The Ed Sullivan Show* and items from that period generate great collector interest. But the King lives on: in addition to frequent Elvis sightings at shopping malls and county fairs, Elvis Presley Enterprises continues to license countless memorial and commemorative items...still takin' care of business.

ELV-2

ELV-3

ELV-1

ELV-1. Fan Photo,
c. 1955. 5x7" glossy bw with facsimile signature, a personal giveaway by him at his home on Audubon Street in Memphis in addition to other forms of distribution. -
$25 $65 $100

ELV-2. "R.C.A. Records" National Fan Club Button,
1956. Black on pink. Litho. Variety - **$50 $75 $150**
Scarcer Cello. Variety - **$75 $150 $225**

ELV-3. Color Photo 3" Cello. Button,
1956. Vendor Item. - **$20 $40 $75**

ELV-4

ELV-5

ELV-4. "TV Guide", September 8,
1956. Issue has first part of three-part article. -
$50 $100 $175

ELV-5. Brass Lipstick Tube,
1956. Store item by Teen-Ager Lipstick Corp. Available in six colors. - **$50 $75 $125**

ELV-6

ELV-7

ELV-6. Jeans Tag,
1956. Elvis Presley Enterprises store item. -
$25 $75 $125

ELV-7. Song Title T-Shirt,
1956. Store item. Elvis Presley Enterprises copyright. -
$75 $175 $250

ELV-8

ELV-8. Fabric Hat,
1956. Store item by Magnet Hat & Cap Corp.
With Tag - **$60 $125 $200**
No Tag - **$40 $80 $125**

ELV-9   ELV-10

ELV-9. Song Titles Handkerchief,
1956. Elvis Presley Enterprises. Includes song titles Hound
Dog, Mystery Train, Blue Moon, Tutti Frutti. 13x13-1/2". -
$100 $250 $400

ELV-10. Glass Tumbler,
1956. Store item. Copyright Elvis Presley Enterprises. -
$50 $80 $140

ELV-11   ELV-13

ELV-12

ELV-11. "Elvis Presley For President" Litho. Tin Tab,
1956. - **$20 $40 $75**

ELV-12. "Love Me Tender" Paper Photo,
1956. Theater hand-out. - **$5 $15 $25**

ELV-13. "Love Me Tender" Litho. Button,
1956. Elvis Presley Enterprises. From set of 10 with pictures, record titles or slogans. Each - **$5 $12 $20**

ELV-14   ELV-15

ELV-14. Metal Charm Bracelet,
1956. Store item. Elvis Presley Enterprises copyright. -
$35 $60 $90

ELV-15. Plastic Picture Frame Charm,
c. 1956. Vending machine item. - **$10 $25 $50**

ELV-16   ELV-17

ELV-16. Metal Ring With Photo Under Plastic Dome,
c. 1956. Elvis Presley Enterprises store item. Two different
color photos. Each - **$75 $150 $250**

ELV-17. Gold Record Litho. Button,
c. 1956. Known with seven different record titles.
Each - **$15 $25 $50**

ELV-18   ELV-19

ELV-18. Fabric And Paper 6" Badge,
c. 1957. Pleated fabric border around paper disk portrait,
possibly designed for movie usher use. - **$25 $50 $75**

ELV-19. "Elvis Presley Photo Folio",
1957. Elvis Presley Enterprises. From concert tour. -
$20 $40 $75

ELV-21

ELV-20

ELV-22

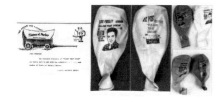

ELV-26

ELV-26. "Follow That Dream" Movie Balloons With Promotion Letter,
1962. Rubber balloons with cover form letter from Thomas A. Parker, Elvis' manager. Letter - **$15 $25 $50** Each Balloon - **$3 $8 $15**

ELV-20. Christmas Card,
1958. Red, green and white 5-1/2x8-1/2" including inset photo of Colonel Parker as Santa. - **$15 $30 $45**

ELV-21. Elvis In Army Uniform 4" Cello. Button,
c. 1958. No markings other than "U.S. Army" patch pictured above left pocket and part of "Presley" name patch visible above right pocket. - **$100 $250 $400**

ELV-22. "King Creole" Wallet Card,
1958. Movie promotion. - **$25 $50 $90**

ELV-28

ELV-27

ELV-29

ELV-27. Movie Coloring Contest Sheet,
1962. Paramount Pictures for local stores. Promotion for "Girls! Girls! Girls!" movie. - **$20 $40 $75**

ELV-28. Girls! Girls! Girls! Album Insert,
1963. - **$10 $20 $30**

ELV-29. Fan Club Booklet,
1967. - **$10 $20 $35**

ELV-23

ELV-23. Christmas Postcard,
1959. - **$15 $25 $50**

ELV-24

ELV-24. "G.I. Blues" Paper Army Hat,
1960. Advertises movie and record album. - **$15 $35 $75**

ELV-30

ELV-31

ELV-30. "Elvis' Gold Car On Tour" RCA Postcard,
1960s. - **$8 $12 $20**

ELV-31. Elvis Concert Program,
1977. Souvenir Folio Concert Edition, Volume 6. Boxcar Enterprises. - **$10 $15 $25**

ELV-25

ELV-25. "Blue Hawaii" Movie Promotion Lei,
1961. Tissue paper lei with 5" cardboard disk. - **$25 $50 $100**

ELV-32

ELV-32. "Elvis' Lisa Marie" Airplane Pen,
c. 1970s. Plastic ballpoint with liquid in upper barrel around image of Elvis' jet plane that moves when pen is tilted. Other images include him and gates of Graceland. Possible souvenir for passengers on Elvis flights. - **$25 $50 $75**

E.T.

Steven Spielberg's *E.T. The Extra-Terrestrial* opened in mid-1982 and was soon being touted as the most popular movie in Hollywood history. An endearing tale of a 10-year-old boy who befriends an alien creature stranded on earth, the film starred Henry Thomas, Dee Wallace, and Drew Barrymore. The phenomenal success of the movie was matched by a merchandising explosion. Universal City Studios licensed some 50 companies to produce E.T. products, including stuffed dolls (Kamar International), vitamins (Squibb), E.T. cereal (General Mills), trading cards and stickers (Topps), a tie-in promotion with Reese's Pieces (Hershey), and a flood of such items as video games (Atari), T-shirts, ice cream, candy, posters, pins, bed sheets, calendars, an animated alarm clock, a "power" tricycle from Coleco, and countless toys. A profusion of knock-offs and unlicensed items also appeared. An official E.T. Fan Club offered an "E.T. Speaks" record along with a photo, poster, newsletter, membership card and certificate. Following the re-release of *Star Wars* and the 1998 release of James Cameron's *Titanic*, *E.T. The Extra-Terrestrial* holds the record as the third-highest grossing film of all time.

ETT-1

ETT-2

ETT-3

ETT-1. "E.T." 6" Glass Tumbler,
1982. Imprinted for Army & Air Force Exchange Service. Illustration "I'll be right here" from series of four copyright by Universal City Studios. - **$3 $6 $10**

ETT-2. "Reese's Pieces" 29x33" Cardboard Display Sign,
1982. Reese Candy Co. Large diecut image of E.T. eating Reese's Pieces plus text for T-shirt and poster mail premiums. - **$25 $50 $75**

ETT-3. "E.T. Card Set,"
1982. Topps Gum. Set of 87, each with different film scene. Near Mint Set - **$20**

ETT-4

ETT-5

ETT-4. "E.T." Glass Tumblers,
1982. Pizza Hut. From set of four. Each - **$2 $5 $10**

ETT-5. Wristwatch,
1982. Store item by Nelsonic. Metal case with vinyl straps. - **$15 $35 $75**

ETT-6

ETT-7

ETT-6. Figural Plastic Ring With Box,
1982. Store item by Naum Bros. Plastic head on adjustable metal band. Boxed - **$25**
Ring Only - **$10 $15 $20**

ETT-7. "E.T." 20x28" Video Cassette Display Sign,
1988. Pepsi-Cola sponsorship. Molded thin plastic for MCA Home Video Inc. designed for attachment to a light box or hung in window to enhance 3-D effect. - **$15 $30 $50**

FAWCETT COMICS

Fawcett Publications began with *Capt. Billy's Whiz Bang*, a digest-sized somewhat bawdy magazine of the 1920s. The mix of girlie photos, stories, and cartoons (later Donald Duck artist Carl Barks being a regular contributor) was successful enough that Fawcett would expand into a major magazine publisher in the 1930s. Titles included *True Confessions*, *Motion Picture*, and *Mechanix Illustrated*.

Late in 1939 Roscoe Fawcett announced the company's entry into the comic book field with *Whiz Comics*, dated February, 1940. Captain Marvel was the lead feature, ably drawn by C.C. Beck and his assistants Pete Costanza and Kurt Schaffenberger. The success of Captain Marvel spawned a number of spin-offs including Captain Marvel Jr., Mary Marvel, and Hoppy the Marvel Bunny.

By 1943 Fawcett was also publishing *Captain Midnight, Bulletman, Spy Smasher*, and *Don Winslow*. In the later 1940s the line was expanded to westerns (including *Hopalong Cassidy, Tom Mix Western*, and *Gabby Hayes Western*) as well as romance, humor, sports, horror, and science fiction titles. Fawcett had become a major comic book publisher, with a yearly circulation of 50 million copies in the mid 1940s which grew to over 70 million by 1949. A 1941 DC Comics lawsuit alleging Captain Marvel was an imitation of Superman was settled in DC's favor in 1953. This, combined with lost sales due to the popularity of TV, brought an end to the Fawcett comic book empire.

They re-entered the field with *Dennis the Menace* in 1958 and published that title until 1980.

FAW-1

FAW-1. "American Alphabet" Song Book,
1944. Patriotism song pages with cover art of Hoppy the Marvel Bunny and other Fawcett characters. -
$15 $35 $50

FAW-2

FAW-2. "Funny Animals Acrobats" Punch-Out,
c. 1944. Store item and probable club issue.
Unpunched - **$35 $50 $75**

FAW-3 FAW-4

FAW-3. "Tippy Toy" Punch-Out Sheet With Envelope,
1945. Store item and club premium. For assembly of 3-D rocker toy featuring Hoppy the Marvel Bunny and Millie Bunny. Unused - **$5 $10 $15**

FAW-4. "Comic Stamps" Perforated Sheet,
c. 1945. Pictures 24 Fawcett comic book characters. -
$15 $35 $60

FAW-5 FAW-6

FAW-5. Captain Marvel Club Offer Sheet,
c. 1945. Offers 18 action toys, games, puzzles, etc. for Captain Marvel and other Fawcett characters. 8-1/2x11" black on yellow printed both sides. - **$10 $20 $30**

FAW-6. "Funny Animals Coloring Book",
1946. Store item by Abbott Publishing Co. Features Hoppy the Marvel Bunny and other Fawcett characters. -
$25 $40 $65

FAW-7

FAW-7. "Funny Animal Paint Books" With Box,
c. 1946. Store item by Abbott Publishing Co. Set of six including Hoppy the Marvel Bunny and five other Fawcett animals. Boxed - **$50 $90 $150**
Hoppy Book - **$10 $25 $50**
Others Each - **$5 $10 $15**

FAW-8

FAW-8. Coco-Wheats "Tattoo Transfers" Kit With Mailer Envelope,
1956. Transfer sheets picture 22 Fawcett characters.
Mailer - **$10 $15 $25**
Illustrated Inner Envelope With Two Sheets - **$25 $50 $75**

FELIX THE CAT

Felix has been called one of the great creations of comic art...a supercat...an animation superstar...the Charlie Chaplin of cartoon characters. Alienated, alone, a heroic and resourceful battler against fate, Felix was created by cartoonists Otto Messmer and Pat Sullivan shortly after World War I. His first animated appearance came in 1919 and by the mid-1920s he was an international star, most notably in England. Sullivan was quick to license the character and many early merchandised items were produced. A Sunday comic strip from King Features Syndicate debuted in August 1923 and a daily strip followed in May 1927. Comic book appearances began in the 1930s and Felix has had his own books from the 1940s into the 1990s. Hundreds of the silent shorts were distributed to television in 1953 by Pathe Films. New color episodes, produced for television by the Joe Oriolo Studios, appeared in 1960. Felix now had a magic bag of tricks to rely on in place of his talented and multifunctional tail.

FLX-1

FLX-2

FLX-1. "Felix Meets His Match" English Cartoon Booklet,
c. 1925. Sportex clothing. Printed in England for distribution with clothing items locally and abroad. Eight-page story about Felix adopted by a tailor to dissatisfaction of both. - **$50 $125 $200**

FLX-2. English Cream Toffee Candy Tin,
c. 1920s. Scarce. Store item. - **$300 $800 $2000**

FLX-3

FLX-4

FLX-3. Tin Pull Toy,
1930s. Store item by Nifty Toys. - **$150 $300 $600**

FLX-4. "Katz Kitten Klub" Cello. Button,
1930s. Unknown sponsor. Felix image not identified. - **$15 $50 $100**

FLX-5

FLX-6

FLX-7

FLX-5. "Herald & Examiner" Litho. Button,
1930s. Chicago newspaper. From "30 Comics" series featuring various characters. - **$10 $20 $40**

FLX-6. "Warner Bros. State" Theater Cello. Button,
1930s. Obvious Felix image although "Krazy Kat Klub" designation. - **$30 $75 $150**

FLX-7. "Evening Ledger Comics" Cello. Button,
1930s. Philadelphia newspaper. From set of 14 various characters. - **$60 $150 $300**

FLX-8

FLX-9

FLX-10

FLX-8. Aviation Shield Badge,
1940s. Scarce. - **$75 $125 $225**

FLX-9. "Felix The Cat" Litho. Button,
1950s. From set of various King Features Syndicate characters. - **$10 $20 $30**

FLX-10. "Felix The Cat Candy And Toy" Product Box,
1960. Phoenix Candy Co. - **$20 $50 $100**

FIBBER McGEE & MOLLY

Jim and Marian Jordan were veterans of small-time vaudeville before they ventured into radio comedy in Chicago, first as *The O'Henry Twins* in 1924, then as *The Smith Family* in 1925, as *The Air Scouts* in 1927 and in *Smackout* from 1931 to 1935. Finally along with writer Don Quinn, they created *Fibber McGee and Molly* for Johnson's Wax. The show premiered on the NBC Blue network in April 1935 and developed into one of the most popular radio comedies of all time.

From their home at 79 Wistful Vista, McGee, the blundering windbag, and Molly, his long-suffering, forgiving wife, presided over one domestic disaster after another. Listeners waited each week for Fibber to open his closet door, whereupon the stacked contents would crash to the floor. The show featured a number of regular supporting characters: their neighbor Gildersleeve, Beulah the maid, henpecked Wallace Wimple, the Old Timer, Mayor La Trivia and Myrt, the telephone operator whose voice was never heard.

After Johnson's Wax dropped the show in 1950, Pet milk sponsored it until 1952, then Reynolds Aluminum until 1953, when the half-hour format was replaced by a 15-minute weekday series that ran until 1957. There was a comic book in 1949, the Jordans made some movies in the 1940s and a television series had a brief run on NBC in 1959-1960, but nothing equaled the McGee success on radio.

FIB-1

FIB-2

FIB-3

FIB-1. Cast Photo,
c. 1935. Shown at "NBC" microphone. - **$15 $30 $45**

FIB-2. Fibber Cello. Spinner Top On Wood Peg,
1936. Scarce. Johnson's Wax Polishes. - **$75 $200 $500**

FIB-3. Molly Cello. Spinner Top With Wood Peg,
1936. Scarce. Johnson's Wax Polishes. - **$60 $175 $450**

FIB-4

FIB-5

FIB-4. "Johnson Glo-Coat Floor Polish" 8x14"
Cardboard Display Sign ,
1937. - **$50 $150 $250**

FIB-5. Cardboard 9x15" Store Display Sign,
c. 1937. Designed for holding sample can of Johnson's
Wax - **$75 $150 $300**

FIB-6

FIB-7

FIB-8

FIB-6. Cardboard 11x16" Store Display Sign,
c. 1937. Designed for holding sample can of Johnson's
Wax. - **$60 $125 $250**

FIB-7. Johnson Products 11x15" Countertop Sign,
c. 1937. Johnson's auto wax and cleaner. Diecut cardboard with easel back. - **$50 $125 $200**

FIB-8. Cast Photo,
1930s. - **$15 $30 $50**

FIB-9

FIB-10

FIB-9. Cardboard Advertising Blotter,
1930s. Prudential Insurance. - **$15 $30 $50**

FIB-10. Fan Photo,
c. 1940s. - **$15 $30 $50**

THE FLASH

The fastest man alive, a superhero of the Golden Age
of comic books, made his first appearance in *Flash
Comics* #1 of January 1940. The book was disconti-
ued in 1949 after 104 issues and was revived with
issue #105 in March 1959. The speedster also
appeared in *All-Flash* comics from 1941 to 1948 and
showed up in early issues of *All-Star Comics* and
Comic Cavalcade and in various DC Comics collections. He was revived in *Showcase* #4 of October 1956.
Among the colorful villains confronted by The Flash
were The Fiddler and his magic Stradivarius, Mirror
Master and Captain Cold, each with special evil powers. A 1946 giveaway comic book was distributed
taped to boxes of Wheaties and a comics club offered
a membership card and button as premiums.

FLA-1

FLA-2

FLA-1. "The Flash/Fastest Man Alive" Litho. Button,
1942. Rare. Flash Comics. Sent to everyone submitting a
reader survey coupon printed in All-Flash #6 (July, 1942).
The first thousand respondents also received a free copy
of All-Flash #7. - **$300 $1200 $3200**

FLA-2. "Flash Comics" Wheaties Purchase Comic
Book,
1946. As taped to two-box purchase, highest grade is fine.
Good - **$350**
Fine - **$1050**

FLASH GORDON

Flash Gordon first blasted into space in January 1934
in a Sunday comic strip created by Alex Raymond for
King Features. Since then, along with his companions
Dale Arden and Dr. Zarkov, Flash has done violent battle with Ming the Merciless on the planet Mongo and
with an assortment of interplanetary menaces in every
possible medium. The Sunday strip, an immediate success, generated many comic book appearances--the
first in *King Comics* #1 of April 1936; a radio series on
the Mutual network in 1935-1936; an original novel
published in 1936; three chapter plays for Universal
starring Buster Crabbe between 1936 and 1940; a daily
comic strip that ran from 1940 to 1944 and was revived
in 1951; a syndicated live-action television series in
1953-1954; hardback reprints of early strips in 1967
and 1971; a Filmation animated cartoon for NBC in
1979-1980 and a lavish Technicolor movie in 1980.
"Steady, Dale!"

FGR-1

FGR-2

FGR-3

FGR-1. "Flash Gordon" Litho. Button,
1934. From set of seven showing various King Features Syndicate characters. - **$25 $50 $85**

FGR-2. "Dale Arden" Litho. Button,
1934. From set of seven showing various King Features Syndicate characters. - **$25 $50 $85**

FGR-3. Buster Crabbe Dixie Ice Cream Lid,
1936. - **$12 $20 $40**

FGR-4

FGR-4. "Flash Gordon Strange Adventure Magazine" Vol. 1 #1,
1936. - **$200 $400 $750**

FGR-5

FGR-6

FGR-7

FGR-5. "Buster Crabbe" Dixie Ice Cream Picture,
c. 1936. He is pictured as Flash Gordon from "New Universal Serial" described on reverse. - **$35 $100 $175**

FGR-6. "Buster Crabbe" Dixie Ice Cream Picture,
c. 1936. He is pictured as Flash Gordon from "New Universal Serial" described on reverse. - **$35 $100 $175**

FGR-7. "Flash Gordon Vs. The Emperor Of Mongo" Book,
1936. 4x5" hardcover otherwise similar format to Fast-Action Book. - **$75 $150 $200**

FGR-8

FGR-9

FGR-10

FGR-8. "Flash Gordon/Buster Crabbe Movie Club" Cello. Button,
c. 1938. - **$250 $700 $1200**

FGR-9. "Flash Gordon Adventure Club" Cello. Button,
1938. Rare. Universal Pictures. For 12-chapter movie serial "Flash Gordon Conquers The Universe" starring Buster Crabbe and Carol Hughes, both pictured. - **$250 $600 $1000**

FGR-10. Movie Serial Club Member Card,
c. 1938. Scarce. Buster Crabbe pictured as Flash Gordon. - **$200 $350 $750**

FGR-11

FGR-13

FGR-12

FGR-11. "Chicago Herald And Examiner" Club Litho. Button,
1930s. - **$75 $125 $250**

FGR-12. "World Battle Fronts" World War II Folder Map,
1943. Macy's department store "Flash Gordon Headquarters". Map opens to 20x27" sheet picturing global areas on both sides. - **$40 $75 $140**

FGR-13. "S.F. Call-Bulletin" Cardboard Disk,
c. 1940s. San Francisco newspaper. From series of contest disks, match number to win prize. - **$10 $25 $40**

FGR-14

FGR-14. "Flash Gordon Comics",
1951. Gordon Bread Give-Away. Two issues of strip reprints. Each - **$2 $5 $10**

FGR-15

FGR-16

FGR-15. "March Of Comics No. 133" Booklet,
1955. Poll-Parrot Shoes. From series by K.K.
Publications. - **$12 $36 $85**

FGR-16. "Puck" 10x10" Paper Store Sign,
1950s. Puck The Comic Weekly and Sunday Comics.
From series for drugstore use picturing various King
Features characters. - **$25 $60 $100**

FGR-17

FGR-17. "Puck" 15x40" Paper Store Sign,
1950s. Puck The Comic Weekly and Sunday Comics. For
drugstore use picturing King Features characters. -
$35 $75 $125

FGR-18

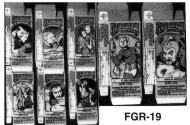

FGR-19

FGR-18. Dale Arden Litho. Button,
1960s. From set of King Features characters marked only
by copyright symbol. - **$10 $20 $35**

FGR-19. Candy Boxes,
1978. Phoenix Candy Co. Set of eight. Each - **$5 $10 $25**

THE FLINTSTONES

Hanna-Barbera's Flintstones started life as the first
adult prime-time television cartoon, went on to
become the longest running such animated series in
TV history and spawned numerous reruns, specials,
spinoffs and adaptations--as well as a merchandising
bonanza. *The Flintstones* premiered on ABC in
September 1960 and ran uninterrupted for six years,
was rebroadcast on NBC Saturday mornings from
1967 to 1970 and has been around in one form or
another ever since. A major film starring John
Goodman was released in 1994.

Fred and Wilma Flintstone and their friends Barney
and Betty Rubble are a prehistoric parody of the
Kramdens and Nortons of *The Honeymooners,* complete with marital bickering, get-rich-quick schemes,
bowling nights out and lodge membership. As added
attractions, Dino, their pet dinosaur, was joined in
1963 by a baby daughter, Pebbles and by the Rubbles'
adopted son, Bamm-Bamm. The kids spun off on their
own show in 1971.

Comic book appearances began in 1961 and continued
into the 1990s. The characters have been merchandised extensively, with several thousand tie-in items

licensed. Post's Pebbles cereal and Flintstones chew-
able vitamins were promotional successes. "Yabba
dabba doo!"

FLN-1

FLN-2

FLN-1. "Stone Age Candy" Boxes,
1962. Store item. Each - **$5 $10 $15**

FLN-2. "March Of Comics" #243,
1963. Various retail sponsors. - **$10 $25 $50**

FLN-3

FLN-4

FLN-3. 1964-1965 New York World's Fair Comic Book,
1964. Officially licensed souvenir published by JW Books
With Hanna-Barbera copyright. - **$10 $20 $45**

FLN-4. Dino Litho. Button,
1960s. Hanna-Barbera copyright. From 1960s Flintstone
character set. - **$10 $20 $30**

FLN-5

FLN-6

FLN-5. "History Of Bedrock" 23x28" Poster,
1970. Miles Laboratories. - **$25 $45 $75**

**FLN-6. Flintstone Jewelry Display With 36 Character
Rings,**
1972. Store item by Cartoon Celebrities Inc.
Complete - **$150 $250 $350**
Each Ring - **$3 $5 $8**

FLN-7

FLN-8

FLN-7. Fred Flintstone "Powell Valves" Pencil Eraser,
1972. Wm. Powell Co. - **$15 $30 $50**

FLN-8. Vending Machine Litho. Button Set,
1973. Set of 12, various color combinations.
Each - **$3 $5 $15**

FLN-9

FLN-9. Litho. Buttons,
1973. Store item. Set of 10. Each - **$5 $10 $15**

FLN-10

FLN-11

FLN-10. Vending Machine Header Card,
c. 1970s. Includes generic rings, generic Dino figure and
rubber Flintstones figures. Complete - **$75**

**FLN-11. "Flintstick" Plastic/Metal Miniature Cigarette
Lighter,**
c. 1970s. Flintstones Multiple Vitamins. - **$50 $100 $150**

FLN-12

**FLN-12. Flintstones Brand Multiple Vitamins Plastic
Mugs,**
1970s. Each - **$5 $8 $15**

FLN-13

FLN-14

FLN-13. Flintstone Land/Sea Vehicle,
1970s. Probable Post's Fruity Pebbles. Unassembled In
Cellophane Wrapper - **$20**
Assembled - **$5 $10 $15**

FLN-14. Fred On Dino Digger Toy,
c. 1970s. Pebbles Cereal. Plastic mechanical action toy. -
$8 $15 $20

FLN-15

FLN-16

FLN-15. Fruit Drinks Litho. Tab,
c. 1970s. Yabba Dabba Dew. - **$8 $12 $20**

FLN-16. "Post" Plastic Cereal Box Banks,
1984. Cocoa Pebbles and Fruity Pebbles.
Each - **$8 $12 $20**

FLN-17

FLN-17. Fred & Barney Ceramic Figurines,
1990. Post Cereals. Boxed - **$15 $30 $50**
Loose Pair - **$5 $15 $25**

FLYING ACES CLUB

One of the many 1930s aviation-themed clubs inspired
in part by the accomplishment of Charles Lindbergh.
Sponsored by *Flying Aces Magazine*, most premiums
carry the initials "FAC."

FAC-1

FAC-2

FAC-1. Club Membership Card,
1932. Logo of wings only, no propeller. - **$10 $25 $50**

FAC-2. Gold Cadet Wings,
1932. - **$30 $60 $90**

| FAC-3 | FAC-4 |

FAC-3. Silver Pilot Wings,
1932. - **$30 $60 $90**

FAC-4. "Pilot/FAC" Wings Badge,
1932. Propeller on top of wings.
Silver version. - **$10 $20 $30**
Gold version - **$30 $60 $90**

FAC-5

FAC-6

FAC-5. "Cadet/FAC" Wings Rank Badge,
1932. Propeller on top of wings.
Silver version. - **$15 $30 $50**
Gold version - **$30 $60 $90**

FAC-6. "Ace/FAC" Star Badge,
1932. Scarce. - **$35 $70 $140**

FAC-7

FAC-7. "Flying Aces" Silvered Brass Bracelet,
1932. Link bands with top plate in wing and propeller
design. - **$20 $45 $100**

FAC-8

FAC-8. Club Membership Card,
1932. Logo of wings mounted by propeller. - **$10 $25 $50**

FAC-9

FAC-10

**FAC-9. "F.A.C. Distinguished Service Medal" Brass
Medal With Ribbon ,**
1932. Rare. Back inscription "Awarded By Flying Aces
Club". - **$65 $150 $250**

FAC-10. FAC Propeller Pins,
1932. Rare. For placement on "Service Medal" ribbon.
Each - **$15 $30 $50**

FAC-11

FAC-11. "FAC" Stitched Fabric Wings Patch,
1932. Scarce. Flying Aces magazine. - **$20 $75 $100**

THE FLYING FAMILY

This children's adventure program aired briefly on
NBC in 1932-1933. The program dramatized the true-
life story of Colonel George Hutchinson, his wife
Blanche, and their daughters Kathryn and Janet.
Accompanied by Sunshine, their lion cub mascot, the
flying family found adventure in all parts of the country. Cocomalt sponsored the series, and young listeners could obtain their Flight Commander wings by
drinking Cocomalt for at least 30 days and mailing in a
statement witnessed and signed by a parent.

FLY-1

**FLY-1. Puzzle, Flight Commander Folder And
Envelope,**
1932. Complete - **$10 $15 $25**

FLY-2

FLY-3

**FLY-2. "Flight Commander/Flying Cubs" Brass Wings
Rank Badge,**
1932. Highest rank depicting tiger head. - **$15 $30 $50**

FLY-3. "Flying Cubs" Brass Wings Badge,
1932. Depicts tiger head. - **$15 $25 $40**

FLY-4

FLY-5

FLY-4. Family Picture Wheaties Box Back,
c. 1932. - **$10 $20 $30**

FLY-5. "Cub" Brass Wings Pin,
c. 1932. Association with this program is uncertain. -
$10 $30 $50

FLY-6

FLY-7

FLY-6. "Cub" Silvered Brass Lapel Stud,
c. 1932. Association with this program is uncertain. -
$10 $30 $50

FLY-7. Family Adventures Map,
c. 1932. Cocomalt. Pictures various global regions plus listing of air times on NBC radio stations. - **$10 $15 $25**

FOODINI

They started out in 1948 as the bumbling villains of the
Lucky Pup series on CBS but Foodini and his dimwit
accomplice Pinhead eventually took over the show and
by 1951 were starring in their own series, *Foodini the
Great*, on ABC. The hand puppets, created by Hope and
Morey Bunin, were fated never to accomplish their swin-
dling schemes, defeated by the Pup's pal Jolo the clown
as well as by their own ineptitude. Sponsors of the two
series (1948-1951) included Ipana toothpaste, Good and
Plenty candy, Sundial shoes and Bristol-Myers.
Licensed items are normally copyrighted R. P. Cox.

FOO-1

FOO-1. Paper Portraits,
c. 1948. Scarce. CBS-TV. Set of four: Doris Brown with
Lucky Pup, Foodini, Pinhead, Jolo. Each - **$15 $25 $35**

FOO-2

FOO-3

FOO-2. "Jolo" Metal Pin On Card,
1949. Store item. Pins or bracelets, also seen for Foodini.
Each Carded - **$20 $40 $60**
Each Loose - **$10 $25 $50**

FOO-3. Plastic Microscope With Instructions,
1950. Ipana Toothpaste. Includes six slides for microscope. Instruction Folder - **$10 $15 $25**
Microscope - **$15 $30 $50**
Slides Each - **$1 $3 $5**

FOO-4

FOO-5

FOO-6

FOO-4. Cardboard Mask,
c. 1950. Scarce. Punch-out from unknown source. -
$50 $150 $250

FOO-5. "Foodini" As Magician Dexterity Puzzle,
1951. Plastic over tin frame puzzle. - **$20 $50 $75**

FOO-6. "Jolo" Juggling Dexterity Puzzle,
1951. Plastic over tin frame puzzle. - **$20 $50 $75**

FOO-7

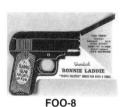

FOO-8

FOO-7. "Pinhead" Dexterity Puzzle,
1951. Plastic over tin frame puzzle. - **$30 $65 $100**

FOO-8. Cardboard Pop Gun,
c. 1951. Sundial Bonnie Laddie Shoes. - **$25 $65 $100**

FOO-9

FOO-9. "Television Studio" Cardboard Kit With Mailer, c. 1951. Sundial Bonnie Laddie Shoes. Includes stage, figures and accessories. Near Mint In Mailer - **$250**

FOXY GRANDPA

Cartoonist C. E. Schultze created his *Foxy Grandpa* comic strip for the Sunday New York Herald in 1900. The strip, which showed Grandpa consistently outwitting a pair of young tormentors, was an instant success with readers, but its popularity waned over the years. It moved to the New York American in 1902, then to the New York Press, where it ran until 1918. A series of nature tales, *Foxy Grandpa's Stories*, ran in newspapers during the 1920s. Hardcover reprints of the strip were published in the early years and a musical comedy based on the strip opened on Broadway in 1902. Schultze typically signed his drawings Bunny, with an appropriate sketch.

FOX-1

FOX-2

FOX-1. Comic Strip Announcement 15x20" Paper Poster, 1902. New York Sunday Journal. - **$75 $150 $250**

FOX-2. "Foxy Grandpa's Grocery Store" Cut-Out Supplement, 1902. New York American & Journal newspaper. Uncut - **$25 $50 $75**

FOX-3

FOX-4

FOX-3. "Six Months In New York" Cello. Button, 1902. For theater version based on comic strip. - **$15 $30 $50**

FOX-4. "Foxy Grandpa" Cello. Button, c. 1902. Hearst's Chicago American. Promotes start of comic strip by that newspaper. - **$15 $30 $50**

FOX-5

FOX-5. Foxy Grandpa Song Sheet, c. 1902. Scarce. Newspaper supplement. - **$20 $60 $120**

FOX-6

FOX-7

FOX-8

FOX-6. Foxy Grandpa Song Sheet, c. 1902. Scarce. Newspaper supplement. - **$20 $60 $120**

FOX-7. "Foxy Grandpa/Chicago American" Diecut White Metal Stickpin, c. 1902. Lightly tinted, depicts him and both boys. - **$25 $40 $60**

FOX-8. "Foxy Grandpa Second Year Of The Musical Comedy" Diecut Cello. Figure, c. 1903. 2-1/2" tall full color thin cello. figure by Whitehead & Hoag Co. - **$10 $20 $30**

FOX-9

FOX-10

FOX-11

FOX-9. Bisque Figure, c. 1905. Store item. - **$50 $100 $150**

FOX-10. Composition Figure, c. 1905. Store item. Jointed arms and legs. - **$50 $120 $200**

FOX-11. Flocked Composition Candy Container, c. 1905. Store item. - **$75 $150 $250**

FOX-12

FOX-12. Postcard, 1906. Boston Sunday American premium. Has heat-applied tattoo transfer on front. - **$8 $15 $25**

FRANK BUCK

Animal hunter and trapper Frank Buck (1884-1950) achieved international fame after World War I as a jungle explorer whose claim that he never intentionally harmed a wild animal led to his motto "Bring 'Em Back Alive." Buck went around the world more than a dozen times collecting animals, giving lectures, making movies and writing magazine articles and books, and at one point owned the world's largest private zoo in Amityville, New York. He appeared as himself in two brief radio series: on NBC in 1932 sponsored by A. C. Gilbert toys and on the Blue network in 1934 sponsored by Pepsodent toothpaste. Buck and his animals were featured at the 1933-1934 Century of Progress Exposition in Chicago and the 1939-1940 New York World's Fair. A 1932 documentary film followed him through the Malay jungles as he collected various animals and Buck played an adventurer in Columbia Pictures' first chapter play, *Jungle Menace*, in 1937. CBS-TV aired a *Bring 'Em Back Alive* fiction series in 1982-1983 starring Bruce Boxleitner as the legendary hunter.

FRB-1

FRB-2

FRB-1. A.C. Gilbert Christmas Ad Photo,
1932. Frank Buck inscription "I Hope You Get An Erector Set For Christmas". - **$20 $40 $60**

FRB-2. Club Manual,
1934. Pepsodent toothpaste. - **$35 $100 $175**

FRB-3

FRB-4

FRB-3. Mailer,
1934. For Club manual. Rare. - **$35 $75 $100**

FRB-4. World's Fair Promo,
1934. Chicago Century of Progress giveaway. Eight pages. - **$25 $35 $50**

FRB-5

FRB-6

FRB-7

FRB-5. "A Century Of Progress" Chicago World's Fair Litho. Button,
1934. From exhibit, dated for second year of fair. - **$35 $75 $125**

FRB-6. "Adventurers Club-Member" Brass Button,
1934. Pepsodent toothpaste. - **$5 $12 $25**

FRB-7. "Frank Buck" Brass Lucky Piece,
1934. Pepsodent toothpaste. Back pictures leopard head with inscription "Tidak Hilang Berani". Copy of Hindu hunter's charm carried by Ali, Frank Buck's Number 1 Boy. - **$30 $100 $150**

FRB-8

FRB-9

FRB-8. Film Supplement,
1934. Sixteen page premium. Promotes the film "Wild Cargo." - **$25 $50 $75**

FRB-9. "Adventurers Club" Fabric Neckerchief,
1934. Pepsodent toothpaste. - **$40 $80 $150**

FRB-10

FRB-11

FRB-10. Prize Checklist,
1935. Pepsodent prize list. - **$10 $20 $30**

FRB-11. "Frank Buck Club" Cello. Button,
1936. - **$25 $50 $100**

FRB-12

FRB-12. "Frank Buck's Jungleland" New York World's Fair Card,
1939. Briefly described his exhibit in the amusement area. - **$8 $12 $20**

(CLOSE-UP)   **FRB-14**
FRB-13

FRB-15

FRB-13. "Jungle Camp" Metal Letter Opener/Bookmark,
1939. From exhibit at New York World's Fair. - **$25 $50 $90**

FRB-14. "Frank Buck's Jungle Camp" Cello. Button,
1939. From exhibit at 1939-1940 New York World's Fair. - **$15 $30 $50**

FRB-15. "Bring 'Em Back Alive" Ivory Initial Ring,
1939. Ivory Soap. Brass with personalized initial ivory-colored insert. - **$175 $300 $500**

FRB-17

FRB-16

FRB-16. "Frank Buck's Jungleland" New York World's Fair Brass Ring,
1939. Rare. Tiny "NYWF" initials rather than traditional Frank Buck's Adventurers Club inscription. - **$1200 $3500 $6500**

FRB-17. Cello./Steel Pocketknife,
1939. Ivory Soap. White grips with facsimile signature on one. - **$50 $100 $160**

FRB-18   **FRB-19**

FRB-18. World's Fair Promo,
1939. New York World's Fair premium. Four pages. Promotes Jungleland exhibit. - **$20 $30 $40**

FRB-19. Coin,
1939. Jungleland premium with hole for chain. New York World's Fair Coin. Scarce. - **$35 $70 $125**

FRB-20

FRB-20. Pennant,
1939. New York World's Fair Jungleland exhibit pennant. Scarce. - **$75 $150 $250**

FRB-21

FRB-22

FRB-21. "Bring 'Em Back Alive" Map And Game 14x22",
1930s. Two versions: premium from "Scott's Emulsion" or store item by "Funland Books & Games". - **$60 $150 $200**

FRB-22. Buckhorn Rifle Manual,
1930s. Twelve page premium. Shows Frank testing the gun, as well as various photos of the gun. - **$15 $25 $45**

FRB-24

FRB-23

FRB-23. Postcard,
1930s. Premium for exhibition in New York - **$10 $25 $40**

FRB-24. "Frank Buck Explorer's Sun Watch",
1949. Jack Armstrong/Wheaties. - **$20 $35 $65**

FRB-25

FRB-25. Wheaties Caribbean Cruise Contest And Sun Watch Leaflets,
1949. Contest Sheet - **$5 $15 $25**
Sun Watch Order Form - **$5 $10 $15**

FRB-26

FRB-26. "Frank Buck Explorer's Sun Watch" Instruction Leaflet,
1949. Wheaties. Folder opening to four panels w/instructions printed on both sides. - **$10 $20 $35**

FRANK MERRIWELL

Dime novels, the forerunner of pulp magazines, became popular in the 1880s. Colorful covers highlighted text stories embellished with daring deeds and the triumph of good over evil. Writer Gilbert Patten, under various pseudonyms, had been doing stories for several years when approached by the large publishing company Street & Smith to come up with a character for their new magazine *Tip Top Library*. Using "Frank" for frankness, "Merri" for happy disposition and "Well" for good health, he came up with Frank Merriwell.

Written under the pen name Burt L. Standish, Frank's first adventure was published on April 18, 1896. Author Patten imbued Frank Merriwell with a Yale education, a sharp mind, physical fitness, an honest demeanor and a penchant for hard work. Merriwell became an inspiration to boys and girls nationwide. He was not only a role model, but an imaginary friend they could trust. Patten went on to author 208 Frank Merriwell books, which sold over 100 million copies.

Merriwell's adventures remained popular well in the 1940s in a comic strip, a Big Little Book title, a movie serial and a radio program with Lawson Zerbe in the title role. Frank Merriwell's adventures and personality set the tone for one of radio's most popular characters, the next "All-American Boy," Jack Armstrong.

FRM-1

FRM-2

FRM-1. Tip Top Weekly #242,
1900. Frank Merriwell's Tip Top League Badge pictured with application for 1st premium badge. - **$25 $50 $75**

FRM-2. Frank Merriwell Tip Top League Brass Badge,
1900. Tip Top Magazine premium. First character badge. - **$100 $200 $400**

FRM-3

FRM-4

FRM-3. "Frank Merriwell At Yale" BLB,
1935. Store item. Whitman #1121. - **$12 $25 $50**

FRM-4. "Club Member/Follow The Adventures Of Frank Merriwell" Cello . Button,
1936. Scarce. Universal Pictures. For 12-chapter movie serial "The Adventures Of Frank Merriwell". - **$40 $100 $150**

FREAKIES

Ralston Purina Company introduced Freakies cereal--crunchy, sugary puffs--in 1973, along with a gang of seven creatures also called Freakies. The creatures, ugly little characters covered with bumps, were named Boss Moss, Cowmumble, Gargle, Goody-Goody, Grumble, Hamhose, and Snorkledorf. In-package premiums included PVC Freakies, stickers, holograms, and a set of rubber air bulb-powered vinyl race cars. The cereal was an initial success but failed to win repeat customers. An attempt to revive Freakies as Space Surfers in 1987 also failed.

FRK-1

FRK-2

FRK-1. "Freakie Car" Set Of Seven Vinyl Racers,
1974. Each is 2-1/2" long plus rubber air bulb to launch car. Top edge of front bumper names each as "Goody Goody, Hamhose, Cowmumble, Boss Moss, Snorkledorf, Gargle, Grumble."
Near Mint Boxed With Instructions - **$125**
Each With Air Bulb - **$5 $8 $12**

FRK-2. Fabric Iron-On Patches,
1975. Pictured are Gargle, Cowmumble, Hamhose from probable set of seven. Each - **$5 $10 $15**

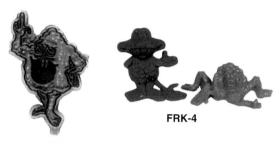

FRK-4

FRK-3

FRK-3. Freakies Rubber Magnet,
1970s. At least five different characters seen in a small version about 1" to 1-1/2" and a larger version about 1-1/2" to 2". Each - **$3 $6 $10**

FRK-4. Freakies Vinyl Figures,
1970s. At least seven different in various single colors, each about 1-1/2" to 2". Each - **$3 $5 $10**

FRK-5

FRK-5. Freakies Boats,
1970s. Soft plastic figures of Hamhose, Cowmumble, Grumble, each designed to hold balloon to propel in water by air loss after inflation. Each - **$3 $10 $15**

FRED ALLEN

Fred Allen (1894-1956) was a vaudeville juggler and standup comic who became one of the legendary radio comedians of the 1930s and 1940s. From his first show on CBS in 1932 to his last on NBC in 1949, hardly a week went by without a Fred Allen program of one sort or another. Allen wrote his own material and his "feud" with Jack Benny was a successful running gag from 1936 to 1949. Also memorable was Allen's Alley, a mythical street he developed in 1942, inhabited by Mrs. Nussbaum, Titus Moody, Ajax Cassidy and Senator Claghorn. Sponsors over the years included Linit bath oil, Hellmann's mayonnaise, Sal Hepatica, Ipana toothpaste, Texaco gasoline, Tenderleaf tea and Ford automobiles. Allen made a number of television appearances in the 1950s on comedy and quiz shows but his biting wit and literate humor were better suited to radio.

FRD-1

FRD-1. Fred Allen's "Town Hall Tonight" Audition Notice Postcard,
1935. Notification to entertainer hopeful granting radio audition at NBC Studios, New York. - **$5 $10 $15**

FRD-2   **FRD-3**

FRD-2. "Town Hall Tonight" Fan Postcard,
1937. Radio show title on back. - **$10 $15 $25**

FRD-3. Fred Allen & Portland Hoffa Fan Photo,
c. 1937. Ipana toothpaste and Salhepatica Stomach Relief. Back names "Town Hall Tonight" radio show. - **$8 $15 $30**

FRIENDS OF THE PHANTOM

Between 1933 and 1953 Richard Curtis Van Loan-- alias the Phantom--solved over 150 crimes in the pages of the pulp magazine *Phantom Detective*. Created by D.L. Champion writing under the name Robert Wallace, the Phantom was a genius of disguise and a physical marvel. During the 1930s, readers who joined his crime-fighting club would receive a Friends of the Phantom badge.

FPH-1   **FPH-2**

FPH-1. "Friends Of The Phantom" Letter And Membership Card,
1930s. Phantom Detective magazine.
Card - **$75 $125 $250**
Letter - **$50 $100 $150**

FPH-2. "Friends Of The Phantom" Brass Shield Badge,
1930s. Phantom Detective magazine. Phantom depicted in mask and top hat. - **$75 $175 $400**

FU MANCHU

Master scientist and brilliant prince of evil, Fu Manchu was created by novelist Sax Rohmer in 1911. He appeared in a series of silent films in the 1920s and in talkies from 1929 to 1980 played by Warner Oland, Boris Karloff, Henry Brandon, Christopher Lee or Peter Sellers. The evil oriental, who was either avenging the death of his wife and son or out to conquer or destroy the world, starred in several radio serials: on *The Collier Hour*, sponsored by Collier's magazine, on the Blue network in 1927; on CBS in 1932-1933 sponsored by Campana Balm and in *The Shadow of Fu Manchu*, a syndicated 1939-1940 serial. A syndicated television series had a brief run in 1956.

FUM-1

FUM-2

FUM-3

FUM-1. Paper Mask,
1932. Rare. Various theaters. - **$50 $150 $200**

FUM-2. "Mask Of Fu Manchu" Movie Herald,
1932. Folder for M-G-M movie starring Boris Karloff in title role. - **$25 $50 $70**

FUM-3. "Shadow Of Fu Manchu" Radio Promo Matchbook Cover,
1939. - **$10 $40 $50**

FUM-4

FUM-5

FUM-4. "The Shadow Of Fu Manchu" Radio Serial Cello. Button,
1939. - **$35 $75 $150**

FUM-5. "Shadow Of Fu Manchu" Keys Trick With Envelope,
c. 1939. Dodge Motors Co. "Mystic Keys" dexterity trick of two interlocking 2" metal keys in envelope imprinted for WFBR Radio, Baltimore. Envelope - **$50 $100 $150**
Key Set - **$40 $75 $125**

FUM-6

FUM-7

FUM-8

FUM-6. "Drums Of Fu Manchu" Movie Serial Cello. Button,
1940. Scarce. - **$50 $125 $350**

FUM-7. "Drums Of Fu Manchu" 41x77" Three-Sheet Poster,
1940. Republic Pictures. 15-chapter movie serial. - **$200 $400 $750**

FUM-8. "Drums Of Fu Manchu" 27x41" Movie Serial Poster,
1940. Republic Pictures. - **$200 $400 $600**

FUM-9

FUM-9. "Drums Of Fu Manchu" 14x22" Window Card,
1940. Republic Pictures. - **$30 $50 $75**

Fury was a black stallion and the star attraction on NBC-TV's Saturday morning lineup from 1955 to 1966. His human co-stars in this extremely popular series were Bobby Diamond as a young orphan and Peter Graves as the rancher who adopted the boy and gave him the horse as a means of teaching him responsibility. The show received a number of awards from various civic and service groups for its non-violent handling of problems of right and wrong. Post cereals was an early sponsor but merchandising was not extensive. Items are normally copyrighted Vision Productions Inc., Television Programs of America Inc. or Independent Television Corp. The show has been syndicated under the title *Brave Stallion*. Dell published a series of *Fury* comic books between 1957 and 1962.

FUR-1

FUR-1. Cast Member Photo,
c. 1955. Glossy black and white with facsimile signatures of Bobby Diamond, Peter Graves, William Fawcett, Ann Robinson. - **$10 $20 $30**

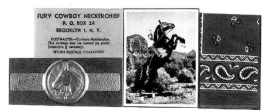

FUR-2

FUR-2. "Fury Cowboy Neckerchief" Kit With Envelope,
c. 1955. Mail premium of fabric bandanna, metal clasp, color photo. Near Mint In Mailer - **$100**
Photo - **$5 $10 $20**
Bandanna - **$5 $10 $15**
Clasp - **$15 $30 $55**

FUR-3

FUR-3. "Fury's Western Roundup" Party Kit,
c. 1955. Borden Co. Extensive paper items including eight punch-out sheets. Unused - **$20 $40 $75**

FUR-4

FUR-4. "Fury Adventure Kit",
1960. Post Alpha-Bits. Multi-purpose plastic including weather indicator, flashlight, whistle, pen and miniature writing tablet. - **$75 $150 $250**

GABBY HAYES

George "Gabby" Hayes (1885-1969) acted in a traveling repertory company and played burlesque and vaudeville before he went to Hollywood for a film career that spanned more than 30 years. Known as Windy, then Gabby, the whiskered, ornery, toothless geezer played sidekick to Hopalong Cassidy, Roy Rogers, Gene Autry, Bill Elliott, Randolph Scott and John Wayne in well over 100 Westerns. Hayes was a regular on radio's *Roy Rogers Show* in the 1940s and had his own program on the Mutual network in 1951-1952, sponsored by Quaker cereals. Adventure and Western comic books appeared between 1948 and 1957. On television, two separate series--both called *The Gabby Hayes Show*--ran concurrently. One was a weekly educational program about episodes in American history (NBC 1950-1951), the other a fictional series of tall tales and Western film clips (NBC 1950-1954 and ABC 1956). Sponsors were Quaker cereals and Peter Paul candy.

GAB-1

GAB-2

GAB-1. "George 'Gabby' Hayes" Dixie Ice Cream Picture,
1947. - **$50 $100 $250**

GAB-2. "George 'Gabby' Hayes" Cello. Button,
c. 1948. - **$10 $20 $30**

GAB-3

GAB-4

GAB-3. Prospector's Hat 16x21" Paper Store Sign,
1951. Quaker Cereals. - **$50 $100 $175**

GAB-4. Prospector's Black Felt Hat,
1951. Quaker Cereals. - **$25 $50 $100**

GAB-5

GAB-5. "Shooting Cannon Ring" Instruction Sheet,

1951. Quaker Cereals. Opposite side offers Miniature Western Gun Collection. - **$75 $88 $100**

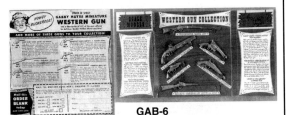

GAB-6

GAB-6. "Gabby Hayes Miniature Western Gun Collection",

1951. Quaker Cereals. Set of six: Buffalo Rifle, Colt Revolver, Flintlock Dueling Pistol, "Peacemaker" Pistol, Remington Breech-Loader Rifle, Winchester 1873 Rifle.
Gun Set - **$25 $50 $100**
Display Folder - **$30 $75 $100**
Order Sheet - **$15 $30 $40**

GAB-7

GAB-8

GAB-7. Quaker Cereal Comic Booklets With Mailing Envelopes,

1951. Set of five. Each Book Or Mailer - **$9 $26 $65**

GAB-8. Quaker Cannon Ring,

1951. Puffed Wheat & Puffed Rice. Large ring with brass base and spring-loaded barrel in either brass or aluminum. - **$50 $150 $250**

GAB-9

GAB-9. Quaker "Five Western Wagons" Cereal Box,

1952. Quaker Puffed Rice.
Complete Box - **$50 $175 $275**

GAB-10

GAB-10. Gabby Hayes Western Wagon Kits,

1952. Quaker Cereals. Five different kits: Buckboard, Chuck Wagon, Covered Wagon, Great Plains Freighter, Wells Fargo Stagecoach. Each Boxed - **$20 $50 $75**

GAB-11

GAB-11. Movie Viewer Set,

1952. Quaker Cereals. Filmstrip with five titles, instruction slip, mailer. Near Mint Boxed - **$200**

GAB-12

GAB-12. Quaker "Pocket-Sized Movie Viewer" Newspaper Ad,

1952. - **$5 $10 $15**

GAB-13

GAB-13. Gabby Hayes Metal Automobiles,
1952. Quaker Cereals. Set of six.
Near Mint Boxed - **$180**
Each - **$5 $15 $30**
Instructions - **$15 $25 $35**

GANG BUSTERS

Marching against the underworld, proving each week that crime does not pay, *Gang Busters* was based on case files of the FBI and local police and proved so popular that it ran on network radio for 21 years. The show premiered on CBS in 1936 sponsored by Palmolive. Succeeding sponsors including Cue magazine (1939-1940), Sloan's liniment (1940-1945), Waterman pens (1945-1948), Tide soap (1948), Grape-Nuts cereal (1949-1954) and Wrigley's gum (1954-1955). The show was last aired in 1957. Descriptions of actual criminals, broadcast at the end of each program, apparently resulted in the capture of hundreds of fugitives. A television series with the same format had a nine-month run on NBC in 1952. *Gang Busters* comic books were published from 1938 to 1959.

GNG-1

GNG-2

GNG-1. "Phillips H. Lord's Gang Busters" Badge,
c. 1935. Brass luster on embossed tin. - **$75 $150 $275**

GNG-2. "Stop Thief" 22x30" Paper Game Board Map,
1937. Palmolive. Came with nine metal cars.
Game - **$30 $75 $100**
Each Car - **$5 $10 $15**

GNG-3

GNG-4

GNG-5

GNG-3. Member's Badge,
c. 1937. - **$20 $50 $75**

GNG-4. "Green's Gang Busters Crime Crusaders" Enameled Brass Badge,
c. 1937. "Phillips H. Lord's" copyright. - **$50 $100 $150**

GNG-5. Enameled Belt Buckle,
c. 1937. Rare. - **$65 $150 $250**

GNG-6

GNG-7

GNG-6. Tie,
1937. Scarce. - **$65 $150 $250**

GNG-7. "Gang Busters" Game,
1938. Store item by Lynco Inc. - **$100 $200 $350**

GNG-8

GNG-8. Whitman Boxed Board Game,
1939. Store item. - **$60 $100 $150**

GENE AUTRY

America's favorite singing cowboy was born in 1907 on a small ranch in Texas and grew up in Oklahoma, where he worked as a railroad telegraph operator and began his career singing and composing. Local performances as a yodeling cowboy led to national radio spots on the *National Barn Dance* and *National Farm and Home Hour* programs in the 1930s. Autry began recording cowboy songs in 1929 and had phenomenal success both as a composer and as a singer. He moved to Hollywood in 1934 and a year later starred in *Phantom Empire*, a 12-episode chapter play for Mascot. Over the years Autry was to write more than 250 songs and act in more than 100 Westerns.

Gene Autry's Melody Ranch, a program of Western songs and stories told around a campfire, premiered on CBS radio in 1940 and ran continually until 1956, interrupted only by Autry's service in the Army Air Corps from 1942 to 1945. The program, sponsored by Wrigley's gum, featured bearded sidekick Pat Buttram for comic relief, along with a variety of musical groups.

On television, also sponsored by Wrigley's gum, *The Gene Autry Show* aired on CBS from 1950 to 1956. Filmed at his 125-acre Melody Ranch and produced by his Flying A Productions company, the program put

Autry back in the saddle again each week to do battle with assorted villains. Riding his wonder horse Champion and accompanied by saddle-partner Buttram, Autry set a consistently high moral tone for his young fans. A spinoff series, *The Adventures of Champion*, which ran for a season (1955-1956) on CBS, featured young Barry Curtis and his dog Rebel along with the hero horse.

A *Gene Autry* Sunday comic strip from General Features Syndicate was begun in 1940 and revived from 1952 to 1955, and Autry comic books from Dell and Fawcett--including giveaways from Pillsbury (1947) and Quaker Oats (1950)--appeared from 1941 through the 1950s. Autry and Champion made countless personal appearances at fairs, parades, Wild West shows, and rodeos, and Flying A Productions did extensive merchandising of Autry-related items ranging from 10-cent club membership cards to complete buckskin outfits.

In the 1950s Autry began a career in business that mirrored his show-business success. He invested in oil and real estate, bought a radio-TV chain and a major league baseball team, served as chairman of the Cowboy Hall of Fame, and created a Western Heritage Museum in Los Angeles.

GAU-4. Photo,
1930s. Radio premium shows Gene Autry playing guitar with foot on bench next to toy dog. - **$20 $50 $80**

GAU-5. Composition Statue,
c. 1930s. Rare. Store item. - **$150 $300 $500**

GAU-6

GAU-7

GAU-6. Fan Photo With Insert Sheet,
1940. Republic Studio. Near Mint In Mailer - **$35**
Photo Only - **$8 $12 $20**

GAU-7. Rodeo Handbill,
c. 1940. World Championship Rodeo, Boston Garden. - **$25 $50 $85**

GAU-1

GAU-2

GAU-3

GAU-8

GAU-9

GAU-10

GAU-8. "Boston Garden Rodeo" Litho. Button,
c. 1940. Single event issue. - **$20 $40 $75**

GAU-9. "Gene Autry" Friendship Ring,
1941. Brass and silvered brass varieties issued by American Specialty Co. of Lancaster, PA for selling seed packs or Christmas cards. An aluminum variety with gold lustre on portrait is c. 1950, issuer unknown.
Brass or Silvered Brass - **$75 $115 $150**
Aluminum - **$85 $135 $185**

GAU-1. Movie Serial Club Member Button,
1935. Rare. Name of club formed by kids in Mascot serial The Phantom Empire. - **$200 $400 $600**

GAU-2. Wheaties Box Back,
c. 1937. For Republic Picture "The Big Show" released late 1936. - **$10 $20 $35**

GAU-3. Photo,
1930s. Radio premium shows Gene Autry in a business suit. - **$20 $40 $50**

GAU-10. "Adventure Comics And Play-Fun Book",
1947. Pillsbury Pancake Mix. - **$20 $60 $220**

GAU-4

GAU-5

GAU-11

GAU-12

GAU-11. Gene Autry Dixie Ice Cream Picture,
1948. - **$10 $25 $50**

GAU-12. Clothing Manufacturer Photo And Cover Note,
1948. J. M. Wood Mfg. Co., maker of Autry shirts and jeans. Set - **$20 $35 $50**

GAU-13

GAU-14

GAU-13. Gene Autry/Lone Ranger Plastic Ring,
c. 1948. Dell Comics. U.S. flag pictured under plastic dome, offered for comic book subscription for each character. - **$60 $100 $150**

GAU-14. "Gene Autry/Champ Crackshot Cowboy" Metal Badge,
c. 1948. Store item by Daniel Smilo & Sons, New York City. Hanger bar has "Deputy" inscription, linked pendant includes words "Valor/Honor Merit."
Medal - **$75 $125 $250**
Card - **$25 $60 $100**

GAU-15

GAU-16

GAU-15. Dell Publishing Co. Picture Strip,
1949. Folder strip of five color photos. - **$25 $50 $80**

GAU-16. Cello. Button,
1940s. Probably a rodeo souvenir. - **$15 $25 $45**

GAU-17   **GAU-18**   **GAU-19**

GAU-17. "Minneapolis Aquatennial Rodeo" Cello. Button,
1940s. Souvenir button. - **$50 $100 $150**

GAU-18. Official Club Badge Cello. Button,
1940s. - **$15 $25 $40**

GAU-19. "Republic's Singing Western Star" Cello. Button,
1940s. - **$25 $50 $75**

GAU-20   **GAU-21**

GAU-20. Store Owner's 10x12" Cardboard Sign,
1940s. Wrigley Doublemint Gum. Signifies sponsorship of "Doublemint Melody Ranch" radio show. - **$40 $60 $125**

GAU-21. "March Of Comics" #25,
1940s. Various sponsors. - **$25 $75 $175**

GAU-23

GAU-22

GAU-22. "Columbia Records" Listing Card,
1940s. Black and white photo with facsimile signature, reverse lists album and individual record titles. -
$8 $15 $25

GAU-23. Portrait Ring,
c. 1940s. Brass frame holds black and white photo under clear plastic cover. - **$35 $65 $100**

GAU-24

GAU-24. Fan Letter With Photo,
c. 1950. Letter includes references to Columbia Pictures, Melody Ranch radio program, fan club address. Photo has facsimile signature. Letter - **$5 $10 $15**
Photo - **$10 $15 $25**

GAU-25

GAU-25. Quaker Comic Booklets,
1950. Puffed Wheat/Rice box inserts. Set of five.
Each - **$10 $25 $60**

GAU-27

GAU-28

GAU-26

GAU-26. "Sunbeam Bread" Color Photo,
c. 1950. - **$10 $18 $30**

GAU-27. "Sunbeam Bread" Cardboard Gun,
c. 1950. - **$25 $40 $65**

GAU-28. Sunbeam Bread Litho. Button,
c. 1950. 1-3/8" size, also as 1-1/4" cello.
Each - **$10 $15 $20**

GAU-30

GAU-29

GAU-29. Sunbeam Bread "Gene Autry Show" 3-1/2" Cello. Button,
c. 1950. - **$20 $40 $75**

GAU-30. Plastic Ring,
c. 1950. Store item. Gold finish with inset paper photo. -
$10 $15 $20

GAU-31

GAU-32

GAU-31. "March Of Comics No. 120",
1954. Poll-Parrot Shoes. - **$10 $30 $75**

GAU-32. "Hit Show" Live Performance 14x22" Cardboard Poster,
1955. - **$50 $125 $200**

GAU-34

GAU-33

GAU-33. Rodeo Souvenir Photo,
1957. - **$5 $12 $20**

GAU-34. Flying A Cardboard Wrist Cuffs,
1950s. Scarce. Probable premium. - **$50 $150 $250**

GAU-35

GAU-35. Horseshoe Nail Ring On Card,
1950s. Store item. Complete - **$200**
Ring Only - **$10 $22 $35**

GAU-36

GAU-37

GAU-36. Plastic Ring With Photo,
1950s. Store item, from card of rings featuring various personalities. Plastic cover over photo. - **$10 $20 $35**

GAU-37. School Tablet,
1950s. Clothing stores. - **$15 $25 $50**

GAU-39

GAU-40

GAU-38

GAU-38. "Adventure Story Trail Map",
1950s. Stroehmann's Bread. Large folder to hold 16 color photo bread end labels telling story of "Gene Autry And The Black Hat Gang!". Folder - **$30 $60 $100**
Each Mounted Label - **$3 $6 $10**

GAU-39. Bread Labels,
1950s. Various bread companies. Numbered photos in at least five different series. Each - **$5 $10 $15**

GAU-40. Publicity Photo,
1950s. Columbia Records. - **$5 $10 $18**

GAU-41

GAU-42

GAU-41. Rain Boots Merchandise Card,
1950s. Servus Rubber Co. - **$10 $15 $25**

GAU-42. English Fan Club Badge On Card,
1950s. Gene Autry Comics, Silvered tin with insert photo.
Near Mint On Card - **$125**
Loose - **$25 $50 $75**

GAU-43

GAU-43. Dell Picture Strip,
1950s. Unfolds with five photos. - **$25 $50 $75**

GAU-44

GAU-45

GAU-44. Litho. Tin Club Tab,
1950s. - **$15 $30 $60**

GAU-45. "Gene Autry & Champion" Cello. Button,
1950s. Star design in gold or silver. - **$15 $25 $35**

GAU-46

GAU-47

GAU-46. Flying A Symbol Brass Wings Badge,
1950s. - **$20 $40 $75**

GAU-47. Ranch Symbol Cigarette Lighter,
1950s. Promotional item by Penguin. Chrome metal with plastic wrapper, other side has "Melody Ranch". - **$25 $45 $80**

GAU-48

GAU-49

GAU-48. Photo,
1950s. Black & white premium photo of him playing guitar. - **$10 $20 $30**

GAU-49. Photo,
1950s. Radio premium for radio show featuring Doublemints Melody Ranch on CBS. - **$25 $50 $95**

GAU-50

GAU-51

GAU-50. "Gene Autry Deputy Sheriff",
1950s. Issuer unknown. Large embossed brass badge. - **$50 $125 $200**

GAU-51. "Western Story Round-Up And Picture Map" Album,
1950s. Sunbeam Bread. Paper folder for mounting 16 numbered bread loaf end pictures. Album - **$40 $85 $135** Each Mounted Label - **$3 $6 $10**

GAU-52

GAU-53

GAU-52. Gene Autry Small Photo Button,
1950s. British Commonwealth. 1-1/4". Black on yellow with red accents on vest and bandanna. - **$25 $65 $100**

GAU-53. Gene Autry Large Photo Button,
1950s. US version. 1-3/4". Pink Gene with red accents on saddle. - **$15 $30 $50**

GENERAL MILLS MISC.

This mammoth food and related products company, born and still based in Minneapolis, was a mid-1920s pioneer in national radio advertising via a powerful transmitter provided jointly by an immediate preceding company, Washburn Crosby Co. and other business interests in the Minneapolis-St. Paul Twin Cities area. The first three programs--*Betty Crocker, The Wheaties Quartet, The Gold Medal Fast Freight*--were of home-maker nature and offered a few premiums in like style. The premium heyday for youngsters, however, began in the early 1930s through the *Skippy and His Pals* pro-gram based on the Percy Crosby comic strip. Skippy was followed in 1933 by *Jack Armstrong, The All-American Boy*. Both offered premiums by sponsor Wheaties, a very popular Depression era cereal that continues to the present. General Mills through the years has offered hundreds of premiums for purchase of food products, principally breakfast cereals. Various General Mills brands are represented in this section while Cheerios, Wheaties and major characters they sponsored are covered in separate sections.

GEN-1

GEN-1. "Gen'l Mills/Five Star Hour" Plaster Figurine,
c. 1938. Rare. Probably issued to retailers, base lists six radio programs. - **$250 $600 $1000**

GEN-2

GEN-2. Kix Plastic Planes,
1946. 24 planes in set. Booklet - **$20 $50 $75** Each Plane - **$3 $7 $10**

GEN-3

GEN-4

GEN-3. "General Mills Map Of The Old West" 20x28",
c. 1940s. - **$15 $50 $75**

GEN-4. General Mills Airplanes/Missile Launchers,
1950s. At least eight different planes in various colors and missile launchers. Each - **$2 $7 $10**

 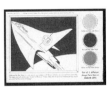

GEN-6

GEN-7

GEN-5

GEN-5. Toytimer,
1950s. Stop watch with mailer. - **$30 $50 $75**

GEN-6. Tex-Son Cowhand Badge,
1950s. General Mills premium. - **$20 $60 $120**

GEN-7. Major Jet Magic Paint Set Book 1,
1950s. Sugar Jets premium. Coloring book.- **$20 $30 $45**

GEN-8

GEN-9

GEN-10

GEN-8. Franken Berry 2-3/4" Tall Figural Plastic Pencil Sharpener,
1960s. - **$5** **$10** **$15**

GEN-9. "Franken Berry" Vinyl Doll With Box,
1975. Near Mint Boxed - **$150**
Loose - **$25** **$40** **$75**

GEN-10. "Count Chocula" Vinyl Doll With Box,
1975. Near Mint Boxed - **$150**
Loose - **$25** **$40** **$75**

GEN-11   GEN-12

GEN-11. "Fruit Brute" Vinyl Squeeze Doll,
1975. Near Mint Boxed - **$150**
Loose - **$25** **$40** **$75**

GEN-12. "Boo Berry" Vinyl Squeeze Doll,
1975. Near Mint Boxed - **$150**
Loose - **$25** **$40** **$75**

GEN-14

GEN-13

GEN-13. Secret Compartment Plastic Ring Set,
1976. Four rings with Hasbro name in four colors depicting Franken Berry, Boo Berry, Count Chocula, Fruit Brute. Each - **$100** **$190** **$275**

GEN-14. "Stampos" Printing Kit,
1970s. Ink stampers with portraits of Franken Berry, Count Chocula, Boo Berry. Each - **$15** **$30** **$50**

GEN-15

GEN-15. Big Monster Flicker Rings,
1970s. Five of six shown: two feature the Count and Franken Berry, two feature the Count only, two feature Franken Berry only. Each - **$50** **$100** **$150**

GEN-16   GEN-17

GEN-18

GEN-16. Count Chocula Vinyl Flat Figure,
1970s. Finished image front and back, molded small base. - **$8** **$15** **$25**

GEN-17. Franken Berry Vinyl Flat Figure,
1970s. Finished image front and back, molded small base. - **$8** **$15** **$25**

GEN-18. Count Chocula Toothbrush Holder,
1970s. 3" tall soft plastic with raised portrait design looped on back to hold toothbrush. - **$10** **$20** **$30**

GEN-19

GEN-19. Character Card Games,
1981. Two sets of cards featuring Lucky Charms, Cocoa Puffs, Trix, Franken Berry, Count Chocula, Boo Berry. Complete With Mailer - **$15** **$25** **$40**

GEN-20

GEN-20. "Raiders Of The Lost Ark" Packaged Action Figures,
1982. Set of "Indiana Jones Four Pack" of him, Toht, Cairo Swordsman, Marian Ravenwood.
Near Mint Complete - **$175**

GEN-21

GEN-21. "Count Chocula" Cereal Box And Disguise Stickers,
1987. Box art depicts necklace on Dracula's neck with design similar to Star of David. Box was quickly redesigned. Box - **$25 $75 $150**
Stickers - **$5 $15 $30**

GEN-22

GEN-22. "Count Chocula" Cereal Box,
1987. Box art altered to remove Dracula's necklace that resembled Star of David. - **$25 $75 $150**

GEN-23

GEN-23. Franken Berry Cereal Box With Spooky Shape Maker Offer,
1987. Three different to emboss paper with images of Franken Berry, Count Chocula, Fruity Yummy Mummy.
Box - **$20 $35 $50**
Each Shape Maker - **$5 $10 $20**

GEN-24

GEN-24. Fruity Yummy Mummy Cereal Box,
1987. Packaging introduces the character and the cereal to the public while back panel introduces the new character to the established monsters. - **$100 $150 $250**

GEN-25

GEN-25. Boo Berry Cereal Box With Monster Poster And Crayons Offer,
1988. Last premium issued for monster cereals. Crayons shaped like monsters in their correct colors.
Box - **$10 $25 $50**
Poster And Crayons - **$20 $35 $60**

GEN-26

GEN-26. Franken Berry Mask,
1980s. Thin shell plastic with high relief design. - **$5 $10 $15**

GI JOE

Hasbro's creative director of product development Don Levine was approached by independent toy designer Stanley Weston in March of 1962. Weston was selling merchandising rights to the TV show *"The Lieutenant,"* based on a Marine, and thought Hasbro would be interested in doing combat action figures for boys similar in design to what the Mattel Co. was doing with Barbie figures for girls. Levine and the people at Hasbro decided to go with a more universal appeal, basing the name on a 1945 Robert Mitchum war movie *The Story of G.I. Joe*. Hasbro claimed the trademark and christened the new product GI Joe.

Test marketing began in New York stores in August, 1964 and the figures sold out in one week. By early fall the figures were selling out nationwide. The GI Joe Club started in December and soon had 150,000 members. 1965 saw the introduction of a black action soldier into the line of American Army, Air Force, Navy and Marine figures.

1966 brought the introduction of Action Soldiers of the World, offering soldiers from six countries. In 1969 GI Joe's hard core military image was softened to an "Adventurer" concept which would expand the merchandising even further. 1975 saw the introduction of the 11-1/2" Atomic Man.

The oil shortage of 1976 halted production due to lack of petroleum used in manufacturing the figures. In 1982 Joe was re-introduced in a new 3 and 3/4" size. In 1991 Hasbro brought out the first original 12-inch action figure since 1976, Master Sergeant Duke, based on the *GI Joe, A Real American Hero* cartoon series.

Over the years, the company has sold hundreds of millions of the ever-popular GI Joe dolls and associated figures, vehicles and gear.

GIJ-1

GIJ-2

GIJ-1. "Command Post News" Newspaper. Vol. 1 #1, April, 1965. - **$25 $40 $75**

GIJ-2. "Command Post News" Newspaper #4, April, 1966. - **$5 $12 $25**

GIJ-3

GIJ-4

GIJ-3. Catalogue, 1967. Came only with the 1967 series of talking GI Joe figures. - **$3 $8 $15**

GIJ-4. "Command Post Yearbook", 1967. - **$20 $40 $75**

GIJ-5

GIJ-6

GIJ-5. GI Joe Letter With Transfer, 1960s. Letter - **$3 $6 $12**
Transfer - **$5 $10 $20**

GIJ-6. Cello. Button, c. 1970s. Probably Hasbro promotional button. - **$5 $10 $20**

GIJ-7

GIJ-8

GIJ-7. "Commando" Enameled Metal Badge, 1982. Store item. - **$8 $15 $25**

GIJ-8. "GI Joe Shuttle Crew" Plastic Ring, 1980s. Image of space shuttle high above world globe. - **$5 $8 $10**

THE GOLDBERGS

The Goldbergs, the first memorable Jewish radio comedy, was the brainchild of Gertrude Berg, who wrote, produced, directed, and starred as Molly, the benevolent matriarch of a working-class family in the Bronx. With husband Jake, children Sammy and Rosalie, and Uncle David, Molly was a fixture on the NBC, CBS, or Mutual networks from 1929 to 1945 and again in 1949-1950. Sponsors included Pepsodent (1931-1934), Colgate (1936), Oxydol (1937-1945), and General Foods (1949-1950). A successful television series aired from 1949 to 1954, a Broadway play (Molly and Me) was produced in 1948, and a movie (Molly) was released in 1951. "Yoo-Hoo, Mrs. Bloom!"

GLD-1

GLD-1. Goldbergs Puzzle, 1932. Pepsodent Co. 8x10" full color jigsaw puzzle. - **$15 $30 $50**

GLD-2

GLD-3

GLD-2. Molly Goldberg Fan Photo, 1930s. - **$8 $15 $30**

GLD-3. Gertrude Berg 11x14" Frame Tray Jigsaw Puzzle, 1952. Store item by Jaymar. - **$15 $35 $50**

GONE WITH THE WIND

One of the most popular films of all time, Gone with the Wind premiered in Atlanta, Georgia, on December 15, 1939, won 10 Academy Awards, and remains a perennial smash in theaters, on television, and in video rentals. This Civil War saga, based on Margaret Mitchell's novel, starred Clark Gable, Vivien Leigh, an all-star cast--and the burning of Atlanta. Merchandising, including portrait dolls, collector plates, and porcelain figurines, continues to this day.

GON-1

GON-2

GON-1. Book Publishing House Summary Booklet, 1936. Macmillan Co. - **$35 $70 $125**

GON-2. Movie Theater Herald, 1940. Various theaters. - **$15 $30 $60**

GON-3

GON-4

GON-5

GON-3. "I've Seen Gone With The Wind" Cello. Button,
1940. - **$30 $60 $90**

GON-4. "Clark Gable/Gone With The Wind" Cigarette Series Card,
c. 1940. Turf Cigarettes. Card #34 from series of 50 "Famous Film Stars" with photo head on illustrated body. - **$8 $15 $25**

GON-5. "Scarlett O'Hara" Handkerchief,
c. 1940. Store item. Sheer fabric with design image repeated on all four quadrants. - **$35 $60 $100**

GON-6

GON-7

GON-8

GON-6. "Scarlett O'Hara Perfume" Novelty Container,
1940. Store item. - **$50 $85 $150**

GON-7. Scarlett O'Hara "Yesteryear" Perfume Glass Vial,
1940. Babs Creations. Figure image within vertical dome. - **$60 $150 $250**

GON-8. Cardboard String Tag From Clothing Dress,
1940. Mae Delli's Originals. - **$40 $100 $150**

GON-9

GON-10

GON-11

GON-9. Brass Heart-Shaped Jewelry Pin,
1940. Store item. - **$40 $85 $150**

GON-10. "Gone With The Wind" Brass Charm Locket Designed In Book Image,
1940. Opens to hold two miniature pictures. - **$50 $100 $175**

GON-11. Gone With The Wind Brass/Cello. Cameo Brooch,
1940. Lux Toilet Soap. Replica of brooch worn by Scarlett in movie, offered originally for 15 cents and three soap wrappers. - **$40 $100 $200**

GON-12

GON-12. Scarlett's Brooch,
1940. Lux Soap. Movie jewelry replica in brass accented by simulated pearls around single simulated turquoise stone. - **$40 $100 $200**

GON-13

GON-14

GON-13. Cookbook,
1940. Pebeco Toothpaste premium. - **$35 $65 $100**

GON-14. Cookbook Store Display From Pebeco Toothpaste,
1940. Scarce. - **$100 $150 $275**

THE GREAT GILDERSLEEVE

Throckmorton P. Gildersleeve started life as a character on the *Fibber McGee and Molly* radio series in the 1930s. Created and played by actor Harold Peary, Gildy was a pompous windbag who was spun off successfully to his own program on NBC in 1941. He was a small-town water commissioner, but the show centered on his life as the bachelor uncle of Leroy and Marjorie and his romantic encounters as the town's most prominent eligible man. Willard Waterman stepped into the role in 1950, and the program ran until 1958. Kraft Foods was the sponsor. There was a brief television series and a 1942 RKO movie of the same name.

GIL-1

GIL-3

GIL-2

GIL-1. Litho. Tin 2-1/4" Jar Lid,
c. 1941. - **$15 $25 $45**

GIL-2. Radio Show Studio Audience Ticket,
1947. Parkay margarine. Pictured example for December 24 Christmas Eve broadcast. - **$10 $20 $35**

GIL-3. Great Gildersleeve Record w/Sleeve,
1940s. Radio premium. Titled "Name My Song Contest" part 1& 2. - **$20 $40 $75**

GREEN GIANT

The Green Giant was born in 1925 as the trademark for a new variety of peas by the Minnesota Valley Canning Company. The original illustration of a giant wrapped in fur, created to satisfy trademark requirements, was redesigned 10 years later into the character we now recognize--a smiling green giant clothed in leaves. Little Sprout was added in the early 1970s, and the company has merchandised both characters.

GNT-1

GNT-1. 20th Anniversary Birthday Record With Envelope,
1949. In Mailer - **$5 $15 $30**
Loose - **$2 $7 $15**

GNT-2

GNT-3

GNT-2. Earliest Cloth Doll,
1966. - **$10 $20 $35**

GNT-3. Campaign Kit,
1968. Voter card, litho. badge, sticker, 26x38" poster. Set - **$12 $20 $35**

GNT-4   GNT-5

GNT-4. Little Sprout Cloth Doll,
c. 1970. - **$5 $10 $15**

GNT-5. "Speakin' Sprout" Talking Cloth Doll,
1971. Contains battery operated tape recorder. - **$25 $50 $75**

GNT-6   GNT-7

GNT-6. Little Sprout Vinyl Doll,
1970s. - **$10 $15 $30**

GNT-7. "Little Sprout Radio" With Box,
1980s. Hard plastic battery operated figural radio 9-1/2" tall. Near Mint Boxed - **$50**
Loose - **$10 $20 $30**

THE GREEN HORNET

Accompanied by his faithful valet Kato, the Green Hornet matched wits with the underworld on the radio from 1936 to 1952, first on WXYZ in Detroit, then on the Mutual network in 1938, on NBC in 1939, on the ABC Blue network in 1940, and finally back on Mutual in 1952. Sponsors included General Mills in 1948 and Orange Crush in 1952. Under his mask the Hornet was Britt Reid, crusading newspaper publisher and grand-nephew of the Lone Ranger, and his crime-fighting exploits in the big city resembled those of his relative in the West. (Both shows were created by George W. Trendle and written largely by Fran Striker.) Also featured was Miss Case, secretary and love interest, along with Black Beauty, the Hornet's supercharged limousine, and his non-lethal gas gun. Kato, originally Japanese, became a Filipino after Pearl Harbor.

Two Green Hornet chapter plays were released by Universal in 1940, with Keye Luke as Kato, and a souped-up television series aired for a season (1966-1967) on ABC, with Van Williams in the title role and Bruce Lee as Kato. Comic books appeared more or less regularly from 1940 to 1949, followed by a one-shot in 1953, three issues in 1966-1967 timed to coincide with the television series, and a revival in 1989.

GRN-1

GRN-1. Postcard,
1936. Golden Jersey Milk. Radio premium-
$100 $200 $300

GRN-2

GRN-2. Radio Fan Club Photo,
1938. Golden Jersey Milk. Pictures Britt Reid (Al Hodge) as Green Hornet with back ad text. - **$75 $200 $300**

GRN-3

GRN-4

GRN-3. Radio Fan Club Photo,
1938. Golden Jersey Milk. Pictures Miss Case (Lee Allman) with back ad text, from G-J-M Club photo series of several cast members. - **$60 $150 $200**

GRN-4. "Kato" Portrait Photo,
1938. Golden Jersey Milk. - **$50 $150 $200**

GRN-5

GRN-5. "Mike Oxford" Portrait Photo,
1938. Golden Jersey Milk. - **$50 $150 $200**

GRN-6

GRN-7

GRN-6. Membership Card,
1938. Golden Jersey Milk. - **$50 $175 $250**

GRN-7. Green Hornet Glass,
c. 1938. Scarce. Golden Jersey Milk. - **$40 $200 $300**

GRN-8

GRN-9

GRN-8. Kato And Black Beauty Glass,
c. 1938. Scarce. Golden Jersey Milk. - **$40 $200 $300**

GRN-9. Radio Show Postcard,
1939. - **$75 $175 $250**

GRN-10

GRN-11

GRN-12

GRN-13

GRN-10. "The Green Hornet Adventure Club" Cello. Button,
1940. Rare. Universal Pictures. For 13-chapter movie serial. - **$150 $500 $750**

GRN-11. "The Green Hornet Strikes Again" Movie Serial Cello. Button,
1940. Rare. Universal Serial/Adventure Club. For 13-chapter serial. - **$150 $500 $750**

GRN-12. "Green Hornet Loyalty Club" Cello. Button,
c. 1940. - **$125 $250 $500**

GRN-13. Secret Compartment Glow-In-Dark Ring,
1947. General Mills. Brass with hinged lid over glow plastic compartment. - **$300 $750 $1200**

GRN-14

GRN-15

GRN-14. "Green Hornet Night Signaling Ring" Enclosure Slip,
c. 1947. Betty Crocker Cereal Tray offer. Instructions are on one side, order coupon for additional rings on reverse. - **$100 $125 $150**

GRN-15. "Newspaper Reporter" Recruitment Letter,
1940s. Union Biscuit Co. Offers reporter's kit described in full over radio broadcasts on KWK, St. Louis. - **$50 $125 $200**

GRN-16

GRN-17

GRN-16. Green Hornet Sting Whistle,
1966. Scarce. Chicken Of The Sea Tuna (Required Two Labels). Two-piece plastic slide whistle with small name mark on handle. Newspaper Ad - **$25 $50 $100** Whistle - **$200 $500 $1000**

GRN-17. Battery Operated "Signal Ray",
1966. Store item by Colorforms. Display card is 10x11". Display With Toy - **$300 $600 $1000**

GRN-18

GRN-19

GRN-20

GRN-18. "The Green Hornet/Kato" Glass,
1966. Probable food product container. - **$40 $80 $125**

GRN-19. Vernors Plastic "Trick Or Treat Bag",
1966. Vernors Ginger Ale. - **$20 $40 $75**

GRN-20. "Agent" 4" Litho. Button,
1966. Store item. - **$10 $20 $35**

GRN-21

GRN-22

GRN-21. Pennant 28 1/2",
1966. Promotes TV show. - **$25 $60 $85**

GRN-22. Green Hornet Character Plastic Flicker Rings,
1966. Set of 12, each with double image when tilted.
Silver Base Each - **$10 $15 $25**
Blue Base Each - **$8 $14 $20**

GRN-23

GRN-24

GRN-25

GRN-26

GRN-23. Litho. Buttons,
1966. Vending machine set of nine. Two color styles, with or without yellow. Each - **$5 $10 $15**

GRN-24. Rubber Figural Ring,
1966. Vending machine issue. - **$5 $7 $10**

GRN-25. Green Hornet Pez Dispenser,
c. 1966. Several hat variations, grey & brown hats worth more. - **$75 $150 $250**

GRN-26. 3-1/2" Cello. Button,
c. 1966. Store item by Button World Mfg. - **$10 $20 $30**

GRN-27

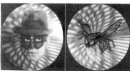

GRN-28

GRN-27. Flicker Button 3",
1967. Store item. - **$10 $25 $40**

GRN-28. Flicker Disk 7",
1967. Store item. - **$20 $40 $60**

GRN-29

GRN-30

GRN-29. Flicker Picture Plastic Ruler,
1967. Store item by Vari-Vue. 6" length. - **$50 $100 $150**

GRN-30. Green Hornet Large Rubber Ring,
1970s. Vending machine issue. Thin band of green rubber attached to matching 2x2-1/4" hornet image. - **$7 $10 $15**

THE GREEN LAMA

The first appearance of the Green Lama was in *Prize Comics* #7 in 1940. He then appeared in his own book for eight issues from 1944 to 1946. For a dime readers could join the *Green Lama Club* and receive a membership card, the key to the Lama's secret code, and an Escapo folding trick that showed victory over Fascist rats. The character was revived on CBS radio for the summer of 1949 as a New York-based crime fighter with special powers acquired after 10 years of study in a Tibet monastery.

(INSTRUCTIONS)

(CARD AND MAILER)

(VARIATION 2)

GLM-1

GLM-1. Club Kit,
1945. Victory Game. Club Card - **$75 $120 $200**
Mailer - **$20 $40 $80**
Escape Trick with Instructions, Two Variations,
Each - **$50 $125 $250**

GLM-2

GLM-3

GLM-2. Code Letter,
1940s. M.L.J. Magazines. Came with kit. "Green Lama Code Chart" with instructions concluding by translated "Buy Bonds" message. - **$100 $250 $400**

GLM-3. Radio Episode Script,
1949. For June 26 broadcast "Million Dollar Chopsticks". - **$50 $100 $150**

GULLIVER'S TRAVELS

Jonathan Swift's masterpiece, published in 1726, has retained its satirical thrust and fairy-tale aura for almost three centuries. The voyages of Lemuel Gulliver to Lilliput, Brobdingnag, and the land of the Yahoos continue to enchant readers and viewers to this day. In addition to the many print editions of the classic, the tales have been adapted in various media, including: a full-length animated film by the Fleischer studios (1939); a Japanese animated feature that sent Gulliver into outer space (1966); a part live-action British film with Richard Harris (1977); *The 3 Worlds of Gulliver* (British, 1960); a Hanna-Barbera animated series, *The Adventures of Gulliver* (ABC, 1968-1970); a Hanna-Barbera feature for CBS, sponsored by Kenner toys (1979); Saban's *Gulliver's Travels*, syndicated in 1992; a Classic Comics edition first published in 1943; and Dell Comics editions in 1956 and again in 1965-1966. Ted Danson starred in a filmed version on NBC-television in 1996. Even the BBC tried its hand with a four-part adaptation for radio.

GLL-1

GLL-1. "Gulliver's Travels" Booklet,
1939. Macy's department store. - **$20 $40 $75**

(BACK OF MASK)

GLL-2

GLL-2. Character Masks,
1939. Hecker's Flour. Diecut stiff paper full color masks of Princess Glory, Prince David, King Bombo, Snitch, Gabby. Each **$10 $15 $25**

GLL-4

GLL-3

GLL-3. Boxed English Card Deck,
1939. Store item copyright Paramount Pictures Inc.,
England. Set of 44 playing cards picturing various film
scenes in color. - **$25 $50 $100**

GLL-4. Cereal Bowl,
1939. White glass picturing characters from Fleischer animated film around perimeter. - **$15 $25 $40**

GLL-5   GLL-6

GLL-5. "Snoop" Glass Tumbler,
1939. Probably distributed as dairy product container.
Reverse has descriptive verse. - **$10 $20 $30**

GLL-6. "Snitch" Glass Tumbler,
1939. Probably distributed as dairy product container.
Reverse has descriptive verse. - **$10 $20 $30**

GLL-7   GLL-8

GLL-7. Child's China Cup,
c. 1939. Pictures Gabby, Snitch and bird character from
Fleischer animated cartoon movie. - **$12 $25 $35**

GLL-8. China Pitcher,
c. 1939. Store item by Hammersley & Co., England.
Pictures two scenes and five characters. -
$50 $100 $150

THE GUMPS

The Gumps, one of the most popular comic strips of
the 1920s, was created by Sidney Smith for the
Chicago Tribune. The story of Andy and Min, son
Chester, and rich Uncle Bim began as a daily strip in
1917 and as a Sunday feature in 1919, and lasted until
1959, some 24 years after Smith was killed in an automobile accident. Comic book reprints appeared from
1918 into the 1940s, and a radio series based on the
strip and sponsored by Pebeco toothpaste was aired
on CBS from 1934 to 1937. The popularity of the
Gumps is reflected by the large variety of licensed
items - toys, games, books, buttons, etc. "Oh Min!"

GMP-2

GMP-1

GMP-1. "Andy Gump" Pictorial Sheet Music,
1923. Store item. Words and music for novelty song illustrated by 15 characters from comic strip by Sidney Smith. -
$10 $20 $35

GMP-2. "The Sunshine Twins" Book,
1925. Sunshine Andy Gump Biscuits by Loose-Wiles
Biscuit Co. Pictured example is designated fourth edition. -
$20 $40 $70

GMP-3   GMP-4

GMP-3. "Chester Gump And His Friends" Booklet,
1934. Tarzan Ice Cream Cups. #5 from series of various
character titles. - **$20 $40 $80**

GMP-4. "The Gumps In Radio Land" Booklet,
1937. Pebeco toothpaste. - **$20 $35 $65**

GMP-6

GMP-5

GMP-5. Malt-O-Meal Cereal Premium Folder,
1938. Four pages of pictures of Andy Gump, Harold Teen, Herby, and cardboard Dummys. - **$30 $60 $120**

GMP-6. "Andy Gump" Die Cut Sign 14x16",
1938. Rare. Malt-O-Meal promotional sign (standee.) Tells how to get comic character dummies. - **$500 $1200 $1600**

GMP-7

GMP-8

GMP-9

GMP-7. "Andy Gump" Dummy Punchout 11x20",
1938. Rare. Malt-O-Meal Cereal premium. - **$150 $300 $500**

GMP-8. "Andy Gump" Wood Jointed Doll,
1930s. Store item. - **$50 $75 $150**

GMP-9. "Andy Gump For Congress" Cello. Button,
1930s. Various newspapers. - **$10 $15 $25**

GMP-10

GMP-11

GMP-12

GMP-10. "Investigator/Gump Charities/Use Solder Seal" Cello. Button,
1930s. - **$15 $25 $40**

GMP-11. "Andy Gump For President" Cello. Button,
1930s. Wonder Milk, various other food products.
$15 $25 $40

GMP-12. "Andy Gump For President" 2" Cello. Button,
1930s. Good Humor Ice Cream Suckers. - **$40 $85 $150**

GMP-13

GMP-14

GMP-13. "The Gumps/Friendly Refreshment" Metal Cap For Soda Bottle,
1930s. Bon-Ton Beverages, Chicago. - **$10 $20 $30**

GMP-14. "Uncle Bim's Roll" Candy Wrapper,
1930s. Voegele & Dinning Co. Waxed paper and design of currency money. - **$8 $12 $20**

GUNSMOKE

Dodge City, Kansas, in the 1880s was the site of this adult Western that premiered on CBS radio in 1952 and on CBS television in 1955 for 20 years until the program ended in 1975. Starring James Arness as Matt Dillon, other continuing characters included the saloon keeper Miss Kitty, old Doc Adams, and the Marshal's deputy Chester, replaced by Festus in 1964. Radio sponsors included Post Toasties (1953), Chesterfield cigarettes (1954), and Liggett & Myers (1954-1957). L & M cigarettes was also a television sponsor. Related comic books appeared from the 1950s to 1970, and two Gunsmoke movies starring James Arness were released in 1987 and 1990. Items usually carry a copyright of CBS Television Enterprises or Columbia Broadcasting System.

GUN-1

GUN-2

GUN-1. "L&M Cigarettes" 21x22" Cardboard Store Sign,
c. 1954. Liggett & Meyers. - **$35 $60 $125**

GUN-2. L&M Cigarettes Cast Card,
c. 1954. - **$8 $15 $30**

GUN-3

GUN-3. Matt Dillon And Miss Kitty 21x21" Cigarette Sign,
c. 1954. L&M Cigarettes of Liggett & Myers Tobacco Co. Stiff cardboard with full color photos. - **$35 $60 $125**

GUN-4

GUN-5

GUN-4. "James Arness Fan Club" Cello. Button, c. 1958. - **$15 $25 $40**

GUN-5. "Matt Dillon/U.S. Marshal" Metal Badge, 1959. Store item. On Card - **$20 $30 $50** Loose - **$10 $15 $25**

GUN-6

GUN-6. "U.S. Marshal" Metal Badge, 1959. Store item. Badge version omits "Matt Dillon" name. On Card - **$20 $30 $50** Loose - **$10 $15 $25**

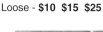

GUN-7

GUN-7. Personal Appearance Souvenir Folder With Photo, c. 1960. - **$15 $25 $50**

GUN-8   GUN-9

GUN-8. "All Star Dairies" Litho. Button, c. 1960. - **$8 $15 $25**

GUN-9. Metal Cuff Links With Bw Photo Inserts, 1960s. Issuer unknown. - **$20 $40 $75**

GUN-10   GUN-11

GUN-10. "Matt Dillon's Favorite" Key Ring, 1960s. Reverse of plastic star reads "Sanders Dairy/All Star". - **$20 $35 $60**

GUN-11. TV Publicity Stills, c. 1972. CBS-TV. 8x10" high gloss black and white photos of cast members. Each - **$1 $3 $5**

HAPPY HOOLIGAN

Happy Hooligan, the ever-innocent optimist, was created by Frederick Opper for the Hearst Sunday comics in 1900 and continued, under a variety of titles, until 1932. The strip, considered a major classic comic, also involved Happy's pet dog Flip and his brothers Gloomy Gus and Lord Montmorency in a series of ill-fated adventures. Happy, with his tin-can hat, and Gus, with his battered top hat, were immensely popular characters, appearing in stage plays, silent animated cartoons, sheet music, and reprints of the strips in book form.

HAP-1   HAP-2

HAP-1. "How To Make Happy Hooligan Dance" Cut-Out Supplement, 1902. New York American & Journal newspaper. Uncut - **$25 $50 $75**

HAP-2. Postcard, 1904. United States Card premium. Shows Happy facing left. Says "You have seen my face before 'Guess where". - **$10 $20 $30**

HAP-3   HAP-4

HAP-3. Valentine Postcard, 1904. Shows Happy fishing. - **$10 $20 $30**

HAP-4. Valentine Postcard, 1904. Shows Happy looking straight ahead. - **$10 $20 $30**

HAP-5

HAP-6

HAP-5. "Shoemakers Fair" Cello. Button, 1905. Figure back view although frontal head for slogan "Are You Goin' Or Comin'?" - **$20 $40 $75**

HAP-6. Happy Hooligan Song Sheet, c. 1905. Rare. Newspaper supplement. - **$50 $100 $200**

HAP-7   HAP-8

HAP-7. Mechanical Postcard,
1906. New York Sunday American & Journal newspaper. Shows picture of cops pulling Hooligan & others out of water. Card folds out to give a 3-D look. - **$30 $65 $100**

HAP-8. Postcard,
1906. American Journal Examiner. Shows Happy watching the Moon. - **$10 $15 $25**

HAP-10

HAP-9

HAP-9. Postcard,
1906. Boston Sunday American newspaper premium. - **$10 $15 $25**

HAP-10. Postcard,
1906. Boston Sunday American newspaper premium. Egyptian police catch Happy & friend trying to steal the Sphinx. - **$10 $15 $25**

HAP-13

HAP-12

HAP-11

HAP-11. Composition Figure,
c. 1910. Store item. Jointed arms and legs. - **$50 $80 $150**

HAP-12. Papier Mache Roly-Poly,
c. 1910. Store item. - **$200 $300 $500**

HAP-13. Happy Hooligan Figural White Metal Stickpin,
c. 1910. - **$15 $25 $40**

HAP-15

HAP-16

HAP-14

HAP-14. "F. Oppers Joke Book,"
1911. New York Sunday American. 10x12" Sunday supplement with 16 pages of Frederick Opper cartoons including Happy Hooligan, Alphonse and Gaston, And Her Name Was Maud. - **$15 $35 $60**

HAP-15. Cello. Button,
c. 1915. - **$10 $18 $30**

HAP-16. Seated Bisque Nodder Figure,
1920s. Store item. - **$50 $100 $200**

HELEN TRENT

The Romance of Helen Trent reigned as the melodramatic queen of the daytime soap operas for over a quarter of a century on CBS radio from 1933 to 1960. Helen, remaining single and 35 through the years, was noble, pure, and pursued by dozens of suitors, most of whom came to a violent end. Sponsors included American Home Products, Affiliated Products, Whitehall Drugs, Pharmaco, Spry, Breeze, and Scott Waldorf tissue.

HLN-2

HLN-1

HLN-1. Radio Replica Mechanical Brass Badge,
1949. Five identified cast members are pictured in sequence through diecut opening by rear disk wheel. - **$20 $50 $75**

HLN-2. Silvered Brass Medallion,
1949. Kolynos dental product. Design motifs on both sides including Sphinx, pyramids, other abstract symbols. - **$10 $18 $30**

THE HERMIT'S CAVE

Produced at Los Angeles radio station KMPC, this syndicated horror show aired from 1940 to 1944, offering ghost stories, weird stories, and mayhem and murders galore. Scary sound effects and the voice of Mel Johnson as the old hermit distinguished these weekly tales of carnage. Olga Coal was the sponsor.

HER-1

HER-1. Cast Pictures,
1940s. Scarce. Each - **$10 $20 $40**

HER-2   HER-3

HER-2. Promo Brochure,
1940s. - **$30 $60 $120**

HER-3. Letter,
1940s. - **$20 $40 $80**

HER-4

HER-4. Radio Show Promotion Mailer, 1940s. Olga Coal of Carter Coal Company. Printed photos include "The Hermit With His Whiskers On." - **$30 $60 $120**

HOBBY LOBBY

From 1937 to 1949 on various networks this popular half-hour program highlighted listeners' unusual hobbies, everything from collecting elephant hairs to talking backwards. Dave Elman created the show, and each week a celebrity guest would show up to "lobby his hobby." Sponsors over the years included Hudson cars, Jell-O, Fels-Naptha soap, Colgate, and Anchor-Hocking glass. A television version with Cliff Arquette (Charley Weaver) as host was broadcast on ABC in 1959-60.

HOB-1   HOB-2

HOB-1. Promotional Ad,
c. 1940s. Rare. - **$30 $60 $100**

HOB-2. "Hobby Lobby" Rocking Horse Charm,
c. 1940s. - **$20 $40 $60**

HOOT GIBSON

Edmund R. Gibson (1892-1962), known as Hoot because as a boy he liked to hunt owls, was born in Nebraska and learned to rope and ride on his father's ranch. He left home as a teenager and worked as a cowboy on the trail and in Wild West shows before arriving in Hollywood in 1910. His first minor film role was in 1911, but he became a star in the 1920s, ultimately appearing in well over 200 silent and talking movies. Gibson's popularity in the late 1920s was second only to Tom Mix. He retired in 1944, then had a few cameo film roles and a brief run as the host of a local television show in Los Angeles. Hoot Gibson comic books appeared in 1950.

HGB-1   HGB-2

HGB-1. "Rope Spinning" Instruction Folder,
1929. Came with Hoot Gibson Rodeo Ropes by Mordt Co., Chicago. - **$10 $18 $30**

HGB-2. Exhibit Cards,
1920s. Vending machine cards by Exhibit Supply Co. Copyright year or movie titles from late 1920s. Each - **$3 $6 $10**

HGB-3

HGB-4

HGB-5

HGB-3. "Robbins Bros. Circus" 14x22" Cardboard Poster,
1930s. - **$50 $100 $150**

HGB-4. Movie Felt Patch,
1930s. - **$30 $75 $150**

HGB-5. Cello. Button,
1930s. Probably circus souvenir. - **$35 $75 $125**

HGB-6

HGB-7

HGB-8

HGB-6. Cello. Button,
1930s. Probably circus souvenir. - **$50 $100 $150**

HGB-7. Litho. Button From Movie Star Set,
1930s. - **$5 $8 $15**

HGB-8. "Ideal Moving Pictures" Flip Booklet,
1930s. Flip sequence pictures Gibson lassoing two fist-fighters. - **$20 $35 $60**

HOPALONG CASSIDY

William Boyd (1898-1972) was born in Ohio, grew up in Oklahoma, and worked at odd jobs before he went to Hollywood in 1919 to look for work in the movies. By the mid-1920s he had become a major star of silent films. Boyd made his first cowboy movie in 1931, and his first as Hopalong Cassidy in 1935. (The original Cassidy character came from the pulp stories and novels of C.E. Mulford in the early 1900s). Dressed in black, with silver spurs and saddle, riding his white stallion Topper, with Andy Clyde or Gabby Hayes as sidekick, Hoppy battled outlaws in a series of movies among the most successful "B" Westerns ever made. Boyd became completely identified with the noble cowboy, and by the time he retired in 1959 he had made more than 100 theatrical and television Cassidy films.

Boyd bought the rights to the Hoppy character in 1948 and released edited versions of the films for syndication to Los Angeles television station KTLA, where they ran from 1948 to 1950. Barbara Ann bread and Wonder bread were sponsors. In 1950 the programs were leased to NBC, with General Foods as sponsor. *The Hopalong Cassidy Show*--the first major television Western series--was a sensation, airing on more than 60 stations and ranking consistently among the top three programs in the country. After two years a new series of half-hour made-for-TV films ran until 1954, with Edgar Buchanan in the sidekick role.

The television success spawned a radio series (1950-1952) on the Mutual and CBS networks, also sponsored by General Foods, and a comic strip drawn by Dan Spiegle that ran in more than 150 newspapers until 1955. Millions of Hoppy comic books appeared from 1943 through the 1950s, including giveaways by White Tower in 1946, Grape-Nuts Flakes in 1950, and several by Bond bread in 1951.

Hoppy's immense popularity with his young audience around the nation also generated an unprecedented merchandising cornucopia. Hundreds of endorsements and licensed products flooded the land, from roller skates to bicycles, watches, pocket knives, toy guns, cowboy outfits, pajamas, peanut butter, candy bars, cottage cheese, bread, cereal, cookies, milk, toothpaste, savings banks, wallpaper--even hair oil became part of the Hopalong Cassidy legend.

HOP-1

HOP-2

HOP-1. "Bill Boyd" Dixie Ice Cream Picture,
c. 1938. - **$25 $45 $90**

HOP-2. Dixie Ice Cream Picture,
1938. - **$20 $40 $85**

HOP-3

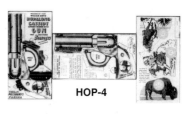

HOP-4

HOP-3. Pillsbury's Promotional 12x24" Sign,
1940. Scarce. Advertises punch-out gun and targets. - **$200 $500 $750**

HOP-4. Punch-Out Gun And Targets Sheet,
1940. Pillsbury's Farina. Boyd/Hoppy identified as "Paramount" star. Unpunched - **$50 $125 $250**

HOP-6

HOP-5

HOP-5. Postcard,
1941.Chrysler Plymouth premium shows Hoppy in suit in front of car. Ads for cars on back. - **$20 $45 $65**

HOP-6. "Bill Boyd/For Democracy 100%" Cello. Button,
c. 1942. Rare. From patriotism series picturing various cowboys. - **$100 $200 $350**

HOP-7

HOP-7. Fan Club Form Letter With Envelope,
1946. Hopalong Cassidy Productions. Promotes new film series, photo on folder reverse.
With Envelope - **$50 $75 $150**
No Envelope - **$40 $60 $100**

HOP-8

HOP-9

HOP-8. Cole Bros. Circus Pennant,
c. 1948. - **$20 $50 $80**

HOP-9. Round-Up Club "Special Agent Pass" Card,
c. 1948. Probable movie theater give-away. - **$15 $30 $50**

HOP-10

HOP-11

HOP-10. Card,
1948.Special Agents pass. - **$20 $40 $60**

HOP-11. Barclay Knitwear Co. Photo,
1949. Given with sweater purchase. - **$15 $25 $40**

HOP-12

HOP-12. Butter-Nut Bread "Troopers News" Vol. 1 #1,
1949. First issue of periodic newsletter. - **$75 $150 $250**

HOP-13

HOP-14

HOP-13. "Trooper's Club" Application Card,
1949. Various sponsors. - **$15 $25 $40**

HOP-14. "Hopalong Cassidy Official Bar 20 T-V Chair",
1949. Store item and Big Top Peanut Butter premium. Wood and canvas folding chair that opens to 16x16x22" tall. - **$250 $500 $1000**

HOP-15

HOP-16

HOP-15. Troopers Club Card,
1949.Barbara Ann Bread premium. Brown on yellow background with secret code on back. - **$25 $50 $75**

HOP-16. Photo,
1940s.Rare. Early Bill Boyd movie premium with frame. - **$25 $50 $75**

HOP-17

HOP-18

HOP-17. Adult Hat,
1950. Scarce. Premium and store item. Has white picture band and photo button. - **$100 $200 $400**

HOP-18. Child's Hat,
1950. Premium and store item. - **$50 $75 $150**

HOP-19

HOP-20

HOP-19. Bond Bread Loaf End Labels,
1950. Photo style pictures, unnumbered series.
Each - **$3 $6 $12**

HOP-20. Bond Bread Loaf End Labels,
1950. Numbered with perforation around illustration, 16 in set (#17-32). Each - **$5 $8 $12**

HOP-21

HOP-21. Bond Bread "Hang-Up Album",
1950. Folder wall poster for bread loaf end pictures for story "Hoppy Captures The Bank Robbers."
Unused - **$30 $50 $80**

HOP-22

HOP-23

HOP-22. Bond Bread Label Flyer 6x9",
1950. - **$40 $75 $125**

HOP-23. "Bond Bread" Store Hanger Sign 6x7",
1950. - **$100 $175 $250**

HOP-24

HOP-24. Watch Paper Sign 6x24",
1950. Scarce. US Time. - **$100 $225 $400**

HOP-25

HOP-26

HOP-25. "Timex" 16" Painted Latex Store Display,
1950. Rare. Timex Watches. English made. -
$750 $1500 $2500

HOP-26. Metal Pocketwatch,
1950. Store item by US Time. - **$200 $400 $600**

HOP-27

HOP-27. Savings Club Thrift Kit,
1950. Advertised in comic book and sponsored by various banks. Includes certificate, cover letter, color photo, postcard, folder showing club ranks.
Near Mint In Mailer - **$300**
Certificate - **$30 $60 $100**
Letter - **$10 $20 $30**
Photo - **$5 $10 $15**
Postcard - **$5 $12 $20**
Folder - **$25 $50 $75**

HOP-28

HOP-29

HOP-28. Savings Club Membership Card,
1950. Various sponsor banks. - **$35 $60 $90**

HOP-29. Savings Club Postcard,
1950. Various sponsoring banks. - **$15 $25 $40**

HOP-30   **HOP-31**   **HOP-32**

HOP-30. Plastic Bank,
1950. Store item and Hopalong Cassidy Savings Club give-away. Gold Plastic - **$25 $50 $75**
White Plastic (rare) - **$80 $185 $325**
Green - **$50 $125 $250**
Yellow - **$50 $125 $250**
Red - **$50 $125 $250**
Blue - **$75 $175 $300**

HOP-31. Bank Teller's 3" Litho. Button,
1950. - **$15 $25 $40**

HOP-32. Saving Rodeo "Tenderfoot" Canadian Version Litho. Button,
1950. Various Canadian banks. Smaller size than U.S. versions, first five ranks are 1-1/8" litho. while Straw Boss and Foreman versions are 1-3/8". Add 25% To U.S. Version - **$20 $40 $60**

HOP-33   **HOP-34**   **HOP-35**

HOP-33. Saving Rodeo "Tenderfoot" Litho. Button,
1950. Various banks. Awarded for saving $2.00. - **$15 $30 $50**

HOP-34. Saving Rodeo "Wrangler" Litho. Button,
1950. Various banks. Awarded for saving $10.00. - **$10 $18 $25**

HOP-35. Saving Rodeo "Bulldogger" Litho. Button,
1950. Various banks. Awarded for saving $25.00. - **$12 $25 $35**

HOP-36   **HOP-37**   **HOP-38**   **HOP-39**

HOP-36. Saving Rodeo "Bronc Buster" Litho. Button,
1950. Various banks. Awarded for saving $50.00. - **$15 $35 $50**

HOP-37. Saving Rodeo "Trail Boss" Litho. Button,
1950. Fifth highest of seven ranks. - **$20 $40 $75**

HOP-38. Saving Rodeo "Straw Boss" 2-1/4" Litho. Button,
1950. Scarce. Honor circle rating awarded for saving $250.00, also Canadian issue in smaller cello. version. - **$75 $125 $225**

HOP-39. Saving Rodeo"Foreman" 2-1/4" Litho. Button,
1950. Scarce. Highest rank Honor Circle rating awarded for saving $500, also Canadian issue in smaller cello. version. - **$75 $150 $250**

HOP-40   **HOP-41**

HOP-40. "Hopalong Cassidy's Western Magazine" First Issue,
1950. Vol. 1 #1 quarterly pulp magazine. - **$50 $100 $150**

HOP-41. Candy Bar Wrapper,
1950. Foil paper with mail offer for "Hopalong Cassidy Cowboy Neckerchief With Stone Set Metal Steerhead Loop" expiring June 30. See HOP-131. - **$40 $80 $140**

HOP-42   **HOP-43**   **HOP-44**

HOP-42. "Timex Watches" Cello. Button,
c. 1950. English made. - **$40 $75 $125**

HOP-43. Newspaper Strip Promotion Cello. Button,
c. 1950. Sun-Telegram. - **$20 $50 $75**

HOP-44. Milk Bottle Cap,
c. 1950. Jo-Mar Milk. Foil paper with inner cardboard liner. - **$10 $20 $30**

HOP-45

HOP-45. Christmas Card With Cello. Button,
c. 1950. Store item. Folder card from authorized greeting card series by Buzza Cardozo, Hollywood. Inside button is visible through diecut opening on front cover.
With Button - **$25 $45 $75**
Card Only - **$15 $30 $45**

HOP-46

HOP-47

HOP-46. Australian Candy Tin,
c. 1950. Bester's Sweets Ltd., Melbourne. Litho. tin box and lid with color portrait. Side panels list eight rules of "Hopalong Cassidy's Troopers Creed For Boys And Girls." - **$75 $150 $300**

HOP-47. "Hopalong Cassidy" Large Doll,
c. 1950. Store item and promotional award from Chicago Sun-Times news paper. 22" tall stuffed cloth and plush fabric body with thin vinyl boy image face with felt hat holding title headband. - **$250 $500 $750**

HOP-48

HOP-48. "Buzza Cardozo Greeting Cards" 15x27" Store Sign,
c. 1950. Diecut cardboard for officially licensed Hoppy greeting card series. - **$500 $1000 $1800**

HOP-49

HOP-50

HOP-51

HOP-49. "Hoppy's Favorite" Litho. Button,
1950. Issued with names of various sponsors. Each - **$10 $25 $50**

HOP-50. Postcard,
1950.Beautiful color card of Hoppy with hands on gun. Bill Boyd write up on back. Says he started in films in 1919. - **$25 $50 $75**

HOP-51. Crayon Set In Box,
1950.Crayons- 42 small, 28 large- with stencils and Hoppy pad. Promoted in Life Magazine. - **$100 $250 $375**

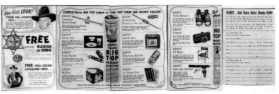

HOP-52

HOP-52. Premium Catalogue With Order Form,
1950. Big Top Peanut Butter. - **$50 $100 $200**

HOP-53

HOP-54

HOP-53. Silvered Brass Identification Bracelet,
1950. Big Top Peanut Butter. Center plate edges have "Hopalong Cassidy-XX Ranch", center is designed for engraving owner's name. - **$50 $100 $150**

HOP-54. Silvered Brass Hair Barrette,
1950. Store item and Big Top Peanut Butter premium. - **$20 $35 $60**

HOP-55

HOP-56

HOP-55. Metal Binoculars,
1950. Store item and Big Top Peanut Butter premium. - **$25 $60 $100**

HOP-56. Boxed Camera,
1950. Store item and Big Top Peanut Butter premium.
Boxed - **$100 $150 $225**
Loose - **$40 $80 $150**

HOP-57

(ENLARGED VIEW)

HOP-58

HOP-57. "Junior Chow Set" Ad Sheet,
1950. Big Top Peanut Butter. - **$15 $25 $50**

HOP-58. Stainless Steel Table Utensils,
1950. Store item and Big Top Peanut Butter premium.
Each - **$10 $20 $30**

HOP-59

HOP-60

HOP-59. Plastic Wrist Compass,
1950. Store item also used as Big Top Peanut Butter and
Popsicle premium. - **$25 $50 $75**

HOP-60. Glass Mugs,
1950. Big Top Peanut Butter. Set of four in black, green,
blue, red on white. Each - **$10 $18 $30**

HOP-61

HOP-61. "Bar 20 Chow Set" Boxed Glassware,
1950. Store item and Big Top Peanut Butter premium. Set
for "Gun Totin' Buckaroos". Near Mint Boxed - **$350**
Each - **$30 $50 $75**

HOP-62

HOP-63

HOP-64

HOP-62. Metal Thermos,
1950. Store item by Aladdin Industries and Big Top Peanut
Butter premium. - **$25 $70 $150**

HOP-63. Metal Lunch Box,
1950. Store item by Aladdin Industries and Big Top Peanut
Butter premium. Rectangular decal. - **$60 $125 $300**

HOP-64. Metal Lunch Box,
1950. Store item by Aladdin Industries. Cloud-shaped
decal. - **$60 $125 $300**

HOP-65

HOP-65. Wallet With Coin & Papers,
1950. Store item and Big Top Peanut Butter premium.
Complete - **$75 $125 $200**
Coin Only - **$5 $10 $15**

HOP-66

HOP-67

HOP-66. "Good Luck From Hoppy" Aluminum Medal,
1950. Earliest version with Hoppy image on each side was
produced in 1948 for a Hoppy rodeo in Hawaii. The 1950
version for inclusion with wallets by Pioneer has a four-leaf
clover within a horseshoe on the reverse. A heavy pewter-
like version is a reproduction. Rodeo Version -
$10 $20 $30
Wallet Style - **$8 $12 $20**

HOP-67. Burry's Cookies Cut-Out Box Panel,
1950. #1 panel from 24 different packages with "The
Continued Story Of Hopalong Cassidy's Bar-20 Ranch
Adventures". Each Uncut Panel - **$20 $40 $60**

HOP-68

HOP-69

**HOP-68. "Hopalong Cassidy Picture Card Gum" Waxed
Paper Wrapper,**
1950. Topps Chewing Gum. - **$20 $50 $100**

HOP-69. Candy Bag,
1950. Topps Candy Division. - **$25 $50 $75**

HOP-70

HOP-71

HOP-70. Litho. Tin Potato Chips Can,
1950. Kuehmann Foods Inc. - **$60 $125 $200**

HOP-71. Grape-Nuts Flakes Comic Book,
1950. - **$11 $34 $90**

HOP-72

HOP-73

HOP-72. Boxed Drinking Straws,
1950. Various pictures on reverse.
Complete - **$50 $80 $140**

HOP-73. Hard Plastic Figures,
1950. Store item by Ideal Corp.
Boxed - **$75 $150 $250**
Loose - **$30 $60 $100**

HOP-74

HOP-74. "Hair Trainer" 8x22" Paper Poster With Picture,
1950. Poster - **$75 $150 $250**
Picture - **$5 $12 $18**

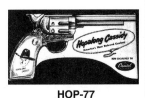

HOP-77

HOP-75

HOP-76

HOP-75. Pocketknife,
1950. Store item by Hammer Brand. - **$30 $65 $125**

HOP-76. Vinyl Pocketknife Loop,
1950. Store item. - **$25 $50 $90**

HOP-77. Cardboard Noisemaker Gun,
1950. Capitol Records. - **$30 $60 $100**

HOP-78

HOP-79

HOP-80

HOP-78. "Hopalong Cassidy Bikes And Skates" Ad Card,
1950. Rollfast Co. - **$25 $60 $100**

HOP-79. New York Daily News 10x13" Cardboard Poster,
1950. Announces start of daily comic strip. -
$80 $175 $250

HOP-80. "Hopalong Cassidy In The Daily News" 2" Cello. Button,
1950. - **$15 $30 $50**

HOP-81

HOP-82

HOP-83

HOP-81. Hopalong Cassidy Western Badge,
1950. Post's Raisin Bran. From set of 12 including titles Calamity Jane, General Custer, Wild Bill Hickok, Rodeo Trick Rider, Sheriff, Ranch Boss, Bull Dogging Champ, Annie Oakley, Chief Sitting Bull, Roping Champ, Indian Scout. Hoppy Tab - **$12 $25 $50**
Others Each - **$5 $12 $20**

HOP-82. Radio Show 9x11" Handbill,
c. 1950. Grape-Nuts Flakes. Probable grocery bag insert. -
$40 $75 $125

HOP-83. "Strawberry Preserves" Glass,
c. 1950. Ladies Choice Foods. With Label - **$35 $75 $120**

HOP-84

HOP-85

HOP-84. "Hoppy's Favorite" Bond Bread Cards,
c. 1950. Some fronts advertise bread loaf seals. Reverse caption "Ways Of The West." Unnumbered, set of 16.
Each - **$3 $6 $12**

HOP-85. Bond Bread Postcard,
c. 1950. - **$8 $15 $25**

HOP-86

HOP-87

HOP-86. Bond Bread Book Cover,
c. 1950. - **$12 $20 $35**

HOP-87. Bond Bread Book Cover,
c. 1950. - **$12 $20 $35**

HOP-88

HOP-88. "Ranch House Race" Game,
c. 1950. Stroehmann's Sunbeam Bread. - **$35 $65 $100**

HOP-89

HOP-90

HOP-89. TV Show "Special Guest" 11x16" Cardboard Store Sign,
c. 1950. Wonder Bread. - **$40 $125 $200**

HOP-90. Dairylea Milk 13x20" Paper Store Poster,
c. 1950. Various dairies. - **$40 $100 $150**

HOP-91

HOP-91. Dairylea Ice Cream Carton,
c. 1950. Offers neckerchief and t-shirt. - **$40 $75 $150**

HOP-92

HOP-93

HOP-92. "Dairylea Milk" Glass Inscribed "Do As Hoppy And Miss Dairylea Do/Drink Dairylea Milk",
c. 1950. - **$75 $150 $300**

HOP-93. "1 Cent Play Money" Cardboard Milk Bottle Cap,
c. 1950. - **$8 $12 $20**

HOP-94

HOP-94. Product Box And Premium Order Coupon,
c. 1950. Scarce. Honey Roll Sugar Cones.
Box - **$200 $300 $450**
Coupon - **$20 $40 $75**

HOP-95

HOP-96

HOP-95. Waxed Cardboard Ice Cream "Hoppy Cup",
c. 1950. - **$15 $30 $60**

HOP-96. "Hopalong Cassidy Bar 20" Vectograph Brass Clip,
c. 1950. Hopalong Cassidy Ice Cream Bar and others. Plastic mechanical insert reveals Hoppy picture, although image almost always gone. Used as belt or pocket clip. No Image - **$15 $40 $75**

HOP-97

Meadow Gold Butter

HOP-97. "Bob Atcher's Meadow Gold Song" TV Show Music Folder,
c. 1950. Meadow Gold Butter. - **$20 $40 $75**

HOP-99

HOP-98

HOP-98. "All-Star Milk" Pint Glass Bottle,
c. 1950. Local imprint for "McClellan's". - **$30 $65 $100**

HOP-99. Vinyl Tumbler,
c. 1950. Cloverlake Cottage Cheese.
With Lid - **$25 $60 $100**
No Lid - **$20 $40 $70**

HOP-101

HOP-102

HOP-100

HOP-100. Popsicle "Hopalong Cassidy" Silvered Tin Badge,
c. 1950. Various sponsors. Sold carded in stores. -
$20 $40 $75

HOP-101. "HC" Silvered Metal Portrait Ring,
c. 1950. Popsicle and various sponsors. - **$20 $40 $60**

HOP-102. Miniature Plastic TV With Hoppy Film,
c. 1950. Hole on side for key chain, film has four color pictures of Hoppy. - **$35 $75 $110**

HOP-103

HOP-103. "Dudin'-Up Kit",
c. 1950. Fuller Brush Co. Hair treatment set with two trading cards on box back. Complete - **$200 $350 $550**

HOP-104

HOP-105

HOP-104. "Daily News" Cardboard Clicker Gun,
c. 1950. Various sponsors. - **$30 $60 $125**

HOP-105. Color Photo,
c. 1950. Came with gun to project filmstrips. -
$15 $25 $40

HOP-106

HOP-107

HOP-108

HOP-106. "Hopalong Cassidy/Sheriff" Cello. Button,
c. 1950. From Arizona radio station. For Mutual Network broadcasts. - **$30 $60 $100**

HOP-107. Double Sponsor Cello. Button,
c. 1950. Filene's department store, Boston and Loew's State Theater. Dark red/black featuring Hoppy portrait. -
$100 $200 $300

HOP-108. Encased Penny With Coded Message,
1951. Reads "Member Hopalong Cassidy Savings Club/Security-First National Bank." Coded message and good luck symbols on rim. Code was printed on member's club card. - **$25 $60 $100**

HOP-109

HOP-110

HOP-109. Wild West Trading Cards,
1951. Post Cereals. Set of 36. Each - **$5 $10 $20**

HOP-110. Bond Bread "The Strange Legacy" Comic Booklet,
1951. 3-1/2x7" format. Titles also in series "The Mad Bomber" and "Meets The Brend Brothers, Bandits."
Each - **$10 $30 $65**

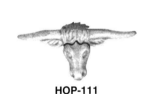

HOP-111

HOP-112

HOP-111. Concho/Branding Iron,
c. 1951. Post's Grape-Nuts Flakes. Plastic steer head with tie slide loop on back, used as ring or tie clip. Front has steer head cover over "HC" initials for printing paper. See HOP-113. - **$100 $175 $250**

HOP-112. "Hopalong Cassidy's Western Magazine" Second Issue,
1951. Vol. 1 #2 quarterly pulp magazine. Believed to be final issue. - **$75 $125 $175**

HOP-113

HOP-113. Concho/Branding Iron Instruction Leaflet,
c. 1951. Post's Grape-Nuts Flakes. See HOP-111. - **$30 $40 $50**

HOP-114

HOP-114. "Western Badges" 9x20" Paper Sign,
1952. Shows set of 12 litho. tin tabs, but Hoppy is not pictured. Possibly the star design picturing a "Ranger" was never produced, or if it was, a "Hopalong Cassidy" image was soon substituted and produced using the identical border design of a horse head, four pistols and arrowhead. When the set with Hoppy was issued, the reverses were marked "Post's Raisin Bran," but the Post's name does not appear on this sign. - **$40 $90 $175**

HOP-115

HOP-116

HOP-115. Hoppy Savings Club "Honor Member" Litho. Button,
c. 1952. Rare. Highest ranking award for early 1950s youthful bank savings program. Club folder from 1950 (HOP-27) does not show this button, which is likely the final in series. Rarest of all in series. - **$100 $250 $400**

HOP-116. Hat/Compass Ring,
1952. Post cereal. Brass bands, removable metal hat over plastic magnetic compass. - **$100 $150 $225**

HOP-117

HOP-117. All-Star Dairy Products Folder,
c. 1956. Pictured premiums include those for Hoppy as well as baseball stars Mickey Mantle and Stan Musial. - **$40 $80 $125**

HOP-118

HOP-119

HOP-118. Autographed Photo,
1950s. Pictured holding supplement to Philadelphia Sunday Bulletin. - **$50 $100 $150**

HOP-119. Secretarial Autographed Photo,
1950s. Signed by secretary or similar representative. - **$15 $30 $50**

HOP-120

HOP-121

HOP-120. "Hoppy's Bunkhouse Clothes Corral" Wood Rack,
1950s. Northland Milk. - **$75 $150 $200**

HOP-121. Melville Milk 11x42" Cardboard Store Sign,
1950s. Various dairies. Simulated wood grain. - **$60 $150 $250**

HOP-122

HOP-123

HOP-124

HOP-122. Photo Postcard,
1950s. Shows Hoppy from the waist up in cowboy outfit. - **$15 $25 $35**

HOP-123. Pin Back,
1950s. Scarce. Harmony Farms Dairies. - **$25 $50 $75**

HOP-124. Pin Back,
1950s. Scarce. Med-O Pure Dairy. - **$25 $50 $75**

HOP-125

HOP-125. Paper Mask in Realistic Color,
1950s. - **$75 $150 $250**

HOP-126

HOP-126. "Hopalong Cassidy Fan Club" English Black And White Photo Postcards,
1950s. Each - **$10 $18 $30**

HOP-127   HOP-128   HOP-129

HOP-127. Portrait Photo,
1950s. Various sponsors. - **$12 $25 $40**

HOP-128. Restaurant Ad Postcard,
1950s. Sherman Skipalong Club, Hotel Sherman, Chicago. Also pictures manager "Skipalong Tattler". - **$25 $40 $65**

HOP-129. Quart Milk Carton,
1950s. Various sponsors. - **$40 $75 $150**

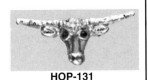

HOP-131

HOP-130

HOP-130. Western Series Glass,
1950s. Probably held food product. At least four in the set. - **$40 $80 $125**

HOP-131. "Hopalong Cassidy" Silvered Metal Kerchief Slide,
1950s. Steer head has rhinestone eyes, his name is across the horns. See HOP-41. - **$15 $30 $60**

HOP-132

HOP-133

HOP-132. Sterling Silver Ring,
1950s. Portrait framed by horseshoe, non-adjustable band. - **$60 $125 $250**

HOP-133. "Hopalong Cassidy Bar 20 Ranch" 2" Silvered Metal Badge,
1950s. English made store item with "Sheriff" under inset bw photo. - **$30 $50 $80**

HOP-134

HOP-135

HOP-134. Topper Bracelet,
1950s. Scarce. Anson Jewelry, gold finish. - **$30 $60 $120**

HOP-135. Bar 20 Bracelet,
1950s. Rare. Anson Jewelry, gold finish. - **$40 $80 $160**

HOP-136   HOP-137

HOP-136. "People and Places" Magazine,
1950s. Scarce. Car premium. - **$30 $60 $120**

HOP-137. Poster,
1980s. Promotes tapes of old films. - **$10 $20 $30**

HOP HARRIGAN

America's ace of the airways, Hop Harrigan made his debut in *All-American Comics* #1 in 1939, complete with Flying Club wings, patch, and other membership paraphernalia. On the ABC and Mutual radio networks from 1942 to 1948, Hop and his mechanical pal Tank Tinker conquered the Axis powers during the war years and fought assorted American villains once the war ended. The program was locally sponsored for much of its run; network sponsors included Grape-Nuts Flakes (1944-1946) and Lever Brothers (1947-1948). Columbia Pictures released a 15-episode Hop Harrigan chapter play in 1946.

HPH-1

HPH-2

**HPH-1. "Hop Harrigan All American Flying Club"
Copper Finish Brass Wings Badge,**
c. 1940. - **$25 $60 $100**

HPH-2. Certificate of Membership,
1940. All American Comics premium- **$75 $150 $300**

HPH-3

HPH-4

HPH-3. Photo,
1940. All American Comics. DC premium-
$75 $100 $150

HPH-4. Letter and Mailer For Badge,
1940. All American Comics premium.
Letter - **$50 $75 $90**
Mailer - **$50 $60 $75**

HPH-5

HPH-5. "All-American Flying Club" Kit.
c. 1942. Membership letter, card, stickers, fabric patch.
Near Mint In Mailer - **$250**
Patch - **$20 $60 $100**
Card - **$15 $35 $70**

HPH-6

HPH-7

HPH-6. Club Fabric Patch,
c. 1942. - **$20 $60 $100**

HPH-7. Plastic Movie Viewer With Films,
c. 1942. Includes three films. Near Mint Boxed - **$200**
Viewer And Films - **$40 $100 $150**

HPH-8

HPH-9

HPH-8. Jolly Junketeers Badge,
1942. Jolly Junketeers Flying Club. Canada. -
$25 $50 $75

HPH-9. Patch,
1942. "Keep 'Em Flying" American Observation Corps
patch. - **$20 $50 $85**

HPH-10

HPH-10. Grapenuts Flakes Sign 13x18",
1944. Rare. Promotes radio show and shows Para-plane
offer. - **$100 $250 $325**

HPH-11

HPH-12

**HPH-11. "Para-Plane With Parachutists" 15x16" Diecut
Cardboard Store Sign,**
c. 1944. Rare. Grape-Nuts Flakes. Sign is three-dimen-
sional and has open center to display cereal box.
Sign - **$250 $500 $1200**
Para-Plane Complete - **$100 $250 $500**

HPH-12. Superfortress Grape Nuts Flakes Sign,
1944. Scarce. - **$200 $400 $500**

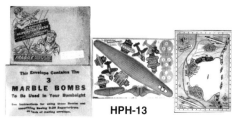

HPH-13

**HPH-13. "Boeing B-29 Superfortress Model Plane And
Target Game",**
c. 1944. Scarce. Grape-Nuts Flakes. Includes target, two
punch-out sheets, marbles. Complete - **$150 $350 $500**

HOWDY DOODY

It aired on NBC-TV from 1947 to 1960, starting out as *The Puppet Playhouse*, created and hosted by Buffalo Bob Smith. It was one of television's all-time successes, winner of the first Peabody award, attracting millions of devoted young viewers and responsible for millions of dollars in licensed merchandise. It was *Howdy Doody Time*, a combination of fantasy, music, films, and slapstick played out by puppets and humans in front of a screaming studio audience of 40 kids for more than 2,300 performances.

Howdy, with voice supplied by Buffalo Bob, consorted with a long list of characters, including Clarabell the clown (played originally by Bob Keeshan); Mr. Bluster, the mayor of Doodyville; Flub-A-Dub, a fantastic animal crossbreed; Dilly-Dally, a big-eared carpenter; Indian Princess Summerfall-Winterspring; and many others. The original Howdy puppet was replaced with a new design in 1948.

Among the program's many sponsors: Wonder Bread, Colgate tooth powder, Ovaltine, Poll-Parrot shoes, Mars candy, Tootsie Rolls, Welch's grape juice, Marx and Ideal toys, Kellogg's and Nabisco cereals, and Royal pudding. Character licensees were barely able to meet the huge demand for toys, dolls, lunch boxes, clothes, marionettes, wristwatches, mugs, piggy banks, figurines, records, T-shirts, even a musical rocking chair. Items were copyrighted Bob Smith (1948-1951), Kagran Corp. (1951-1959), or NBC (1960 on).

A Sunday *Howdy Doody* comic strip appeared from 1950 to 1953, and Dell published comic books from 1950 to 1957. A radio version of the show aired on NBC from 1952 to 1958, and the TV series was revived briefly on NBC in 1976, but, sadly, it was no longer *Howdy Doody Time*.

HOW-1

HOW-1. Photo Doody,
Late 1940s. First advertising piece to sell for more than $100,000. This marionette was the third Howdy Doody to be created, and was used strictly for promotional purposes, It is virtually identical to the Howdy Doody we remember except for the lack of strings (to allow for easier use in photo shoots). Sold at Leland's 1997 auction for **$113,431**

HOW-2

HOW-3

HOW-2. "I'm For Howdy Doody" Cello. Button,
1948. First item and premium offered March 23, 1948 as part of Howdy Doody for President campaign. Five stations carried the show and the offer was made seven times. NBC was astonished by 60,000 requests. Colgate, Continental Baking, Ovaltine and Mars candy quickly signed as sponsors. - **$20 $50 $85**

HOW-3. "The Billboard" Magazine With Cover Photo,
November 27, 1948. Early item from second year of Howdy show. - **$20 $30 $50**

HOW-4

HOW-5

HOW-4. Howdy Doody Newspaper #1,
1950. Poll-Parrot. Scarce. - **$50 $150 $250**

HOW-5. Thank-You Letter,
1950. Rare. Recipient awarded box of Snickers for poem selected from a contest. - **$75 $150 $250**

HOW-6

HOW-7

HOW-8

HOW-6. Wood Jointed Doll,
c. 1950. Store item. Includes leather belt and fabric bandanna. - **$150 $275 $450**

HOW-7. Ovaltine Plastic Mug With Decal,
c. 1950. - **$20 $24 $75**

HOW-8. Ovaltine Plastic Shake-Up Mug,
c. 1950. - **$25 $50 $90**

HOW-9

HOW-10

HOW-9. Cardboard Store Sign,
c. 1950. Colgate Dental Cream.
Large (About 24") Size - **$150 $300 $600**
Small (About 6") Size - **$20 $50 $80**

HOW-10. "Magic Trading Card" 14x21" Proof Sheet,
1951. Issued individually in boxes of Burry's Howdy Doody
Cookies. Uncut - **$80 $200 $350**
Each Card - **$2 $5 $8**

HOW-11

HOW-12

HOW-11. "Howdy Doody Talkin' Tag",
1951. Wonder Bread/Hostess Cupcakes. Disk turns to
form four mouth expressions. - **$20 $50 $75**

HOW-12. "Poll Parrot's" Comic Book #4,
1951. Series of four. Each - **$10 $30 $70**

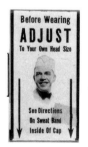

HOW-14

HOW-13

HOW-13. Store Clerk Paper Cap,
c. 1951. Wonder Bread. - **$15 $30 $50**

HOW-14. "American History" Bread Label Album, c.
1951. Wonder Bread. Holds 19 label cut-outs depicting
Howdy Doody characters in historial situations such as
"Landing Of The Pilgrims." Album Only - **$20 $40 $60**
Each Uncut Label - **$5 $10 $15**
Each Cut Label - **$3 $8 $12**

HOW-15

HOW-16

HOW-15. "Circus Album" 5-1/2x8" Ad Sheet,
c. 1951. Wonder Bread. - **$50 $100 $150**

HOW-16. T.V.-Merrimat Paper Place Mat,
1952. Store item. Placematters, Inc. - **$20 $45 $75**

HOW-17

HOW-18

HOW-17. T.V.-Merrimat Plastic Place Mat,
1952. Store item. Placematters, Inc. - **$20 $50 $85**

HOW-18. "Howdy Doody For President" Cello. Button,
1952. Wonder Bread. - **$25 $50 $85**

HOW-19

HOW-20

HOW-19. "Campaign Cap",
c. 1952. Poll-Parrot Shoes. Paper punch-out assembled by
slots and tabs. Unpunched - **$25 $60 $100**
Assembled - **$15 $50 $90**

HOW-20. Welch's Cookbook,
1952. Welch's Grape Juice. - **$15 $50 $80**

(BOTTOM
OF BOTTLE)

HOW-21

HOW-22

HOW-21. Welch's Grape Juice Glass Bottle,
c. 1952. Various character portraits embossed on bottom.
Each - **$10 $25 $40**

HOW-22. Welch's Grape Juice Tin Cap From Bottle,
c. 1952. - **$5 $10 $15**

HOW-23

HOW-23. "Howdy Doody Ice Cream Circus" Puzzle,
c. 1952. Howdy Doody Frozen Treat products. 10-1/2x14"
jigsaw puzzle comprised of 42 numbered pieces obtained
individually by product purchase.
Complete - **$100 $200 $300**

HOW-24

HOW-25 **HOW-26**

HOW-24. Kellogg's "Free Cut-Out Masks" 15x20" Paper Store Sign,
c. 1953. Corn Flakes and Rice Krispies. Offers masks on box rear panels. - **$30 $60 $100**

HOW-25. Kellogg's Howdy Doody Oversized Sample Mask,
c. 1953. Diecut 12x15" paper promotion for masks offered on back panels of Corn Flakes and Rice Krispies boxes.
Howdy Doody - **$100 $150 $250**
Pirate, Witch Or Devil - **$35 $60 $85**

HOW-26. Kellogg's "Free Cut-Out Masks" 15x20" Paper Store Sign,
c. 1953. Corn Flakes and Rice Krispies. Advertises pirate mask from series on box back panels.
Howdy Doody - **$100 $150 $250**
Pirate, Witch Or Devil - **$35 $60 $85**

HOW-27

HOW-28

HOW-27. Welch's Grape Juice 3" Tin Lid From Glass Jelly Jar,
1953. - **$8 $15 $25**

HOW-28. Welch's Grape Jelly Glasses,
1953. Six designs, various colors, character faces on bottom. Each - **$5 $10 $15**

HOW-29

HOW-29. "Doodyville" Cardboard Houses,
1953. Welch's Grape Juice. Set of eight.
Each Unused - **$20 $40 $75**
Each Assembled - **$10 $25 $40**

HOW-30

HOW-31

HOW-32

HOW-30. "Coloring Comics" Sheet #1,
1953. Blue Bonnet Margarine. From numbered series of box inserts. Each - **$5 $10 $20**

HOW-31. "Snap-A-Wink" Target,
1953. Poll-Parrot Shoes. - **$25 $45 $60**

HOW-32. "Comic Circus Animals" Picture Toy,
1954. Poll-Parrot Shoes. - **$30 $75 $125**

HOW-33

HOW-33. Kellogg's Rice Krispies Flat,
1954. Box (9 1/2 oz.) features Howdy on front and large mask of Howdy on back. - **$250 $500 $900**

HOW-34

HOW-34. "Big Prize Doodle List" Sheet,
1954. Howdy Doody Ice Cream Club. Premium listing for 1954-1955. - **$10 $20 $30**

HOW-35

HOW-36

HOW-35. Kellogg's Rice Krispies Box Panel Masks,
1954. One of a set: Howdy, Clarabell, Dilly Dally, The
Princess. Each Uncut Box Back - **$10 $25 $40**

HOW-36. Merchandise Manual,
1954. Rare. - **$100 $300 $500**
1955. Rare. - **$75 $250 $400**

HOW-37

HOW-38

HOW-37. Ice Cream Cup Lid,
1955. Doughnut Corp. of America. Lid and 25 cents used
to order "Howdy Doody Magic Talking Pin." - **$10 $20 $35**

HOW-38. "Clarabell Dangle-Dandy" Box Back,
c. 1955. Kellogg's. One of a series.
Uncut Each - **$20 $50 $75**
Assembled Each - **$10 $25 $50**

HOW-39

HOW-40

HOW-39. Jumble Joy Book,
1955. Scarce. Poll Parrot shoe premium. 16 pages in
color. - **$40 $100 $150**

HOW-40. "Twin-Pop" 7x14" Paper Store Sign,
1956. - **$20 $50 $75**

HOW-41

HOW-42

HOW-41. "Jackpot Of Fun" Comic Book,
1957. DCA Food Industries. - **$15 $25 $45**

HOW-42. Ceramic Piggy Bank,
1950s. Store item. - **$100 $175 $300**

HOW-44

HOW-43

HOW-43. Mobile Pictures,
1950s. Scarce. Clarabell, Howdy, Gabby and Tom Corbett
featured. - **$50 $125 $175**

HOW-44. TV Set Instructions,
1950s. Rare. Colgate premium. - **$35 $75 $100**

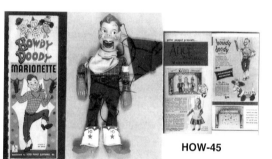

HOW-45

HOW-45. Composition Marionette,
1950s. Store item by Peter Puppet Playthings.
Boxed - **$100 $150 $300**
Loose - **$50 $100 $150**

HOW-47

HOW-48

HOW-46

HOW-46. Large Glazed Ceramic Bust Bank,
1950s. Store item. - **$250 $350 $700**

HOW-47. Photo Glow Ring,
1950s. Ring name implies image glows in dark but all
examples seen do not glow. - **$100 $150 $250**

HOW-48. Flicker Picture Ring With Brass Base,
1950s. Portrait of Howdy alternates with image of Poll
Parrot on a perch. - **$75 $100 $125**

HOW-50

HOW-49

HOW-51

HOW-49. Poll-Parrot TV Plastic Ring With Flicker Picture,
1950s. Frame image of TV screen, image alternates between Howdy and parrot. - **$100 $150 $200**

HOW-50. Plastic Ring With Paper Insert Picture,
1950s. - **$75 $110 $150**

HOW-51. Illuminated Head Ring,
1950s. Palmolive Soap. Brass bands holding plastic head lighted by bulb and battery. - **$75 $140 $200**

HOW-52   HOW-53   HOW-54

HOW-52. Newspaper Comic Strip Litho. Button,
1950s. - **$20 $35 $75**

HOW-53. "Howdy Doody Safety Club/CBC" Cello. Button,
1950s. Canadian Broadcasting Company. Canadian issue by Toronto maker. - **$35 $75 $125**

HOW-54. "Sunday Post-Dispatch" Litho. Button,
1950s. Issued for newspaper comic strip. - **$30 $60 $100**

HOW-55   HOW-56   HOW-57

HOW-55. Jack-In-The-Box Plastic Ring,
1950s. Poll-Parrot Shoes. Lid lifts over miniature 3-D plastic Howdy head. - **$500 $1500 $3500**

HOW-56. "Poll-Parrot" Plastic Ring,
1950s. Raised portrait. - **$25 $50 $75**

HOW-57. Clarabell's Horn Ring,
1950s. Scarce. Brass bands picture Clarabell and Howdy, top has aluminum horn that works by blowing. - **$150 $335 $525**

HOW-58

HOW-58. "Poll-Parrot's Howdy Doody Photo Album",
1950s. Includes four blank pages to mount four photos. Complete - **$75 $150 $200**

HOW-59

HOW-59. Tuk-A-Tab Mask,
1950s. Poll-Parrot. Masks of Howdy and Clarabell. Each Unpunched - **$20 $30 $50**

HOW-60   HOW-61   HOW-62   HOW-63

HOW-60. Poll-Parrot Coloring Book,
1950s. - **$20 $75 $100**

HOW-61. Jointed Cardboard Puppet,
1950s. Wonder Bread. 13" tall. - **$15 $35 $60**

HOW-62. Jointed Cardboard Puppet,
1950s. Wonder Bread. 7-1/2" tall. - **$15 $35 $60**

HOW-63. Princess Cardboard Jointed Puppet,
1950s. Wonder Bread. 7-1/2" tall. - **$15 $35 $60**

HOW-64

HOW-64. Howdy Doody Periscope,
1950s. Rare. Wonder Bread. - **$125 $350 $500**

HOW-65

HOW-66

HOW-65. Bread Labels,
1950s. Wonder Bread. From two different sets.
Each - **$5 $8 $12**

HOW-66. "Wonder-Land Game" Sheet,
1950s. Wonder Bread. With spinner and 16 spaces for cut-outs from bread end labels. Unused - **$20 $40 $75**
Complete - **$75 $100 $200**

HOW-67

HOW-67. "Wonder Bread Circus Album" Label Sheet,
1950s. - **$30 $75 $100**

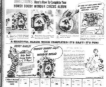
HOW-68

HOW-68. "Wonder Bread Balloon Parade" Label Sheet,
1950s. - **$30 $75 $100**

HOW-69   HOW-70   HOW-71

HOW-69. "Howdy Doody's Favorite Doughnuts" Cellophane Package,
1950s. Tom Thumb. - **$15 $35 $60**

HOW-70. "Wonder Bread Zoomascope",
1950s. Opens to 3-1/2x51". - **$25 $50 $85**

HOW-71. Cardboard Disk Flipper Badge,
1950s. Wonder Bread. Disk flips by pulling string to complete phrase "The Princess Says...Eat Wonder Bread". From set picturing various Howdy Doody characters.
Each - **$10 $20 $30**

HOW-72

HOW-72. "Fudge Bar" Waxed Paper Bag,
1950s. Offers talking pin and ice cream club membership. - **$5 $12 $20**

HOW-73   HOW-74   HOW-75

HOW-73. "Hostess" Cupcake Package Tag,
1950s. Continental Baking Co. - **$50 $75 $100**

HOW-74. Litho. Tab,
1950s. Ten tabs were collected for free "Twin Pop Or Fudge Bar". - **$15 $25 $40**

HOW-75. Ice Cream Waxed Cardboard Cup,
1950s. - **$20 $35 $50**

HOW-76

HOW-76. Packaged Wood Ice Cream Spoon,
1950s. - **$5 $10 $15**

HOW-77

HOW-77. Christmas Cards,
1950s. Mars Candy. Set of 8 with 8 blank envelopes.
Each - **$10 $15 $25**

HOW-78   HOW-79

HOW-78. "Mason Candy Words To The 'Howdy Doody' Song" Sheet,
1950s. - **$10 $18 $30**

HOW-79. "Howdy Doody Animated Puppet" Punch-Out With Envelope,
1950s. Three Muskateers/Mars candy bars.
Near Mint In Mailer - **$150**

HOW-80

HOW-81

HOW-80. "Clarabell Animated Puppet" Punch-Out With Envelope,
1950s. Mars Coconut Bar. Near Mint In Mailer - **$150**

HOW-81. "E-Z DO Junior Space Saver" 2-1/4" Tin Tab,
1950s. - **$15 $25 $45**

HOW-82

HOW-82. "Royal Trading Card",
1950s. Royal Pudding. Set of 14.
Each Complete Box - **$10 $20 $40**
Each Cut Card - **$5 $10 $15**

HOW-83

HOW-84

HOW-85

HOW-83. Princess Face Mask With Glassine Envelope,
1950s. Royal Desserts. Issued for additional characters.
With Envelope - **$20 $50 $75**
Loose - **$10 $25 $40**

HOW-84. Silver Plate Iced Tea Spoon,
1950s. Sponsor unknown. - **$8 $15 $30**

HOW-85. "Howdy Doody Climber" Cardboard Figure,
1950s. Luden's Wild Cherry Cough Drops.
Near Mint In Mailer - **$60**
Loose - **$10 $20 $35**

HOW-86

HOW-87

HOW-86. "Magic Kit" With Envelope,
1950s. Luden's, makers of Fifth Avenue candy bar. Tricks on punch-out sheets. Near Mint In Mailer - **$100**

HOW-87. Cereal Box Mask,
1950s. Wheaties. Cut Mask - **$15 $20 $40**

HOW-88

HOW-88. Blue Bonnet Margarine Box Panels,
1950s. Waxed cardboard set of 12 for "Play TV" stage offered separately as mail premium.
Each Uncut Panel - **$10 $20 $35**

HOW-89

HOW-89. Four-Sided Mask,
1950s. Philco TV depicting Howdy, Gabby Hayes and National/American League baseball players to promote World Series on Philco TV. - **$50 $125 $175**

HOW-90

HOW-91

HOW-90. "Howdy Doody Napkins" Trading Card Sheet,
1950s. Colonial Paper Products Co. At least two different sheets. Each Uncut - **$20 $40 $75**

HOW-91. "Princess Summerfall Winterspring" Photo,
1950s. Pictures Judy Tyler. - **$20 $40 $75**

HOW-92

HOW-93

HOW-92. Hat,
1950s. Store bought. - **$10** **$20** **$30**

HOW-93. Large Postcard,
1950s. - **$30** **$75** **$100**

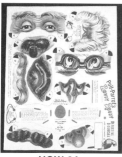

HOW-94

HOW-95

HOW-94. Detective Disguise Punch-Out Sheet,
1950s. Poll-Parrot Shoes - **$20** **$40** **$60**

HOW-95. Air-O-Doodle Rocket Beanie with Mailer,
1950s. Rare. Kellogg's Rice Krispies premium. -
$35 **$100** **$150**

HOW-96

HOW-97

HOW-98

HOW-96. "Revival Show" Local Cello. Button,
1971. Towson State College. Single day issue for May 5
event. - **$3** **$6** **$10**

HOW-97. "Howdy Doody For President" Litho. Tin Tab,
c. 1976. National Broadcasting Corp. - **$10** **$20** **$30**

HOW-98. "A 40-Year Celebration" 3" Cello. Button,
1987. National Broadcasting Co. - **$5** **$12** **$25**

HOWIE WING

The air adventures of ace Howie Wing were heard on
CBS radio five times a week in 1938 and 1939, with
William Janney battling evil as young Howie. Kellogg's
cereals sponsored the program and issued a number of
aviation-related premiums, including wings, a weather
forecaster ring, decoder, model airplane kits, and membership paraphernalia for the Cadet Aviation Corps.

HWN-1

HWN-2

**HWN-1. "Kellogg's Cadet Aviation Corps" Club
Manual,**
1938. - **$15** **$40** **$75**

HWN-2. Premium Order Sheet,
c. 1938. Offers Cadet Aviation Corp. button, Flying Guide
and Pilot Test Card. - **$10** **$20** **$40**

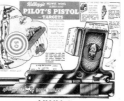

HWN-3

HWN-4

**HWN-3. "Kellogg's Rubber Band Pilot's Pistol And
Targets",**
c. 1938. Unpunched - **$50** **$125** **$200**

HWN-4. "Kellogg's Moving Picture Machine",
c. 1938. Unpunched - **$50** **$125** **$200**

HWN-5

HWN-6

HWN-5. Cadet Aviation Corps News,
c. 1938. - **$25** **$50** **$75**

HWN-6. Kellogg's Corn Flakes Box - 8 oz.,
1939. Cereal box features Wings Over America. Vultee V-
12 plane pictured. Premium offer of ring, plane model kit,
and handbook pictured on side of box.
Complete - **$75** **$150** **$250**

HWN-7

HWN-8

HWN-7. Kellogg's Corn Flakes Box Back,
1939. Wings Over America series. Brewster F2A-1 plane pictured. Premium offer for membership kit pictured on side of box. - **$20 $30 $45**

HWN-8. Kellogg's Corn Flakes Box -13 oz.,
1939. Wings Over America series. Curtiss SBC-40 plane pictured. Premium offer for club material on side of box. Shows badge at top. Complete - **$50 $100 $175**

HWN-9

HWN-10

HWN-9. "Official Handbook",
1939. Kellogg's. - **$25 $40 $75**

HWN-10. "Howie Wing/Cadet Aviation Corps" Club Membership Card,
1939. Kellogg's. - **$15 $30 $50**

HWN-11

HWN-12

HWN-11. "Kellogg's Cadet Aviation Corps" Club Member Certificate,
1930s. - **$10 $20 $30**

HWN-12. "Howie Wing's Adventures On The Canadian Lakes" Map,
1930s. Kellogg's of Canada. 11x16" opened. - **$75 $200 $300**

HWN-13

HWN-14

HWN-13. Ventriloquist Dummy Cardboard Fold-Out,
1930s. Kellogg's premium. - **$75 $150 $225**

HWN-14. Instructions For Dummy,
1930s. Kellogg's premium. - **$10 $15 $25**

HWN-16

HWN-15

HWN-17

HWN-15. "Howie Wing/Kellogg's" Holed Aluminum Coin,
1930s. - **$10 $15 $25**

HWN-16. "Howie Wing Cadet" Silvered/Enameled Brass Badge,
1930s. - **$5 $10 $15**

HWN-17. "Pilot CAC" Aluminum Wings Badge,
1930s. For Howie Wing Cadet Aviation Corps. Probably Canadian issue. - **$20 $50 $75**

HWN-18

HWN-19

HWN-18. Weather Forecast Ring,
1930s. Brass bands with metal clip holding slip of litmus paper. - **$150 $300 $450**

HWN-19. "Cadet" Cello. Button,
1930s. Distributed to Canadian members. - **$10 $20 $35**

HWN-20

HWN-20. "Kellogg's Cadet Aviation Corps" Pamphlet Set,
1930s. Set of 17. Each - **$3 $5 $8**

H.R. PUFNSTUF

This Saturday morning children's television series, which used both live actors and puppets, aired on NBC from 1969 to 1971 and was repeated on ABC from 1972 to 1974. The program told, with songs and dances, the adventures of young Jimmy and his golden talking flute Freddie as they try to escape the clutches of the wicked Witchiepoo on Living Island. A movie version was released by Paramount in 1970, and comic books appeared from 1970 to 1972.

HPF-1

HPF-1. Soundtrack Record Album and Photo,
1970. Kellogg's. With Mailer - **$40 $100 $150**
No Mailer - **$25 $75 $100**

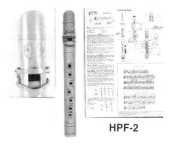

HPF-2

HPF-2. "Freddie The Flute" Musical Toy With Instructions,
1970. Kellogg's. Flute - **$100 $250 $350**
Instruction Sheet - **$25 $50 $75**

HPF-3   HPF-4

HPF-3. "Pufnstuf" Translucent Plastic Ring,
1970. Copyright Sid & Marty Krofft Prod. Inc. Slightly raised character image from seven different versions also picturing Witchipoo, Cling and Clang, Jimmy and Freddie, Orson, two unknown. Each - **$40 $60 $80**

HPF-4. "Witchipoo" Translucent Plastic Ring,
1970. Copyright Sid & Marty Krofft Prod. Inc. From series of seven different also picturing Pufnstuf, Cling and Clang, Jimmy and Freddie, Orson, two unknown.
Each - **$40 $60 $80**

HPF-5   HPF-6   HPF-7

HPF-5. H.R. Pufnstuf Vinyl Hand Puppet,
1970. Store item by Remco. - **$25 $50 $75**

HPF-6. Jimmy Vinyl Hand Puppet,
1970. Store item by Remco. - **$25 $50 $75**

HPF-7. Cling Or Clang Vinyl Hand Puppet,
1970. Store item by Remco. - **$25 $50 $75**

HUCKLEBERRY HOUND

Huckleberry Hound, the first animated cartoon to win an Emmy, was Hanna-Barbera's first major television hit and the source of hundreds of licensed products. The syndicated series, sponsored by Kellogg's cereals, aired from 1958 to 1962 and was watched by millions of viewers all over the world. Huck was a noble-hearted bloodhound who remained untroubled no matter what misfortunes plagued him. Other cartoon segments on the show: Pixie and Dixie, a pair of carefree mice who tormented the affable tomcat Mr. Jinks ("I hate those meeces to pieces!"); Yogi Bear, who debuted on the show and went on to his own major series in 1961; and Hokey Wolf, a Sgt. Bilko-like con artist whose pal was Ding-a-Ling, a fox. *Huckleberry Hound* comic books appeared from 1959 into the 1970s.

HUC-1   HUC-2

HUC-1. "Fun Cards" Box Back,
1959. Kellogg's Corn Flakes. Back Panel Only - **$10 $15 $25**

HUC-2. Plush Doll With Vinyl Face,
1960. Store item by Knickerbocker and Kellogg's premium. - **$25 $40 $65**

HUC-3

HUC-3. "Huck Hound Club" Kit,
1960. Kellogg's. Includes letter, member card, two color pictures, club button, Breakfast Score Card (not shown). Complete - **$75 $150 $250**

HUC-4   HUC-5   HUC-6

HUC-4. "Huckleberry Hound For President" 3" Litho. Button,
1960. - **$15 $30 $60**

HUC-5. "The Great Kellogg's TV Show" Record Album,
c. 1960. - **$8 $12 $20**

HUC-6. Plastic Bank,
c. 1960. Store item by Knickerbocker. - **$15 $25 $35**

HUC-7   HUC-8   HUC-9

HUC-7. "Huck Hound Club" Enameled Brass Ring,
c. 1960. Kellogg's. - **$30 $78 $125**

HUC-8. "Huck Hound Club" Brass Ring Copyrighted,
1961. Kellogg's. Variety without enamel paint accents. -
$30 $78 $125

HUC-9. Club Card,
1962. Scarce. Certified as TopDog. - **$20 $35 $45**

HUC-10

HUC-11

HUC-12

HUC-10. "Kellogg's Special K" 17x41" Cardboard Hanger String Sign,
1960s. - **$75 $125 $200**

HUC-11. Huck Hound/Mr. Jinks Plastic Flicker Ring,
1960s. Kellogg's Cereal. Believed to be set of six. -
$45 $110 $175

HUC-12. Cereal Box Plastic Figures,
1960s. Kellogg's OK Cereal. Miniatures of Huck Hound, Pixie and Dixie, Mr. Jinks, Yogi Bear, Boo Boo Bear, Tony the Tiger. Each - **$4 $8 $12**

INNER SANCTUM

The memorable squeaking door and the sinister voice of "Raymond, your host" introduced the macabre *Inner Sanctum* mysteries on radio from 1941 to 1952, first on the Blue network, then on CBS (1943-1950), and ABC. The morbid anthology featured such film veterans as Boris Karloff, Peter Lorre, and Claude Raines in ghostly tales of murder and mayhem. Sponsors included Carter's Little Liver Pills (1941-1943), Colgate-Palmolive shaving cream (1943-1944), Lipton tea and soup (1945), Bromo-Seltzer (1946-1950), and Mars candy (1950-1951). A number of second-feature Inner Sanctum movies were made in the 1940s by Universal, most starring Lon Chaney Jr.

INN-1

INN-1. Cardboard Ink Blotter,
1945. Scarce. Lipton tea and soup. - **$20 $50 $75**

INSPECTOR POST

General Foods created Post's Junior Detective Corps in 1932-1933 to promote its line of cereals. The club was advertised in Sunday newspaper comic sections and on the cereal boxes, offering its young members manuals edited by Inspector General Post and badges for detective ranks up to the level of Captain.

INS-1   INS-2   INS-3

INS-1. "Inspector Post's Case Book" Manual,
1933. Post Toasties. Includes 10 mysteries solved by
answers on back. - **$10 $30 $50**

INS-2. Junior Detective Corps" Club Manuals,
1933. Set of four. Each - **$10 $30 $50**

INS-3. Headquarters To Lieutenants Letter,
1933. Announces lowering of requirements to advance
from Sergeant to Lieutenant. - **$15 $25 $40**

INS-4   INS-5   INS-6   INS-7

INS-4. "Detective/Post's J.D.C." Silvered Tin Badge,
1933. - **$15 $30 $50**

**INS-5. "Detective Sergeant/Post's J.D.C." Brass Rank
Badge,**
1933. - **$10 $30 $50**

**INS-6. "Lieutenant Post's J.D.C." Silvered Brass Rank
Badge ,**
1933. - **$15 $35 $60**

INS-7. "Captain/Post's J.D.C." Brass Rank Badge,
1933. Scarce. - **$20 $50 $90**

JACK ARMSTRONG

Jack Armstrong hit the air in July 1933 and ruled the
late-afternoon airwaves until 1951, one of the most
popular and longest-running radio adventure series
ever--and, thanks to Wheaties' sponsorship, one of the
most bountiful sources of premiums. Jack started as a
sports hero at Hudson High School, but within a year
he and cousins Billy and Betty were seeking adventure
with Uncle Jim in exotic spots all over the world. They
were still waving the flag for Hudson High, but the
intrepid four were tackling Tibet, searching out the elephants' graveyard in darkest Africa, recovering sunken
uranium in the Sulu Sea, always looking for something
lost or stolen or buried.

Jack Armstrong premiums were frequently linked to
the program's story line--a Hike-O-Meter just like the
one Jack used to measure how far he'd walked, a torpedo flashlight or explorer telescope, a signaling mir-

ror or secret whistle ring to send messages, a bombsight, a bracelet just like Betty's, and, of course, club
memberships. During World War II listeners were
urged to buy war bonds, collect scrap, and write letters to servicemen, and to stay strong by eating their
Wheaties. In 1950 the program was renamed
Armstrong of the SBI and Jack, Billy, and Betty began
working for the Scientific Bureau of Investigation. The
series went off the air in 1951.

Jack Armstrong comic strips and a series of 13 comic
books were published from 1947 to 1949, all drawn by
Bob Schoenke. Also in 1947, Columbia Pictures
released a 15-episode chapter play.

JAC-1

JAC-1. Wheaties Box With 1st Premium Offer On Back,
1933. Rare. Offers hand exercise grips.
Complete - **$100 $300 $500**

JAC-2   JAC-3   JAC-4

JAC-2. "Johnny (Tarzan) Weissmuller" Photo,
1933. Rare. One of earliest Jack Armstrong Wheaties premiums. - **$40 $125 $200**

**JAC-3. Wheaties "How To Hit A Home Run" Flip
Booklet,**
1933. Scarce. Photo pages in sequence of batting stance,
complete swing, follow-through. - **$75 $250 $400**

JAC-4. Armstrong On Horse Blackster Photo,
1933. - **$10 $15 $25**

JAC-5

JAC-5. "Shooting Plane" With Directions And Mailer,
1933. Made by Daisy Mfg. Co. Metal gun and two spinner
wheels. Near Mint Boxed - **$175**
Gun - **$50 $75 $100**
Each Spinner - **$10 $20 $30**

JAC-6

JAC-6. "Wee-Gyro" Flying Ship, Instruction Paper,
1934. Sheet came with a balsa model similar to autogyro. -
$25 $75 $125

JAC-7

JAC-8

JAC-7. Jack Armstrong Wee-Gyro,
1934.General Mills Cereal premium. Includes Wee gyro,
mailer, and instructions. Gyro - **$75 $125 $250**
Mailer - **$15 $30 $50**
Instructions - **$25 $75 $125**

JAC-8. All American Team Photo,
1934. Radio premium. - **$10 $20 $30**

JAC-9   JAC-10

JAC-9. Jack Armstrong Photo,
1934. Radio premium. - **$10 $20 $30**

JAC-10. Betty Fairfield Photo,
1934. Radio premium. - **$10 $20 $30**

JAC-11   JAC-12

JAC-11. Box Back Panel,
1935. - **$10 $30 $50**

JAC-12. Box Back Panel,
1935. - **$10 $30 $50**

JAC-13   JAC-14   JAC-15

JAC-13. Box Back Panel,
1935. - **$10 $30 $50**

JAC-14. Betty Fairfield Box Back Panel,
1935. - **$10 $30 $50**

JAC-15. Betty Fairfield Box Back Panel,
1935. - **$10 $30 $50**

JAC-16

JAC-16. Stamp Collecting Items,
1935. Includes booklet and pamphlets about stamp collecting with offer of oriental stamps. Each - **$10 $20 $35**

JAC-17

**JAC-17. "Jack Armstrong's Chart Game/Adventures
With The Dragon Talisman" Map Game,**
1936. Map Game Only - **$35 $75 $150**
Spinner and Game Markers (4) - **$10 $20 $40**
Dragon Talisman - **$20 $35 $75**

JAC-18

JAC-23

JAC-24

JAC-23. "Hike-O-Meter" Aluminum Pedometer,
1938. Blue painted rim. - **$20 $40 $75**

JAC-24. "Treasure Hunt" Instruction Booklet,
1938. Came with Hike-O-Meter pedometer. - **$15 $25 $35**

JAC-18. "Big Ten Football Game",
1936. Near Mint In Mailer - **$250**
Board Only - **$10 $20 $50**
Booklet Only - **$10 $20 $30**

JAC-19

JAC-20

JAC-19. Milk Glass Bowl,
1937. - **$10 $25 $35**

JAC-20. Movie Viewer With Filmstrip,
1937. Film title is "Graveyard Of Elephants".
Box - **$10 $20 $35**
Viewer And Film - **$40 $75 $125**

JAC-25

JAC-26

JAC-25. "Baseball Centennial" Brass Ring,
1938. Offered as Jack Armstrong premium by General
Mills Wheaties and Corn Kix from 7/27/38-10/28/38.
Company recorded 46,501 responses. Manufacturer's
remainder offered by Quaker Puffed Rice in 1939. -
$250 $500 $750

**JAC-26. "Jack Armstrong Ped-O-Meter" Variety With
Mailer,**
c. 1938. 2-5/8" dia. scarce version metal pedometer in
chrome finish case rather than traditional blue rim plus title
variation from traditional "Hike-O-Meter" title.
Near Mint In Mailer - **$125**
Ped-O-Meter Only - **$30 $50 $100**

JAC-21

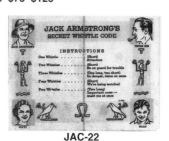

JAC-22

JAC-21. Secret Whistling Brass Ring,
1937. Egyptian symbols on sides. - **$40 $95 $150**

JAC-22. "Secret Whistle Code" Instruction Sheet,
1937. Paper (not cardboard). For Egyptian Whistle Ring. -
$60 $70 $80

JAC-27   JAC-28

JAC-27. Explorer Telescope,
1938. Cardboard tube with metal caps holding glass lenses. - **$8 $15 $25**

JAC-28. Heliograph And Distance Finder,
1938. Scarce. Brass multi-function premium for land and
water measurements, message sender, secret compartment, Morse Code. Scarce test premium. -
$250 $550 $1100

JAC-29

JAC-29. "Jack Armstrong Magic Answer Box",
1938. Complete Boxed - **$50 $75 $150**
Answer Box Only - **$30 $50 $75**

JAC-30

JAC-30. "Adventures Of Jack Armstrong" Box Backs,
1938. Wheaties. Set of six.
Each Back Panel - **$15 $30 $50**

JAC-31

JAC-32

JAC-31. "Lie Detektor" Metal Answer Box,
c. 1938. Supposed first version of "Magic Answer Box"
quickly redesigned because parents objected to children
telling lies. - **$75 $150 $300**

JAC-32. All American Boy Ring Lead Proof,
1939. Unique - **$2250**

JAC-33

JAC-34

JAC-35

JAC-33. Decoder Lead Proof,
1939. Designed by Orin Armstrong for Robbins Company.
Never produced. Unique - **$2000**

JAC-34. Pedometer,
1939. Version with unpainted aluminum rim. -
$15 $25 $40

JAC-35. Torpedo Flashlight Set,
1939. Set of three in red, blue, or black cardboard barrels
with metal nose and rear cap.
Blue - **$15 $25 $40**
Red - **$15 $30 $50**
Black - **$20 $35 $60**

JAC-36

JAC-36. Serial - "Return To Mars,"
1939. American Boy Magazine which features ad for Jack
Armstrong promoting Wheaties and serial adventure
"Return To Mars." Also shown is inside front cover featuring Armstrong ad. - **$15 $30 $50**

JAC-37

JAC-37. How to Fly Promo Sign,
1930s. - **$30 $75 $100**

JAC-38

JAC-38. Windfair W. J. A. C. Club Lead Proof,
1930s. Unique. - **$1200**

JAC-39

JAC-39. Sentinel Junior Ace First Aid Kit Complete with Mailer ,
1930s. Complete With Mailer and Contents -
$100 $300 $400
Tin Box Only - **$30 $60 $100**

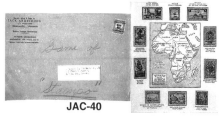

JAC-46   **JAC-48**
JAC-47   **JAC-49**

JAC-40

JAC-40. Wheaties "Stampo" Game With Mailer Envelope,
1930s. Two sheets to be cut and four leaflets for game devised by H. E. Harris Co., domestic and foreign postage stamps dealer of Boston. Uncut In Mailer - **$50 $100 $150**

JAC-46. "Lieutenant/Listening Squad" Brass Whistle Badge,
1940. Scarce. Test premium, small quantity distributed. -
$200 $500 $850

JAC-47. Lieutenant/Listening Squad Whistle Lead Proof,
1940. Unique - **$1200**

JAC-41   **JAC-42**

JAC-48. "Captain/Listening Squad" Sample Brass Whistle Badge,
1940. Rare. Test premium, even scarcer than Lieutenant version. - **$300 $1000 $1500**

JAC-49. Captain/Listening Squad Whistle Lead Proof,
1940. Unique - **$1750**

JAC-41. Bicycle Safety Kit,
c. 1930s. Booklet with generic light, battery, reflector and possibly more. Complete - **$100 $200 $300**

JAC-50

JAC-42. Fan Card,
1930s. "To My Friend" is imprinted followed by personalized inked first name of recipient above facsimile signature. - **$25 $60 $90**

JAC-50. Crocodile Glow in the Dark Plastic Whistle,
1940. Rare. Test premium with three known. -
$1000 $3000 $4500

JAC-51

JAC-44

JAC-43

JAC-45

JAC-51. "Dragon's Eye Ring" Instructions/Order Blank Sheet,
1940. Order coupon for additional rings expired January 2, 1941. - **$125 $150 $175**

JAC-43. Betty's Luminous Gardenia Bracelet,
1940. Rare. Glows in the dark. - **$75 $150 $350**

JAC-44. Sky Ranger Plane,
1940. - **$50 $175 $300**

JAC-45. Listening Squad Membership Card,
1940. Rare. Test premium. - **$150 $300 $400**

JAC-52

JAC-53

JAC-52. Dragon's Eye Ring With Instruction Paper,
1940. White glow plastic ring topped by dark green stone. Ring - **$300 $800 $1300**

JAC-53. "Sound Effects Kit" and Instruction Sheet,
1941. "Spy Hunt" mystery script utilizing sound effects. Complete - **$150 $250 $400**

JAC-55

JAC-54

JAC-54. "Write A Fighter Corps" Kit,
1942. Includes manual, stencils (6), star sticker sheets (6), insignia patches (6). Near Mint In Mailer - **$250**
Manual Only - **$25 $50 $75**

JAC-55. Press Release Photo Picturing Wood Bombsight,
1942. Mutual Broadcasting System. Pictures radio cast members Uncle Jim and Jack Armstrong holding Wheaties premium. - **$20 $40 $85**

JAC-57

JAC-56

JAC-56. Wheaties Secret Bombsight,
1942. Wood/litho. paper bomb release holding three wooden bombs. Bombsight Only - **$50 $100 $200**
Each Bomb - **$20 $30 $40**

JAC-57. "Secret Bomb Sight Instruction Manual",
1942. Scarce. Includes cut-out ships for use with bomb sight. Uncut - **$60 $150 $300**

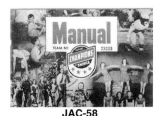

JAC-58   **JAC-59**

JAC-58. "Future Champions Of America" Club Manual,
1943. - **$20 $40 $75**

JAC-59. "Future Champions Of America" Fabric Patch,
1943. - **$5 $12 $20**

JAC-60

JAC-60. Model Planes 16x36" Paper Store Sign,
1944. - **$75 $150 $250**

JAC-61

JAC-61. Wheaties Tru-Flite Warplane Paper Model Kit With Envelope,
1944. Seven sets (A-G), each with two cut-out airplanes and instructions. Each Uncut Set In Mailer - **$25 $60 $90**

JAC-62   **JAC-63**

JAC-62. Tru-Flite News Vol. 1 #1 Newspaper,
Sept. 1944. - **$15 $35 $60**

JAC-63. Tru-Flite News Vol. 1 #2 Newspaper,
Oct. 1944. - **$15 $30 $55**

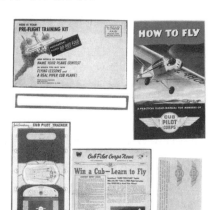

JAC-64

349

JAC-64. Pre-Flight Training Kit,
1945. Mailer holds "How To Fly" booklet, "Cub Pilot Corps. News" first issue newspaper, three-fold punch-out "Trainer" with short cardboard dowel "stick," and sheet of club logo transfers.
Complete Near Mint in Mailer - **$600**
Booklet - **$25 $50 $75**
Newspaper - **$15 $35 $60**
Punch-Out With Stick - **$100 $200 $300**
Transfers - **$10 $20 $30**

JAC-65

JAC-65. "Cub Pilot Corps" Contest Newspaper With I.D. Tag And Envelope,
1945. Includes newspaper #3 and metal "G.I. Identification Tag". Near Mint In Mailer- **$175**
Newspaper - **$15 $35 $60**
Tag - **$20 $40 $85**

JAC-66

JAC-66. Jack Armstrong Sign,
1945. Scarce. 17x22" sign promotes radio show and advertises joining Cub Pilots Corps. Talks about contest and how to get Piper Cub Pre-Flight Kit. Sponsored by Wheaties. - **$150 $300 $550**

JAC-67   JAC-68

JAC-67. Announcement,
1945. Announces 3 new books available for order from Library of Sports Books. - **$10 $20 $30**

JAC-68. Book 1,
1945. Wheaties. Library of Sports book premium. - **$15 $30 $50**

JAC-69   JAC-70

JAC-69. Book 2 - Type 1 (Offense),
1945. Wheaties. Library of Sports book premium. Features Bucky Walters, Bob Feller, Joe Cronin, the late Lou Gehrig and others. - **$20 $45 $75**

JAC-70. Book 2 - Type 2 (Defense),
1946. Wheaties. Library of Sports book premium. Cover and interior are different than 1045 cdition. Also features Bucky Walters, Bob Feller, Joe Cronin, the late Lou Gehrig and others. - **$20 $45 $75**

JAC-71   JAC-72

JAC-71. Book 3,
1945. Wheaties. Library of Sports book premium. - **$10 $20 $40**

JAC-72. Book 4,
1945. Wheaties. Library of Sports book premium. - **$10 $20 $40**

JAC-73   JAC-74

JAC-73. Book 5,
1945. Wheaties. Library of Sports book premium. - **$10 $20 $40**

JAC-74. Book 6,
1945. Wheaties. Library of Sports book premium. - **$10 $20 $40**

JAC-75

JAC-76

JAC-75. Book7,
1945. Wheaties. Library of Sports book premium. -
$10 $20 $40

JAC-76. Book 8,
1945. Wheaties. Library of Sports book premium. -
$10 $20 $40

JAC-77

JAC-78

JAC-77. Book 10,
1945. Wheaties. Library of Sports book premium. -
$10 $20 $40

JAC-78. Book 11,
1945. Wheaties. Library of Sports book premium. -
$10 $20 $40

JAC-79

JAC-80

JAC-79. Book 12,
1945. Wheaties. Library of Sports book premium. -
$10 $20 $40

JAC-80. Book14,
1945. Wheaties. Library of Sports book premium. -
$10 $20 $40

JAC-81

JAC-82

JAC-81. Book 15,
1945. Wheaties. Library of Sports book premium. Features
Marty Marion, Johnny Mize, Mel Ott, Lou Boudreau and
others. - **$20 $45 $75**

JAC-82. Book 16,
1945. Wheaties. Library of Sports book premium. -
$10 $20 $40

JAC-83

JAC-83. Library Of Sports Mailer,
1945. General Mills. - **$15 $25 $35**

JAC-84

JAC-84. "Parachute Ball" With Instructions And Mailer,
1946. Aluminum ball with paper parachute.
Near Mint Boxed - **$200**
Ball And Parachute Only - **$35 $60 $100**

JAC-85

JAC-86

JAC-85. Jack Armstrong #1 Comic,
1947. Odd size. - **$40 $100 $300**

JAC-86. "Explorer's Sun Watch" With Glow-In-Dark Dial,
1948. Version without "Frank Buck" name with insert compass and movable pointer. Also offered by "Rocky" Lane,
sponsored by Carnation Malted Milk, in 1951. -
$20 $30 $50

JAC-87

JAC-88

JAC-87. Armstrong & Betty Fairfield Photo Cards,
c. 1940s. Each - **$20 $40 $75**

JAC-88. Pictorial Pedometer,
1940s. Metal with lt. green rim picturing six golfers. -
$50 $100 $150

JAC-89

JAC-89. Record,
1973. Wheaties. Volume One with sleeve. - **$15 $25 $50**

JACK BENNY

Jack Benny (1894-1974) started in show business at the age of eight as a combination usher and violinist in a theater in Waukegan, Illinois. Thirty years later, when his program debuted on radio, he was a major star of stage and vaudeville. For 23 years on radio (1932-1955) and for 15 years on television (1950-1965) Benny was a Sunday night comic institution. His long-running feud with Fred Allen, his penny-pinching, his blue eyes, his ancient Maxwell car, his vault in the basement, his violin, his age--always 39--became part of the country's pop culture. Also featured over the years were his wife Mary Livingston, Rochester the valet, Don Wilson, Dennis Day, Phil Harris, Mel Blanc, and a host of others. Long-term radio sponsors were Jell-O (1934-1942) and Lucky Strike cigarettes (1944-1955); others included Canada Dry ginger ale (1932-1933), Chevrolet (1933-1934), General Tire (1934), and Grape-Nuts Flakes (1942-1944). Benny also appeared on numerous other television shows and made a number of movies.

JBE-1

JBE-2

JBE-3

JBE-1. Fan Photo,
c. 1934. Jell-O. - **$5 $12 $25**

JBE-2. Jell-O Recipe Book,
1937. Inside covers have Jack Benny and Mary Livingston comic strips. - **$10 $20 $35**

JBE-3. Photo,
1937. Philadelphia Record newspaper premium. -
$8 $15 $25

JBE-4

JBE-5

JBE-4. "Benny Buck" Movie Theater Play Money,
1939. Local theaters. For film "Buck Benny Rides Again" picturing supporting stars Ellen Drew and Andy Devine on back. - **$10 $20 $30**

JBE-5. Dixie Ice Cream Picture,
1930s. - **$5 $10 $15**

JBE-6

JBE-6. "Grape-Nuts Flakes" Endorsement Box, c. 1942. Back panel pictures him with balloon statement "Take It From Benny They're Better Than Any!" - **$30 $60 $90**

JBE-7

JBE-7. Radio Show Program,
c. 1944. Lucky Strike cigarettes. - **$20 $40 $60**

JBE-8

JBE-9

JBE-8. "Rochester" Fan Photo,
c. 1940s. Store item, probable sample from dime store picture frame. Pictured is Jack Benny's long-time valet on radio show, played by Eddie Anderson. - **$8 $12 $20**

JBE-9. "Friars Luncheon/Jack Benny" Gold Luster Metal Money Clip,
c. 1950s. Dinner event souvenir. Raised design of his violin. - **$15 $25 $45**

THE JACK PEARL SHOW

A veteran comic of vaudeville and burlesque, Jack Pearl (1895-1982) brought his dialect character Baron Munchausen to radio in 1932. When straight man Cliff Hall expressed doubts about one of the Baron's tall tales, the inevitable response, "Vas you dere, Sharlie?" brought down the house. Sponsors of *The Jack Pearl Show* included Chrysler (1932), Lucky Strike cigarettes (1932-1933), Royal gelatin (1934), Frigidaire (1935), and Raleigh and Kool cigarettes (1936-1937). Comeback attempts in 1942 and 1948 were not successful.

JPL-1   JPL-2

JPL-1. "Baron Munchausen" Map Of Radioland 19x24",
c. 1932. Scarce. - **$50 $100 $200**

JPL-2. "Jack Pearl As Dectective Baron Munchausen" Book,
1934. Store item published by Goldsmith Co. with endorsement of Juvenile Educators League. - **$10 $20 $30**

JACK WESTAWAY UNDER SEA ADV. CLUB

Membership in Jack Westaway's U.S.A.C. entitled young fans of the 1930s to wear the club badge (shaped like a diving helmet) and to a member's identification card that spelled out the club rules--including, whenever possible, eating a breakfast of Malt-O-Meal hot puffed wheat and puffed rice cereal.

(FRONT)

JWS-1   JWS-2   (BACK)

JWS-1. "Under Sea Adventure Club News" Vol. 1 #1 Newspaper With Envelope,
1930s. Malt-O-Meal. Newspaper - **$15 $40 $60**
Mailer - **$3 $5 $10**

JWS-2. Club Membership Card,
1930s. Malt-O-Meal. - **$20 $40 $75**

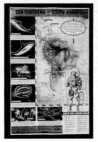

JWS-3

JWS-3. Member Recruitment Brochure,
1930s. Malt-O-Meal. Cover features letter from Jack Westaway, center depicts "Sea Denizens of South America" with map and back cover tells how to order diver's badge and membership card. - **$35 $75 $150**

JWS-4

JWS-4. Shark's Tooth Story Letter,
1930s. Malt-O-Meal. Front describes shark's tooth premium with coupon for a friend. Reverse recruits new member with coupon for diver's badge and membership card. - **$15 $25 $40**

JWS-5

JWS-5. "Jack Westaway Under The Sea/U.S.A.C." Brass Diver's Helmet Badge,
1930s. - **$3 $15 $25**

JAMES BOND

English novelist Ian Fleming (1908-1964) created James Bond, the fabled Agent 007 of the British secret service, in a series of thrillers beginning with *Casino Royale* in 1953 and continuing until his death. But it was the film versions of the novels, starting with *Dr. No* in 1963, that made Bond an international hero. Sean Connery first embodied the cool but deadly Bond for millions of fans around the world. Licensed to kill, carrying a Baretta or Walther PPK, drinking his martinis shaken not stirred, and enjoying success with the ladies, Bond has defeated a string of unlikely villains in the most exotic of settings. Connery and Roger Moore each played Bond in seven films. Others who played the smooth commander: David Niven in the

1967 spoof (with Peter Sellers playing his replacement as James Bond and Woody Allen playing his evil nephew Jimmy), *Casino Royale*; George Lazenby in *On Her Majesty's Secret Service* (1969); Timothy Dalton in *The Living Daylights* (1987) and *Licence to Kill* (1989); and Pierce Brosnan in *Goldeneye* (1995) and *Tomorrow Never Dies* (1997).

Bond comic books appeared in the 1980s and 1990s, and the novels were adapted as a comic strip for the *London Daily Express* from 1957 into the 1960s. *James Bond Jr.*, a syndicated half-hour television cartoon, aired in 1991-1993. Merchandising of Bond items has been extensive, with most toys of the 1960s era produced by Gilbert and Corgi.

JBD-1

JBD-2

JBD-1. "Agent 007" 3-1/2" Cello. Button,
c. 1964. Design includes image of woman painted gold from Goldfinger movie. - **$5 $15 $25**

JBD-2. Dell "James Bond 007" Magazine,
1964. - **$20 $35 $60**

(FRONT VIEW)

(SIDE VIEW)

JBD-3

JBD-3. "James Bond Secret Agent 007 Attache Case,"
1965. Store item by Multiple Products. Black plastic case holding gun and attachments, black flexible plastic dagger (frequently missing), code and decoder items, wallet with passport, business cards, play money. Case itself has trick-firing mechanism. Near Mint Complete - **$700**

JBD-4

JBD-4. "James Bond's Aston-Martin" Toy Car With Box,
1965. Store item by Gilbert Co. Battery operated metal replica including design feature that ejects passenger in addition to other mechanical features.
Near Mint Boxed - **$350**
Loose - **$75 $150 $250**

JBD-5

JBD-6

JBD-7

JBD-5. "007 Coming Soon!" 3" Cello. Button,
1960s. Probably worn by movie theater employees. - **$10 $20 $30**

JBD-6. "James Bond's Brew/007 Special Blend" 2-1/2" Cello. Button,
1960s. For apparently unauthorized beverage. - **$8 $15 $25**

JBD-7. "Agent 007" Bond-Inspired 3" Cello. Ad Button,
1960s. "Wilton Vise Squad" issue picturing example bench vise. - **$10 $20 $30**

JBD-8

JBD-9

JBD-8. Sean Connery Fan Photo,
1960s. - **$5 $10 $15**

JBD-9. "007" Replica Pistol Ring in Package,
1960s. Store item, unauthorized. Gold luster or aluminum.
Packaged - **$10 $20 $30**
Loose - **$5 $15 $20**

JBD-10

JBD-11

JBD-12

JBD-10. James Bond Plastic Snow Dome,
1960s. Store item. - **$50 $125 $200**

JBD-11. James Bond "Agent 007 Espionage" Litho. Button,
1960s. Vending machine issue. - **$5 $10 $15**

JBD-12. James Bond "Goldfinger's Death Derby" Litho. Button,
1960s. Vending machine issue. - **$5 $10 $15**

JBD-13   JBD-14   JBD-15

JBD-13. James Bond "Laser Beam/Goldfinger's Ray Machine" Litho. Button,
1960s. Vending machine issue. - **$3 $8 $12**

JBD-14. James Bond "Calling Agent 007" Litho. Button,
1960s. Vending machine issue. - **$5 $10 $15**

JBD-15. James Bond "Agent 007" Plastic Ring,
1960s. Vending machine issue. - **$10 $30 $50**

JBD-16   JBD-17   JBD-18   JBD-19

JBD-16. "007" Plastic Ring,
1960s. Vending machine item depicting shield symbol. From set of five. Each - **$10 $20 $30**

JBD-17. "007" Plastic Ring,
1960s. Vending machine item depicting face silhouette. From set of five. Each - **$10 $20 $30**

JBD-18. "007" Plastic Ring,
1960s. Vending machine item picturing car. From set of five. Each - **$10 $20 $30**

JBD-19. "007" Plastic Flicker Ring,
1960s. Vending machine issue from set of 12. Images are James Bond portrait and "007" numeral partially formed by image of pistol as the third numeral.
Each Silver Base - **$10 $22 $35**
Each Blue Base - **$5 $15 $25**

JBD-20   JBD-21

JBD-20. Movie Promotion Cello. English Buttons,
1981. Eon Productions Ltd. For release of movie "For Your Eyes Only." Each - **$2 $4 $8**

JBD-21. "Michelin Dealers' 007 Sweepstakes" 3-1/2" Cello. Button,
1985. Michelin tires. Art pictures Roger Moore as James Bond posed beside Michelin Man. - **$10 $25 $40**

JAMES DEAN

The untimely and tragic death of this young actor in 1955 evoked an international outpouring of anguish and disbelief by his fandom. His brief acting career epitomized the moody, brooding, casual restlessness of young adulthood. Due to this brevity, related memorabilia from the 1950s is scarce. A few buttons were produced before his death but the most frequently encountered 1950s item is a memorial brass medalet offered by *Modern Screen Magazine* in October 1956.

JDN-2

JDN-1

JDN-1. "James Dean's" Denim Jeans,
1955. Store item by J.S.B. Adult sized, likened to those worn in his movies Rebel Without a Cause, East of Eden, Giant. With Tag - **$40 $65 $100**

JDN-2. Cello. 3-1/2" Photo Button,
1955. Store item. Issued before his death. - **$15 $35 $75**

JDN-3   JDN-4

JDN-3. Cello. 3-1/2" Button,
c. 1955. Store item. Issued before his death. -
$15 $35 $75

JDN-4. Color Portrait 2-1/2" Cello. Button,
c. 1955. Photo with facsimile signature. - **$15 $25 $40**

JDN-5

JDN-5. Commemorative Brass Necklace Medallion,
c. 1955. "Modern Screen" magazine. Inscription "In Memory Of James Dean 1931-1955". - **$5 $12 $25**

JDN-6

JDN-7

JDN-6. Commemorative China Plate,
c. 1956. Store item. - **$30 $50 $85**

JDN-7. "I, James Dean" Paperback Biography,
1957. Store item published by Popular Library. First published biography after his death. - **$8 $15 $30**

JIMMIE ALLEN

The Air Adventures of Jimmie Allen thrilled its young radio listeners from 1933 to 1943. Jimmie was a 16-year-old messenger at the Kansas City airport, taught to fly by veteran pilot Speed Robertson. Together they courted danger, searched for lost treasure, and competed in international air races. The series was syndicated, sponsored initially by the Skelly Oil company in the Midwest, then by Richfield Oil on the West Coast and by bakeries and many other companies eager to share in the show's large audience.

Premiums were an integral part of the program from the beginning, starting with a free jigsaw puzzle offer during the third week of broadcasting and available only at Skelly gas stations. The *Jimmie Allen Flying Club* and the *Weather-Bird Flying Club* attracted thousands of applicants, all of whom received membership cards, wings, emblems, patches, flight charts, and personal letters from Jimmie. Members could pick up weekly flying lessons and model airplane kits at their local gas stations.

Other promotional items followed in great profusion: photo albums, stamp albums, road maps, whistles, ID bracelets, model planes, Flying Cadet wings. Since sponsors were free to design and mark their own premiums, many varieties were produced. Jimmie Allen Air Races were held throughout the Midwest, with thousands of fans gathering to watch the young contestants piloting their model planes.

Paramount Pictures released a Jimmie Allen movie, *The Sky Parade*, in 1936. Transcriptions of the original broadcasts were re-released in 1942-1943.

JMA-1

JMA-1. Club News Chapter 2 - "The Strange Mist",
May 1933. Richfield Oil Co. Radio premium. -
$20 $40 $75

JMA-2

JMA-2. "Map Of Countries Visited In 'Air Adventures Of Jimmie Allen ' 11x25",
1934. Skelly Oil Co. - **$50 $150 $200**

JMA-3

JMA-3. Skelly Oil Holiday Newsletter,
1934. - **$20 $40 $60**

JMA-4

JMA-5

JMA-4. "Flight Lesson" Sheet,
1934. Various sponsors. Five lessons in set.
Each - **$5 $10 $15**

JMA-5. "Merry Christmas" Photo,
1934. Skelly Oil Co. - **$10 $20 $30**

JMA-6

JMA-6. "B-A Flying Cadet" Canadian Flight Wings Pin,
c. 1934. British-American Oil. Embossed Brass. -
$25 $60 $100

JMA-7

JMA-8

JMA-7. Richfield Flight Wings,
1934. - **$15 $25 $50**

JMA-8. Richfield I.D. Bracelet,
1934. - **$15 $50 $75**

JMA-9

JMA-9. Radio Listener Letter With Photos,
c. 1934. Skelly Oil Co. Letter thanks listener for name of
gasoline dealer not handling Skelly products. Photos are
Allen and Speed Robertson. Letter - **$15 $30 $50**
Each Photo - **$10 $20 $40**

JMA-10

JMA-10. Radio Listener Letter With Picture And Mailer,
c. 1934. Skelly Oil Co. Letter urges trial of Skelly products,
picture is "Monsoon 800" aircraft.
Near Mint In Mailer - **$125**
Letter Only - **$15 $30 $50**
Picture Only - **$15 $30 $50**

JMA-12

JMA-11

**JMA-11. "What's On The Air" Pacific Coast Schedule
Book,**
1934. Richfield Oil Co. - **$15 $30 $60**

**JMA-12. Skelly "Jimmie Allen Flying Cadet" Brass
Airplane Badge,**
1934. - **$10 $20 $35**

JMA-14

JMA-13

JMA-13. Skelly Club Membership Card,
c. 1934. - **$10 $25 $40**

JMA-14. "Speed Robertson" Photo,
c. 1934. Skelly Oil Co. - **$10 $20 $30**

JMA-15

JMA-16

**JMA-15. Skelly "Jimmie Allen Flying Cadet" Bronze
Luster Brass Wings Badge,**
c. 1934. - **$15 $25 $35**

**JMA-16. "Jimmie Allen/Skelly Flying Cadet" Brass
Wings Badge,**
c. 1934. - **$35 $75 $110**

JMA-17

JMA-18

**JMA-17. "Jimmie Allen Cadet/Fairmont Air Corps"
Brass Wings Badge,**
c. 1934. - **$60 $150 $200**

JMA-18. "B-A Flying Cadet" Canadian Flight Wings,
c. 1934. British-American Oil. Red on silvered metal. -
$50 $100 $150

JMA-19

JMA-20

JMA-19. Membership Card,
c. 1934. Richfield Oil Co. - **$15 $30 $45**

JMA-20. Club Creed Certificate,
c. 1934. Richfield Oil. - **$15 $35 $50**

JMA-21

JMA-22

JMA-21. Photo,
c. 1934. Richfield Oil. - **$5** **$12** **$20**

JMA-22. Felt Fabric Aviator Cap,
c. 1934. Scarce. Richfield Oil. - **$35** **$70** **$125**

JMA-23

JMA-23. Postcard,
c. 1934. Log Cabin Bread. - **$10** **$20** **$40**

JMA-24

JMA-25

JMA-24. "Jimmie Allen Flying Cadet/Log Cabin" Brass Wings Badge,
c. 1934. Log Cabin Syrup. - **$20** **$45** **$75**

JMA-25. "Speed Robertson" Photo Card,
c. 1934. Hi-Speed Gasoline of Hickok Oil Corp. Pictured is comrade aviator of Jimmie Allen. - **$12** **$20** **$30**

JMA-26

JMA-26. Richfield Oil Travel Map,
1935. Paper folder that opens to 18x24" map of California with panel ad for Jimmie Allen radio show. - **$10** **$30** **$40**

 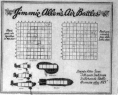

JMA-27

JMA-27. Skelly "Jimmie Allen's Air Battles" Booklet,
1935. Contents include game pages plus comic strips. - **$20** **$50** **$75**

JMA-28

JMA-29

JMA-28. Postcard,
1935. Richfield Oil Co. Radio premium. - **$15** **$30** **$45**

JMA-29. Road Map,
1935. Skelly Oil Co. Map of U.S. and Kansas. - **$20** **$40** **$50**

JMA-30

JMA-31

JMA-30. "Jimmie Allen Air Races" Sterling Silver Bracelet With Silvered Brass Chain,
c. 1935. Skelly Oil. - **$60** **$125** **$175**

JMA-31. "Jimmie Allen/Pilot" Silvered Brass Bracelet,
c. 1935. Skelly Oil. - **$60** **$125** **$175**

JMA-32

JMA-33

JMA-32. "Jimmie Allen Air Races" Silvered Brass Bracelet,
1935. Skelly Oil. - **$75** **$175** **$250**

JMA-33. Kansas City Air Races Enameled Bracelet,
1935. Rare. Skelly Oil. - **$125** **$350** **$500**

JMA-34

JMA-34. Browntone Photos,
1936. Skelly Oil Co. Numbered set of six.
Each - **$3 $6 $12**

JMA-35

JMA-35. Club Card,
1936. Scarce. Skelly Oil Co. Membership card with pledge
on back. Blue trim, plane on left. - **$30 $70 $100**

JMA-36

JMA-37

JMA-36. "Flying Club Stamp Album",
1936. Richfield Oil Co. Near Mint With Stamps - **$75**
Album Only - **$20 $50 $75**

JMA-37. Richfield Gasoline Cardboard Ink Blotter,
1936. - **$12 $30 $40**

JMA-38

JMA-39

JMA-40

**JMA-38. "Official Jimmie Allen Secret Signal" Brass
Whistle,**
1936. - **$50 $85 $150**

JMA-39. Movie Cast Photo,
1936. For movie "The Sky Parade" picturing Jimmie Allen,
Grant Withers, Katherine DeMille, Kent Taylor. -
$15 $25 $40

JMA-40. "Jimmie Allen Air Races" Silvered Brass Pin,
1936. Skelly Oil. - **$60 $100 $150**

JMA-41

JMA-42

JMA-41. "Flying B-A Cadet" Certificate,
1939. British-American Oil. Canadian certificate received
with Squadron Commander Badge. - **$25 $50 $100**

**JMA-42. "Squadron Commander" Canadian Brass
Badge,**
1939. British-American Oil. - **$50 $100 $200**

JMA-44

JMA-45

JMA-43

JMA-43. "Jimmie Allen" Bone Handle Pocketknife,
1930s. Sponsor unknown. Grip has silvered metal club
symbol. - **$50 $100 $150**

JMA-44. "Official Outing Knife" With Sheath,
1930s. Sponsor unknown. - **$100 $200 $300**

**JMA-45. "Jimmie Allen Model Builder Merit Award"
Brass Badge,**
1930s. Scarce. Richfield Oil. Also designated "Richfield Hi-
Octane Flying Cadet". - **$75 $175 $250**

JMA-47

JMA-46

JMA-46. Blue Flash Brass Wings Badge,
1930s. Blue Flash. Says "Jimmie Allen Flying Cadet". -
$35 $75 $110

JMA-47. Certified Flying Cadet Brass Wings Badge,
1930s. - **$25 $50 $75**

JMA-48

JMA-49

JMA-48. Cleo Cola Brass Wings Badge,
1930s. Cleo Cola. - **$20 $45 $65**

JMA-49. Colonial Brass Wings Badge,
1930s. Colonial. - **$15 $35 $50**

JMA-50   JMA-51

JMA-50. Duplex Brass Wings Badge,
1930s. Duplex. - **$15 $35 $50**

JMA-51. Fair-Maid Brass Wings Badge,
1930s. Fair-Maid. - **$20 $45 $65**

JMA-52   JMA-53

JMA-52. Rain-Bo Brass Wings Badge,
1930s. Rain-Bo. - **$20 $45 $65**

JMA-53. Richfield Brass Wings Badge,
1930s. Richfield. - **$15 $35 $50**

JMA-54   JMA-55

JMA-54. Richfield Silver Wings Badge,
1930s. Richfield. - **$30 $65 $100**

JMA-55. Sawyer Brass Wings Badge,
1930s. Sawyer. - **$30 $65 $100**

JMA-56   JMA-57

JMA-56. Skelly Gold Wings Badge,
1930s. Skelly Oil. - **$35 $75 $110**

JMA-57. Town Talk Bread Brass Wings Badge,
1930s. Town Talk Bread. - **$30 $65 $100**

JMA-58   JMA-59

JMA-58. Weatherbird Brass Wings Badge,
1930s. Weatherbird Shoes. - **$20 $45 $65**

JMA-59. "Jimmie Allen Hi-Speed Flying Cadet" Brass Wings Badge,
1930s. - **$15 $30 $40**

JMA-60

JMA-61

JMA-60. Gummed Paper Sticker,
1930s. Hi-Speed Gasoline. - **$20 $60 $90**

JMA-61. Hi-Speed Photo Card,
1930s. Hickok Oil Co. - **$10 $20 $35**

JMA-63

JMA-62

JMA-62. Cloth "Mail Pouch",
1930s. Cleo Cola. For saving bottle caps. - **$35 $75 $125**

JMA-63. Club Membership Card,
1930s. Hi-Speed Gasoline. - **$10 $25 $45**

JMA-64

JMA-64. Flying Club Aviation Lesson Newspapers,
1930s. Republic Motor Oil. Map inside lesson #1.
Each - **$10 $20 $35**

JMA-66

JMA-65

JMA-65. "Certificate In Aviation",
1930s. Republic (Oil) Air Corps. Awarded for completion of advanced aviation course. - **$20 $30 $50**

JMA-66. "Jimmie Allen/Republic Pilot" Brass Wings Badge,
1930s. - **$30 $50 $75**

JMA-67

JMA-67. Skelly Oil Club Album,
1930s. Booklet of photo pages.
Album Only - **$10 $15 $25**
Each Photo Page - **$2 $4 $6**

JMA-69

JMA-68

JMA-68. Jimmie & Barbara Photo,
1930s. Skelly Oil. - **$10 $15 $25**

JMA-69. "Yellow Jacket" Model Airplane Construction Kit,
1930s. Skelly Oil. Balsa parts with instructions and insignia cut-outs. - **$50 $100 $150**

JMA-70

AIR CADETS

JMA-71

JMA-70. "Thunderbolt" Model Airplane Construction Kit,
1930s. Skelly Oil. Balsa parts with instruction sheet and insignia cut-outs. - **$50 $100 $150**

JMA-71. "J.A. Air Cadets" Cello. Button,
1930s. Canadian issue. - **$60 $100 $150**

JMA-73

JMA-72

JMA-72. "J.A. Air Cadets" Brass Ring,
1930s. Rare. Canadian issue. - **$100 $200 $350**

JMA-73. "J.A. Air Cadets" Brass Wings Badge,
1930s. Canadian issue. - **$30 $75 $100**

JMA-74

JMA-75

JMA-74. Flying Club Membership Card,
1930s. Skelly Oil Co. Brown trim on white. Propeller at top & bottom on front. - **$25 $50 $75**

JMA-75. Coin,
1930s. Bond Bread premium. - **$50 $100 $150**

JMA-76

JMA-76. Diploma,
1930s. Hi-Speed Gasoline. - **$40 $80 $100**

JMA-77

JMA-77. Season's Greetings Card,
1930s. Richfield Oil Co. - **$30 $60 $90**

JMA-78

JMA-78. Flight Lesson #4,
1930s. Colonial Bread. - **$20 $30 $50**

JMA-79

JMA-79. Flight Lesson #1-6 Lessons,
1930s. Weather Bird Shoes.
Each - **$20 $50 $75**

JMA-80

JMA-80. Membership Card,
1930s. Weather Bird Shoes. -
$25 $60 $90

JMA-81

JMA-81. Membership Certificate,
1930s. Weather Bird Shoes. -
$40 $80 $100

JMA-82

JMA-82. "Jimmie Allen Listening Post" Member Kit,
1944. Re-broadcast of shows sponsored by Bamby Bread,
Atlanta, Georgia. Includes cover letter, photo, member
card, charter, song sheet, application, "Listening Post" tag.
Each Item - **$10 $20 $30**

JIMMIE MATTERN

An actual aviator in the early 1930s era of personal
and mechanical endurance flying, Mattern is best
remembered for his June 3 to August 3, 1933 solo
flight around the world begun in his "Century of
Progress" single engine aircraft (crashed en route)
and finished by other borrowed planes. Premiums
were typically aviation theme booklets and photo
albums by sponsor Pure Oil.

JMT-1

JMT-2

JMT-1. "The Diary Of Jimmie Mattern" Paper Folder,
1935. Pure Oil Co. "Diary Sheet" insert pages issued separately, probably weekly. Folder Only - **$10 $20 $35**
Each Insert Page - **$3 $5 $10**

JMT-2. "Book One 'Cloud Country/Wings Of Youth'",
1936. Pure Oil Co. hardcover. - **$5 $15 $25**

JMT-3

JMT-4

JMT-3. "Book 2 'Hawaii To Hollywood'",
1936. Pure Oil Co. Hardcover. - **$5 $15 $25**

JMT-4. "Air-E-Racer" Figural Rubber Eraser,
c. 1936. Pure Oil Co., also marked "Tiolene Motor Oil". -
$20 $35 $60

JIMMY DURANTE

At the age of 17 Jimmy Durante (1893-1980) was playing piano in a Coney Island beer garden. By his mid-thirties, after years in vaudeville and burlesque, he was playing Broadway and making movies. In 1943, when he and Gary Moore appeared together on NBC in the *Camel Comedy Caravan*, Durante was on the road to national stardom. With his joyful mangling of the language, his legendary nose, his mythical friends Umbriago and Mrs. Calabash, Durante charmed his radio audience for seven years, first for Camel cigarettes (1943-1945), then for Rexall drugs (1945-1948), then again for Camel (1948-1950). A couple of Durante comic books appeared in the late 1940s, and from 1950 to 1957 Durante was a regular on television for such sponsors as Buick, Colgate, and Texaco.

JIM-5

JIM-6   JIM-7

JIM-5. "Gimme Jimmy! The Candidate" Button,
1952. Issued with booklet of same title.
Cello. - **$5 $12 $20**
Litho. - **$5 $10 $15**

JIM-6. Rubber/Fabric Hand Puppet,
1950s. Store item. - **$15 $25 $ 50**

JIM-7. "Children's Fund" Metal Portrait Pin On Card,
1950s. - **$8 $15 $25**

JIM-1

JIM-2

JIM-8

(FRONT)   JIM-9   (BACK)

JIM-1. "Schnozzle Durante/Vice-President" Cello. Button,
1932. Paramount Pictures. Based on movie "Phantom President" that year. - **$15 $30 $50**

JIM-2. Song Book - Inka Dinka Doo,
1933. Store bought. - **$15 $40 $50**

JIM-8. Portrait Pen,
c. 1950s. Plastic and metal ballpoint with miniature bronze luster metal portrait attached on pocket clip. -
$10 $20 $30

JIM-9. Corn Flakes Box With Testimonial From Durante,
1965. Gary Lewis and the Playboys record offer on side of box. Complete - **$30 $60 $100**

JIM-3

JIM-4

JIM-3. "My Friend Umbriago" Litho. Button,
c. 1940s. Durante holds hand puppet. - **$8 $15 $25**

JIM-4. "The Candidate" Book,
1952. Publisher Simon & Schuster. - **$8 $12 $18**

JOE E. BROWN

Show-business veteran Joe E. Brown (1892-1973), noted for the contortions of his big mouth, started out as a circus acrobat at the age of 10, was a featured comedian in burlesque and vaudeville in his mid-twenties, graduated to musical comedies, and started making movies in 1927. He made dozens of films, with memorable roles in *You Said a Mouthful* (1932), *Alibi Ike* (1935), and *Some Like It Hot* (1959). Quaker Oats issued the *Joe E. Brown Bike Club* premiums in 1934. In 1936, Post cereal sponsored the *Joe E. Brown Club* through newspapers and packaging offers. On radio, the *Joe E. Brown Show*, a musical variety program, ran for a season (1938-1939) on CBS, sponsored by Post Toasties cereal.

JOE-1

JOE-2

JOE-1. "Joe E. Brown's Funny Bike Book",
1934. Quaker Oats. - **$10 $30 $40**

JOE-2. "Member/Joe E. Brown Bike Club" Cello. Button,
1934. Quaker Oats. - **$5 $15 $25**

JOE-3

JOE-4

JOE-3. Bicycle Contest 15x20" Store Sign,
1934. Quaker Oats. Diecut cardboard display also picturing Joe E. Brown Bike Club button and book plus advertises his new film "6-Day Bike Rider." - **$75 $175 $300**

JOE-4. Premium Folder Sheet,
1936. Grape-Nuts Flakes. Offers about 30 premiums with expiration date December 31. - **$10 $20 $35**

JOE-6

JOE-5

JOE-7

JOE-5. Club Member Brass Badge With Three Award Bars,
1936. Grape-Nuts Flakes. Bars in different colors individually marked by 1, 2, or 3 stars denoting club ranks of Sergeant, Lieutenant, or Captain.
Portrait Badge Only - **$5 $15 $25**
For Each Bar Add - **$5 $15 $25**

JOE-6. Brass Club Member Ring,
1936. Grape-Nuts Flakes. Features small portrait. -
$50 $125 $200

JOE-7. Radio Fan Photo,
c. 1936. Probable Grape-Nuts Flakes. - **$8 $15 $25**

JOE-8

JOE-9

JOE-8. "Smiler's Club" Cello. Button,
1930s. - **$10 $25 $50**

JOE-9. "You Said A Mouthful" Booklet,
1944. Doughnut Corp. of America with local dealer imprint. Contents include World War II tour photos plus mention of radio quiz show "Stop Or Go". - **$8 $15 $20**

JOE-10

JOE-10. Joe E. Brown "How To Play Baseball" Record Album,
1940s. Store item by RCA Victor. - **$20 $30 $50**

JOE LOUIS

Joe Louis (1914-1981) was born in Alabama but made Detroit his home for many years. Louis won the world heavyweight championship by knocking out James J. Braddock in 1937 and successfully defended the title 24 times in 12 years. Known as the "Brown Bomber," he won 68 of his 71 bouts, 54 by knockouts. He was elected to the Boxing Hall of Fame in 1954. Louis enlisted in the U.S. Army in 1942 and gave many exhibition bouts for troops around the world. He retired undefeated as champion in 1949, then returned to the ring the following year, without success. Louis is buried in Arlington Cemetery.

JLO-1

JLO-2

JLO-1. "Braddock Or Louis" Puzzle In Envelope, 1937. Green River Whiskey. Novelty cardboard puzzle based on upcoming June 22 bout between champion James J. Braddock and contender Joe Louis. Assembled puzzle is about 2-1/2x4" consisting of four pieces to form image pictured on envelope. - **$35 $60 $90**

JLO-2. "Louis-Schmeling Fight" 14x22" Tavern Poster, 1938. Martin's Scotch Whiskey. Cardboard sign promoting radio listenership of return bout between Joe Louis and Max Schmeling of Germany with cartoon art by O. Soglow. - **$30 $50 $75**

| JLO-3 | JLO-4 | JLO-5 |

JLO-3. Joe Louis "Heavyweight Sensation" Cello. Button, c. 1938. Sponsored by Valmor Products Co., Chicago. - **$25 $50 $85**

JLO-4. "Joe Louis Good Luck Club" Litho. Button, c. 1938. Bottom rim design includes tiny four-leaf clover symbol. - **$25 $50 $75**

JLO-5. "Joe And Me For Willkie" Cello. Button, 1940. Endorsement attributed to Joe Louis for U.S. Presidential candidate Wendell L. Willkie. - **$10 $20 $40**

| JLO-6 | JLO-7 |

JLO-8

JLO-6. "Joe Louis Punch" Cello. Button, c. 1940s. For soda beverage product also inscribed "It's A Knockout." - **$10 $20 $30**

JLO-7. "Joe Louis Punch" Soda Bottle Tin Cap, c. 1940s. For carbonated beverage. - **$15 $25 $40**

JLO-8. "Joe Louis Punch" Soda Bottle, c. 1940s. All American Drinks Corp. Reverse slogan is "It's A Knockout." - **$10 $25 $40**

JOE PALOOKA

Ham Fisher (1901-1955) created the *Joe Palooka* comic strip, the most successful sports strip of all time. It started small, appearing in a handful of papers in 1928, but a decade later the strip was running in hundreds of papers. Joe was sweet, innocent, clean-cut, and given to uttering clichés about home, mother, and fair play. He was also a top boxer, winning the World Heavyweight Championship in 1931. Joe joined the army in 1940 and married his longtime girlfriend Ann Howe in 1949--two events that generated great reader interest and sent circulation soaring. Other characters included the Palooka's daughter Joan and Joe's sidekicks Humphrey Pennyworth and (mute) Little Max. The strip outlived Fisher, surviving until 1984.

A *Joe Palooka* radio series aired on CBS in 1932, sponsored by Heinz, with Ted Bergman as Joe. *Palooka*, a feature film based on the strip, was released in 1934 with Stu Erwin as Joe and Jimmy Durante as his manager Knobby Walsh. Two series of comic books were published, the first in 1942-1944, the second in 1945-1961. A live-action television series, *The Joe Palooka Story*, with Joe Kirkwood as Joe, was syndicated in 1952.

| JPA-1 | JPA-2 |

JPA-1. "Joe Palooka" Wood Jointed Doll, 1930s. Store item. - **$40 $60 $125**

JPA-2. Red Cross Cartoon Booklet, 1949. Softcover 12-page color booklet featuring Joe explaining work of American Red Cross. - **$8 $15 $20**

| JPA-3 | JPA-4 |

JPA-3. "Joe Palooka Championship Belt" Metal Buckle, 1940s. Store item by Ham Fisher Belt Rite Leather Goods. Buckle - **$25 $50 $75** With Belt - **$40 $75 $125**

JPA-4. Joe Palooka "Tangle Comics" Cello. Button, 1940s. Philadelphia Sunday Bulletin. - **$10 $20 $35**

JPA-5

JPA-6

JPA-7

JPA-5. "Joe Palooka Cap" Litho. Button,
1940s. Sponsor not indicated. Pictures Joe as he appeared in early years of comic strip. - **$10 $20 $30**

JPA-6. Newspaper Strip Cello. Button,
1940s. Philadelphia Bulletin. - **$20 $40 $80**

JPA-7. "Hi!-Humphrey" Cello. Button For Doll,
1940s. Ideal Novelty & Toy Co. for character doll of Palooka sidekick Humphrey Pennyworth. - **$15 $35 $75**

JPA-8

JPA-9

JPA-8. Club Medal,
1940s. New York Daily Mirror. Aluminum with portrait front and horseshoe/boxing glove design on reverse. -
$8 $15 $25

JPA-9. "The Art Of Self Defense" Booklet,
1952. Store item by Ideal Toy Corp. Came with "Bop Bag" punching toy. - **$5 $15 $25**

JPA-10

JPA-10. "Joan Palooka" Boxed Doll/Hand Puppet,
c. 1952. Store item by National Mask & Puppet Corp. Replica doll of Joe and Ann's daughter plus flannel blanket, paper birth certificate and instruction sheet.
Near Mint Boxed - **$150**
Doll - **$25 $50 $75**
Certificate - **$10 $15 $25**

JOE PENNER

"Wanna buy a duck?" Perhaps no other comedian is so well remembered for such a single phrase as Joe Penner. Penner's trademark prop, of course, from vaudeville days into radio and 1930s to early 1940s films, was the inevitable live duck carried in a basket. His wacky repartee style ended with his death in 1941 at the early age of 37 years with his duck remaining unbought.

JOP-1

JOP-1. "Wise Quacks" Fan Newsletter Vol. 1 #4,
November 1934. - **$10 $15 $25**

JOP-2

JOP-2. "Don't Never Do-o-o That" Sheet Music,
1934. Six pages of words and music for novelty song subtitled "You Nasty Man" featuring cover art of Penner and his duck. - **$5 $12 $20**

JOP-3

JOP-4

JOP-5

JOP-3. "Cocomalt Big Book Of Comics",
1938. Featuring Joe Penner, various comic characters. -
$190 $575 $1700

JOP-4. "Raisin Bread/Radio Special" Cello. Button,
1930s. Unknown bakery or bakeries. From series listing
various types of breads or rolls. - **$5 $10 $20**

JOP-5. "I'm A Joe Penner Quacker" Cello. Button,
1930s. - **$5 $10 $15**

JOP-7

JOP-6

JOE-6. First Issue "Joe Penner Songs" Folio,
1941. - **$5 $15 $25**

JOE-7. Photo/Dexterity Game Brass Ring,
c. 1940s. Scarce. - **$300 $500 $750**

JOHN WAYNE

Born Marion Morrison in Iowa, John Wayne (1907-1979) was to grow from a football player at the University of Southern California to become one of the legendary giants of American film. After bit parts in silent films in the 1920s, he played the lead in *The Big Trail* (1930) and three chapter plays for Mascot Pictures (1932-1933). He achieved stardom with his role as the Ringo Kid in John Ford's *Stagecoach* in 1939. Wayne was to appear in more than 250 films over half a century, the most memorable directed by Ford or Howard Hawks, and most of them westerns. He won an Academy Award for *True Grit* (1969). The Duke, who came to symbolize the rugged courage of the American West, was one of the greatest box office attractions of all time. He was awarded a Congressional Medal of Freedom posthumously.

John Wayne Adventure Comics was published from 1949 to 1955. Wayne made scattered appearances in other comic book series between 1948 and 1967, mostly associated with his movie roles, and in one of a set of six pocket-size giveaways from Oxydol-Dreft in 1950. Commemorative items appear to this day.

JWA-1

JWA-1. "Raoul Walsh's The Big Trail" Cello. Button,
1930. Contest or club member promotion for movie of John Wayne's first starring role. - **$50 $75 $150**

JWA-2

JWA-2. "The Fighting Seabees" Movie Postcard,
1944. Republic Pictures. - **$8 $12 $20**

JWA-3 **JWA-4** **JWA-5**

JWA-3. John Wayne Cello. Button,
1940s. Black and white photo on blue background. -
$15 $30 $60

JWA-4. John Wayne Photo Charm,
c. 1950. Vending machine item. Red plastic frame with black and white glossy photo. - **$5 $10 $15**

JWA-5. John Wayne Photo Charm,
c. 1950. Vending machine item. Silver plastic frame with black and white glossy photo. - **$5 $10 $15**

JWA-6   **JWA-7**

JWA-6. "John Wayne/The Cowboy Troubleshooter" Comic Booklet,
1950. Procter & Gamble wrappers or boxtops from Dreft, Oxydol or Ivory Soap. - **$15 $40 $105**

JWA-7. John Wayne Photo Ring,
c. 1950. Silvered plastic base with inset glossy black and white paper photo. - **$20 $32 $45**

JWA-8

JWA-9

JWA-8. John Wayne Photo Charm,
c. 1950. Vending machine item. White plastic frame with glossy black and white photo. Example shown missing top edge loop. - **$5 $10 $15**

JWA-9. "The Searchers" 11x14" Cardboard Sign For Book Store,
c. 1956. Popular Library. Announces release of paperback novel by Alan Lemay "soon to be a great motion picture starring John Wayne." - **$25 $50 $90**

JWA-10   JWA-11

JWA-10. Transfer Picture Sheet,
1950s. Store item. 4-1/2x5-1/2" paper with full color reverse image portrait for application to fabric. - **$10 $20 $30**

JWA-11. Leather Billfold,
c. 1950s. Store item. Zippered wallet with color portrait on front. - **$75 $150 $250**

JWA-12   JWA-13

JWA-12. John Wayne And Ronald Reagan Cello. Button,
c. 1968. Rim curl names "Big Little Store" of San Francisco. - **$15 $25 $40**

JWA-13. "McQ" Movie Mug,
1974. Ceramic mug belived given to cast members of the film starring him as modern-day detective policeman. 3-1/2" tall with facsimile signature. - **$10 $20 $30**

JWA-14

JWA-15

JWA-14. Commemorative 3-1/2" Cello. Button,
1979. - **$3 $6 $10**

JWA-15. Boxed Commemorative Doll,
1982. Store item by Effanbee Doll Corp. 18" vinyl in fabric cavalry outfit from limited "Legend Series."
Near Mint Boxed - **$150**
Loose - **$35 $60 $100**

JONNY QUEST

Jonny Quest, a prime-time animated adventure series from the Hanna-Barbera studios, premiered on ABC in 1964 and aired for a year. The series was repeated on Saturday mornings on CBS (1967-1970), on ABC (1970-1972), and on NBC, first as part of the *Godzilla Power Hour* (1978), then on its own (1979-1981). Created by comic book artist Doug Wildey, Jonny and his scientist father traveled to exotic places in their supersonic plane, fought mythical beasts, confronted unsolved mysteries, and triumphed over danger wherever they found it.

JNY-1

JNY-2

JNY-1. Boxed Card Game,
1965. Store item by Milton Bradley. - **$20 $25 $75**

JNY-2. "Magic Ring" 21x22" Cardboard Store Sign,
1960s. P.F. footwear of B.F. Goodrich. Shows gold plastic decoder ring (Pictured in Rings, Miscellaneous section). - **$30 $75 $150**

JUNIOR BIRDMEN OF AMERICA

Hearst newspapers sponsored this club for young aviation enthusiasts in the 1930s, offering membership cards and manuals along with pins and patches. Club activities included flying model airplanes, with medals awarded to contest winners.

JRB-2

JRB-1   JRB-3

JRB-1. Champion Award Medal In Presentation Box,
1934. Rare. Near Mint Boxed - **$300**
Unboxed - **$35 $100 $200**

JRB-2. Second Place Award Medal In Presentation Box,
1934. Scarce. Near Mint Boxed - **$150**
Unboxed - **$35 $60 $90**

JRB-3. "Eagle Membership Test" Brochure And Membership Card,
1938. Brochure - **$15 $30 $50**
Card - **$15 $30 $50**

JRB-4

JRB-4. "Flight Squadron Plan" Folder,
1930s. Contents include depiction of rank insignia pins for Commander, Captain, Eagle. - **$15 $25 $40**

JRB-5

JRB-6

JRB-7

JRB-5. Hearst Newspapers Club Card,
1930s. For various newspapers of Hearst Syndicate with facsimile signature of George Hearst, National Commander. - **$15 $35 $50**

JRB-6. "Field Day" Felt Fabric Pennant,
1930s. 22" long. - **$25 $90 $125**

JRB-7. Hearst Newspapers "Flight Squadron" Charter Certificate,
1930s. For various newspapers of Hearst Syndicate with facsimile signature of George Hearst, National Commander. - **$25 $50 $75**

JRB-8

JRB-9

JRB-8. Membership Card,
1930s. Shows boy and girl on front. - **$25 $50 $75**

JRB-9. Rule Book,
1930s. Also lists newspapers where Junior Birdmen column appears. - **$25 $50 $75**

JRB-10   **JRB-11**

JRB-10. Felt Fabric Emblem,
1930s. Large 2-1/2x8" size. - **$35 $125 $200**

JRB-11. "Jr. Birdmen Of America" Enameled Brass Wings Badge,
1930s. - **$15 $30 $50**

JRB-12

JRB-12. "Eagle" Enameled Brass Wings Badge With Rank Bar,
1930s. Scarce. - **$35 $100 $150**

JUNIOR JUSTICE SOCIETY OF AMERICA

The Justice Society of America began in the DC Comics publication *All Star* #3 published in the fall of 1940. During its existence members included the Flash, the Spectre, Hawkman, Sandman, the Green Lantern and Hourman. Wonder Woman was club secretary as well as a member. The December 1942 *All Star* #14 announced the formation of the *Junior Justice Society of America,* a comic book club for readers. The 15¢ membership fee included: a welcome letter from Wonder Woman, a silver plated membership badge (later replaced by a cloth sew-on patch), a cardboard decoder, a four-page war bond comic *The*

Minute Man Answers the Call, and a four color membership certificate which encouraged the recipient to keep the country united despite differences in cultural or ethnic backgrounds.

JUN-1

JUN-2

JUN-1. Solid Brass Badge,
1942. Rare. In-house prototype with tie-tac fastener. - **$500 $1500 $2500**

JUN-2. Club Member Fabric Patch,
1942. Replaced large letter badge because of metal shortage. - **$150 $400 $700**

JUN-3 (BACK)

(BACK) JUN-4

JUN-3 (CLOSE-UP)

JUN-4 (CLOSE-UP)

JUN-3. Silver Finish Club Badge,
1942. Scarce. Large letter style only offered for two months. - **$100 $450 $900**

JUN-4. Silver Finish Club Badge,
1948. Small letter style. Badge also existed with variation of pin on back running across. - **$100 $350 $600**

JUN-5

JUN-6

JUN-7

JUN-5. Club Kit Envelope,
1942. - **$20 $40 $60**

JUN-6. Club Kit Envelope,
1945. - **$30 $75 $100**

JUN-7. Club Kit Envelope,
1948. - **$30 $75 $100**

JUN-8

JUN-9

(CLOSE-UP)

(CLOSE-UP)

JUN-8. Club Kit Certificate,
1942. Type 1. - **$100 $275 $425**

JUN-9. Club Kit Certificate,
1942. Type 2. - **$75 $250 $375**

JUN-10

JUN-11

JUN-10. Club Kit Certificate,
1945. Note Wildcat photo. - **$200 $500 $650**

JUN-11. Club Kit Certificate,
1948. Note Black Canary & Atom pictured. - **$100 $400 $500**

JUN-12

JUN-13

JUN-12. The Minute Man Answers the Call,
1942. EC comic included in Type 1 and Type 2 club kits. -
$30 $60 $90

JUN-13. Club Kit Letter and Brochure,
1942. - **$70 $100 $150**

JUN-15

JUN-14

JUN-14. Club Kit Letter,
1948. - **$70 $100 $150**

JUN-15. Club Kit Decoder,
1942. - **$50 $125 $250**

(CLOSE-UP)

JUN-16

JUN-16. Club Kit Decoder,
1945. Note Wildcat in window. - **$75 $325 $450**

JUN-17

JUN-18

JUN-17. Club Kit Decoder,
1948. Black rectangle design. - **$75 $225 $350**

JUN-18. Comic Book Ad for Club,
1948. Original art. - **$250**

KATE SMITH

Kate Smith (1909-1986) had a brief stage career on Broadway before she moved to radio and became a beloved American institution. Guided throughout by her partner and friend Ted Collins, she broadcast continually from 1931 to 1959, mainly on CBS. Known as the Songbird of the South, she was a large woman, with voice and personality to match. She made her opening theme, *When the Moon Comes Over the Mountain*, practically her own, and for a time she had exclusive rights to Irving Berlin's *God Bless America*. Audiences loved her, and sponsors followed: La Palina cigars (1931-1933), Hudson cars (1934-1935), Philip Morris (1947-1951), and Reader's Digest (1958-1959). During World War II her patriotic efforts sold millions of dollars in war bonds. On television, she had an afternoon show (1950-1954) and two evening variety programs, in 1951-1952 on NBC and in 1960 on CBS.

KAT-2

KAT-1

KAT-3

KAT-1. Fan Photo,
c. 1931. La Palina Cigars. - **$10 $15 $25**

KAT-2. "Kate Smith La Palina Club" Litho. Button,
c. 1931. La Palina cigars. - **$12 $20 $35**

KAT-3. "Philadelphia A & P Party" 2-1/2" Cello. Button,
1935. Great Atlantic & Pacific Tea Co. (grocery chain).
Single day issue for November 4. - **$20 $35 $60**

KAT-4

KAT-5

KAT-6

KAT-4. Photo,
1937. Philadelphia Record newspaper premium. -
$10 $25 $45

KAT-5. Recipe Folder - Christmas,
1937. CBS. Radio premium. - **$15** **$35** **$45**

KAT-6. Recipe Folder - New Years,
1938. CBS. Radio premium. - **$15** **$35** **$45**

KAT-7

KAT-8

KAT-7. Bracelets With Mailer And "Kate Smith Speaks" Reference,
1940. Swan's Down Cake Flour and Calumet Baking Powder. Brass bracelets with enclosure slip naming Kate Smith program plus another sponsored daytime program "My Son And I." Near Mint Boxed - **$40**

KAT-8. Recipe Book - 16 pages,
1945. Swans Down. Radio premium. - **$20** **$40** **$55**

KATZENJAMMER KIDS

Considered by some to be the first true comic strip, *The Katzenjammer Kids* premiered in December 1897 in the *New York Journal*. Created by Rudolph Dirks (1877-1968), this seminal work has been called the single most important creation in the history of the comic strip. The hell-raising kids, Hans and Fritz, and their long-suffering Mamma, were joined by der Captain in 1902 and by der Inspector in 1905. As the result of a legal battle, Harold Knerr (1882-1949) took over the strip in 1914, while Dirks started a new strip, *The Captain and the Kids*, for the *New York World*. A stage adaptation appeared in 1903, and over the years the strips have been reprinted frequently in comic books. Both strips had their own comic books from the 1930s to the 1950s. Animated cartoon versions were directed by Gregory LaCava in 1916-1918 and by Friz Freleng for MGM in 1938-1939, and the Kids appeared on television in *MGM Cartoons* (ABC, 1960) and *The Fabulous Funnies* (NBC, 1978-1979).

KAZ-1

KAZ-2

KAZ-1. "The Katzies" Comic Strip Folder,
1904. King Features copyright but no sponsor indicated. 2x3" folder that opens to 13-panel story. - **$15** **$25** **$40**

KAZ-2. Katzenjammers Heat Image Cartoon Postcard,
1906. American Journal Examiner. Hidden image appears when heat is applied. - **$5** **$10** **$15**

KAZ-3

KAZ-4

KAZ-3. Katzenjammers Heat Image Postcard,
1906. Hidden image appears when heat is applied. - **$5** **$10** **$15**

KAZ-4. Katzenjammer Heat Image Postcard,
1906. Hidden image appears when heat is applied. - **$5** **$10** **$15**

KAZ-5

KAZ-6

KAZ-5. Captain And The Kids Postcard,
1907. Hearst's Boston Sunday American Newspaper Premium. Includes water color paint to paint comic. - **$20** **$50** **$80**

KAZ-6. "Jungle Joke Book" With R. Dirks Cover,
1912. New York Sunday American. 10x12" Sunday supplement with cover cartoon by Katzenjammer artist Rudolph Dirks and 16 pages by various contemporary cartoonists. - **$15** **$35** **$60**

KAZ-7

KAZ-8

KAZ-7. Hot Air Balloon Picture Puzzle,
c. 1915. Newspaper Feature Service. 4x4-1/2" cardboard jigsaw with eight interlocking pieces. - **$15 $30 $50**

KAZ-8. Mama And Kids Figurine,
c. 1920. Store item. German made, hand-painted hollow bisque group figure. - **$60 $100 $150**

KAZ-9

KAZ-10

KAZ-9. "Comicaps" Bottle Caps,
c. 1935. Golden Rod Beer. 1" diameter full color litho. tin believed set of six. Each - **$10 $15 $30**

KAZ-10. Syroco Figures,
1944. Store items. Painted wood composition.
Captain - **$30 $100 $150**
Hans - **$25 $75 $125**
Fritz - **$25 $75 $125**

KAZ-12

KAZ-11

KAZ-11. "Hingees" Punch-Out Kit With Envelope,
1945. Store item. Contains two sheets of punch-out body parts for assembly into 3-D figures of major characters. Unpunched In Envelope - **$15 $30 $50**

KAZ-12. Katzenjammer Character Litho. Buttons,
1946. Kellogg's Pep. From box insert set picturing total of 86 comic characters. Each - **$5 $10 $15**

KAYO

Frank Willard's *Moon Mullins*, one of the most successful comic strips of all time, first appeared in 1923. Four years later Moon was joined by kid brother Kayo, a brat in a derby hat. Together with Lord Plushbottom, Emmy, Uncle Willie, and Mamie, the Mullins boys were to hang out at carnivals and in pool rooms for decades. The Kayo name and character were licensed to promote a chocolate-flavored drink in the 1930s and 1940s. *Moon Mullins* comic books appeared from 1927 to 1933 and through the 1940s. After Willard's death in 1958 the strip was continued by long-time assistant Ferd Johnson.

KAY-1

KAY-2

KAY-1. "Kayo And Moon Mullins-'Way Down South"
Booklet,
1934. Lemix & Corlix Desserts. Book #7 from Whitman series. - **$15 $30 $60**

KAY-2. Yellow Mug,
1930s. Mug pictures Kayo and promotes Kayo Hot Chocolate. - **$25 $50 $75**

KAY-3

KAY-4

KAY-5

KAY-3. Club Member Cello. Button,
1930s. Kayo Chocolate. - **$10 $20 $35**

KAY-4. "Kayo Comics Club" Litho. Button,
1930s. San Francisco Chronicle newspaper. -
$15 $25 $40

KAY-5. "Park Theater Kayo Club" Cello. Button,
1930s. - **$20 $30 $65**

(FRONT)   KAY-6   (BACK)

KAY-6. Cloth Doll,
1930s. - **$30 $100 $150**

(BOTTOM VIEW
SHOWING DICE)

KAY-7

KAY-7. Statue with Dice Salesman's Premium,
1930s. - **$200 $400 $800**

KAY-8

**KAY-8. "Kayo/The Real Chocolate Malted Drink"
Jigsaw Puzzle,**
1930s. - **$35 $75 $125**

KAY-9

KAY-10

KAY-9. "Drink Kayo Chocolate" Transfer Picture,
c. 1940s. Kayo Chocolate Drink. Image is reversed in
unused condition. - **$20 $40 $75**

KAY-10. Promo Chocolate Drink Sign,
1940s. Holed for display on bottle. - **$30 $90 $150**

KELLOGG'S CEREAL MISC.

Dr. John Harvey Kellogg was at the center of a vegetarian health-food craze in Battle Creek, Michigan, in
the late 19th century. The experimental kitchen at his
Battle Creek Sanitarium created a number of meat sub-
stitutes for his patients, including Protose, Nuttose,
Nuttolene, Granola, and Caramel Coffee. With his
brother, W.K. Kellogg, he devised a wheat flake cereal
in 1894 and, four years later, a variety made from corn,
which he sold by mail as Sanitas Corn Flakes.

W.K. Kellogg struck out on his own in 1903, adding fla-
vorings to the cereal, naming it Kellogg's Toasted
Corn Flakes, and promoting it heavily with advertising
and free samples. The cereal became, and remains, a
breakfast staple in millions of homes. Over the years
the company has used a variety of promotional symbols, starting with the Sweetheart of the Corn in 1907.
With new cereals came the need for new personalities:
Snap, Crackle, and Pop in 1933 to promote Kellogg's
Rice Krispies, Tony the Tiger in 1953 for Kellogg's
Sugar Frosted Flakes, and Toucan Sam in 1964.

Kellogg's sponsored many programs such as *Tom
Corbett, Howdy Doody, Superman,* and *Huckleberry
Hound* but the items in this section focus on characters specifically created for Kellogg's advertising and
a sampling of the many non-character premiums they
offered over the years. See separate sections devoted
to Snap, Crackle, and Pop, as well as Tony the Tiger.

KEL-1

**KEL-1. "Kellogg's Funny Jungleland Moving-Pictures"
Booklet,**
1909. Among the earliest premium booklets (3-1/2x4-3/4")
but re-issued in 6x8" and available for many years.
Earliest Version - **$20 $40 $75**
Later Version - **$12 $20 $50**

KEL-2

KEL-2. "Cereal League" Baseball Game Box Panels,
1910. Three panels from same box of Kellogg's Toasted Corn Flakes, possibly the earliest cereal box game.
Complete - **$400**
As Shown - **$100 $200 $300**

KEL-3   KEL-4

KEL-3. "My Visit To Kellogg's" Factory Visit Souvenir Book,
c. 1924. - **$12 $20 $35**

KEL-4. Johnny Bear Uncut,
1925. Kellogg's Corn Flakes premium. Goldilocks & The Three Bears cloth series. - **$40 $60 $100**

KEL-5

KEL-6

KEL-5. "Kellogg's Toasted Corn Flakes" Cello. Button,
c. 1920s. - **$10 $20 $35**

KEL-6. Corn Flakes Blotter,
1920s. Art deco blotter. Premium. - **$8 $15 $30**

KEL-7   KEL-8   KEL-9

KEL-7. Stamp Games #1,
1931. 12 page book of fairy tales and games. Includes spinner and paper chips. - **$25 $45 $60**

KEL-8. Stamp Games #3,
1931. 12 page book of fairy tales and games. Includes spinner and paper chips. - **$25 $45 $60**

KEL-9. Stamp Games #4,
1931. 12 page book of fairy tales and games. Includes spinner and paper chips. - **$25 $45 $60**

KEL-11

KEL-10

KEL-10. Diet Book,
1933. All Bran premium. 33 pages. "Keep On The Sunny Side Of Life." - **$10 $20 $30**

KEL-11. "Junior Texas Ranger Force" Member Certificate,
1933. Facsimile signatures of commanding officer Colonel Louis and W. K. Kellogg. - **$20 $50 $75**

KEL-12

KEL-12. "Junior Texas Ranger" Club Kit,
1936. Five paper items: Two premium folders, card that held badge, survey postcard, leaflet promoting Mother Goose stories by Kellogg's Singing Lady plus mailer.
Each - **$10 $25 $40**

KEL-14   **KEL-15**

KEL-14. Die Cut Aeroplane Sign,
1930s. Rare. Die cut standee promotes Corn Flakes and free planes. - **$175 $350 $525**

KEL-15. Premium Plane 13-1/2x20",
1930s. Rare. Features Avion Cauldron cut-out plane. - **$50 $100 $150**

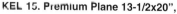

KEL-16   **KEL-17**

KEL-16. Premium Plane 13-1/2x20",
1930s. Rare. Features Empire Flying Boat cut-out plane. - **$50 $100 $150**

KEL-17. Premium Plane 13-1/2x20",
1930s. Rare. Features U.S. Stinson Reliant cut-out plane. - **$50 $100 $150**

KEL-13

KEL-13. Corn Flakes Box Backs,
1935. Features Kellogg's adventure stories on back. Tells plane stories about famous aviators like Admiral Byrd, Floyd Bennett, Cy Armstrong, Jack Traywick, and others. Titles: Parachutes; Desperation and Science; Old Jonah (1936 on); The Flying Dog; Bennett's Last Flight; Do-X The Flying Giant; Army Acrobatics; Mountain Mystery; An Unsung Hero; A Matter of Routine; The Red Dash Warning; Mid-AirTransfer; Night Wings.
Each - **$10 $25 $35**

KEL-18   **KEL-19**

KEL-18. Premium Plane 13-1/2x20",
1930s. Rare. Features Brewster Scout Planecut-out. - **$50 $100 $150**

KEL-19. Premium Plane 13-1/2x20",
1930s. Rare. Features Seversky Convoy Fighter Plane cut-out. - **$50 $100 $150**

KEL-21

KEL-20

KEL-22

KEL-20. Fairy Tales Wall Plaques Premium Sign 12x18",
1930s. Rare. Designed by Vernon Grant, picturing six plaques. Sign - **$200 $400 $600**
Each Plaque - **$25 $50 $100**

KEL-21. Baseball Hat with Mailer,
1930s. - **$20 $45 $65**

KEL-22. Beamy Beanie with Mailer,
1942. Scarce. - **$25 $75 $100**

KEL-23

KEL-23. "Kellogg's Pep Model Warplanes" 16x43" Advertising Poster,
c. 1942. Scarce. - **$75 $200 $400**

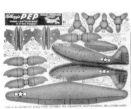

KEL-24

KEL-25

KEL-24. "Kellogg's Pep Model Warplane" Punch-Out,
c. 1942. Set of 28 as follows:
Series "A": A1 - Vought SB2U "Vindicator" U.S. Dive Bomber
A2 - Boulton Paul "Defiant" British Night Fighter
A3 - Lockheed P-38 "Lightning" U.S. Fighter
A4 - Sikorsky VS-300 U.S. Helicopter
A5 - Douglas A-20C or A-20 "Havoc" U.S. Attack Bomber
A6 - Grumman F6F "Hellcat" U.S. Fighter
A7 - North American B-25 "Mitchell" U.S. Attack Bomber.
Series "B": B1 - Westland "Whirlwind" British Fighter
B2 - YAK-4 Russian Fighter/Bomber
B3 - Douglas A-24 "Dauntless" U.S. Dive Bomber
B4 - Curtiss P-40F "Warhawk" U.S. Fighter
B5 - Short "Sunderland" British Patrol Bomber
B6 - Vought JR2S "Excalibur" U.S. Navy Transport
B7 - Consolidated Vultee B-24 "Liberator" U.S. Heavy Bomber
Series "C": C1 - Boeing B-17E "Flying Fortress" U.S. Heavy Bomber
C2 - De Havilland "Mosquito" British Medium Bomber

C3 - Grumman F4F "Wildcat" U.S. Navy Fighter
C4 - Republic P-47 "Thunderbolt" U.S. Fighter
C5 - Doulgas A-17A U.S. Attack Bomber
C6 - "Mosca" Russian Fighter
C7 - Supermarine "Spitfire" British Fighter
Series "D": D1 - Lockheed C-69 "Constellation" U.S. Transport Plane
D2 - Curtiss SB2C-1C "Helldiver" U.S. Dive Bomber
D3 - Douglas C-54 "Skymaster" U.S. Transport
D4 - Handley-Page "Hampden" British Bomber
D5 - Avro "Lancaster" British Heavy Bomber
D6 - Lockheed B-34 "Ventura" U.S. Bomber
D7 - I-18 Russian Fighter
Each Unpunched - **$15 $25 $40**

KEL-25. "Pep Model Warplane" Balsa Sheet In Envelope,
c. 1942. Numbered series, some envelopes mention Superman radio show. Each In Envelope - **$15 $25 $40**

KEL-27

KEL-26

KEL-26. Pep Aluminum Wings,
1943. Each Pep box contained an aluminum wing for turbo jet cut-out planes on back. Ten wings pictured for the ten plane set shown. Each - **$5 $10 $15**

KEL-27. Pep Cereal Back For Turbo Jet Plane Cut-Outs,
1943. Strato Streak cut-out plane. - **$10 $25 $40**

KEL-28

KEL-29

KEL-28. Pep Cereal Back For Turbo Jet Plane Cut-Outs,
1943. Sky Chaser cut-out plane. - **$10 $25 $40**

KEL-29. Pep Cereal Back For Turbo Jet Plane Cut-Outs,
1943. Red Demon cut-out plane. - **$10 $25 $40**

KEL-30   KEL-31

KEL-30. Pep Cereal Back For Turbo Jet Plane Cut-Outs,
1943. Red Arrow cut-out plane. - **$10 $25 $40**

KEL-31. Pep Cereal Back For Turbo Jet Plane Cut-Outs,
1943. Cloud King cut-out plane. **$10 $25 $40**

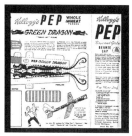

KEL-32   KEL-33

KEL-32. Pep Cereal Back For Turbo Jet Plane Cut-Outs,
1943. Green Flash cut-out plane. - **$10 $25 $40**

KEL-33. Pep Cereal Back For Turbo Jet Plane Cut-Outs,
1943. Green Danger cut-out plane. - **$10 $25 $40**

KEL-34   KEL-35   KEL-36

KEL-34. Pep Cereal Back For Turbo Jet Plane Cut-Outs,
1943. Thunder-Jet cut-out plane. - **$10 $25 $40**

KEL-35. Pep Cereal Back For Turbo Jet Plane Cut-Outs,
1943. Flying Tiger cut-out plane. - **$10 $25 $40**

KEL-36. Pep Cereal Box,
1943. Promotes Turbo Jet Plane program. Each box shows cut-out. Sky Streak plane pictured.
Complete Box - **$50 $75 $150**

KEL-37

KEL-37. "Pep Military Insignia Buttons" 16x44" Paper Store Banner,
1943. Scarce. Reverse offers beanie cap as mail premium for pinning box insert insignia and aircraft litho. buttons. - **$100 $250 $400**

KEL-38   KEL-39

KEL-38. "Kellogg's Pep" Felt Beanie,
1943. Orange and white. With Tag - **$25 $60 $85**
Missing Tag - **$15 $25 $50**

KEL-39. Pep Beany/Military Insignia Buttons 16x44" Paper Store Poster,
1943. Scarce. - **$100 $250 $400**

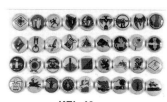

KEL-40

KEL-40. Pep Military Insignia Litho. Buttons,
1943. Set of 36. Paint very susceptible to aging and wear, most examples grade fine or worse. Each - **$3 $8 $15**

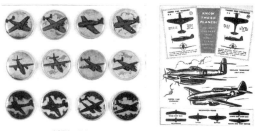

KEL-41   KEL-42

KEL-41. Pep Airplane Litho. Buttons,
1943. Set of 12. Four planes in green, four planes in brown with photo-style artwork and same four planes in brown with hand illustrated style artwork. Paint very susceptible to wear. Each - **$30 $80 $120**

KEL-42. Pep "Plane Spotter" Box Card,
c. 1944. Two cards on each back, at least 42 cards in set.
Uncut Back - **$10 $15 $25**

KEL-43

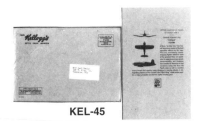

KEL-44

KEL-47

KEL-48

KEL-43. Pep Large Diecut Cardboard Sign,
1945. 38" x 26". Features Pep buttons and boy wearing
Pep beanie. Three known. - **$750 $3000 $5000**

KEL-44. Pep Comic Character Litho. Button Set,
1945. Complete set of 86.
Most Characters - **$5 $10 $15**
Felix - **$15 $30 $50**
Phantom - **$25 $50 $75**

KEL-47. Pep Beanie,
1945. Black and white. With Tag - **$25 $60 $85**
Missing Tag - **$15 $25 $50**

KEL-48. "Metal Pin-On Comic Buttons" Ad,
c. 1945. Comic book page ad for Kellogg's Pep box insert
buttons although indicating complete set of 18 as opposed
to eventual final set of 86. - **$3 $6 $10**

KEL-45

KEL-49

**KEL-45. Pep Punch-Out Warplane Pictures With
Envelope,**
c. 1945. Set of six. Near Mint In Mailer - **$300**

**KEL-49. "Kellogg's Pep Real Photos" 16x20" Paper
Sign,**
c. 1947. Pictures example movie and sports stars miniature photos offered individually as box inserts. -
$75 $150 $250

KEL-50

KEL-50. Pep Comic Character Buttons Ad Sheet,
1947. Canadian issue. - **$75 $150 $250**

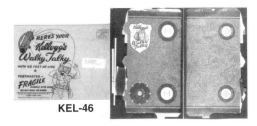

KEL-46

KEL-46. "Kellogg's Walky Talky" Punch-Out,
c. 1945. Near Mint In Mailer - **$375**
Complete Assembled Pair - **$50 $125 $200**
Promotional Sign (Not Shown) - **$100 $250 $375**

(CLOSE-UP)

KEL-51

KEL-51. "Flight Control Sabre Jet Plane",
c. 1948. Unused In Mailer - **$20 $50 $75**

KEL-52

KEL-53

KEL-54

KEL-52. Auto Cut-Outs,
1948. Corn Flakes box back shows cut-out of 1948 Packard. - **$25 $40 $50**

KEL-53. Auto Cut-Outs,
1948. Corn Flakes box back shows cut-out of 1948 Frazer. - **$25 $40 $50**

KEL-54. Super Jet Racer
1949. Rare. Yellow racer with red wheels, instructions, spring, mailer, and Rice Krispies ad.
Complete - **$50 $75 $150**

KEL-55

KEL-56

KEL-57

KEL-55. Presidents Album,
1949. Kellogg's Premium. 36 page stamp album. -
$10 $20 $40

KEL-56. Presidents Album Mailer,
1949. Kellogg's Premium. - **$5 $12 $20**

KEL-57. Presidents Album - The Stamps,
1949. Kellogg's Premium. 32 different large stamps (cereal box contained 1 stamp). Each - **$2 $4 $6**

KEL-58

KEL-58. Punch-Out Airport in Mailer,
1940s. - **$30 $90 $120**

KEL-59

KEL-59. Kellogg's Pep "Photo Album",
1940s. 10 pages for mounting miniature premium photos of sports and entertainment stars.
Near Mint With Mailer - **$150**
Album Only - **$35 $60 $100**

KEL-60

KEL-61

KEL-60. Pin Premium On Card,
1940s. Metal name pin premium for 2 Corn Flakes box tops and10¢. - **$15 $25 $35**

KEL-61. Pennant ,
1940s. Cereal premium, 17" long. - **$25 $60 $90**

KEL-62

KEL-63

KEL-62. College Prom Photo Sign,
1940s. Pep On The Air - N.B.C. Blue Network. -
$15 $25 $35

KEL-63. "Stagecoach" Toy With Mailer And Coupon,
1950. Sugar Frosted Flakes, Sugar Smacks, Sugar Pops.
7" long replica plastic toy with order coupon in mailer carton. Near Mint Box - **$75**
Stagecoach - **$10 $25 $40**

KEL-64

KEL-64. "Kellogg's Pep" Box With Ring Ads,
1950. Complete Box - **$75 $175 $250**

KEL-65

KEL-66

KEL-65. Sugar Smacks Flat,
1951. Soldier premium offer. Maxie the seal on front. -
$50 $200 $300

KEL-66. Soldiers in Mailer,
1951. 12 total. Complete - **$35 $100 $150**

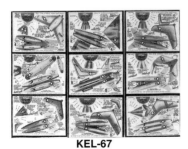

KEL-67

KEL-67. "Flying Model Jet Planes" Punch-Outs,
1951. Ten in the set. Unpunched Each - **$10 $15 $25**

KEL-68

KEL-68. Sugar Frosted Flake Insignia Box Back,
1953. Armed Forces shoulder patch insignia. Box back
with patch premium offer. Each Patch - **$5 $10 $15**
Box Back - **$15 $30 $50**

KEL-69   **KEL-70**   **KEL-71**

KEL-69. Baking Soda Frogman 3-1/2" Size,
1954. Obstacles Scout. Depicts scuba diver holding knife.
Various colors. - **$10 $25 $40**

KEL-70. Baking Soda Frogman 3-1/2" Size,
1954. Demolitions Expert. Depicts diver holding mine.
Various colors. - **$10 $25 $40**

KEL-71. Baking Soda Frogman 3-1/2" Size,
1954. Torch Man. Depicts diver holding cutting torch.
Various colors. - **$10 $25 $40**

KEL-73

KEL-72

KEL-72. U.S. Army Swamp Glider,
1955. Sugar Frosted Flakes premium. Includes glider,
instructions, and box. - **$30 $75 $125**

KEL-73. Jumbly Jungle Book with Mailer,
1950s. - **$20 $30 $40**

KEL-74

KEL-75

KEL-74. "Famous Guns of History" Sets,
1950s. Pep Wheat Flakes premium. 8 different, 2 to a set.
Each Set - **$10 $20 $40**

KEL-75. "Famous Guns of History" Box Back,
1950s. Famous guns of history pictured. - **$10 $20 $30**

KEL-77. Pep Whirl-Erang,
1950s. Scarce. Discontinued because children were
injured. - **$10 $20 $40**
Box Back with Ad - **$50**

KEL-78

KEL-79

KEL-78. Old West Trail Booklet,
1968. Kellogg's premium. 16 pages history of the Old
West.- **$15 $30 $50**

KEL-79. Postcard,
1960s. Postcard features many cartoon and cereal characters like Yogi Bear and Tony the Tiger. - **$8 $15 $25**

KEL-80

KEL-80. "U.S. Navy PT Boat",
c. 1960s. Includes boat, jet race way, package of propel-
lant and instruction sheet. Near Mint Boxed - **$125**
Boat Only - **$15 $30 $60**

KEL-76

KEL-81

KEL-76. U.S.S. Nautilus Submarine Toy With Mailer,
1950s. Sugar Smacks or Sugar Corn Pops. 4-1/2" toy powered by "Atomic Fuel" of baking powder. Pictured instruction sheet is earliest version. Near Mint Boxed - **$125**
Nautilus Only - **$10 $30 $50**

KEL-81. Cereal Box With "Pin-Me-Ups" Back,
1960s. Set of eight featuring Hanna-Barbera characters.
Complete Box - **$20 $40 $75**

KEL-82

KEL-82. "U.S.S. Nautilus" Plastic Atomic Sub,
c. 1960s. Later issue than KEL-76 with different box label
and small differences on instructions.
Near Mint In Box - **$125**
Sub Only - **$15 $25 $40**

KEL-77

KEL-83

KEL-84

KEL-83. "Dig 'Em" Metal Wind-Up Alarm Clock,
1979. - **$15 $35 $50**

KEL-84. "Toucan Sam" Plastic Secret Decoder,
1983. Movable disk code wheel. Comes in different colors -
$5 $12 $20

KEN MAYNARD

An all-around sagebrush hero, cowboy actor Maynard was first an accomplished trick rider and rodeo championship rider. Pre-movie years included performances at King Ranch, Texas; Buffalo Bill's Wild West Show, Ringling Bros. Wild West Show, Tex Rickard's World's Champion Cowboy competition (first place in 1920). He was introduced into silent movies by Tom Mix and best remembered for his First National films of the mid-1920s and following decade, also featuring his talented horse Tarzan. He is credited by many as the first to introduce song to the western movie. His 1938-1948 years were mostly a return to live performances and he continued to draw audiences even into his fifties. Maynard died March 23, 1973 at 87 years of age.

KEN-2

KEN-1

KEN-1. "First National Films" Studio Matchbook,
1929. Reverse lists six film titles from that year. -
$12 $20 $30

KEN-2. "Ken Maynard Club/First National Pictures"
Cello. Button,
c. 1929. - **$10 $20 $30**

KEN-4

KEN-3

KEN-3. Paper Mask,
1933. Einson-Freeman movie promo. - **$50 $100 $250**

KEN-4. "Round Up/Buckaroo Club" Card,
1930s. Various radio stations. - **$15 $30 $50**

KEN-5

KEN-6

KEN-5. Portrait Cello. Button,
1930s. Probably circus souvenir. - **$30 $60 $100**

KEN-6. "Cole Bros. Circus" Cello. Button,
1930s. - **$50 $100 $150**

KEN-7

KEN-8

KEN-7. "Ken Maynard's Wild West And Indian Congress" Performance Ticket,
1930s. Printed identically on both sides including small title for Diamond K Ranch. - **$10 $25 $40**

KEN-8. "Ken Maynard's Wild West Circus And Indian Congress" Contract Agreement Pass,
1930s. Paper perforated into billing contract on left for right to post advertising entitling free admission pass on right. Complete - **$20 $40 $60**

KING FEATURES MISC.

King Features Syndicate, the country's largest newspaper comic-strip syndicator, has been the agency of such legendary giants as Popeye, Flash Gordon, Felix the Cat, Krazy Kat, Beetle Bailey, Henry, Skippy, Betty Boop, Barney Google, and dozens of other major comic characters. In 1915 King Features became the sales agent for all the combined Hearst Newspapers syndicate operations. Over the years it has issued a number of items promoting various combinations of its comic characters.

KIN-1

KIN-2

KIN-1. "Polar Lark" Metal Paperweight,
1926. 10 King Features character heads form North Pole in homage to Commander Byrd's flight over pole. - **$150 $300 $600**

KIN-2. The Comic Club Stamps,
1934. Wrigley's Gum. 18 stamps on sheet. - **$60 $125 $175**

KIN-3

KIN-3. Christmas Card Folder To Media Customers,
1935. Authorized Hallmark Card publication with 24 full color pages featuring prominent King Features comic strip characters illustrating story theme "T'was The Night Before Christmas." - **$250 $500 $800**

KIN-4

KIN-5

KIN-6

KIN-4. "Sunday Examiner" Newspaper Contest Litho. Button,
1930s. Part of a set. - **$10 $20 $30**

KIN-5. "A Christmas Carol Holiday Greetings" Book With Slipcase,
1946. Christmas theme hardcover with 160 pages picturing virtually all King Features comic strip characters. Art is repeated on slipcase and book cover.
With Slipcase - **$75 $150 $225**
No Slipcase - **$50 $100 $150**

KIN-6. "Sing With King At Christmas" Book,
1949. Pictures numerous Christmas caroles sung by various syndicate characters. - **$20 $40 $60**

KIN-7

KIN-7. "King Features Syndicate Famous Artists & Writers" Book,
1949. Biographies of those represented by K.F.S. - **$50 $85 $140**

KIN-8

KIN-8. "Popular Comics" Boxed Christmas Cards,
1951. Set of 16. - **$35 $90 $150**

KIN-9

KIN-9. "King Features Syndicate Blue Book",
1955. Full color sample pages of strips represented by K.F.S. - **$75 $150 $225**

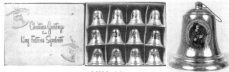

KIN-10

KIN-10. Plastic Ornament Set Showing 12 Characters,
c. 1950s. Boxed - **$50 $125 $175**

KIN-11

KIN-11. Comic Strip Character Lighter,
1950s. Metal case cigarette lighter picturing total of eight characters on both sides. Probably an executive or salesman giveaway. - **$20 $40 $60**

KIN-12

KIN-13

KIN-12. Glass Ashtray,
1950s. Pictures 14 comic strip characters. - **$15** **$30** **$50**

KIN-13. Plastic Pen Holder,
1964. - **$20** **$35** **$50**

KISS

In 1971, Gene Simmons and Paul Stanley gave birth to a modern rock legend by playing their first show as Wicked Lester. In August of 1973, after a name change and the addition of new personnel, Kiss took the stage at the Grand Ballroom of the Diplomat Hotel in New York, shortly resulting in a record deal. Gene Simmons (bass player), Paul Stanley (guitarist), Ace Frehley (guitarist), and Peter Criss (drummer) had transformed themselves into The Demon, Starchild, Space Ace, and The Cat, respectively, through makeup. By mixing a hard rock edge with glam rock theatrics, Kiss took the world by storm as evidenced by their legion of followers, known as The Kiss Army. The group spawned best selling albums, action figures, a made-for-TV movie (*Kiss Meets the Phantom of the Park*—1978), a comic book, and scores of other merchandise.

Over the years, the band's line-up would change (Ace and Peter left, and Vinnie Vincent and Eric Carr would join), with Simmons and Stanley remaining at the core. In 1983, Kiss took a major chance and removed their make-up, thus shattering the illusion of their rock personas for scores of followers while still maintaining a loyal fan base with The Kiss Army. During this time period, two other guitarists would try to fill the shoes left by Frehley—Mark St. John and Bruce Kulick. In 1991 Eric Carr died of cancer and Eric Singer took his seat behind the drums.

In 1996, a reunited Kiss in full makeup appeared at the Grammy Awards. In April they announced a 1996-1997 reunion tour which would go on to become the music industry's most successful tour of the year. Like magic, the Kings of the Nighttime World were once again back on top, launching new merchandise like best-selling action figures from McFarlane Toys, and a comic line, and entertaining thousands of fans who only wanted to "rock 'n' roll all night and party every day."

KIS-1

KIS-2

KIS-1. Kiss Bracelet,
1977. Aucoin. Gold with red logo on Love Gun display card. - **$10** **$15** **$25**

KIS-2. Kiss Army Selective Service Notification,
1970s. - **$10** **$15** **$25**

KIS-3

KIS-4

KIS-3. Colorform Set,
1970s. Colorforms. - **$50** **$75** **$125**

KIS-4. "Destroyer" Puzzle,
1970s. By Casse-tete. - **$25** **$40** **$55**

KIS-5

KIS-6

KIS-5. Kiss Make-Up Kit,
1970s. By Remco. First issue. - **$75** **$150** **$225**

KIS-6. Window Sign,
1970s. Blue Gene face. Creatures of the Night. - **$2** **$5** **$10**

KIS-7

KIS-8

KIS-9

KIS-7. View-Master Special Subjects Series,
1970s. 21 3-D pictures on 3 reels in photo envelope. - **$10** **$15** **$20**

KIS-8. Rub 'N' Play Magic Transfer Set,
1970s. 8 stand-up play figures by Colorforms. - **$50** **$100** **$175**

KIS-9. Kiss Signature Necklace,
1970s. One of four featuring Ace, Gene, Paul, and Peter. Ace Frehely version pictured. Each - **$35** **$65** **$95**

KIS-10

KIS-11

KIS-10. Kiss Promo Card,
1970s. 4x5" card says "Compliments of Kiss." -
$10 $20 $30

KIS-11. "Kiss Meets the Phantom of the Park" Video,
1986. World Vision Home Video. Tape of a 1978 Hanna Barbera production in association with Kiss/Aucoin Productions. 96 minute made-for-TV movie also starred Anthony Zerbe, Carmine Caridi, and Deborah Ryan. - **$50**

KIS-12   (SIDE VIEW)

KIS-12. Kiss Rings,
1997. Three different plastic rings with a filigree metal base. Gene, Paul and the group. Each - **$5 $10 $20**

KRAZY KAT AND IGNATZ

George Herriman (1880-1944), creator of the comic strip *Krazy Kat*, has been ranked with Chaplin as one of the giants of American popular art. The strip, which began as a minor part of a daily strip called *The Dingbat Family* in the *New York Journal* in 1910, came into its own in 1913, and a Sunday page debuted in 1916. For the next 28 years the complex saga of Krazy Kat, the brick-throwing Ignatz Mouse, and Offissa Pupp unfolded against ever-changing backgrounds. Animated cartoons based on the strip were produced in the 1920s and 1930s and later as part of the King Features Trilogy and Screen Gems Theatrical Cartoon Package. Dell published a series of *Krazy Kat* comic books in the 1950s. The strip was retired upon Herriman's death.

KRA-1

KRA-2

KRA-1. "Krazy Kat" Stuffed Doll,
c. 1915. Store item by Averill Co. - **$300 $600 $1000**

KRA-2. "Don't Be A Krazy Kat" Cello. Button,
c. 1915. Cigarette purchase give-away. Art by character creator George Herriman. - **$20 $35 $50**

KRA-3

KRA-4

KRA-3. "Ignatz" Flexible Figure,
c. 1930. Store item. Composition/wood/wire by Cameo Doll Co. - **$150 $250 $400**

KRA-4. "Krazy Kat Kiddies Klub" Member Card,
c. 1920s. Art is unsigned, issuer is unknown. -
$100 $350 $400

KRA-5

KRA-5. "All Star Comics" Boxed Playing Card Game,
1934. Store item by Whitman. Card characters also include those from "Just Kids" and "Captain And Kids" comic strips. - **$50 $100 $150**

KRA-6   KRA-7

KRA-6. Krazy Kat Enameled Brass Figural Pin,
1930s. Accents are four enamel colors and tiny rhinestone eyes. - **$15 $25 $40**

KRA-7. Krazy Kat Enameled Brass Figure Pin,
1930s. Sign inscription is "If You Can Read This You're Too Darn Close." - **$20 $35 $50**

KRA-8　　　**KRA-9**　　　**KRA-10**

KRA-8. "Krazy Kat/New York Evening Journal" Cello. Button,
1930s. From series of newspaper contest buttons, match number to win prize. - **$25 $50 $75**

KRA-9. "Krazy Kat/New York Evening Journal" Cello. Button,
1930s. From series of newspaper contest buttons, match number to win prize. - **$10 $25 $50**

KRA-10. "Ignatz Mouse/New York Evening Journal" Cello. Button,
1930s. From series of newspaper contest buttons, match number to win prize. - **$10 $25 $50**

KUKLA, FRAN AND OLLIE

Puppeteer Burr Tillstrom created Kukla, a chronic worrier, and Ollie, a one-tooth dragon, in Chicago in the late 1930s. Along with singer-actress Fran Allison, the Kuklapolitans were to produce one of early television's most beloved long-running successes, first as *Junior Jamboree* on WBKB (1947-1948), then as *Kukla, Fran & Ollie* on NBC (1948-1954), on ABC (1954-1957), again on NBC (1961-1962), on public television (1970-1971), and in syndication (1975-1976). Sponsors included RCA Victor, Sealtest, Ford and Pontiac automobiles, National Biscuit, Life magazine, Procter & Gamble, and Miles Laboratories. Promotional items are normally copyrighted Burr Tillstrom. A radio version aired on NBC in 1952-1953.

KUK-1

KUK-1. "Kuklapolitan Courier" Newsletter With Envelope,
1949. One of series sent to fans.
With Envelope - **$25 $75 $100**
Without Envelope - **$10 $35 $60**

KUK-2

KUK-2. Fan Postcard,
1950. Announces August 8 starting day for third season of TV show. - **$15 $30 $50**

KUK-3

KUK-3. "Kuklapolitan Courier Year Book",
1951. - **$25 $50 $100**

KUK-4　　　　　**KUK-5**

KUK-4. "TV Guide" Cover Article,
1953. Weekly issue for October 30 with two-page Kukla, Fran & Ollie article titled "Beulah Witch's Halloween." - **$10 $20 $30**

KUK-5. Vinyl On Cardboard Postcard Record,
c. 1957. Curtiss Candy Co. Several versions. - **$15 $30 $55**

KUK-6

KUK-6. Curtiss Candy Co. Vinyl Cardboard Record,
1950s. - **$15 $50 $75**

(KUKLA)　　**KUK-7**　　(OLLIE)

KUK-7. Spoon Set Of Two,
1950s. Rare. - **$75 $150 $300**

LASSIE

The story of the courageous, intelligent collie first appeared in Erick Knight's 1938 short story and 1940 best-selling novel *Lassie Come Home*--the start of an odyssey that was to continue for some 35 years: the 1943 MGM movie, followed by a half-dozen sequels over eight years; the radio serial sponsored by Red Heart dog food on ABC (1947-1948) and NBC (1948-1950); three decades of comic books beginning in 1949; and ultimately the CBS television saga, from 1954 to 1971, followed by three years of syndication under various titles (1972-1975), all sponsored by Campbell's soup. Lassie's human companions were played by Tommy Rettig (1954-1957) and Jon Provost (1957-1964), and by Robert Bray (1964-1969) as an adventurous forest ranger. *Lassie's Rescue Rangers*, an animated series, ran on ABC from 1973 to 1975. The 50th anniversary of the original movie was celebrated in 1994 with the release of a new movie (*Lassie*), a TV program, a new book (*Lassie: A Dog's Life*), and numerous deals for spinoff products. Items bear the copyright of Wrather Corp., Rankin & Bass Productions, or Jack Wrather Productions.

LAS-1　　　　LAS-2　　　　LAS-3

LAS-1. Color Premium Picture - Red Heart, Large,
1949. Scarce. - **$20 $50 $75**

LAS-2. Comic Book Premium - Red Heart,
1949. Scarce. - **$15 $45 $160**

LAS-3. Postcard,
1940s. Thank you postcard for entering contest. -
$10 $25 $35

LAS-4　　　　　　　LAS-5

LAS-4. "Jeff's Collie Club" Member Card,
c. 1954. Virginia Dairy Co., probable others. No direct Lassie reference but obviously based on early version of TV series. - **$10 $25 $40**

LAS-5. Lassie Friendship Silvered Brass Ring,
c. 1955. Campbell Soup Company. Initial "L" on each side with high relief portrait on top. - **$90 $135 $200**

LAS-6

LAS-7

LAS-6. "Lassie Club" Savings Bond Certificate,
1956. - **$20 $40 $60**

LAS-7. "Tim Magazine For Boys" Issues With Lassie,
1957-1958. Each has cover article featuring Tommy Rettig as youthful star of Lassie TV series. Issues are for September 1957 and November 1958 with imprint for local Tim store. Each - **$5 $12 $20**

LAS-8　　　　　　LAS-9

LAS-8. "Have You Voted For Lassie?" Cello. Button,
1950s. 1-3/4" size. - **$10 $15 $30**

LAS-9. "I Voted For Lassie" Cello. Button,
1950s. 1" version. - **$8 $12 $20**

LAS-10

LAS-10. Wallet With Membership Card,
c. 1950s. Campbell's Soups. Card reads "Lassie-Get-Up-And-Go Club". - **$15 $25 $40**

LAS-11

LAS-11. "Lassie Forest Ranger" Vinyl Wallet With Contents,
1964. Campbell's Soups. Includes white metal badge and Lassie photo. Complete - **$20 $40 $60**

LAS-12.

LAS-12. "Forest Ranger Handbook",
1967. Authored by "Corey Stuart And Lassie." -
$10 $20 $35

LAS-13

LAS-14

LAS-13. TV Patch,
1960s. - **$20 $40 $60**

LAS-14. Lassie/Corey Stuart TV Photo,
1960s. - **$20 $40 $60**

LAS-15

LAS-16

LAS-15. Fan Card,
1960s. Recipe Brand Dinners. Back has facsimile paw
print of Lassie and signature of trainer Rudd Weatherwax. -
$10 $20 $30

LAS-16. "A Friend Of Lassie" Brass Dog Tag,
c. 1970s. Probable dog food sponsor. Back identification
inscription to be completed by dog owner. - **$10 $20 $35**

LAUGH-IN

Rowan & Martin's Laugh-In was the psychedelic con-
coction of Dan Rowan and Dick Martin, a classic comic
team of straight man and foil. The program, which
aired on NBC television from 1968 to 1973 was a free-
wheeling, frenetic mix of sight gags, low humor, and
political satire. Among the supporting cast: Goldie
Hawn, Lily Tomlin, Henry Gibson, Arte Johnson, Ruth
Buzzi, and Judy Carne. Catch phrases from the show
such as "You bet your bippy," "Look that up in your
Funk & Wagnall's," and "Sock it to me," became part
of the nation's vocabulary. *Laugh-In* was the No. 1 television show during its first two seasons, winning
numerous awards. A dozen issues of *Laugh-In Magazine*
were published in 1968-1969. Verrry interesting!

LAU-1   **LAU-2**   **LAU-3**   **LAU-4**

LAU-1. Laugh-In Flicker Ring,
1968. Store item made by L. M. Becker Co., Appleton,
Wisconsin. This and the next 11 rings comprise a set of 12.
Images are slogan "Here Comes The Judge" and photo of
Pigmeat Markham. - **$10 $15 $25**

LAU-2. Laugh-In Flicker Ring,
1968. Images are Henry Gibson as Indian and Priest. -
$10 $15 $25

LAU-3. Laugh-In "Beauty/Beast" Flicker Ring,
1968. Images are Dan Rowan and Ruth Buzzi. -
$10 $15 $25

LAU-4. Laugh-In Joke Flicker Ring,
1968. Text images are "If Minnehaha Married Don
Ho/She'd Be Minne Ha Ha Ho." - **$10 $15 $25**

LAU-5   **LAU-6**   **LAU-7**   **LAU-8**

LAU-5. Laugh-In Phrase Flicker Ring,
1968. Images are text "Flying Fickle Finger Of Fate Award"
to winged hand featuring pointed index finger. -
$10 $15 $25

LAU-6. Laugh-In Flicker Ring,
1968. Alternate image is Dan Rowan and Dick Martin. -
$10 $15 $25

LAU-7. Laugh-In Goldie Hawn Flicker Ring,
1968. Images are close-up of her in black hat and as bikini
dancer. - **$10 $15 $25**

LAU-8. Laugh-In Ruth Buzzi Flicker Ring,
1968. Images are close-up of her in hair net and another in
wig. - **$10 $15 $25**

LAU-9   **LAU-10**   **LAU-11**   **LAU-12**

LAU-9. Laugh-In "Good Night, Dick" Flicker Ring,
1968. Images are Dan Rowan to Dick Martin with caption
"Who's Dick?" - **$10 $15 $25**

LAU-10. Laugh-In Judy Carne Flicker Ring,
1968. Images are "Sock It To Me" text to photo of her in striped sweater. - **$10 $15 $25**

LAU-11. Laugh-In Joanne Worley Flicker Ring,
1968. Images are photo of her screaming to another with sad face. - **$10 $15 $25**

LAU-12. Laugh-In Arte Johnson Flicker Ring,
1968. Images are "Verry Innteresting" slogan picturing him as German soldier to slogan "But Stupid" picturing him in different style German helmet. - **$10 $15 $25**

LAU-14

LAU-13

LAU-13. "Laugh-In Magazine" First Issue,
1968. Laufer Publishing Co. Vol. 1 #1 for October. - **$10 $15 $25**

LAU-14. "Laugh-In" Gum Pack Box,
1968. Topps Gum. Box Only - **$20 $50 $80**

LAU-15

LAU-16

LAU-15. "Rowan And Martin's Laugh-In" Book,
1969. Store item by World Publishing Co. Hardcover 160-page assortment of photos, fold-outs, sayings and jokes. - **$8 $15 $25**

LAU-16. "Laugh-In" 17x26" Fabric Banner,
1970. Copyright by George Schlatter-Ed Friendly Productions and Romart Inc. - **$10 $20 $30**

LAU-17

LAU-17. "Here Come The Judge" Pendants,
c. 1970. Store items. Cast metal in silver or gold finish featuring one of the popular humor slogans from the show. Each - **$5 $10 $15**

LAU-18

LAU-19

LAU-18. "Rowan & Martin Laugh-In" Cello. Button,
c. 1970. For "Westbury Music Fair" related appearance or event. - **$5 $10 $15**

LAU-19. Laugh-In Vending Machine Display,
c. 1970. Paper insert on styrofoam with two plastic rings with Laugh-In slogans, other generic rings and novelties. - **$18 $45 $70**

LAUREL AND HARDY

Stan Laurel (1890-1965), the British-born thin one, and Oliver Hardy (1892-1957), the pompous fat one, teamed in 1926 to become one of the screen's finest comedy teams. In silent two-reelers, and in feature films between 1929 and 1950, the slapstick misadventures of Laurel, scratching his head, and Hardy, fiddling with his tie, found them in "one fine mess" after another. A British comic strip ran in *Film Fun* (1930-1942), and *Laurel and Hardy Comics* appeared in the U.S. from 1949 to 1956 and in 1962-1963. Vintage films were edited and cut for syndication to television in 1948 and ran locally for over three decades. Five-minute animated episodes based on the films, co-produced by Hanna-Barbera and Larry Harmon, were syndicated to television in 1966 with limited success. Merchandising in the 1960s and 1970s was extensive, with the pair used to promote a wide variety of products--toys, dolls, games, coloring books, watches, spray deodorants-- and film clips used in television commercials in the 1970s. Items associated with the animated cartoons are usually copyrighted either by the co-producers or by Wolper Productions Inc.

L&H-3

L&H-2

L&H-1

L&H-1. Laurel & Hardy "Old Gold Cigarettes" 31x42" Cardboard Sign,
1934. - **$500 $800 $1500**

L&H-2. Laurel And Hardy Metal Figures,
1930s. Store item by Mignot of France, maker of lead soldier toys. Paint and detailing on front and back of each figure standing on small base. Pair - **$20 $40 $60**

L&H-3. Derby Hats Enameled Metal Pin,
c. 1930s. English made without markings. - **$15 $30 $50**

L&H-4

L&H-5

L&H-4. Figural Caricature Ceramic,
c. 1930s. Store item made in Japan for use as pencil holder or planter . - **$35 $75 $125**

L&H-5. Salt And Pepper Set,
1930s. China figural pair by Beswick of England. - **$75 $125 $200**

L&H-9

L&H-10

L&H-9. Esco Products Large Statuettes,
1971. Set of 17" tall painted solid plaster figures colorfully painted. Each - **$15 $25 $50**

L&H-10. Figure Set By Dakin,
c. 1974. Store items by R. Dakin Co. Painted hard plastic figures with movable arms, soft vinyl movable heads, fabric jackets. Each is about 8". Each - **$15 $30 $50**

L&H-12

L&H-13

L&H-11

L&H-11. Oliver Hardy "TV Pals" Plastic Candy Dispenser,
1970s. - **$30 $60 $90**

L&H-12. "Ask Me About My Partner" 2-1/4" Cello. Button,
c. 1980s. Ziyad Printers. - **$3 $8 $12**

L&H-13. "Together We're A Team" 2-1/2" Cello. Button,
c. 1980s. Ziyad Printers. - **$3 $8 $12**

L&H-6

L&H-6. "Mickey Mouse With The Movie Stars" Gum Card,
1930s. Gum, Inc. Card #120 from series featuring Mickey and various stars. - **$50 $100 $150**

L&H-7. "Join The Laurel And Hardy Laff Club!" 3-1/2" Button,
1960s. Larry Harmon's Pictures Corp. - **$15 $25 $45**

L&H-7

LIGHTNING JIM

U.S. Marshal Lightning Jim Whipple was the hero of a Western adventure radio series broadcast on the West Coast in the 1940s and syndicated in the 1950s. Meadow Gold dairy products sponsored the program. Membership in Lightning Jim's Special Reserve entitled the young listener to wear the Meadow Gold Round-Up Badge. Whitey Larsen served as Jim's sidekick and deputy.

L&H-8

L&H-8. Donuts 9x13" Diecut Cardboard Store Signs,
1960s. Various users. Depict Laurel and Hardy.
Each - **$30 $50 $90**

LGH-1

LGH-1. "Meadow Gold Round-Up" Photo,
1940s. - **$10 $20 $35**

LGH-2

LGH-3

LGH-2. Membership Card,
1940s. Scarce. - **$10 $50 $75**

LGH-3. Membership Brass Badge,
1940s. Scarce. - **$30 $75 $125**

LGH-4

LGH-5

LGH-4. Mailer,
1940s. Scarce. - **$10 $20 $40**

LGH-5. Drinking Glass,
1940s. Rare. - **$40 $100 $200**

LGH-6

LGH-7

LGH-6. "Round-Up" Radio Broadcast Ad Paper,
1940s. Meadow Gold Dairies. 3x5-1/2" imprinted for
WMBC Radio, Columbus, Mississippi with text including
names of Marshal "Lightning" Jim Whipple and his Deputy
Whitey Larson. - **$10 $20 $30**

LGH-7. "Lightning Jim Posse" Litho. Tin Tab,
1950s. Sponsor is NuGrape Soda. Other inscriptions are
"Learning-Justice-Power." - **$20 $40 $60**

LI'L ABNER

Al Capp created *Li'l Abner* for United Features as a
daily comic strip in 1934 and as a Sunday page in
1935. Along with the handsome hillbilly from Dogpatch
has come a string of unforgettable characters: Daisy
Mae, Mammy and Pappy Yokum, Marryin' Sam, Sadie
Hawkins, Sir Cecil and Lady Cesspool, Hairless Joe,

Lonesome Polecat, Fearless Fosdick, the bountiful
Shmoos, the Kigmys, Kickapoo Joy Juice, and many
others. Comic books appeared from the 1930s into the
1950s. A *Li'l Abner* radio show on NBC in 1939-1940
featured John Hodiak as Abner; a brief run of five animated shorts was released in 1944-1945; a musical
comedy ran on Broadway for almost 700 performances in 1956-1957; and a Paramount film was
released in 1959.

LIL-1

LIL-2

LIL-1. "Tip Top Comics" 11x14" Store Sign,
c. 1938. - **$50 $75 $125**

LIL-2. "Buy War Stamps" 14x18" Poster,
c. 1944. U.S. Government. - **$40 $75 $125**

LIL-3

LIL-4

LIL-5

LIL-3. Li'l Abner Beanie with Tag,
1948. Cereal premium. - **$30 $60 $90**

LIL-4. High Relief Brass Badge,
c. 1948. - **$20 $35 $60**

LIL-5. "Shmoo Club Member" Litho. Button,
c. 1948. - **$20 $40 $75**

LIL-7

LIL-6

LIL-6. Shmoo Paddle Ball,
1948. Scarce. - **$50 $100 $200**

LIL-7. Shmoo Plastic Wall Clock,
c. 1948. Store item by Lux Clock Co.
Near Mint Boxed - **$350**
Loose - **$50 $100 $150**

LIL-8

LIL-9

LIL-16

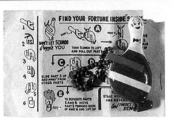

LIL-17

LIL-8. Shmoos Savings Bond Certificate,
1949. - **$25 $50 $75**

LIL-9. Shmoo "Snow Week" Cello. Button,
1949. University of Minnesota. Rim curl has 1948 copyright. - **$35 $75 $150**

LIL-10

LIL-11

LIL-12

LIL-13

LIL-10. Shmoo Club 2-1/4" Litho. Tab,
1949. Sealtest ice cream. - **$10 $20 $35**

LIL-11. Shmoo Club 2-1/4" Litho. Tab,
1949. Sealtest ice cream. - **$10 $20 $35**

LIL-12. Shmoo Club 2-1/4" Litho. Tab,
1949. Sealtest ice cream. - **$10 $20 $35**

LIL-13. Shmoo Club 2-1/4" Litho. Tab,
1949. Sealtest ice cream. - **$10 $20 $35**

LIL-14

LIL-14. Shmoo Character Litho. Buttons,
c. 1949. United Features Syndicate copyrights. Pictured examples from series of about 12 are Captain Kidd, Sailor, Joe. Each - **$10 $20 $30**

LIL-15

LIL-15. Decal Sheet With Envelope,
1940s. Orange-Crush. - **$10 $20 $35**

LIL-16. "Tangle Comics" Cello. Button,
1940s. Philadelphia Sunday Bulletin. - **$10 $20 $35**

LIL-17. Shmoo Figure Puzzle,
1940s. Red, white, and green puzzle with instructions. - **$10 $20 $40**

LIL-18

LIL-19

LIL-20

LIL-18. Shmoo Ad,
Sept, 1940s. - **$5 $10 $20**

LIL-19. Shmoo Ad,
Nov, 1940s. Shows 8 different glasses. - **$5 $10 $20**
Each Glass - **$5 $15 $25**

LIL-20. "Shmoo Girls" Felt Patch,
c. 1950. 5x8" diecut fabric. - **$25 $60 $100**

LIL-21

LIL-22

LIL-21. "Shmoo Lucky Rings" 12x13" Cardboard Store Display Sign,
c. 1950. Store item by Jarco Metal Products.
Empty Card - **$50 $125 $200**
Brass Ring - **$30 $45 $60**

LIL-22. "Li'l Abner" Cello. Button,
c. 1950. - **$15 $30 $50**

LIL-23

LIL-24

LIL-23. Civil Defense Comic Book,
1956. Features Civil Defense comic figure created by Al Capp. - **$5 $12 $20**

LIL-24. Kigmy Plastic Charm,
1950s. Scarce. - **$30 $60 $90**

LITTLE LULU

Mischievous Little Lulu Moppet, the brainchild of Marjorie H. Buell (Marge), started life as a single-panel cartoon in the *Saturday Evening Post* in 1935. She began her comic book career as a one-shot in 1945 and as a regular series in 1948, scripted by John Stanley. A newspaper strip ran from 1955 to 1967, and from 1944 to 1960 Lulu was featured in advertising campaigns for Kleenex tissues. She also appeared, along with boyfriend Tubby Tompkins and little Alvin, in an animated cartoon series from Paramount Pictures in 1944-1948. The series was syndicated on television in 1956, and other series were produced in the 1970s. A short-lived animated series with Tracey Ullman as the voice of Little Lulu debuted on HBO in 1995.

LUL-1

LUL-2

LUL-1. "Tubby Tom And Flipper" Glass,
1940s. Dairy product container, from set of six. - **$30 $60 $125**

LUL-2. Annie And Mops Glass,
1940s. Dairy product container, from set of six. - **$25 $50 $85**

LUL-3

LUL-4

LUL-3. Wilbur Van Snobbe Glass,
1940s. Dairy product container from set of six. - **$25 $50 $85**

LUL-4. Gloria And Tipper Glass,
1940s. Dairy product container from set of six.- **$25 $50 $85**

LUL-5

LUL-6

LUL-5. Little Lulu Mask,
1952. Kleenex. - **$20 $40 $60**

LUL-6. Tubby Mask,
1952. Kleenex. - **$25 $50 $75**

LUL-7

LUL-8

LUL-7. Kleenex Cut-Out Doll 11x14" Cardboard Store Sign,
1952. - **$20 $40 $60**

LUL-8. March of Comics Booklet,
1964. Various retail stores. - **$10 $35 $80**

LITTLE NEMO

Winsor McCay (1869-1934), widely considered the greatest of the comic strip artists, created his master-piece, *Little Nemo in Slumberland,* out of dreams and visions, exploring the unconscious with grace and fairy-tale beauty through the dazzling nocturnal voyages of his little hero. The strip ran in the *New York Herald* from 1905 to 1911 and from 1924 to 1927. From 1911 to 1914 the adventures appeared as *The Land of Wonderful Dreams* in the Hearst newspapers. A musical with a score by Victor Herbert was produced in 1908, and the following year McCay started a parallel career in film cartoons with the release of a hand-colored version of *Nemo.* Scattered comic book reprints of the strips were published from 1905 to 1970.

LNE-1

LNE-2

LNE-1. "Little Nemo In Slumberland" First Comic Strip Reprint Book,
1906. Store item by Duffield & Co. 11x16" with 58 pages of Winsor McCay strips printed one side to a page. - **$500 $1880 $3300**

LNE-2. "Won't You Be My Playmate" Sheet Music,
1908. New York Herald Co. Words and music for song by Victor Herbert from "Little Nemo" stage play. From series of various song titles. Each - **$30 $60 $100**

LNE-3

LNE-3. Little Nemo Postcard,
1900s. From a series. Scarce. - **$30 $60 $120**

LNE-4

LNE-5

LNE-6

LNE-4. "Doctor Pill" Painted Bisque Figure,
c. 1910. Store item. 4-3/4" tall figure from Little Nemo comic strip, one of the rarest comic character bisques. - **$400 $1200 $2000**

LNE-5. "Little Nemo Child's Set" Boxed Place Setting,
c. 1910. Silver plate metal knife, fork and spoon with matching generic handle design. Box art is not attributed to Nemo creator Winsor McCay. Boxed - **$50 $100 $150**

LNE-6. "Little Nemo" Brass Clothing Buttons,
c. 1910. 1/2" diameter with profile bust relief image of him. Each - **$5 $10 $15**

LNE-7

LNE-8

LNE-7. Flip Of Little Nemo Bobbing Head Figure,
c. 1910. 6-1/2" tall painted composition with spring-mounted head on wooden rod neck. - **$100 $250 $400**

LNE-8. Bell Ringer Metal Toy,
c. 1910. Pull or push toy on turning wheels causing ringing of bell chimes by figures of Nemo and Flip. - **$300 $600 $900**

LITTLE ORPHAN ANNIE

Orphan Annie was the life work of cartoonist/storyteller Harold Gray. From her comic strip debut in the *New York Daily News* in 1924 until Gray's death in 1968, the curly-haired pre-teen with blank eyes survived one thrilling adventure after another, accompanied by her faithful dog Sandy (Arf!), saved when necessary by billionaire Daddy Warbucks and his enforcers the Asp and Punjab.

The strip, consistently among the most popular of its time, gave rise to the classic radio serial that captivated its young fans on NBC from 1931 to 1942, sponsored by Ovaltine (1931-1940), then by Quaker Puffed Wheat and Rice Sparkies (1941-1942). With the new sponsor, Annie's pal Joe Corntassel was replaced by heroic combat pilot Captain Sparks, but the program could not survive the change and was soon dropped.

Merchandising of Annie premiums during the Ovaltine years was extensive, producing a seemingly endless stream of mugs, masks, decoders, games, books, pins, dolls, toys, dishes, rings, photos, whistles, and membership gear for *Radio Orphan Annie's Secret Society*. Premiums during the Puffed Wheat years included membership in the Secret Guard and the Safety Guard, along with aviation-related items.

A string of artists and writers continued the Annie comic strip after Gray's death, with little success, and in 1974 the strip was replaced by reprints of the original strip. Comic books, hardcover reprints of the newspaper strips, and giveaway books proliferated from 1926 through the 1940s.

Two movies added to the legend: the 1932 *Little Orphan Annie* from RKO and the 1982 *Annie* from

Columbia Pictures, the latter based on the successful 1977 Broadway musical. In 1995 an animated series, *Annie & the Tomorrow Team*, was announced by Tribune Media Services.

LAN-1

LAN-2

LAN-3

LAN-1. "Little Orphan Annie/Her Story By Harold Gray" Convention Booklet,
1927. Chicago Tribune Newspaper Syndicate. 32 pages of "Her Adventures To Date" given away at convention of American Newspapers Publishers Association. - **$75 $175 $350**

LAN-2. "Some Swell Sweater" Cello. Button,
1928. Given with sweater purchase. - **$25 $75 $150**

LAN-3. Song Sheet Giveaway,
1928. Scarce. Chicago Tribune. - **$50 $100 $200**

LAN-4

LAN-5

LAN-4. "Little Orphan Annie Candy Bar" Ad,
1931. Monthly issue for September of "The Northwestern Confectioner" trade magazine for candy makers and retailers with cover art introducing new candy bar by Shotwell Mfg. Co., Chicago. - **$50 $100 $200**

LAN-5. "Little Orphan Annie" Candy Bar Wrapper,
1931. Waxed paper cover for product of Shotwell Mfg. Co. also offering Orphan Annie doll and coloring book as mail premiums. - **$60 $125 $225**

LAN-6

LAN-6. "Little Orphan Annie's Song" Sheet Music,
1931. Probably 1st Ovaltine Annie premium.
Near Mint in Mailer - **$175**
Letter Only - **$25 $50 $100**
Music Only - **$15 $25 $50**

LAN-7

LAN-8

HERE'S YOUR VOTERS BUTTON

FOR YOU TO WEAR

Showing That You Like
JOE CORNTASSEL'S WAY
Of Making
ICE COLD OVALTINE BEST
LAN-9

LAN-10

LAN-7. "Orphan Annie" Cello. Button,
1931. Scarce. Known as Voter's Button issued as companion pair with Joe Corntassel version, awarded respectively for vote preferring Ovaltine with ice or Ovaltine with ice cream. - **$200 $400 $800**

LAN-8. "Joe Corntassel" Cello. Button,
1931. Known as Voter's Button with companion Orphan Annie button issued respectively for voters preferring Ovaltine with ice cream or simply ice. - **$100 $250 $500**

LAN-9. Joe Corntassel "Voters Button" Card,
1931. Also issued for Annie. Each - **$40 $100 $175**

LAN-10. Beetleware Shake-Up Mug,
1931. - **$20 $40 $75**

LAN-11

LAN-11. "Shake-Up Game" Instruction Folder,
1931. Came with Shake-Up mug. - **$20 $40 $60**

LAN-12

NEW PENN THEATRE
LAN-13

LAN-12. Ceramic Mug,
1932. - **$25 $50 $75**

LAN-13. "Mitzi Green As Little Orphan Annie" Movie Photo,
1932. Imprinted for local theaters. - **$25 $60 $100**

LAN-14   LAN-15

LAN-14. "Shirley Bell" Radio Show Photo,
1932. Pictured is Radio Orphan Annie portrayer. -
$20 $45 $60

LAN-15. "Joe Corntassel/Allan Baruck" Radio Show Photo,
1932. - **$15 $35 $50**

LAN-16

LAN-16. "Tucker County Fair" Jigsaw Puzzle With Mailer Box,
1933. Near Mint In Mailer - **$100**
Loose - **$25 $50 $75**

LAN-17   LAN-18

LAN-17. Paper Face Mask,
1933. - **$20 $50 $65**

LAN-18. Beetleware Plastic Cup,
1933. - **$15 $25 $50**

LAN-19

LAN-19. "Treasure Hunt" Game With Paper Boats,
1933. With Four Sailboats. Brown & yellow cover variations. Set - **$60 $125 $250**
Board Only - **$20 $30 $75**
Mailer - **$20 $40 $60**

LAN-21

LAN-20   LAN-22

LAN-20. "Secret Society" Manual,
1934. - **$20 $40 $75**

LAN-21. Secret Society Bronze Badge,
1934. - **$10 $15 $25**

LAN-22. Bandanna Ring Slide Offer Sheet,
1934. "Face" ring also used as bandanna holder. -
$20 $50 $80

LAN-23

LAN-24   LAN-25

LAN-23. Annie Portrait Ring and Bandanna Slide,
1934. - **$50 $75 $100**

LAN-24. "Flying W" Bandanna,
1934. - **$20 $50 $75**

LAN-25. "Flying W" Bandanna Explanation Card,
1934. Explains the 26 brands pictured on bandanna. -
$25 $50 $75

LAN-26

LAN-26. "Identification Bureau" Bracelet With Mailer Envelope,
1934. Silver finish, personalized with initial.
Near Mint In Mailer - **$160**
Bracelet Only - **$20 $50 $75**

LAN-27   LAN-28

LAN-29

LAN-27. "Good Luck" Brass Medal,
1934. Includes "Ovaltine 3 Times A Day" with back "Good Luck" in several languages. - **$10 $20 $35**

LAN-28. Silver Star Club Badge,
1934. Silvered brass. - **$15 $30 $45**

LAN-29. "Silver Star Member" Manual,
1934. Near Mint In Mailer - **$85**
Loose - **$20 $40 $60**

LAN-30

LAN-30. Adventure Books & Contest Winner Sheet,
1934. One side lists winners of "Shake-Up Naming Contest". - **$15 $30 $50**

LAN-31 **LAN-32** **LAN-33**

LAN-31. Pronunciation Card For "Good Luck" Medal,
1934. Offers correct phonetic pronunciation for each of the seven foreign language "Good Luck" inscriptions on medal reverse. Slotted to hold medal. - **$20 $40 $75**
Medal Only - **$10 $20 $35**

LAN-32. Club Manual,
1935. - **$25 $60 $100**

LAN-33. Brass Decoder,
1935. Silver flashing often worn off outer rim. - **$15 $35 $125**

LAN-34

LAN-34. Premium Catalogue Folder With Envelope,
1935. Opens to 4x22" with May 15 expiration date, envelope has NRA symbol of Depression era.
Near Mint In Mailer - **$325**
Folder - **$75 $150 $275**

LAN-35 **LAN-36** **LAN-37**

LAN-35. Beetleware Cup,
1935. Green circle background. - **$15 $30 $75**

LAN-36. Beetleware Plastic Shake-Up Mug,
1935. Orange lid. Shows Annie from waist up. - **$25 $50 $80**

LAN-37. Ovaltine Apology Postcard,
1935. Form message for delay in shipment of Orphan Annie Identification Disk postmarked January 5. - **$25 $50 $75**

LAN-38 **LAN-39**

LAN-38. Magic Transfers and Instruction Sheet,
1935 Scarce. - **$50 $150 $210**

LAN-39. Club Manual,
1936. - **$15 $30 $65**

LAN-40 **LAN-41** **LAN-42**

LAN-40. Secret Compartment Brass Decoder,
1936. - **$15 $25 $85**

LAN-41. Dog-Naming Contest Notice,
1936. Thank you notice for entering contest to name Bob Bond's new dog. - **$10 $25 $50**

LAN-42. "Book About Dogs",
1936. Contents include Annie characters in various activities plus photo descriptions of various dog breeds. - **$15 $30 $65**

LAN-44

LAN-43

LAN-43. "Silver Star Member" Secrets Folder,
1936. For Silver Star Ring, shown on cover. -
$25 $50 $75

LAN-44. Silver Star Ring,
1936. Silvered brass design of crossed keys over star. -
$200 $325 $450

LAN-45

LAN-45. "Birthday Ring" With Folder And Envelope,
1936. Birthstones in various colors. Offer appeared
October, 1935. Near Mint In Mailer - **$500**
Ring - **$125 $260 $400**
Folder - **$50 $55 $60**

LAN-46

**LAN-46. "Welcome To Simmons Corners" 19x24"
Paper Map,**
1936. - **$25 $75 $125**

LAN-47

LAN-48

LAN-47. "Little Orphan Annie Circus" Punch-Out Book,
1936. Six pages including more than 30 punch-outs.
Unpunched - **$150 $300 $500**

LAN-48. Glassips Package In Mailer,
1936. Rare. Contents are cellophane drinking straws. -
$100 $300 $425

LAN-49

**LAN-49. Club Manual with Mailer and Silver Star Ring
Order Form,**
1937. Manual - **$20 $35 $60**
Other Items - **$5 $10 $20**

LAN-52

LAN-50

LAN-51

LAN-50. Sunburst Brass Decoder Badge,
1937. - **$15 $50 $125**

**LAN-51. "Silver Star Members" Folder With Mailer
Envelope,**
1937. Includes code for Silver Star Ring.
Folder - **$65 $140 $225**
Envelope - **$10 $20 $30**

LAN-52. Silver Star Member Secret Message Ring,
1937. Silvered brass with coded message to be decoded
by that year's decoder. - **$150 $225 $300**

LAN-53

LAN-54

LAN-53. Two Initial Signet Brass Ring,
1937. Ring was customized with recipient's initials. -
$50 $75 $100

LAN-54. Foreign "Coin Collection" Folder,
1937. - **$15 $30 $50**

LAN-55

LAN-55. "Talking Stationery",
1937. Diecut paper mouths open and close, came with 12 letter sheets and envelopes. Near Mint Complete - **$250** Each Sheet - **$5 $10 $15**

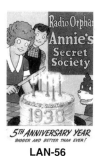

LAN-57

LAN-56

LAN-58

LAN-56. Club Manual,
1938. - **$20 $50 $75**

LAN-57. Telematic Brass Decoder Badge,
1938. - **$25 $60 $110**

LAN-58. Silver Star Manual,
1938. - **$90 $300 $400**

LAN-59

LAN-60

LAN-61

LAN-59. Silver Star Triple Mystery Secret Compartment Ring,
1938. Silvered brass with removable cap covering member's serial number. - **$300 $600 $1200**

LAN-60. Miracle Compass Sun-Watch,
1938. - **$20 $50 $100**

LAN-61. School Brass Badge,
1938. Customized with two initials. - **$15 $50 $75**

LAN-62

LAN-63

LAN-62. Beetleware Shake-Up Mug,
1938. Light blue with orange top, dancing scene. - **$35 $80 $175**

LAN-63. "Little Orphan Annie Gets Into Trouble" Booklet,
1938. J. C. Penney Co. - **$12 $25 $40**

LAN-64

LAN-64. "Snow White And The Seven Dwarfs Cut-Out Book" With Envelope ,
1938. Scarce. Ovaltine as Radio Orphan Annie premium, also store item. Published by Whitman with six punch-out sheets. Near Mint In Mailer - **$650**
No Mailer, Unpunched - **$150 $400 $500**

LAN-65

LAN-66

LAN-65. Silver Plated Foto-Frame,
1938. Scarce. Metal base inscribed on front "To My Best Friend". - **$100 $250 $400**

LAN-66. "Shadowettes" Mechanical Paper Portraits,
1938. Set of six. Sandy, Annie, Warbucks, Joe Corntassel, Mr. Silo, Mrs. Silo. Near Mint In Mailer - **$300**
Each Assembled - **$10 $20 $35**

LAN-67

LAN-67. "Snow White And The Seven Dwarfs Paperdolls" Book With Envelope And Replacement Notice Slip,
1938. Ovaltine Orphan Annie premium letter reads "even more expensive book" with full color cover sent as replacement due to depleted supply of lesser quality book originally offered as Christmas premium. Originally offered version had blue and yellow cover. Enclosed replacement slip explains details. Doll book is copyright Walt Disney Enterprises, 1938. Christmas Insert - **$25 $50 $100**
Unpunched Book - **$300 $750 $1000**
Mailer - **$50 $100 $150**

LAN-68

LAN-69

LAN-75

LAN-76

LAN-70

LAN-68. Ann Gillis Photo,
c. 1938. Little Orphan Annie radio portrayer of late 1930s. -
$20 $55 $75

LAN-69. Manual with Mailer,
1939. Manual - **$20 $40 $75**
Mailer - **$5 $10 $20**

LAN-70. Mysto-Matic Brass Decoder Badge,
1939. - **$25 $50 $100**

LAN-75. Mystic-Eye Detective (Look-Around) Ring,
1939. Brass ring with American eagle cover cap over look-
in mirror. Also issued for Captain Midnight and The Lone
Ranger. - **$75 $115 $150**

**LAN-76. "Mystic-Eye Detective Ring" Instruction
Sheet,**
1939. - **$15 $30 $60**

LAN-78

LAN-71

LAN-72

LAN-77

LAN-71. "Goofy Gazette" First Issue,
1939. Ovaltine. Vol. 1 #1 issue of eight-page newspaper
including information on two contests closing June 15. -
$40 $80 $125

**LAN-72. Greater Boston Community Fund Campaign
13x22" Cardboard Poster,**
1939. Orphan Annie and Sandy art by Harold Gray. -
$40 $80 $150

**LAN-77. "Initial Identification Disc And Chain" Order
Sheet,**
1939. Back explains how Identification Bureau works
above order coupon. Brass finish. - **$20 $40 $60**

LAN-78. Identification Bracelet,
1939. Brass version with American flag in bow design, personalized by single initial designated by orderer. -
$25 $50 $85

LAN-79

LAN-80

LAN-73

LAN-74

LAN-79. Beetleware Plastic Shake-Up Mug,
1939. Brown mug with orange lid. - **$50 $100 $175**

LAN-73. Code Captain Secret Compartment Badge,
1939. Silvered finish. Sometimes found with link chain on
back to fasten to that year's decoder badge. -
$35 $80 $120

LAN-74. "Code Captain Secrets" Folder,
1939. - **$50 $85 $175**

**LAN-80. "Goofy Gazette" Newspaper #3 With
Envelope,**
1939. Last of three issues. Newspaper - **$35 $60 $100**
Mailer - **$5 $15 $25**

LAN-81

LAN-81. "Goofy Circus" Punch-Out Kit With Mailer Envelope,
1939. Mailer - **$15** **$50** **$60**
Unpunched - **$200** **$350** **$700**

LAN-83

LAN-84

LAN-82

LAN-82. Little Orphan Annie Oilcloth Doll,
1930s. Premium, unknown sponsor. - **$100** **$200** **$300**

LAN-83. Sandy Oilcloth Doll,
1930s. Premium, unknown sponsor. - **$75** **$150** **$225**

LAN-84. Cello. Button,
1930s. Cunningham Ice Cream. - **$75** **$125** **$200**

LAN-86

LAN-87

LAN-85

LAN-85. Heart's Desire Dress Clip,
1930s. Ovaltine. Offered as Orphan Annie unmarked premium with her name on order form of "Costume Jewelry Gifts" Ovaltine folder. Also issued by radio show "Girl Alone/Patricia Roberts" on a pink card. See LAN-133. - **$100** **$250** **$400**

LAN-86. "Pittsburgh Post-Gazette" Newspaper Contest Cello. Button,
1930s. Part of a set showing other characters in the newspaper. - **$40** **$75** **$150**

LAN-87. "Funy Frostys Club" Cello. Button,
1930s. Two styles: "Member" in straight or curved type. - **$75** **$150** **$250**

LAN-88

LAN-89

LAN-88. "Funy Frostys" Waxed Paper Wrapper,
1930s. Funy Frostys Ice Cream. Bottom has cardboard finger hole card for holding ice confection bar. - **$25** **$50** **$80**

LAN-89. "Sunshine Biscuits" Box,
1930s. Loose-Wiles Biscuit Co. - **$100** **$300** **$400**

LAN-90

LAN-91

LAN-92

LAN-90. "Word Building Contest" Acknowledgement Letter,
1930s. Response to entrant in contest to see how many different words can be made from single word Ovaltine plus Christmas greeting from Shirley Bell, ROA portrayer. - **$20** **$50** **$90**

LAN-91. "Los Angeles Evening Express" Cello. Button,
1930s. From set of newspaper characters, match number to win prize. - **$30** **$50** **$75**

LAN-92. Bisque Toothbrush Holder,
1930s. Store item. - **$60** **$90** **$175**

LAN-94

LAN-93

LAN-95

LAN-93. Club Manual,
1940. - **$50** **$80** **$150**

LAN-94. Speed-O-Matic Brass Decoder Badge,
1940. - **$30** **$60** **$125**

LAN-95. Beetleware Plastic Shake-Up Mug,
1940. Green with red lid. - **$40** **$80** **$150**

LAN-96

LAN-98

LAN-97

LAN-96. Shake-Up Mug Leaflet,
1940. Came with green mug. - **$25 $50 $75**

LAN-97. Sandy 3-Way Dog Whistle,
1940. 3-1/4" brass tube whistle that extends to 5-1/4"
length. - **$20 $35 $75**

LAN-98. "3 Way Mystery Dog-Whistle" Instruction Leaflet,
1940. - **$20 $30 $50**

LAN-99

LAN-100

LAN-101

LAN-99. Metal Puzzle,
1940. Four metal ball puzzle tin. Store bought. -
$30 $90 $150

LAN-100. "Code Captain" Brass Buckle With Fabric Belt,
1940. Complete - **$100 $225 $350**
Buckle Only - **$50 $125 $200**

LAN-101. Card,
1940. Card premium from the radio show. "How to Become a Code Captain." - **$20 $40 $80**

LAN-102

LAN-103

LAN-102. "Slidomatic Radio Decoder",
1941. Quaker Cereals. Cardboard slide with instructions on back. - **$25 $60 $100**

LAN-103. "Safety Guard" Application Blank for Captain's Commission,
1941. Quaker Cereals. Also see item LAN-116. -
$10 $20 $35

LAN-104

LAN-105

LAN-104. Secret Guard Double-Sided Sign,
1941. - **$500 $750 $1100**

LAN-105. Club Manual,
1941. Quaker Cereals. - **$60 $175 $250**

LAN-106

LAN-106. Quaker Rice Sparkies Shipping Carton,
c. 1941. 11x16x25" long corrugated cardboard box originally holding 24 boxes of cereal plus 12 comic books. -
$75 $150 $250

LAN-107

LAN-108

LAN-107. Secret Guard Mysto-Snapper,
1941. Quaker Cereals. Litho. tin clicker. - **$25 $75 $110**

LAN-108. "Captain's Secrets" Folder Manual,
1941. Quaker Sparkies. - **$50 $175 $300**

LAN-109

LAN-109. Secret Guard Member Letter With Quaker Cereal Leaflet,
1941. Both explain "Vitamin Rain" additives to Quaker cereals. Each - **$10 $20 $35**

LAN-110   LAN-111

LAN-110. Secret Guard Wood Handle Rubber Stamp With Mailer,
1941. Rare. Quaker Cereals.
Stamp Only - **$150 $300 $400**
Mailer - **$50 $100 $200**

LAN-111. Brass Slide Dog Whistle,
1941. Scarce. Quaker Cereals. End has Orphan Annie head. - **$100 $200 $300**

LAN-112

LAN-112. "The Adventures Of Little Orphan Annie" Comic Book,
1941. Quaker Puffed Wheat & Rice Sparkies. "...Kidnappers/Magic Morro..." stories. - **$15 $40 $100**

LAN-113   LAN-114

LAN-113. "The Adventures Of Little Orphan Annie" Comic Book,
1941. Quaker Puffed Wheat & Rice Sparkies. "...Rescue/Magic Morro..." stories. - **$15 $40 $100**

LAN-114. Quaker "How To Fly" Manual,
1941. - **$30 $75 $125**

LAN-115

LAN-115. "Captain Sparks Airplane Cockpit" Cardboard Assembly Kit,
1941. Quaker Cereals. 6x27" assembled with him pictured at center. Unassembled - **$150 $300 $500**
Assembled - **$100 $225 $350**

LAN-116   LAN-117   LAN-118

LAN-116. "SG/Captain" Glow-In-Dark Plastic Badge,
1941. Quaker Cereals. Also see item LAN-103. - **$65 $250 $400**

LAN-117. Secret Guard Magnifying Ring,
1941. Quaker Cereals. Offered briefly in 1941 with 8/31/41 expiration date "before Orphan Annie comes back on the air next Fall". - **$500 $1200 $3000**

LAN-118. "SG" Secret Guard Brass Ring,
1941. Scarce. Quaker Cereals. Also inscribed "Bravery/Health/Justice" and personalized with initial. - **$750 $1500 $4000**

LAN-119

LAN-119. "S.G." Secret Guard 3" Metal Flashlight,
1941. Scarce. Quaker Cereals. - **$100 $175 $250**

LAN-120

LAN-120. "Little Orphan Annie Scribbler" Canadian Booklet,
1941. Quaker Puffed Wheat And Puffed Rice. Canadian issue. - **$35 $60 $100**

LAN-121

LAN-121. Captain Sparks Box Cut-Outs,
c. 1941. Quaker Sparkies cereal. From "Home Defense Series" set of 12. Each Panel Cut-Out - **$5 $10 $15**

LAN-122

LAN-122. "Safety Guard" Membership Kit,
1942. Quaker Cereals. Included tin whistle not shown (see item LAN-123). Set Near Mint - **$600**
Decoder - **$50 $100 $150**
Whistle - **$20 $40 $75**
Handbook - **$60 $150 $300**

LAN-123

LAN-124

LAN-123. "Safety Guard" Captain Application Blank,
1942. Quaker Cereals. Also see item LAN-128. -
$10 $20 $35

LAN-124. "Safety Guard" Tri-Tone Signaler Badge,
1942. Quaker Cereals. Litho. tin whistle from member's kit (see item LAN-122). - **$20 $40 $75**

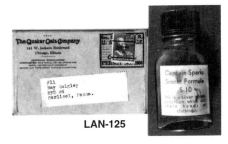

LAN-125

LAN-125. Quaker "Detector-Kit" With Mailer Box,
1942. Many items for photo printing, "Captain Sparks Secret Formula S-10" on bottle label.
Boxed - **$100 $150 $300**

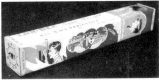

LAN-126

LAN-126. "3 In 1 Periscope",
1942. Scarce. Quaker Cereals. No Annie name but offered in 1942 Safety Guard handbook. - **$60 $200 $300**

(OPEN)   LAN-127   (CLOSED)

LAN-127. Altascope Ring,
1942. Rare. Quaker Cereals. Several moveable brass plates for sighting airplanes and estimating their altitudes. -
$3000 $8000 $21250

LAN-128   LAN-129

LAN-130

LAN-128. "SG Captain" Safety Guard Magic Glow Bird Badge,
1942. Rare. Quaker Cereals. Also see item LAN-123. -
$150 $400 $850

LAN-129. "SG Captain" Glow-In-Dark Canadian Club Brass Badge,
1942. Rare. Quaker Cereals. Design includes Canadian maple leaf symbol. - **$150 $350 $600**

LAN-130. "Super Book Of Comics-Little Orphan Annie",
c. 1943. Pan-Am gasoline. Book #7 from numbered series featuring various characters. - **$15 $30 $75**

LAN-131   LAN-132

LAN-131. "Super-Book Of Comics Featuring Little Orphan Annie",
1946. Omar Bread. Book #23 from numbered series featuring various characters. - **$12 $20 $45**

LAN-132. Quaker Puffed Wheat Comic Book,
1947. - **$2 $4 $8**

LAN-133

LAN-139

LAN-140

LAN-133. "Beautiful Costume Jewelry Gifts" Folder,
1930s. Annie name on order coupon. See LAN-85. -
$50 $125 $175

LAN-134

LAN-135

LAN-136

**LAN-134. "Orphan Annie's Parents Smoked" Litho.
Tin Tab,**
1968. "Truth About Smoking" group. - **$10 $20 $40**

LAN-135. Plastic Cup,
1980. Ovaltine. - **$15 $25 $40**

LAN-136. Ceramic Anniversary Mug,
1981. Ovaltine. - **$10 $20 $30**

LAN-137

LAN-138

LAN-137. Movie Plastic Shake-Up Mug,
1982. Ovaltine. - **$10 $20 $30**

LAN-138. Plastic 50-Year Anniversary Shake-Up Mug,
1982. Ovaltine. - **$15 $30 $60**

LAN-139. "Annie" Cloth Doll With Order Form,
1982. Ivory, Zest, Camay soaps and others. Offered April
15 to September 30. Doll - **$5 $10 $25**
Order Form - **$2 $4 $6**

**LAN-140. "In Person At Kennedy Center" Litho.
Button,**
1980s. Related to stage play. - **$10 $20 $35**

LITTLE PINKIES

A series of product insert buttons made by Whitehead
& Hoag around 1896 featured cartoon drawings of
Little Pinkies in various guises. Including varieties, the
set totals 21: The Actor, The Bad Boy, The Ball Player
(with and without a period), the Boot Black, Boy
Orator, The Clown, The Colonel, The Drum Major, The
Dude, The Dunce, The Fireman, Greenie, Just Landed,
The Letter Carrier, The News Boy, The Policeman, The
Sailor, The Soldier (with sabre or with toy sword), and
Uncle Sam. The buttons are usually found with back
papers for American Pepsin gum, sometimes for Old
Gold cigarettes or Whitehead & Hoag. Nothing else is
known about Little Pinkies. They seem to be the
briefly popular creation of an unknown Whitehead &
Hoag staff artist, possibly inspired by Palmer Cox's
Brownie characters.

LPS-1

LPS-1. Little Pinkies Button Set,
1896. American Pepsin Gum or less frequently Old Gold
Cigarettes. Each - **$5 $10 $15**

THE LONE RANGER

The legend of the Lone Ranger was born on Detroit radio station WXYZ in January 1933, the product of station owner George W. Trendle and writer Fran Striker. The program was a success from the start, and within a year was also being heard on WGN in Chicago and WOR in New York--in effect forming the nucleus of the new Mutual network. By 1937, "Hi-Yo Silver!" was echoing nationwide. Initially sustained by the station, the program was sponsored by Silver Cup bread starting in November 1933. Bond bread took over as sponsor in 1939 except in the Southeast states, where Merita bread retained its franchise. General Mills became the sponsor in 1941, tying the masked rider to such cereals as Kix and Wheaties until the radio series went off the air in 1955. Cheerios sponsored rebroadcasts until 1956, ending some 23 years and over 3,000 episodes of Western radio thrills and adventure.

Jack Deeds was the first actor to play the Lone Ranger, followed within weeks by George Seaton, and then in May 1933 by Earl Graser, who kept the role until his death in 1941. Probably best remembered is Brace Beemer, who played the part from 1941 to 1955.

On television, the Lone Ranger rode for more than 30 years on the networks and in syndication. The series, sponsored by General Mills (and Merita bread), premiered on ABC in 1949 and aired in prime time until 1957. Reruns were shown on all three networks: CBS (1953-1960 and 1966-1969), ABC (1957-1961 and 1965), and NBC (1960-1961). Syndication began in 1961. Clayton Moore played the lead for most of the series (John Hart covered the years 1952-1954) and Jay Silverheels, a Mohawk Indian, was Tonto, his faithful companion.

Republic Pictures released two 15-episode chapter plays; *The Lone Ranger* (1938), with Lee Powell as the lead, and *The Lone Ranger Rides Again* (1939), with Robert Livingston. Wrather Productions made three full-length films, *The Lone Ranger* (1955) and *The Lone Ranger and the Lost City of Gold* (1958), both with Clayton Moore and Jay Silverheels, and *The Legend of the Lone Ranger* (1981), with Klinton Spilsbury and Michael Horse.

A Saturday morning animated Lone Ranger series aired on CBS from 1966 to 1969, with the Ranger and Tonto battling mad scientists as well as conventional Western villains. The animated defenders of law and order surfaced again on CBS in 1980-1981 as part of *The Tarzan/Lone Ranger Adventure Hour*.

A Sunday comic strip distributed by King Features appeared from 1938 to 1971 and was revived from 1981 to 1984--one of the longest running of the Western strips. Comic books, including giveaways, novels, coloring books, photo albums, and scrapbooks appeared in great numbers from the 1940s on.

It would be hard to overestimate the number of items licensed and merchandised in the name of the Lone Ranger, especially during the years the program ruled the air on radio and television. Items may be copy-righted by Lone Ranger Inc., Lone Ranger Television Inc., or, starting in 1954, Wrather Corp.

LON-1

LON-2

LON-1. Photo,
1933. First premium photo for the Lone Ranger Show. Shows Lone Ranger on Silver with head tilted down. Michigan Radio Network printed on left and signed bottom right. - **$50 $75 $100**

LON-2. Photo On Horse,
1934. Early Silvercup radio premium.- **$25 $35 $60**

LON-3

LON-3. Silvercup Bread "Chief Scout" Qualification Cards Set,
1934. Scarce. Fifth card (shown first) came with "Chief Scout" brass badge, others denoted "Degree" rank advancements to the badge.
1st - **$30 $80 $125**
2nd - **$30 $80 $125**
3rd - **$40 $90 $160**
4th - **$50 $100 $200**
5th - **$60 $110 $250**

LON-4

LON-5

LON-4. Silvercup Bread Safety Club Folder,
c. 1934. - **$50 $125 $200**

LON-5. Radio Sponsorship Brochure Opens To 19x25",
c. 1934. Silvercup Bread. - **$50 $100 $150**

LON-6   LON-7

LON-8

LON-12

LON-13

LON-6. Safety Scout Member's Badge,
1934. Silvercup Bread. - **$10 $20 $50**

LON-7. Silvercup Bread "Chief Scout" Enameled Brass Badge,
1934. Also inscribed "Lone Ranger Safety Scout/Silvercup". - **$100 $225 $350**

LON-8. "Oke Tonto" Photo Card,
1934. Various bread company radio sponsors. - **$15 $25 $50**

LON-12. "How The Lone Ranger Captured Silver" Booklet, 1936. Silvercup Bread. - **$25 $60 $100**

LON-13. "Lone Ranger Safety Sentinel" Brass Badge, 1936 Miami Maid Dread. - **$60 $150 $250**

LON-14

LON-9

LON-10

LON-14. "Lone Ranger Target Game",
1936. Morton's Salt. Punch-out cardboard parts include gun and six targets. Near Mint Unpunched - **$400**
Loose - **$100 $200 $300**

LON-9. Safety Scout Badge Mailer,
1935. Silvercup Safety Scout premium. Rare.-
$50 $75 $100

LON-10. Scout Badge Offer Card With Pledge,
1935. Silvercup Bread radio premium.- **$35 $70 $100**

LON-15

LON-16

LON-15. Silvercup Bread Picture,
1936. - **$12 $20 $30**

LON-16. Cobakco Bread Story Booklet,
c. 1936. "How The Lone Ranger Captured Silver" seven-page story collected over seven weeks. - **$60 $125 $200**

LON-11

LON-17

LON-18

LON-11. Campfire Photo,
1935. Tonto and Lone Ranger at campfire with horses in background. - **$25 $50 $75**

LON-17. "The Lone Ranger Magazine" Vol. 1 #1,
1937. Trojan Publishing Corp., Chicago. -
$100 $250 $450

LON-18. Silvercup Lone Ranger Personalized Letter,
1937. Silvercup Bread. Response from Gordon Baking Co. to youngster who adopted kitten and wished Lone Ranger to know of it. - **$25 $60 $90**

LON-19

LON-20

LON-21

LON-19. "Republic Picture" Horseshoe Enameled Brass Badge,
1938. - **$40 $75 $125**

LON-20. "V-Bev Lone Ranger News" First Issue,
1938. V-Bev soda beverage. - **$60 $125 $200**

LON-21. Safety Club Membership Card,
1938. Cobakco Bread. Back has code alphabet. - **$100 $200 $300**

LON-22

LON-23

LON-24

LON-22. Merita "Lone Ranger Salesmen's Club" Badge,
c. 1938. Merita Bread. White enamel and silvered brass. - **$75 $150 $200**

LON-23. Gately's Enameled Brass Star Badge,
c. 1938. Gately's Bread. - **$35 $75 $125**

LON-24. Master Bread Enameled Brass Star Badge,
c. 1938. - **$35 $75 $125**

LON-25

LON-26

LON-25. Republic Serial Club Brass Badge,
1938. Republic Pictures. Badges are serially numbered. - **$40 $75 $125**

LON-26. Movie Discount Card,
1938. Republic Pictures. Admits child for 5 cents to Saturday matinee. - **$40 $75 $100**

LON-27

LON-28

LON-29

LON-27. Strong Box Bank,
1938. Sun Life Insurance. - **$40 $80 $160**

LON-28. Bat-O-Ball,
1938. Scarce. Pure Oil premium. WOR Radio. - **$30 $60 $120**

LON-29. Bond Bread Promo,
1938. Scarce. WOR Radio. - **$30 $60 $120**

LON-30

LON-31

LON-32

LON-33

LON-34

LON-30. Glass,
1938. - **$20 $50 $100**

LON-31. Republic Serial Promo,
1938. Scarce. 15 episodes. - **$40 $85 $150**

LON-32. Detroit Sunday Times Comic Strip Announcement,
1938. Strip began September 11. - **$20 $40 $75**

LON-33. Star Badge Used On Large Composition Doll,
1938. Rare. Dollcraft Novelty Doll Co. - **$25 $60 $150**

LON-34. Radio WOR Promo,
1938. - **$20 $40 $60**

LON-35

LON-36

LON-41

LON-42

LON-43

LON-35. Composition/Cloth Doll With Fabric Outfit,
1938. Store item as well as premium. 16" tall.
Lone Ranger - **$500 $1000 $1800**
Matching Tonto - **$400 $800 $1600**

LON-36. Sign for Lone Ranger Gun Offer,
1938. - $250 **$500 $750**

LON-41. Sheet Music - Hi Yo Silver
1938.Six pages. Store bought. - **$15 $40 $75**

LON-42. Bread Wrapper,
1938. Blue Ribbon Bread. Very colorful wrapper.-
$30 $60 $90

LON-43. High Gloss Photo,
1938. Shown on horse with name at bottom right. Blank
back. - **$25 $50 $75**

LON-38

LON-37

LON-44

LON-37. Safety Scouts Letter,
1938. Silvercup Bread premium.
Mailer - **$20 $30 $40**
Letter - **$25 $40 $60**

LON-38. Certificate/Pledge,
1938. Safety Club Bread premium. - **$50 $125 $250**

LON-44. Wright Bread Picture,
1938. - **$20 $40 $60**

LON-40

LON-39

LON-45

LON-39. Silvercup Bread Picture,
1938. - **$10 $20 $35**

LON-40. Cardboard Mask,
1938. Schultz Butter-Nut Bread and Dolly Madison
Cakes. - **$35 $75 $125**

LON-45. Ho-Ling Recipes Pamphlet and Letter,
1938. Silvercup Bread. Mailer also shown.
Pamphlet - **$30 $60 $90**
Letter - **$25 $50 $60**
Mailer - **$20 $30 $40**

LON-46

LON-46. "White Cross" First Aid Booklet,
1938. - **$25 $50 $100**

LON-47

LON-47. "Lone Ranger Safety Club" Membership Card,
1938. Merita Bread. - **$15 $50 $75**

LON-48

(CARD #1
WITHOUT
MASK)

(CARD #1
WITH
MASK)

LON-49

LON-48. Tin Litho. Wind-Up,
1938. Store item by Marx Toys.
"Silver" In White - **$100 $250 $400**
"Silver" In Silver - **$150 $300 $500**

LON-49. Gum Wrappers Mail Picture,
1938. Scarce. Lone Ranger Bubble Gum. Card #1 of five collected by sending wrappers. 8x10" size. Card #1 came with and without mask on Lone Ranger's face.
Card Without Mask - **$125 $250 $500**
Others - **$100 $200 $350**

LON-50   **LON-51**

LON-50. Bond Bread 9x13" Paper Poster,
1938. Scarce. Announces local radio broadcast times. - **$50 $110 $175**

LON-51. "Bond Bread Lone Ranger Safety Club" Enameled Brass Star Badge,
1938. - **$10 $25 $40**

LON-52

LON-53

LON-52. "Lone Ranger Cones" Paper Wrapper,
1938. Offers comic book, bracelet, Lone Ranger Ring, Tonto Ring with October 31, 1940 expiration date. - **$20 $50 $75**

LON-53. "Lone Ranger Cones" Matchbook,
1938. - **$10 $20 $40**

LON-54

LON-55

LON-54. Lone Ranger Ice Cream Cones Enameled/Silvered Metal Picture Bracelet,
1938. Rare. - **$300 $1000 $1500**

LON-55. Tonto Lucky Ring,
1938. Rare. Lone Ranger Ice Cream Cones. Green plastic to simulate onyx with paper portrait, also issued for Lone Ranger. Tonto - **$800 $1750 $3250**
Lone Ranger - **$1000 $2250 $4500**

LON-56

LON-57

LON-56. Blue Beanie With Red Trim,
1938. Rare. Lone Ranger Ice Cream Cones. - **$100 $200 $400**

LON-57. Silvercup Bread Photo,
c. 1938. - **$15 $30 $75**

LON-58 **LON-59** **LON-60**

LON-64 **LON-65** **LON-66**

LON-58. Cobakco Bread Picture Card,
c. 1938. - **$15 $30 $50**

LON-59. "Friend Of The Lone Ranger" Photo Card,
c. 1938. Cobaco Bread. Pictured is "Your Friend, U.S. Marshal" from radio series. - **$15 $30 $50**

LON-60. Cobakco Bread "Chuck Livingston" Picture Card,
c. 1938. Pictures "Outlaw On Lone Ranger Dramas". - **$15 $30 $50**

LON-64. Merita Bread Photo,
c. 1938. - **$20 $50 $75**

LON-65. "Dr. West's Tooth Paste" Cello. Club Button,
c. 1938. - **$35 $65 $110**

LON-66. "Silver's Lucky Horseshoe" Enameled Brass Badge,
c. 1938. Smaller 1-1/4" size. - **$20 $40 $75**

LON-61 **LON-62**

LON-67

LON-61. "Cobakco Safety Club" Enameled Brass Badge,
c. 1938. Cobakco Bread. - **$30 $60 $100**

LON-62. 7up Personalized Picture,
c. 1938. Black/white print personalized in white ink "To" recipient's first name. - **$15 $30 $50**

LON-67. "Lone Ranger/Hi-Yo Silver" Brass Good Luck Medal,
1938. Reverse design and inscription "Silver's Lucky Horseshoe". Sent in Detroit station WXYZ mailer with medal in rwb stiff card.
Near Mint Complete - **$200**
Card Only - **$25 $50 $100**
Medal Only - **$15 $25 $50**

LON-63

LON-68 **LON-69**

LON-63. Silvercup Bread 13x17" "Lone Ranger Hunt Map" With Envelope,
c. 1938. With Envelope - **$75 $150 $250**
Map Only - **$50 $100 $175**

LON-68. "Silver's Lucky Horseshoe" Enameled Brass Badge,
c. 1938. Larger 1-3/4" size. - **$20 $40 $75**

LON-69. "WFIL/Daily News Safety Club" Cello. Button,
c. 1938. Philadelphia radio station. - **$40 $75 $135**

LON-70   **LON-71**   **LON-72**

LON-70. "Lee Powell/Original Motion Picture" Cello. Button,
c. 1938. Scarce. Republic Pictures. -
$75 $175 $300

LON-71. "Supplee Lone Ranger Club" Enameled Brass Badge,
c. 1938. - **$35 $75 $125**

LON-72. Merita Enameled Brass Star Badge,
c. 1938. Merita Bread. - **$20 $50 $75**

LON-73   **LON-74**   **LON-75**

LON-73. "The Lone Ranger" Cello. Button,
c. 1938. Possibly Merita Bread Safety Club. -
$20 $50 $75

LON-74. Rath's Enameled Brass Star Badge,
c. 1938. Rath's Bread. - **$35 $75 $125**

LON-75. Bestyett Enameled Brass Star Badge,
c. 1938. Bestyett Bread. - **$35 $75 $125**

LON-76   **LON-77**   **LON-78**

LON-76. A. B. Poe Enameled Brass Star Badge,
c. 1938. Poe Bread. - **$35 $75 $125**

LON-77. "The Lone Ranger Radio Station" Cello. Button,
c. 1938. WCSC, Charleston, South Carolina. -
$20 $40 $75

LON-78. "Sunday Herald And Examiner" Litho. Button,
c. 1938. - **$15 $25 $40**

LON-79

LON-79. Movie Serial Ticket With Sears Offer,
c. 1938. Scarce. Ticket for 15-episode serial, reverse promotes cowboy suits at Sears, Roebuck. - **$50 $125 $200**

LON-80

LON-80. "The Lone Ranger Comic Book No. 1",
1939. Rare. Lone Ranger Ice Cream Cones. -
$800 $2400 $4000

LON-81

LON-81. "Ice Cream Cone Coupons" Envelope To Merchant,
1939. Lone Ranger Cones. Originally held 100 mail coupons expiring Jan. 1, 1940.
Envelope Only - **$25 $60 $100**
Each Coupon - **$1 $2 $4**

LON-82   **LON-83**   **LON-84**

LON-82. "Lone Ranger Cake Cones" Matchbook,
c. 1939. - **$10 $20 $40**

LON-83. "Lone Ranger Cones" Matchbook Cover,
c. 1939. Inscribed "Lone Ranger Ice Cream Cone Campaign." - **$10 $20 $40**

LON-84. "Lone Ranger Ice Cream Cones" Dealer Sheet,
1939. Reprinted ad from November issue of ice cream trade magazine for upcoming promotion in 1940. -
$25 $50 $75

LON-86

LON-85

LON-85. Safety Club Letter,
1939. Weber Bread premium. - **$70 $100 $125**

LON-86. Creed Postcard And Mailer,
1939. Weber Bread premium. Postcard is used to join club.- **$50 $95 $110**

LON-87

LON-88

LON-87. Post Card,
1939. Weber Bread. Back of postcard is an order form for 2 book covers. Radio premium.- **$25 $50 $75**

LON-88. Photo,
1939. Rare. Premium from New York World's Fair. Sponsored by Gimbel's Lone Ranger Show. - **$30 $75 $100**

LON-90

LON-89

LON-89. Bond Bread Safety Club "Lone Ranger Roundup" Vol. 1 #1 Newspaper,
August 1939. Rare. At least nine issues through Vol. 2 #3.
First Issue - **$50 $150 $200**
Other Issues - **$25 $100 $150**

LON-90. World's Fair Bond Bread Premium,
1939. Rolled penny. - **$20 $40 $60**

LON-92

LON-91

LON-93

LON-91. "Lone Ranger Secret Code" Cardboard Decoder,
1939. Dr. West's Toothpaste. Came boxed with two bottles of "Invisible Writing Ink" and "Ink Developer" plus cotton swab. Complete Boxed - **$125 $250 $450**
Decoder Only - **$75 $150 $300**

LON-92. Membership Card,
1939. Dr. West's Toothpaste. Came with club newsletter. - **$50 $100 $175**

LON-93. Membership Certificate,
1939. Dr. West's Toothpaste. Came with club newsletter. - **$65 $150 $250**

LON-94

LON-94. Dr. West's Lone Ranger News,
1939. Dr. West's Toothpaste. Vol.1 #1 newsletter with 8 pages. Back cover offers Secret Writing Set that includes cardboard "Official Lone Ranger Automatic Decoder." (See LON-91). - **$100 $200 $400**

LON-95

LON-95. Weber's Bread Club Manual,
1939. - **$50 $85 $175**

LON-96

LON-97

LON-96. Calendar,
1939. Cobakco Bread. - **$75 $150 $200**

LON-97. Pony Contest 11x14" Cardboard Poster,
c. 1939. Cobakco Bread. - **$50 $100 $200**

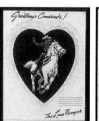

LON-98

LON-99

LON-100

LON-98. Merita Safety Club Radio Card,
1939. Merita Bakers. Card sent by WBT Radio, Charlotte, North Carolina. Code translates: "Be Sure To Obey My Ten Safety Rules Always And Remember That You Help To Make My Great Safety Drive Possible By Eating Merita Bread And Cakes. So Be Sure To Ask Mother To Always Buy Merita Products!" - **$60 $125 $200**

LON-99. Roundup Paper,
1939. Bond Bread. Vol. 1 #2. 8 pages.- **$25 $50 $75**

LON-100. Roundup Paper,
1939. Bond Bread. Vol. 1 #3. 8 pages.- **$25 $50 $75**

LON-101

LON-102

LON-101. Leather Watch Fob Holster With Miniature Gun,
1939. Came with some issues of New Haven pocketwatches. - **$35 $50 $100**

LON-102. Horlick's Malted Milk Picture,
1939. "Over Station WGN-Chicago". - **$15 $30 $50**

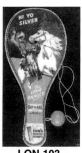

LON-103

LON-104

LON-103. "Bat-O-Ball" Toy,
1939. Scarce. Tom's Toasted Peanuts. Cardboard paddle with rubber band and ball. With Ball - **$40 $125 $175**
No Ball - **$20 $100 $150**

LON-104. Bond Bread Color Cellophane Picture Sheet,
c. 1939. 6x9" probably for window display. - **$35 $75 $125**

LON-105

LON-105. "Safety Club" Application Postcard,
1939. Bond Bread. - **$10 $35 $50**

LON-106

LON-106. "Bond Bread Safety Club" Letter And Membership Card,
1939. Card - **$15 $40 $80**
Letter - **$20 $50 $75**

LON-107

LON-108

LON-107. Bond Bread Contest Card Stub,
c. 1939. - **$15 $30 $65**

LON-108. May Co. Activity Booklet,
1939. May department store. Christmas issue. - **$35 $125 $200**

LON-109

LON-109. "Lapel Watch" Boxed Pocketwatch,
1939. Store item by New Haven Time Co. as well as premium. Near Mint Boxed - **$800**
Watch Only - **$100 $200 $400**

LON-110

LON-110. Bond Bread 8x12" Cardboard Store Sign,
1940. Scarce. - **$100 $200 $300**

LON-111

LON-111. "Cloverine Salve" Premium Catalogue With Watch Ads,
c. 1940. - **$10 $25 $40**

LON-112   LON-113

LON-112. "Hi-Yo Supplee Lone Rangers" Newsletter,
1940. Supplee Milk. First anniversary issue. -
$25 $50 $75

LON-113. "Orange Pops" 6x12" Cardboard Store Sign,
1940. Scarce. - **$100 $300 $500**

LON-114

LON-114. "Lone Ranger Posse" Club Papers,
c. 1940. Philadelphia Record. Letter and membership card
for comic strip promotion. Letter - **$20 $40 $60**
Card - **$25 $50 $75**

LON-115   LON-116

LON-115. Bond Bread Wrapper,
1940. - **$20 $40 $65**

LON-116. Color Photo,
c. 1940. Bond Bread. - **$15 $25 $50**

LON-117

LON-118

LON-117. Merita "The Life Of Tonto" Story Chapter,
1940. Merita Bread of American Bakeries Co. 11-chapter
newspaper ad/feature jointly sponsored by various radio
stations. Pictured example is Chapter 10 co-sponsored by
WDBJ, Roanoke, Virginia. Each - **$35 $65 $100**

LON-118. Roundup Paper,
1940. Bond Bread. Vol. 11 #3. 8 pages.- **$25 $50 $75**

LON-119

LON-120

LON-119. "Lone Ranger Cones" Paper Wrapper,
c. 1940. Offers same premiums as 1938 wrapper without
expiration date. - **$20 $50 $75**

**LON-120. Kix Cereal "Name Silver's Son" 16x20"
Contest Poster,**
1941. Rare. - **$1000 $2000 $3000**

LON-121

LON-121. Photo With Insert And Envelope,
1941. Came with insert announcing Kix as new radio sponsor. Complete - **$40 $80 $150**
Photo Only - **$10 $15 $30**

LON-122

LON-122. "National Defenders Secret Portfolio" Manual,
1941. - **$75 $150 $250**
Mailer - **$20 $40 $60**

LON-123

LON-124

LON-123. Glow-In-Dark Brooch 3" Plastic Pin,
1941. General Mills. Offered in the Lone Ranger National Defenders Portfolio from Kix cereal as "something for mother" along with matching earrings. Also offered on soap operas sponsored by General Mills and in the southeastern states as a Whistling Jim premium. Not associated with Jack Armstrong as previously believed.
Brooch - **$50 $100 $150**
Earring Set - **$60 $125 $175**

LON-124. "Silver Bullet Defender" Leaflet With 45-Caliber Silver Bullet,
1941. Contains silver ore. Bullet - **$20 $40 $75**
Folder - **$15 $35 $65**

LON-125

LON-125. Kix Luminous Blackout Plastic Belt,
1941. Near Mint Boxed With Insert Folder - **$200**
Belt Only - **$50 $75 $150**

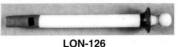

LON-126

LON-127

LON-126. National Defenders Danger-Warning Siren,
1941. Scarce. Came with carrying cord. Offered as bounce back premium with Gardenia Brooch. - **$200 $500 $1000**
Tube Mailer - **$20 $40 $60**

LON-127. National Defenders Look-Around Brass Ring,
1941. No inscription but offered in Lone Ranger premium advertisements. Also issued for Captain Midnight and Radio Orphan Annie. - **$75 $115 $150**

LON-129

LON-128

LON-128. "Danger-Warning Siren" Offer Ad,
1941. Kix Cereal. Sunday comics one-half page color ad offering premium as part of Lone Ranger National Defenders Club kit. - **$15 $30 $75**

LON-129. Safety Club Card,
1941. Rare. Felber Biscuit Co. Shows Silver, Lone Ranger, and Tonto on front. Secret code on back. - **$50 $75 $100**

LON-130

LON-130. Merita Safety Club Card,
1941 Merita Bakers. - **$20 $50 $75**

LON-132

LON-131

LON-131. Victory Bread Wrapper,
1942. Weber's White Bread. - **$20 $40 $60**

LON-132. Victory Corps Club Promo,
1942. - **$50 $100 $200**

LON-133

LON-139

LON-138

LON-133. "War Album Of Victory Battles" With Mailer Envelope,
1942. General Mills. No Lone Ranger mention but offered on radio show, came with battle scene stamps.
Complete With Mailer - **$35 $60 $100**
Complete Album - **$25 $40 $60**
Album No Stamps - **$10 $20 $30**

LON-138. Safety Club Letter,
1942. Merita Bread premium. - **$50 $75 $100**

LON-139. "Lone Ranger VC" Victory Corps Cello. Button,
1942. - **$30 $60 $100**

LON-134. Sailor Hat,
1942. - **$50 $75 $100**

LON-140

LON-141

LON-135

LON-136

LON-135. Military Hat with Metal Button,
1942. Rare. - **$100 $250 $400**

LON-136. "Lone Ranger Victory Corps" Brass Tab,
1942. - **$15 $30 $60**

LON-140. Kix Army Air Corps Ring,
1942. Interior ring photos of Lone Ranger and Silver often missing. Ring Complete - **$375 $590 $800**
Ring, No Photos - **$100 $210 $320**

LON-141. Secret Compartment Ring Instruction Paper,
1942. Leaflet opens to four panels with other Lone Ranger radio and club notes. - **$40 $75 $150**

LON-143

LON-142

LON-144

LON-137

LON-137. "Victory Corps" Membership Kit,
1942. Cheerios/Kix. Includes cover letter with membership/I.D. folder plus brass tab (see item LON-136).
Envelope - **$20 $50 $75**
Letter - **$15 $60 $100**
Member Card - **$15 $25 $50**
Folder - **$30 $85 $125**

LON-142. Marine Corps Brass Ring,
1942. Two inside photos of Lone Ranger and Silver often missing. Complete - **$400 $625 $900**
No Photos - **$110 $225 $340**

LON-143. Army Insignia Secret Compartment Brass Ring,
1942. Two inside photos of Lone Ranger and Silver often missing. Complete - **$400 $625 $900**
No Photos - **$110 $225 $340**

LON-144. "USN" Navy Photo Ring,
1942. Brass, two inside photos of Lone Ranger and Silver often missing. Complete - **$500 $800 $1200**
No Photos - **$135 $270 $400**

LON-146

LON-145

LON-145. Kix "Blackout Kit" With Envelope,
1942. Contents include luminous paper items.
Near Mint In Mailer - **$300**

LON-146. Meteorite Ring,
1942. Scarce. Kix bounce back offer with Lone Ranger military rings April, 1942. Company recorded 85 requests. Brass with plastic dome over tiny "meteorite" granules. Following General Mills (Kix) offer, also offered briefly by Kellogg's as Gold Ore ring. - **$1175 $2350 $5000**

LON-147 **LON-148**

LON-147. Merita Bread Standee,
1942. 10x17-1/2" diecut cardboard shown framed with Merita Club Member's Application.
Standee - **$500 $1000 $2000**
Application - **$25 $50 $75**

LON-148. Lone Ranger Safety Club Calendar And Membership Application Pad Holder,
1942. Merita Bread. 17x25". Boy shown wearing Lone Ranger Merita Bread Brass Club Badge. Example shown without application and calendar pads.
Complete - **$750 $1500 $2000**
Without Pads - **$500 $1000 $1500**

LON-150

LON-149. "Victory Corps" Postcard To Member,
1942. Acknowledgement to "Dear Ranger" thanking member for letter describing Victory Corps activities. Pictured example has reverse August 5 postmark from Minneapolis. - **$20 $40 $60**

LON-150. Merita "Tonto" Headband,
1942. Merita Bakers. Tonto name on one side and "Merita" on other side of fabric band holding insert feather. - **$50 $100 $150**

LON-151

LON-152

LON-151. "V" Toy Gun,
c. 1942. 7" composition play gun with "Lone Ranger" name on right side and "V" letter symbol on both sides, symbolizing Lone Ranger Victory Corps. - **$100 $200 $300**

LON-152. Merita Safety Club Card,
1943. Merita Bakers. - **$20 $50 $75**

LON-153

LON-153. Lone Ranger And Tonto Color Prints,
1943. Merita Bread. Each about 9x11" with artist's name Sheffield. Each - **$40 $75 $125**

LON-154

LON-155

LON-154. Weber's Decoder Folder,
1943. Rare. - **$100 $250 $350**

LON-155. Kix Decal Sheet,
1944. Set #5 sheet from series with water transfer decals of Lone Ranger and other western subjects. -
$15 $30 $50

LON-156

LON-156. "Kix Airbase" 27x27" Play Sheet Map With Envelope,
1945. No Lone Ranger inscription but offered on his show. Used with 32 warplane cut-outs from four Kix cereal boxes.
With Envelope - **$50 $100 $200**
No Envelope - **$25 $50 $100**

LON-157

LON-158

LON-157. Merita Safety Club Card,
1946. Merita Bakers. - **$15 $40 $65**

LON-158. Lone Ranger Safety Club Calendar And Membership Application Pad Holder,
1946. Merita Bread. 16-1/2x25-1/2" cardboard. Example shown without application and calendar pads.
Complete - **$750 $1500 $2000**
Without Pads - **$500 $1000 $1500**

LON-159

LON-160

LON-159. Weather Forecasting Ring,
1946. Brass with clear lucite cover over small litmus paper. - **$60 $90 $150**

LON-160. Merita Bread Portrait Picture,
1946. Artist signature appears to be Frederic Myer. Also issued as a calendar. Picture - **$100 $200 $400**
Calendar - **$300 $750 $1200**

LON-161

LON-161. Punch-Out Sheet,
1947. American Bakeries Co. - **$35 $75 $110**

LON-162

LON-163

LON-162. Atomic Bomb Ring,
1947. Kix cereal. Brass with plastic bomb cap. - **$50 $100 $200**

LON-163. "Atomic Bomb Ring" Newspaper Ad,
1947. Kix Cereal. 10x14" clipping from Sunday newspaper comic section. - **$10 $20 $40**

LON-164

LON-165

LON-164. Six-Gun Ring,
1947. Brass with plastic gun holding flint. - **$60 $110 $165**

LON-165. "Lone Ranger 6-Shooter Ring" 17x22" Store Poster,
1947. - **$75 $115 $150**

LON-166.
LON-167.

LON-166. "Lone Ranger .45" Secret Compartment Bullet,
1947. Aluminum with removable cap. - **$25 $50 $90**

LON-167. Merita Bread Safety Club Calendar,
1948. Rare. 16"x24". With calendar tablet pages and club application forms. - **$300 $750 $1600**
Smaller version without calendar - **$100 $200 $400**

LON-171.

LON-172.

LON-171. Flashlight Ring,
1948. Brass with lightbulb and battery. - **$25 $50 $100**

LON-172. "Flashlight Ring" Instruction Sheet,
1948. Cheerios. Reverse includes "Good Deed Order Blank" for friend. - **$50 $55 $60**

LON-168.

LON-169.

LON-168. Tonto Set Of Two Metal Bracelets,
1948. Scarce. No character name on the bracelets, each has Indian symbols. Complete With Mailer -
$50 $150 $225

LON-169. Gift Subscription Christmas Card With Envelope,
1948. Dell Comics. - **$15 $30 $60**

LON-173.

LON-174.

LON-173. Cheerios Aluminum Pedometer With Fabric Strap,
1948. Near Mint Boxed - **$75**
Loose - **$15 $30 $50**

LON-174. Lone Ranger/Gene Autry Flag Ring,
c. 1948. Dell Comics. Plastic with dome over flag image, for one-year subscription to comic book for either. -
$60 $100 $150

(MAP) **LON-170** (BUILDING SECTION)

LON-170. "Lone Ranger Frontier Town" Punch-Outs And Maps,
1948. Four separate maps and four separate unpunched Building sections.
Each Unpunched Section With Mailer - **$400**
Complete Punched Section - **$250**
Each Map - **$75 $125 $200**

LON-175.

LON-175. Merita Safety Club Card,
1948. Merita Bakers. Dark blue or dark green variations.
Either - **$15 $40 $65**

LON-176

LON-177

LON-181

LON-182

LON-176. Merita Bread Safety Club Large Color Picture,
1948. Smaller version of 1948 calendar with application forms. Sent to new member. - **$100 $200 $400**

LON-177. "Lone Ranger Frontier Town" Newspaper Ad,
1948. Cheerios. 10x14" clipping from Sunday newspaper comic section. - **$10 $20 $40**

LON-181. Flashlight Gun With Secret Compartment Handle and Lenses,
1949. Battery operated with clear, red and green lenses. - **$50 $150 $200**

LON-182. General Mills Outfit,
1949. Rare. Includes shirt, mask, neckerchief, cardboard tag with official seal. Set - **$100 $350 $500**

LON-179

LON-178

LON-184

LON-183

LON-178. "Frontier Town" Cheerios Box,
1948. Set of nine. Complete Box Each - **$100 $350 $500**
Each Back Panel Used to Complete Lone Ranger Town - **$25 $50 $75**

LON-179. Lone Ranger Movie Film Ring,
1949. Brass bands with aluminum viewing tube, came with 25-frame 8mm color filmstrip titled "U.S. Marines".
Ring - **$50 $90 $125**
Film - **$50 $62 $75**

LON-183. Cheerios "Deputy Secret Folder",
1949. - **$15 $30 $50**

LON-184. "Lone Ranger Deputy" 2" Brass Badge With Secret Compartment,
1949. - **$25 $50 $100**

LON-180

LON-185

LON-186

LON-180. "Movie Film Ring" Instruction Sheet,
1949. Cheerios. Reverse has order blank and description of Marine Corps film. - **$50 $60 $75**

LON-185. "Lone Ranger" Waxed Paper Bread Loaf Liner,
1940s. Harris-Boyer Bakeries. - **$25 $50 $90**

LON-186. Child Labor Law Folder,
1940s. New York State Department of Labor. Lone Ranger endorsement for labor laws affecting boys and girls aged 14-17. - **$20 $35 $60**

LON-187

LON-188

LON-187. Lone Ranger "Captain" Star Button,
1940s. - **$30 $60 $100**

LON-188. Lone Ranger "Deputy" Star Button,
1940s. - **$30 $60 $100**

LON-189

LON-190

LON-191

LON-189. Color Photo Card,
1940s. Madison Square Garden promo (#A6181 at bottom.).Shows Lone Ranger riding horse. - **$25 $50 $75**

LON-190. Silver Bullet Offer,
1940s. Kix Cereal. Explains how to order a silver bullet for 15¢ and 1 box top.- **$10 $20 $30**

LON-191. Note Paper,
1940s (pre-1945). Rare. Test program for Victory Corps note paper. Shows 3 men firing cannon on left and says "Let's Go U.S.A." Put out during WWII. Each -
$25 $50 $75

LON-192

LON-193

LON-192. Lone Ranger Calendar,
1940s. Merita Bread. 16x28". Example shown without pad.
Bread wrapper design includes children wearing masks and Indian headbands. Complete - **$500 $1000 $1500**
Without Pad - **$400 $800 $1200**

LON-193. Dan Reid With Lone Ranger And Tonto Color Picture,
1940s. Issuer unknown, possibly Merita Bread. About 7x9". - **$50 $125 $200**

LON-194

LON-195

LON-194. Pocketknife,
1940s. Store item with grips in black, red or white. -
$35 $75 $110

LON-195. Buchan's Bread Cello. Button,
c. 1940s. 12 known in either 7/8" or 1-1/4" size, various Lone Ranger slogans. Each - **$15 $35 $60**

LON-196

LON-197

LON-198

LON-196. Seal Print Face Ring,
1940s. Unmarked believed Lone Ranger premium tin ring designed to press face image into soft material. -
$150 $225 $300

LON-197. Merita Bread Safety Club 8x15" Cardboard Wall Calendar,
1950. Scarce. - **$75 $150 $250**

LON-198. "Lone Ranger Lucky Piece" Silvered Brass 17th Anniversary Key Ring Fob Medal,
1950. Cheerios. - **$15 $25 $40**

LON-199

LON-199. Bandanna Order Blank,
1950. General Mills.- **$10 $15 $25**

LON-200

LON-201

LON-200. Fabric Bandanna,
1950. Offered by Betty Crocker Soups. - **$25 $60 $90**

LON-201. Lone Ranger Calendar,
1950. Merita Bread 16x28". Example shown without pad.
Complete - **$500 $1000 $1500**
Without Pad - **$400 $800 $1200**

LON-202

LON-203

LON-202. Photo Card,
1950. TV premium.- **$10 $20 $30**

LON-203. Cheerios Contest Postcard,
1951. Back text for coloring contest. - **$8 $15 $30**

LON-204   **LON-205**

LON-204. Cheerios Crayon Offer Box Back,
1951. #1 from set of four. - **$10 $20 $30**

LON-205. Cheerios Crayon Offer Box Backs,
1951. #2 and #4 shown, from set of four offering free crayon set for crayoned box picture sent to General Mills. -
$10 $20 $30

LON-206

**LON-206. Cheerios Saddle Ring With Filmstrip,
Paper And Box,**
1951. Near Mint Boxed - **$300**
Ring Only - **$75 $110 $150**
Film Only - **$25 $37 $50**

LON-207

LON-207. Cheerios Paper Mask,
c. 1951. Back text "See The Lone Ranger And Silver In
Person At Minneapolis Aquatennial". - **$25 $60 $100**

LON-208

LON-208. Cheerios Box With Comic Book Advertising,
1954. - **$100 $250 $400**

LON-209

**LON-209. "The Lone Ranger And The Story Of Silver"
Comic,**
1954. Cheerios. - **$10 $35 $75**

LON-210

LON-210. Merita Bread Coloring Book,
1955. - **$10 $20 $35**

LON-211

**LON-211. Merita Bread Safety Club "Branding"
Booklet,**
1956. Cattle branding explained by Lone Ranger. -
$20 $50 $100

LON-212

LON-213

LON-212. Deputy Card,
1956. Wheaties premium. Schedule on back.-
$15 $25 $45

LON-213. Merita Safety Club Card,
1956. Merita Bakers. - **$10 $35 $60**

LON-214

LON-215

LON-214. Cheerios "Lone Ranger Fun Kit" Sign,
1956. Diecut 6x8" paper display sign. - **$30 $60 $100**

LON-215. Wheaties "Lone Ranger Hike-O-Meter" Sign,
1956. Diecut 6x8" paper display sign. - **$25 $40 $60**

LON-216

LON-217

LON-216. Sugar Jets "Lone Ranger Six-Shooter Ring" Sign,
1956. Diecut 6x8" paper display sign. - **$25 $40 $60**

LON-217. Trix "Tonto Belt" Sign,
1956. Diecut 6x8" paper display sign. - **$25 $40 $60**
Belt with Mailer - **$30 $60 $120**

LON-218

LON-218. "Lone Ranger Ranch Fun Book",
1956. Cheerios. - **$20 $50 $90**

LON-219

LON-220

LON-219. Kix "Lone Ranger Branding Iron" Sign,
1956. Diecut 6x8" paper display sign. - **$30 $50 $75**

LON-220. Lone Ranger With Guns 6' Standee,
1957. Rare. General Mills. - **$1000 $2500 $3100**

LON-221

LON-222

LON-221. Wheaties Box With Posters Offer,
1957. Complete Box - **$200 $300 $500**
Box Back - **$20 $60 $75**

LON-222. Wheaties Life-Sized Posters,
1957. Set of two 25x75" paper posters.
Lone Ranger - **$80 $175 $300**
Tonto - **$75 $150 $250**

LON-223

LON-224

LON-223. Life-Sized Uncut Poster Sheet (not separated),
1957. Used in lobby at General Mills headquarters. Unique - **$1250**

LON-224. Cheerios "Wild West Town" Figures With Sheet And Box,
1957. Scarce. Set of 22 figures including Lone Ranger, Tonto, three horses, nine cowboys, eight Indians. Near Mint Complete - **$400**

LON-225

LON-225. Cheerios "Movie Ranch Wild West Town" Ad Sheet,
1957. Box insert 3x4". - Set Complete - **$100 $200 $400**
Sheet - **$15 $40 $60**

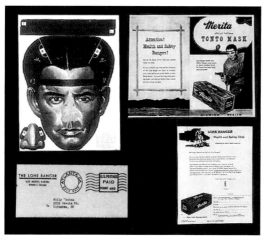

LON-226

LON-226. Merita "Tonto Mask" Kit,
1957. Mailer with Lone Ranger Health And Safety Club letter including order form for Lone Ranger Growth Chart, punch-out face mask. Near Mint In Mailer - **$350**
Letter - **$25 $50 $75**
Mask Unpunched - **$50 $100 $200**
Mask Assembled - **$35 $75 $150**

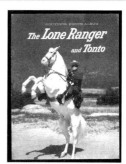

LON-227

LON-227. Photo Album,
1957. General Mills, Nestle, Swift, and Merita Bread. Contains 12 black and white photos plus 2 front and back color photos. Has the history of the Lone Ranger and promotes the next year's 25th silver anniversary of his program. TV premium.- **$50 $100 $150**

LON-228   LON-229

LON-228. Calendar,
1958. Premium calendar. Shaped like a loaf of bread.- **$20 $30 $45**

LON-229. Merita Bread "Lone Ranger Peace Patrol" Aluminum Token,
1959. Sponsored in conjunction with U.S. Treasury Department. Promotion for savings bonds. - **$40 $75 $125**

LON-230

LON-230. "Peace Patrol" Member Card,
c. 1959. U.S. Treasury Department. Encourages savings bond purchase, back has creed and pledge. - **$5 $15 $25**

LON-232

LON-231

LON-231. "Join The Peace Patrol" 11x14" Paper Poster,
c. 1959. U.S. Treasury Department. Encourages savings bond purchase. - **$60 $150 $250**

LON-232. Full Color 1-1/4" Cello. Button,
c. 1959. Unmarked but probably related to Treasury Department campaign to promote sales of U.S. Savings Bonds. - **$10 $20 $35**

LON-233

LON-234

LON-233. Litho. Button With Bw Photo On Lt. Blue,
c. 1959. Same design as full color 1-1/4" cello. button but rare 1-3/8" litho. - **$75 $150 $300**

LON-234. Deputy Chief Badge,
1950s. Rare. Detail of paper also shown. - **$100 $200 $300**

LON-235

LON-236

LON-235. "Merita Bread" Color Picture,
1950s. - **$15 $30 $60**

LON-236. Merita Bread Aluminum Silver Bullet Pencil Sharpener,
c. 1950s. - **$20 $50 $75**

LON-237

LON-237. Dell Comics Picture Strip,
1950s. Strip folio of five pictures. - **$50 $80 $150**

LON-238

LON-238. Smoking Click Plastic Pistol,
1950s. Store item by Marx Toys.
Boxed - **$75 $175 $250**
Loose - **$50 $120 $200**

LON-239

LON-239. "Magic Lasso" With Brass Badge,
1950s. Store item by Round-Up Products.
Near Mint Boxed - **$450**
Badge Only - **$60 $175 $300**

LON-240   LON-241   LON-242

LON-240. Litho. Tin Tab Star Badge,
1950s. Pictures Clayton Moore. - **$15 $30 $50**

LON-241. "Lone Ranger Deputy" 2-1/4" Silvered Metal Badge,
1950s. Red and black painted versions. Store Item.
Card with 12 Badges - **$500**
Each - **$10 $20 $30**

LON-242. "Lone Ranger Deputy" Gold Finish Metal Badge,
1950s. Store item. - **$15 $25 $40**

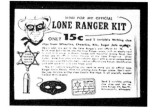

LON-243

LON-243. "Lone Ranger Junior Deputy" Gold Luster Tin Star Badge,
1950s. From Junior Deputy kit. Badge - **$20 $30 $45**
Coupon - **$10 $15 $25**

LON-244   LON-245

LON-244. Merita Bread Loaf End Labels,
1950s. Three examples from 11 seen.
Each - **$10 $20 $35**

LON-245. Silver Bullet,
1950s. Probably General Mills premium. 1-1/2" metal replica in silver finish with his name in cursive lettering on side. TLR Inc. copyright. - **$15 $30 $50**

LON-246

LON-247

LON-246. "The Dodge Boys" Silver Bullet,
c. 1950s. Dodge Motors Corp. 1-1/2" silver luster metal bullet issued for TV sponsor. - **$20 $40 $60**

LON-247. Coloring Book,
1950s. Cheerios. Large two page premium featuring the Cheerios Kid and Tonto.- **$10 $25 $45**

LON-248   LON-249

LON-250

LON-248. English Cookie Tin,
1961. Huntley & Palmers Biscuits. - **$40 $85 $150**

LON-249. English Cookie Tin,
1961. Huntley & Palmers Biscuits. Version pictures Tonto only. - **$40 $85 $150**

LON-250. "The Legend Of The Lone Ranger" Comic Book,
1969. Chain restaurant promotion. Identifies him as "The Good Food Guy". - **$2 $5 $12**

LON-251

LON-252

LON-251. "The Good Food Guy" Cello. Button,
c. 1969. Chain restaurant promotion. - **$10 $18 $25**

LON-252. "The Dodge Boys" TV Sponsor Card,
1960s. 9x11" counter card for agency of Dodge Motors Corp. Facsimile Clayton Moore signature. - **$10 $20 $35**

LON-253

LON-254

LON-255

LON-253. Record,
1972. Coca Cola premium with sleeve.- **$15 $25 $50**

LON-254. Autographed Clayton Moore Photograph,
1977. Lynn Wilson's Convenient Fun Food. Design includes Lone Ranger Creed. Signed - **$15 $30 $60**
Unsigned - **$8 $15 $25**

LON-255. Amoco Gas Station "Ride With Silver" 44x70" Vinyl Sign,
1970s. "Amoco Silver" lead-free gasoline. - **$35 $60 $125**

LON-256

LON-256. "Lone Ranger Deputy Kit",
1980. Cheerios. Contains Deputy certificate, "Legend" story folder, punch-out mask, 2-1/2" plastic Deputy badge and 17x22" color poster. Complete - **$10 $20 $35**

LON-257

LON-258

LON-257. Cheerios Box Back "Deputy Kit" Offer,
1980. Complete Box - **$15 $25 $40**
Back Only - **$5 $8 $15**

LON-258. Movie Press Kit,
1981. Contains saddle bag mailer with 14 photos & script. -
$20 $75 $100

LON-259   LON-260

LON-259. Movie Lone Ranger Rocking Book,
1981. Lone Ranger on front cover, Tonto on back cover. -
$10 $20 $30

LON-260. Hallmark Christmas Ornament,
1997. Shaped like a Lone Ranger lunchbox. - **$35**

LONE WOLF TRIBE

Wrigley's gum sponsored this children's program on
CBS in 1932-1933. The series offered dramatized versions of the American Indian way of life, told by Chief
Wolf Paw to the tribe members "with the voice that
flies (radio)." Listeners could obtain premiums by
sending in "wampum" (Wrigley's wrappers). Most premiums were marked with the imprint of a wolf paw.
The club ring, sterling silver and non-adjustable, is
considered the earliest issued premium ring.

LWF-1   LWF-2

LWF-1. Wrigley's Chewing Gum Samples Folder,
1932. Held three sticks of gum, reverse lists radio times
and offers Lone Wolf Tribe Book.
With Gum - **$25 $100 $175**
Folder Only - **$15 $30 $75**

LWF-2. Club Manual,
1932. Wrigley Gum. - **$15 $25 $75**

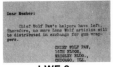

LWF-3

LWF-3. New Member Letter,
1932. Wrigley Gum. - **$15 $25 $40**

**LWF-4. "Treasure Of The Lone Wolf" 11x17" Paper
Map,**
1932. Scarce. Wrigley Gum. - **$50 $100 $150**

LWF-5

**LWF-5. "Lone Wolf Tribe Tom-Tom" Leather And Thin
Rubber Drum With Beater Stick,**
c. 1932. Rare. Wrigley's Gum. Boxed - **$50 $150 $200**
Loose - **$25 $80 $125**

LWF-6

LWF-7

LWF-8

LWF-6. Chief Wolf Paw Sterling Ring,
1932. Wrigley's Gum. Considered the first radio premium
ring. - **$60 $140 $225**

LWF-7. Tribe Bracelet,
1932. Wrigley Gum. Silvered metal expansion bracelet
with tribal code symbols. - **$30 $90 $125**

LWF-8. Arrowhead Silvered Brass Member's Badge,
1932. On Card - **$30 $75 $125**
Loose - **$15 $30 $50**

LWF-9   LWF-10

LWF-9. Lone Wolf Arrowhead Pin Mailer,
1932. Wrigley's Gum. - **$20 $50 $75**

LWF-10. Lone Wolf Letter (Goes With Pin),
1932. Wrigley's Gum. - **$10 $20 $30**

LWF-11

LWF-17

LWF-18

LWF-19

LWF-11. Chief Wolf Paw/Lone Wolf Tribe Arrowhead With Mailer,
c. 1932. Wrigley's Gum. Stone arrowhead held in flap pocket of 3x5-1/2" mailer card.
Arrowhead With Mailer - **$35 $75 $150**

LWF-17. Lone Wolf Tribe Postcard,
1932. Wrigley's Gum. - **$40 $50 $60**

LWF-18. Lone Wolf Closing Mailer,
1933. Wrigley's Gum. - **$20 $40 $60**

LWF-19. Lone Wolf Tribe Trading Post Closing Folder,
1933. Wrigley's Gum. Four page folder with 3 sticks of gum. - **$100 $200 $350**

LWF-12

LWF-13

LWF-12. Cow Head Tie Holder,
1932. Actual bone tie slide from "Vertebra Of A Range Animal". - **$20 $40 $60**

LWF-13. "Sitting Bull" Picture,
c. 1932. Lone Wolf Tribe premium with back text "How Sitting Bull Got His Name". - **$15 $50 $75**

LWF-20

LWF-21

LWF-22

LWF-14

LWF-15

LWF-16

LWF-14. Tribe Necklace,
1932. Scarce. - **$100 $250 $350**

LWF-15. Chief Wolf Paw Arrowhead Fob,
1932. Wrigley Gum. Thin silvered brass picturing paw and arrow designs. - **$20 $75 $100**

LWF-16. Lone Wolf Silvered Brass Pin,
1932. Thunderbird broach. - **$25 $50 $75**

LWF-20. Lone Wolf Arrowhead Chain,
1933. Unmarked - Hunt Buffalo sign. - **$20 $30 $40**

LWF-21. Lone Wolf Pin,
1933. Unmarked - Horse symbol for journey. - **$20 $30 $40**

LWF-22. Out Of Business Paper,
c. 1933. Wrigley Gum. Paper reads "Dear Member: Chief Wolf Paw's Helpers Have Left. Therefore, No More Lone Wolf Articles Will Be Distributed In Exchange For Gum Wrappers." - **$25 $50 $100**

LOST IN SPACE

"Never fear, Smith is here!" This cult sci-fi TV series, created by Irwin Allen for 20th Century Fox Television and aired on CBS from 1965-1968, ran up against another memorable science fiction show with its own following--something called *Star Trek*. It was *Lost in Space* that was the first-run success, though, and to this day its three seasons remain popular in syndication and on the Sci-Fi Channel. Following the exploits of the intrepid Robinson family--Professor John Robinson, wife Maureen, daughters Judy and Penny, son Will, their pilot Major Don West, their Robot...called "Robot," and a stock villain stowaway known as Dr. Smith originally sent to sabotage the ship--the series was a campy hit that mixed cheap special effects, excessive over-acting, and a wild sense of fun to produce a show enjoyed by both children and adults.

Originally sent from Earth to colonize the nearby star system of Alpha Centauri, the family finds themselves encountering a bizarre collection of aliens thanks to the bumbling malevolence of Dr. Smith, who often attempts to exploit opportunities to return home at the expense of the family's safety. *Lost in Space* has now enjoyed a resurgence of popularity thanks to several anniversary celebrations, including a Sci-Fi Channel tribute aired on October 16th, 1997 (the date on which the Robinson's spacecraft, the Jupiter II, was supposedly launched) as well as the 1998 New Line feature film of the same name, starring William Hurt, Mimi Rogers, and Gary Oldman taking over for Jonathan Harris as Dr. Smith. Most items are copyright 20th Century Fox. "Oh the pain, the pain!"

LIS-2

LIS-1

LIS-1. "March Of Comics" Booklet #352,
1964. Various sponsors. "Space Family Robinson/Lost In Space" story. - **$13 $40 $90**

LIS-2. "Lost In Space" Cast Photo,
c. 1966. CBS-TV fan card. - **$20 $40 $75**

LIS-3

LIS-3. "Lost In Space" Battery Operated Robot,
1966. Store item by Remco. Boxed - **$200 $400 $600**
Loose - **$100 $200 $400**

LIS-4

LIS-4. Lost in Space Metal Lunch Box With Thermos,
1967. King Seeley Thermos. . - **$125 $300 $500**

LIS-5

LIS-6

LIS-5. "Lost In Space" Battery Operated Robot,
1977. Store item by Ahi. Boxed - **$75 $175 $250**
Loose - **$50 $125 $175**

LIS-6. Lost in Space Talking Environmental Robot B-9,
1997. Trendmasters, Inc. and Newline Productions. 10" tall Robot with two recorded sayings (delivered by the original Robot voice, Dick Tufeld): "Danger, Danger Will Robinson!" and "My sensors indicate an intruder is present." Comes with removable laser pistol, retractable arms, light-up dome and pull-back tread action. - **$40**

LUCILLE BALL

Lucille Ball (1911-1989) developed the character of the wacky housewife on radio in *My Favorite Husband*, which ran for three years (1948-1951) on CBS, sponsored by General Foods. But it was on CBS television that she became a comic star, first on *I Love Lucy* (1951-1957). The show, an instant hit, also featured Lucy's husband, Desi Arnaz, as bandleader Ricky Ricardo, and Vivian Vance and William Frawley as neighbors Ethel and Fred Mertz. The birth of little Ricky on the show in 1953--on the same night Lucille Ball was actually giving birth--was a major national event. A radio adaptation aired briefly in 1952, sponsored by Philip Morris cigarettes. Other television shows on CBS followed: *The Lucille Ball-Desi Arnaz Show* (1957-1959), *The Lucy Show* (1962-1968), *Here's Lucy* (1968-1974), and *Life With Lucy* on ABC in 1986. Syndicated reruns are still being widely broadcast to this day.

Lucille Ball also appeared in a number of forgettable movies, including the title role in a disastrous *Mame* for Warner Bros. in 1974. Comic book versions of the television series include *I Love Lucy Comics* (1954-1962), *The Lucy Show* (1963-1964), and *I Love Lucy* (1990-1991). Licensed items are usually copyrighted Lucille Ball and Desi Arnaz or Desilu, the name of their production studio.

LUC-1

LUC-2

LUC-1. Footwear 12x17" Countertop Display Sign,
c. 1949. Summerettes Shoes by Ball-Band. Cardboard easel back with replica ad from Life magazine. - **$100 $200 $300**

LUC-2. "I Love Lucy" 3-D Picture Storybook,
1953. Store item by 3 Dimension Publications Inc. 24-page photo magazine includes four pages printed in process for viewing by "Foto Magic 3-D Spex" eyeglasses.
With Glasses - **$100 $200 $300**
Without Glasses - **$75 $150 $250**

LUC-3

LUC-4

LUC-3. "TV Guide" Vol. 1 #1,
April 3, 1953. First national issue with cover article "Lucy's Fifty Million Dollar Baby". - **$200 $500 $1000**

LUC-4. "TV Guide" Cover Article,
1953. Weekly issue for July 17 with three-page article on Lucy and Desi movie "The Long-Long Trailer." - **$25 $60 $100**

LUC-5

LUC-5. Lucy & Desi Ad Postcard,
1955. Pontiac Motors. - **$12 $20 $40**

LUC-6

LUC-7

LUC-6. "Pocket Encyclopedia Of Alaska" With Lucy/Desi Cover,
1959. Westinghouse Corp. TV show sponsor folder opening to 20x25" featuring map and text about newly-admitted 50th state. - **$10 $20 $30**

LUC-7. "I Love Lucy" Cigarette Sponsor Display Card,
1950s. Philip Morris Cigarettes. Cardboard hinge card for countertop or merchandise use with color photo lower half geared to Father's Day cigarette gifts. - **$75 $150 $275**

LUC-8

LUC-9

LUC-10

LUC-8. "Desi's Conga Drum",
1950s. Store item by A&A American Metal Toy Co. Came with wooden beater. - **$250 $450 $800**

LUC-9. "I Love Lucy" Doll With Apron,
1950s. Store item. - **$150 $300 $450**

LUC-10. "Lucy's Notebook",
1950s. Philip Morris cigarettes. 40-page recipe booklet with Lucy/Desi photos. - **$20 $40 $60**

LUC-11

LUC-12

LUC-13

LUC-11. "Wildcat" Broadway Production 3" Cello. Button,
c. 1961. For "Musical Smash Hit" at Alvin Theater. - **$20 $40 $60**

LUC-12. "Lucy Day" New York World's Fair 3-1/2" Cello. Button,
1964. Macy's department store. Single day issue for August 31. - **$40 $80 $125**

LUC-13. "Lucy Day" New York World's Fair 3-1/2" Cello. Button,
1964. Single day issue for August 31 event designated for "Press" representative. - **$40 $80 $125**

LUM AND ABNER

For 22 years on various radio networks and for a long list of sponsors, Lum Edwards and Abner Peabody ran the Jot 'Em Down Store in the mythical town of Pine Ridge, Arkansas. The show was conceived by Chester Lauck and Norris Goff, boyhood friends in rural Arkansas who played not only the title roles but also most of the other characters in a continuing mixture of dialect comedy and rustic soap opera. The program premiered on Hot Springs station KTHS in 1931 and soon moved to Chicago and went national. Sponsors included Quaker Oats (1931), Ford automobiles (1933), Horlick's malted milk (1934-1938), Postum (1938-1940), Alka-Seltzer (1941-1948), and Frigidaire (1948-1949). The final broadcast was in 1953. (In 1936, in honor of the show, the town of Waters, Arkansas, officially changed its name to Pine Ridge).

LUM-1

LUM-2

LUM-1. Horlick's Drink Mixer With Letter,
1933. 6-1/2" tall glass and aluminum malted milk drink mixer prize with letter informing a contest winner.
Letter - **$5 $15 $25**
Mixer - **$35 $70 $140**

LUM-2. "Pine Ridge News" Vol. 1 #1 Newspaper, November
1933. Ford Motor Co. - **$25 $50 $80**

LUM-3

LUM-4

LUM-3. "The Pine Ridge News" Newspaper With Envelope,
1936, Spring. Horlick's Malted Milk.
Near Mint In Mailer- **$75**
Loose - **$15 $25 $50**

LUM-4. "Lum And Abner's Almanac",
1936. Horlick's Malted Milk. - **$5 $20 $40**

LUM-5

LUM-6

LUM-7

LUM-5. Lum Edwards For President Cello. Button,
1936. Horlick's Malted Milk. - **$5 $15 $25**

LUM-6. "Walkin' Weather Prophet" Brass Badge,
1936. Horlick's Malted Milk. Litmus paper insert changes color with humidity but almost always inactive due to age. - **$10 $50 $75**

LUM-7. Letter,
1936. Premium letter explains how the Weather Prophet Badge works.- **$5 $10 $15**

LUM-8

LUM-9

LUM-10

LUM-8. Glass Shake-Up Decanter With Aluminum Lid,
c. 1936. For preparing Horlick's Malted Milk. Lid has pouring spout. - **$40 $75 $150**

LUM-9. "Family Almanac",
1937. Horlick's Malted Milk. - **$10 $25 $40**

LUM-10. "Lum And Abner's Family Almanac",
1938. Horlick's Malted Milk. - **$10 $25 $40**

LUM-11

LUM-12

LUM-13

LUM-11. Postcard,
1938. Shows Lum and Abner in and out of costume. Bottom card says "Mena, Arkansas Home of Lum and Abner." - **$10 $25 $40**

LUM-12. Promo,
1930s. Postum Cereal. Promotes radio show.- **$10 $20 $30**

LUM-13. Mailer For Photo,
1930s. Horlick's Malted Milk. - **$10 $20 $30**

LUM-14

LUM-15

LUM-16

LUM-14. Tour Book,
1930s. Ten page premium. Gives a tour of the town. - **$15 $25 $35**

LUM-15. Fan Photo,
1930s. Inset photo of radio portrayers Chester Lauck and Norris Goff. - **$20 $35 $60**

LUM-16. Movie Postcard,
1946. Various theaters. Announces upcoming movie "Partners In Time". - **$5 $20 $35**

MAD MAGAZINE

What started as an irreverent little comic book in August 1952 has grown into what was once the nation's leading humor magazine. Early issues, edited by Harvey Kurtzman, satirized popular comic strips with features such as *Little Orphan Melvin* and *Batboy and Rubin*. With issue #24 in 1955 publisher Bill Gaines changed the format from comic book to magazine. Alfred E. Neuman, a cartoon rendering of a 19th century icon, made his debut on the cover of issue #21 and has become the magazine's (What--Me Worry?) trademark. Annual issues of *More Trash from MAD* and *The Worst from MAD* appeared from 1958 to 1969, *MAD Follies* from 1963 to 1969, and *MAD Specials* from 1970 on. Licensed merchandise includes clothing, food products, games, trading cards, and greeting cards. *MAD TV*, a late-night comedy show, debuted on the Fox television network in October 1995. In 1997 *MAD* underwent an extensive editorial makeover with the addition of many new artists and writers. *Tales Calculated To Drive You MAD*, a limited series reprinting *MAD*'s first 23 full-color issues in magazine format, is presently appearing quarterly.

MAD-1

MAD-2

MAD-3

MAD-1. "Comfort Soap" Cello. Button,
c. 1901. Very strong early character resemblance to later Alfred E. Neuman. - **$150 $350 $800**

MAD-2. Birthday Card,
c. 1930s. - **$50 $125 $200**

MAD-3. "Me Worry?" Cello. Button,
1941. "Superior" unknown sponsor. - **$100 $250 $400**

MAD-4

MAD-4. Get Well Card,
c. 1940s. - **$25 $60 $100**

MAD-5

MAD-6

MAD-5. "EC Fan-Addict Club" Patch And Bronze Badge,
1953. Part of membership kit. Re-issue patch includes copyright symbol. Original Patch - **$50 $125 $175** Reissue Patch - **$25 $50 $75** Badge - **$75 $175 $250**

MAD-6. Figurine,
1960. Glazed base with unglazed white bust to be painted by recipient. Small 3-3/4" Size - **$100 $175 $300** Large 5-1/2" Size - **$150 $300 $500**

MAD-7

MAD-8

MAD-7. "For President" 2-1/2" Cello. Button,
1960. - **$40 $75 $140**

MAD-8. "Me Worry??" Composition Bust Figure,
c. 1960. Unlicensed. With Tag - **$75 $150 $250**
No Tag - **$50 $125 $200**

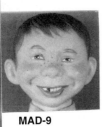

MAD-10

MAD-9

MAD-11

MAD-9. "What Me Worry?" Doll,
1961. Unlicensed store item by Baby Barry. -
$400 $1000 $1800

MAD-10. "For President" 2-1/2" Cello. Button,
1964. - **$20 $40 $75**

MAD-11. "Alfred E. Neuman For President" Litho. Tin Tab,
1964. - **$10 $20 $35**

MAD-13   MAD-14

MAD-12

MAD-12. "Alfred E. Neuman" Aurora Plastics Model Kit,
1965. Store item. Boxed And Unbuilt - **$150 $200 $250**

MAD-13. Alfred E. Neuman Plastic Portrait Pin,
c. 1960s. Store item. Vending machine issue, unlicensed, marked "Hong Kong". - **$10 $25 $40**

MAD-14. "What Me Worry?" Dark Gold Luster Metal Necklace Pendant,
c. 1960s. Store item. Depicts Alfred E. Neuman riding bomb. - **$40 $75 $125**

MAD-15

MAD-16

MAD-15. Movie Promotion 3" Cello Button,
1980. Warner Brothers. MAD Magazine name was removed from the film after initial release but some versions now restore the full title and opening and closing cameo by a live-action Alfred E. Neuman. - **$8 $12 $20**

MAD-16. Magazine Subscription Promotion Buttons,
1987. E. C. Publishing Inc. Set of 24 cello. 1" pin-backs reproducing art from MAD Magazine covers 1950s-1980s. Each - **$8 $15 $25**

MAJOR BOWES ORIGINAL AMATEUR HOUR

Edward Bowes (1874-1946), a major in U.S. Army intelligence in World War I and a show-business veteran, introduced his amateur hour on New York radio station WHN in 1934. The following year, sponsored by Chase & Sanborn coffee, it aired on the NBC network, and from 1936 to 1946, sponsored by Chrysler automobiles, it was a Thursday night institution on CBS. 'Round and 'round she goes, and where she stops nobody knows--so went the wheel of fortune, each week drawing thousands of amateur performers looking for the big break. For most, it was a dream that didn't come true.

MJB-1   MJB-2

MJB-1. First Fan Newsletter #1,
1935. Chase & Sanborn Coffee. - **$15 $30 $50**

MJB-2. Second Fan Newsletter #2,
1935. Chase & Sanborn Coffee. - **$12 $20 $30**

MJB-3

MJB-4

MJB-3. Fan Photo,
1936. Chrysler Corp. Radio show title on back. -
$10 $15 $25

MJB-4. "Major Bowes Amateur Parade" Photo Newsletter,
June 1937. Chrysler Corp. - **$8 $25 $40**

MJB-5

MJB-6

MJB-7

MJB-5. Gong Alarm Clock,
c. 1930s. Made by Ingersoll. - **$75 $150 $250**

MJB-6. Home Broadcasting Microphone With Box,
1930s. Store item by Pilgrim Electric Corp. Metal actual working device for household radio set.
Boxed - **$100 $300 $400**
Loose - **$50 $175 $250**

MJB-7. Major Bowes Gong With Hammer Clasp,
1930s. Prize from radio show. Sterling Silver. -
$50 $100 $150

MJB-8

MJB-8. "Capitol Theatre Family" Fan Photo Card,
1930s. Pictures Capitol Radio orchestra of radio broadcasts. - **$5 $12 $20**

MJB-9

MJB-9. Fan Postcards,
1930s. Each - **$5 $8 $12**

MAJOR JET

A mid-1950s character created to promote Sugar Jets cereal of General Mills, Major Jet was an otherwise unidentified individual although always appearing in his jet-age flight helmet snappily accented by voltage bolt symbols centered by a "J" symbol denoting speed. His resemblance to an established comic strip jetting hero of the era, Milton Caniff's *Steve Canyon*, may have been more than coincidental. Actor Roger Pace portrayed Major Jet in TV commercials. His motto, "Jet Up And Go With Sugar Jets," accompanied premium offer--notably a mail premium Rocket-Glider kit of styrofoam and plastic but "made for high, jet-speed flying." The Rocket-Glider was offered by a May 1, 1955 Sunday comic section ad "while supplies last" and probably by cereal box as well.

MAJ-1

MAJ-1. Magic Paint Set Booklet,
1954. Sugar Jets cereal. #1 from set of three.
Each - **$8 $15 $25**

MAJ-2

MAJ-2. "Magic Paint Set" Book #2,
1954. Sugar Jets cereal. From set of three.
Each - **$8 $15 $25**

MAJ-3

MAJ-4

MAJ-3. Sugar Jets "Filmo Vision" Box Back,
1954. Cut-out parts for assembly of spaceship viewer for watching two cut-out films. Uncut Back - **$10 $20 $30**

MAJ-4. Rocket-Glider With Launcher,
1955. Sugar Jets cereal. Near Mint Boxed - **$50**
Loose - **$10 $15 $20**

MANDRAKE THE MAGICIAN

Created by writer Lee Falk and artist Phil Davis, Mandrake debuted as a daily comic strip in 1934 and as a Sunday page in 1935. Distributed by King Features, the adventures of the top-hatted magician with supernatural and hypnotic powers was an immediate success. Assisted by his faithful companion Lothar, an African king with enormous strength, and Princess Narda, Mandrake triumphed over earthly enemies and extraterrestrial invaders. He made his first comic book appearance in *King Comics* #1 in 1936 and has appeared in numerous collections in the decades since. Columbia Pictures released a 12-episode chapter play in 1939 with Warren Hull as Mandrake, and a syndicated radio series aired on the Mutual network from 1940 to 1942. A pilot made-for-TV movie was broadcast in 1979.

MAN-1

MAN-2

MAN-3

MAN-1. "Member Mandrake's Magic Club" Litho. Button,
1934. - **$50 $100 $175**

MAN-2. "Mandrake Magicians' Club/Taystee Bread" Enameled Brass Pin,
1934. - **$30 $75 $175**

MAN-3. Club Kit Card,
1934. Taystee Bread. Accompanied membership card and enameled brass member's pin. - **$35 $75 $125**

MAN-4

MAN-5

MAN-4. "New Magic Tricks" Sheet,
c. 1940. Taystee Bread and WOR (New York City). Sheet has earlier 1934 King Features copyright. - **$20 $40 $65**

MAN-5. Magic Kit Leaflet,
1948. Suchard Chocolate Bars. Offers trick premiums with expiration date of January 31, 1949. - **$10 $15 $25**

MAN-6

MAN-7

MAN-8

MAN-6. Christmas Card,
1950s. King Features Syndicate. From series featuring various syndicate characters. - **$10 $20 $35**

MAN-7. Plastic Gumball Charm,
c. 1950s. Store item. Clear plastic with insert paper picture, from vending machine series. Second character on reverse. - **$8 $12 $20**

MAN-8. Sponge,
c. 1960s. Store item. - **$5 $12 $20**

MA PERKINS

Beginning in 1933, Oxydol's own Ma Perkins solved her neighbors' problems and dished out her homespun philosophy from her lumber yard in Rushville Center for a total of 27 years. The program, first heard on Cincinnati radio station WLW, went national on NBC four months after its debut. From 1942 to 1948 it was broadcast on both the NBC and CBS networks, and from 1948 until it went off the air in 1960 it aired exclusively on CBS. Virginia Payne played the part of the widowed Ma for the entire run of over 7,000 episodes, and Procter & Gamble's Oxydol was the long-term sponsor.

MPK-1

MPK-2

MPK-1. Garden Planner,
1935. Oxydol. 3 pages. Letter came with flower seeds. Radio premium. - **$10 $25 $40**

MPK-2. Seeds and Mailer,
1935. Oxydol. Cultivation instructions on packets. Radio premium. Seeds - **$5 $10 $25**
Mailer - **$5 $10 $25**

MPK-4

MPK-3

MPK-3. Oxydol Fan Photo,
1930s. - **$12 $25 $35**

MPK-4. "Ma Perkins-Your Radio Friend" Photo,
1930s. Oxydol. - **$8 $20 $30**

MPK-5   MPK-6   MPK-7   MPK-8

MPK-5. Seed Pack,
1946. Oxydol.Zinnia. - **$10 $20 $30**

MPK-6. Seed Pack,
1946. Oxydol.Morning Glory. - **$10 $20 $30**

MPK-7. Seed Pack,
1946. Oxydol.Gourds. - **$10 $20 $30**

MPK-8. Seed Pack,
1946. Oxydol.Sweet Alyssum. - **$10 $20 $30**

MPK-9

MPK-9. Garden Planner,
1948. Oxydol. 6 pages. - **$10 $25 $40**

MARVEL COMICS

Marvel began in 1939 with a firm known as Timely Publications operated by Martin Goodman who began publishing pulp magazines in 1932. Science fiction, western, crime and horror were steady sellers and Goodman became very astute at publishing and distribution. Superman had created quite a splash in 1938 and Goodman took notice. Funnies Inc. was a comic book shop, a business with artists, writers and editors who would produce comic books for others to publish. Their art director, Bill Everett, had created Prince Namor, The Sub-Mariner for another title and co-worker Carl Burgos came up with the Human Torch. Both characters made their debut in Goodman's *Marvel Comics* #1, October 1939. Martin Goodman was in the comic book business.

Joe Simon was Goodman's first editor and he and fellow artist Jack Kirby came up with *Captain America Comics*, the company's biggest seller. Super heroes waned in the 1950s but Goodman told editor Stan Lee that they should consider a revival in 1961. Shortly thereafter Jack Kirby's Fantastic Four appeared followed by Steve Ditko's Spider-Man, The Hulk, Daredevil and others. A risky venture into a new field in 1939 formed the foundation for what is today the best selling comic book company in the world.

Items in this section promote Marvel Comics in general and a variety of their superhero characters. Captain America and Spider-Man are in separate sections.

MAR-2

MAR-1

MAR-1. "Marvel Action Rings" Vending Machine Display Card,
1966. Promotes set of 12 flicker rings and features Jack Kirby signed art. - **$40 $55 $75**

MAR-2. Vending Machine Flicker Rings,
1966. Set of 12. Each Silver or Gold Base - **$10 $18 $30**
Each Blue Base - **$8 $12 $20**

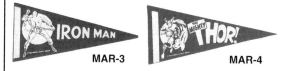

MAR-3   MAR-4

MAR-3. Marvel Pennant Iron Man,
1966. 6 1/2" sold through comic books. - **$10 $20 $30**

MAR-4. Marvel Pennant Thor,
1966. 6 1/2" sold through comic book. - **$10 $20 $30**

MAR-11

MAR-5

MAR-6

MAR-7

MAR-12

MAR-5. "Daredevil" 3-1/2" Cello. Button,
1966. Store item. #4 from numbered series.
Near Mint Bagged - **$35**
Loose - **$10 $15 $25**

MAR-6. "The Incredible Hulk" 3-1/2" Cello. Button,
1966. Store item. #5 from numbered series.
Near Mint Bagged - **$35**
Loose - **$10 $15 $25**

MAR-7. "The Invincible Iron Man" 3-1/2" Cello. Button,
1966. Store item. #7 from series.
Near Mint Bagged - **$35**
Loose - **$10 $15 $25**

MAR-11. "Mini-Books" Vending Machine Insert Paper,
1966. Advertises tiny 1" tall, 48 page books for Captain
America, Incredible Hulk, Millie the Model, Sgt. Fury,
Spider-Man, Thor. Insert Paper - **$8 $15 $25**
Each Book - **$5 $12 $30**

**MAR-12. "Merry Marvel Marching Society"
Membership Kit,**
1967. Envelope with letter, card, record, etc.
Complete Near Mint - **$180**
Each Paper Piece - **$5 $20 $40**
Record - **$10 $40 $60**

MAR-13

MAR-14

MAR-15

MAR-13. "Make Mine Marvel" 3-1/2" Cello. Button,
1967. Issued with Marvel Marching Society club kit. -
$10 $20 $35

MAR-14. Club Member 3" Cello. Button,
1967. - **$10 $20 $30**

MAR-15. "Convention '75" 3" Cello. Button,
1975. - **$10 $20 $30**

MAR-8

MAR-9

MAR-10

MAR-8. "Sub-Mariner" 3-1/2" Cello. Button,
1966. Store item. #8 from series.
Near Mint Bagged - **$35**
Loose - **$10 $15 $25**

MAR-9. "The Mighty Thor" 3-1/2" Cello. Button,
1966. Store item. #9 from series.
Near Mint Bagged - **$35**
Loose - **$10 $15 $25**

MAR-10. "The Avengers" 3-1/2" Cello. Button,
1966. Store item. #10 from series.
Near Mint Bagged - **$35**
Loose - **$10 $15 $25**

MAR-16

MAR-16. "Marvel Comics Convention" Shopping Bag,
1975. 13x16" plastic bag with drawstring top given away at
comic book collectors convention. - **$3 $6 $10**

MAR-17

MAR-17. The Incredible Hulk Game with The Fantastic Four,
1978. Milton Bradley. - **$5 $10 $25**

McDONALD'S

What began as a simple hamburger joint in southern California has become an international symbol of American initiative and drive. At last count there were more than 18,000 McDonald's fast-food restaurants in some 89 countries--the busiest of all in Pushkin Square, Moscow. It all started in 1937 when the McDonald brothers, Maurice and Richard, opened a small stand near Pasadena. Two years later they opened a second spot, fine-tuning their fast-food philosophy in a building with two yellow arches poking through the roof. A character called Speedee, with a hamburger for a head, courted drive-in customers atop another arch. Franchising the successful operation began in 1953, and Ray Kroc opened his first franchise in 1955. Six years later, with more than 200 stores licensed, Kroc bought out the entire operation. Speedee was retired in 1962 and replaced by the Ronald McDonald character in 1963. Other characters--Big Mac, the Hamburglar, Grimace, Mayor McCheese, Captain Crook, and the Professor--were introduced in the 1970s. Toys, games, premiums, licensed products, and promotional items continue to proliferate.

McD-1

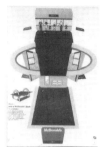

McD-2

McD-1. "Speedee" Litho. Button,
c. 1955. Pictures trademark character used from beginnings until his retirement c. 1962. - **$25 $60 $100**

McD-2. Cardboard Drive-In Punch-Out Sheet,
c. 1962. Design intent of coin bank. Unpunched - **$25 $50 $100**

McD-3

McD-4

McD-3. "Let's Go To McDonald's" Plastic/Tin Palm Puzzle,
1964. Pictured is "Archie" serving character. - **$20 $40 $75**

McD-4. "Let's Eat Out!" Storybook,
1965. Issued for 10th anniversary, stiff covers. - **$35 $75 $150**

McD-5

McD-6

McD-5. "Ronald McDonald Goes To The Moon" Coloring Book,
1967. Story and art about his victorious race to the moon against rival Mr. Muscle to establish a McDonald's restaurant there. - **$35 $65 $100**

McD-6. Model Kit,
c. late 1960s. Store item made by Life-Like Products (H.O. scale). - **$50 $125 $200**

McD-7

McD-8

McD-7. Captain Crook Bubble Boat,
1979. Vacuum form plastic punch-out 2-1/2x2-1/2" toy that runs on baking powder. Near Mint Unassembled - **$75** Assembled - **$10 $25 $50**

McD-8. Ronald Cloth Doll,
1970s. First 1971 version designed with black zipper pull. Later 1970s versions have zipper design without pull.
First Style - **$8 $15 $30**
Later Style - **$5 $10 $15**

McD-9   McD-10

McD-11

McD-9. Ronald Litho. Tin Tab,
c. 1970s. - **$3 $8 $15**

McD-10. Mayor McCheese Litho. Tin Tab,
c. 1970s. - **$3 $8 $15**

McD-11. Employee Doll,
c. 1970s. Jointed vinyl 11" doll in brown uniform. -
$20 $35 $50

McD-13   McD-14

McD-12

McD-12. Ronald Wristwatch,
1970s. - **$15 $25 $40**

**McD-13. Employees Glasses Promotion 3-1/2" Cello.
Button,**
c. 1970s. McDonald's and Coca-Cola Canadian issue. -
$8 $12 $20

McD-14. Captain Crook Orange Vinyl Ring,
c. 1980. - **$5 $7 $10**

McD-17

McD-15   McD-16

McD-15. Big Mac Yellow Vinyl Ring,
c. 1980. - **$5 $7 $10**

McD-16. Grimace Purple Vinyl Ring,
c. 1980. - **$5 $7 $10**

McD-17. Hamburglar Plastic Siren Whistle,
1986. - **$5 $8 $12**

MELVIN PURVIS

The story of FBI agent Melvin Purvis (1903-1960) is a mixture of fact and legend. Purvis, a South Carolina lawyer, joined the FBI in 1927 and chased minor criminals in Texas and Oklahoma, eventually ending up in the Bureau's Chicago office. In 1934, with the help of a "woman in red," Purvis and other agents ambushed and killed the notorious John Dillinger as he left the Biograph movie theater in Chicago. Three months later Purvis, again acting on a tip, led a raid on an Ohio farm that ended in the killing of Pretty Boy Floyd. Purvis left the FBI in 1935, wrote a book about his experiences, and worked in law and broadcasting. In 1960, in poor health, he committed suicide.

As the embodiment of law and order and the implacable enemy of criminals, Purvis was heavily promoted in the 1930s by Post cereals in newspapers, on cereal boxes, and in magazine advertising. His *Junior G-Man Corps* and *Law and Order Patrol* enlisted kids by the thousands with a profusion of premiums--a variety of badges, ID cards, rings, flashlights, knives, fingerprint kits, manuals, pen and pencil sets, even separate badges for members of the Girls Division. Dale Robertson played Purvis in a 1974 television movie.

MLV-2

MLV-1   MLV-3

MLV-1. Club Manual Of Instructions,
1936. - **$20 $30 $50**

**MLV-2. Junior G-Man Corps "Chief Operative"
Certificate,**
1936. - **$25 $75 $125**

MLV-3. Premium Folder,
1936. - **$15 $40 $65**

MLV-5

MLV-4

MLV-4. "Chief Operative" Brass Shield Badge,
1936. - **$20 $40 $75**

MLV-5. "Girls Division" Brass Club Badge,
1936. - **$15 $30 $50**

MLV-6

MLV-7

MLV-8

MLV-6. "Melvin Purvis Junior G-Man Corps" Brass Ring,
1936. - **$25 $50 $75**

MLV-7. "Junior G-Man Corps" Brass Badge,
1936. - **$15 $25 $40**

MLV-8. "Roving Operative" Brass Badge,
1936. - **$20 $40 $75**

MLV-9

MLV-10

MLV-9. "Special Agent" Metal Flashlight Gun,
1936. Battery operated. - **$40 $100 $150**

MLV-10. "Junior G-Man Corps" Member Card In Leather Wallet,
1936. Wallet - **$20 $60 $90**
Card - **$15 $40 $65**

MLV-11

MLV-12

MLV-11. "Junior G-Men Secret Passport",
1936. Envelope - **$5 $15 $25**
Card - **$20 $50 $85**

MLV-12. Junior G-Men Fingerprint Set With Mailer Envelope,
1936. Cardboard folder containing fingerprint powder, ink pad, instruction booklet. Mailer - **$10 $20 $30**
Set - **$25 $75 $125**

MLV-13

MLV-13. Wood Pencil With "G-Man" Metal Clip,
c. 1936. Scarce. No Purvis markings.
Pencil - **$20 $50 $75**
Clip - **$20 $50 $75**

MLV-14

MLV-15

MLV-16

MLV-14. "G-Men" Brass Watch Fob,
c. 1936. Unmarked for Purvis but pictured in his premium catalogues. Came with unmarked dark brown leather strap.
Fob Only - **$25 $50 $80**
With Correct Strap - **$50 $100 $175**

MLV-15. Club Manual,
1937. Pictures 33 premiums. - **$15 $30 $60**

MLV-16. Premium Catalogue Folder Sheet,
1937. Pictures 12 premiums. - **$15 $30 $50**

MLV-17

MLV-18

MLV-19

MLV-17. Scarab Ring,
1937. Scarab in green. Also issued for Captain Frank Hawks. - **$250 $500 $1200**

MLV-18. Secret Operator/Law & Order Patrol Brass Ring,
1937. - **$75 $125 $175**

MLV-19. "Secret Operator" Brass Badge,
1937. - **$20 $40 $60**

MLV-20

MLV-21

MLV-22

MLV-20. "Lieutenant" Brass Rank Badge,
1937. - **$20 $40 $75**

MLV-21. "Captain" Brass Rank Badge,
1937. - **$25 $50 $85**

MLV-22. "Secret Operators/Girls Division" Brass Badge,
1937. - **$20 $60 $75**

MLV-24

MLV-23   **MLV-25**

MLV-23. "Secret Operator" Grained Leather Wallet,
1937. Inside has two slot pockets and small note pad. -
$20 $60 $90

MLV-24. "Inter-District Pass" Club Card,
1937. - **$20 $50 $85**

MLV-25. Prize Folder,
1937. Junior G-Man premium folder. 4 pages. -
$25 $50 $75

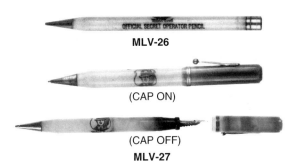

MLV-26

(CAP ON)

(CAP OFF)
MLV-27

MLV-26. "Melvin Purvis Official Secret Operator Pencil",
1937. Scarce. 5-1/2" bakelite mechanical pencil with
inscription plus portrait. - **$50 $100 $200**

MLV-27. "Melvin Purvis Official Secret Operator Combination" Bakelite Pen/Mechanical Pencil,
1937. Rare. - **$100 $400 $750**

MLV-28

MLV-29

MLV-28. "Secret Operator" Pocketknife,
1937. Steel with cello. grips. Pictured in premium catalogue for Secret Operators. - **$50 $100 $200**

MLV-29. G-Man Tin Whistle,
1930s. No Purvis markings. - **$20 $50 $75**

MICKEY MANTLE

Oklahoma-born Mickey Mantle (1931-1995) joined the
New York Yankees in 1951 and soon succeeded Joe
DiMaggio in center field. A powerful switch-hitter,
Mantle hit 536 home runs in his 18 seasons with the
team. The Mick won the Triple Crown in 1956, was
voted the American League's Most Valuable Player in
1956, 1957, and 1962, and played in every All-Star
game between 1951 and 1968, when he retired. He was
elected to the Baseball Hall of Fame in 1974. One of
the most popular athletes of his time, Mantle slugged
his way into the hearts of sports fans everywhere.

MKM-1   **MKM-2**

MKM-1. "I Love Mickey" Sheet Music,
1956. Words and music for fan song popularized by
songstress Teresa Brewer. - **$20 $40 $65**

MKM-2. "Boys' Life" Cover Article,
1959. Monthly issue for August with color photos cover for
article "Star Of The Stadium" with 11 more photos. -
$10 $20 $40

MKM-4

MKM-3   **MKM-5**

MKM-3. "Mickey Mantle" Cello. Button,
1950s. Probable stadium souvenir with fabric ribbon and
plastic charms. -
$40 $60 $125

MKM-4. "I Love Mickey" Cello. Button,
1950s. Promotion for tribute song to Mickey Mantle
inspired and sung by songstress Teresa Brewer. -
$20 $40 $60

MKM-5. Mickey Mantle Cello. Button,
1950s. Youthful photo image with attachments of fabric ribbon plus plastic charms on keychain. - **$75 $150 $250**

MKM-6

MKM-7

MKM-12

MKM-13

MKM-6. "Playing Major League Baseball" Booklet,
1950s. Karo Syrup. 6x9" with 32 pages including baseball tips attributed to Mickey Mantle plus similar tips from various other major league stars. - **$20 $40 $60**

MKM-7. "Louisville Sluggers" 11x17" Paper Sign With Mantle And Others,
1950s. Hillerich & Bradsby Co. Poster by bat maker company with facsimile signatures of dozens of well-known batters featuring "Mickey Mantle" signature on depicted baseball bat writing pen. - **$15 $30 $60**

MKM-12. Mickey Mantle Guest Appearance Cello. Button,
1982. For local mall visit in his retirement years. - **$5 $10 $15**

MKM-13. Mickey Mantle Personal Appearance Cello. Button,
1982. For local mall visit in his retirement years. - **$5 $10 $15**

MICKEY MOUSE

Mickey Mouse has been called a legend, a national symbol, a worldwide celebrity, a work of art, a merchandising monarch, the successor to Charlie Chaplin, the keystone of the Walt Disney empire. Mickey's career took off in 1928 with *Steamboat Willie*, the first animated cartoon with sychronized sound. Ub Iwerks did the animation, Walt Disney did the voice of Mickey, and success was immediate.

Over the next 25 years the studio turned out some 120 cartoons starring Mickey. Supporting characters included Minnie Mouse, Pluto the Pup, Donald Duck, Goofy, Horace Horsecollar, and Clarabelle Cow. The Mickey daily comic strip, distributed by King Features, began in 1930 and the Sunday pages in 1932, scripted and drawn by Floyd Gottfredson for the next 45 years.

1930 also saw the first Mickey book published by Bibo and Lang followed by a continuing flood of magazines, collections, reprints, albums, specials, and hardbacks, along with feature appearances in other Disney books.

Mickey and his pals had a brief run on NBC radio in 1938, sponsored by Pepsodent toothpaste. *The Mickey Mouse Club*--the most popular afternoon children's network television series ever--was broadcast on ABC from 1955 to 1959, with reruns syndicated in 1962-1965, 1975-1976, and as *The New Mickey Mouse Club* in 1977-1978. The series, hosted by the Mouseketeers, was a mix of music, cartoons, serialized adventures, children's news features, and visits by guest celebrities. In 1995 *Runaway Brain*, the first Mickey cartoon short in more than 40 years, was released to theaters.

Mickey's popularity continues undiminished, as does the merchandising and licensing of Mickey Mouse items of all shapes and sizes.

MKM-8

MKM-9

MKM-8. "Life" Magazine With Post Cereals Card Ad And Insert, 1962. Weekly issue for April 13 with full page ad for cereal box cards plus example bound insert card picturing Mantle on one side and Roger Maris on other side. Magazine With Insert Intact - **$25 $50 $75**

MKM-9. "Mickey Mantle" 3" Cello. Button,
c. 1962. Full color photo with facsimile signature, image is 1955 Dormand postcard photo. - **$15 $30 $50**

MKM-10

MKM-11

MKM-10. Closeup Photo,
1963. Phillies cigars. 6-1/2x9" black and white with facsimile signature. - **$15 $35 $60**

MKM-11. "All Star" Wristwatch With Mantle, Others,
1960s. Store item. Dial face has facsimile signatures of Mickey Mantle, Roger Maris, Willie Mays. - **$50 $75 $100**

MCK-1

MCK-1. "Chief Mickey Mouse" 2-1/8" Cello. Button,
Copyright 1928-1930. High rank award from series of various officer ranks of Mickey Mouse Clubs organized in movie theaters. Copyright is by W. E. Disney. - **$500 $1500 $2500**

MCK-2

MCK-2. First "Mickey Mouse Book",
1930. Published by Bibo & Lang, several printings. The first Disney publication, pages 9-10 often missing due to children cutting out game pieces.
Complete - **$1000 $5000 $10000**
Missing Pages 9-10 - **$200 $800 $1500**

MCK-4   MCK-5

MCK-3

MCK-3. "Theme Song" Music Sheet,
1930. Movie theater hand-out. Song title "Minnie's Yoo Hoo." - **$25 $50 $75**

MCK-4. Movie Club Cello. Button,
1930. Inscribed "Copy. 1928-1930 By W. E. Disney". - **$60 $100 $175**

MCK-5. "Mickey Mouse Club" Cello. Button,
1930. 1928-1930 W. E. Disney copyright. - **$50 $90 $150**

MCK-6   MCK-8

MCK-7

MCK-6. "Meets Every Saturday" Club Member Cello. Button,
1930. Standard image with 1930 Disney copyright and name on bottom edge but uncommon imprint. - **$75 $150 $200**

MCK-7. "Mickey Mouse" Wood Jointed Figure,
1930. Scarce. Store item. 4-1/2" tall with flat disk hands to allow balancing in various positions. - **$200 $400 $800**

MCK-8. Mickey In Santa Outfit Cello. Button,
c. 1930. Several imprints but usually "Meet Me At Hank's Toyland." - **$300 $600 $1200**

MCK-9

MCK-9. Mickey Mouse Illustrated Movie Stories,
1931. David McKay Co. Hardcover. Store item. 190 pages of black & white story pages with art taken from eleven of Mickey's earliest cartoons. 6-1/4x8-3/4."
With Dust Jacket. - **$400 $650 $1100**
Without Jacket. - **$250 $400 $750**
With 2" Red Wraparound Banner With Instructions add $150

MCK-11   MCK-12

MCK-10

MCK-10. First Newspaper Premium Picture Card,
May 1931. Various newspapers. 3-1/2x5-1/2" bw. - **$100 $400 $750**

MCK-11. Mickey Mouse Paper Face Mask,
1933. Store and theater give-away, published by Einson-Freeman Co. - **$25 $50 $75**

MCK-12. Minnie Mouse Paper Mask,
1933. Store and theater give-away. - **$15 $25 $50**

MCK-13

MCK-13. "Mickey Mouse Magazine" Vol. 1 #1,
January 1933. Rare #1. Various dairies, stores. "Published
By Kamen-Blair, Inc." on front cover. Nine issues, first few
had 5 cents on cover. First Issue - **$350 $1050 $3000**
Other Issues - **$115 $350 $900**

MCK-14

MCK-15

MCK-14. "Mickey Mouse Magazine",
1933. #1 Rare. Various dairies, Nov. 1933-Oct. 1935.
"Edited By Hal Horne" on cover.
1st Issue - **$125 $375 $1000**

MCK-15. "Mickey Mouse Magazine",
1933. Various dairies, Nov. 1933-Oct. 1935.
Nos. 2-12 Each - **$45 $130 $350**

MCK-16

MCK-16. "Mickey Mouse Bubble Gum" Example Cards,
1933. Gum Inc. #1-96 first series plus #97-120 titled
"Mickey Mouse With The Movie Stars".
First Series Each - **$5 $12 $25**
Movie Stars Each - **$35 $75 $150**

MCK-17

MCK-17. Picture Card Album Vol. 2,
1933. For cards #49-96. Volume 1 holds cards #1-48.
Unused #1 - **$50 $200 $200**
Unused #2 - **$75 $150 $250**

MCK-18

MCK-19

**MCK-18. "Mickey Mouse Bubble Gum" Waxed Paper
Wrapper,**
1933. Store item, used for cards #1-96 of Gum Inc. card
set. - **$60 $150 $200**

**MCK-19. "Mickey Mouse With The Movie Stars" Gum
Wrapper,**
1933. Gum Inc. Wrapper for cards #97-120. -
$150 $300 $600

MCK-20

MCK-21

MCK-20. "Mickey Mouse The Mail Pilot" BLB,
1933. American Oil Co. Softcover version. - **$40 $90 $150**

MCK-21. Cello. Button 3-1/2",
c. 1933. Worn by store employees. - **$250 $1000 $2000**

MCK-22

MCK-22. "Mickie Mouse Animal Crackers" Box,
c. 1933. Rare. Apparent unauthorized item (or printing
error) with misspelled name. Near Mint Flat - **$1500**
Folded - **$150 $400 $750**

MCK-24

MCK-23

MCK-23. "Micky Maus" 17x24" German Film Poster,
1934. Rare. - **$500 $2000 $3500**

MCK-24. Card Game,
1934. Hoffman's Ice Cream. 24 cards. 8 page instruction sheet and box. - **$75 $150 $175**

MCK-25

MCK-25. Post Toasties Box,
1934. Rare. Mickey pictured on front. Several versions.
Each Complete - **$750 $1500 $2550**

MCK-26

MCK-26. Post Toasties Box,
1935. Scarce. Mickey pictured on front. Several versions.
Each Complete - **$500 $1000 $2100**

MCK-27

MCK-27. First "Mickey Mouse Magazine" Vol. 1 #1,
1935. Later became "Walt Disney's Comics & Stories". Kay Kamen Publications/Western Publishing Co., size 10-1/4x 13-1/4". - **$1100 $3300 $11000**

MCK-28

MCK-28. "Mickey Mouse And The Magic Carpet" Book,
1935. Various sponsors, and used as a Mickey Mouse Magazine premium as late as 1938. - **$150 $250 $400**

MCK-29   MCK-30   MCK-31

MCK-29. "Mickey Mouse And Minnie March To Macy's" Booklet,
1935. Rare. Macy's department store. Published by Whitman in format of Big Little Book. - **$300 $750 $1000**

MCK-30. "Mickey Mouse Hose" Cello. Button,
c. 1935. - **$60 $100 $175**

MCK-31. Litho. Button,
c. 1935. Comes with back paper reading "Mickey Mouse Gloves And Mittens". - **$75 $150 $350**

MCK-32

MCK-32. "Magic Movie Palette",
1935. Store give-away. Mechanical paper. -
$75 $150 $300

MCK-34

MCK-33

MCK-33. Glazed Ceramic Toothbrush Holder,
c. 1936. Store item by S. Maw & Son, London.-
$250 $450 $700

MCK-34. "The Atlanta Georgian's Silver Anniversary" Litho. Button,
1937. Named newspaper. From set of various characters. -
$150 $350 $750

MCK-35

MCK-35. Pepsodent 10x40" Paper Poster,
1937. For NBC radio show. - **$125 $250 $400**

MCK-36

MCK-36. Post Toasties Mickey Box,
1937. - **$100 $200 $300**

MCK-37

MCK-37. "The Mickey Mouse Globe Trotter Weekly" Vol. 3 No. 3 Example ,
1937. Various bakeries and dairies. Each - **$20 $40 $60**

MCK-38   MCK-39

MCK-38. "Globe Trotter Club" Membership Card,
1937. Various sponsors. - **$20 $40 $75**

MCK-39. "Mickey Mouse Globe Trotters/Member" Cello. Button,
1937. Imprints of various bakeries and dairies. -
$20 $40 $75

MCK-40

MCK-40. "Round The World" Map,
1937. Issued by various bread companies. Opens to 20x27" for mounting 24 "Globe Trotters" picture cards. Without Pictures - **$50 $125 $250**

MCK-41

MCK-41. "Mickey Mouse Globe Trotters" 11x23" Paper Store Sign,
1937. Imprinted for Peter Pan Bread. Mickey is pictured holding May 1937 issue of Mickey Mouse Magazine. - **$200 $400 $600**

MCK-42

MCK-42. Sunoco Oil Advertising Booklet,
1938. - **$40 $60 $125**

MCK-43

MCK-43. "Mickey Mouse Magazine" Gift Subscription Card With Envelope ,
1938. With Envelope - **$50 $125 $200**
Loose - **$35 $75 $150**

MCK-44

MCK-44. Dental Appointment Envelope, Card And Certificate,
c. 1938. Envelope - **$5 $10 $15**
Card - **$15 $25 $40**
Certificate - **$25 $60 $90**

MCK-45   MCK-46

MCK-45. Mickey Mouse Cello. Button,
1938. Offered for subscription to Mickey Mouse Magazine. - **$35 $75 $125**

MCK-46. "Mickey Mouse Travel Club" Map,
1938. Various sponsors, example is for Star Bakery. Opens to 16-1/2x24" from series featuring various states. - **$100 $200 $300**

MCK-47

MCK-48

MCK-47. "Mickey Mouse-Good Teeth" Cello. Button,
c. 1938. Back paper for Bureau of Public Relations/American Dental Association. - **$50 $110 $175**

MCK-48. Christmas Giveaway for Shoes,
1939. Rare. - **$175 $525 $1600**

MCK-49

MCK-49. Cereal Box,
1939. Mickey not on front. - **$100 $200 $300**

MCK-50

MCK-50. "All-Star Parade Glasses" Brochure,
1939. Includes order blank for cottage cheese filled glasses. - **$40 $75 $125**

MCK-51

MCK-51. "Mickey's And Donald's Race To Treasure Island" 20x27" Paper Map.
1939. Standard Oil of California. Pictures from "Travel Tykes" weekly newspapers go around border.
Unused - **$100 $200 $450**

MCK-52

MCK-52. Sunoco Winter Oil Postcard,
1939. Pictures Mickey as pilgrim. - **$20 $30 $50**

MCK-53

MCK-54

MCK-53. Blue Sunoco Cardboard Ink Blotter,
1939. Pictures Minnie and Mickey as bride and groom. -
$25 $50 $75

MCK-54. Pocket Mirror,
1930s. Black/white/red printed on ribbed paper with satin-
like finish. Only authentic 1930s design known, fantasy
mirrors include Chicago 1933 and New York 1939 World's
Fair reference. - **$75 $150 $300**

MCK-55

MCK-56

MCK-55. "Mickey Mouse Scrapbook",
1930s. Various bakery imprints. The first bread card book.
Designed to hold 24 large sized cards, see next item. -
$75 $125 $250

MCK-56. Large Recipe Cards,
1930s. Photo shows 16 of 24 in set for previous item.
Each - **$8 $12 $20**

MCK-57

MCK-57. "Mickey Mouse Recipe Scrapbook",
1930s. Various bakery and dairy company imprints.
Designed to hold 48 cards, see next item. - **$40 $75 $125**

MCK-58

MCK-58. Small Recipe Cards,
1930s. Photo shows 35 of 48 in set for previous item.
Each - **$5 $10 $15**

MCK-60

MCK-59

MCK-61

MCK-59. Bread Loaf Waxed Paper Insert Band,
1930s. Various breads. Offers free Recipe Scrapbook for
bread pictures. - **$50 $125 $200**

MCK-60. Mickey Mouse 7-1/2" Bavarian China Plate,
1930s. Used as movie theater give-aways, various
designs. 7-1/2" Size - **$150 $300 $600**
6" Size - **$100 $200 $400**

MCK-61. Mickey Mouse Bavarian China Cream Pitcher,
1930s. Used as movie theater give-aways, various
designs. - **$100 $200 $400**

MCK-62   MCK-63

MCK-64

MCK-62. German Bisque Figures,
1930s. Store item. Pair - **$150 $300 $600**

MCK-63. Hard Rubber Figure,
1930s. Store item by Seiberling Rubber Co. Thin rubber tail usually gone. No Tail - **$35 $75 $150**
With Tail - **$75 $150 $300**

MCK-64. Cardboard String Climbing Toy,
1930s. Store item by Dolly Toy Co. - **$200 $400 $650**

MCK-65   MCK-66

MCK-65. Cardboard Figural Pencil Case,
1930s. Store item by Dixon Pencil Co. - **$125 $225 $350**

MCK-66. "Dixon's Mickey Mouse Map Of The United States" 10x14",
1930s. Came in pencil boxes. - **$25 $60 $100**

MCK-68

MCK-67

MCK-67. "Mickey Mouse Globe Trotters" Door Hanger,
1930s. Pictured example imprinted for Pevely Dairy Co. Diecut stiff paper for door knob suspension including offer for membership button and world map. - **$75 $150 $225**

MCK-68. "Mickey Mouse Beverages" Felt Cap,
1930s. Fabric garrison-style cap with designated area on headband for mounting six bottle caps issued with brass pins. See MCK-79. - **$75 $150 $250**

MCK-69   MCK-70

MCK-69. "Mickey Mouse Club" Cello. Button,
1930s. W. E. Disney copyright plus back paper for Kay Kamen Distributorship. - **$40 $75 $125**

MCK-70. "Post Toasties" Stationery Sheet,
1930s. Letterhead art offering "Mickey Mouse And Other Walt Disney Cut-Outs On Back And Sides Of Package." Pictured example is letterhead only of 8-1/2x11" sheet. - **$50 $125 $200**

MCK-71

MCK-71. Mickey Mouse Bread 9x16" Paper Poster,
1930s. Advertises "A New Picture Card Every Day With Every Loaf." - **$250 $600 $1200**

MCK-72   MCK-73

MCK-72. Mickey & Minnie Bisque Toothbrush Holder,
1930s. Store item. - **$75 $150 $250**

MCK-73. Paper Hat,
1930s. Mickey Mouse Comic Cookies. - **$50 $100 $200**

MCK-74   MCK-75

MCK-74. Play Money $1.00 Bill,
1930s. Southern Dairies Ice Cream premium. -
$10 $20 $35

MCK-75. Play Money $10.00 Bill,
1930s. Southern Dairies Ice Cream premium. -
$10 $20 $35

MCK-76

MCK-77

MCK-82

MCK-76. Toasted Nut Chocolate Candy Wrapper,
1930s. Wilbur-Suchard Chocolate Co. - **$30 $60 $100**

MCK-77. Dixie Ice Cream Cup Lid,
1930s. Southern Dairies. - **$25 $60 $100**

MCK-82. Dodge Motors Advertising Flip Booklet,
1930s. Story title "Mickey Takes Minnie For A Ride". -
$35 $75 $150

MCK-78

MCK-78. Post Cereal Spoon,
1930s. Near Mint In Mailer With Instructions - **$200**
Spoon Only - **$8 $15 $30**

MCK-83

MCK-84

MCK-83. Movie Theater Club Card,
1930s. Back has club creed. - **$40 $85 $150**

**MCK-84. "Penney's For Back To School Needs" Cello.
Button,**
1930s. - **$35 $65 $100**

MCK-79

MCK-80

MCK-85

MCK-86

MCK-87

MCK-79. Mickey Mouse Bottle Cap Set Of Six,
1930s. Stores supplied a felt hat for bottle caps that had
brass pins for mounting. Usually found without the spring
pins. See MCK-68. Each - **$15 $30 $60**

**MCK-80. "Mickey And Oswald Shake Hands"
Department Store Card,**
1930s. Boston store. Christmas "Toytown" give-away with
unauthorized art. - **$25 $50 $80**

MCK-85. Minnie Mouse "Good Teeth" Cello. Button,
1930s. Kern County Health Department, California. -
$300 $800 $1750

MCK-86. "Southern Dairies Ice Cream" Cello. Button,
1930s. Scarce. - **$300 $700 $1500**

**MCK-87. "California Mickey Mouse Club" Cello.
Button,**
1930s. - **$60 $100 $175**

MCK-81

MCK-88

MCK-89

MCK-90

**MCK-81. "Mickey Mouse's Midnight Adventure"
Folder,**
1930s. Accompanied "USA Lites" flashlights. -
$35 $75 $125

MCK-88. "Evening Ledger Comics" Cello. Button,
1930s. Philadelphia newspaper. From set of 14 various characters. - **$200 $400 $700**

MCK-89. "Evening Ledger Comics" Cello. Button,
1930s. Philadelphia newspaper. From set of 14 various characters. - **$150 $300 $600**

MCK-90. "Mickey Mouse Undies" Cello. Button,
1930s. - **$50 $90 $150**

MCK-91

MCK-92

MCK-91. "Ask For Mickey Mouse Undies" Paper Tag,
1930s. Stamp nature but example seen had ungummed back, other inscriptions "Make Children Happier" and "Undergarments Of Quality". - **$35 $60 $100**

MCK-92. Goodyear Tires Mailing Brochure,
1940. Canadian issue, opens to 11x20". - **$35 $75 $125**

MCK-93

MCK-94

MCK-93. Mickey Mouse "Nu-Blue Sunoco" Cardboard Ink Blotter,
1940. Example pictures him in speeding car. - **$20 $40 $60**

MCK-94. "Sunheat Furnace Oil" Cardboard Ink Blotter,
c. 1940. Sun Oil Co. Mickey hanging wall plaque. - **$12 $25 $40**

MCK-95

MCK-96

MCK-95. Sunoco Oil Cardboard Ink Blotter,
c. 1940. Pictures Donald listening for motor knocks. - **$20 $40 $60**

MCK-96. Sunoco Oil Ink Blotter,
1941. Depicts Mickey and Donald in military outfits. - **$50 $100 $150**

MCK-97

MCK-97. Sunoco Oil Ink Blotter,
1942. Mickey by artillery gun with oil bottle body. - **$10 $20 $45**

MCK-98

MCK-99

MCK-98. "Mickey Mouse...On The Home Front" Newspaper,
April 1944. Beechcraft Aviation Corp. - **$35 $75 $150**

MCK-99. "Mickey Mouse" Weekly English Newspaper,
1945. Long running publication, seldom better than Fine condition. 1930s Each - **$10 $20 $30**
1940s Each - **$8 $15 $25**

MCK-100

MCK-100. "US Time" Comic With Mickey Watch Ad,
c. 1947. - **$25 $50 $80**

MCK-101

MCK-102

MCK-101. Beanie,
1940s. Scarce. - **$100 $200 $300**

MCK-102. "March Of Comics" #60,
1950. Various sponsors. - **$35 $105 $245**

MCK-103

MCK-103. 78 RPM Record,
1956. General Mills, Inc. #3 from series of four.
Each With Sleeve - **$10 $15 $25**

MCK-104

MCK-105

MCK-104. Mickey Mouse And His Pals Plastic Rings,
1956. Sugar Jets cereal. Peter Pan example from set of
eight: Mickey, Minnie, Donald, Pluto, Snow White,
Pinocchio, Dumbo, Peter Pan. Each - **$40 $60 $80**

MCK-105. Picture Sheet For Bread Label Cut-Outs,
1950s. NBC Bread. Blank - **$40 $60 $80**

MCK-106

**MCK-106. "Mickey Mouse Club Magic Kit" Punch-Out
Set,**
1950s. Mars candy. Near Mint In Mailer - **$75**

MCK-107

MCK-108

MCK-107. Mouseketeer Doll,
1950s. Scarce. Mickey Mouse Club. Store bought
marionette on roller skates. - **$50 $150 $300**

MCK-108. Punch-Out Paper Puppet,
1950s. Donald Duck Bread. Unpunched - **$10 $20 $35**

MCK-109

**MCK-109. Pillsbury "Mickey Mouse Club" Ring Offer
Box,**
1950s. Offered set of five aluminum rings: Donald, Goofy,
Jiminy, Bambi, Cinderella. Box - **$25 $50 $75**
Each Ring - **$10 $20 $35**

MCK-110

MCK-111

MCK-112

MCK-110. "KVOS-TV 12" Cello. Club Button,
1950s. Unidentified but TV station of Bellingham,
Washington. - **$15 $25 $40**

**MCK-111. "Member Mickey Mouse Club" Litho. Tin
Tab,**
1950s. - **$8 $15 $25**

MCK-112. Club Membership Card,
1950s. Channel 12 TV premium. - **$15 $30 $50**

MCK-113

MCK-113. "Mars/Mickey Mouse Club Magic Manual"
Booklet,
1950s. - **$10 $20 $30**

MCK-114

MCK-114. "Mickey Mouse Club/Disneyland
Headquarters" Membership Card And Litho. Tab,
1963. Card - **$15 $30 $50**
Tab - **$20 $40 $60**

MCK-116

MCK-115

MCK-115. "Mickey Mouse Explorers Club Coloring
Book",
1965. Kroger food stores. - **$8 $12 $20**

MCK-116. "Seed Shop" 3" Cello. Button,
1976. Promotion for garden seeds in packages featuring
Disney characters. - **$35 $85 $150**

MCK-117

MCK-118

MCK-117. "Around The World In 80 Days" Hardcover
Book,
1978. Crest Toothpaste. - **$5 $10 $20**

MCK-118. "Mickey And Goofy Explore The Universe Of
Energy" Comic Book,
1985. Exxon. - **$1 $2 $3**

MIGHTY MOUSE

The rodent equivalent of Superman, Captain Marvel
and other humanoid cloaked flying heroes, Mighty
Mouse was probably the best-known Terrytoons character and certainly one of the most prolific in animated
episodes. Originally dubbed Supermouse in his 1942
creation year by Paul Terry, the battler of villainous
cats was renamed Mighty Mouse in 1944. He starred in
about 80 television episodes between 1955 and 1967,
frequently saving girlfriend Pearl Pureheart from her
perils. In addition to animated adventures, Mighty
Mouse starred also in numerous comic books by various publishers, including Gold Key and Dell, from the
mid-1940s into the early 1990s.

 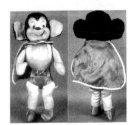

MGH-1

MGH-2

MGH-1. Mighty Mouse 12" Stuffed Oilcloth Doll,
1942. Rare. Rubber head, star designs on cape. -
$200 $500 $750

MGH-2. Vinyl/Plush/Fabric Doll,
c. 1950. Store item by Ideal Toys. Tag inscriptions include
"CBS". - **$50 $100 $150**

MGH-3

MGH-4

MGH-3. Post Cereals "Merry-Pack" Punch-Outs With
Envelope,
1956. Post Treat-Pak and Post Alpha-Bits. Consists of
three sheets to form about 20 items.
Unpunched - **$15 $50 $75**

MGH-4. Club Member Paper Wallet,
1956. Part of previous punch-out set. - **$3 $7 $12**

MGH-5

MGH-5. "Post Cereals Mighty Mouse Mystery Color Picture" Cards,
1957. Set of six. Water makes invisible character appear.
Unused Set - **$30 $50 $75**
Used Set - **$20 $35 $50**

MGH-6

MGH-6. Cereal Box With Cut-Out,
c. 1957. Post Sugar Crisp. Back panel printed for cutting and assembly of action scene toy from set of four.
Uncut - **$50 $100 $150**

MGH-7

MGH-7. Cereal Pack Wrapper,
1950s. Post. Advertises Naval Battles Trading Card. Back panel printed for cutting and assembly of action scene toy from set of four. Uncut - **$50 $100 $150**

MGH-8

MGH-8. Terrytoons Store Hankies,
1950s. Store item. Mighty Mouse opens display. Six hankies with all the Terrytoons characters featured. -
$50 $100 $175

MGH-9   MGH-10   MGH-11

MGH-9. Rubber Squeaker Figure,
1950s. Store item. Comes with red felt cape. -
$20 $60 $100

MGH-10. Terrytoons Fabric Scarf,
1950s. Store item. - **$15 $25 $40**

MGH-11. "Mighty Mouse In Toyland" Record,
1960. Store item by Peter Pan Records. - **$10 $20 $35**

MISTER SOFTEE

Sales of soft ice cream dispensed from a spigot blossomed in the 1950s, not only from ice cream trucks but also from drive-in retail outlets. Thousands of these outlets were opened on the nation's highways by such retail chains as Dairy Queen, Tastee Freeze, and Carvel. By the end of the decade hard ice cream was making a comeback, but the soft ice cream chains had established themselves as a continuing roadside fixture. Dairy Queen issued a few premiums (see Dennis the Menace rings), but Mister Softee was the leader, and issued premiums through the "Mister Softee Club," probably established in the late 1950s.

MSF-1   MSF-2   MSF-3   MSF-4

MSF-1. "Mister Softee Safety Club" Litho. Button,
c. 1950s. Softee Ice Cream. - **$5 $8 $15**

MSF-2. "Mister Softee" Enameled Brass Keychain Tag,
c. 1960s. - **$10 $25 $40**

MSF-3. "Mister Softee" Plastic Ring,
c. 1960s. - **$10 $15 $20**

MSF-4. "I Like Mister Softee" Logo Figure Plastic Ring,
1960s. Mister Softee cones, shakes, sundaes. -
$50 $80 $115

MSF-5

MSF-5. "Adventures Of Captain Chapel" Space Cards, 1960s. Mister Softee. Cards 1-10 are numbered, following cards are unnumbered from unknown set total. - **$1 $2 $3**

THE MONKEES

Four "insane" boys--actors Mickey Dolenz (formerly Mickey Braddock of the TV series *Circus Boy*) and Davy Jones, and musicians Peter Tork and Mike Nesmith--picked from hundreds of hopefuls who answered an audition call, comprised the Monkees, a fictional rock group that nevertheless enjoyed considerable success on records and on network television. The show, inspired stylistically by the Beatles' 1964 film *A Hard Day's Night*, featured surrealistic camera work and comic or melodramatic story lines. The series ran on the three television networks, originally on NBC (1966-1968), and repeated on CBS (1969-1972) and ABC (1972-1973). *Monkees* comic books appeared from 1967 to 1969. Merchandising was extensive, and a custom-built Monkeemobile was created for appearances at automobile shows and shopping centers. After years of obscurity, a resurgence of popularity in Japan and a re-airing of the original television episodes on MTV in 1985 and 1986 sparked a 20th anniversary reunion that produced multiple live performances (a handful including Nesmith, now a successful video production entrepeneur) and a new album in 1987. In 1996, Mike reformed the group yet again to film a special 30th anniversay "episode" of the series and record another new album. Plans are currently in the works for a feature film. Items are usually copyrighted by Raybert Productions or Screen Gems. "Listen to the band!"

MON-1 MON-2

MON-1. Celluloid 3-1/2" Button, 1966. Vendor item. - **$10 $20 $35**

MON-2. "Official Monkees Fan" Cello. Button, 1966. Raybert Productions. - **$15 $30 $45**

MON-3

MON-4

MON-3. Fan Club Postcard, 1967. - **$5 $8 $12**

MON-4. Tour Sign 29x22", 1967. Promotional sign for performance at the Cow Palace in San Francisco. - **$150 $350 $500**

MON-5 MON-6 MON-7

MON-5. Official Fan Club Button, 1967. Litho. 2-1/4". - **$5 $10 $15**

MON-6. Kellogg's "Mike" Flicker Ring, 1967. Set of 12 silvered plastic with insert alternating picture of individual for group. Each - **$20 $40 $65**

MON-7. Monkees Litho. Button, 1967. Vending machine issue set of six. Four with single portraits, two with group portraits. Each - **$3 $5 $10**

MON-8

MON-8. "Monkee Coins", 1967. Kellogg's. Set of 12 color photos in yellow plastic frames. Canadian issue with reverse text in English and French. Each - **$3 $6 $12**

MON-9

MON-9. Photo Flip Booklets, 1967. Store item. Set of 16. Each - **$3 $8 $12**

MON-10

MON-10. "Monkees" Cereal Box Cut-Out Record,
c. 1970. Kellogg's. Series of four box backs.
Each - **$5 $8 $12**

MOVIE MISC.

The first known moving pictures on a public screen
were shown at Koster and Bial's Music Hall in New
York City April 23, 1896. The program included films of
two blonde girls performing an umbrella dance, a
comic boxing exhibition and a view of surf breaking on
a beach. Movies remained only a novelty until shortly
after the turn of the century. 1903 released two pioneer
efforts, *The Passion Play* and *The Great Train Robbery*
and movies as mass entertainment were born.

The 1920s added dimensions of sound plus color
experimentation; full-length features were soon followed by the popular episode serial or "chapter play"
that remained popular to the mid-1950s. Premiums followed a few individual stars of universal acclaim such
as Charlie Chaplin, Our Gang, Shirley Temple.

Generally, movies produced souvenirs of only non-
premium original purpose, e.g., heralds and programs,
lobby cards, posters and similar that since have
matured to status paralleling premiums. Notable
exceptions, of course, are classic films such as *Gone
With The Wind*, Disney creations from the early 1930s
Mickey Mouse to the 1990s *Dick Tracy* version, other
animated cartoons plus premiums resulting from the
most popular of the adventure hero serials.

Movie premiums after the advent of television were
very limited for a time but recent years have seen frequent tie-ins between movies aimed at family audiences and fast food restaurants.

MOV-1

Buttons for
"MIKE and IKE"
"OSWALD"
(The Lucky Rabbit)
"KEEPING UP WITH
THE JONESES"

MOV-2

MOV-1. "Snookums" Cello. Button On Card,
1927. Universal Exchange (Movie Publicity Agency).
Pictured is toddler star of comedy based on "Newlyweds
And Their Baby" comic strip. Button maker is Philadelphia
Badge Co. Complete - **$40 $90 $150**
Button Only - **$25 $60 $100**

MOV-2. "Oswald The Lucky Rabbit" Cello. Button,
1927. Universal Exchange (Movie Publicity Agency).
Pictured is animated cartoon character in Disney art. -
$75 $150 $300

MOV-3

MOV-4

MOV-3. "Jackie Coogan Club" Cello. Button,
1920s. - **$10 $20 $35**

MOV-4. Roscoe "Fatty" Arbuckle Cello. Button,
1920s. - **$15 $30 $50**

MOV-5

MOV-6

MOV-5. "'Freaks' Metro-Goldwyn-Mayer's Amazing
Picture" Cello. Button,
1932. Scarce. Movie was quickly withdrawn from
distribution. - **$200 $600 $1200**

MOV-6. "Tom Tyler/Clancy Of The Mounted" Movie
Club Cello. Button,
1933. Universal Pictures. For 12-chapter serial. -
$75 $175 $250

MOV-7

MOV-8

MOV-7. "Mae West" 17x30" Cardboard Store Sign,
1934. Old Gold cigarettes. Text includes "Goin' To Town"
movie title. - **$350 $600 $1200**

MOV-8. Mae West-Inspired China Ashtray,
c. 1934. Store item. - **$30 $50 $75**

MOV-9

MOV-10

MOV-9. Frankie Darro Stamp Album,
1935. Tootsie Roll. Movie Club premium. Holds 24
stamps. - **$30 $60 $120**

MOV-10. Frankie Darro Stamps,
1935. Large premium stamp given at each movie.
Each - **$10 $20 $30**

MOV-11

MOV-11. Hollywood Snapshots,
1935. Booklet with actual photos of stars inside. Photos
taken by an editor of the L.A. Evening Herald. -
$25 $50 $75

MOV-12

MOV-12. Rio Theatre Photo Folder,
1938. Theatre premium. 16 photos (folder & two photos
shown). Photos - **$2 $4 $10**
Folder - **$5 $10 $20**

MOV-13

**MOV-13. "The Black Falcon Of The Flying G-Men"
Game,**
1939. Store item by Ruckelshaus Game Corp. Based on
Columbia Pictures movie serial. - **$100 $250 $350**

MOV-14

MOV-14. Junior Cagney Club Litho. Buttons,
1930s. Theater patrons collected set of 11, each with single letter of James Cagney name, to gain free admission.
Each - **$5 $10 $15**

MOV-16

MOV-15

MOV-17

**MOV-15. Park Drive Album Cards For Series 1 & 2 -
Spencer,**
1930s.Cigarette premium from England. 96 total cards.
Each Card - **$1 $3 $5**

MOV-16. Park Drive Album Series 1,
1930s.Cigarette premium from England. Album for 48
cards. U.S. stars. Album Only - **$5 $10 $20**

MOV-17. Park Drive Album Series 2,
1930s.Cigarette premium from England. Album for 48
cards. Album Only - **$5 $10 $20**

MOV-19

MOV-18

MOV-18. Churchman's Card Album,
1930s. Cigarette premium from England. Holds 50
cards. Album Only - **$10 $20 $30**

MOV-19. Churchman's Card Album - The Cards,
1930s. Famous U.S. movie stars on cards.
Each Card - **$1 $3 $5**

MOV-21

MOV-20

MOV-27

MOV-20. Film Star Album,
1930s. Cigarette premium from England. Holds cards for 53 stars from U.S. movies. Album Only - **$10 $20 $30**

MOV-21. Film Star Album Cards,
1930s. Cigarette premium from England. 53 different colorful cards. 3rd series. Each Card - **$1 $3 $5**

MOV-27. Cardboard Stand-Up,
1941. Two piece 6x9" promo from "The Outlaw" starring Jane Russell. - **$75 $125 $200**

MOV-22 MOV-23 MOV-24

MOV-28 MOV-29

MOV-22. "The Terrytooners Music And Fun Club" Cello. Button,
1930s. Pictures Farmer Alfalfa and Little Wilbur. - **$20 $45 $75**

MOV-23. "George O'Brien Outdoor Club" Cello. Button,
1930s. - **$20 $35 $65**

MOV-24. "Sabu Club" Cello. Button,
1940. Inscribed for "The Thief Of Baghdad" movie of that year. - **$8 $5 $25**

MOV-28. "Perils Of Nyoka" 27x41" Movie Serial Poster,
1942. Republic Pictures. Poster is for Chapter 1. - **$200 $400 $750**

MOV-29. "Perils Of Nyoka" 27x41" Movie Serial Poster,
1942. Republic Pictures. Same art for Chapters 2-15. Each - **$100 $250 $ 400**

MOV-26

MOV-25

MOV-30 MOV-31

MOV-25. "Citizen Kane" Program,
1941. Souvenir of RKO Radio Pictures classic film directed by and starring Orson Welles. - **$40 $80 $125**

MOV-26. Citizen Kane "Souvenir Of Xanadu" Card Deck,
c. 1941. Playing cards with box art picturing seaside mansion Xanadu of William Randolph Hearst, the pattern for 1941 Orson Welles film "Citizen Kane." - **$100 $200 $300**

MOV-30. "Secret Service In Darkest Africa" 27x41" Movie Serial Poster,
1943. Republic Pictures. - **$40 $75 $125**

MOV-31. "International Reno Browne Fan Club" Newsletter And Membership Card,
c. 1946. Issued by Canadian headquarters.
Near Mint In Mailer - **$35**
Newsletter - **$5 $10 $15**
Card - **$5 $10 $15**

MOV-32   **MOV-33**

MOV-32. Betty Grable Movie Promo,
1947. Chunky Candy Premium. Ten pages of highlights of stars. - **$25 $50 $75**

MOV-33. Hollywood Star Stamps,
1947. Set Y - 12 stamps on uncut sheet in mailer. -
$10 $25 $35

(ENLARGED VIEW OF HOPPY STAMP)

MOV-34   **MOV-35**

MOV-34. Hollywood Star Stamps,
1947. Set Q - 12 stamps on uncut sheet in mailer. -
Eleven Stamps - **$10 $25 $35**
Hoppy Stamp - **$10 $20 $30**

MOV-35. Hollywood Star Stamps,
1947. Set H - 12 stamps on uncut sheet in mailer. -
$10 $25 $35

MOV-37

MOV-36

MOV-36. "The Black Widow" 27x41" Movie Serial Poster,
1947. Republic Pictures. - **$75 $250 $500**

MOV-37. "The Sea Hound Club" Movie Serial Card,
1947. For admission to 15-episode Columbia Pictures serial starring Buster Crabbe. - **$50 $100 $150**

MOV-38

MOV-38. Martin & Lewis Fan Club Member Card And Cello. Button,
1949. Card - **$15 $40 $50**
Button - **$10 $30 $40**

MOV-39

MOV-39. Susan Hayward Puzzle,
1940s. Esquire Magazine premium includes puzzle and mailer. - **$25 $50 $100**

MOV-40   **MOV-41**

MOV-40. "Ginger Rogers" Cigarette Ad Paper Standup,
1940s. Lucky Strike Cigarettes. Lunch place card holder also designed to hold two cigarettes, one of a series. -
$10 $18 $25

MOV-41. "Reno Browne/Queen Of The Westerns" Cello. Button,
1940s. - **$15 $25 $40**

MOV-42

MOV-42. "Little Women" Movie Premium Plastic Jewel Box with Mailer,
1940s. Scarce. - **$40 $100 $150**

MOV-43

MOV-43. "Glance" Magazine With Monroe,
May 1950. Features Marilyn Monroe by her original name, Norma Jean Dougherty. - **$50 $100 $175**

MOV-45

MOV-44

MOV-44. "The Day The Earth Stood Still" 5' Standee,
1951. Rare. - **$1500 $3500 $5500**

MOV-45. Martin & Lewis 21x22" Cardboard Sign,
1951. Chesterfield cigarettes. - **$50 $90 $150**

MOV-46   **MOV-47**

MOV-46. "Jungle Drums Of Africa" Republic Serial, 27x41",
1952. Starred Clayton Moore. - **$15 $25 $50**

MOV-47. "Radar Men From The Moon" 27x41" Movie Serial Poster,
1952. Republic Pictures. - **$150 $275 $400**

MOV-48

MOV-48. Marilyn Monroe Movie Postcard,
1953. For movie "Niagara." - **$25 $60 $125**

MOV-49

MOV-49. "Buster Crabbe Western Club" Photo Card And Button,
1953. Black and white photo card with facsimile autograph plus litho. "Official Badge" pin-back button.
Card - **$10 $15 $25**
Button - **$20 $40 $65**

MOV-51

MOV-52

MOV-50

MOV-50. "The Seven Year Itch" 39x80" Theater Lobby Standee,
1955. - **$750 $1500 $3000**

MOV-51. Martin & Lewis Ceramic Salt & Pepper Set,
1950s. Store item by Napco Ceramic Japan. - **$125 $250 $400**

MOV-52. Jerry Lewis Watch,
1950s. Store item. - **$30 $60 $85**

MOV-53

MOV-54

MOV-53. Marilyn Monroe Pocket Mirror,
1950s. Store item. Full color paper photo with cello. rim. - **$30 $65 $85**

MOV-54. Sunbeam Bread Movie Star Loaf End Labels,
1950s. Each - **$5 $10 $15**

MOV-55

MOV-56

MOV-55. "Walkie-Talkie Set" Offer Folder,
1950s. Campbell's tomato products. Promotional folder for distributors or retailers featuring endorsements of Abbott & Costello, Howdy Doody TV shows. - **$10 $20 $30**

MOV-56. "Melody Time" Promotional Brochure (Disney),
1950s. - **$20 $40 $80**

MOV-57

MOV-58

MOV-59

MOV-57. "Alfred Hitchcock's The Birds" Movie Theater Mask,
1963. - **$10 $20 $30**

MOV-58. "Tom Thumb" Standee,
1960s - **$20 $50 $100**

MOV-59. "Alien" Poseable Plastic Figure,
1979. Store item by Kenner. Came with poster in box. Often missing fangs from mouth. Near Mint Boxed - **$450**
Figure Only - **$100 $200 $300**

MOV-60

MOV-61

MOV-60. "Ghostbusters Ectomobile" Die-Cast Vehicle,
1988. Carded offer with two film rolls from Fuji Film.
Carded - **$40 $75 $125**
Loose - **$10 $20 $30**

MOV-61. "Independence Day" Patch,
1996. Premium notes "Restricted Access" to "Area 51." - **$150**

MR. MAGOO

Near-sighted, stubborn, crotchety Mr. Magoo first stumbled into view in 1949 in the UPA animated cartoon *Ragtime Bear*, and over the next 10 years he starred in more than 50 theatrical cartoons. He went to television on Los Angeles station KTTV in 1960 and to prime-time network television on NBC in *The Famous Adventures of Mr. Magoo* in 1964-1965. Other televised specials followed, and in 1977-1979 the old-timer reappeared in *What's New, Mister Magoo?* on CBS. A theatrical film, *1001 Arabian Nights*, was released by UPA in 1959. Jim Backus (1913-1989) was the voice of Magoo from the beginning. Comic books appeared between 1953 and 1965. General Electric has featured Mr. Magoo in various promotions, and Magoo films have been made for the National Heart Association, Timex, General Foods, Rheingold beer, Ideal toys, Dell Publishing, Colgate-Palmolive, and other advertisers.A 1997 Disney feature film starred Leslie Nielsen as Magoo.

MGO-1

MGO-2

MGO-1. Figural Metal Badge,
1960. GE Lightbulbs. On Card - **$15 $25 $35**
Badge Only - **$8 $15 $20**

MGO-2. General Electric Flicker Plastic Keychain Tag,
1961. - **$10 $18 $25**

MGO-3

MGO-4

MGO-3. Vinyl/Cloth Doll,
1962. Store item. - **$40 $80 $150**

MGO-4. Hand Puppet,
1962. Store item. Soft vinyl head with fabric body. -
$20 $40 $60

MGO-5

MGO-6

MGO-5. Glass Ashtray,
1960s. General Electric. - **$10 $20 $35**

MGO-6. Plastic Ring Kit,
1960s. Store item. Comes with attachment heads of
Magoo, Waldo or Charlie. Near Mint Bagged - **$25**
Each Complete Ring - **$4 $6 $8**

MGO-7

MGO-7. "Big Pop Birthday Bash" Party Kit,
1960s. GE/Hershey's numerous paper items of circus
theme. Near Mint In Mailer - **$90**

MR. PEANUT

The corporate symbol for the Planters Nut and
Chocolate Company was the inspiration of a 13-year-
old schoolboy in a 1916 company-sponsored contest.
Decked out in top hat, monocle, and cane, Mr. Peanut
has been promoting the products of this Suffolk,
Virginia, company ever since. The design has been
refined from the original figure, first in 1927 and again
in 1962. Mr. Peanut has appeared in the form of a wide
variety of promotional items, from lamps to salt and
pepper sets, peanut dishes, banks, buttons, pins,
bookmarks, figures and dolls of wood, plastic, bisque,
and cloth, silverware, cigarette lighters, and mechanical pencils, as well as in a series of children's story
and paint books first published in 1928 and available
from the company in exchange for product wrappers.

MRP-1

**MRP-1. "Mr. Peanut Book No. 1" Canadian Version
Coloring Book,**
c. 1928. Pictured example shows cover and sample coloring page. - **$40 $75 $150**

MRP-2

MRP-3

MRP-4

MRP-5

MRP-2. New York World's Fair Cardboard Bookmark,
1939. - **$5 $12 $20**

MRP-3. Laminated Wooden Pin As Santa,
c. 1939. - **$35 $60 $115**

MRP-4. Laminated Wood Pin,
c. 1939. - **$20 $40 $75**

MRP-5. Wood Jointed Figure,
1930s. Frequently missing his cane. - **$125 $225 $350**

MRP-6

MRP-7

MRP-8

MRP-6. Bisque Ashtray,
1930s. - **$35 $70 $100**

MRP-7. New York World's Fair Wood Figure Pin,
1940. Dated on Trylon either 1939 or 1940.
Each - **$25 $50 $85**

MRP-8. "Spooky Picture" Optical Illusion Card,
c. 1940. Believed insert for Planter's Jumbo Block Bar. -
$5 $15 $25

MRP-9

MRP-10

MRP-9. "The People's Choice" Litho. Button,
c. 1940s. - **$10 $20 $35**

MRP-10. Paperweight Figure,
c. 1940s. 7" tall painted metal figural weight with inscription on rear base "Compliments Planters Nut & Chocolate Co." - **$200 $400 $600**

MRP-11   MRP-12

MRP-13

MRP-11. 50th Anniversary Metal Tray,
1956. - **$20 $40 $60**

MRP-12. Composition Bobbing Body Figure,
1960s. - **$60 $90 $150**

MRP-13. Mr. Peanut Metal Ring,
c. 1960s. Gold luster with raised image of him. -
$10 $20 $30

MR. ZIP

The U.S. Post Office inaugurated its system of ZIP Codes (Zone Improvement Program) on July 1, 1963, to help speed delivery of increasing volumes of mail. A wide-eyed, cheerful character, Mr. ZIP was created to help popularize the program. He zipped along in advertising and at postal conventions between 1963 and July 1986, when he was officially retired.

MRZ-1

MRZ-2

MRZ-1. Service Introduction 32x56" Paper Poster,
1963. Large Mr. ZIP image on post office department poster issued in May. - **$25 $50 $75**

MRZ-2. "Zip Code" Game,
1964. Store item by Lakeside Toys. Game is based on actual post office and zip code operations. - **$10 $20 $35**

MRZ-3   MRZ-4   MRZ-5

MRZ-3. "Mr. ZIP" Cello. Button,
1960s. U.S. Postal Service. -
$5 $10 $15

MRZ-4. "Use Zip Code" Cello. Button,
1960s. U.S. Postal Service. - **$5 $10 $15**

MRZ-5. "Mr. ZIP" Figure Pin,
1960s. U.S. Postal Service. Gold luster figure image in salute pose with "US Mail" pouch over one shoulder. -
$5 $10 $15

MRZ-6

MRZ-7

MRZ-6. Mail Box Bank,
1960s. Store item. 6" tall litho. tin replica of mail drop box with coin savings chart on back panel. - **$10 $20 $30**

MRZ-7. "Zip Code System" First Day Commemorative Cover,
1974. Probably a 10th anniversary issue postmarked January 4 from Washington, D.C. - **$10 $20 $30**

MUHAMMAD ALI

He was born Cassius Clay in Louisville, Ky., in 1942, began amateur boxing at age 12, and burst into boxing prominence in 1960, when he won the Amateur Athletic Union light-heavyweight title, the National Golden Gloves heavyweight title, and an Olympic gold medal as a light-heavyweight. Then he turned professional, and four years later defeated Sonny Liston to win the world heavyweight championship. Clay changed his name to Muhammad Ali and embraced the Muslim religion. In 1967 he refused induction into the army as a conscientious objector and was stripped of his title and banned from boxing. In 1971 his refusal was upheld in a unanimous decision of the Supreme Court. Ali regained his title in 1974, knocking out George Foreman in "The Rumble in the Jungle" in Zaire, then lost it in 1978 to Leon Spinks, and won it back from Spinks seven months later. Ali retired in 1979, then returned to the ring and lost bouts in 1980 and 1981, after which he again retired.

Always a popular and beloved champion, Ali lent his name and image to a variety of commercial products, including shoe polish, potato chips, cookies, barbecue sauce, candy bars, cologne, shaving cream, Knockout shampoo, roach traps, dolls and games. He played himself in a 1977 biographical movie, *The Greatest*, and provided his voice for the 1977 NBC-television animated series, *I Am the Greatest: The Adventures of Muhammad Ali*. In 1996, Ali lit the torch at the summer Olympics in Atlanta. Also, a 1997 documentary, *When We Were Kings*, about Ali's "Rumble in the Jungle" with Foreman, has garnered many awards and much critical praise.

MUH-1

MUH-1. Cassius Clay "The Champ Sings!" Record, c. 1962. 7x7" sleeve holding 45 rpm record sung by him of song titles "Stand By Me" and "I Am The Greatest." - **$20 $40 $60**

MUH-2

MUH-2. Ali-Joe Frazier Championship Fight Pennant, 1971. 8x21" felt fabric for undated but March 8 bout at Madison Square Garden. - **$15 $25 $50**

MUH-3

MUH-3. Ali-Jimmy Ellis Fight Promotion Photo, 1971. 8x10" black and white print of 10 Ali facial expressions and contortions with inscriptions including upcoming July 26 closed circuit telecast bout from Houston Astrodome. - **$10 $20 $30**

MUH-4

MUH-4. Ali-George Foreman Championship Fight Pennant, 1974. 8-1/2x27" felt fabric for October 29 bout in Zaire, Africa. - **$15 $30 $45**

MUH-5

MUH-6

MUH-5. Ali-Joe Frazier 14x22" Fight Poster, 1974. For closed circuit telecast of January 28 "Super Fight II" bout. - **$40 $80 $125**

MUH-6. Ali Exhibition Match 14x23" Paper Poster, c. 1976. For closed circuit TV 15-round specialty match between him and Antonio Inoki, Japanese heavyweight wrestling champion, televised from Tokyo. - **$25 $40 $60**

MUH-7

MUH-8

MUH-7. Ali/Charity Event 3" Cello. Button,
1979. Promotion for exhibition match between him and
"The Urban Fighter" Mayor Tommie Smith of Jersey City,
New Jersey. - **$15** **$30** **$50**

MUH-8. Ali/Charity Event 3-1/2" Cello. Button,
1979. For same event as preceding item also picturing
New Jersey Governor Byrne and apparent Ali unnamed
body guard to prevent thrashing by Mayor Smith. -
$15 **$30** **$50**

MUH-9   MUH-10

MUH-9. "Muhammad Ali" Belt Buckle,
c. 1970s. Everlast boxing equipment. Bronze luster finish
on thick metal with image and inscriptions in raised relief. -
$15 **$40** **$75**

**MUH-10. Ali-Larry Holmes Championship Fight 4"
Cello. Button,**
1980. For employee of hosting Caesar's Palace, Las
Vegas prior to October 2 match. - **$10** **$20** **$30**

THE MUPPETS

Jim Henson (1936-1990) introduced his Muppets on
local television in Washington, D.C. in 1955, with *Sam
and Friends*. The creatures (the name is a combination
of marionette and puppet) found use in commercials
and gained national exposure in periodic guest
appearances on a number of variety shows.

They debuted as regulars in 1969 on *Sesame Street*,
the phenomenally successful children's television
series, where Big Bird, Oscar the Grouch, Bert and
Ernie, and the Cookie Monster have enchanted millions. *The Muppet Show* (syndicated, 1976-1981) was
hosted by Kermit the Frog, who managed to avoid the
persistent romantic advances of the divine Miss Piggy.
The show garnered three Emmys. In 1975-1976, during
the first season of *Saturday Night Live*, Jim Henson's
creations—The Scred (lizard-like muppets that became
the prototypes for the characters featured in the 1982
film *The Dark Crystal*)—appeared alongside the Not
Ready For Prime Time Players. *Muppet Babies*, the animated series sponsored by Campbell soups and
Sears, premiered on CBS in 1984 and went on to win
numerous Emmy awards.

New Muppet characters were introduced on *Fraggle
Rock* (cable, 1983). The creatures also made movies:
The Muppet Movie (1979), *The Great Muppet Caper*
(1981), *The Muppets Take Manhattan* (1984), and
Muppet Treasure Island (1996). *Muppet-Vision 3D*
opened in 1991 at Walt Disney World's Disney/MGM
Studios Theme Park. Kermit and pals also returned to

TV, but less successfully than before. Jim Henson died
on May 16, 1990. Despite the passing of this gifted
man, his legacy lives on--Henson's son Brian continues to guide the Muppets through a variety of all-new
adventures. Merchandising of the Muppet characters
has become a multi-million-dollar industry.

MUP-1   MUP-2

MUP-1. "The Muppet Show" Lunch Box With Bottle,
1978. Store item by King-Seeley Co. Metal box and plastic
bottle. Box - **$10** **$20** **$30**
Bottle - **$5** **$10** **$15**

MUP-2. Kermit The Frog Figural Container,
1978. Store item. Ceramic holder and lid by Sigma. -
$25 **$50** **$75**

MUP-3   MUP-4   MUP-5

MUP-3. Miss Piggy Wristwatch,
1979. Store item. By Picco with Henson Associates Inc.
copyright. - **$10** **$20** **$30**

MUP-4. Fozzie Bear Enameled Brass Figure Pin,
c. 1970s. Satchel inscription is "Jaycee Kids." -
$5 **$10** **$15**

MUP-5. Kermit Frog Enamel Brass Figure Pin,
c. 1970s. Local sponsor is "NJ Jaycees." - **$5** **$10** **$15**

MUP-6   MUP-7   MUP-8

MUP-6. Miss Piggy Ceramic Mug,
1970s. Store item by Sigma. - **$10 $20 $30**

MUP-7. Miss Piggy Ceramic Figural Bank,
1970s. Store item by Sigma. - **$20 $40 $75**

MUP-8. Kermit The Frog Ceramic Mug,
1970s. Store item by Sigma. - **$5 $12 $20**

MUP-9

MUP-10

MUP-9. "The Great Muppet Caper" Glass Tumblers,
1981. McDonald's. From set of four. Each - **$2 $4 $6**

**MUP-10. "Miss Piggy's Calendar Of Calendars" 2-1/4"
Cello. Promo Button,**
1983. Alfred A. Knopf Publishing Co. with Henson
Associates copyright. - **$8 $15 $25**

MUP-11

MUP-11. Kermit The Frog Telephone,
1983. Store item by American Telecommunications Corp.
copyright Henson Associates Inc. Hard plastic actual function telephone 8x8x11". - **$30 $50 $100**

MUSIC MISC.

Great vocalists, instrumentalists or instruments do not
necessarily great premiums make. Vocalists, other
than Elvis and the Beatles, have created little furor in
premiums throughout the years, other than a small
flurry of pin-back buttons picturing crooner stars of
the 1940s-1950s. Rock music groups beginning in the
1960s have inspired some very attractively designed
buttons, although mainly of retail nature. Music instruments and premiums seldom mingle. Possibly a kazoo
here, a harmonica there and--by considerable leeway -
bird calls, sirens, etc. Still, music in its broadest sense
has produced a modest assortment of premiums such
as songbooks, records and novelty items.

MUS-2

MUS-3

MUS-1

**MUS-1. "Lucky Strike Presents Your Hit Parade
Starring Frank Sinatra" Cardboard Fan,**
1943. Scarce. Lucky Strike cigarettes. 12" tall diecut tobacco leaf replica inscribed on back "A Fan For My Fans-
Frank Sinatra". - **$25 $60 $100**

MUS-2. "Four Aces" Cello. Button,
c. 1940s. Philadelphia Fan Club. - **$10 $15 $25**

**MUS-3. Tony Bennett "Bennett Tones Fan Club" Litho.
Button,**
1940s. - **$10 $20 $35**

MUS-5

MUS-4

MUS-6

**MUS-4. "Liberace" Gold Luster Metal Link Charm
Bracelet,**
c. 1956. Store item. Miniature framed photo plus charms
depicting hands on keyboard, grand piano, candleabra,
piano lid. - **$15 $35 $60**

MUS-5. "Pat Boone/4th Anniversary" Litho. Button,
1959. Dot Records. - **$5 $10 $15**

MUS-6. "Pat Boone Fan" Litho. Button,
c. 1959. - **$5 $10 $15**

MUS-7

MUS-8

MUS-9

MUS-7. "Picture Patches",
1950s. Store item. Probable set of eight. Includes Ricky Nelson, Dave Nelson, Bobby Darin, Frankie Avalon, Tommy Sands, Jimmie Rodgers, Fabian.
Each Packaged - **$3 $6 $10**

MUS-8. Fabian And Frankie Avalon 3-1/2" Cello. Buttons,
1950s. Store item. Matching designs, possibly issued for others. Each - **$8 $15 $25**

MUS-9. "Everly Brothers Fan Club" Litho. Button,
1950s. - **$12 $20 $35**

MUS-10

MUS-11

MUS-12

MUS-10. "Bill Haley And His Comets Fan Club" Cello. Button,
1950s. - **$15 $30 $60**

MUS-11. Tony Bennett Fan Club 2" Cello. Button,
1950s. - **$8 $15 $25**

MUS-12. "Pat Boone" Brass Heart Charm,
1950s. Dot Records. Reverse inscription "Always Your Boy, Pat Boone." - **$5 $12 $20**

MUS-13

MUS-14

MUS-15

MUS-13. "Herman's Hermits" 3-1/2" Cello. Button,
c. 1965. Store item. - **$8 $15 $25**

MUS-14. "The Rolling Stones" 3-1/2" Cello. Button,
c. 1966. Probably sold at concerts. - **$20 $35 $60**

MUS-15. "The Supremes Official Fan" 2-1/2" Cello. Button,
1968. - **$15 $30 $50**

MUS-16

MUS-17

MUS-16. "Woodstock" Celebration Litho. Button,
1969. Issued for 1970 live-action movie filmed during four-day concert. - **$10 $15 $25**

MUS-17. Jackson 5 Groovie Push-Out Buttons,
1970. Frosted Rice Krinkles. Strip of three 1-1/2" thin vacuum form sticker buttons. Set of 10 different titles.
Each Near Mint Strip - **$10**
Each Used Button - **$1 $2 $3**

MUS-18

MUS-19

MUS-18. 5th Dimension Club Card,
1970s. Card for official fan member. - **$5 $10 $20**

MUS-19. "Elton John" Ecology 3" Cello. Button,
1980. Also inscribed "Central Park-Keep It Green." - **$10 $20 $35**

MUTT AND JEFF

Bud Fisher's *Mutt and Jeff*, the first continually published six-day-a-week comic strip, was to become one of the best known, funniest, and most popular strips in America. It started as a horseracing cartoon called *A. Mutt* in the *San Francisco Chronicle* in 1907. Jeff showed up the following year but it wasn't until 1916 that the strip was titled *Mutt and Jeff*. A Sunday color strip was added in 1918. There were many early collections of reprints starting around 1910, hardback books, and comic books into the 1960s. A series of *Mutt and Jeff* musicals toured the country from about 1911 to 1915, and from 1918 to 1923 Bud Fisher Productions turned out animated cartoons, typically at a pace of one a week.

MUT-2

MUT-3

MUT-1

MUT-8

MUT-9

MUT-1. Postcard,
1910. New York American newspaper premium. -
$25 $50 $75

MUT-2. Stage Show Cardboard Ink Blotter,
1912. - **$10 $20 $35**

MUT-3. "Mutt And Jeff In Mexico" Cardboard Blotter,
c. 1912. For musical comedy stage production. -
$10 $20 $30

MUT-8. "Mutt And Jeff Play Croquet" Dexterity Puzzle,
1928. Tin and glass 2-1/2x4" skill game by Herbert Special
Mfg. Co., Chicago with instructions on underside. -
$75 $125 $200

MUT-9. Composition/Steel Jointed Flexible Figures,
1920s. Store item. With fabric outfits.
Each - **$100 $225 $400**

MUT-4

MUT-5

MUT-10

MUT-11

MUT-4. "Mutt And Jeff In College" Cardboard Blotter,
c. 1913. For musical comedy stage production. -
$10 $20 $30

MUT-5. Cast Iron Bank,
c. 1915. Store item. - **$60 $150 $200**

MUT-10. Bronze Statue of Jeff,
1920s. 5 3/4" - Premium /Award. - **$50 $100 $150**

MUT-11. Jeff Stick Pin,
1920s. Issued in brass or silver finish. Shows bust of Jeff.
Probably store bought. - **$75 $100 $125**

MUT-6

MUT-7

MUT-12

MUT-13

MUT-14

MUT-6. "Join The Evening Telegraph" Cello. Button,
c. 1915. Promotion for strip beginning and "Mutt & Jeff
Club". - **$25 $50 $75**

MUT-7. "Cut That Stuff" Cartoon Litho. Button,
c. 1916. Various cigarette sponsors. Example from set featuring art by Bud Fisher and other cartoonists. Paint easily
worn. Fisher Cartoons - **$5 $12 $20**
Other Artists - **$3 $8 $15**

MUT-12. "Meet Us At Forest Park" Cello. Button,
c. 1920s. - **$25 $50 $85**

MUT-13. "Buffalo Evening News" Cello. Button,
1930s. From series of newspaper contest buttons, match
number to win prize. - **$10 $20 $35**

MUT-14. "Tangle Comics" Cello. Button,
1940s. Philadelphia Sunday Bulletin. - **$10 $20 $35**

NABISCO MISC.

The giant National Biscuit Company was formed in 1898 by the merger of a number of smaller companies and independent bakers. The following year its sales totaled 70% of all the crackers and cookies sold in America. Adolphus Green, company chairman, set about to create a new product and a national brand. He named it the Uneeda biscuit, developed a carton (In-er-Seal) to keep it fresh, chose a picture of a boy wrapped in rain gear as a symbol, and invested heavily in advertising. In 1900 the company sold 100 million boxes of Uneeda biscuits. Then quickly came Oysterettes, Zu Zu ginger snaps, Fig Newtons, sugar wafers, and Barnum's Animal Crackers. Nabisco, always a heavy advertiser, issued a number of promotional items over the years and has sponsored such children's television classics as *The Adventures of Rin-Tin-Tin, Jabberwocky, Kukla, Fran & Ollie,* and *Sky King*. In the mid-1980s the company was acquired by R.J. Reynolds and became part of RJR Nabisco.

NAB-1

NAB-1. Flying Circus Cards,
1948. Shredded Wheat premium. Card set of 25 model planes and 12 card set of index and preparation of flight. Since cards were made of cardboard, they were to be cut out and assembled into planes and used like gliders. Cards were obtained in cereal boxes. The 12 card set tells how to fold, cut, and assemble the 25 card set of planes.
Each - **$4 $8 $10**

NAB-2. Picture Story Album,
1940s. Seven card set of classic fairy tales found in boxes of Shredded Wheat. Cards were used as a coloring book.
Each - **$2 $4 $6**

NAB-3

NAB-4

NAB-3. Picture Story Album,
1940s. 28 card set of boys and girls of all nations Each card tells the story of children in each foreign country.
Each - **$2 $4 $6**

NAB-4. Toytown Cards,
1940s. Rare. Shredded Wheat premiums. 36 card set which when assembled makes a toytown. Includes cutouts of buildings like firehouses, stores, bank, church, general store, ice cream parlor and gas station. Also includes bus, car, trees, and of all things, an antique store. Yes, collecting was very popular in the 1940s. Each - **$4 $8 $10**

NAB-5

NAB-5. Plastic Dinosaurs With Guide Folder And Box,
1957. Near Mint In Mailer - **$150**

NAB-6

NAB-6. Wheat Honeys Store Promotional Kit With Plastic Dinosaurs,
1957. Set of 10. Box Only - **$50 $125 $200**
Each Figure - **$3 $5 $10**

NAB-7

NAB-7. "Munchy The Spoonman" Pillow,
1958. 3x9-1/2x15" stuffed fabric figure. - **$150 $300 $600**

NAB-8   NAB-9   NAB-10

NAB-8. "Munchy" Vinyl Attachment For Spoon Handle,
1959. One of three Nabisco Spoon Men. Three rows of buttons. **$15 $25 $50**

NAB-9. "Crunchy" Vinyl Attachment For Spoon Handle,
1959. Two rows of buttons. - **$15 $25 $50**

NAB-10. "Spoon Size" Vinyl Attachment for Spoon Handle,
1959. One row of buttons and smaller size than Munchy and Crunchy. - **$25 $35 $60**

NAB-11   NAB-12   NAB-13

NAB-11. "Rocket Man" Paper Mask,
1950s. - **$15 $30 $60**

NAB-12. Rice Honey Bee,
1961. Designed to perch on edge of cereal bowl. -
$5 $12 $20

NAB-13. Rice Honey Clown,
c. 1961. Vinyl figure designed to perch on edge of cereal bowl. - **$5 $12 $20**

NAB-14

NAB-14. Defenders Of America Cards,
1950s. Shredded Wheat. 24 cards in the set. 8 of the 24 are Rocket cards. 7 pictured. Full color.
Eight Rocket cards. Each - **$6 $12 $20**
Other sixteen cards. Each - **$4 $8 $12**

NANCY AND SLUGGO

Nancy, a stubby little girl with a perpetual hair arrangement resembling black steel wool held by a white bow, was created in 1933 by cartoonist Ernie Bushmiller, originally as a niece and periodic visitor to her aunt, the established Fritzi Ritz. By the late 1930s, niece and aunt had reversed their featured roles. Nancy's equally-stubby platonic boyfriend & sidekick, Sluggo, came into her life and the pair remains an inseparable cartoon strip duo to this day.

NAN-1

NAN-2

NAN-1. "Fritzi Ritz Spinner",
1930s. United Features Syndicate. Cello. over metal disk that has underside center bump for spinning. -
$50 $100 $150

NAN-2. "Journal-Transcript Funnies Club" Litho. Button,
c. 1930s. From set of various characters, also has radio call letters for station in Peoria, Illinois. - **$10 $25 $45**

NAN-3   NAN-4

NAN-3. "Nancy And Sluggo" BTLB,
1946. Store item. Whitman Better Little Book #1400. -
$10 $20 $40

NAN-4. Nancy 7-1/2" Hard Plastic Doll,
1940s (late). Rare. Post Grape-Nuts Flakes. -
$500 $1000 $1650

NAN-5

NAN-6

NAN-5. Sluggo 7-1/2" Hard Plastic Doll,
1940s (late). Rare. Post Grape-Nuts Flakes. -
$400 $1000 $1500

NAN-6. "Comic Capers Club" 2-1/8" Cello. Button,
1940s. Sun-Times (newspaper). - **$250 $500 $1000**

NAN-7

NAN-8

NAN-7. Nancy Rubber/Vinyl Doll,
1954. Store item by S&P Doll and Toy Co.
Near Mint Boxed - **$500**
Loose - **$75 $150 $300**

NAN-8. Sluggo Rubber/Vinyl Doll,
1954. Store item by S&P Doll and Toy Co.
Near Mint Boxed - **$500**
Loose - **$75 $150 $300**

NEW FUN COMICS

Former pulp magazine writer and cavalry officer Major
Malcolm Wheeler-Nicholson came up with the idea of a
comic book containing all original material in late
1934. The 10x15" tabloid size magazine *New Fun*, with
color covers and black and white interiors, appeared
on newsstands with a cover date of February 1935.
Pages were laid out in a Sunday comic page format
with continuing stories, humor pages, text stories and
games. Subsequent issues were titled *More Fun*. The
magazine added more color and adapted to the standard comic book size and format by 1936. Historically,
More Fun not only was one of the first comic books
with original material but also the first to publish work
by Walt Kelly of later *Pogo* fame and Siegel and
Shuster of *Superman* fame. *New Fun* formed the cor-
nerstone of the DC Comics publishing empire. The
title ran through issue #127 dated November-
December 1947.

NEW-1

NEW-1. "New Fun Club" Cello. Button,
1935. Rare. - **$250 $600 $1000**

NEWSPAPER CLUBS

During the 1930s newspapers reached out to younger
readers by means of loosely organized clubs, usually
associated with comic strip characters featured in
their pages. Pinback buttons were a favored means of
promotion; some papers offered buttons with a variety
of different characters, while syndicated characters
appeared with imprints from dozens of newspapers.
Often the buttons were serially numbered for use in
prize-winning contests designed to boost circulation.

NES-1

NES-1. Comic Strips Promotion Postcard,
1929. Imprinted for Buffalo Courier-Express. For member
of "Jolly Junior Sunshine Club" birthday greeting featuring
group image of characters. - **$15 $30 $50**

NES-2

NES-3

NES-2. "Bud Billiken Club" Cello. Button,
c. 1920s. Chicago Defender. - **$5 $10 $15**

**NES-3. Moon Mullins "Order Of The Fish" Litho.
Button,**
1930s. No sponsor but probably a newspaper issue. -
$10 $20 $40

NES-4

NES-5

NES-6

**NES-4. "Reg'lar Fellers Legion Of Honor" Litho.
Button,**
1930s. No sponsor but probably a newspaper issue. -
$15 $25 $50

NES-5. Evening Ledger Comics "Relentless Rudolph" Cello. Button,
1930s. Philadelphia Evening Ledger. From colorful series in 1-1/4" size with Evening Ledger promotional back paper. - **$25 $40 $75**

NES-6. Evening Ledger Comics "Connie" Cello. Button,
1930s. Philadelphia Evening Ledger. - **$20 $35 $60**

NES-7   NES-8   NES-9

NES-7. Evening Ledger Comics "Harold Teen" Cello. Button,
1930s. Philadelphia Evening Ledger. - **$25 $40 $75**

NES-8. Evening Ledger Comics "Bobby Thatcher" Cello. Button,
1930s. Philadelphia Evening Ledger. - **$20 $35 $60**

NES-9. Evening Ledger Comics "Babe Bunting" Cello. Button,
1930s. Philadelphia Evening Ledger. - **$15 $30 $50**

NES-10   NES-11   NES-12

NES-10. Evening Ledger Comics "Smitty" Cello. Button,
1930s. Philadelphia Evening Ledger. - **$20 $35 $60**

NES-11. "Just Kids Safety Club" Cello. Buttons,
1930s. Imprinted for at least 48 different newspapers. Set includes 11 characters in 18 picture variations. Pictured examples are "Mush" and "Marjory." Each - **$10 $18 $30**

NES-12. Bronco Bill Litho. Button,
1930s. Example is imprinted for media of Peoria, Illinois. From set of at least 15 different characters. - **$12 $25 $40**

NICK CARTER, MASTER DETECTIVE

Nick Carter, hero of hundreds of dime novels, began life in 1886 in the pages of Street & Smith's *New York Weekly*. The stories, signed by "Nicholas Carter," were written by a number of different authors. Following decades of pulp magazine appearances, the master detective came to the Mutual radio network in 1943 and was broadcast until 1955. Sponsors included Lin-X Home Brighteners (1944-1945), Cudahy meats (1946-

1951), and Old Dutch cleanser (1946-1952). Walter Pidgeon played Carter in a 1939 MGM movie. *The Nick Carter Club* was a 1930s Street & Smith promotion.

NCK-1   NCK-2

NCK-1. "Nick Carter Magazine" Store Window 10x13" Ad Card,
1933. Pictures cover of May issue. - **$50 $100 $150**

NCK-2. "Nick Carter Magazine" Pulp Vol. 1 #3,
May 1933. Published by Street & Smith. - **$20 $40 $85**

NCK-3

NCK-3. "Nick Carter Fingerprint Set",
1934. Store item by New York Toy & Game Co. Includes "Nick Carter 999 Club" instruction book with Street & Smith club enrollment form. Complete - **$35 $75 $125**
Book Only - **$15 $30 $50**

NCK-4

NCK-5   NCK-6

NCK-4. Club Shield Badge,
c. 1934. - **$40 $75 $125**

NCK-5. Club Card,
c. 1934. Nick Carter Magazine. Came with badge. -
$25 $60 $100

NCK-6. "Nick Carter Magazine" Gummed Envelope Sticker,
1930s. Street & Smith Publications. -**$20 $40 $75**

OG, SON OF FIRE

The prehistoric adventures of Og and his companions--Ru, Nada and Big Tooth--were broadcast for a year (1934-1935) on CBS radio, sponsored by Libby. Alfred Brown played the primeval hero of the series, written by Irving Crump, the author of the original Og stories.

OGS-1

OGS-1. "Adventures Of Og, Son Of Fire" 15x20" Map,
1935. Rare. Libby. - **$150 $300 $450**

OGS-2   OGS-3   OGS-4

OGS-2. "Og" 2-1/4" Painted Metal Figure,
c. 1935. Marked under base "Made For Libby's Milk By Lincoln Logs USA." Six figures in set. For each mailing canister with metal lid add $10-20-30. - **$40 $60 $100**

OGS-3. "Ru" Metal Figure,
c. 1935. Part of Og set. - **$40 $60 $100**

OGS-4. "Nada" Metal Figure,
c. 1935. Part of Og set. - **$40 $60 $100**

OGS-5   OGS-6   OGS-7

OGS-5. "Big Tooth" Metal Figure,
c. 1935. Part of Og set. - **$40 $60 $100**

OGS-6. "Three Horn" Metal Figure,
c. 1935. Part of Og set. - **$60 $100 $150**

OGS-7. "Rex" Metal Figure,
c. 1935. Part of Og set. - **$50 $75 $125**

OGS-8

OGS-8. "Og, Son Of Fire" Adventure Game,
1930s. Store item. Whitman game licensed by Stephen Slesinger Inc. "Based On The Famous Stories By Irving Crump" rather than radio premium by sponsor Libby Foods. - **$50 $125 $200**

OMAR THE MYSTIC

Also known as O*mar the Wizard*, this radio series ran for a year (1935-1936) on the Mutual radio network, sponsored by Taystee bread. M.H. Joachim played Omar.

OMR-1

OMR-1. "The Secrets Of Omar The Mystic" Book,
1936. Scarce. Taystee Bread. - **$35 $50 $100**

OMR-2   OMR-3

OMR-2. Taystee Bread Code Card,
1936. Back has instructions for using "Mystic Wheel". -
$20 $40 $75

OMR-3. Taystee Bread Code Bookmark,
1936. Cardboard marker printed by code numerals on one side. - **$15 $30 $50**

ONE MAN'S FAMILY

The saga of the Barbour family, written lovingly by Carlton E. Morse, was the longest running serial drama in the history of radio. The program debuted in 1932 on NBC's San Francisco station KGO and a year later went to the NBC network, where it continued until 1959. The family tree series told the stories of Henry and Fanny Barbour, their five children (Paul, Hazel, the twins Claudia and Clifford, and Jack), and succeeding generations of Barbours as they lived and died, married, had children, and faced family crises against the backdrop of a changing world. Sponsors included Wesson Oil (1932-1933), Kentucky Winner tobacco (1933-1935), Royal gelatin (1935-1936), Tenderleaf tea (1936-1949), Miles Laboratories (1950-1954), and Toni Home Permanents (1954-1955). A television version ran on NBC prime time from 1949 to 1952 and as a daytime serial in 1954-1955.

ONE-1

ONE-2

ONE-1. "One Man's Family History In Words And Pictures" Folder,
1935. Standard Brands Foods. - **$12 $20 $35**

ONE-2. "Scrapbook" Yearbook,
1936. Tenderleaf Tea. Published in graphic style of personally kept album. - **$10 $20 $30**

ONE-3

ONE-4

ONE-3. Teddy Barbour "Diary" Book,
1937. Standard Brands Foods. Family events in simulated handwriting. - **$5 $20 $30**

ONE-4. "One Man's Family" Book,
1938. Title look at life. Had cast phots. Radio premium. - **$10 $20 $35**

ONE-5

ONE-6

ONE-5. Fanny Barbour "Memory Book",
1940. Standard Brands Foods. Family photos, notes, etc. in simulated scrapbook form. - **$5 $20 $30**

ONE-6. "I Believe In America" Album,
1941. Standard Brands Foods. Style of family scrapbook heavily emphasizing early war years. - **$20 $30 $60**

ONE-7

ONE-8

ONE-7. Barbour Family Scrapbook,
1946. Standard Brands Foods. Format of simulated family photos, news clippings, telegrams, etc. - **$8 $25 $40**

ONE-8. "One Man's Family" Broadcast Highlights Record Album,
c. 1947. Store item. Vol. 1 hardcover album of three 78 rpm records of selected excerpts from episodes between 1940-1946 on NBC Radio sponsored by Standard Brands Inc. - **$10 $20 $35**

ONE-9

ONE-9. TV Cast Photo,
c. 1949. - **$8 $15 $25**

ONE-10

ONE-11

ONE-10. "Barbour Family Album",
1951. Miles Laboratories. - **$10 $20 $35**

ONE-11. "Mother Barbour's Favorite Recipes" Booklet,
c. 1951. Miles Laboratories. 20th anniversary souvenir picturing cast members over the years. - **$10 $20 $35**

OPEN ROAD FOR BOYS

The Open Road for Boys, a popular magazine of the 1920s and 1930s, organized The Open Road Pioneers Club in 1927 for boys and young men who loved the outdoor life and were willing to live up to the ideals of the old pioneers: courage, self-reliance, honesty, determination, endurance, progress, and meeting obstacles squarely. For 35¢ (in coins or stamps) sent to Deep-River Jim, members received a pin, certificate, and sweater emblem. The Club boasted over 3,000 chapters and lasted well into the 1950s.

OPN-1

OPN-2

OPN-3

OPN-1. Open Road For Boys Magazine,
1934. Has write-up for club & application for pin -
$8 $15 $30

OPN-2. "Open Road Pioneers Club" Certificate,
1935. - **$15 $30 $50**

OPN-3. "Open Road Pioneers" Cello. Button,
1930s. - **$5 $10 $15**

OPN-4

OPN-5

OPN-6

OPN-4. "Open Road Pioneers" Brass Badge,
1930s. - **$8 $15 $25**

OPN-5. "Open Road Pioneers" 4-1/2" Fabric Patch,
1930s. - **$25 $50 $75**

OPN-6. Leader's Certificate,
1954. Different wording than member's certificate and "Deep-river Jim" no longer titled as "The Campfire Chief." -
$15 $30 $50

OPERATOR #5

America's Undercover Ace, handsome young Jimmy Christopher, fought spies and foreign agents from 1934 until the outbreak of World War II as Secret Service Operator #5 in the pages of the pulp magazine of the same name. His task, month after month, was to save the United States from destruction. A 1934 offer of a replica Operator #5 skull ring must have been short-lived as the ring is quite scarce.

OPR-1

OPR-2

OPR-1. Enameled Silvered Metal Club Ring,
1934. Rare. Operator 5 Magazine. Silvering easily worn off. - **$3500 $8500 $22500**

OPR-2. "Secret Service Operator #5" Pulp Magazine,
June-July 1936. Published by Popular Publications. -
$20 $40 $100

OUR GANG

Between 1922 and 1944 the Hal Roach Studios and MGM produced 221 *Our Gang* comedies. The short films, one- or two-reelers, were immensely successful, with the little rascals--Alfalfa, Farina, Buckwheat, Spanky, Darla Hood, Baby Jean, Mickey, Waldo, and their dogs Pete the Pup, Pal, and Von--joyfully getting into and out of mischief, playing hooky, putting on musicals, and generally doing no harm and having lots of fun. The films were syndicated on television as *The Little Rascals* (1955-1965), as *Our Gang Comedies* (1956-1965), and as *Mischief Makers* (1960-1970). *The Little Rascals* series was re-edited and televised again in the 1970s. A prime-time animated cartoon, *The Little Rascals Christmas Show*, aired on NBC in 1979. *Our Gang* comic books were published in the 1940s.

OUR-1

OUR-2

OUR-1. "Pete" With Child Photo,
c. 1920s. Child's souvenir of Steel Pier, Atlantic City. -
$15 $25 $40

OUR-2. Cardboard Ad Blotter,
1920s. Various sponsors. - **$15 $35 $60**

OUR-4

OUR-5

OUR-3

OUR-3. "Hal Roach's Rascals" Photo,
1920s. - **$20 $40 $75**

OUR-4. Joe Cobb China Mug,
1920s. Store item by Sebring Pottery Co. -
$60 $125 $175

OUR-5. Scooter Lowry China Mug,
1920s. Store item by Sebring Pottery Co. -
$75 $125 $250

OUR-6

OUR-7

OUR-6. "Majestic Electric Radio" Cardboard Ink Blotter,
1920s. - **$12 $35 $60**

OUR-7. Dickie Moore Mask,
c. 1932. U.S. Caramel Co. One of a set. - **$10 $25 $40**

OUR-8

OUR-9

OUR-10

OUR-8. "Pete" Cello. Button,
c. 1932. From "Member Spanky Safety Club" series with Hal Roach copyright. - **$40 $85 $140**

OUR-9. "Buckwheat" Cello. Button,
c. 1932. From "Member Spanky Safety Club" series with Hal Roach copyright. - **$40 $90 $150**

OUR-10. "Alfalfa" Cello. Button,
c. 1932. From "Member Spanky Safety Club" series with Hal Roach copyright. - **$35 $75 $125**

OUR-11

OUR-12

OUR-11. "Darla Hood" Cello. Button,
c. 1932. From "Member Spanky Safety Club" series with Hal Roach copyright. - **$30 $65 $115**

OUR-12. Fan Photo,
1934. Hal Roach Studios. - **$10 $20 $45**

OUR-13

OUR-14

OUR-13. Puzzle,
1932. McKesson's Milk of Magnesia. - **$40 $75 $125**

OUR-14. Puzzle Mailer,
1932. McKesson's Milk of Magnesia. - **$15 $25 $50**

OUR-15

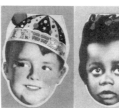

OUR-16

OUR-15. Jackie Cooper Photo,
1936. Philadelphia Record newspaper premium. -
$8 $15 $25

OUR-16. Fan Photo,
1937. Hal Roach Studios. - **$10 $20 $45**

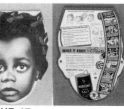

OUR-17

OUR-17. "Fun Kit" Diecut Booklet,
1937. Morton's Salt. Features colored mask-like photos, activity pages, rules for their "Eagles Club". - **$35 $125 $175**

OUR-18   **OUR-19**

OUR-20

OUR-18. "Our Gang Painting Book",
1937. Sears, Roebuck. Copyright by Hal Roach Studios. - **$30 $60 $100**

OUR-19. Spanky Fan Photo,
c. 1937. Hal Roach Studios. - **$10 $18 $35**

OUR-20. Our Gang Calendar,
1939. Taystee bread. Cardboard sheet issued monthly. Each - **$20 $40 $80**

OUR-22

OUR-23

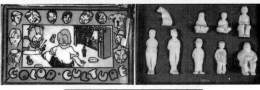

OUR-24

OUR-21

OUR-21. Our Gang Comedy Blatz Gum,
1930s. - **$20 $40 $60**

OUR-22. "Contestant" Cello. Button,
1930s. Probable theater or newspaper contest. - **$15 $35 $60**

OUR-23. "Our Gang Club" Cello. Button,
1930s. Superba Theatre by Chicago button maker. Matinee inscription plus "Watch For Your Color". - **$25 $50 $75**

OUR-24. Figure Mold Play Kit,
1930s. Store item by Jem Clay Forming Co. for Louis Wolf Co. Eight hollow plaster figures for painting plus backdrop panel. Near Mint Boxed - **$350**
Each Painted Figure - **$8 $20 $30**

OUR-25

OUR-25. Bisque Nodders,
1930s. German made store item. Set of six as shown: Pete, Chubby Chaney, Wheezer, Jackie Cooper, Farina, Mary Ann Jackson. Each - **$75 $125 $200**

OUR-26   **OUR-27**

OUR-28

OUR-26. "Safety First" Cello. Button,
1930s. Probable Our Gang member club button, rim curl copyright "Hal Roach Studios". - **$12 $25 $40**

OUR-27. "King Carl 'Alfalfa' Switzer" 2-1/2" Cello. Button,
1930s. National Ice Cream Week. His name is followed by "Of Hal Roach's Our Gang-A MGM Release". - **$75 $150 $300**

OUR-28. "Spanky's Safety Patrol" 14x28" Sample Wall Calendar,
1943. - **$50 $100 $150**

OUR-29

OUR-29. "The Little Rascals' Club" Member Card, c. 1955. WHUM-TV Channel 61. - **$15 $40 $50**

OVALTINE MISC.

Ovaltine was created in 1904 by Swiss physician Dr. George Wander as a flavored milk additive, and the original combination of malt, eggs, vitamins, and minerals is still in use in Europe. The Wander Company brought Ovaltine to the United States in 1905, using the same mix of ingredients except for the addition of sugar. Ovaltine found wide use as a tasty health food for children and adults. (The Red Cross shipped Ovaltine to Allied prisoner-of-war camps as a nutritional supplement during both World Wars.) The Sandoz Pharmaceutical Company acquired the Wander Company in 1967 and Ovaltine is now sold in "chocolate malt" (introduced in the 1960s) and "rich chocolate" (introduced in the 1980s) flavors, as well as the "original malt" version. In addition to the many premiums the company issued as the sponsor of such classic radio programs as *Radio Orphan Annie* and *Captain Midnight*, Ovaltine has produced promotional items not related to specific programs.

OVL-1

OVL-2

OVL-1. "Lecture On Nutrition And Digestion By The Wonder Robot" Booklet, 1934. Issued at Century of Progress Hall of Science. - **$40 $80 $150**

OVL-2. "Betty The Nail Biter" Sunday Comics Ad, 1936. One-half page with coupon for Orphan Annie cup with green background decal. Text promotes Ovaltine as cure for nervousness. - **$5 $10 $15**

OVL-3

OVL-4

OVL-3. Litho. Tin Canister, 1939. 9" tall "Hospital Size". - **$15 $25 $40**

OVL-4. Glass Shaker with Mixer, 1930s. - **$20 $45 $85**

OVL-5

OVL-6

OVL-5. English "Delicious Ovaltine" China Mug, 1930s. - **$15 $25 $45**

OVL-6. English "Delicious Ovaltine" China Mug Designed Without Handle, 1930s. - **$15 $25 $40**

OVL-7

OVL-8

OVL-7. Sample Size Tin Container, 1930s. Miniature 2-1/4" diameter by 2" tall. With Lid - **$15 $30 $55**

OVL-8. "School Size" Sample Tin Container, 1930s. English issue miniature 1-1/2" diameter by 1-3/4" tall. Pictures Johnnie, Winnie, Elsie. Complete - **$20 $35 $55** Opened - **$15 $25 $40**

OVL-9

OVL-10

OVL-9. Plastic Mug, 1940s. Sandy Strong. - **$20 $50 $75**

OVL-10. "Ding Dong School" Plastic Mug, 1950s. Decal pictures "Miss Frances," the teacher on 1952-1956 TV educational series. - **$15 $40 $60**

PEANUTS

Probably the most successful comic strip of all time, Charles Schulz's *Peanuts* appeared for a couple of years as *Li'l Folks* in the St. Paul *Pioneer Press* before it was syndicated under its new name by United Features in 1950. The antics of Charlie Brown, the strip's unlikely hero, Snoopy the wonder dog, Lucy van Pelt, Linus, Schroeder, and Pigpen have become part of American culture. There have been numerous reprint books, feature-length animated films, prime-time television specials, a musical comedy, and extensive merchandising and licensing of the major characters. Items are usually copyrighted Charles M. Schulz or United Features Syndicate. Copyright dates on items relate to character designs and are usually unrelated to the date an item was issued.

PEA-1   PEA-2

PEA-1. College Football Homecoming 2-1/4" Litho. Button,
1960. Minnesota Star and Sunday Tribune. For University of Minnesota vs. University of Illinois game with rim curl authorizations by Peanuts and United Features Syndicate. - **$10 $20 $35**

PEA-2. Daily Comic Strip Introduction 11x28" Promotion Card,
c. 1960. United Features Syndicate. Imprinted for (New York) Daily News. - **$25 $50 $75**

PEA-3

PEA-3. Pre-School Child's Eye Exam Promotion Booklet,
1967. Imprinted for Detroit Department of Health. Eight pages of comic strips illustrating vision information by members of Peanuts gang. - **$10 $20 $35**

PEA-4   PEA-5   PEA-6

PEA-4. Charlie Brown Composition Bobbing Head,
1960s. Store item. Other characters also issued. - **$30 $75 $125**

PEA-5. Lucy Composition Bobbing Head,
1960s. Store item, other characters also issued. Each - **$30 $75 $125**

PEA-6. Charlie Brown Enameled Metal Necklace Charm,
1960s. Store item. United Features Syndicate copyright. From character series. - **$12 $25 $50**

PEA-7   PEA-8   PEA-9

PEA-7. Plastic Clip-On Badge,
1970. Millbrook Bread. Five or more characters in set.
Carded - **$5 $8 $12**
Loose - **$3 $5 $8**

PEA-8. "Snoopy's Spotters Club" 2" Litho. Tab,
c. 1970. Millbrook Bread. - **$5 $10 $15**

PEA-9. Litho. Tab,
c. 1970. Restaurant issue. - **$3 $5 $8**

PEA-10

PEA-10. "Peanuts Patches",
1971. Interstate Brands. Set of five with envelope and order coupon. Set With Mailer - **$10 $20 $50**

PEA-11

PEA-13

PEA-12

**PEA-11. "Colonial Capers Cartoon Comics" 2-1/2"
Cello. Button,**
1971. Probable newspaper issue. - **$5 $12 $20**

PEA-12. "Red Baron's Albatross" Punch-Out,
1973. Coca-Cola. - **$25 $50 $75**

PEA-13. "Happy Birthday, America!" Cello. Button,
1976. Bicentennial issue. - **$8 $12 $20**

PEP BOYS

The Pep Boys--Manny, Moe and Jack--were three pals
who opened an auto supply store in Philadelphia in
1921. The store prospered and eventually grew into a
chain of operations in the Eastern states, watched
over through the years by the smiling cartoon faces of
the founders.

PEP-1

PEP-1. U.S. Sesquicentennial Exposition 6x8" Decal,
1926. Pep Auto Supply Co. copyright. Full color patriotic
art water transfer decal with "Pep Boys" glassine envelope.
Decal reverse inscription includes "All Over Philadelphia
And Camden." Near Mint With Envelope - **$90**
Loose - **$20 $40 $75**

PEP-2

PEP-3

PEP-2. Manual,
1930. 72 pages and front and back cover. - **$25 $50 $75**

PEP-3. Mailer For Manual,
1930. - **$10 $20 $30**

PEP-4

PEP-5

PEP-4. Manual,
1931. 96 pages and front and back cover. - **$25 $50 $75**

PEP-5. "Pep Boys Dawn Patrol" Postcard,
1933. Response to listener over WIP Radio w/facsimile
signature of announcer Fred Wood. - **$30 $60 $100**

PEP-6

PEP-7

PEP-6. Catalogue,
1938. - **$20 $50 $75**

PEP-7. Catalogue,
1939. - **$20 $50 $75**

PEP-8

PEP-9

PEP-10

PEP-11

PEP-8. Patch,
1930s. Red outline with yellow background premium
patch. - **$10 $20 $40**

PEP-9. Brass Match Cover Holder,
1940s.Brass match holder which has opening for Pep Boy
logo at bottom. - **$15 $35 $50**

PEP-10. Matches,
1940s. No name printed at bottom. - **$5 $10 $15**

PEP-11. Matches,
1940s. "Pep Boys" printed at bottom. - **$5 $10 $15**

PEP-12

PEP-12. Boxed Playing Cards,
1940s. - **$25 $50 $90**

PEP-13

PEP-14

PEP-15

PEP-13. Catalogue,
1954. Store premium. - **$10 $25 $40**

PEP-14. Catalogue,
1955. Store premium. - **$20 $40 $60**

PEP-15. Plastic Cigarette Holder,
c. 1950s. - **$25 $50 $85**

PETE RICE

Pistol Pete Rice was the sheriff of Buzzard Gap, Arizona, in a series of Street and Smith pulp westerns. Written by Ben Conlon under the name Austin Gridley, *Pete Rice Western Adventures* appeared from November 1933 to June 1936. For a dime, readers could get a *Pete Rice Club* deputy badge and a members' pledge card.

PTR-1

PTR-2

PTR-1. "Pete Rice" Gummed Paper Envelope Sticker,
c. 1934. Street & Smith Co., publishers of Pete Rice pulp magazine. - **$15 $30 $50**

PTR-2. Deputy Club Metal Badge,
c. 1934. Badge - **$25 $50 $100**
Envelope - **$5 $10 $15**

PETER PAN

The story of Peter Pan, the boy who lived in Never-Never land and refused to grow up, was created in 1904 by British novelist and playwright Sir James M. Barrie (1860-1937). The fantasy of Peter, Wendy, Tinkerbell, and the evil Captain Hook was given new life in 1953 with the release of the full-length Disney animated feature, and in 1991 Tri-Star Pictures released *Hook*, a revised version of the beloved tale directed by Steven Spielberg and starring Dustin Hoffman and Robin Williams.

PAN-1

PAN-1. "Animated Coloring Book",
1943. Derby Foods. Non-Disney with punch-out sheet to animate the pictures. - **$15 $25 $40**

PAN-2

PAN-2. Soap Bar With 18x24" Paper Map,
c. 1953. Colgate-Palmolive. Map - **$35 $75 $150**
Soap Bar - **$5 $12 $20**

PAN-3

PAN-4

PAN-3. Coasters 11x14" Paper Store Sign,
c. 1953. Peter Pan Peanut Butter. - **$30 $60 $90**

PAN-4. "Peter Pan Peanut Butter" Tin Lids,
c. 1953. Examples from set. Each - **$3 $8 $15**

PAN-5

PAN-6

PAN-5. "Get Your Peter Pan Picture Puzzle" Litho. Button,
c. 1953. Disney copyright. - **$20 $40 $60**

PAN-6. Bread Labels,
c. 1953. Various bread companies. Examples from set of 12. Each - **$3 $6 $10**

PAN-7

PAN-7. "Hallmark Pirate Ship" Kit With Mailer Envelope,
c. 1953. Store item, Hallmark Cards. Includes 21x29" map and four punch-out sheets to assemble pirate ship.
Near Mint In Envelope - **$85**
Map Only - **$15 $25 $45**

PAN-8

PAN-9

PAN-8. Litho. Button,
1950s. Hudson's department store, Detroit. No Disney copyright. - **$10 $20 $40**

PAN-9. Coloring Book,
1963. Peter Pan Peanut Butter, non-Disney. - **$5 $15 $25**

PETER RABBIT

The characters in Thornton Burgess's children's books were adapted by Harrison Cady for the *Peter Rabbit* Sunday comic strip, which appeared in the *New York Tribune* starting in 1920. The strip, however, soon became more Cady than Burgess, featuring an essentially new rabbit family and slapstick humor. Comic book reprints appeared in the 1940s and 1950s. The strip ceased publication in 1956.

PET-1

PET-2

PET-1. "Quaddy Note Paper" Box,
1916. Store item. Stationery box copyright by Harrison Cady. - **$25 $50 $75**

PET-2. Peter Rabbit Child's Sterling Silver Ring,
c. 1920s. Miniature figure image in clothing outfit. - **$50 $100 $175**

PET-3

PET-4

PET-5

PET-3. Peter Rabbit "Bedtime Stories Club" Cello. Button,
c. 1920s. Newspaper sponsor name specified. - **$40 $75 $125**

PET-4. Peter Rabbit "Bedtime Stories Club" Cello. Button,
c. 1920s. Newspaper sponsor unspecified. - **$30 $65 $100**

PET-5. Newspaper Club Cello. Button,
1920s. - **$40 $75 $125**

PET-6

PET-6. "Peter Rabbit" Tin Canister,
c. 1920s. Store item. 4" dia. by 2" tall can and lid, both with full color Peter Rabbit family art. - **$30 $60 $90**

PET-7

PET-8

PET-7. Paint Book,
1937. Store item. Whitman book with 36 pages of Harrison Cady art in comic strip panel format. - **$10 $25 $45**

PET-8. "Peter Rabbit Club" Cello. Button,
c. 1930s. Sponsor "Wisconsin News." - **$40 $75 $125**

PEZ

This peppermint candy originated in Austria in 1927. Edward Haas, the inventor, shortened the German word for peppermint, *pfeffermintz*, to Pez. Sales were slow until the company, Pez Candy Inc., entered the United States in 1952 targeting the children's market with a figural head on the dispenser and a cherry flavored candy. Collectors are now willing to spend four-figure amounts for a rare example. In addition to the classic dispensers featuring cartoon figures, animals, superheroes, and Disney characters, PEZ watches, jewelry, keychains, and clip-ons have been produced.

PEZ-1

PEZ-2   (ENLARGED VIEW)

PEZ-1. Litho. Tin Clicker,
c. 1948. - **$150 $300 $450**

PEZ-2. Tin Rotating Store Rack,
1950s. 16" tall. - **$125 $250 $400**

PEZ-3

PEZ-4

PEZ-3. Space Gun,
1950s. Candy shooter gun. - **$40 $75 $100**

PEZ-4. Litho. Tin Yo-Yo,
1950s. - **$60 $175 $250**

PEZ-5

PEZ-6

PEZ-5. Tin Clicker,
c. 1960s. - **$15 $30 $50**

PEZ-6. Dispenser Cardboard Costumes,
c. 1960s Three examples and one back panel from 12 in series "A". Each - **$5 $10 $20**

PEZ-7

PEZ-8

PEZ-7. Miniature Duck Plastic Dispenser Stick Pin,
1960s. Premium. - **$10 $20 $30**

PEZ-8. Silver Coin,
1960s. Pez premium coin given to employees. -
$25 $50 $75

PEZ-9

PEZ-9. Disney Pez Dispenser Display Card,
c. 1960s. Card fits into the back of a display box. -
$10 $18 $30

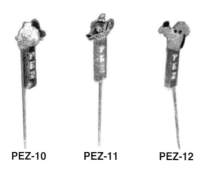

PEZ-10   **PEZ-11**   **PEZ-12**

**PEZ-10. Donald Duck Miniature Plastic Dispenser
Replica On Brass Stickpin,**
c. 1960s. From European made Disney character series. -
$10 $20 $35

**PEZ-11. Bambi Miniature Plastic Dispenser Replica On
Brass Stickpin,**
c. 1960s. From European made Disney character series. -
$10 $25 $40

**PEZ-12. Pluto Miniature Plastic Dispenser On Brass
Stickpin,**
c. 1960s. From European made Disney character series. -
$10 $20 $30

PEZ-13

PEZ-13. "Pez Premium Club" Paper,
1970s. - **$8 $12 $20**

PEZ-14

PEZ-14. Insert Paper,
1970s. Paper slip illustrating different dispensers plus
reverse ad for Golden Glow candy dispenser and Pez
Costume Fun Books. - **$10 $20 $35**

PEZ-15   **PEZ-16**

PEZ-15. Spider-Man Cardboard Mask,
1970s. - **$20 $40 $60**

PEZ-16. Hulk Cardboard Mask,
1970s. - **$15 $35 $50**

PEZ-17

PEZ-17. Make-A-Face on Card,
1970s. German version. One of the most sought-after Pez
dispensers. - **$1000 $1800 $2500**

PHANTOM PILOT PATROL

Langendorf baked goods sponsored this regionally broadcast radio adventure series on the West Coast in the 1930s. The brass and black enamel paint membership badge is the only premium known.

PLT-1

PLT-1. Black Enamel On Brass Member's Badge,
1930s. - **$10 $25 $75**

THE PHANTOM

The legendary ghost-who-walks was created by writer Lee Falk and artist Ray Moore as a daily comic strip for King Features in 1936. A Sunday page was added in 1939. Aided by Guran, the leader of the Bandar pygmies, and by his wolf Devil, the masked crime fighter with the sign of the skull has been battling evil and pursuing his fiancee Diana Palmer in comic strips in the U.S. and overseas ever since. Comic book reprints were first published in 1939, with new material added starting in 1951. A 15-episode chapter play starring Tom Tyler was released by Columbia Pictures in 1943. In 1996, Paramount Pictures released a big screen version of *The Phantom* staring Billy Zane. Despite a poor box office showing, the film received favorable word of mouth from fans and has done well on cable.

PHN-1

PHN-2

PHN-3

PHN-1. Amoco Gas Station Display,
1930s. Prototype, one of 4 diff. known to exist. Poster shows 5 diff. Phantom trading cards that would be available for 1¢ with the purchase of a tankful of gas. Yellow background, 1¢ logo and red lettering. - **$500 $750 1000**

PHN-2. One-Sheet Spanish Poster,
1943. To coincide with the release of the Tom Tyler serial. - **$350 $500 $750**

PHN-3. Comic Strip Characters Tattoo Pack,
c. 1948. Classic Comics, published by Gilberton Co. Store item packet of 20 tattoo transfers with The Phantom and other examples pictured on envelope. - **$40 $80 $150**

PHN-4

PHN-5

PHN-6

PHN-4. Portrait Ring,
c. 1948. Gold plastic bands with clear cover over color picture. - **$75 $115 $150**

PHN-5. Exhibit Card,
1949. Postcard stock and size. Vending machine item sold for one penny. - **$50 $70 $90**

PHN-6. "The Phantom Club Member" Australian Cello. Button,
1940s. Scarce. - **$150 $500 $850**

PHN-7

PHN-8

PHN-7. "S.F. Call-Bulletin" Cardboard Disk,
c. 1940s. San Francisco newspaper. From series of contest disks, match number to win prize. - **$8 $20 $35**

PHN-8. Three-Sheet,
1940s. Columbia Pictures. 80" by 40". -
$2000 $4000 $6000

PHN-9

PHN-10

PHN-9. Radio Show Billboard Poster,
1940s. Produced in cooperation for the intended Phantom radio show to be heard on WEBR/Canada. One of two. -
$1000 $1500 $2000

PHN-10. Amoco Gas Station Premium Card,
1940s. The earliest of all Phantom trading cards. On light cardboard, these 3"x3" black and white cards each depicted a different comic panel from the original Lee Falk/Ray Moore story from 1936. The reverse had an ink-stamped logo. Each - **$75 $100 $150**

PHN-11

PHN-12

PHN-11. Australian Brass Stickpin,
1953. Comic book premium. Embossed skull symbol with red eye accents. - **$75 $150 $250**

PHN-12. China Portrait Mug,
1950s. Store item. - **$35 $75 $125**

PHN-13

PHN-14

PHN-15

PHN-13. Litho. Tab,
1950s. - **$25 $60 $100**

PHN-14. "The Phantom" Litho. Button,
1950s. From set of various King Features Syndicate characters. - **$15 $30 $50**

PHN-15. Plastic Frame Picture Charm,
1950s. Store item. Gumball vending machine issue. - **$10 $20 $35**

PHN-16

PHN-17

PHN-16. Board Game With Plastic Skull Ring,
1966. Store item by Transogram.
Near Mint Boxed With Ring - **$250**
Ring Only - **$50 $100 $150**

PHN-17. Comic Book Fan Reply Card,
1967. King Features Syndicate. Color postcard with reverse message from King Comics thanking recipient for ideas and suggestions. - **$25 $60 $125**

PHN-18

PHN-19

PHN-18. Soda Cardboard Display,
1960s. Swedish. Two-sided, for the promotion of carbonated lemon drink. - **$700 $1000 $1200**

PHN-19. Soda Lemon Drink Bottle,
1960s. Store item. Phantom pictured in blue garb. - **$40 $50 $60**

PHN-20

PHN-21

PHN-22

PHN-20. Australian Ink Stamp Ring,
1960s. Rubber with raised skull symbol as ink stamp, "Phantom" name on ring band. - **$1000 $1500 $2000**

PHN-21. Australian Brass Ring,
1960s. Depicts raised skull symbol with red eye sockets. - **$250 $525 $800**

PHN-22. Sticker,
1975. King Features. - **$5 $10 $20**

PILLSBURY

The Pillsbury Company was formed in 1869 when 27-year-old Charles Alfred Pillsbury bought a flour mill in Minneapolis and set about improving the milling process and producing a finer flour. Pillsbury's Best XXXX, a conversion of the historic bakers' XXX symbol for premium bread, was adopted as a company trademark in 1872. The Pillsbury Doughboy, created by animator Hal Mason, was introduced in television commercials in 1966 and named Poppin' Fresh in 1971. He was soon joined by Poppie Fresh, and the two characters have been successfully merchandised as corporate symbols.

In 1964, Pillsbury introduced the Funny Face products, a sugar-free drink mix for children. There were six flavors originally. The line went national in 1965 and more flavors were added throughout the 1970s. The brand faded in the late 1970s with stiff competition from market leader Kool-Aid. Pillsbury sold the line in 1980 to Brady Enterprises. The new owners test marketed Chug A Lug Chocolate in 1983 and offered the final plastic cup premium. Limited distribution makes this the scarcest of the nine cups in the Funny Face series.

PLS-1

PLS-1. Funny Face Masks,
c. 1964. Set of five diecut paper images of Goofy Grape, Loud-Mouth Lime, Rootin' Tootin' Raspberry, Chinese Cherry, Injun Orange. Latter two were subsequently renamed Choo Choo Cherry and Jolly Olly Orange.
Each - **$100 $200 $300**

PLS-2

PLS-3

PLS-2. "Funny Face Fun Book",
1965. Full color 5x7" self-mailer booklet with 20 pages of games, puzzles, jokes, rhymes, etc. - **$35 $75 $150**

PLS-3. Funny Face Finger Puppets,
c. 1965. 2x4" plastic sheeting set of five: Chinese Cherry, Goofy Grape, Loud-Mouth Lime, Injun Orange, Rootin' Tootin' Raspberry. Each - **$25 $50 $75**

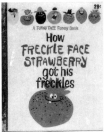

PLS-4

PLS-5

PLS-4. "How Freckle Face Strawberry Got His Freckles" Book,
1965. - **$25 $40 $75**

PLS-5. "Crash Orange" Book,
1967. - **$30 $60 $95**

PLS-6

PLS-6. Funny Face Mugs,
1969. First three of nine in set. Chug A Lug Chocolate introduced in 1983. First Eight Each - **$10 $20 $35**
Chug A Lug - **$15 $25 $50**

PLS-7

PLS-8

PLS-9

PLS-7. Choo Choo Cherry Cloth Pillow Doll,
1970. Pillsbury Co. - **$15 $30 $60**

PLS-8. Lefty Lemon Cloth Pillow Doll,
1970. Grape and Strawberry also issued.
Each - **$15 $30 $60**

PLS-9. "Lefty Lemonade" Funny Face Iron-On Fabric Patch,
c. 1970. - **$10 $20 $30**

PLS-10

PLS-10. Funny Face Plastic Walkers,
1971. Set of four, each with plastic weight.
Each - **$50 $75 $125**

PLS-11

PLS-12

PLS-11. "Poppin' Fresh Doughboy",
c. 1971. Full figure color label on plastic can holding vinyl figure. - **$30 $60 $100**

PLS-12. "Poppin' Fresh Doughboy",
c. 1971. Closeup portrait label on plastic can holding vinyl figure. - **$30 $60 $100**

PLS-13

PLS-14

PLS-15

PLS-13. "Poppin' Fresh" & "Poppie" Plastic Salt & Pepper Shakers,
1974. - **$12 $18 $25**

PLS-14. "Poppin' Fresh" Vinyl Playhouse,
1974. Complete with four figures. - **$60 $100 $150**

PLS-15. "Pillsbury" Cloth Doll,
c. 1970s. - **$5 $10 $18**

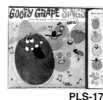

PLS-16

PLS-17

PLS-16. Goofy Grape Plastic Pitcher,
1974. Pillsbury Co. Two versions: Single face or face on each side of pitcher. - **$20 $40 $85**

PLS-17. "Goofy Grape Sings" Record,
1970s. - **$15 $30 $50**

THE PINK PANTHER

This slinky, bulgy-eyed pantomime creature first appeared in the opening credits of the 1964 live-action feature film of the same title starring actors David Niven and Peter Sellers. The catchy animated antics, abetted by Henry Mancini theme music, prompted a spin-off single cartoon short that evolved into a career of other performances in theaters, TV cartoons and comic books. Creators were animators DePatie-Freleng Enterprises. Early adventures typically pitted Pink Panther against his traditional inept, dim-witted foil Inspector Clouseau. Later animations added other characters and the 1985 *Pink Panther And Sons* (Pinky, Panky, Punkin) TV series was produced in association with Hanna-Barbera Studios.

PNK-1

PNK-2

PNK-1. Inspector Clouseau 3" Cello. Button,
c. 1965. Issued following original 1964 Pink Panther film starring Peter Sellers as Clouseau. - **$5 $12 $20**

PNK-2. RPX Race Car,
1973. Pink Panther Cereal. Styled after George Barris car. - **$50 $80 $150**

PNK-3

PNK-4

PNK-3. 5-1 Spy Kit,
1973. Pink Panther Cereal. - **$50 $75 $125**

PNK-4. "Pink Panther Painless Pin" Litho. Tin Tab,
1970s. Issued by Clean 'N Treat Medicated First Aid Pads. One of a series. Each - **$5 $10 $15**

PNK-5

PNK-6

PNK-5. "One Man Band" Battery Toy With Box,
c. 1980. Store item by Illco Toys. Plush/vinyl/metal action movement toy. Boxed - **$40 $75 $100**
Loose - **$25 $50 $75**

PNK-6. Albertson's 3-1/2" Cello. Button,
1984. - **$5 $10 $15**

PINOCCHIO

Italian author Carlo Collodi wrote the children's tale *Pinocchio: the Story of a Puppet* in 1880. The classic adventure of a wooden marionette who wants to become a real boy was first translated into English in 1892 and given new life as a full-length animated feature by the Disney studio in 1940. The film was a huge success, and the characters were merchandised extensively. Pinocchio, his tiny conscience Jiminy Cricket, Figaro the cat, Cleo the goldfish, the Blue Fairy, Monstro the whale, and the other creations were produced in a great variety of materials and formats, and Pinocchio was licensed to a long list of manufacturers of foods, candy, gum, paint, salt, razors, mouthwash, clothing, watches, etc. Comic book appearances began in 1939, animated sequels were released in 1964 and 1987, and a television special using a stop-motion process was aired on ABC in 1980.

PCC-1

PCC-2

PCC-1. "Walt Disney's Pinocchio" Book,
1939. Store item and Cocomalt premium.
Premium Edition - **$15 $40 $115**
Store Edition - **$10 $30 $90**

PCC-2. Cocomalt "Walt Disney's Pinocchio" 10x16"
Book Ad Poster,
1939. - **$50 $100 $150**

PCC-3

PCC-3. Post Toasties Box,
1939. Various boxes with cut-outs.
Each Complete - **$150 $300 $600**

PCC-4

PCC-5

EPPETTO & PINOCCHIO · MONSTRO · COACHMAN · LAMPWICK · HONEST JOHN · TICKET OFFICE

PCC-4. "Pinocchio Circus" 32x51" Linen Sign,
1939. Various sponsors. - **$300 $1200 $2000**

PCC-5. "Pinocchio's Circus" Cut-Out Sheet,
1939. Various bread companies. Came with 60 cards.
Uncut Tent - **$50 $75 $100**
Each Uncut Card - **$1 $3 $5**

PCC-6

PCC-7

PCC-6. "Pinocchio Masks Free" Newspaper Ad,
1939. Gillette Blue Blades. - **$10 $20 $35**

PCC-7. Pinocchio Paper Mask,
1939. Gillette Blue Blades. From set of five characters:
Pinocchio, Jiminy Cricket, Geppetto, Figaro, Cleo.
Each - **$5 $12 $18**

PCC-8

PCC-8. "Save Pinocchio Lids From Ice Cream Cups"
6x18" Paper Sign,
1939. - **$60 $100 $150**

PCC-9

PCC-9. "Pinocchio's Christmas Party" Department Store Give-Away Book,
1939. Various stores. - **$15 $25 $50**

PCC-10

PCC-11

PCC-10. "Good Teeth Certificate",
1939. American Dental Association. - **$25 $60 $100**

PCC-11. "Good Teeth" Cello. Button,
1939. Back paper for Bureau of Public Relations/American Dental Association. - **$75 $150 $275**

PCC-13

PCC-12

PCC-12. Catalin Plastic Thermometer,
1939. Store item. - **$40 $80 $150**

PCC-13. Studio Issued Fan Card,
1940. - **$30 $50 $75**

PCC-14

PCC-14. Theater Give-Away Sheet,
1940. - **$35 $60 $125**

PCC-15

PCC-15. "Poster Stamps" Booklet,
1940. Independent Grocers Alliance of America. Holds 32 stamps. Booklet - **$15 $60 $80**
Each Glued Stamp - **$2 $4 $6**

PCC-16

PCC-17

PCC-16. Envelope,
1940. IGA premium. Envelope for 4 stamps. - **$10 $20 $35**

PCC-17. Stamp Set,
1940. IGA premium. Set of 4 stamps. Not glued to book. - **$20 $40 $60**

PCC-18

PCC-19

PCC-18. "Pinocchio Candy Bar" Box,
1940. Schutter Candy Co. Originally held 24 bars. - **$50 $150 $250**

PCC-19. "Pinocchio Chewing Gum" Paper Wrapper,
1940. Store item by Dietz Gum Co. - **$15 $30 $60**

PCC-20

PCC-21

PCC-22

PCC-20. "Jiminy Cricket Official Conscience Medal" Brass Badge,
1940. - **$40 $85 $150**

PCC-21. "Walt Disney's Pinocchio" Cello. Button,
1940. Back paper has Kay Kamen distributorship name. Used by toy stores and others as giveaway. - **$15 $30 $45**

PCC-22. Victor Records Cello. Button,
1940. Phonograph record design inscribed "Pinocchio Comes To Town On Victor Records". - **$200 $500 $1000**

PCC-23

PCC-24

PCC-25

PCC-32

PCC-33

PCC-34

PCC-23. Jiminy Cricket Wood Jointed Doll,
c. 1940. Store item by Ideal. - **$150 $250 $450**

PCC-24. Figaro 6" Figure,
1945. Store item by Multi Products, Chicago. -
$40 $110 $175

PCC-25. Geppetto Sitting 6" Figure,
1945. Store item by Multi Products, Chicago. -
$60 $150 $275

PCC-32. Figaro 2" Figure,
1945. Store item by Multi Products, Chicago. -
$40 $125 $250

PCC-33. Geppetto 2" Figure,
1945. Store item by Multi Products, Chicago. -
$40 $110 $175

PCC-34. Giddy 2" Figure,
1945. Store item by Multi Products, Chicago. -
$40 $110 $175

PCC-26

PCC-27

PCC-28

PCC-35

PCC-36

PCC-26. Geppetto Standing 6" Figure,
1945. Store item by Multi Products, Chicago. -
$40 $90 $125

PCC-27. Giddy 6" Figure,
1945. Store item by Multi Products, Chicago. -
$40 $80 $200

PCC-28. Jiminy Cricket 6" Figure,
1945. Store item by Multi Products, Chicago. -
$40 $110 $225

PCC-35. Lampwick 2" Figure,
1945. Store item by Multi Products, Chicago. -
$40 $110 $175

PCC-36. Pinocchio 2" Figure,
1945. Store item by Multi Products, Chicago. -
$40 $80 $200

PCC-29

PCC-30

PCC-31

PCC-37

PCC-38

PCC-29. Jiminy Cricket United Fund 6" Figure,
1945. Store item by Multi Products, Chicago. -
$40 $125 $250

PCC-30. Lampwick 6" Figure,
1945. Store item by Multi Products, Chicago. -
$30 $100 $150

PCC-31. Pinocchio 6" Figure With Hands Down,
1945. Store item by Multi Products, Chicago. -
$40 $80 $200

PCC-37. Jiminy Cricket "United Way" Countertop Sign,
1940s. Diecut cardboard 5x7" with easel back. -
$40 $65 $100

PCC-38. Pinocchio Silver Spoon Premium,
1940s. - **$20 $40 $75**

PCC-39

PCC-40

PCC-39. Tell The Truth Ring,
1954. Weather-Bird Shoes. Brass with rubber nose. -
$250 $400 $600

PCC-40. "Tell The Truth Club" Membership Card,
1954. Weather-Bird Shoes. - $15 $22 $30

PCC-41

PCC-41. Cardboard Punch-Out Puppet Sheets With Envelope,
1950s. Campbell's Pork and Beans plus "Rex Allen" names on mailer. Near Mint In Mailer - $50

PCC-42

PCC-43

PCC-42. "I've Seen Pinocchio At Hudson's" Cello. Button,
1950s. Sponsored by Detroit department store. -
$35 $75 $100

PCC-43. "United/Official Conscience" Litho. Button,
c. 1950s. United Way. - $20 $40 $75

PLANET OF THE APES

First released in 1968, the intensely popular sci-fi film *Planet of the Apes*, starring Charlton Heston, Roddy McDowall, and Kim Hunter, is appreciated by science fiction and pop culture fans worldwide, with Heston's hammy dialogue still quoted and parodied to this day. Heston's Colonel Taylor is a hapless astronaut who crash-lands on a planet ruled by talking apes, only to discover that it is in fact the Earth of the far future. The simple morality play with a *Twilight Zone*-like twist (no surprise, since it was scripted from the original Pierre Boulle novel by Rod Serling) also featured some heavy-handed political commentary, which would become a regular ingredient in the sequels: *Beneath the Planet of the Apes* (1970), with Heston in only a brief appearance at the beginning and end of the film, *Escape From the Planet of the Apes* (1971), *Conquest of the Planet of the Apes* (1972), and *Battle for the Planet of the Apes* (1973). All but *Beneath* featured Roddy McDowall as chimpanzee scientist Cornelius, and later Cornelius' son Caesar, the leader of the new ape civilization.

Thinly-veiled protests against the Vietnam war and racial tensions at home gave the films a political identity unusual for "sci-fi" films of the time. A short-lived TV series also starring McDowall as another chimpanzee named Galen aired in 1974, and a cartoon spin-off lasted one season as well. *Planet of the Apes* celebrates its 30th anniversary this year, and with recent buzz on a planned remake or sequel, as well as near-continual airings of the original films on the Sci-Fi Channel (often hosted by McDowall himself), the series is experiencing renewed interest among collectors. Most items are copyright 20th Century Fox. "Clever ape!"

PLA-1

PLA-2

PLA-1. Planet of the Apes Novel,
1968. By Pierre Boulle. This edition was released with a photo cover to promote the film. - $8 $15 $25

PLA-2. Colorforms Adventure Set,
1960s. Full color box with plastic clinging figures and coated color backgrounds. - $10 $25 $50

PLA-3

PLA-4

PLA-5

PLA-3. "Battle for the Planet of the Apes" Novelization,
1973. Award Books. Written by David Gerrold, the book is one of several novelizing the five films in the series (see also PLN-1). - $5 $7 $10

PLA-4. Planet of the Apes Coloring Book,
1974. Authorized edition by Artcraft. One of several coloring and activity books. - $10 $20 $30

PLA-5. Planet of the Apes Press Book,
1974. 14x8-1/2" U.S. press book. In 1974, all 5 films in the series were released on a marathon bill. Press books were supplied to theaters with ads, stories, photos, and mock newspaper front pages. Unclipped - **$15 $25 $40**

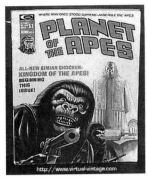

PLA-6

PLA-7

PLA-6. Planet of the Apes Magazine,
1975. Volume 1 #9 shown. Published by Magazine Managment Co. - **$3 $5 $9**

PLA-7. Planet of the Apes Toy Rings,
1975. Stan Toy Co., England. Scarce. 5 rings in set: Dr. Zaius, Galen, Zira, Urko, and Cornelius or Caesar. Galen and Dr. Zaius rings shown. Came in gold, silver, green or black on iodized aluminum base. Similar rings were made in Japan in recent years. Each - **$700**

POGO

Walt Kelly chose the Okefenokee Swamp as home for his characters making their debut in *Animal Comics*, which ran briefly in the early 1940s. The strip then ran in the *New York Star* in 1948 and moved to the *New York Post* and syndication in 1949. Pogo the wise possum and his contrary pal Albert the alligator thrived for more than 25 years, dealing with the eccentricities of a cast of characters that included such creatures as Howland Owl, Churchy la Femme the turtle, Beauregard the retired veteran bloodhound, Porky Pine, and P.T. Bridgeport the scheming bear. Comic books appeared in the 1940s and 1950s and Simon & Schuster published more than 30 Pogo books between 1951 and 1976. An animated cartoon aired on NBC in 1969 and an animated "claymation" film was produced by Warner Brothers in 1980, starring the voices of Skip Hinnant, Vincent Price and Jonathan Winters. The strip itself was discontinued in 1975, but enjoyed a brief revival in the late 1980s.

POG-1

POG-2

POG-1. "The Little Fir Tree" Storybook,
1942. W. T. Grant Co. Christmas giveaway with color cover and eight pages of bw unsigned Walt Kelly art. - **$200 $400 $800**

POG-2. "Peter Wheat News" Comic Book With Kelly Art,
1949. Peter Wheat Bread, Bakers Associates Inc. Issue #21 including cover and three pages of art by Walt Kelly, Pogo creator. - **$15 $30 $45**

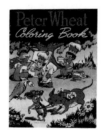

POG-3

POG-3. "Peter Wheat" Coloring Book With Kelly Art,
1951. Peter Wheat Bread, Bakers Associates Inc. Sixteen pages including art examples by Walt Kelly, Pogo creator. - **$40 $75 $150**

POG-4

POG-4. "Peter Wheat" Cut-Out Circus,
1951. Bakers Associates. Designed by Walt Kelly.
Near Mint Uncut - **$250**
Cut - **$40 $100 $150**

POG-5

POG-6

POG-5. "I Go Pogo" Litho. Button,
1952. 7/8" version, similar button issued for 1956. -
$5 $10 $18

POG-6. Pogomobile Kit,
1954. Store item published by Simon and Schuster.
Cardboard assembly parts for ceiling mobile.
Near Mint In Envelope - **$250**

POG-7   POG-8

POG-7. 4" Diameter Litho. Button,
1956. Probably sent by Post-Hall Syndicate to newspapers
carrying the strip. **$35 $60 $100**

POG-8. "I Go Pogo" Litho. Button,
1956. 7/8" version. - **$8 $15 $25**

POG-9

POG-10

POG-11

POG-9. Walt Kelly Christmas Card,
1958. His own personal issue. Unsigned. - **$35 $75 $125**

POG-10. Walt Kelly Christmas Card,
1960. His own personal issue. Unsigned - **$35 $75 $125**

POG-11. Walt Kelly Christmas Card,
1961. His own personal issue. Unsigned - **$35 $75 $125**

POG-12

POG-13

POG-12. Cello. Button,
1968. One of 30 known designs with Walt Kelly facsimile
signature on each. - **$10 $20 $40**

POG-13. Vinyl Figures,
1968. Poynter Products, distribution method unknown.
Includes Beauregard, Albert, Churchy, Howland, Hepzibah,
Pogo. Often missing are Pogo's hat and flowers, Churchy's
fish on end of string. Each - **$50 $100 $150**

POG-14

POG-14. "Jack And Jill" Magazine With Cover Article,
1969. Monthly issue of child's magazine for May with specialty cover art related to four-page historic article about
Pogo plus promotion for NBC-TV Pogo cartoon. -
$10 $20 $35

POG-15

POG-15. Vinyl Figures,
1969. Procter & Gamble. Six in set: Pogo, Beauregard
Hound, Churchy La Femme, Howland Owl, Albert Alligator,
Porky Pine. Each - **$5 $10 $15**

POG-17

POG-16

POG-16. Pogo Characters Plastic Mug Set,
1969. Procter & Gamble. Set of six: Pogo, Albert, Churchy,
Porky Pine, Howland, Beauregard. Each - **$5 $10 $15**

POG-17. "Sunday Newsday" 2-1/2" Cello. Button,
1972. Long Island newspaper promotion. Further inscribed
"Try It/You'll Like It". - **$35 $75 $150**

POLL-PARROT SHOES

Paul Parrot, owner of the Parrot Shoe Company, decided to christen his products Poll-Parrot Shoes in 1925. Extensive use of advertising and appropriate giveaways for boy and girl customers--carrying the parrot trademark--were successful marketing tools for the company's shoes and replacement parts. From 1947 to 1950 the company sponsored the *Howdy Doody* program on NBC television, resulting in a number of paper premiums and rings linking the puppet and the parrot.

POL-1   POL-2   POL-3

POL-1. Litho. Tin Spinner Top With Wood Peg, c. 1920s. - **$12 $20 $35**

POL-2. Litho. Tin Top with Wood Peg, 1930s. - **$8 $15 $25**

POL-3. Litho. Tin Disk Spinner, c. 1930s. - **$10 $18 $30**

POL-4

POL-5

POL-4. "Pre-Tested Poll-Parrot Shoes" Litho. Button, 1930s. - **$5 $12 $20**

POL-5. "The Cruise Of The Poll-Parrot" Radio Show Paper, 1930s. Store hand-out slip imprinted for WSVA Radio, Harrisonburg, Virginia, also offering shoe purchase premium of magnetic compass. - **$5 $10 $15**

POL-6

POL-7   POL-8

POL-6. "Poll Parrot Shoe Money", 1930s. Various denominations and colors. - **$3 $5 $10**

POL-7. Litho. Tin Whistle, 1930s. - **$10 $20 $30**

POL-8. Litho. Tin Clicker, 1930s. - **$10 $15 $25**

POL-9

POL-9. Baseball Game, 1944. Premium includes cardboard baseball game with spinner, mailer, wooden pegs, holder, and scoreboards. Also promotes the War Bond drive. - **$50 $100 $150**

POL-10

POL-10. "Uncle Sam" Paper Over Tin Bank, c. 1945. - **$25 $50 $75**

POL-12   POL-13

POL-11

POL-11. Flying Parrot Plastic Flicker Ring, 1950s. - **$25 $50 $70**

POL-12. "Poll-Parrot Shoes" Symbol Brass Ring, c. 1950s. - **$20 $30 $40**

POL-13. "Poll-Parrot Shoes" Symbol Aluminum Ring, c. 1950s. - **$20 $30 $40**

POPEYE

Popeye was introduced to the world in E.C. Segar's *Thimble Theatre* comic strip in 1929 and within a year was the strip's most popular character. The adventures of the spinach-chomping sailor, Olive Oyl, the hamburger-mooching Wimpy, Jeep, Swee'pea, and a host of other characters proved to be a phenomenal success. Comic book reprints appeared as early as 1931, and in 1933 the Fleischer Studios released the first of what would eventually add up to more than 450 animated cartoon shorts for theaters and television. A *Popeye* radio series aired on NBC and CBS from 1935 to 1938, sponsored by Wheatena (1935-1937) and Popsicle (1938). Early cartoon shorts were syndicated on television starting in 1956, new films were added in 1961, plus a further series from Hanna Barbera on CBS in 1978. Robin Williams and Shelley Duvall starred in the 1980 Paramount film. The Popeye characters have been merchandised extensively since the 1930s.

PPY-1   PPY-2

PPY-1. Character Painted Cast Iron Figurines,
c. 1929. Store items. Each - **$60 $125 $200**

PPY-2. Popeye/Wimpy Glass Tumbler,
1929. Probably held dairy product. From believed set of eight picturing two characters on each. - **$50 $120 $175**

PPY-3

PPY-3. "Popeye Comic" Gum Folders,
1933. Tattoo Gum by Orbit Gum Co. From numbered set. Each - **$8 $15 $30**

PPY-4   PPY-5

PPY-4. Sheet Music For Cartoon "Popeye The Sailor",
1934. Six pages. Store bought. - **$20 $40 $75**

PPY-5. Large Sign,
1935. Promotes Magic Transfer picture premiums. IGA Rolled Oats sponsor. - **$300 $500 $800**

PPY-6   PPY-7   PPY-8

PPY-6. Pipe Toss Game,
1935. Store item by Rosebud Art Co. Also used as Popsicle premium. - **$30 $65 $100**

PPY-7. "Penney's 'Back To School Days' With Popeye" Cello. Button,
1935. J. C. Penney Co. - **$10 $20 $30**

PPY-8. Popeye/Jeep Glass Tumbler,
1936. From same series as PPY-2 but later copyright year. - **$60 $140 $200**

PPY-9

PPY-9. "State Theatre Popeye Club" Membership Certificate,
1938. Paper document for theater in Kingsport, Tennessee with affixed foil paper seal. Local particulars are inked including member name and August 27 effective date of membership. - **$30 $60 $100**

PPY-10   PPY-11

PPY-10. "Popeye The Sailor Man" 9x13" Cardboard Book Sign,
c. 1937. Grosset & Dunlap. - **$125 $250 $500**

PPY-11. Popsicle-Fudgsicle-Creamsicle 13x18" Cardboard Store Sign,
1938. Scarce. Pictures premiums and announces Popeye "On The Radio After May 1st". - **$125 $250 $500**

PPY-12

PPY-13

PPY-14

PPY-12. Bisque Toothbrush Holder,
1930s. Store item. Has moveable arm. - **$75 $175 $300**

PPY-13. Painted White Metal Lamp With Pipe,
1930s. Store item. - **$75 $150 $300**

PPY-14. Poll-Parrot Shoes Photo Ad Card,
c. 1930s. Probable unauthorized use of Popeye character by local store owner. - **$12 $20 $30**

PPY-15

PPY-15 Enameled Metal Pin,
1930s. Wheatena cereal. Set of three: Popeye, Olive Oyl, Wimpy. Each On Card (Two Varieties) - **$75 $125 $200**
Popeye Pin - **$20 $40 $80**
Olive Pin - **$30 $60 $100**
Wimpy Pin - **$30 $60 $100**

PPY-16

PPY-16. Theatre Club Card And Cello. Button,
1930s. Various theaters.
Button - **$10 $20 $35**
Card - **$15 $50 $75**

PPY-17

PPY-18

PPY-19

PPY-17. Olive Oyl Enamel On Silvered Brass Pin,
1930s. Wheatena cereal.
On Card - **$75 $125 $200**
Pin Only - **$30 $60 $100**

PPY-18. Jeep Enamel On Brass Pin,
1930s. Apparent store item, similar to Wheatena give-aways and used as premium by Popsicle. -
$75 $150 $250

PPY-19. "New York Evening Journal" Club Card,
1930s. - **$15 $40 $75**

PPY-20

PPY-20. "The Popeye Line Of Hats & Caps" Store Carton,
c. 1930s. Unidentified clothing maker. 16x19x24" long carton with lid. - **$200 $400 $600**

PPY-21

PPY-22

PPY-23

PPY-21. "I Yam Strong For King Comics" Cello. Button,
1930s. One of earliest buttons to advertise comic books. -
$15 $25 $40

PPY-22 "Sunday Examiner" Litho. Button,
1930s. From "50 Comics" set of various newspaper characters, match number to win prize. - **$20 $30 $60**

PPY-23. "S. F. Examiner" Litho. Button,
1930s. San Francisco newspaper. From set of various characters, match number to win prize. - **$20 $35 $65**

PPY-24

PPY-25

PPY-24. Wimpy Color Picture Silvered Brass Ring,
1930s. - **$75 $125 $175**

PPY-25. Coca-Cola Postcards With Wrapper,
1942. Set of four. Near Mint With Wrapper - **$90**
Each Card - **$5 $10 $15**

PPY-26

PPY-27

PPY-26. "Buy War Stamps" 14x18" Poster,
c. 1944. U.S. Government. - **$50 $100 $150**

PPY-27. Popcorn Bank,
1949. Van Camp premium. 20 oz. popcorn can which converts into bank. - **$20 $40 $60**

PPY-28

PPY-28. Ruler,
1940s. 7 inch ruler. Came with pencil box. Store bought. - **$10 $25 $40**

PPY-29

PPY-29. Popeye Sailor's Cap,
1940s. Probable premium. - **$75 $125 $250**

PPY-30

PPY-31

PPY-30. Popeye 8x14" Diecut Cardboard Display,
1940s. Glows in dark and holds 12 Magic Nite Glo flashlights with whistles. Display Card - **$50 $100 $200**
Each Glow In Dark Flashlight - **$20 $40 $60**

PPY-31. "Sunshine Popeye Cookies" Cardboard Tab,
c. 1940s. - **$20 $45 $75**

PPY-32

PPY-33

PPY-34

PPY-32. "Popeye: The First Fifty Years" 2-1/4" Cello. Button,
1959. Workman Publishing Co. For book promotion with King Feautures copyright. - **$5 $10 $15**

PPY-33. Popeye Cello. Button,
1950s. Comes in 3-1/2" size and scarcer 1-3/4" size.
Larger Size - **$10 $20 $35**
Smaller Size - **$25 $50 $75**

PPY-34. Cloth/Vinyl Doll,
1950s. Store item by Gund Mfg. Co. - **$50 $80 $150**

PPY-35

PPY-35. "Crew Club" 16-Page Comic Booklets,
1989. Instant Quaker Oatmeal. Photo shows set of four different plus one back. Each - **$3 $6 $12**

POPSICLE

Add some flavor and coloring to water, freeze it around a pair of flat sticks, and the result is a Popsicle, a popular alternative to ice cream promoted as a frozen drink on-a-stick. In addition to flavored ice, the producers created Popsicle Pete, a comic book character that started on a long run in *All-American Comics* in 1939. *The Popsicle Pete Fun Book* (1947) and *Adventure Book* (1948) contained stories, games, and cut-outs, and the company sponsored two short-lived television variety shows: *The Popsicle Parade of Stars* on CBS in 1950 and *Popsicle Five-Star Comedy* on ABC in 1957.

PSC-1

PSC-2

PSC-1. Uncle Don Club Card Popsicle Premium,
1932. Rare. - **$25 $50 $75**

PSC-2. "Popsicle" Premium Sheet,
1937. - **$5 $12 $20**

PSC-3

PSC-3. Sign,
1930s.Very early die-cut cardboard sign for Popsicle when they were offered one stick for 5¢. Young girl promoter was later replaced by Popsicle Pete. - **$50 $100 $150**

PSC-4

PSC-5

PSC-4. "Jo-Lo Creamsicles" Waxed Paper Bag,
1930s. Popsicles with Joe Lowe Corp. copyright for various local retailers. Bags were saved for gifts. - **$8 $12 $20**

PSC-5. "Adventurer's Popsicle Club" Litho. Button,
1930s. - **$10 $30 $50**

PSC-6

PSC-7

PSC-6. Popsicle Pete Cheerio Bag,
1941. Cheerio bags were used as coupons to get gifts. - **$5 $10 $25**

PSC-7. Popsicle Pete Gift News,
1941. 8 page flyer for gifts. Popsicle Pete pictured upper left. - **$15 $30 $45**

PSC-8

PSC-9

PSC-8. Paper Store Sign 9x19",
1946. - **$20 $50 $80**

PSC-9. Paper Store Sign 11x14",
1946. - **$30 $60 $85**

PSC-10

PSC-10. "Popsicle Pete Free Gift News",
1947. - **$15 $30 $45**

PSC-11

PSC-12

PSC-11. "Giant Gift List" Catalogue,
1949. - **$15** **$40** **$60**

PSC-12. "Popsicle Pete Jo-Lo-Fone",
1940s. Assembled Pair - **$15** **$25** **$40**

PSC-13

PSC-14

PSC-13. Popsicle Pete's "Mystery Box With Mystery Prize",
c. 1940s. Held prize and stick good for free Popsicle.
Complete - **$100**
Empty - **$37** **$56** **$75**

PSC-14. Cowboy Boot Plastic Ring,
1951. Popsicle. Top has magnifier lens, compass, secret compartment. Boot holds "Cowboy Ring Secret Code" symbols paper. Also offered by Bazooka Joe and shown in his premium catalog as late as 1966. - **$25** **$50** **$100**

PSC-15

PSC-16

PSC-15. Popsicle Pete Gift List,
1952. Paper sheet opening to 11x15" printed on both sides including illustration of 34 premium offers for 1952-1953 years. - **$15** **$25** **$45**

PSC-16. "Giant Gift List" Sheet,
1953. For 1953-1954 premium offers. - **$15** **$25** **$45**

PSC-17

PSC-18

PSC-17. Abbott And Costello Paper Sign,
1954. 11x15". - **$20** **$50** **$100**

PSC-18. "Giant Gift List" Sheet,
1954. For 1954-1955 premium offers. - **$15** **$25** **$45**

PSC-19

PSC-20

PSC-19. "5 Star Comedy Party" 8x15" Paper Poster,
1957. For short-lived May-July ABC-TV program. - **$25** **$50** **$75**

PSC-20. "Popsicle Gift List" Catalogue,
1958. Eight-page color booklet picturing more than 40 premiums offered 1958-1959 for various coupon quantities. - **$10** **$20** **$35**

PSC-21

PSC-21. Popsicle Gift List,
1959. 1959-1960 list of prizes. 8 pages. Children riding train on front. - **$10** **$20** **$30**

PSC-22

PSC-22. Popsicle Gift List,
1961. 8 page premium. Has Bob Hope on the front and promotes his new film inside. - **$15** **$25** **$40**

PORKY PIG

Porky Pig, one of the star cartoon characters created by the Warner Brothers studio in the 1930s, made his screen debut in 1935 and had his first feature role the following year. From then until the mid-1960s the stuttering little porker appeared in more than 100 cartoon shorts, frequently paired with Daffy Duck, Sylvester the cat, or his girlfriend Petunia. Porky went through several early design changes, and from 1937 on was given voice by Mel Blanc. Porky made his comic book debut in issue #1 of *Looney Tunes & Merrie Melodies* in 1941, had his own book by 1943, and over the years has appeared in numerous special issues and as a guest star in other Warner character books. On television the *Porky Pig Show* aired on ABC from 1964 to 1967 and *Porky Pig and His Friends* was syndicated to local stations starting in 1971. "Tha- Tha- That's All Folks!"

PRK-1

PRK-2

PRK-1. Bisque Bank,
c. 1936. Store Item - **$30 $75 $150**

PRK-2. Coloring Book,
1938. Store item by Saalfield Publishing Co. Probably first Porky coloring book. Sixteen pages of art by Ralph Wolfe involving Porky and Petunia in various activities. -
$50 $100 $150

PRK-3

PRK-4

PRK-3. "Porky's Book Of Tricks" Activity Booklet,
1942. K. K. Publications. - **$40 $125 $300**

PRK-4. "Petunia" Wood Jointed Doll,
1940s. Store item. - **$40 $75 $140**

PRK-5

PRK-5. Warner Bros. Character Place Mats,
c. 1940s. Probable store item. "Rhyme-A-Day Series" set of seven. Each - **$15 $30 $50**

PRK-6

PRK-7

PRK-6. Dell Comic Pictures,
1940s. Version in top hat with Warner Bros. copyright, second version Leon Schlesinger copyright.
Each - **$15 $30 $50**

PRK-7. "March Of Comics" #175,
1958. Various sponsors. - **$5 $10 $20**

POST CEREALS MISC.

Charles W. Post, a patient at Dr. John Kellogg's Battle Creek Sanitarium, was introduced to the benefits of a vegetarian diet in 1891. His enthusiasm for Kellogg's Caramel Coffee led him to develop his own formula and by 1895 he was marketing Postum Cereal Food Drink, a coffee substitute that "Makes Red Blood." Within two years he had created Grape-Nuts, a cold breakfast cereal that was also promoted as a health food. Post advertised his products as if they were medicines under the theme "There's a Reason." The company flourished, expanded, and took the name of General Foods in the late 1920s.

PST-1

PST-1. Comic Rings Store Shelf Display,
1948. Post's Raisin Bran. Cardboard assembly display for litho. tin ring box inserts. Twelve character rings are identified. - **$100 $175 $350**

PST-2

PST-3

PST-2. Andy Gump Litho. Tin Ring,
1948. This and the next 11 rings are from the 1948 Post Raisin Bran set. The Near Mint price is for unbent examples with no rust. - **$5 $20 $35**

PST-3. Dick Tracy Litho. Tin Ring,
1948. - **$20 $60 $100**

PST-4

PST-5

PST-4. Harold Teen Litho. Tin Ring,
1948. - **$5** **$20** **$35**

PST-5. Herby Litho. Tin Ring,
1948. - **$5** **$20** **$35**

PST-6   **PST-7**

PST-6. Lillums Litho. Tin Ring,
1948. - **$5** **$20** **$35**

PST-7. Orphan Annie Litho. Tin Ring,
1948. - **$10** **$35** **$60**

PST-8   **PST-9**

PST-8. Perry Winkle Litho. Tin Ring,
1948. - **$5** **$20** **$35**

PST-9. Skeezix Litho. Tin Ring,
1948. - **$5** **$20** **$35**

PST-10   **PST-11**

PST-10. Smilin' Jack Litho. Tin Ring,
1948. - **$10** **$35** **$60**

PST-11. Smitty Litho. Tin Ring,
1948. - **$5** **$20** **$35**

PST-12   **PST-13**

PST-12. Smokey Stover Litho. Tin Ring,
1948. - **$5** **$20** **$35**

PST-13. Winnie Winkle Litho. Tin Ring,
1948. - **$5** **$20** **$35**

PST-14   **PST-15**

PST-14. Alexander Litho. Tin Ring,
1949. This and the next 23 rings are from the 1949 Post
Toasties set. The Near Mint price is for unbent examples
with no rust. - **$5** **$20** **$35**

PST-15. Blondie Litho. Tin Ring,
1949. - **$5** **$20** **$35**

PST-16   **PST-17**

PST-16. Captain Litho. Tin Ring,
1949. - **$5** **$20** **$35**

PST-17. Casper Litho. Tin Ring,
1949. - **$5** **$20** **$35**

PST-18   **PST-19**

PST-18. Dagwood Litho. Tin Ring,
1949. - **$10** **$30** **$50**

PST-19. Felix The Cat Litho. Tin Ring,
1949. - **$20** **$70** **$125**

PST-20   **PST-21**

PST-20. Flash Gordon Litho. Tin Ring,
1949. - **$20** **$70** **$125**

PST-21. Fritz Litho. Tin Ring,
1949. - **$5** **$20** **$35**

PST-22   **PST-23**

PST-22. Hans Litho. Tin Ring,
1949. - **$5** **$20** **$35**

PST-23. Henry Litho. Tin Ring,
1949. - **$5** **$20** **$35**

PST-24   **PST-25**

PST-24. Inspector Litho. Tin Ring,
1949. - **$5** **$20** **$35**

PST-25. Jiggs Litho. Tin Ring,
1949. - **$5** **$20** **$35**

PST-26   **PST-27**

PST-26. Little King Litho. Tin Ring,
1949. - **$10** **$30** **$50**

PST-27. Mac Litho. Tin Ring,
1949. - **$5** **$20** **$35**

PST-28   **PST-29**

PST-28. Maggie Litho. Tin Ring,
1949. - **$5** **$20** **$35**

PST-29. Mama Litho. Tin Ring,
1949. - **$5** **$20** **$35**

PST-30   **PST-31**

PST-30. Olive Oyl Litho. Tin Ring,
1949. - **$10** **$30** **$50**

PST-31. The Phantom Litho. Tin Ring,
1949. - **$20** **$70** **$125**

PST-32   **PST-33**

PST-32. Popeye Litho. Tin Ring,
1949. - **$20** **$70** **$125**

PST-33. Snuffy Smith Litho. Tin Ring,
1949. - **$10** **$30** **$50**

PST-34   **PST-35**

PST-34. Swee' Pea Litho. Tin Ring,
1949. - **$10** **$30** **$50**

PST-35. Tillie The Toiler Litho. Tin Ring,
1949. - **$5** **$20** **$35**

PST-36   **PST-37**

PST-36. Toots Litho. Tin Ring,
1949. - **$10** **$30** **$50**

PST-37. Wimpy Litho. Tin Ring,
1949. - **$10** **$30** **$50**

PST-38   **PST-39**

PST-38. "Turbo Jet Pilot" 3-1/2" Plastic Badge,
1949. Center has built-in siren whistle. - **$10** **$30** **$75**

PST-39. Air Speed Indicator,
1940s. Premium for bike with mailer. - **$25** **$50** **$75**

PST-40

PST-41

PST-40. "Viking Rockets" Toy With Instructions And Mailer,
1952. Post's Krinkles. Set of plastic spring launcher and three 2-3/4" plastic rockets. Near Mint Boxed - **$150**
Launcher and Three Rockets - **$25** **$50** **$75**

PST-41. Sugar Crisp Order Form for Puppets (Handy, Dandy, Candy),
1953. Post Cereal. - **$10** **$20** **$30**

PST-42

PST-42. Sugar Crisp Puppets,
1953. Post Cereal. With accesories add $20 each. -
$10 **$20** **$40**

PST-43

PST-43. Railroad Tin Signs,
1954. 28 different tin signs of railroad companies logos and mailer.Complete - **$150** **$300** **$600**
Each - **$5** **$10** **$20**

PST-44

PST-49

PST-50

PST-44. Grape-Nuts Flakes Cars,
1954. Plastic cars of models, Ford County Sedans, Ford Tudors, Ford Crown Victorias. Various colors: red, dark blue, turquoise, yellow, and brown. 8 cars pictured.
Each - **$8 $20 $40**

PST-49. Rocket Racer,
1950s. Scarce. Orange battery powered plastic rocket racer. With mailer and instructions. - **$35 $75 $125**

PST-50. Post Race Car Premium (Speed Town) with Mailer,
1950s. - **$30 $70 $100**

PST-45

PST-46

PST-51

PST-52

PST-45. Sugar Crisp Bears Mug & Bowl Set,
1954. With instructions & mailer. Blue & Pink. Post Cereal. - **$30 $50 $100**

PST-46. Plastic Cars,
1955. Eight different colors and models.
Each - **$8 $20 $40**

PST-51. Railroad Fun Book - Sugar Crisp,
1950s. 36 page premium which promotes trains. - **$10 $35 $45**

PST-52. Spy Master Belt Set,
1950s. Includes command belt which lights up, with camera, signal mirror, magnifying glass, sundial, compass, a measure with glasses and plastic mustache. With mailer and instructions. - **$35 $65 $100**

PST-47

PST-48

PST-53

PST-47. Sugar Crisp Tractor Trailers,
1955. Grey and orange color pictured. Freuhauf written on top of trailers. Each - **$10 $15 $25**

PST-48. Grape-Nuts Flakes Plastic Tanker Set,
1956. Ford/Freuhauf Oil. Set contained a red, yellow, orange, and grey tanker. Each - **$15 $30 $50**

PST-53. Plymouth Plastic Cars,
1960. Post Rice Krinkles. Red, blue, and turquoise colors. Features convertible, hard top, and station wagon.
Each - **$10 $25 $40**

PST-54

PST-54. Football Booklet Set,
1962. Each - **$2 $6 $10**

PST-55

PST-55. "Linus The Lion Fun Book" With Play Scene Card,
1964. Near Mint In Mailer - **$100**
Book Only - **$20 $40 $75**

PST-56   PST-57

PST-56. Plastic Cars,
1966. Ford Mustang, Ford hardtop, fastback and convertible. All yellow. Each - **$8 $20 $40**

PST-57. Rice Krinkles Plastic Cars,
1967. Premium cars. Mercury Cougar. Green, dark blue, light blue, brown, red, and yellow. Each - **$8 $20 $40**

PST-58

PST-59

PST-58. Checkers Game and Mailer,
1960s. Premium. Complete- **$10 $25 $40**

PST-59. 3-D Poster (Honeycomb Cereal),
1970s. Kirby art. Premium with 3-D glasses. -
$15 $20 $30

POT O' GOLD

A thinly-disguised lottery radio show hosted by Horace Heidt and sponsored by Tums from 1939-1941 on NBC, although briefly revived for one season by ABC in 1946. A "Wheel of Fortune" was spun three times during each broadcast to determine: (1) a telephone directory from a random city, (2) a page from it, and (3) a specific home telephone number from that page. The number, then called by Heidt, rewarded the answerer $1,000 by Western Union. Obviously people listened in hopes of being selected, probably with no concept of the millions-to-one odds against it. The wheel selections were interspersed by musical entertainment by Heidt's Musical Knights. The show left the air as a result of a ruling by the Federal Communications Commission.

PGL-2

PGL-1

PGL-1. "Pot O' Gold" Game,
1939. Store item. Large 13x20" box reading "America's Newest Radio Game Craze As Played Over NBC Network". - **$40 $80 $110**

PGL-2. "Tums Pot-O-Gold" 3" Metal Pocket Flashlight,
c. 1939. Inscription continues "With Horace Heidt On Your Radio Thursday Night". - **$30 $60 $100**

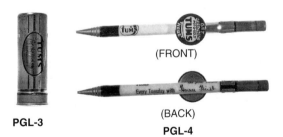

(FRONT)

(BACK)

PGL-3   PGL-4

PGL-3. Tums Metal Container With Show Logo,
c. 1939. Rare. - **$50 $100 $200**

PGL-4. Metal Pencil With Logo On Attached Cello. Pencil Clip,
c. 1939. - **$25 $50 $100**

PRETTY KITTY KELLY

The story of a young Irish immigrant girl who arrived in New York with amnesia, no friends, and charged with murder, aired on CBS radio from 1937 to 1940. Kitty managed to make friends and had a number of spirited adventures during her three-year run. Continental Baking Company's Wonder bread and Hostess cupcakes were sponsors.

PKK-1

PKK-2

PKK-1. "Pretty Kitty Kelly" 12x17-1/2" Paper Store Sign,
c. 1937. Wonder Bread. - **$10 $15 $25**

PKK-2. "Pretty Kitty Kelly Balloon" 11x15" Paper Store Sign,
c. 1937. Wonder Bread. - **$5 $8 $15**

PKK-3

PKK-4

PKK-3. "Kitty Kelly" Enameled Brass "Perfume Pin" On Card,
c. 1937. Wonder Bread. Complete - **$25 $40 $60**
Pin Only - **$10 $25 $40**

PPK-4. Cello. Button,
c. 1937. Columbia Broadcasting System. - **$3 $5 $8**

PULP MAGAZINE MISC.

Pictured is sampling of 1930s to 1940s membership cards. "Pulps" derived the name from inexpensive paper used for publication of fantasy and adventure magazines produced at low cost; very few pulps made the leap to producing a badge, ring or other premiums.

PUL-1

PUL-2

PUL-1. "Weird Tales Club" Member Card,
1930s. - **$50 $150 $200**

PUL-2. "Black Arts Club" Member Card,
1930s. - **$20 $60 $75**

PUL-3

PUL-4

PUL-3. "The Futuremen" Club Card,
1930s. Captain Future magazine. - **$20 $60 $75**

PUL-4. "The Lone Eagles Of America" Member Card,
1930s. Lone Eagle magazine. Back has club Ten Commandments. See ADV 22-23. - **$20 $60 $85**

PUL-5

PUL-6

PUL-7

PUL-5. "Science Fiction League" Club Card With Metal Lapel Stud,
1930s. Thrilling Wonder Stories magazine.
Card - **$10 $35 $60**
Lapel Stud - **$15 $75 $100**

PUL-6. "The Science Fictioneers" Club Card,
1930s. Facsimile signature of executive secretary "Ascien Cefictionist". - **$10 $35 $50**

PUL-7. "Globe Trotters Club" Member Card,
1930s. Thrilling Adventures magazine. - **$15 $75 $100**

PURPLE PEOPLE EATER

For six weeks in 1958 this novelty tune featuring a one-eyed, one-horned creature was the No. 1 record on the charts in America. The song was written by Sheb Wooley, a Western band leader with an MGM recording contract. Wooley also had an acting career, appearing in some 50 movies (he was the killer Ben Miller in *High Noon*) and on television as Pat Nolan in *Rawhide* (CBS, 1959-1965) and in the cast of *Hee Haw* (CBS, 1969) for which he also wrote the theme song.

PUR-2

PUR-1

PUR-3

PUR-1. Stuffed Fabric Figure,
1958. Store item copyright by Cordial Music Co. Features include jiggle eyeball in single eye. - **$20 $40 $60**

PUR-2. "I Am A Purple People Eater" Litho. Button,
1950s. Probably a vending machine issue. - **$5 $10 $15**

PUR-3. Plastic Figure,
1950s. Store item by J. H. Miller Mfg. Co. 5" tall. - **$50 $100 $200**

PUR-4

PUR-4. Plastic Hat On Store Card,
1950s. Store item by Spec-Toy-Ulars, Inc. Thin shell plastic purple hat designed with single eye on front plus markings "One-Eyed, One-Horned Purple People Eater."
Carded - **$20 $40 $60**
Hat Only - **$10 $20 $30**

PUR-5

PUR-6

PUR-5. "I'm A Purple People Eater" Litho. Button,
1950s. Probably a vending machine issue. - **$3 $8 $12**

PUR-6. Cello. 3-1/2" Button,
1950s. Store item. Purple and white art. - **$8 $15 $25**

QUAKER CEREALS MISC.

The Quaker Oats Company got its start in 1877 when an oatmeal processor named Henry D. Seymour opened his Quaker Mills Company in Ravenna, Ohio, and registered a likeness of a somber Quaker as his trademark. The company was sold in 1879 and by 1890 was part of the giant American Cereal Company. With the Quaker as the symbol of its principal product, the company sold its rolled oats in cardboard boxes rather than in bulk, making it one of the first packaged foods. Heavy advertising and promotion--including cross-country trains distributing free samples--made Quaker Oats a national success. The company entered the cold cereal market with Puffed Wheat and Puffed Rice, "shot from guns." The Quaker logo was revised in 1945 and further modernized in 1971. This section shows Quaker premiums not associated with the many major characters they sponsored over the years.

QKR-1

QKR-2

QKR-1. Trade Card,
1883. Shows Quaker cereal assembly line. - **$20 $40 $60**

QKR-2. "Quaker Rolled White Oats" Cello. Button,
c. 1905. - **$10 $20 $35**

QKR-3

QKR-4

QKR-3. Quaker Oats Doll,
1930. Rare. Cloth uncut mascot doll for Quaker Crackels Cereal. - **$75 $200 $300**
Assembled Doll - **$35 $75 $150**

QKR-4. "Phil Cook/The Quakerman" With Doll Photo,
c. 1930. Quaker Crackels. Black and white photo of radio show host at NBC microphone while displaying 'Crackels Boy' assembled stuffed fabric cut-out premium doll.
Photo - **$8 $12 $20**

QKR-5

QKR-5. "Jake's Glider" Kit With Envelope,
c. 1931. Quaker Oats/Quaker Crackels/Mother's Oats. Instructions envelope holding balsa assembly parts for 12x12" glider toy propelled by rubber band. Offered on "Quaker Early Birds" NBC radio program that began December 29, 1930. Envelope Only - **$10 $25 $40** Glider Only - **$15 $30 $45**

QKR-7

QKR-6

QKR-6. Muffets Biscuits Humming Rocket Premium Sign 12x15",
1930s. - **$40 $80 $160**

QKR-7. Muffets Biscuits Humming Rocket,
1930s. - **$20 $40 $65**

QKR-9

QKR-8

QKR-10

QKR-8. Humming Rocket Ship Promo Manual,
1930s. - **$30 $60 $90**

QKR-9. "Betty Lou" Silver Plate Spoon With Mailer,
1930s. Quaker Oats. Handle tip is figural depiction of young girl in polka dot dress. With Mailer - **$10 $20 $30** Spoon Only - **$5 $10 $15**

QKR-10. "Milton Berle's Jumbo Fun Book",
1940. Pre-TV era. - **$10 $15 $25**

QKR-11

QKR-12

QKR-11. "Maple Leaf Bantam Hockey Club" Certificate,
1946. Canadian youth pledge certificate for club affiliated to professional Toronto Maple Leafs 1946-1947 season. - **$15 $25 $40**

QKR-12. "Veronica Lake" Litho. Button,
1948. Quaker Puffed Wheat & Rice. From set of 20 movie stars, each including studio name in inscription. Each - **$5 $10 $15**

QKR-13

QKR-14

QKR-13. Lizabeth Scott Litho. Button,
c. 1948. Similar to photographic set of 20 distributed in America by Quaker Puffed Wheat & Rice but this is Canadian version with line drawings and back inscription "Quaker Puffed Wheat And Rice Sparkies." Eleven different known, all marked "A PARAMOUNT STAR". Each - **$10 $20 $35**

QKR-14. Plastic Mug,
c. 1950. - **$5 $10 $15**

QKR-15

QKR-15. "Space Flight To The Moon" Box Backs #1-5,
1953. Quaker Puffed Rice. From set of eight. Each Complete Box - **$35 $75 $150** Each Uncut Back - **$10 $25 $40**

QKR-16

QKR-17

QKR-16. Indian Picture Cards (18) & Mailer,
1950s. - **$50 $100 $190**

QKR-17. Indian Bead Rings Unassembled With Mailer,
1962. Frosty-O's cereal premium. Rare. - **$50 $100 $150**

QUISP AND QUAKE

Quaker Oats Company introduced a pair of competing new cereals in 1965--Quisp, for quazy energy, and earthquake-powered Quake. The Quisp character was a propeller-headed pink alien who promoted "the biggest selling cereal from Saturn to Alpha Centauri," and Quake was a spelunking superhero in a hard hat and logging boots who could swim through bedrock. Initial promotions included battery-operated helmets as premiums for grocers. Though the two cereals were virtually identical, Quake was dropped in the early 1970s, while Quisp still survives in selected areas.

QSP-1

QSP-2

QSP-1. "Adventures Of Quake And Quisp" Comic Book,
1965. - **$5 $10 $20**

QSP-2. Quisp Cloth Doll,
1965. - **$35 $100 $150**

QSP-3

QSP-4

QSP-3. Quake Cloth Doll,
1965. - **$30 $90 $125**

QSP-4. "Quisp Flying Saucer" With Instruction Sheet,
1966. Battery operated plastic toy.
Near Mint In Generic Box - **$300**
Saucer Only - **$50 $125 $200**

QSP-5

QSP-6

QSP-7

QSP-8

QSP-5. "Quisp Beanie",
1966. Battery operated plastic with turning propeller. - **$75 $150 $300**

QSP-6. Quisp Friendship Figural Plastic Ring,
1960s. Rare. - **$1000 $1550 $2100**

QSP-7. Space Disk Whistle Plastic Ring,
1960s. - **$250 $425 $600**

QSP-8. Meteorite Plastic Ring,
1960s. - **$250 $425 $600**

QSP-9

QSP-10

QSP-11

QSP-9. Space Gun Plastic Ring,
1960s. - **$250 $425 $600**

QSP-10. Quake Figural Plastic Ring,
1960s. - **$250 $500 $750**

QSP-11. Quake Volcano Plastic Ring,
1960s. - **$250 $425 $600**

QSP-12

QSP-13

QSP-12. Quake World Plastic Ring,
1960s. - **$750 $1150 $1500**

QSP-13. "Quazy Moon Mobile" Punch-Out Assembly Sheet,
c. 1960s. Assembly parts glow in the dark.
Complete/Unpunched - **$50 $90 $135**

QSP-14

QSP-15

QSP-14. Quisp Gyro Trail Blazer,
c. 1960s. - **$20 $40 $75**

QSP-15. Smoke Gun,
1960s. Plastic inscribed "Quisp" on each side. - **$75 $175 $300**

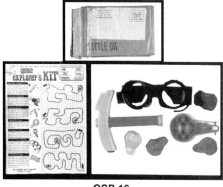

QSP-16

QSP-16. "Quake Explorer's Kit,"
1960s. Quaker Oats. Boxed mail premium of plastic play parts, paper maps and diagrams. Includes hammer, 4 color plastic rocks, Geiger counter, magnifying glass, tweezers and stand, goggles with mirrors, exploration maps, instructions and mailer. Near Mint Boxed - **$200**

QSP-17

QSP-17. Quisp 2-In-1 Fun Bowl With Instructions,
1972. Quaker Oats. Hinged plastic game bowl and with four orange "X" and four blue "O" playing disks for game "Quispity Winks" or "Quanga-Tac-Toe." Near Mint Complete - **$300**
Bowl Only - **$50 $90 $150**

QSP-18

QSP-19

QSP-18. "Quake" Plastic Miner's Helmet,
1970s. Features include battery operated light bulb housing. - **$50 $100 $150**

QSP-19. "Quake Super Spinner" Toy,
1970s. Cellophane pack holds plastic disk ship and launcher with rubber band. Near Mint Sealed - **$40**
Loose - **$5 $15 $25**

QSP-20

QSP-20. Cereal Box,
1985. Two panels have "Space Trivia" game parts. Complete Box - **$10 $15 $30**

A panel of juvenile experts (from as young as 4 to as old as 16) answering questions submitted by listeners, the *Quiz Kids* had a successful 13-year run on network radio from 1940 to 1953. The program was heard initially on NBC, then on the Blue Network (1942-1946), and again on NBC (1946-1951)--sponsored throughout by Alka-Seltzer. For its final season it was sustained on CBS. The show was simulcast on television starting in 1949 and continued on NBC or CBS until 1953, sponsored by Alka-Seltzer (1949-1951) and Cat's Paws Soles (1952-1953). Show-business veteran Joe Kelly served as moderator and quizmaster. A brief television revival in 1956 was hosted by Clifton Fadiman.

QIZ-1

QIZ-2

QIZ-1. "Quiz Kids" Game,
1940. Store item by Parker Brothers. - **$10 $15 $20**

QIZ-2. Red Book,
1941. 31 page book of popular questions and answers from radio show. - **$25 $50 $75**

QIZ-3   **QIZ-4**

QIZ-3. Photo Postcard,
c. 1949. Alka-Seltzer. - **$3 $6 $10**

QIZ-4. Photo Postcard,
c. 1949. Alka-Seltzer. - **$3 $6 $10**

QIZ-5

QIZ-6

QIZ-7

QIZ-8

QIZ-5. "Quiz Kids" Cello. Button,
1940s. - **$8 $12 $20**

QIZ-6. "Quiz Kids" Cello. Button,
1940s. Kaynee. - **$5 $10 $15**

QIZ-7. Tin Badge,
1940s. - **$5 $20 $35**

QIZ-8. "Quiz Kids" Gold Finish Metal Figural Badge,
1940s. Quiz Kid figure suspends miniature metal book that opens to pull-out paper listing questions and answers. - **$20 $60 $100**

RADIO MISC.

Radio of the 1930s to early 1950s has little resemblance to the typical formats offered today's listeners. Newspapers and other periodicals could be perused as time or leisure allowed but radio program timing was firm if "live" household entertainment was desired. There was little casual listening, no lengthy spans of similar format. Program nature differed distinctively from one time slot to the next and the intervening commercial breaks could be as creative as the program itself. The earliest and infrequently offered radio premiums were usually tailored to adult listeners. The early 1930s ushered in premiums for youngsters--ever mindful that mom or other adult was still necessary for product purchase--and the subsequent flourishing of club badges, manuals, secret devices, etc. is a matter of record. This section is a sampling of shows, some admittedly obscure, whose sponsors issued at least one imaginative premium.

RAD-1

RAD-2

RAD-1. Real Folks Radio Show,
1925. Vaseline Hair Tonic. Thompson Corner Enterprise newspaper premium. - **$15 $25 $35**

RAD-2. True Story Hour Book,
1931. True Story hardcover. 196 pages. "Mary and Bob Radio Show" started in 1929. - **$25 $50 $75**

RAD-3

RAD-4

RAD-3. Old Time Songs & Mountain Ballads,
1931. WLW Radio premium. - **$10 $15 $25**

RAD-4. Radio Pictorial Log Book, 34 Pages,
1932. Photos of stars and listing of radio stations. - **$15 $30 $45**

RAD-5

RAD-5. "Just Plain Bill" Puzzle With Mailer Envelope,
1933. Koloynos toothpaste. Puzzle pictures the three major radio cast members.
Envelope - **$3 $5 $10**
Puzzle - **$10 $15 $25**

RAD-6

RAD-6. "Maverick Jim's Runko Race Game" With Letter,
1934. Runkel Bros. Co. 14x20" full color map includes images of Maverick Jim, Amy, Sam, Aunt Sarah Hardy, Sackfull Wilkes. Map printer is Einson-Freeman Co. Letter urges listenership over WOR, New York City and sampling of new "Runko With Malt". Letter - **$5 $10 $15**
Game Sheet - **$20 $40 $75**

RAD-7

RAD-7. Buck Owens "Pals Of The Prairie" Membership Card,
c. 1934. Curtiss Candies. Imprinted for KSD, St. Louis. -
$8 $15 $25

RAD-8

RAD-8. Congo Bartlett's "Ethiopia" 21x29" Paper Map,
1935. Karl's White Bread. - **$40 $75 $150**

RAD-9   RAD-10

RAD-9. Radio Explorers Club Kit,
1935. American-Bosch radios. Contents of certificate and
folder sheet that opens to 17x22" including picture of
Captain James P. Barker, master mariner and club commander.
Folder - **$15 $25 $35**
Certificate - **$10 $18 $30**

RAD-10. "Radio Explorers Club" Metal Globe,
c. 1935. American-Bosch, made by J. Chein Co. -
$25 $60 $90

RAD-11

RAD-11. Happy Hollow Promo With Mailer,
1936. Network feature. Flyer with recipes.. - **$10 $20 $30**

RAD-12   RAD-13

RAD-12. Lucky Strike Hit Parade Six Page Contest Flyer,
1936. Radio premium which allowed you to pick hits for
radio's Top 15 songs. Includes self addressed postcard still
attached with 1¢ stamp. - **$35 $70 $100**

RAD-13. Lucky Strike Hit Parade Four Page Contest Flyer,
1936. Radio contest flyer that was handed out with business reply card still attached. - **$25 $50 $75**

RAD-14   RAD-15

RAD-14. Monk And Sam Radio Show Kit,
1936. Features photo, mailer, song book, and 1936 calendar called Monkalendar. Complete - **$25 $50 $75**

RAD-15. Sara And Aggie's Cook Book,
1936. 32 page radio premium from "The Tuttle Parlor
Show." - **$10 $20 $30**

RAD-16 **RAD-17** **RAD-18**

RAD-24 **RAD-25** **RAD-26**

RAD-16. Mary Marlin Cast Photo Of David Post,
1936. Kleenex. Radio premium from "The Story of Mary Marlin" show. - **$5 $10 $20**

RAD-17. Mary Marlin Cast Photo Of Joe Marlin,
1936. Kleenex. Radio premium from "The Story of Mary Marlin" show. - **$5 $10 $20**

RAD-18. Mary Marlin Cast Photo Of Sally Gibbons,
1936. Kleenex. Radio premium from "The Story of Mary Marlin" show. - **$5 $10 $20**

RAD-24. Alka Seltzer Song Book,
1937. 16 pages of songs featuring radio stars. - **$10 $20 $30**

RAD-25. Stars Of Radio Book,
1937. 16 pages of stars like Kate Smith, Orphan Annie and others. - **$15 $30 $50**

RAD-26. Rudy Vallee Photo,
1937. Philadephia Record newspaper premium. - **$8 $12 $20**

RAD-19 **RAD-20** **RAD-21**

RAD-27

RAD-28

RAD-19. Mary Marlin Letter,
1936. Kleenex. Talks about the cast pictures that were ordered. - **$10 $25 $35**

RAD-20. Mary Marlin Photo Of Actress Joan Gaine,
1936. Kleenex. Radio premium from "The Story of Mary Marlin" show. - **$10 $20 $30**

RAD-21. Mary Marlin Photo Of Wedding,
1936. Kleenex. - **$5 $10 $15**

RAD-27. "The Woman In White" Photo Book,
1938. Pillsbury Flour Co. 9-1/2x11-3/4" cast member and information promotion for hospital drama radio show beginning January 3 that year. - **$10 $20 $30**

RAD-28. "I Want A Divorce" Radio Show Game & Mailer,
1938. Large colorful game with punch-outs and game spinner. Called S&W "Happy Marriage Game." - **$75 $150 $225**

RAD-23

RAD-22

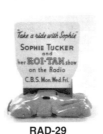 

RAD-29 **RAD-30**

RAD-22. Mary Marlin Photo With Station Attachment,
1936. Kleenex. Holds letter and 5 cast photos from "The Story of Mary Marlin" show. - **$25 $65 $125**

RAD-23. Thrilling Moments,
1936. Sun Oil Co. Lowell Thomas - news voice on the air. - **$10 $20 $30**

RAD-29. Roi-Tan Cigars Contest Novelty,
1939. Miniature metal car with mounted litho. tin sign for contest offering 1939 Chevrolet daily prize with added inscription for Sophie Tucker CBS radio show. - **$35 $100 $200**

RAD-30. "Voodoo Eye" Metal Pendant With Envelope,
1930s. Wheato-Nuts. Pendant designed as look-around device. Envelope - **$50 $100 $125**
Pendant - **$75 $200 $300**

RAD-32

RAD-31

RAD-31. Jolly Joe's Radio Club Book,
1930s. Co Co Wheat. Booklet for youth program utilizing partial code lettering. - **$10 $20 $30**

RAD-32. "The Whistler" Blotter Card,
1930s. Household Finance Corp. Cardboard ink blotter for weekly drama suspense detective program. Pictured example is imprinted for WBBM Radio, Chicago. - **$50 $120 $175**

RAD-34

RAD-33

RAD-33. WLW Radio Photo Postcard Of Lullaby Boys,
1930s. Big Ford & Little Glenn pictured. - **$5 $10 $15**

RAD-34. New Bachelor Cigar Cutter,
1930s. Brass cutter premium for cigars. - **$20 $50 $75**

RAD-35

RAD-36

RAD-35. Radio Folks Brochure,
1930s. Keystone Steel. Barn Dance Party, 16 pages, features George Gobel, Red Foley, and others. - **$10 $20 $35**

RAD-36. Sohio Radio Puzzle,
1930s. Boxed puzzle from "In Dutch" radio show. Bought at gas station. - **$15 $25 $40**

RAD-37

RAD-37. Fife - Musical Instruments In Mailer,
1930s. Symphony Hour sponsored by Malt O'Meal. Includes instructions and mailer. - **$50 $75 $100**

RAD-39

RAD-38

RAD-38. Rudy Vallee Photo,
1930s. Fleischmann's Yeast. Radio premium with story of life folder. Complete - **$20 $40 $75**

RAD-39. Uncle Bob Birthday Card,
1930s. Hydrox premium for "Curb is the Limit Radio Show." Shows Mr. & Mrs. Uncle Bob on front. - **$10 $18 $30**

RAD-40

RAD-42

RAD-41

RAD-40. Family Hour of Stars Blotter,
1940. Prudential. Radio premium from sponsor. - **$20 $40 $60**

RAD-41. Truth Or Consequences Brochure,
1940. Thirty-two pages. Radio show premium. - **$25 $50 $75**

RAD-42. "The Aldrich Family" Schedule Sheet,
c. 1940. Jell-O Puddings. Picture sheet of Ezra Stone as Henry Aldrich of NBC radio comedy series with listing on reverse of more than 75 stations coast to coast offering Thursday evening episode. - **$12 $20 $30**

RAD-43

RAD-43. "Horton's Bulldog Drummond Bomber",
c. 1941. Cardboard punch-out that releases marble bombs onto four small battleships.
Unused In Mailer - **$75 $200 $300**

RAD-44

RAD-45

RAD-44. "The Sea Hound" Paper Map,
1942. Blue Network. Pictures "Captain Silver's Sea Chart". - **$35 $75 $100**

RAD-45. "David Harum" Seed Packets,
1943. Jermin Seed & Plant Co., Los Angeles. Contents are actual flower seeds "Packed For Season Of 1943".
Each - **$5 $15 $25**

RAD-46

RAD-47

RAD-46. WFBL Radio Stars Cook Book With Mailer,
1945. Featured Aunt Jenny, Lionel Barrymore, Milton Berle, Fanny Brice, Major Bowes, Burns & Allen, Danny Kaye, Frank Sinatra, and many others. - **$25 $40 $75**

RAD-47. Big Brother Radio Kit with Mailer,
1945. KMBC radio, Kansas City, Kansas. - **$25 $50 $100**

RAD-48

RAD-48. NBC "On The Air" Comic Book,
1947. National Broadcasting Co. Full color 16-page illustrated description of network operations. Photo example shows front cover and final frame of story. - **$20 $60 $150**

RAD-49

RAD-50

RAD-49. Spike Jones Souvenir Program,
1949. 16 page program premium for RCA. - **$25 $50 $75**

RAD-50. "David Harum Handprint" Folder,
c. 1940s. Bab-o Cleanser. Cover pictures "Homeville" community and cast members, inside "Handprint" is apparent clue to ongoing serial mystery. - **$10 $15 $25**

RAD-51

RAD-52

RAD-51. Texaco Star Theater Sign ,
1940s. 13x9-1/2" sign for ABC radio show featured famous stars. - **$25 $60 $90**

RAD-52. "Meet The Misses" Radio Game & Mailer,
1940s. Automatic Soap Flakes. 48 cards and 19"x19" playing paper board with mailer. - **$65 $125 $200**

RAD-53

RAD-54

RAD-53. Dinah Shore Postcard,
1940s. Promotes her RCA radio show "Up In Arms." -
$15 $30 $50

RAD-54. Ken Murray Promo - NBC Radio,
1940s. The Brown Derby. "RKO Theatre of the Air" program review. - **$15 $25 $35**

RAD-55

RAD-56

RAD-55. Radio Syd & Suzie's Scrapbook,
1940s. Gas & Electric radio premium. Shows photo of
cast. - **$10 $20 $30**

RAD-56. Captain Hal's Membership Card,
1940s. Radio Rangers premium for radio show. -
$10 $20 $30

RAD-57

RAD-58

RAD-57. Big Jon Arthur & Sparkie Fan Card,
1950s. American Broadcasting Corp. - **$15 $25 $50**

RAD-58. WOR Radio 25 Year Anniversary Gold Tie Tack,
1950s. Gold Tie Tack with diamond set in radio mike. - **$150**

THE RANGE RIDER

An early 1950s television weekly series, *The Range
Rider* starred Jock Mahoney in the title role and Dick
Jones as his youthful sidekick Dick West. The two
wandered the West, apparently for the sole purpose of
correcting local injustices. Both actors were accomplished stuntmen, a skill well displayed in each
episode. The show was produced by Gene Autry's
Flying A Productions and ran 1951-1953 on CBS-TV
before syndication. Premiums were issued by bread
companies in addition to non-premium coloring books
and Dell comic books.

RAN-1

RAN-2

RAN-3

RAN-1. Langendorf Bread Photo,
c. 1951. - **$8 $15 $30**

**RAN-2. Sunbeam Bread "Range Rider's Brand" Cello.
Button,**
c. 1951. Pictures Jock Mahoney. - **$20 $50 $75**

**RAN-3. "TV Guide Cowboy Album" Celluloid Covered
Wall Plaque,**
1953. From series of TV Guide promotional plaques sent
to stations. - **$50 $75 $125**

RAN-4

RAN-5

RAN-4. Cello. Button 2-1/4",
1950s. Peter Pan Bread. - **$25 $65 $90**

RAN-5. Philadelphia TV Program Promotion Card,
1950s. Pictures Jock Mahoney, Sally Starr and Gene
Autry. Back has an offer for Oldsmobile "Wild West Fun
And Game Booklet". - **$8 $15 $25**

RAN-6

RAN-7

RAN-6. ButterKrust Bread Label Folder,
1950s. Opens to 11x17" for mounting 16 labels. -
$25 $50 $75

RAN-7. "The Range Rider And Dick West" Mini-Flashlight,
1950s. Store item by Bantam Lite. Metal case with plastic cap plus vinyl carrying cord. - **$15 $25 $40**

RANGER JOE

Ranger Joe Honnies began in 1939, a creation of Jim Rex for the Philadelphia area. A new owner extended distribution throughout the east and south, operating as Ranger Joe, Inc. from Chester, Pennsylvania, a suburb southwest of Philadelphia. Despite this limited Western exposure, the cereal box depicted him as an authentic cowboy with horse; glassware premiums of "Ranch Mug" and cereal bowl repeated his image plus cowboy scenes. The other known Ranger Joe premium is a wood and cardboard gun designed for shooting rubber bands. Product and premiums were apparently tied into local telecasts of *Ranger Joe*, a 1951-1952 NBC-TV Saturday morning adventure show for youngsters.

Rice Honnies joined the original Wheat Honnies product in 1951. Nabisco bought the company in 1954 replacing Ranger Joe with Buffalo Bee, changing Honnies to Honeys and initiating national distribution.

RJO-1

RJO-2

RJO-1. Rubber Band Cardboard Gun,
c. 1940s. - **$25 $50 $75**

RJO-2. Fan Card,
c. 1951. - **$8 $12 $20**

RJO-3

RJO-4

RJO-3. Glass Cup,
c. 1951. Blue & red. - **$5 $10 $15**

RJO-4. Glass Cereal Bowl,
c. 1951. Blue & red. - **$8 $15 $25**

RJO-5

RJO-5. Free Gift Coupon,
1952. - **$5 $8 $12**

RJO-6

RJO-7

RJO-6. "Ranger Joe Ranch Money" Premium Currency Bill,
1952. Ranger Joe Cereal. Box insert to be accumulated for ordering premiums pictured on reverse. - **$3 $8 $12**

RJO-7. "Wheat Honnies" Cereal Box,
1950s. Complete Box - **$35 $65 $100**

REDDY KILOWATT

The friendly little fellow with a lightbulb for a nose and a lightning-bolt torso was created in 1926 by A.B. Collins of the Alabama Power Company. Designed to personify the electric power industry, Reddy was licensed freely to local power companies for promotional use, and his image has adorned a wide variety of items from ashtrays to soap, pinback buttons to comic books. A competing figure, Willie Wiredhand, was created in 1951 by the National Rural Electric Cooperative.

RKL-1

RKL-2

RKL-3

RKL-1. Early Silvered Metal Badge With Red Accent,
c. 1938. - **$75** **$150** **$200**

RKL-2. Translucent Plastic Figure,
1940s. Earliest design style. Pink - **$85** **$150** **$250**
1950s-60s design style. Red - **$75** **$125** **$200**

RKL-3. "25th Anniversary Public Service" Cello. Button,
1951. Public Service Co. of New Hampshire. - **$20** **$40** **$75**

RKL-4

RKL-4. "Your Favorite Pin-Up" Enameled Brass Pin On Card,
1952. On Card - **$10** **$15** **$20**
Loose - **$3** **$5** **$10**

RKL-5

RKL-6

RKL-5. "Light's Diamond Jubilee" Cello. Button,
1954. - **$35** **$75** **$120**

RKL-6. Cuff Links,
c. 1950s. Color image under glass dome with brass frame and shaft. - **$20** **$40** **$75**

RKL-7

RKL-8

RKL-7. Fabric 8-1/2x11" Jacket Patch,
1950s. Diecut flannel with stitched fabric image of Reddy Kilowatt as bowler. - **$35** **$75** **$125**

RKL-8. Cello. Button,
c. 1950s. Canadian. - **$20** **$50** **$80**

RKL-9

RKL-9. Plastic Cookie Cutter With Card,
c. 1950s. Boxed - **$10** **$20** **$35**
Loose - **$5** **$15** **$20**

RKL-10

RKL-11

RKL-10. Service Counter Figure,
c. 1950s. 11" tall jigsawed wood figure in finished image both sides and wire spring clip on raised fingertip for holding card or leaflet. - **$125** **$250** **$400**

RKL-11. Figural Vinyl Bank,
c. 1960. 3-1/2x5-1/2" tall by 6-1/2" wide 3-D image of him dashing through clouds with coin slot in rear, trap in bottom. Near Mint With Both Plastic Lightning Bolt Head Accents - **$1000**
Missing Accents - **$200** **$400** **$600**

RKL-12

RKL-13

RKL-12. Glow-In-The-Dark Plastic Figure,
1961. 1961 copyright on base. - **$75** **$125** **$200**

RKL-13. "The Mighty Atom" Comic Book,
1966. Back cover may designate sponsoring electric utility company. - **$8** **$20** **$40**

RKL-16

RKL-14   RKL-15

RKL-14. "Reddy" Composition Bobbing Head,
1960s. - **$250 $400 $750**

RKL-15. Employee Bowling Trophy,
1960s. Metal figure and award plate on wood base. -
$500 $1200 $2000

**RKL-16. "Courteous Personal Attention To Every
Customer" Litho. Button,**
1960s. - **$15 $25 $50**

RKL-17

**RKL-17. "Inspectors Club Big Rock Point Nuclear
Plant",**
1970s. Consumers Power Company. - **$10 $15 $25**

RED RYDER

Artist Fred Harman created the *Red Ryder* comic strip
as a Sunday feature in 1938 and added a daily version
the following year. The strip, which ran until the late
1960s, told the story of rancher Ryder and his Navajo
ward Little Beaver as they ranged the West of the
1890s, battling bandits and rustlers and settling frontier quarrels. Comic book reprints first appeared in
1939 and continued through most of the 1950s, and
more than 20 "B" Westerns from Hollywood chronicled
the popular hero's adventures. A radio series aired on
the Mutual network--primarily on the West Coast--from
early 1942 to 1949, sponsored by Langendorf bread
and other bakeries. A television adaptation was syndicated in 1956. The Red Ryder character was used
extensively for many years to promote Daisy air rifles.

RYD-1

RYD-1. Red Ryder Target Game with Box,
1939. Store item. - **$100 $200 $400**

RYD-2

RYD-2. "Daisy Air Rifles" Catalogue,
1940. Near Mint In Mailer - **$250**
Loose - **$50 $125 $175**

RYD-4

RYD-3

RYD-3. Victory Patrol Member Card,
1943. Included in membership kit. Back has Red Ryder
radio listings. - **$20 $40 $60**

RYD-4. Victory Patrol Magic V-Badge,
1943. Scarce. Luminous cardboard badge. Ordered by
sending coupon from membership kit. - **$50 $150 $300**

RYD-5

**RYD-5. Membership Kit Promotion Sheet for Magic V-
Badge,**
1943. Example shown has coupon to order and membership card trimmed off the bottom.
As Shown - **$20 $40 $75**

RYD-6

RYD-6. "Rodeomatic Radio Decoder",
c. 1943. Rare. Cut out and assembled from "Victory Patrol" kit. Assembled - **$200 $400 $600**

RYD-7

RYD-11

RYD-7. Victory Patrol Membership Kit With Comic,
1943. Langendorf Bread. Scarce. Includes cut-out "Rodeomatic" decoder, order coupon for "Magic V-Badge", cut-out membership card and membership certificate, comic book. Complete - **$425 $1275 $3600**

RYD-11. Victory Patrol Membership Kit With Comic,
1944. Scarce. Includes membership card, map, comic book, code card and regular cards.
Complete - **$350 $1075 $3200**

RYD-8

RYD-9

RYD-12

RYD-13

RYD-8. "Victory Patrol" Paper Store Signs,
1944. Scarce. Langendorf Bread. Larger sign 7x15", smaller oval 4x5". Picture Sign - **$50 $125 $200**
Oval Sign - **$20 $65 $100**

RYD-9. "Red Ryder Victory Patrol" Copper Luster Metal Badge,
1944. - **$35 $65 $125**

RYD-12. "Bobby Blake/Little Beaver" Dixie Ice Cream Picture,
1945. - **$25 $40 $75**

RYD-13. Plastic Horse Statue,
c. 1947. Saddle inscribed "Red Ryder" on each side. Believed to be one of 100 second place prizes in glove selling contest sponsored by Wells Lamont Corp., maker of Red Ryder gloves. - **$50 $90 $175**

RYD-10

RYD-14

RYD-10. Postcard,
1944. Langendorf Bread. Promotes Red Ryder Victory Patrol comic book and shows how to get other premiums. - **$25 $50 $75**

RYD-14. "Daisy Handbook No. 2",
1948. - **$35 $100 $275**

RYD-15

RYD-16

RYD-17

RYD-15. Air Rifle Safety Litho. Button, c. 1948. Daisy Mfg. Co. Given with Red Ryder rifle and handbook. - **$10 $18 $30**

RYD-16. Pocketknife, 1940s. Store item by Camco USA. Steel with plastic grips. - **$75 $150 $250**

RYD-17. "Red Ryder Fighting Cowboy" Certificate, c. 1940s. Wells Lamont Corp., maker of Red Ryder gloves. Text details 10 qualities of character for youthful members. - **$20 $35 $50**

RYD-18

RYD-18. Salesman's Fiberboard Glove Case, 1940s. Wells-Lamont Co. - **$100 $200 $300**

RYD-19

RYD-20

RYD-21

RYD-19. Radio Sponsor Handbill, 1940s. N.B.C. Bread, probably others. Imprint includes local broadcast times. - **$35 $60 $100**

RYD-20. "Red Ryder" Cello. Button, 1940s. - **$15 $30 $50**

RYD-21. "Little Beaver" Cello. Button, 1940s. - **$15 $30 $50**

RYD-22

RYD-23

RYD-24

RYD-22. "Red Ryder Patrol" Silvered Metal Badge, 1940s. - **$30 $50 $100**

RYD-23. "I Have Entered The Red Ryder Pony Contest" Litho. Button, 1940s. - **$8 $15 $25**

RYD-24. Penney's "Red Ryder Lucky Coin", 1940s. J. C. Penney Co. Brass, holed for keychain. Back slogan "Penney's For Super Value". - **$8 $12 $20**

RYD-25

RYD-26

RYD-27

RYD-25. "Red Ryder Gloves" Silvered Tin Whistle, 1940s. Wells-Lamont Co. - **$35 $75 $135**

RYD-26. "Red Ryder Gloves/Red Ryder Sheriff" Silvered Metal Star Badge, 1940s. Probable Wells-Lamont Co. - **$60 $150 $200**

RYD-27. Red Ryder/Little Beaver Fan Card, c. 1950. Fred Harman art. - **$10 $20 $35**

RYD-28

RYD-28. "Howdy Compadre" Photo and Letter,
1950. Langendorf Bread. 5x7" photo with "Dear Compadre" letter as a thank-you for promising to eat Langendorf Bread. Mailer - **$5 $15 $25**
Letter - **$15 $30 $50**
Photo - **$25 $50 $75**

RYD-29

RYD-30

RYD-31

RYD-29. Trading Cards Sheet,
1952. Wells-Lamont Corp. Uncut. - **$15 $25 $40**

RYD-30. "Daisy Gun Book",
1955. Daisy Mfg. Co. - **$25 $65 $175**

RYD-31. "Good Luck/Red Ryder" Plastic Arrowhead Keychain Charm,
1955. Daisy Mfg. Co. - **$35 $80 $160**

RENFREW OF THE MOUNTED

Inspector Douglas Renfrew of the Royal Canadian Mounties, the hero of a dozen adventure novels by Laurie York Erskine, came to CBS radio in 1936. Sponsored by Wonder bread for two years, the series then moved to the Blue network, where it was sustained until it went off the air in 1940. Renfrew movies, produced by Grand National Pictures and Monogram in the late 1930s and early 1940s, were edited into 30-minute tales for television syndication in 1953. While he lasted, the strong, silent Renfrew always got his man.

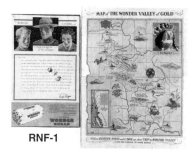

RNF-1

RNF-1. "Renfrew Of The Mounted" 17x22" Premium Map,
1936. Wonder Bread. - **$40 $75 $125**

RNF-2

RNF-3

RNF-2. "Lost Wonder Valley Of Gold" Map Order Postcard,
1936. Wonder Bread. Used to order previous item. - **$10 $20 $30**

RNF-3. "Around The Camp Fire With Carol And David" Leaflet,
c. 1936. Wonder Bread. Illustrated magic tricks including "Tricks That Fooled Renfrew". - **$12 $20 $30**

RNF-4

RNF-5

RNF-4. Renfrew Sign 9 1/2 x 20",
1936. Wonder Bread. Promotes radio show. - **$50 $100 $175**

RNF-5. Renfrew Radio Sponsor Folder,
c. 1936. Wonder Bread. Four-page ad leaflet with mention on back for daily radio show. - **$10 $15 $25**

RNF-6

RNF-6. Fan Postcard,
c. 1936. Wonder Bread. - **$20 $40 $65**

RNF-7

RNF-8

RNF-7. Renfrew Adventure Store Window Signs,
c. 1936. Wonder Bread. Paper "Wanted" and "Missing" posters, each 11x17" from radio episode "The Sunken City Of The Arctic." Each - **$15 $40 $75**

RNF-8. Radio Program Debut Folder,
c. 1936. Columbia Broadcasting System. Four-page leaflet previewing "Coming Thrills" plus mention of premium map and member badge. Card Only - **$25 $50 $75**

RNF-10

RIN-1

RIN-2

RIN-3

RNF-9

RNF-9. Wonder Bread Radio Show Paper Sign 10x17",
c. 1936. - **$50 $100 $200**

RNF-10. "Renfrew Of The Mounted" Cello. Button,
c. 1936. Wonder Bread. - **$3 $6 $10**

RIN-TIN-TIN

The Wonder Dog was introduced to the world by Warner Brothers in 1923 and the talented German shepherd, an instant success, proved to be the studio's first major film star. There were a number of Rintys over the years, but the canine hero consistently battled villains and the elements, rescued those in danger, preserved his good name, turned into a noteworthy "actor"--and saved the studio from bankruptcy. Rinty starred in 19 films for Warner Brothers between 1923 and 1930, and went on to make a series of chapter plays for the Mascot studios.

On radio, *Rin-Tin-Tin* aired on the Blue network (1930-1933) and CBS (1933-1934), sponsored by Ken-L-Ration, and returned for a season on the Mutual network in 1955, sponsored by Milk Bone.

On television, Rinty joined young Corporal Rusty and the troopers of the 101st Cavalry, the Fighting Blue Devils, in maintaining law and order in the West of the 1880s. The hit series, sponsored by the National Biscuit Company, aired in prime time on ABC from 1954 to 1959 and was the source of a wide variety of premiums and licensed products. Reruns were broadcast on ABC (1959 to 1961) and CBS (1962 to 1964), and sepia-tinted episodes were offered briefly for syndication in 1976. Comic books appeared during most of the 1950s and early 1960s.

RIN-1. "The Lone Defender" Cello. Button,
1930. For Mascot Pictures 12-chapter movie serial. - **$15 $25 $40**

RIN-2. "The Lightning Warrior" Movie Serial Cello. Button,
1931. Mascot Pictures. Comes in 7/8" or 1-1/4" sizes. - **$15 $25 $40**

RIN-3. Ken-L-Ration Photo,
1931. - **$8 $12 $20**

RIN-4

RIN-5

RIN-4. Fan Club Notice,
1931. Flyer for button premium - **$20 $40 $50**

RIN-5. Photo With Mailer,
1931. Fan Club movie premium. Photo of two dogs. - **$15 $25 $45**

RIN-6

RIN-7

RIN-6. "What Every Dog Should Know" Booklet,
c. 1931. Ken-L-Ration. - **$12 $20 $35**

RIN-7. Advertising Litho. Button,
1930s. Atwater Kent Radios. - **$25 $50 $75**

RIN-8

RIN-8. Rin Tin Tin III Postcard,
1940s. Premium promotes Camp Haan Training Center. - **$10 $20 $30**

RIN-9

RIN-9. Club Membership Kit,
1954. Nabisco. Includes fabric banner, membership card, white metal badge.
Complete Near Mint - **$400**
Banner - **$60 $100 $200**
Card - **$10 $25 $50**
Badge - **$20 $50 $75**

RIN-10   RIN-11

RIN-10. Shredded Wheat Box,
1954. Nabisco. Lt. Rip Masters on front. Offers insignia patch. Back of box shows picture of all seven patches. - **$50 $100 $175**

RIN-11. Shredded Wheat Box,
1954. Nabisco. Shows Rin Tin Tin and Rusty on front. Back shows cast and promotes radio and TV show. - **$50 $100 $175**

RIN-12

RIN-12. Stereo Cards With Viewer,
1954. Nabisco. Set of 24 cards.
Viewer - **$10 $20 $35**
Card Set - **$30 $50 $80**

RIN-14

RIN-13

RIN-15

RIN-13. Nabisco "Wonda-Scope",
c. 1954. Components include compass, mirror, magnifying lenses. Dial marked "Rin-Tin-Tin". - **$20 $40 $75**

RIN-14. "Bugle Calls" Vinyl Cardboard Record,
c. 1954. Nabisco. Came with plastic bugle premium. - **$15 $25 $40**

RIN-15. Felt Cavalry Hat,
c. 1954. Nabisco. Fabric patch on brim front. - **$50 $100 $150**

RIN-16

RIN-16. Magic Brass Ring,
c. 1954. Nabisco. Portrait cover opens over two miniature felt pads. Came with magic pencil and chemically treated paper strips. Complete - **$250 $500 $750**
Ring Only - **$150 $250 $350**
Magic Pencil Only - **$40 $105 $170**
Instructions Only - **$110 $135**

RIN-17

RIN-18

RIN-17. Nabisco Plastic Rings,
1955. Set of 12, various characters. Each - **$10 $15 $20**

RIN-18. Nabisco Cast Photo,
c. 1955. - **$10 $18 $25**

RIN-19

RIN-20

RIN-19. English Postcard,
c. 1955. - **$10 $20 $30**

RIN-20. Nabisco Box Insert Cards,
1956. At least 12 different examples. Each - **$3 $6 $12**

RIN-21

RIN-22

RIN-21. "Rusty" Tin/Plastic Palm Puzzle,
1956. From "Nabisco Juniors" set of 12.
Each - **$5 $10 $15**

RIN-22. Gun And Holster,
1956. Nabisco. Includes gun and leather holster with belt
and buckle. Belt - **$20 $40 $75**
Holster - **$30 $80 $175**
Gun - **$50 $100 $200**

RIN-23

RIN-23. Leather Belt With Metal Buckle,
1956. Complete - **$20 $40 $75**
Buckle Only - **$10 $20 $35**

RIN-24   **RIN-25**

RIN-24. Plastic Mug,
1956. - **$15 $25 $40**

RIN-25. Plastic Cup,
1956. - **$15 $25 $40**

 **RIN-26**

RIN-26. Cavalry Rifle Ballpoint Pen,
1956. Nabisco. Near Mint In Mailer - **$50**
Rifle Pen Only - **$8 $15 $25**

RIN-27   **RIN-28**

RIN-27. Cast Member Photo,
c. 1956. - **$8 $12 $20**

RIN-28. Color Litho. Button,
c. 1956. Sent to participants in Nabisco's 'Name The
Puppy Contest.' - **$5 $12 $20**

RIN-29

RIN-29. Rin-Tin-Tin Related Vacuum-Form Medals,
c. 1956. Nabisco. Offered while Nabisco sponsored the
show but no reference to Rin-Tin-Tin on items or cereal
box. Set of eight with four in "Indian Wars" series, four in
"Frontiersmen" series. Each - **$5 $12 $20**

RIN-30

RIN-30. Cereal Box With Medal Ads,
c. 1956. Nabisco Rice Honeys. Front and back panels picture and describe "Indian Wars Medal" and "Frontier Hero" medals offered as box inserts. - **$25 $50 $80**

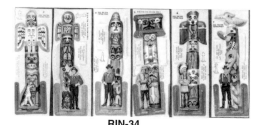

RIN-31   RIN-32   RIN-33

RIN-31. Miniature Plastic Telegraph Set,
c. 1956. Nabisco. Tapper key makes clicking sound. - **$10 $15 $25**

RIN-32. "101st Cavalry" Plastic Canteen With Strap,
1957. Nabisco. - **$10 $20 $35**

RIN-33. Plastic On Steel Pocketknife,
c. 1957. Store item. - **$25 $60 $100**

RIN-34

RIN-34. Totem Pole Plastic Punch-Outs,
1958. Nabisco. Set of eight.
Each Unpunched - **$5 $15 $20**

RIN-35

RIN-35. Insignia Patch,
1958. Nabisco, paper peel-off stickers. Set of seven: Cochise, Fort Apache, Lt. Rip Masters, Major Swanson, Rin Tin Tin, Rusty, and Sgt. O'Hara.
Each Unused - **$3 $10 $15**

RIN-36

RIN-36. Plush And Vinyl Toy Dog,
1959. Smile Novelty Co. Store item, about 15" long. - **$40 $80 $160**

RIN-37

RIN-38

RIN-37. Cereal Box,
1950s. Nabisco Shredded Wheat premium. Shows walkie talkie offer for 25¢ and box top. - **$50 $125 $250**

RIN-38. Walkie Talkies And Mailer,
1950s. Nabisco Shredded Wheat premium. Also enclosed plastic belt for wrist to hold walkie tallkies - **$75 $150 $300**

RIN-39

RIN-39. Cast Photo,
1950s. Movie premium. - **$25 $50 $75**

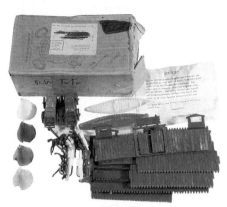

RIN-40

RIN-40. Fort Set,
1960. Honeycomb Cereal premium. Plastic Ft. Apache with horses, wagons, teepees, canoes, instruction letter and box. Has printed name mistake at top on front of plastic fort. Says Fort Boone instead of Fort Apache. - **$50 $100 $150**

RINGS MISC.

Kids love to wear rings, and the sponsors of radio programs and their merchandisers, particularly cereal makers, learned that offering a ring related to their heroes was sure to bring in a flood of box tops. Hardly a radio character in the 1930s and 1940s could get through a season without a special ring premium offer. There were rings with secret compartments, glow-in-the-dark rings, flashlight rings, magnifying-glass rings, whistle rings, saddle rings, compass rings, magnet rings, rocket rings, decoder rings, baseball rings, movie rings, microscope rings, treasure rings, cannon rings, weather rings, and membership rings, along with rings bearing photos, faces, and logos. Collecting premium rings has become a specialty of its own. (For more information, refer to *The Overstreet Toy Ring Price Guide*, 3rd edition.)

RGS-1   RGS-2   RGS-3

RGS-1. "Kewpie" Sterling Silver Ring,
c. 1920s. Store item. Depicts single Kewpie with raised hands and kicking one foot. - **$75 $110 $150**

RGS-2. "Rosalie Gimple" Brass Ring,
1936. Rare. Pabst-ett cheese food. Depicts air hostess. - **$200 $300 $400**

RGS-3. "Huskies Club" Brass Ring,
1937. Post's Huskies Cereal. Top depicts discus thrower, bands picture various sports equipment. - **$300 $450 $600**

RGS-4   RGS-5   RGS-6

RGS-4. "Murray-Go-Round Ring" Folder,
1937. Radio sponsor Fleischmann's Yeast. - **$20 $40 $60**

RGS-5. "Murray-Go-Round" Brass Spinner Ring,
1937. Fleischmann's Yeast for Arthur Murray Dance Studios. Disk pictures male dancer on one side, female on other. They appear to unite in dance when disk is spun. - **$100 $165 $225**

RGS-6. "Base Ball Centennial" Brass Ring,
1939. Quaker Puffed Rice. Also offered in 1938 by General Mills as Jack Armstrong premium from July 27, 1938 to October 28, 1938 with company recording 46,501 responses. Quaker offered manufacturer's remainder in 1939. - **$250 $500 $750**

RGS-7   RGS-8   RGS-9   RGS-10

RGS-7. Kool-Aid "Treasure Hunt" Brass Ring,
1930s. - **$100 $150 $200**

RGS-8. Chicago "Cubs" Gold Luster Metal Ring,
1930s. Cubs name accented in blue, bands have baseball motifs. - **$75 $165 $250**

RGS-9. Lucky Sheik Brass Ring,
1930s. Catalogue item from Johnson & Smith Novelty Co. Coiled snake design around Pharoh's head plus tiny accent stones. - **$75 $110 $150**

RGS-10. "Junior Broadcasters Club" Brass Ring,
1930s. Top depicts radio microphone, bands depict radio transmission towers. - **$50 $100 $150**

RGS-11   RGS-12

RGS-11. Viking Magnifying Ring,
1941. Rare. Kellogg's All Rye Flakes. Brass with magnifying glass to view Prince "Valric Of The Vikings". Very limited distribution. - **$1750 $3500 $7500**

RGS-12. Kix Pilot's Ring,
1945. Brass secret compartment ring with slide-off top. Also issued in 1942 as Capt. Midnight ring. See item CMD-41. Envelope - **$10 $25 $50**
Ring - **$75 $115 $200**

RGS-13

RGS-14

RGS-13. "His Nibs Compass Ring" On Card,
1947. Nabisco. Ring - **$15 $25 $60**
Card - **$20 $40 $60**

RGS-14. Roger Wilco Rescue Ring,
1948. Power House Candy. Brass base with glow-in-dark plastic top which fits over brass whistle. - **$75 $150 $250**

RGS-15

RGS-16

RGS-15. Roger Wilco Magni-Ray Brass Ring,
1948. Power House candy bar. Paper insert under hinged cover glows in dark. - **$30 $60 $90**

RGS-16. F-87 Super Jet Plane Ring.
1948. Kellogg's Corn Flakes. Black plastic plane on nickel-plated ring. Advertised on Superman radio program but no other association. Ring - **$125 $190 $250**
Instructions - **$125 $135 $150**

RGS-17

RGS-18

RGS-19

RGS-17. Jet Plane Ring,
1948. Kellogg's Pep. Brass bands, metal airplane shoots off ring by spring lever. Advertised on Superman radio program but no other association. - **$125 $190 $250**

RGS-18. Fireball Twigg Explorer's Ring,
1948. Post Cereals. Brass bands hold glow-in-dark plastic sundial under clear plastic dome. - **$50 $100 $150**

RGS-19. "Ted Williams Baseball Ring" Newspaper Ad,
1948. Nabisco Shredded Wheat. - **$10 $20 $30**

RGS-21

RGS-23

RGS-20

RGS-22

RGS-20. "Ted Williams" Mechanical Ring,
1948. Nabisco. Plastic batter figure moves by spring in brass base. - **$325 $650 $1000**

RGS-21. "Andy Pafko" Baseball Scorer Brass Ring,
1949. Muffetts cereal. Named for Chicago Cubs star, top has three turning wheels for counting balls, outs, strikes - **$75 $150 $250**

RGS-22. "Scorekeeper Baseball Ring" Order Blank,
1949. Mechanical ring featuring Andy Pafko of Chicago Cubs. - **$25 $40 $65**

RGS-23. Baseball Game Mechanical Ring,
1949. Kellogg's. Silvered metal capped by diamond-shaped plastic compartment with lever action for game of miniature palm puzzle nature. - **$50 $150 $250**

RGS-24

RGS-25

RGS-26

RGS-24. Your Name Ring,
1949. Kellogg's Rice Krispies. Brass bands with good luck symbols hold plastic dome over paper with personalized first name designated by orderer. - **$20 $35 $50**

RGS-25. Glow-In-Dark "Flying Tigers Rescue Ring",
c. 1949. Red or yellow plastic base with glow-in-dark top featuring secret compartment holding tiny brass whistle. - **$115 $200 $300**

RGS-26. "Flying Tiger Rescue Ring" Leaflet,
c. 1949. Power House candy bar. - **$20 $40 $60**

RGS-27

RGS-28

RGS-29

RGS-30

RGS-27. "Billy West Club" Silvered Brass Ring,
1940s. Depicts cowboy on horseback. - **$50 $110 $175**

RGS-28. Cap-Firing Brass Ring,
1940s. Store item. Cover snaps down to fire single cap.
On Card - **$65**
Loose - **$12 $15 $20**

RGS-29. Glow-In-Dark Whistle Ring,
c. 1940s. Rare. Probable candy sponsor. Very similar to Kix atom bomb ring but varies by glow white plastic cap, whistle element is aluminum. - **$600 $1250 $2500**

RGS-30. "Arthur Murray" Watch Ring,
c. 1940s. Brass bands pronged at top to hold actual miniature watch in brass case. - **$100 $200 $300**

RGS-31   **RGS-32**   **RGS-33**

RGS-31. Basketball Action Brass Ring,
1940s. Scarce. Holds back board with tiny hoop and chained basketball to throw through it. - **$75 $150 $300**

RGS-32. "Joe DiMaggio Sports Club" Member Card,
1940s. M&M's Candies. Probably came with club ring. - **$25 $40 $75**

RGS-33. "Joe DiMaggio Sports Club" Brass Ring,
1940s. Scarce. M & M's candies. Bands have club name and picture sports equipment. - **$300 $575 $850**

RGS-34   **RGS-36**   **RGS-37**

RGS-35

RGS-34. Knights Of Columbus Secret Compartment Glow-In-Dark Metal Ring,
1940s. Rare. Same base as Green Hornet version except initials "GH" altered to "HG" (Holy Ghost). - **$750 $2000 $4000**

RGS-35. "Red Goose Shoes" Glow-In-Dark Secret Compartment Ring,
c. 1940s. Metal and plastic with swing-out disk over paper lapel in glow compartment. - **$115 $170 $225**

RGS-36. Skelly Oil Co. Red Checkmark Brass Ring,
1940s. Top has stamped-in red enameled checkmark, possible Captain Midnight association but no documentation seen. - **$75 $165 $250**

RGS-37. Sundial Brass Ring,
c. 1950. Sundial Shoes. Top has plastic dome over sundial. - **$30 $45 $60**

RGS-38   **RGS-39**

RGS-38. "Magno-Power '50 Ford Mystery Control" Ring With Instruction Slip,
1950. Kellogg's Pep. Magnetized plastic ring and car.
Ring - **$200 $250 $300**
Instructions - **$75 $90 $100**

RGS-39. Ralston Wheat Chex "Magic Pup" Ring,
1951. Magnet ring moves pup's magnetized head.
Complete - **$60 $90 $120**

RGS-41

RGS-40

RGS-40. "Western Saddle Ring" Offer Ad,
1951. Smith Brothers Cough Drops. Comic book ad for finely detailed replica saddle expansion ring. - **$1 $3 $5**

RGS-41. "The Range Rider" Aluminum Ring With Paper Tag,
c. 1951. Tag names TV show title produced by Autry Flying A Productions. Near Mint With Tag - **$550**
No Tag - **$75 $135 $200**

RGS-42

RGS-43

RGS-42. Rocket-To-The-Moon Ring,
1951. Kix cereal. Brass bands with plastic top for launching three glow-in-dark rockets.
Ring Only - **$100 $200 $400**
Each Rocket Near Mint - **$150**

RGS-43. "Rocket-To-The-Moon Ring" Instruction Sheet,
1951. Kix Cereal. - **$50 $100 $150**

RGS-44

RGS-44. "Major Mars Rocket Ring" Kit,
1952. Popsicle. Mailer holds plastic rocket with brass chain, ring base, instruction folder, strip with four negatives, envelope with 12 light-sensitive paper strips. A strip of four different negatives, 24 papers could be ordered separately. Near Mint Complete - **$1500**
Rocket With Base - **$300 $600 $1000**
Rocket Without Base - **$200 $400 $600**

RGS-45

RGS-46

RGS-45. "Steve Donovan Western Marshal" Aluminum Ring,
1955. Sponsor unknown. For syndicated western TV show. - **$50 $85 $150**

RGS-46. Quaker Cereals "Crazy Rings" Set,
1957. Set of 10 plastic rings of assorted nature.
Near Mint In Mailer - **$350**
Each - **$15 $20 $30**

RGS-47

RGS-48

RGS-47. (Buffalo) Bill Jr. Brass Ring,
1950s. Sides depict bucking horse and holster gun with buffalo on top. Probably from Mars Candy. - **$30 $45 $60**

RGS-48. Bazooka Joe Initial Ring,
1950s. Topps Chewing Gum. Gold luster metal expansion ring with personalized single initial. Issued as late as 1966. - **$75 $175 $275**

RGS-49

RGS-50

RGS-51

RGS-49. "Jets Super Space Ring",
c. 1950s. Ball-Band. One of the few rings that actually decodes. Near Mint In Package - **$40**
Assembled - **$12 $20 $30**

RGS-50. "U.S. Keds" Space Symbols Silvered Brass Ring,
c. 1962. Keds footwear. Depicts "K" space capsule, band has atomic symbol. - **$60 $90 $120**

RGS-51. Bazooka Joe Brass Initial Ink Stamp Ring,
1962. Bazooka Joe Gum. Personalized by rubber stamp single initial designated by orderer. - **$60 $120 $175**

RGS-52

RGS-53

RGS-52. "Smokey Stover" Assembly Ring,
1964. Sugar Jets Cereal and Cracker Jack. From plastic series including Kayo, Smilin' Jack, Terry and the Pirates, others. Each Near Mint On Tree - **$100**
Each Assembled - **$15 $25 $50**

RGS-53. Bazooka Comics Premium Order Sheet,
1966. Topps Chewing Gum. Paper folder opening to 9x14" picturing total of more than 30 items on both sides including Bazooka Joe Magic Circle Initial Stamp Club Ring, Gold-Plated Initial Ring and Cowboy Boot Ring. - **$10 $20 $40**

RGS-54

RGS-54. Old West Trail Club Kit,
1968. Old West Trail Foundation. Includes map, member card, ring. Complete Near Mint - **$125**
Ring Only - **$25 $50 $80**

RGS-55 **RGS-56** **RGS-57**

RGS-55. "Cousin Eerie" Brass Ring,
1969. Warren Publishing Co., publisher of Eerie Comics. - **$30 $60 $100**

RGS-56. "Uncle Creepy" Gold Finish Metal Ring,
1969. Warren Publishing Co., publisher of Eerie Comics. - **$100 $150 $225**

RGS-57. P.F. Magic Decoder Ring With Card,
1960s. P.F. footwear. Also used as Jonny Quest premium. Gold plastic ring with several functions.
Card - **$10 $20 $30**
Ring - **$25 $45 $70**

RGS-58 **RGS-59**

RGS-58. "Miss Dairylea" Plastic Ring,
1960s. Dairylea Products. Domed plastic trademark girl image. - **$20 $30 $40**

RGS-59. Flying Jet Ring With Envelope And Instructions,
1960s. Cereal premium by unknown issuer.
Near Mint In Envelope - **$50**
Ring Only - **$15 $22 $30**

RGS-60 **RGS-61** **RGS-62**

RGS-60. Ralston "Chex's Agent" Decoder Ring,
c. 1960s. Plastic base topped by two cardboard dials. - **$5 $7 $10**

RGS-61. "Wonder" Bread Loaf Plastic Ring,
c. 1970s. - **$5 $7 $10**

RGS-62. Tekno Comix Logo Secret Compartment Ring,
1994. Silvery-gray metal. - **$5 $10 $15**

Robert L. Ripley's Believe It or Not! started life as a newspaper cartoon for the *New York Globe* in 1919 and was ultimately syndicated in as many as 300 newspapers. The focus was on bizarre or freakish events and people and human oddities, all of which, Ripley claimed, could be substantiated. In 1930 he took the show to radio, where it aired in various formats on NBC or CBS for 18 years. Sponsors included Colonial Oil, Esso, General Foods, Royal Crown Cola and Pall Mall cigarettes. A television version ran on NBC in 1949-1950, with other hosts after Ripley's death in 1949 and resurfaced on CBS in 1982 with Jack Palance as host. Collections were published in book form around 1930 and as comic books in the 1960s.

RPY-1

RPY-1. "Disk-O-Knowledge" Cardboard Diecut Mechanical Wheel,
1932. Oddities appear in diecut openings on both sides. - **$10 $20 $30**

RPY-2

RPY-2. "Electric Flash" Game,
1933. Store item by Meccano Co. of America. Battery operated game flashes miniature light bulb for correct response to question of Ripley nature. - **$25 $50 $80**

RPY-3

RPY-3. "Odditorium" Exhibit Souvenir,
1936. From Texas Centennial exposition. Booklet and 12 postcards. Set - **$25 $50 $90**

RPY-4

RPY-5

RPY-4. Oddities Fabric Bandanna,
1930s. - **$8** **$15** **$25**

RPY-5. "Believe It Or Not/Ripley" Diecut Metal Miniature Charm,
1930s. Usually in green antiqued copper finish. -
$10 **$20** **$35**

RPY-6

RPY-6. Oddities Fold-Out Card,
1940. Various local sponsors as Christmas premium. Opens to 13x19" sheet illustrated on both sides. -
$15 **$35** **$60**

RPY-7

RPY-8

RPY-7. Cardboard Ink Blotters,
1948. Various local sponsors. Examples from monthly series dated October, November, December.
Each - **$5** **$10** **$15**

RPY-8. Stamp,
1940s. Scarce. Royal Crown Cola radio premium. -
$25 **$40** **$50**

ROCKY JONES, SPACE RANGER

This early television space opera was two years in preparation and survived only one season of 39 episodes before it was syndicated. The series premiered in December 1953 on KNXT in Los Angeles, in February 1954 on WNBT in New York, and late in 1954 on WBKB in Chicago. Richard Crane played Rocky, chief of a 21st century security patrol force charged with maintaining peace in the galaxies. Silvercup bread was a sponsor, and Space Ranger toys, uniforms, and comic books were licensed to promote the series.

RKJ-1

RKJ-2

RKJ-1. Two Stills,
c. 1954. Each - **$5** **$12** **$25**

RKJ-2. Color Photo,
c. 1954. Possible school tablet cover. - **$10** **$20** **$30**

RKJ-3

RKJ-4

RKJ-3. "Official Space-Ranger" Metal Wings Pin On Card,
c. 1954. Space Rangers Enterprises.
On Card - **$12** **$20** **$30**
Loose - **$8** **$12** **$20**

RKJ-4. Cardboard Rubber Band Gun,
c. 1954. Johnston Cookies And Crackers. - **$15** **$30** **$75**

RKJ-5

RKJ-6

RKJ-5. "Rocky Jones, Space Ranger" Billfold,
1954. Space Ranger Secret code card & billfold with seal on right. - **$25** **$50** **$75**

RKJ-6. Code Card,
1954. Mickelberry's Meats. - **$30** **$75** **$100**

RKJ-7

RKJ-8

RKJ-9

RKJ-7. "Johnston Cookies" Litho. Button,
c. 1954. Also comes with "Silvercup Bread" imprint. -
$10 $20 $35

RKJ-8. Silvercup Bread Litho. Button,
c. 1954. - **$10 $20 $35**

RKJ-9. "Rocky Jones-Space Ranger" Cello. Button,
c. 1954. - **$10 $20 $30**

ROCKY LANE

Harold Albershart (1904-1973), as Allan Rocky Lane, was a longtime actor in adventure films. He made dozens of "B" Westerns, Royal Mountie serials, and jungle epics for Republic Pictures between 1938 and 1961. Lane took over the film role of Red Ryder around 1944 and continued as a star for the studio into the 1950s. *Rocky Lane* comic books were published between 1949 and 1959, and Lane was the television voice of Mr. Ed, the talking horse, from 1961 to 1965.

RLN-1   RLN-2

RLN-1. "Allan 'Rocky' Lane" Cello. Button,
c. 1950. Store item. - **$10 $20 $30**

RLN-2. "Member 'Rocky' Lane Posse" Decal Club Patch,
1950. Rare. Carnation Malted Milk.
Patch - **$50 $275 $350**
Mailer - **$25 $50 $100**

RLN-4

RLN-3

RLN-3. "Posse Shoulder Patch" Premium Offer Ad,
1950. Carnation Malted Milk. Comic book page ad for clothing patch available until January 30, 1951. - **$1 $3 $5**

RLN-4. "Rocky Lane Posse" Cello. Button,
1950. Carnation Malted Milk. - **$50 $100 $150**

RLN-6

RLN-5

RLN-5. "Explorer's Sun Watch" Ad,
1951. Carnation Malted Milk. Comic book page ad with product endorsement by "Rocky" Lane. - **$1 $3 $5**

RLN-6. Dixie Ice Cream Picture,
c. 1952. - **$8 $15 $25**

ROOTIE KAZOOTIE

Who is the lad who makes you feel so glad? He was Rootie Kazootie, the little puppet hero who became a giant hit in children's television. The series, known initially as *The Rootie Tootie Club* when it debuted locally in New York in 1950, changed its name to *The Rootie Kazootie Club* and was broadcast nationally on NBC (1951-1952) and ABC (1952-1954). Other puppet charcters were Polka Dottie, El Squeako Mouse, the villainous Poison Zoomack, and the pup Little Nipper, who became Gala Poochie when RCA dropped out as a sponsor. Todd Russell served as host, and Mr. Deetle Doodle, the silent policeman, was the only other human to appear. Sponsors, in addition to RCA, included Coca-Cola, Power House candy, and Silvercup bread. *Rootie Kazootie* comic books were published in the early 1950s.

ROO-1   ROO-2

ROO-1. "Rootie Kazootie Stars" Puppet Punch-Outs,
c. 1952. Coca-Cola. Set of five. Each Unpunched -
$12 $20 $40

ROO-2. "Rootie Kazootie Stars" Animated Punch-Outs,
c. 1952. Coca-Cola. Set of five. Each Unpunched -
$12 $20 $40

ROO-3

ROO-3. "Rootie Kazootie Rooters Club" Membership Card,
c. 1952. - **$10 $20 $35**

ROO-4   **ROO-5**   **ROO-6**

ROO-4. Club Member Litho. Button,
c. 1952. Color (6 characters) or black/white (5 characters) versions. Each - **$5 $12 $20**

ROO-5. "Rootie Kazootie's Lucky Spot" Embossing Ring,
c. 1952. Designed to emboss title and four-leaf clover image on paper. - **$250 $600 $850**

ROO-6. "Rootie Kazootie Rooter" Glow-In-Dark Plastic Disk,
c. 1952. Back has pin fastener. - **$20 $35 $60**

ROO-7

ROO-7. Picture Puzzles Set,
1950s. Store item by E. E. Fairchild Corp. Three-puzzle set featuring Rootie, Polka Dottie, Gala Poochie. Boxed Set - **$30 $65 $100**

ROSCOE TURNER

A real-life aviator hero and successful aviation entrepeneur, Col. Roscoe Turner was idolized in the 1930s much like cowboy fans adored Tom Mix. Turner was a barnstormer flyer and stunt performer of the 1920s following the start of his air career in the Balloon Service during World War I. He was the major test pilot for the DC-2 (Douglas Commercial) first passenger transport aircraft in 1934. In the latter 1930s, his frequent winning of the Thompson Trophy and Bendix Trophy for speed events at annual National Air Races enthralled a nation of speed fans. His enterprises included a passenger run from Los Angeles to Reno to Las Vegas and return, called by some the "Alimony Special" circuit due to frequent use by movie stars. Turner's popularity promoted premiums by several sponsors, notably Gilmore Oil, H. J. Heinz and Wonder Bread (see Sky Blazers). Probably his best remembered gimmick was for Gilmore Oil Co. An actual African lion--a Gilmore trademark lookalike--was acquired and flew with Turner throughout the United States, Canada and Mexico. Despite insistence by humane agencies that the lion be equipped with a parachute, Turner and his lion were welcomed everywhere until the lion died of old age and natural causes.

RTU-1

RTU-1. Flying Corps Certificate,
1934. Heinz Rice Flakes. - **$20 $30 $50**

RTU-2

RTU-2. Membership Card with Mailer,
c. 1934. Heinz Rice Flakes. - **$20 $75 $100**
Mailer - **$15 $30 $50**

RTU-3   **RTU-4**

RTU-3. "Flying Corps" Bronze Wings Badge On Card,
1934. Heinz Co. "Lieutenant" version.
Card - **$10 $25 $35**
Badge - **$10 $25 $35**

RTU-4. "Flying Corps" Silver Wings Badge On Card,
1934. Heinz Co. "Captain" version.
Card - **$15 $30 $40**
Badge - **$15 $30 $40**

RTU-5

RTU-5. "Flying Corps" Gold Wings Badge On Card,
1934. Heinz Co. "Major" version.
Card - **$20 $35 $50**
Badge - **$20 $35 $50**

ROY ROGERS

RTU-6

RTU-6. "Beginning Col. Roscoe Turner's Flying Adventures,"
1934. Full page in May 27 Sunday comic section sponsored by H. J. Heinz Co. - **$10 $20 $30**

RTU-7

RTU-8

RTU-7. Certificate With Booklet and Mailer,
1934. Mailer for Flying Corp Certificate.
Mailer - **$15 $30 $45**
Booklet - **$15 $30 $45**
Certificate - **$20 $30 $50**

RTU-8. "Roscoe Turner" Photo,
1930s. Heinz Rice Flakes. - **$10 $ 25 $40**

RTU-10

RTU-9

RTU-9. "I Want You To Join My Flying Corps" 20x23" Cardboard Store Sign,
1930s. Heinz Rice Flakes. - **$100 $200 $300**

RTU-10. "Col. Roscoe Turner" Cello. Button,
c. 1930s. For "Corinth Airport Dedication". - **$10 $18 $30**

Singing, movies, radio, records, comic books, comic strips, television, rodeos, personal appearances, merchandising--Roy Rogers has done it all, with style and huge success. Born Leonard Slye in Ohio in 1912, he started out organizing cowboy bands and singing in a hillbilly group, and made his first movies--in bit roles or as a member of the Sons of the Pioneers--as Slye or as Dick Weston in the mid-1930s.

His first film as Rogers was Republic Pictures' *Under Western Stars* (1938). He changed his name legally to Roy Rogers in 1942, and went on to make more than 80 Westerns for Republic, pursuing the Happy Trails to stardom as "King of the Cowboys," riding his palomino Trigger ("The Smartest Horse in the Movies") and accompanied by wife Dale Evans ("Queen of the West") on her steed Buttermilk.

On radio, *The Roy Rogers Show* aired on the Mutual or NBC networks from 1944 to 1955, initially as a musical variety show with Dale, the Sons of the Pioneers, and a movie sidekick Gabby Hayes, later as a Western thriller with Pat Brady replacing Hayes. The show was sponsored by Goodyear Tire (1944-1945), Miles Laboratories (1946-1947), Quaker Oats and Mother's Oats (1948-1951), Post Sugar Crisp (1951-1953), and Dodge automobiles (1954-1955).

Roy Rogers comic books were first published in 1944 and continued well into the 1960s, and daily and Sunday strips syndicated by King Features appeared from 1949 to 1961.

On television, *The Roy Rogers Show* was seen on NBC from 1951 to 1957, sponsored by Post cereals. The series was then syndicated for six years, sponsored by Nestle's from 1958 to 1964 and co-sponsored by Ideal Novelty & Toy Corp. from 1961 to 1964. Further syndication followed in 1976. The programs continued the successful mix of adventure, music, and comedy of the Rogers movies, with the usual cast, including Pat Brady and his trick jeep Nellybelle, and Bullet the Wonder Dog. *The Roy Rogers & Dale Evans Show,* a musical variety hour, had a brief run on ABC in 1962.

Merchandising of the Roy Rogers empire and sponsor premiums peaked during the radio and television years. At one point some 400 products were franchised by Roy Rogers Enterprises, earning millions for manufacturers and for the endorsers. A chain of family restaurants opened in the 1960s.

The Roy Rogers Museum in California displays the stuffed remains of Trigger, Buttermilk, Bullet; plus Nellybelle and other relics and memorabilia.

ROY-1

ROY-1. Sons Of Pioneers Photo Card With Roy,
1935. One of earliest items to picture Roy. Text on
reverse. - **$50 $125 $200**

ROY-2
ROY-3

ROY-2. Dixie Ice Cream Picture,
1938. - **$40 $60 $100**

**ROY-3. "Broadway Journal" 12x16" Publicity
Newspaper,**
1938. Republic Studios. "Special Roy Rogers Edition" for
July 16 appearances in New York City. - **$75 $135 $200**

ROY-4
ROY-5
ROY-6

ROY-4. Photo,
1930s. Republic Pictures. Color photo of Roy. -
$10 $25 $35

ROY-5. Souvenir Program,
1930s. Ten pages of stars with descriptions and photos.
Attached to boxes of Wheaties as a premium. -
$25 $50 $75

ROY-6. Dixie Ice Cream Picture,
1940. - **$60 $100 $150**

ROY-7

**ROY-7. "The Roy Rogers Show" Radio Announcement
Brochure,**
c. 1944. Goodyear Tire & Rubber Co. Press kit folder promoting radio series on Mutual Broadcasting System including listing of 67 radio stations.
Complete - **$100 $200 $300**

ROY-8
ROY-9

**ROY-8. "Roy Rogers And Trigger" Dixie Ice Cream
Picture,**
1945. - **$75 $150 $300**

ROY-9. "Dale Evans" Dixie Ice Cream Picture,
1945. - **$30 $75 $150**

ROY-10
ROY-11

**ROY-10. "My Pal Trigger" 13x19" Contest Paper
Poster,**
1946. Republic Pictures for local theaters. -
$50 $150 $250

ROY-11. "Roy Rogers And His Trick Lasso" Photo,
1947. Store item packaged with trick lasso. - **$15 $25 $40**

ROY-12

ROY-12. "Roy Rogers Trick Lasso",
1947. Store item. Came with photo (see item ROY-11) and
game book. Cellophane wrapper very fragile.
Wrapper - **$10 $25 $50**
Lasso - **$10 $15 $25**
Game Book - **$25 $60 $100**

ROY-13
ROY-14

ROY-13. Contest Card,
1948. Quaker Oats. - **$10 $20 $40**

ROY-14. "Roy Rogers And His World Championship Rodeo" Program,
1948. - **$25 $60 $125**

ROY-15

ROY-15. Product Box With "Branding Iron" Ring Offer,
1948. - **$75 $100 $125**

ROY-16

ROY-17

ROY-16. Dixie Ice Cream Picture,
1948. - **$35 $75 $100**

ROY-17. Branding Iron/Initial Brass Ring With Black Cap,
1948. Quaker Cereals. Plastic stamper under brass cover with ink pad was personalized with any requested initial. - **$100 $165 $225**

ROY-18

ROY-19

ROY-18. Sterling Silver Saddle Ring,
1948. Store item by W. G. Simpson Co., Phoenix, Az. Facsimile signature on saddle seat. - **$250 $385 $525**

ROY-19. "Roy Rogers Riders Club" Membership Card,
c. 1948. - **$20 $50 $75**

ROY-20

ROY-20. "Tattoo Transfers" Kit,
c. 1948. Pack #7 with Fawcett Publications copyright, two sheets with 22 transfers. - **$30 $70 $125**

ROY-21

ROY-22

ROY-21. Quaker Contest Postcard,
1949. - **$10 $15 $25**

ROY-22. Fan Club Membership Card,
1949. Washington DC chapter. - **$10 $20 $30**

ROY-23

ROY-23. Quaker Contest Prize 19x26" Poster With Mailer,
1949. Rare. Near Mint With Label On Tube - **$1700**
Poster Only - **$250 $750 $1500**

ROY-24

ROY-24. "March Of Comics" #47,
1949. Various sponsors. Pictured example for Sears merchandise. - **$20 $65 $150**

ROY-25

ROY-26

ROY-25. Microscope Ring/Saddle Ring Newspaper Ad,
1949. Quaker Oats. - **$15 $30 $50**

ROY-26. Quaker Microscope Ring,
1949. - **$50 $80 $125**

ROY-27

ROY-35　　　　**ROY-36**

ROY-28

ROY-27. RCA Victor 18x24" Cardboard Store Sign, c. 1940s. - **$200 $350 $500**

ROY-28. Fan Club Membership Card, 1940s. - **$20 $35 $50**

ROY-35. Photo, 1940s. Quaker Oats. Color photo of Roy on Trigger. - **$20 $40 $65**

ROY-36. Photo, 1940s. Movie premium of Roy and the Sons of the Pioneers. - **$25 $50 $75**

ROY-30　　　　**ROY-31**

ROY-37

ROY-29

ROY-29. Rodeo Souvenir Cello. Button, 1940s. Various attachments. - **$15 $30 $60**

ROY-30. Republic Studios Photo, c. 1940s. - **$10 $20 $30**

ROY-31. Republic Studios Photo, c. 1940s. Includes facsimile signature. - **$10 $25 $40**

ROY-37. Movie Serial Club Card/Ticket With Metal Badge, 1940s. Badge designated "Roy Rogers Deputy". Card - **$20 $50 $75** Badge - **$15 $30 $50**

ROY-38

ROY-39　　　　**ROY-40**

ROY-33

ROY-38. "Roy Rogers" Sterling Silver Child's Ring, c. 1940s. Store item. Image of Roy on rearing Trigger, bands have branding iron design. - **$125 $225 $350**

ROY-39. "Dale Evans Fan Club" Cello. Button, 1940s. - **$35 $60 $100**

ROY-40. Plastic Mug, 1950. Quaker Oats. - **$10 $18 $30**

ROY-32　　　　**ROY-34**

ROY-32. Riders Club Card, 1940s. Scarce. Vertical card with 24 marked stars around card. - **$30 $70 $100**

ROY-33. Postcard, 1940s. Quaker Oats. Radio premium announcing free signed photo. - **$10 $20 $30**

ROY-34. Friendship Club Card, 1940's. Hammond, Ind. Picture of Roy on left, red on white. - **$15 $25 $35**

ROY-41

ROY-41. "Roy Rogers Riders Club" Member's Pack,
1950. Package includes two cover letters, six cards, litho. button on card. Near Mint In Mailer - **$280**
Each Card - **$10 $20 $30**
Loose Button - **$8 $12 $20**

ROY-42

ROY-43

ROY-42. "Souvenir Cup" 15x20" Paper Store Sign,
1950. Quaker Oats. - **$100 $250 $400**

ROY-43 Quaker Canister With "Souvenir Cup" Offer,
1950. - **$35 $85 $125**

ROY-44

ROY-44. Quaker Brass Badge With Sheet And Mailer,
1950. Near Mint Boxed - **$150**
Badge Only - **$25 $60 $100**

ROY-46

ROY-45

ROY-45. Record Album 12x12" Cardboard Store Sign,
c. 1950. RCA Victor. - **$50 $100 $150**

ROY-46. "Thrill Circus" Felt Pennant,
c. 1950. - **$25 $60 $100**

ROY-47

ROY-47. Newspaper Strips Promo,
1951. Rare. Large and colorful. - **$75 $175 $325**

ROY-48

ROY-49

ROY-48. Quaker "Roy Rogers Cookies" Box,
1951. One side panel pictures his gun belt.
Complete - **$200 $400 $600**

ROY-49. Quaker "Roy Rogers Cookies" Newspaper Ad,
1951. Offers Humming Lariat premium. - **$15 $35 $60**

ROY-50

ROY-50. Roy Rogers' Cookies "Crackin' Good" Paper Pop Gun,
1951. - **$15 $30 $50**

ROY-51

ROY-51. Quaker Cereal Box Puzzle Panel,
1951. Back Panel Uncut - **$15 $30 $50**

ROY-52

ROY-52. Bubble Gum Album,
1951. Designed to hold two sets of 24 cards for movies "In Old Amarillo" and "South Of Caliente." Album
Complete - **$75 $150 $250**
Album Empty - **$25 $50 $75**

ROY-53

ROY-60

ROY-61

ROY-54

ROY-53. "March Of Comics" Sears Christmas Book #77,
1951. - **$20 $50 $110**

ROY-54. "Trick Lasso Contestant" Transfer Sheet,
1952. Issued for national lasso contest. - **$25 $50 $75**

ROY-60. Grape Nuts Flakes Wrapper Flat,
1952. Promotes pop-out cards. - **$150 $325 $625**

ROY-61. Lasso Application,
1952. National Trick Lasso contest application. -
$10 $20 $30

ROY-55

ROY-56

ROY-55. "Pop Out Card" Post's Box Wrapper,
1952. Post's 40% Bran Flakes. Waxed paper wrapper offering set of 36 cards issued 1952-1955.
Wrapper - **$150 $300 $600**

ROY-56. Pony Contest Entry Paper,
1952. Post's Krinkles. For four consecutive weekly contests offering first prize pony each week plus other Roy merchandise prizes. - **$5 $12 $20**

ROY-62

ROY-63

ROY-62. "Western Ring" Post's Box Wrapper,
1953. Post's Raisin Bran. Waxed paper wrapper offering set of 12 litho. tin rings. Wrapper - **$150 $300 $600**

ROY-63. "Roy Rogers Western Medals" 17x24" Store Sign,
1953. Post's Raisin Bran. Diecut cardboard with easel back. Pictures six example litho. tin tabs from set of 27 offered as box inserts. - **$250 $600 $900**

ROY-57

ROY-58

ROY-59

ROY-57. "Roy Rogers Riders Club Comics",
1952. From membership kit. - **$25 $75 $175**

ROY-58. Litho. Tin Tab,
1952. Roy Rogers Riders Club. Came with club comic book. - **$20 $40 $65**

ROY-59. Post Cereals Pop-Out Card #22,
1952. From numbered set of 36 issued into 1955.
Each Unpunched - **$8 $15 $25**

(ENLARGED VIEW)

ROY-64

ROY-64. "Post's Grape-Nuts Flakes" Store Window Display,
c. 1953. 18x24" clear thin plastic with brightly colored inscriptions and box art featuring 3x4" Roy image. Top and bottom margins are banded by narrow peel-off adhesive strip for window mounting. - **$75 $200 $400**

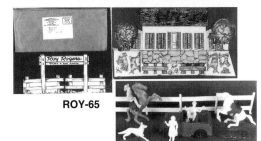

ROY-65

ROY-65. Post Cereals "RR Bar Ranch" Set,
1953. Punch-outs, metal Nellybelle, plastic figures of Roy, Dale, Pat, Trigger, Buttermilk and Bullet.
Complete - **$100 $250 $350**

ROY-67

ROY-66   ROY-68

ROY-66. Post Cardboard Sign 13x18",
1953. Scarce. Pictures all 12 Raisin Bran rings. - **$200 $400 $600**

ROY-67. "Bullet" Post's Raisin Bran Litho. Tin Ring,
1953. This and the next 11 rings comprise a set of 12. The Near Mint price is for unbent examples with no rust. - **$10 $40 $75**

ROY-68. "Dale Evans" Post's Raisin Bran Litho. Tin Ring,
1953. - **$10 $55 $100**

ROY-69   ROY-70

ROY-69. "Dale's Brand" Post's Raisin Bran Litho. Tin Ring,
1953. - **$10 $30 $50**

ROY-70. "Deputy Sheriff" Post's Raisin Bran Litho. Tin Ring,
1953. - **$10 $35 $60**

ROY-71   ROY-72

ROY-71. "Roy Rogers" Post's Raisin Bran Litho. Tin Ring,
1953. - **$10 $55 $100**

ROY-72. "Roy's Boots" Post's Raisin Bran Litho. Tin Ring,
1953. - **$10 $30 $50**

ROY-73   ROY-74

ROY-73. "Roy's Brand" Post's Raisin Bran Litho. Tin Ring,
1953. - **$10 $30 $50**

ROY-74. "Roy's Gun" Post's Raisin Bran Litho. Tin Ring,
1953. - **$10 $30 $50**

ROY-75   ROY-76

ROY-75. "Roy's Holster" Post's Raisin Bran Litho. Tin Ring,
1953. - **$10 $30 $50**

ROY-76. "Roy's Saddle" Post's Raisin Bran Litho. Tin Ring,
1953. - **$10 $30 $50**

ROY-77   ROY-78

ROY-77. "Sheriff" Post's Raisin Bran Litho. Tin Ring,
1953. - **$10 $30 $50**

ROY-78. "Trigger" Post's Raisin Bran Litho. Tin Ring,
1953. - **$10 $30 $60**

ROY-79

ROY-79. "Double R Bar Ranch" Cut-Outs,
c. 1953. Post Grape-Nuts Flakes. Canadian Box, three in set. Each Box - **$100 $200 $400**

ROY-80   ROY-81

ROY-80. "King Of The Cowboys/Roy Rogers" Litho. Button,

1953. Comes in 1-5/8" and 1-1/8" sizes. The 1-5/8" size comes with and without the Post's name on the reverse and was used as the "extra large" button in the U.S.A. along with fifteen 7/8" buttons to make a set of 16. The 1-1/8" button has not been seen with Post's name on the reverse but may have been used at a later time as the "extra large" button in both the U.S.A. and Canadian sets.
Each - **$10 $20 $30**

ROY-81. "Queen Of The West/Dale Evans" Litho. Button,

1953. Seen in 1-1/8" size only. Design matches ROY-80, but seen only with blank reverse. No documentation known indicates this is part of U.S.A. or Canadian set of 16 Post's buttons. - **$15 $25 $40**

ROY-82

ROY-83

ROY-82. Litho. Tin Button Set,

1953. Post's Grape-Nuts Flakes and Rogers copyright text appears on reverse but also issued with blank reverses. Fifteen buttons are 7/8" and "extra large" portrait button inscribed "King of the Cowboys" in 1-5/8" or 1-1/8" size makes 16 in set. Each 7/8" - **$5 $10 $15**
"King of the Cowboys"-1-5/8" or 1-1/8" - **$10 $20 $30**

ROY-83. Canadian Litho. Tin Button Set,

1953. Post's Canadian version of American set with different designs and smaller size. Fifteen small buttons are 3/4". The sixteenth button to complete the set is described as "extra large" and was likely the 1-1/8" version of the "King of the Cowboys" button pictured with item ROY-80.
Each 3/4" - **$15 $30 $50**
Extra Large - **$10 $20 $30**

ROY-84

ROY-85

ROY-84. Roy Rogers Western Medal Litho. Tin Tab,

1953. Post's Raisin Bran. From set of 27.
Each - **$5 $12 $20**

ROY-85. 3-D Photos,

1953. Post's Sugar Crisp. Four photo folder with 3-D glasses, numbered series. Intact - **$8 $15 $25**

ROY-86

ROY-86. "March Of Comics" #105,

1953. Various sponsors. Pictured example for Sears Christmas give-away. - **$10 $35 $75**

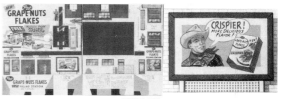

ROY-87

ROY-87. Post Grape-Nut Flakes Box With Roy Billboard,

c. 1953. - **$40 $75 $150**

  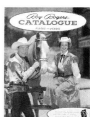

ROY-88

ROY-88. Merchandise Manuals (all rare),

1953 - **$125 $350 $600**
1954-1955 - **$100 $300 $500**
1955-1956 - **$75 $250 $400**

ROY-89

ROY-90

ROY-89. Paint By Number Set,

1954. Post's Sugar Crisp. Three sets, each with two pictures. Each - **$25 $65 $110**

ROY-90. "Roy Rogers Ranch Set" 21x22" Store Poster,

1955. Post Cereals. - **$50 $150 $250**

ROY-91

ROY-92

ROY-91. "Roy Rogers Ranch",
1955. Post Cereals. All cardboard parts. - **$40 $75 $125**

ROY-92. Roy & Dale Golden Records Set With Mail Envelope,
1955. Post's Sugar Crisp "Special Premium" offer not available at retail. Set of two. Near Mint In Mailer - **$150**
Each Record - **$15 $30 $50**

ROY-93

ROY-93. Dodge Motors Comic Booklet,
1955. Ad story "Roy Rogers And The Man From Dodge City". - **$10 $30 $75**

ROY-94

ROY-95

ROY-94. March of Comics #136,
1955. Various sponsors. - **$10 $30 $65**

ROY-95. "San Antonio World Championship Rodeo" Cello. Button,
1955. Admittance serial number. - **$60 $90 $135**

ROY-96

ROY-97

ROY-96. "Tracard" Photo Cards #2-3,
c. 1955. American Tract Society. Examples from Christian message set. Each - **$3 $5 $10**

ROY-97. Roy/Sears Merchandise Handbill,
c. 1955. Sears, Roebuck & Co. Single sheet with black and white photo plus listing on reverse of more than 60 Roy and/or Dale Evans gift items in Sears Christmas catalogue. - **$15 $30 $50**

ROY-98

ROY-99

ROY-98. Schwinn Bicycles Catalogue With Roy And Others,
1956. Folder opening to 18x24" printed on both sides including endorsement photos by Roy Rogers, Bill Williams as TV's Kit Carson, Gail Davis as TV's Annie Oakley. - **$35 $75 $125**

ROY-99. "March Of Comics" #146 Booklet,
1956. Printed for Sears, Roebuck. - **$10 $35 $75**

ROY-100

ROY-100. Post Cereal Puzzles,
1957. Set of six. Each - **$8 $15 $25**

ROY-101

ROY-101. "Flash-Draw" Flip Booklet,
1958. Classy Products Corp. Sequence photo "Movies" pages, came with cap gun set. - **$30 $60 $100**

ROY-102

ROY-102. "Roy Rogers Ranch Calendar",
1959. Unmarked probably Nestle Quik. - **$50 $100 $150**

ROY-103   ROY-104

ROY-103. "Roy Rogers Stop Watch" Box,
1959. Store item by Bradley Time. - **$100 $250 $400**

ROY-104. "Roy Rogers & Trigger" Pocketwatch,
1959. Store item by Bradley. Also functions as a stop-watch. Beware of reproductions with color photocopy dial. - **$200 $300 $400**

ROY-105   ROY-106

ROY-105. "Roy Rogers Trick Lasso" 15x24" Cardboard Store Display,
1950s. Scarce. Equipped with rope lasso on spring wire at center. - **$300 $750 $1800**

ROY-106. Lariat Flashlight On Store Display Card,
1950s. Bantamlite Inc. Carded - **$75 $150 $275**
Light Only - **$15 $35 $75**

ROY-107

ROY-107. Promo Folder with Premium Record,
1950s. Scarce. Sugar Crisp Cereal. - **$175 $300 $400**

ROY-108

ROY-108. "Double R Bar Ranch News" Club Newspaper,
1950s. Issued bi-monthly. - **$25 $50 $75**

ROY-109   ROY-110

ROY-109. "Roy Rogers Riders" Metal/Plastic Harmonica,
1950s. Store item by Harmonic Reed Corp. Also inscribed "King Of The Cowboys".
Boxed - **$40 $75 $100**
Loose - **$10 $20 $35**

ROY-110. Frosted Glass Tumbler With Gold Image,
c. 1950s. Probable store item. On old glass, Trigger's front legs overlap. On Roy Rogers Museum new glass, Trigger's front legs each show without overlap.
Old - **$25 $50 $100**
New - **$3 $5 $8**

ROY-111

ROY-111. Flash Camera With Papers And Box,
1950s. Includes camera club card, press pass card.
Near Mint Boxed - **$250**
Unboxed With Flash - **$40 $75 $100**
Unboxed, No Flash - **$20 $50 $75**
Each Card - **$10 $20 $30**

ROY-112

ROY-113

ROY-112. "Riders Club" Membership Card,
1950s. Back has club rules. - **$10 $30 $60**

ROY-113. "Roy Rogers Riders" Cello. Club Button,
1950s. - **$15 $35 $60**

ROY-114

ROY-115

ROY-116

ROY-114. Fan Club Response Card,
1950s. Club Headquarters. Back includes offer for View-Master reels plus name of TV sponsor Post Cereals. -
$15 $30 $50

ROY-115. Fan Club Response Card,
1950s. Club Headquarters. Back includes ad for store item decals plus name of TV sponsor Post Cereals. -
$15 $30 $50

ROY-116. English Candy Cigarette Box,
c. 1950s. - **$40 $75 $150**

ROY-117

ROY-117. "Wild West Action Toy" Punch-Out Sheet,
1950s. Roy Rogers Cookies.
Unpunched - **$60 $125 $200**

ROY-118

ROY-119

ROY-118. Deputy Tin Star Badge,
1950s. Issued by Post's, Popsicle, and probably others.
Comes in copper, yellow brass, or silver finish. -
$10 $20 $30

ROY-119. Glass,
1950s. Probably held dairy product. - **$50 $80 $150**

ROY-120

ROY-121

ROY-122

ROY-120. "Roy Rogers Riders Lucky Piece",
1950s. 1" brass medalet holed as made for key fob with
Roy pictured facing right. - **$5 $15 $25**

ROY-121. "Roy Rogers Riders Lucky Piece",
1950s. 1-1/16" brass medalet holed as made for key fob
w/Roy pictured facing straight ahead. - **$7 $18 $28**

ROY-122. "Roy Rogers Riders Lucky Piece",
1950s. 1" brass medalet with Roy pictured looking upward
and facing slightly left. - **$10 $20 $30**

ROY-123

ROY-124

ROY-123. "Roy Rogers Riders Lucky Piece",
1950s. 1-3/16" brass medalet picturing Roy with broad
smile facing left. - **$12 $22 $35**

ROY-124. "Roy Rogers Riders Lucky Piece",
1950s. 1-1/8" white metal with copper luster medalet picturing Roy facing straight ahead. Design is in much higher
relief than other medalets with same inscription. -
$12 $22 $35

ROY-125

ROY-125. "Roy Rogers Riders Club" Membership Card,
1950s. Version in red, white and blue front and black, blue
and white reverse. - **$10 $30 $60**

ROY-126

ROY-127

**ROY-126. "Roy Rogers Rodeo" 13x21" Cardboard
Poster,**
1950s. - **$75 $150 $250**

ROY-127. "Roy Rogers Sweaters" Store Postcard,
1950s. - **$10 $20 $30**

ROY-128

ROY-129

ROY-128. Riders Club Membership Card,
1950s. Movie premium from Warwick Theater. -
$10 $30 $60

ROY-129. Riders Club Card,
1950s. Yellow card. Movie premium. - **$15 $30 $60**

ROY-130

ROY-131

ROY-130. Photo,
1950s. Movie premium. Black & white photo featuring Roy
and Gabby Hayes. - **$10 $20 $30**

ROY-131. Photo,
1950s. Movie premium. Black & white photo of Roy and his
gun. - **$10 $20 $30**

ROY-132

ROY-133

ROY-132. Photo,
1950s. Movie premium. Black & white photo of Roy with
two Deputy Sheriffs. - **$10 $20 $30**

ROY-133. Official Cowboy Outfit In Box,
1950s. Shirt, cloth chaps, marked Roy and Trigger, gun,
holster, lariat, and belt. Republic Pictures promoted on colorful box. - **$80 $175 $350**

ROY-134

ROY-135

ROY-134. Dell Comics Photo Strip Folder,
1950s. - **$40 $75 $135**

ROY-135. Sears Toy Town Cards,
1950s. Two Christmas premium cards with holiday verse
on back. Each - **$8 $15 $25**

ROY-136

**ROY-136. "Nestle's Quik" Canister With Premium
Offer,**
1960. Back offers 3-D plastic plaque set with expiration
date June 30. - **$50 $125 $200**

ROY-137

ROY-138

ROY-137. "Roy Rogers Ranch Calendar",
1960. Nestle's Quik. - **$50 $100 $150**

ROY-138. "Roy Rogers Ranch Calendar",
1961. Nestle's Quik. - **$50 $100 $150**

ROY-139

ROY-139. Nestle Candy Coupon,
1961. - **$15 $30 $50**

ROY-140

ROY-141

ROY-140. Litho. Soda Can,
c. 1960s. Continental Beverage Corp., La Jolla, California. - **$60 $130 $200**

ROY-141. Paper Hat,
c. 1970s. Roy Rogers Restaurants. - **$3 $6 $15**

ROY-143

ROY-142

ROY-142. Life-Sized 75" Tall Cardboard Standee,
c. 1980. Thousand Trails Campgrounds. -
$100 $225 $400

ROY-143. "Roy Rogers Family Restaurants" 2" Litho. Button,
1980s. Various locations, pictured example from Maryland. - **$3 $6 $10**

SALLY STARR

Sally Starr, born in Kansas City, Mo., in 1923, was singing on a CBS country radio show at the age of 12. She worked as a radio disc jockey, and in 1950 became hostess of *Popeye Theater* on Channel 6, WFIL, in Philadelphia. Dressed as a cowgirl and calling herself Our Gal Sal, she showed cartoons and *Three Stooges* shorts, read original stories, and chatted with show business visitors. The program became Philadelphia's highest rated children's show and ran until 1972. In the mid-1980s Sal made personal appearances in the tri-state area and in 1993 she was named Grand Marshal of the 84th Annual Baby Parade in Ocean City, New Jersey.

SAL-1

SAL-2

SAL-1. Full Color 3-1/2" Cello. Button,
1950s. - **$5 $15 $25**

SAL-2. "Sally Starr" Outfitted Doll,
1950s. 10" tall vinyl doll with fabric cowgirl outfit patterned after actual performance outfit. - **$25 $60 $95**

SAL-3

SAL-3. "Cowgirl Outfit" With Photo,
1950s. Store item by Herman Iskin & Co. 8x10" photo accompanies youngster's denim and suede-like fabric colorful jacket and skirt. Near Mint Boxed - **$125**
Photo Only - **$5 $10 $15**
Outfit Only - **$30 $50 $75**

SAL-4

SAL-4. Performance Ticket With Record Offer,
1950s. Photo ticket with reverse offer for child's Easter song record by her. - **$3 $8 $12**

SCOOP WARD

Laddie Seaman, alias Scoop Ward, narrated dramatizations of the news for his teenage audience in *News of Youth* on CBS radio from late 1935 to 1937. The program was sponsored by Ward's Soft Bun bread and Silver Queen pound cake.

SCW-1

SCW-2

SCW-3

SCW-1. Club Newsletter With Envelope,
1936. Ward's Bread and Silver Queen Pound Cake.
Mailer - **$3 $5 $10**
Newsletter - **$10 $20 $30**

SCW-2. "Official Reporter" Brass Shield Badge,
1936. Ward's Soft Bun Bread. - **$5 $12 $25**

SCW-3. Member Recruitment Brochure With Typewriter Offer,
c. 1936. Ward's Bread/Silver Queen Pound Cake. - **$10 $20 $30**

SECKATARY HAWKINS

This children's program was developed from a comic strip of the same name by Robert F. Schulkers. Hawkins was the leader of a boys' club that spent its time helping to round up bad boys. The club's motto was "Fair and Square." The radio series, sponsored by Ralston Purina, was broadcast on NBC in 1932-1933.

SKH-1

SKH-1. Club Kit,
1929. With pin, card, and mailer. Set - **$25 $50 $75**

SKH-2   SKH-3

SKH-2. Birthday Card,
1929. Newspaper premium from the Milwaukee Journal. - **$12 $20 $30**

SKH-3. Birthday Card Mailer,
1929. Premium mailer for card. - **$5 $10 $15**

SKH-4   SKH-5   SKH-6

SKH-4. "Fair And Square" Member's Cello. Button,
1932. 7/8" size. Red rim. - **$5 $12 $20**

SKH-5. "Fair And Square" Cello. Club Button,
1932. 7/8" size. Blue rim. - **$4 $8 $12**

SKH-6. "Fair And Square" Litho. Club Button,
1932. 3/4" size. - **$5 $12 $20**

SKH-7   SKH-8

SKH-9

SKH-7. "Fair And Square" Ralston Club Enameled Brass Spinner,
1932. Spinner disk forms club slogan with spun. - **$20 $50 $75**

SKH-8. "Sunday Baltimore American" Cello. Club Button,
c. 1932. - **$10 $20 $30**

SKH-9. Figure Of Hollow Pressed Cardboard,
c. 1932. About 12" tall. - **$35 $60 $100**

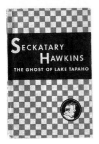

SKH-11

SKH-10

SKH-10. The Ghost of Lake Tapako Book,
1932. Ralston. - **$10 $25 $40**

SKH-11. Good Luck Fair and Square Coin,
1960s. Scarce. - **$15 $30 $50**

SECRET AGENT X-9

Written by Dashiell Hammett and drawn by Alex Raymond, *Secret Agent X-9* was introduced by King Features in January 1934. X-9 is a loner who fights urban criminals by seeming to become part of their evil world. Hammett and Raymond went on to other things in 1935, and the strip was continued by an assortment of writers and artists, evolving in 1967 to *Secret Agent Corrigan*. Comic book reprints of the first eight months of the strip were published in 1934. There was a short-lived radio program, and Universal Pictures made two *Secret Agent X-9* chapter plays, one in 1937 starring Scott Kolk; the other, with Lloyd Bridges starring, in 1945.

SCX-1

SCX-1. Daily Comic Strip Book,
1934. Store item. - **$40 $100 $300**

SCX-2

SCX-2. Secret Agent X-9 Original Comic Strip Art By Alex Raymond,
1935. 7x27" three-panel comic strip art for publication September 19. Examples Of Similar Age And Content - **$250 $500 $750**

SCX-3

SCX-4

SCX-3. Club Membership Card With Envelope,
1930s. With Envelope - **$12 $40 $60**
Card Only - **$8 $20 $40**

SCX-4. "Secret Agent X-9/Chicago Herald And Examiner" Silvered Metal Badge,
1930s. - **$15 $25 $40**

SCX-5

SCX-6

SCX-5. Cello. Button,
1940s. - **$10 $25 $50**

SCX-6. Water Gun,
1950s. Irwin. Store item. Billy club serves as water tank. - **$15 $40 $65**

THE SECRET 3

Murray McLean starred in this serial detective drama sponsored by 3-Minute Oat Flakes and apparently broadcast only regionally in the 1930s. Premiums included a membership badge, a Confidential Code Book, and a variety of generic crime-fighting paraphernalia. The show's main characters were: Ben Potter, Chief of Detectives; Jack Williams, 1st Lieutenant; Mary Lou Davis; 2nd Lieutenant.

SCT-1

SCT-2

SCT-1. Silvered Brass Badge,
1929. Rare. - **$50 $110 $160**

SCT-2. Secret 3 Premium List,
1930s. 3-Minute Oat Flakes Cereal premium. Shows color picture of 12 pieces of equipment on back. Front side lists premiums and how to get them. - **$10 $25 $40**

SCT-3   SCT-4

SCT-3. Club Member Code/Rule Book,
1930s. Rare. 3-Minute Oat Flakes. Includes two pages of detective premiums. - **$25 $125 $200**

SCT-4. Club Headquarters Cover Letter,
1930s. Scarce. P.S. notation on letter is "Burn this letter after you read it." - **$10 $35 $50**

SERGEANT PRESTON OF THE YUKON

Under its original title, *Challenge of the Yukon*, this adventure series of the Royal Canadian Mounties during the gold-rush days of the 1890s was heard initially on Detroit radio station WXYZ from 1938 to 1947. Created by George W. Trendle and Fran Striker after their success with *The Lone Ranger* and *The Green Hornet*, the program centered on the crime-fighting exploits of Sgt. Frank Preston and his malamute partner Yukon King, "the swiftest and strongest lead dog of the Northwest." The series moved to the ABC network in 1947 and then to Mutual in 1950, where it remained until 1955. Quaker Puffed Wheat and Rice were the long-term sponsors. In 1951 the program changed its name officially to *Sergeant Preston of the Yukon*, although it was also popularly known as Yukon King, a reflection of the dog's central role in Preston's always getting his man.

On television, the series was broadcast on CBS from 1955 to 1958, sponsored by Quaker Oats and Mother's Oats. Richard Simmons starred in the title role, riding his black stallion Rex and assisted, as always by Yukon King. Reruns were seen on NBC during the 1963-1964 season.

Sergeant Preston comic books were published between 1951 and 1959, including a set of four giveaways in two sizes from Quaker cereals in 1956. The cereal company also offered a great variety of other premiums, notably a 1955 in-package deed to a one-square-inch tract of land in the Yukon.

SGT-1

SGT-2

SGT-3

SGT-1. Autographed Photo,
c. 1947. Believed to picture Paul Sutton radio voice of Sgt. Preston. - **$75 $125 $200**

SGT-2. Fan Photo,
1947. - **$20 $30 $60**

SGT-3. 2-Way Signal Flashlight,
1949. Plastic disk produces red or green light. - **$25 $60 $90**

SGT-4

SGT-4. Dog Cards,
1949. Set of 35. Each - **$1 $2 $3**

SGT-5

SGT-5. Club Photo,
1949. Radio premium. - **$50 $75 $100**

SGT-6

SGT-6. "Sergeant Preston Gets His Man" Game,
1949. Game board and playing pieces from Quaker cereal boxes. Cut But Complete - **$20 $40 $65**
Complete Box - **$75 $150 $250**

SGT-7

SGT-8

SGT-7. "Dog Sled Race" Quaker Box Back,
1949. From series of three games offered.
Complete Box - **$75 $150 $250**
Uncut Box Back With Side Parts Panel - **$20 $40 $65**

SGT-8. "Great Yukon River Canoe Race" Quaker Box Back,
1949. From series of three games offered.
Complete With Markers - **$20 $40 $65**

SGT-9

SGT-10

SGT-9. "Official Seal" Litho. Button,
c. 1949. Rare.1-3/8" black and red on yellow background. - **$600 $2000 $5000**

SGT-10. Mountie Badge,
1940s. Canada. No documentation as Sgt. Preston item. Came with Toy Clicker Gun Set. - **$25 $50 $75**

SGT-11

SGT-11. Rectangular Bar,
1940s. Canada. No documentation as Sgt. Preston item. Came with Toy Clicker Gun Set. - **$25 $50 $75**

SGT-12

SGT-12. "Yukon Trail" Quaker Puffed Wheat Box Back,
1950. Set of eight. Complete Box - **$100 $200 $350**
Each Uncut Box Back - **$25 $50 $80**

SGT-13

SGT-13. Trading Card/Records Offer Cereal Box,
c. 1950. Quaker Puffed Rice. Back panel offers record series including theme song from TV series.
Complete Box - **$50 $125 $200**

SGT-14   SGT-15

SGT-14. "Sergeant Preston Yukon Adventure Picture Cards",
1950. Set of 36. Each - **$1 $3 $5**
Complete Set With Mailer - **$200**

SGT-15. Quaker Contest Entrant Acknowledgement Postcard,
1950. - **$15 $25 $40**

SGT-17

SGT-16

SGT-18

SGT-16. Dog-Naming Contest 16x22" Award Poster,
1950. Scarce. - **$200 $400 $800**

SGT-17. Mailing Tube For Dog-Naming Contest Award Poster,
1950. Rare. - **$25 $65 $110**

SGT-18. Award Poster Small Version,
1950. - **$20 $35 $60**

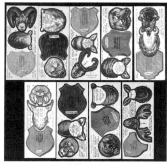

SGT-19

SGT-19. Trophies,
1950. 9 different punch-outs of animal heads.
Each - **$5 $10 $15**

SGT-20

SGT-21

SGT-20. Police Whistle 17x22" Paper Store Sign,
1950. - **$100 $250 $400**

SGT-21. Brass Whistle,
1950. Facsimile signature on side. - **$20 $30 $50**

SGT-22

SGT-23

SGT-22. Portrait Photo,
c. 1950 Probably a Quaker premium. - **$20 $35 $60**

SGT-23. "Quaker Camp Stove" With Folder,
1952. Scarce. Metal items are firebox & cover, oven,
tongs. Set - **$35 $100 $250**
Folder - **$25 $35 $60**

SGT-24

SGT-25

SGT-24. Electronic Ore Detector, Red Variety,
1952. Rare. Quaker Puffed Wheat premium. -
$75 $150 $250

SGT-25. Ore Detector Mailer,
1952. Quaker Puffed Wheat premium. Red Variety. -
$20 $40 $65

SGT-26

SGT-26. Wood Totem Poles,
1952. Set of five. Each - **$10 $18 $30**

SGT-27

SGT-28

SGT-27. Aluminum Pedometer,
1952. - **$20 $40 $75**

**SGT-28. "The Case That Made Preston A Sergeant"
Decca Record #1,**
1952. - **$20 $40 $75**

SGT-29

SGT-30

**SGT-29. "The Case Of The Indian Rebellion" Decca
Record #3,**
1952. - **$20 $40 $75**

**SGT-30. "Sgt. Preston Trail Goggles" Quaker Cereal
Box Cut-Out,**
1952. - Complete Box - **$75 $150 $250**
Cut-out - **$10 $20 $40**

SGT-31

**SGT-31. "Electronic Ore Detector" With Instructions
And Box,**
1952. Plastic battery operated detector, black variety.
Near Mint Boxed - **$225**
Detector Only - **$50 $90 $160**

SGT-32

SGT-33

SGT-32. "Distance Finder",
1954. Metal and paper insert distance gauge. -
$20 $40 $60

SGT-33. Distance Finder Instructions,
1955. Quaker Puffed Wheat premium. - **$15 $25 $35**

SGT-34

SGT-35

**SGT-34. "Klondike Big Inch Land Deed" Certificate
With Cover Sheet,**
1955. Deed - **$10 $15 $20**
Sheet - **$5 $10 $15**

SGT-35. Deed Mailer,
1955. Radio premium. - **$100 $150 $200**

SGT-36

SGT-37

SGT-36. "Map Of Yukon Territory" 8x10",
1955. Quaker Cereals box insert. - **$8 $25 $50**

SGT-37. "Prospector's Pouch Order Blank",
1955. - **$15 $30 $60**

SGT-38

SGT-39

SGT-38. "Klondike Land" Pouch,
1955.
Near Mint Boxed With Klondike Dirt Still In Pouch - **$300**
Pouch Only (pouch is generally cracked) - **$50 $100 $175**

SGT-39. Order Form,
1955. Order form for prospector's pouch & 1 oz. of
Klondike land & deed to 1 square inchof gold rush land. -
$20 $40 $65

SGT-40

SGT-40. "How He Found Yukon King" Comic Booklet,
1956. Quaker box insert. Set of four, each 5" or 7" long. -
$10 $20 $50

SGT-41

**SGT-41. "How Yukon King Saved Him From The
Wolves" Comic Booklet,**
1956. Quaker box insert. Set of four, each 5" or 7" long. -
$10 $20 $50

SGT-42

SGT-42. "How He Became A Mountie" Comic Booklet,
1956. Quaker box insert. Set of four, each 5" or 7" long. -
$10 $20 $50

SGT-43

SGT-44

**SGT-43. "The Case That Made Him A Sergeant" Comic
Booklet,**
1956. Quaker box insert. Set of four, each 5" or 7" long. -
$10 $20 $50

SGT-44. Official Seal Cello. Button,
1956. Full color 1-1/4". White rim. Scarce. -
$500 $1000 $2000

SGT-45   SGT-46

SGT-45. Quaker Cereals T-Shirt,
c. 1956. Scarce. - **$75 $150 $300**

SGT-46. Official Seal Tin Badge,
c. 1956. Seen in copper, silver or matte silver luster, all rare. - **$300 $700 $1200**

SGT-47   SGT-48

SGT-47. Official Seal White Metal Badge With Insert Paper Photo,
c. 1956. Photo is yellow/black. - **$200 $350 $600**

SGT-48. Quaker Cereals Coloring Contest Letter And Photo,
1957. Near Mint In Envelope - **$175**
Photo Only - **$35 $75 $100**

SGT-49

SGT-50

SGT-49. "Sergeant Preston 10-In-1 Trail Kit,"
1958. 6" plastic pen/flashlight/sundial/compass/whistle including Sgt. Preston and King image on mouthpiece.
Box - **$15 $20 $40**
Instructions - **$30 $60 $90**
Device - **$75 $150 $300**

SGT-50. "Richard Simmons" Pencil Tablet,
1950s. Store item. - **$10 $30 $50**

SETH PARKER

Seth Parker was an early radio creation of Phillips H. Lord, who was later to create *Gang Busters* and other adventure programs. In contrast, Seth Parker combined the story of a gentle, kindly Maine philosopher with lots of hymn singing, and it was immensely successful. Also known as *Sunday at Seth Parker* and *Sunday Evenings at Seth Parker*, the series was sustained on NBC from 1929 to 1933, and sponsored by

Frigidaire as *Cruise of the Seth Parker* in 1933-1934. It later aired from 1935 to 1939, sponsored by Vick Chemical for its final three years.

SET-1   SET-2   SET-3

SET-1. "Aboard The Seth Parker" Booklet,
1934. Frigidaire Corp. Includes drawings of the various rooms of global sailing boat. - **$5 $10 $15**

SET-2. Schooner 11x15" Paper Print,
c. 1934. Frigidaire Corp. Pictures world cruise ship used by Phillips H. Lord, creator and radio voice of Seth Parker. - **$12 $20 $30**

SET-3. "Seth Parker's Two-Year Almanac And Party Book",
1939. Vicks Chemical Co. Hardcover edition for 1939-1940. - **$5 $10 $15**

SET-4   SET-5

SET-4. "Seth Parker's Scrapbook",
1930s. Collection of folksy, small-town humor and wisdom. - **$10 $20 $30**

SET-5. Cast Member Fan Photo,
1930s. Pictures family in a parlor hymn sing. - **$5 $8 $15**

THE SHADOW

The Shadow, alias Lamont Cranston, was born in the 1930s, both as a character in Street & Smith publications and by radio sponsor Blue Coal. Written by Walter B. Gibson under the pen name Maxwell Grant, the Shadow fought crime and clouded men's minds not only in the pulps and on the radio but also, along with the lovely Margot Lane, in the movies, in comic books, and in a comic strip.

On the radio, the *Shadow* aired on CBS, NBC, or Mutual from 1932 to 1954, and the programs were resurrected and syndicated in the 1960s and 1970s. There were a number of regional or national sponsors: Blue Coal for most of the years between 1932 and 1949, along with Perfect-O-Lite (1932), Goodrich tires (1938-1939), Grove Laboratories (1949-1950), the Army Air

Force (1950-1951), Wildroot Cream Oil (1951-1953), Carey Salt Company, and Bromo Quinine cold tablets. Both Blue Coal (in 1941) and Carey Salt (in 1945) offered glow-in-the-dark premium rings, and *The Shadow Magazine* offered a club membership lapel emblem and other items.

A *Shadow* comic strip appeared in newspapers from 1938 to 1942, and comic books were published from 1940 to 1950, in 1964-1965 (with the Shadow as costumed superhero), and in 1973-1975. The Shadow made a number of low-budget film appearances in the 1930s and 1940s, notably in a 15-episode chapter play from Columbia Pictures in 1940 with Victor Jory in the title role. In 1994 Alec Baldwin played the lead in a Universal film. "Who knows what evil lurks in the hearts of men?"

SHA-1   SHA-2

SHA-1. "Eyes Of The Shadow" 7x11" Ad Card,
c. 1931. For Maxwell Grant novel. - **$30 $75 $150**

SHA-2. Perfect-O-Lite Radio Broadcast Promotion Folder,
1932. For Perfect-O-Lite sales people. 11x17" folder that opens to 17x22" promoting new radio sponsorship over 29 stations of Columbia network. - **$60 $150 $300**

SHA-3   SHA-4

SHA-3. Radio Broadcasts Schedule Folder With Envelope,
1932. Perfect-O-Lite (automotive accessory). Lists 27 stations in three time zones. Envelope - **$25 $50 $75**
Folder - **$50 $100 $150**

SHA-4. "The Shadow" 11x14" Cardboard Window Poster,
c. 1934. Blue Coal, Shadow magazine. Promotes Monday and Wednesday radio broadcasts on Columbia network. - **$400 $800 $1500**

SHA-5   SHA-6   SHA-7

SHA-5. "Secret Society Of The Shadow" Club Card,
1939. Pledge card originally holding glow-in-dark "Magic Button". - **$75 $175 $275**

SHA-6. "The Shadow" Glow-In-Dark Cello. Magic Button,
1939. Rare not cracked or stained. - **$300 $750 $1500**

SHA-7. Blue Coal Portrait Photo,
1930s. - **$75 $175 $275**

SHA-8   SHA-9

SHA-8. The Shadow Unmasked Photo,
1930s. Blue Coal. - **$60 $150 $200**

SHA-9. The Shadow Club Card,
1930s. Street & Smith Publishers. Originally held Shadow lapel stud. Card - **$100 $200 $300**
Mailer (Pictures The Shadow) - **$75 $150 $275**

SHA-10   SHA-11

SHA-10. "The Shadow Club" Silvered Brass Lapel Emblem,
1930s. Lapel Stud - **$100 $250 $350**
Pin - **$125 $300 $400**

SHA-11. "The Shadow Strikes Again" Paper Folder,
1930s. Blue Coal. Includes listing of radio stations and broadcast times. - **$75 $150 $300**

SHA-12

SHA-13

SHA-12. "Member/The Shadow Club" Rubber On Wood Stamp Block,
1930s. Picture example includes ink stamp image from the block. - **$250 $600 $850**

SHA-13. "Tune In On-The Shadow" Paper Gummed Back Sticker,
1930s. - **$60 $90 $120**

SHA-14

SHA-14. "The Shadow On The Air" Gummed Back Paper Sticker,
1930s. - **$35 $75 $125**

SHA-15

SHA-16

SHA-15. "The Shadow Is Back On The Air" Paper Gummed Back Sticker,
1930s. - **$40 $75 $135**

SHA-16. Pulp Magazine Ad Sticker,
1930s. - **$50 $90 $150**

SHA-17

SHA-18

SHA-17. "The Shadow's Secret Message" Sheet,
1930s. The Shadow pulp magazine. 8-1/2x11" yellow paper sheet treated to reveal message when dipped in water and then disappears when sheet is dry. Rare. - **$125 $250 $400**

SHA-18. "The Shadow" Brown Felt Fabric Hat,
1940. Adult size, offered by The Shadow Magazine. - **$150 $250 $400**

SHA-19

SHA-19. Boxed Board Game,
1940. Store item by Toy Creations. - **$250 $600 $1000**
Board Only - **$75 $175 $300**

SHA-20

SHA-20. Blue Coal Ink Blotter,
1940. - **$15 $25 $50**

SHA-22

SHA-21

SHA-21. "Blue Coal" Ring Instruction Sheet With Mailer Envelope,
1941. Rare. Envelope - **$300 $500 $650**
Instruction Sheet - **$500 $575 $650**

SHA-22. Blue Coal Ring,
1941. Glows in the dark. - **$200 $400 $600**

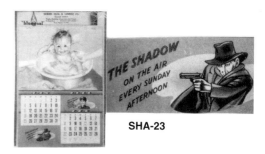

SHA-23

SHA-23. Cardboard 11x16" Ad Wall Calendar,
1942. Picture example shows calendar and corner detail from it. - **$150 $250 $ 400**

SHA-24

SHA-25

SHA-24. Magic Ring,
1945. Carey Salt. Black plastic stone, base glows in dark. - **$500 $850 $1200**

SHA-25. Blue Coal Sticker,
1940s. - **$50 $90 $150**

SHA-26

SHA-26. Matchbook Cover,
1940s. Inside cover has diecut hinged tab that lowers to expose jail cell view.
With Matches - **$40 $80 $150**
Empty - **$30 $60 $100**

SHA-27

SHA-28

SHA-27. Blotter,
1940s. Blue Coal. - **$10 $30 $50**

SHA-28. Blotter,
1940s. Blue Coal. - **$10 $30 $50**

SHA-29

SHA-30

SHA-29. Blotter,
1940s. Blue Coal. - **$10 $30 $50**

SHA-30. Blotter,
1940s. 8" man shows 2 bags of coal on front. - **$25 $50 $75**

SHA-31

SHA-32

SHA-31. Blotter,
1940s. 8" photo of man on right talks about warm home. - **$25 $50 $75**

SHA-32. Full Figure Blotter,
1940s. Scarce. Radio premium. 5" picture of Shadow in middle. - **$50 $100 $150**

SHA-33

SHA-34

SHA-33. Blotter,
1940s. Blue Coal. - **$15 $35 $75**

SHA-34. Blotter,
1940s. Blue Coal. - **$20 $40 $85**

SHA-35

SHA-36

SHA-35. Blotter,
1940s. Blue Coal. - **$30 $60 $125**

SHA-36. Canadian Ink Blotter,
1940s. Various coal companies. - **$30 $60 $125**

SHA-37

SHA-37. The Shadow Hologram Plastic Ring,
1994. Coupon offer from Kenner Toys.
Ring - **$10 $20 $35**
Coupon - **$1 $2 $3**

SHERLOCK HOLMES

The world's most famous detective made his debut in 1887 in Arthur Conan Doyle's story *A Study in Scarlet*. Since then millions of fans have followed the adventures of the brilliant Holmes and his trusted chronicler Dr. John Watson in books, on stage, on the radio, on television, and in numerous films. Holmes solved cases in radio series from 1930 to 1936 and from 1939 to 1950, on various networks, with different sponsors, and through multiple cast changes. Best remembered are Basil Rathbone and Nigel Bruce, who played the radio leads from 1939 to 1946, as well as portraying the characters in a series of films. G. Washington coffee was an early sponsor (1930-1935), followed by Household Finance Corporation (1936), Bromo-Quinine cold tablets (1939-1942), Petri wine (1943-1946 and 1949-1950), and others. Holmes also made scattered comic book appearances from the 1940s to the 1970s. A popular series of one-hour shows and feature-length films from Britain's Granada Television (shown in the US on PBS) starred the late Jeremy Brett as Holmes and won accolades for their attention to detail, setting and performance. "Elementary, my dear Watson."

SHL-1

SHL-1. Sherlock Holmes Game,
1904. Store item by Parker Brothers. - **$40 $80 $150**

SHL-2

SHL-2. Sherlock Holmes Map,
1930s. Rare. Household Finance. - **$80 $250 $400**

SHIELD G-MAN CLUB

Joe Higgins, alias the Shield, was one of the most popular comic book heroes of the 1940s, fighting to protect the American way of life with truth, justice, patriotism, and courage--and a costume that made him invulnerable. He debuted in *Pep Comics* #1 in 1940 and, despite some changes in character, lasted until *Pep* #65 in 1948. Between 1940 and 1944 he also appeared in *Shield-Wizard Comics*. The *Shield G-Man Club*, which offered pins and a membership card, had a short life before becoming the *Archie Club*.

SGM-1

SGM-2

SGM-1. Club Member Card,
1940. Pep Comics, M.L.J. Magazines.
Card - **$50 $125 $200**
Mailer - **$10 $20 $50**

SGM-2. "Shield G-Man Club" Cello. Button (blue border),
c. 1940. Rare. 1-3/4" version. - **$200 $800 $1200**

(badge)

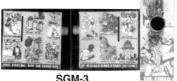

SGM-3

(button)

SGM-4

SGM-3. "The Shield" Cardboard Movie Projector,
c. 1941. Shield Wizard Comics. Filmstrips cut from comic book page by reader to produce "film." Pictured example has replaced viewing tube. - **$200 $400 $800**

SGM-4. Club Member's Cello. Badge and Button
c. 1943. Bar pin behind top folded edge. Also issued as 1-1/4" circular cello. button. Badge - **$15 $30 $60**
Button (no border) - **$75 $300 $550**

SGM-5

SGM-5. The Shield "News Scoop" Postcard,
c. 1945. Announcement of Archie Andrews and his gang returning to radio on Saturday, June 2, Eastern War Time with facsimile signature of Joe Higgins as The Shield. - **$40 $65 $100**

SHIRLEY TEMPLE

America's dimpled sweetheart, the world's darling, Shirley Temple was probably the most popular child prodigy actress ever to come out of Hollywood. Born in 1928, she sang, danced, and acted in 30 movies by the age of 13, was a top box-office star, and charmed the nation. Merchandising during the 1930s was extensive, including Shirley Temple dresses, hats, underwear, mugs, soap, and an estimated 1.5 million Shirley Temple dolls from Ideal Novelty & Toy Corp. She made further films as a teen and as an adult, but could not sustain her immense popularity. There were several short-lived ventures on CBS radio: *Shirley Temple Time* (1939), the *Shirley Temple Variety Show*, sponsored by Elgin watches (1941), and *Junior Miss* (1942). On television, *Shirley Temple's Story Book* was seen in 1958-1959 and *The Shirley Temple Show* aired in 1960-1961.

Married from 1945-49 to actor John Agar, she remarried in 1960, to TV executive Charles Black. In 1967, as Shirley Temple Black, she lost a primary race for a California Congressional seat, but was appointed as a U.S. representative to the United Nations. From 1974 to 1976, Black served as U.S. Ambassador to Ghana, then became Chief of Protocol. She then took the appointment of Ambassador to Czechoslovakia in 1989. She has also authored an autobiography, *Child Star*, in 1988.

SHR-1

SHR-1. "The American Girl" Scout Magazine With Doll Ad,
1936. Doll offered as premium for four subscriptions. - **$8 $10 $20**

SHR-2

SHR-2. Doll Contest Newspaper Advertisement,
1936. - **$15 $30 $50**

SHR-3

SHR-4

SHR-3. 15" Tall Composition Doll,
c. 1936. Store item by Ideal Toy Co. Dress based on 1934 "Bright Eyes" movie costume. - **$200 $350 $650**

SHR-4. Wheaties Box Back Panels,
c. 1936. Set of 12. Each - **$6 $12 $18**

SHR-5

SHR-6

SHR-7

SHR-8

SHR-5. Enameled Brass Figural Pin,
c. 1936. Probable store item. - **$50 $90 $150**

SHR-6. "Shirley Temple's Pet/Rowdy" Enameled Brass Pin,
c. 1936. Pictures her pet dog. Probably store item. - **$60 $100 $175**

SHR-7. "Chicago Times Shirley Temple Club" Litho. Button,
c. 1936. - **$30 $60 $125**

SHR-8. Cello. Button Off Doll,
c. 1936. Ideal Novelty And Toy Co. Many non-authentic doll button designs made in the 1970s-1990s exist. - **$20 $40 $75**

SHR-9

SHR-10

SHR-9. Photo,
1936. Philadelphia Record newspaper premium. - **$12 $20 $35**

SHR-10. Theatre Club Cello. Button,
c. 1936. Also inscribed for WFBR Radio, Baltimore. Beaded brass rim. - **$35 $85 $135**

SHR-11

SHR-12

SHR-11. "Shirley Temple League" Enameled Brass English Pin,
c. 1937. Sunday Referee newspaper. - **$35 $50 $100**

SHR-12. Photo Portrait European Ring,
c. 1937. Store item, "Made In Czechoslovakia". Thin metal band with brass bracket holding black/white photo. - **$75 $150 $250**

SHR-13

SHR-14

SHR-13. Swimsuit Cardboard String Tag,
1930s. Forest Mills. Various photos. - **$20 $40 $60**

SHR-14. Portrait Picture,
1930s. Probably store or theater give-away. - **$8 $12 $20**

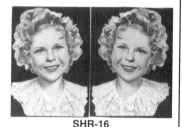

SHR-16

SHR-15

SHR-15. "A Movie Of Me" Flip Book,
1930s. Probably Quaker Cereals. - **$35 $75 $150**

SHR-16. Diecut 12x16" Cardboard Hanger Sign For Theater Lobby,
1930s. Color portrait each side. - **$40 $90 $150**

SHR-17

SHR-18

SHR-17. Photo,
1930s. Sealtest Milk. Promotes the movie "Just Around The Corner" on back of photo. - **$25 $50 $75**

SHR-18. Cardboard Advertising Fan,
1944. Royal Crown Cola. Inscribed for her 1944 movie "I'll Be Seeing You". - **$25 $50 $80**

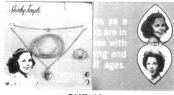

SHR-19

SHR-20

SHR-19. "Picture Locket Jewelry" On Card,
1940s. Store item. Heart-shaped symbol on ring, bracelet, locket. Set - **$75 $150 $250**

SHR-20. Photo Guide,
1960. TV Guide from St. Louis Post Digest. 52 pages. - **$20 $40 $50**

SHOCK GIBSON

Speed Comics began in October 1939 with the origin and first appearance of Shock Gibson in issue #1. Gibson was the cover feature and lead character of the first 15 issues. *Speed Comics* continued through issue #44 in 1947.

SHK-1

SHK-2

SHK-1. Volunteers Club Membership Card,
c. 1939. Brookwood Publishing/Speed Publishing. - **$35 $100 $150**

SHK-2. Volunteers Club Cello. Button,
c. 1939. - **$75 $225 $325**

SHK-3

SHK-3. Mask With Envelope,
1940. Starched black linen generic mask in envelope from "Shock Gibson Volunteers" with New York City address. With Envelope - **$25 $50 $75**

SILVER DOLLAR BRADY

Silver Dollar Brady was a character created to promote Seagram's alcohol. Hoppy, Roy and Gene refused to support projects that used alcohol or cigarettes as sponsors. As a result of this dilemma, these companies had to create their own cowboy heroes. Silver Dollar Brady is a classic example of using in-house characters for this type of advertising. The premium listed was designed to test whether or not you had too much to drink and were off on your own "happy trails."

SIL-1

SIL-1. Test Your Eye Card,
1940s. Includes three different thin metal silver dollar sized play coins with Brady pictured on obverse.
Mailer - **$20 $40 $60**
Card - **$15 $30 $45**
Each Play Dollar - **$10 $20 $30**

SILVER STREAK

Magazine publisher Arthur Bernhard entered the comic book market with *Silver Streak Comics* #1 in December 1939. Jack Cole, later the creator of Plastic Man and a popular Playboy cartoonist, was brought in as artist/editor and drew the first Silver Streak story for issue #3, March 1940. Silver Streak became the second super-speed hero introduced that year, following the debut of The Flash just weeks earlier. The title is notable not only for Silver Streak but for the first appearance of Daredevil and the villainous Claw in issue #6. With issue #22 the title was changed to *Crime Does Not Pay*. Arthur Bernhard sold out to Lev Gleason shortly afterwards and Gleason continued to build a modest success based on the crime comics genre.

SLV-1

SLV-1. Photo,
c. 1941. Rare. - **$100 $200 $300**

THE SIMPSONS

In 1987, a series of 30-second animated shorts appeared on the new Fox network's *The Tracey Ullman Show*. Created by cartoonist Matt Groening, until then best known for his *Life in Hell* comic strip (which currently appears in over 250 newspapers), these short features would soon grow into a pop-culture phenome-

non. On December 17, 1989, *The Simpsons* premiered with their own show on Fox as a half-hour Christmas special, soon followed by a regular series that debuted on January 14, 1990. After becoming Fox's #1 show for children under 17 and #4 for adults 18 to 34, and garnering critical praise and numerous awards including Emmys and a Peabody, *The Simpsons*, in February 1997, dethroned *The Flintstones* as the longest running animated series.

The Simpsons, like *The Flintstones*, concerns the exploits of a family: Homer—the dim-witted father; Marge—the loving wife and mother; Bart—the 10-year old trouble-making son; Lisa—the angst-ridden, intelligent sister; and Maggie—the toddler who communicates via pacifier. Also highlighted on the show are the citizens of Springfield, The Simpsons' hometown, plus guest appearances by a supporting cast of hundreds, voiced by many of Hollywood's top stars, including Dustin Hoffman, Michael Jackson, Mel Brooks, Leonard Nimoy, David Duchovny, Gillian Anderson, Winona Ryder, and many others.

Taking advantage of the popularity of his creations, Groening turned *The Simpsons* into a licensing empire, including comics, videos, CDs, and a string of best selling books. *The Simpsons* continue to be seen in syndication across the country with new episodes airing Sunday nights on Fox. Most items are copyright Twentieth Century Fox or Matt Groening Productions. "D'oh!"

SIM-2   SIM-3

SIM-1

SIM-1. Simpsons Sofa and Boob Tube,
1990. Mattel. Near Mint Boxed - **$80**

SIM-2. Bart Poseable Figure,
1990. Mattel. Near Mint On Card - **$25**

SIM-3. Bartman Poseable Figure,
1990. Mattel. Near Mint On Card - **$25**

SIM-4   SIM-5

SIM-4. Simpsons 3-D Chess Set,
1991. Near Mint Boxed - **$55**

SIM-5. Simpsons 3-D Checker Set,
1994. Near Mint Boxed - **$35**

SIM-6   SIM-7

SIM-6. Bart Figural Cookie Jar,
1990s. Extinct Collectibles. Near Mint - **$45**

SIM-7. Homer Figural Cookie Jar,
1990s. Extinct Collectibles. Near Mint - **$50**

SIM-8

SIM-9

SIM-8. Bart & Lisa Salt & Pepper Set,
1990s. Extinct Collectibles. Bart & Lisa watching TV. 3 piece set. Near Mint - **$25**

SIM-9. Homer & Marge Salt & Pepper Set,
1990s. Extinct Collectibles. Homer & Marge with Maggie on couch. Near Mint - **$30**

SIM-11

SIM-10

SIM-10. Simpsons Toy Display,
1990s. Subway promotion with 4 toys. Near Mint - **$60**

SIM-11. Bartman Watch,
1990s. Nelsonic. Near Mint On Card - **$30**

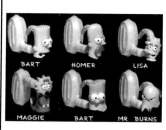

SIM-12

SIM-12. Squirt Rings,
1997. United Kingdom Kellogg's Corn Pops premium. Bart (2 different versions), Homer,Lisa,Maggie, Mr. Burns. Total 6 different. Near Mint Complete Wrapped Set - **$150**
Near Mint Complete Unwrapped Set - **$75**
Box - **$5 $10 $15**

SINCLAIR OIL

Harry F. Sinclair (1876-1956) founded the Sinclair Oil & Refining Corporation in 1916, and the company soon grew to become one of the nation's largest integrated oil companies. (Sinclair himself was caught up in the Teapot Dome oil-lease scandal and served a prison term in 1929 for contempt of the Senate.) The company started using dinosaurs in its advertising in 1930 to illustrate its theme that Sinclair oil was mellowed a hundred million years, and by 1931 had fixed on the brontosaurus as its symbol. Dino was put on signs and oil cans, the company sponsored dinosaur exhibits at the 1933 Century of Progress Exposition in Chicago and Dinoland at the 1964 New York World's Fair, funded dinosaur exploration, and in 1935 started giving out dinosaur stamps and albums at gas stations. Over the years Sinclair issued a number of dinosaur toys and other brontosaurus-oriented promotional items. In 1973 the company became part of the Atlantic Richfield Company.

SNC-1   SNC-2

SNC-1. "Big News" Chicago World's Fair Sinclair Newspaper,
1933. 11x16" photo feature eight-page publication devoted largely to the dinosaurs exhibit. Pictured example is "Second Edition" front and back cover. - **$10 $20 $30**

SNC-2. "Picture News" Issue,
c. 1938. 11x16" monthly four-page news and human interest photo feature publication imprinted on top front and bottom rear page for local Sinclair dealer. - **$5 $12 $20**

SNC-3

SNC-4

SNC-3. "Sinclair Dinoland" New York World's Fair Souvenir Booklet,
1964. Twelve-page picture summary from life-sized dinosaur exhibit. Pictured are front and back cover. - **$10 $20 $35**

SNC-4. "Dinoland" New York World's Fair Glass Tumbler,
1964. Pictures symbolic twins at exhibit. - **$8 $15 $25**

SNC-5   SNC-6

SNC-5. "Sinclair Dinoland" New York World's Fair Figure,
1965. 9" long waxy-plastic dinosaur with inscriptions for Sinclair and second year of the fair. From series of various replicas purchased at the exhibit. Each - **$10 $20 $35**

SNC-6. Dinosaur Vinyl Bank,
1960s. 9" long figure in green hard plastic unmarked but believed Sinclair issue. - **$8 $15 $20**

SNC-7   SNC-8

SNC-7. Dinosaur Toy Pack,
1960s. Six miniature plastic replica figures in cellophane packet naming each plus Sinclair Oil's logo. Near Mint Packaged - **$20**

SNC-8. "Drive With Care" Applique,
c. 1960s. Molded thin shell plastic sign with peel-off adhesive strips on reverse. No Sinclair markings but obvious dinosaur symbol. - **$10 $20 $30**

THE SINGING LADY

Ireene Wicker was the Singing Lady, and for 13 years (1932-1945) she told fairy tales and sang to the nation's children on a highly popular network radio program called *The Singing Story Lady*. The show, loved by parents as well as children, won many major broadcasting awards, including a Peabody. Kellogg's cereals, the long-term sponsor, offered a number of premiums, mostly song and story booklets designed by Vernon Grant. *The Singing Lady* moved to ABC television (1948-1950) with a similar format, using puppets to illustrate fairy tales and historical sketches. In 1953-1954, with Kellogg's again sponsoring, the program returned as *Story Time*.

SNG-1   SNG-2   SNG-3

SNG-1. "Singing Lady Song Book",
c. 1932. Art by Vernon Grant. - **$15 $25 $40**

SNG-2. Singing Lady Punchouts,
1932. Kellogg's. Three cardboard pages of punchouts. Unpunched - **$25 $75 $100**

SNG-3. Kellogg's "Mother Goose" Booklet,
1933. Cover art by Vernon Grant. - **$15 $30 $50**

SNG-4   SNG-5

SNG-4. "Mother Goose" Booklet,
1935. Kellogg's Rice Krispies. Subtitled "Mother Goose As Told By Kellogg's Singing Lady" with artwork over 16 pages by Vernon Grant. - **$10 $20 $30**

SNG-5. Film Stories,
1935. Kellogg's Rice Krispies. Promotes radio show. Has movie film cut-outs that can be played with by running through attached toy theatre. Features Mother Goose stories - **$20 $40 $60**

SNG-6

SNG-6. Punch-Out Paper "Party Kit",
1936. Near Mint With Mailer - **$125**
Book Only - **$20 $50 $100**

SNG-7

SNG-7. "Mother Goose Action Circus" Punch-Out Book With Mailer Envelope,
1936. Six sheets of Vernon Grant illustrations.
Mailer - **$10 $20 $30**
Punch-Out Book - **$100 $250 $350**

SNG-8

SNG-8. "Ireene Wicker" Fan Postcard,
1940. National Broadcasting Co. for her "Musical Stories" radio broadcasts on Blue Network. - **$5 $20 $35**

THE SIX MILLION DOLLAR MAN

Based on a Martin Caidin novel, *Cyborg*, this TV series, which ran from 1973 to 1978, followed the adventures of Steve Austin, a former test pilot and astronaut who is rebuilt with the latest technology after a freak accident ("better, stronger, faster"). He is given replacement limbs which heighten his strength, and a telescopic eye. As the series became a '70s phenomenon, the Bond-like missions of the early episodes gave way to more cartoonish, comic-book adventures, involving stock Arab terrorists, dangerous space probes, and in several memorable episodes, aliens from outer space and a huge robot Bigfoot. A wide variety of toys and action figures were available.

The Bionic Woman, a spin-off based on a story that aired on *The Six Million Dollar Man* in 1975, debuted in 1976 and ran until 1978. Lindsay Wagner played Jamie Summers, Steve's on-and-off girlfriend, and another enhanced government agent working for OSI. When *The Bionic Woman* switched networks, Richard Anderson and Martin E. Brooks (who played Goldman and bionics scientist Rudy Wells) made history as the first actors to play the same characters simultaneously on two different networks. There have been three reunion TV-movies: *Return of the Six-Million Dollar Man and the Bionic Woman* (1987), *Bionic Showdown: The Six-Million Dollar Man and the Bionic Woman* (1989), featuring a young Sandra Bullock, and *Bionic Ever After?* (1994), in which Steve and Jamie were finally wed. A big-screen remake or sequel is planned, with Oscar Goldman himself (actor Anderson) spearheading the project. Most items are copyright Universal City Studios.

SXM-1

SXM-2

SXM-1. Lunch Box,
1974. Aladdin Industries, Inc. Box - **$15 $20 $25**
Thermos - **$6 $8 $12**
Complete - **$30 $40 $50**

SXM-2. Six Million Dollar Man Action Figure,
1975. 13" doll by Kenner. Figure was released in two versions. The first, with telescopic vision and bionic lifting arm with removable modules, came with an engine block. The second featured bionic gripping action and came with an orange I-beam. Box art for first version also shown.
Boxed - **$35 $50 $75**

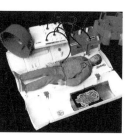

SXM-3

SXM-3. Bionic Transport and Repair Station,
1975. Kenner. Side panel of box also shown. -
$25 $30 $35

SXM-4

SXM-5

SXM-4. Venus Space Probe,
1975. Kenner. Pictured with Steve Austin action figure (see SXM-2). - **$35 $40 $60**

SXM-5. Bionic Action Club Kit,
1975. The kit included a mailing envelope (not pictured), a certificate, wallet card, logo sticker and portrait photo. A comic book ad with a coupon to join the club is also pictured. Complete Kit - **$20 $35 $50**

SXM-7

SXM-6

SXM-6. The Six Million Dollar Man Record,
1975. Peter Pan Industries. Four stories, including "Birth of the Bionic Man," "The Iron Heart," "The Man From the Future," and "Bionic Berserker." - **$3 $5 $8**

SXM-7. Critical Assignment Arms,
1976. Accessories for the action figure. Set comes with three arms (laser, neutralizer, and oxygen supply) and a white T-shirt. Boxed - **$20 $30 $40**

SXM-8

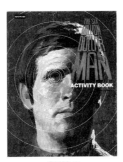
SXM-9

SXM-8. "6 Million Dollar Man Club" Cello. Button,
1977. - **$5 $12 $20**

SXM-9. The Six Million Dollar Man Activity Book,
1977. Rand McNally & Co. - **$10 $15 $20**

SXM-10 **SXM-11**

SXM-10. Book & Record Set,
1977. Peter Pan Industries. Includes "Birth of the Bionic Man" and "The Man From the Future." - **$3 $5 $8**

SXM-11. "Hear 4 Exciting Christmas Adventures" Record,
1978. Peter Pan Industries. Includes "The Toymaker," "Christmas Lights," "The Kris Kringle Caper," and "Elves Revolt." - **$3 $5 $8**

SKEEZIX

The central character of the meandering continuity comic strip *Gasoline Alley*, Skeezix was an exception to the traditional comic style in that he aged accordingly as the strip continued over the years. Skeezix was a doorstep infant foundling left by unknown parents in 1921. He served in World War II and returned to continue his small town, middle-class life so readily identifiable to mass readership. Skeezix was an adult and father in the 1960s but the vast majority of related premiums are from his 1930s happy childhood years with guardian Uncle Walt surrounded by the extensive assortment of relatives, friends and neighbors created by cartoonist Frank King.

SKX-2

SKX-1

SKX-1. Club Letter,
1930s. Wonder Bread. - **$10 $20 $30**

SKX-2. Skeezix Badge,
1930s. Wonder Bread. - **$20 $40 $80**

SKX-4

SKX-5

SKX-3

SKX-3. Litho. Tin Toothbrush Holder,
1930s. Pro-phy-lac-tic Listerine. - **$40 $100 $200**

SKX-4. Birthstone Design "I Wear Skeezix Shoes" 2-1/4" Cello. Pocket Mirror,
1930s. - **$12 $20 $40**

SKX-5. "I Wear Skeezix Shoes" Cello. Button,
1930s. Unidentified sponsor. Added slogan is "Outgrown Before Outworn." - **$15 $25 $40**

SKX-6

SKX-7

SKX-8

SKX-6. "I Like Skeezix Sweaters" Cello. Button,
1930s. - **$15 $25 $45**

SKX-7. "Skeezix Loves Red Cross Macaroni" Cello. Button,
1930s. - **$15 $25 $45**

SKX-8. "Buffalo Evening News" Cello. Button,
1930s. From series of newspaper contest buttons, match number to win prize. - **$10 $20 $35**

SKX-9

SKX-9. "Skeezix Mask",
1940s. Wheaties box panel.
Box Back Mask Uncut - **$15 $30 $45**
Cut Mask - **$5 $10 $15**

SKIPPY

Artist Percy Crosby created the cartoon Skippy Skinner for the old *Life* humor magazine in the early 1920s and began syndicating the strip in 1925. Dressed in shorts, long jacket, and a checked hat, Skippy was the neighborhood pessimist, with a cynical view of the adult world, his humor shadowed by sadness and defeat. Even so, the strip was a popular one and ran until 1943, when Crosby became too ill to continue it. Comic book collections and illustrated Skippy novels appeared in the 1920s and 1930s, and there were two 1931 movies, *Skippy* and *Sooky*, both starring Jackie Cooper. A radio series aired on NBC (1932) and CBS (1932-1935), sponsored first by Wheaties (1932-1933), then by Phillips Magnesia toothpaste (1933-1935). Premiums included membership in *Skippy's Secret Service Society* and the *Skippy Mystic Circle Club*.

SKP-1

SKP-1. Skippy Plate - Boxed,
1931. Large silver plate Skippy plate with price coupon. Store bought. Near Mint Boxed - **$225**
Plate Only - **$40 $75 $125**

SKP-2

SKP-2. Wheaties 9x18" Club Application and Information,
1932. Rare with three perforated pieces intact.
Near Mint Intact - **$300**
Each Piece Loose - **$20 $40 $60**

SKP-3   SKP-4

SKP-3. Wheaties Ceramic Bowl (Sooky),
c. 1932. Rare. Same side view shown for both. Sooky pictured in bottom. - **$75 $135 $300**

SKP-4. Wheaties Ceramic Bowl (Skippy),
c. 1932. Rare. Skippy pictured in bottom. - **$50 $150 $250**

SKP-5

SKP-6

SKP-5. Life Membership,
1932. Certificate for the Secret Service Society, plus 4 page secret code. - **$30 $60 $90**

SKP-6. Plastic Bowl,
1932. Beetleware bowl premium from Wheaties. Comes in green and orange. Each - **$15 $30 $45**

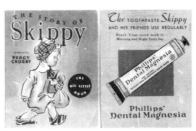

SKP-7

SKP-8

SKP-7. Wheaties Cello. Club Button,
1932. Initialed for Skippy's Secret Service Society. - **$5 $10 $15**

SKP-8. Captain Application Form,
c. 1932. Wheaties. - **$5 $10 $15**

SKP-9

SKP-10

SKP-9. Wheaties "Captain" Cello. Rank Button,
1932. For highest club rank. - **$20 $40 $65**

SKP-10. Wheaties Skippy Letter,
c. 1932. "Dear Captain" form letter in simulated Skippy handwriting certifying rank attained by eating Wheaties "According To The Regulations And Rules". - **$8 $15 $25**

SKP-11

SKP-11. Wheaties "Captain's Commission" Certificate,
c. 1932. Paper award for proven Wheaties consumption. - **$15 $40 $60**

SKP-12

SKP-13

SKP-12. Wheaties "Skippy Racer Club" Cello. Button,
c. 1932. - **$15 $30 $60**

SKP-13. Skippy Cards,
1933. Wheaties premium. Set of 12 different, 6 pictured. Each - **$10 $20 $30**

SKP-14

SKP-14. "The Story Of Skippy" BLB,
1934. Phillips' Dental Magnesia Toothpaste. - **$10 $25 $60**

SKP-15

SKP-15. Christmas Card,
c. 1935. Phillips Dental Magnesia. - **$10 $25 $40**

SKP-16

SKP-16. Mystic Circle Club Folder,
c. 1935. Phillips Toothpaste. Folder opens to 16" length. -
$20 $40 $75

SKP-17

SKP-18

SKP-17. "Skippy Mystic Circle Club" Member Card,
c. 1935. Phillips Dental Magnesia. - **$10 $35 $45**

SKP-18. "Skippy Mystic Circle" Felt Fabric Beanie,
c. 1935. Phillips Dental Magnesia. - **$25 $75 $125**

SKP-19

SKP-20

SKP-19. "The Atlanta Georgian's Silver Anniversary"
Litho. Button,
1937. Named newspaper. From set of various characters. -
$20 $50 $75

SKP-20. "Stories Of Interesting People Who Wear
Glasses Booklet,
1937. Manual for "Skippy Good Eyesight Brigade". -
$15 $20 $40

SKP-21

SKP-22

SKP-23

SKP-21. Skippy Good Eyes Brigade Silvered Badge,
1937. Scarce. - **$30 $80 $150**

SKP-22. Bisque and Celluloid Figures,
1930s. Store item, several versions.
Movable Arms, No Base - **$60 $125 $250**
One Arm Moves, Green Base - **$50 $90 $185**
Celluloid Figure (Not Shown) - **$75 $200 $400**

SKP-23. "Fire Siren" Whistle Toy,
1930s. Wooden tube 1-3/8" long with black image on red
background. - **$10 $20 $40**

SKP-24

SKP-25

SKP-24. Skippy Mazda Lamps Sign,
1930s. 15" by 26". - **$150 $300 $600**

SKP-25. "Fro-Joy Ice Cream" 24x36" Cardboard Store
Sign,
1930s. - **$100 $200 $300**

SKP-26

SKP-27

SKP-28

SKP-26. Paper Mask,
1930s. Socony Oil. From set of "Five Free Funny Faces". -
$10 $35 $50

SKP-27. Fabric Patch,
1930s. Probably Wheaties. Orange/blue/white stitched
design. - **$20 $40 $60**

SKP-28. Skippy Cello. Button From Effanbee Doll,
1930s. - **$20 $35 $60**

SKP-29   SKP-30   SKP-31

SKP-29. Cello. Button,
1930s. Includes artist's name "P. L. Crosby". -
$20 $30 $50

SKP-30. "Saturday Chicago American" Litho. Button,
1930s. From newspaper "16 Pages Of Comics" series of
10 known characters including two Skippy versions. -
$10 $20 $30

SKP-31. "Sunday Examiner" Litho. Button,
1930s. From "50 Comics" set of various newspaper characters, match number to win prize. - **$10 $20 $35**

THE SKY BLAZERS

The Sky Blazers, a radio series that dramatized
episodes in the history of aviation, aired on CBS for a
season (1939-1940), sponsored by Wonder bread. The
show was created by Phillips H. Lord and hosted and
narrated by Colonel Roscoe Turner, an early aviation
hero and holder of various speed records. Each show
closed with Turner interviewing the subject of that
night's episode. Two issues of a *Sky Blazers* comic
book appeared in 1940.

SBZ-1

SBZ-2

SBZ-1. "'Sky Blazers' Wonder Bread" Brass Wings Pin,
c. 1939. - **$15 $25 $40**

SBZ-2. Balsa Airplane In Tube,
c. 1939. - **$60 $200 $300**

SBZ-3

SBZ-4

SBZ-3. Paper Plane,
1939. Wonder Bread premium. Two pieces. -
$30 $65 $95

SBZ-4. "Sky Blazers" Badge,
1940. Silvered brass with red enamel paint. -
$60 $100 $150

SBZ-5   SBZ-6

SBZ-5. Wonder Bread 8x12" Diecut Paper Sign,
1940. Scarce. Promotes 7:00 P.M. CBS radio show. -
$50 $150 $250

SBZ-6. Comic Book #1,
Sept. 1940. - **$50 $150 $450**

SBZ-7
SBZ-8

SBZ-7. "Sky Blazers/Roscoe Turner" Photo,
1940. Wonder Bread. From Sponsor Day Kit at New York
World's Fair. - **$15 $25 $35**

**SBZ-8. "Sky Blazers Model Aircraft Exposition/Roscoe
Turner" Contest Registration Folder,**
1940. Wonder Bread. For Sponsor Day at New York
World's Fair. - **$10 $25 $35**

SBZ-9

**SBZ-9. "Sky Blazers/Roscoe Turner" Waxed Paper
Bread Loaf Inserts,**
c. 1940. Wonder Bread. Each - **$10 $25 $35**

SKY CLIMBERS

The Sky Climbers of America was an aviation-related club sponsored by boys' clothing stores around 1929. Members could qualify as Oiler, Mechanic, Pilot, Ace, or Flight Leader. The symbol of the club was a youthful aviator type known as Pete Weet.

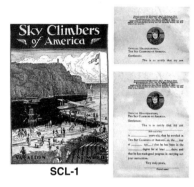

SCL-1

SCL-1. "Sky Climbers Of America" Club Manual,
1929. - **$20 $50 $90**

SCL-2

SCL-2. Fabric Patch,
1929. - **$20 $50 $75**

SCL-3. Club Member Card,
1929. - **$20 $50 $75**

SCL-4

SCL-5

SCL-4. Club Water Transfer Paper Picture,
1929. Rare. - **$30 $90 $150**

SCL-5. "The Sky Climbers" Cello. Button,
1929. - **$10 $20 $40**

SCL-6

SCL-6. "Secret Manual For Sky Climbers Only!",
c. 1930. - **$30 $75 $100**

SCL-7

SCL-8

SCL-7. "Pilot/The Sky Climbers Of America" Brass Bar And Pendant Badge,
c. 1930. "Pilot" designation on pendant. - **$25 $50 $100**

SCL-8. "Ace/The Sky Climbers Of America" Brass Bar And Pendant Badge,
c. 1930. "Ace" designation on pendant is one of higher club ranks. - **$40 $100 $180**

SCL-9

SCL-9. "The Sky Climbers Of America/Flight Leader" Brass Award Bar Badge,
c. 1930. Denotes high rank in club. - **$30 $80 $140**

SCL-10

SCL-10. Last Club Manual,
c. 1930. - **$20 $60 $100**

SKY KING

America's favorite flying cowboy, Sky King aired on ABC radio from 1946 to 1950 and on Mutual from 1950 to 1954, sponsored starting in 1947 by Peter Pan peanut butter. The series centered on the crime-fighting exploits of rancher-pilot Schuyler King and his niece Penny and nephew Clipper. King's Flying Crown Ranch had an airstrip from which he and his young sidekicks flew off in his plane The Songbird to bring criminals to justice. The program made a successful transition to television as *Sky King Theater*, airing on NBC (1951-1952) and ABC (1952-1954), with Peter Pan again sponsoring. A new television series titled *Sky King* was syndicated from 1956 to 1958, then aired on CBS from 1959 to 1966, sponsored by Nabisco. Kirby Grant played King and Gloria Winters was Penny. Both Peter Pan and Nabisco issued program-related premiums, usually copyrighted by Jack Chertok Productions.

SKY-1

SKY-2

SKY-1. Radar Signal Ring,
1946. Top glows in dark. - **$75 $120 $175**

SKY-2. "Secret Signalscope" With Instructions,
1947. Whistle/magnifier held in scope tube.
Near Mint In Mailer - **$175**
Scope - **$35 $75 $100**

SKY-3

SKY-3. Sky King Secret Compartment Belt Buckle,
1948. Prototype designed by Orin Armstrong for Robbins Co. Unique - **$5500**

SKY-4

SKY-5

SKY-6

SKY-4. "Mystery Picture Ring" Instruction Sheet,
1948. - **$75 $90 $100**

SKY-5. Mystery Picture Ring,
1948. Faint image on rectangular plastic sheet under gray plastic top has almost always disappeared.
Complete No Image - **$125 $200 $300**
Near Mint With Image - **$1000**

SKY-6. Magni-Glo Writing Ring,
1949. - **$30 $60 $125**

SKY-8

SKY-7

SKY-7. "Magni-Glow Writing Ring" Instruction Paper,
1949. Peter Pan Peanut Butter. - **$35 $42 $50**

SKY-8. "Spy Detecto Writer",
1949. Elaborate premium that includes decoder. Comes in all brass or brass/aluminum versions. - **$40 $85 $125**

SKY-9

SKY-10

SKY-9. Electronic Television Picture Ring,
1949. Brass and plastic, came with photo strip to be developed and cut showing Jim, Penny, Clipper, Martha.
Ring Only - **$50 $90 $150**
Photo Set - **$75 $90 $100**

SKY-10. "Electronic Television Picture Ring" Instruction Sheet,
1949. Peter Pan Peanut Butter. - **$50 $60 $75**

SKY-12

SKY-17

SKY-11

SKY-13

SKY-17. "Detecto-Microscope" With Accessories,
1952. Cardboard stand and four specimens not shown, map glows in dark. Near Mint Complete - **$500**
Plastic Tube Only - **$25 $50 $75**
Map - **$20 $40 $60**

SKY-11. "2-Way Tele-Blinker Ring" Instruction Sheet,
1949. Peter Pan Peanut Butter. Sheet includes ring order coupon expiring March 13, 1950. - **$60 $68 $75**

SKY-12. Tele-Blinker Ring,
1949. Brass and other metals signal ring. When pressed, ring sides reveal cut-out panels with glow-in-dark inserts. - **$75 $120 $175**

SKY-13. Navajo Treasure Ring,
1950. - **$75 $110 $150**

SKY-18

SKY-19

SKY-14

SKY-15

SKY-18. Detecto Instructions,
1952. Six step instruction sheet for Detecto-Microscope. - **$20 $40 $50**

SKY-19. "Stamping Kit" Newspaper Ad,
1953. - **$8 $15 $20**

SKY-14. "Safety Is No Accident" Litho. Button,
c. 1950. - **$30 $50 $80**

SKY-15. Kaleidoscope Prototype Ring,
c. 1950. Large brass and other metals viewer ring developed in prototype design by Orin Armstrong but never actually offered as premium. Unique - **$11,000**

SKY-20

SKY-21

SKY-16

SKY-16. "Aztec Emerald Calendar Ring" With Instruction Sheet,
1951. Mint Boxed With Instructions - **$1100**
Ring - **$200 $600 $950**
Instructions - **$125 $135 $150**

SKY-20. "Stamping Kit" Order Blank,
1953. - **$15 $25 $40**

SKY-21. Stamping Kit,
1953. Tin container holding ink pad and personalized rubber stamp. Ink often rusts the tin. - **$20 $40 $75**

SKY-22

SKY-22. Figure Set,
1956. Nabisco Wheat & Rice Honeys. Soft plastic in various colors. Sky King, Clipper, Penny, Sheriff, Songbird (plane), Yellow Fury (horse). Each - **$15 $20 $35**

SKY-23

SKY-24

SKY-25

SKY-23. Nabisco Fan Postcard,
c. 1956. - **$10 $20 $35**

SKY-24. "TV Eye" Cover Article,
1956. Weekly television supplement to June 24 newspaper with color cover photo plus one-page Sky King article including three other b&w photos. - **$15 $35 $60**

SKY-25. Kirby Grant Contest Photo,
1957. McGowan Studios. Note on back about search for look-alike to play Kirby's twin in upcoming film. - **$15 $30 $50**

SKY-26

SKY-26. Fan Club Nabisco Contest Postcard,
1959. Oversized 5-1/2x7" card. - **$20 $50 $85**

SKY-27

SKY-27. "Sky King Fan Club" Folder,
1959. Nabisco. 3x5" closed but opens to five panels printed on both sides. Example shown is missing one panel. Includes membership card, good conduct rules, cut-out photos of Sky and Penny plus more. Came with litho. tin tab (SKY-29). Folder Complete - **$40 $75 $125**

SKY-29

SKY-28
SKY-30

SKY-28. Nabisco Fan Club Member Kit,
c. 1959. Includes cut-out Sky King neckerchief ring plus membership card. - **$35 $70 $150**

SKY-29. Nabisco "Sky King Fan Club" Litho. Tin Tab Wings,
1959. - **$40 $100 $150**

SKY-30. Autographed Photo,
1950s. - **$20 $40 $75**

SKY-31

SKY-32

SKY-31. "Cook Out With Sky King" Recipe Folder,
1950s. Nabisco. - **$30 $60 $100**

SKY-32. Cowboy Tie With Envelope,
1950s. Near Mint In Mailer - **$100**
Tie Only - **$15 $30 $50**

SKY RIDERS

Spelled either Sky Riders or Skyriders, this 1930s aviation related club issued celluloid buttons, brass wings badges and lithographed tin wings. The items don't specify a sponsor and research efforts yielded no information.

SRD-1

SRD-2

SRD-1. Club Knife,
1930. Scarce. - **$30 $85 $150**

**SRD-2. "Skyrider Pilot's Club/Certified Pilot" Cello.
Button,**
1930s. - **$20 $40 $75**

SRD-3

SRD-4

SRD-3. "Sky Riders Club" Member Cello. Button,
1930s. - **$20 $40 $75**

**SRD-4. "Lieutenant/Member Skyriders Club" Brass
Wings Badge,**
1930s. Bronze luster. - **$10 $25 $35**

SRD-5

SRD-6

**SRD-5. "Captain/Member Skyriders Club" Brass Wings
Badge,**
1930s. Dark gold luster. - **$15 $40 $60**

**SRD-6. "Colonel/Member Skyriders Club" Brass Wings
Badge,**
1930s. Bronze luster. - **$15 $40 $75**

SRD-7

SRD-8

SRD-7. "General" Brass Wings Badge,
1930s. Highest rank club badge. - **$20 $40 $100**

SRD-8. "Lieutenant" Litho. Tin Rank Badge,
1930s. - **$15 $35 $50**

SRD-9

SRD-9. "Captain" Litho. Tin Rank Badge,
1930s. - **$15 $35 $50**

This pioneer aviation comic strip was created in 1929
by two former pilots and distributed by the John F.
Dille company. Zack Mosley, later creator of Smilin'
Jack, and Russell Keaton, later creator of Flyin' Jenny,
did the artwork, with Keaton taking over and signing
the strip after 1933. Over the years the strip featured a
variety of daredevil pilots dealing with many perils and
romantic adventures. A children's club, the Flying
Legion, offered readers metal badges for Pilot,
Lieutenant, Captain, Major, Colonel, and Ace.
Additional "intermediate ranks" of Aviation Mechanic,
Stunt Flyer, and Combat Flyer were awarded, probably
by letter, but not accompanied by metal badges.
Reprints of the strip appeared in *Famous Funnies*
comic books in the early 1940s and some early
episodes were reprinted in a paperback in 1966. The
strip ended in 1942.

SRO-1

SRO-2

**SRO-1. "Skyroads With Clipper Williams Of The Flying
Legion" BTLB,**
1938. Store item. Whitman Better Little Book #1439. -
$15 $35 $75

SRO-2. "Sky Roads" Cello. Button,
1930s. Buffalo Evening News. From series of newspaper
contest buttons, match number to win prize. -
$10 $15 $30

SRO-3

SRO-4

**SRO-3. "Hurricane Hawk Flying Club" Membership
Card,**
1930s. Certifies "Aerial Machine Gunner" with Skyroads
emblem. - **$10 $20 $35**

SRO-4. "Skyroads Flying Club" Member Card,
1941. Certified member to be "Flying Cadet." Club offered
progressions in rank entitling member to officer pins pictured in next six examples. - **$25 $65 $100**

SRO-5

SRO-6

SRO-7

SRO-5. Skyroads Cadet Litho. Button,
1941. - **$10 $30 $60**

SRO-6. Skyroads Pilot Metal Wings Pin,
1941. - **$20 $40 $75**

SRO-7. Skyroads Lieutenant Metal Bar Pin,
1941. - **$20 $40 $75**

SRO-8

SRO-9

SRO-10

SRO-8. Skyroads Captain Metal Bar Pin,
1941. - **$30 $60 $90**

SRO-9. Skyroads Major Oak Leaf Metal Pin,
1941. - **$40 $75 $100**

SRO-10. Skyroads Colonel Metal Pin,
1941. Highest rank eagle insignia. - **$50 $100 $150**

SMILEY BURNETTE

Lester Smiley Burnette (1912-1967), a bluegrass singer and comic, starred in one movie, Republic's *Call of the Rockies* in 1944, but in floppy black hat and checkered shirt he provided comic relief as Frog Millhouse in a series of "B" Westerns with his pal Gene Autry. Burnette also appeared in a number of chapter plays in the 1930s, and he had his own syndicated radio show in 1950-1953. Smiley Burnette Western comic books were published in 1950.

SMY-1

SMY-2

SMY-1. Fan Club Photo,
c. 1940s. Black and white image of him and horse "Black Eyed Nellie" with club pledge on bottom margin. - **$10 $20 $35**

SMY-2. "Smiley Burnette" Dixie Ice Cream Pictures,
1940s. Back of each includes text for 1940 or 1941 Gene Autry movie. Each - **$5 $12 $20**

SMY-3

SMY-4

SMY-3. "Frog" Autographed Photo,
c. 1940s. Personally signed by nickname only. -
$15 $25 $40

SMY-4. "Checkered Shirt Drive-In Sandwich Shops" Folder,
1955. Self-mailer sheet opening to 11x16" printed on both sides by whimsey art and text seeking individual investors for franchise endorsed by Burnette. - **$15 $25 $40**

SMY-5

SMY-6

SMY-5. "Checkered Shirt Drive-In Sandwich Shops" Signed Letter,
1955. Art letterhead stationery with typewritten information on shop investment venture franchise, personally signed "Smiley." - **$30 $50 $75**

SMY-6. "Checkered Shirt Drive-In Sandwich Shop" Invitation,
1955. Card for grand opening of second shop endorsed franchise by Burnette. - **$5 $10 $15**

SMY-7

SMY-7. "$ellebrity Cash Phoney Money" Currency Bill,
c. 1950s. Hiland Dairy Products. "Auction Points" paper bill picturing him on one side with his product endorsement on reverse. - **$5 $10 $15**

SMILIN' ED McCONNELL

Ed McConnell (1892-1954), singer and banjo picker, moved from vaudeville to local radio in 1922, then to the networks from 1932 to 1941, doing his musical variety shows for a number of sponsors. In 1944 McConnell teamed with Buster Brown shoes to create a children's program combining dramatic tales, music, and listeners' letters. Known variously as *Smilin' Ed's Buster Brown Gang, The Smilin' Ed McConnell Show, The Buster Brown Gang*, or *The Buster Brown Show*, the program aired on NBC radio until 1953 and meantime made a successful move to television in 1950, appearing on all three networks: NBC (1950-1951), CBS (1951-1953), and ABC (1953-1955). The imaginary cast starred Froggy the Gremlin, along with Squeeky the Mouse, Midnight the Cat, and Old Grandie the Piano. Items are normally copyrighted J. Ed. McConnell. After McConnell's death Andy Devine took over and the show was renamed *Andy's Gang*.

SMI-1   SMI-2   SMI-3

SMI-1. Photo,
1920s. Radio premium. - **$15 $25 $35**

SMI-2. "Smilin' Ed McConnell" Autographed Photo,
1932. First year of CBS radio show. - **$25 $50 $75**

SMI-3. "Under His Wing" Theme Song Folder,
1939. Taystee Bread. - **$20 $40 $75**

SMI-4   SMI-5

SMI-4. "Smilin' Ed McConnell/Bill Stewart" Fan Card,
1930s. - **$8 $12 $20**

SMI-5. Froggy Paper Mask,
1946. - **$15 $25 $50**

SMI-6   SMI-7   SMI-8   SMI-9

SMI-6. "Member Buster Brown Gang" Litho. Tin Tab,
1946. From radio show. - **$15 $30 $50**

SMI-7. "Member Buster Brown Gang/Squeeky" Litho. Tin Tab,
1946. From radio show. - **$10 $20 $30**

SMI-8. "Froggy" Litho. Tin Tab,
1946. From radio show. - **$20 $45 $75**

SMI-9. "Mldnight" Litho. Tin Tab,
1946. From radio show. - **$15 $30 $50**

SMI-11   SMI-12

SMI-10

SMI-10. "Smilin' Ed McConnell" Letter
1946. - **$8 $12 $20**

SMI-11. "Smilin' Ed McConnell" Picture
1946. - **$8 $12 $20**

SMI-12. "Smilin' Ed McConnell" Picture
1946. - **$8 $12 $20**

SMI-13   SMI-14

SMI-13. "Smilin' Ed McConnell" Picture
1946. - **$8 $12 $20**

SMI-14. Squeeze Toy,
1948. Store item by Rempel Mfg. Co.
Small 5" Size - **$60 $150 $250**
Large 9-1/2" Size - **$75 $200 $300**

SMI-15   SMI-16

SMI-15. "Smilin' Ed's Buster Brown Comics" #13,
1948. Buster Brown Shoes. Issued between 1945 and
1959. First Issue - **$60 $175 $500**
Second Issue - **$20 $50 $135**
Others - **$10 $20 $45**

SMI-16. Buster Brown Paddle Ball Game,
c. 1948. - **$30 $90 $150**

SMI-17   SMI-18

SMI-17. "Buster Brown Gang" Card With Brass Badge,
c. 1948. Card - **$15 $25 $50**
Badge - **$8 $15 $25**

SMI-18. Buster Brown Gang Brass Ring,
c. 1948. Pictures him and Tige with Froggy and Squeeky
on bands. - **$25 $50 $75**

SMI-19   SMI-20

**SMI-19. "Smilin' Ed McConnell's Buster Brown Gang"
Bandanna,**
c. 1948. - **$25 $50 $80**

SMI-20. "Buster Brown T.V. Theatre" Flicker Card,
c. 1950. Screen area has movement image of Froggy
jumping up and down. - **$30 $100 $125**

SMI-21

SMI-22

SMI-21. "Buster Brown Gang" Card With Litho. Button,
1953. Card - **$10 $30 $50**
Button - **$8 $12 $20**

SMI-22. "Treasure Hunt Game" Shoe Box,
c. 1950s. - **$25 $50 $75**

SMI-23

SMI-23. "Buster Brown Shoes" Periscope,
1950s. 17" long cardboard and mirror lenses toy with
design art including images of Smilin' Ed and various
Buster Brown Gang members. - **$40 $80 $125**

SMOKEY BEAR

Smokey was created for a U.S. Forest Service poster in
1944 to warn of the dangers--and the threat to the
country's wartime lumber supply--of forest fires. Since
then the brown bear with the ranger hat has become
the beloved symbol of the Forest Service and spokes-
bear for the nation's trees. Smokey has been given
special trademark status, had his own zip code,
appeared on a postage stamp in 1984, and in balloon
form has floated in Macy's Thanksgiving Day Parade
since 1968. "Remember--only you can prevent forest
fires!" dates from 1947. In 1950 a four-pound black
bear cub that survived a forest fire in New Mexico was
given the name Smokey, nursed back to health, and
sent to live at the National Zoo in Washington, D.C.
That Smokey died in 1976 but he was promptly
replaced to continue as a symbol of conservation.

The Smokey Bear Show, a half-hour animated cartoon
series, was broadcast on ABC from 1969 to 1971,
stressing the importance of saving natural resources
and protecting wildlife. Smokey comic books appeared
from 1950 into the 1970s, and in 1994 a traveling exhibition and party on the Mall in Washington celebrated
Smokey's golden anniversary.

SMO-1

SMO-1. Slogan Litho. Button,
c. 1950. - **$5 $10 $15**

SMO-2

SMO-3

SMO-2. "Prevent Woods Fires" 12x14" Cardboard Sign,
1955. - **$30 $60 $100**

SMO-3. Calendar,
1956. - **$8 $15 $30**

SMO-4

SMO-4. Letter,
1957. Letter explains Kit, with song sheet on back - **$10 $25 $35**

SMO-5

SMO-6

SMO-5. "Forest Fire Prevention" Award Certificate,
1950s. - **$15 $30 $50**

SMO-6. Cloth Doll With Plastic Hat And Badge,
c. 1950s. Store item by Ideal Toy Corp. - **$25 $50 $75**

SMO-7

SMO-8

SMO-7. "Join Smokey Ranger Club" Litho. Tin Tab,
1950s. - **$15 $25 $40**

SMO-8. Biographical Card,
1965. U.S. Department Of Agriculture-Forest Service. - **$3 $5 $10**

SMO-9

SMO-10   SMO-11

SMO-9. "Soaky" Plastic Soap Bottle,
c. 1965. Colgate-Palmolive Co. - **$5 $12 $20**

SMO-10. Ceramic Salt & Pepper Shakers,
c. 1960s. Store item. - **$15 $30 $50**

SMO-11. Wristwatch,
c. 1960s. Store item. Boxed - **$60 $90 $125**
Loose - **$25 $40 $75**

SMO-12

SMO-13

SMO-14

SMO-12. Plastic Bank,
c. 1960s. Store item. - **$15 $30 $50**

SMO-13. Composition Bobbing Head,
1960s. Store item. - **$60 $125 $175**
Wooden handle on shovel - **$90 $175 $275**

SMO-14. "Junior Forest Ranger/Prevent Forest Fires" Tin Badge,
1960s. Either silver, brass or copper luster. - **$5 $10 $15**

SMO-15

SMO-16

SMO-15. "Smokey's Reading Club" Litho. Button,
1960s. Also says "Keep California Green & Golden." - **$10 $20 $30**

SMO-16. "March Of Comics",
1973. Various Advertisers. - **$5 $8 $15**

SMO-17

SMO-18

SMO-17. Fabric Patch,
c. 1970s. - **$5 $10 $15**

SMO-18. "Smokey" Ring,
1990s. No sponsor. Silver luster finish thin embossed metal expansion ring with name inscription on hat. - **$1 $3 $5**

SNAP, CRACKLE, POP

The Kellogg Company introduced Snap, Crackle, and Pop in 1933 to personify the lively sounds made when a bowl of its Rice Krispies meets cold milk. Originally drawn by Vernon Grant, the cartoon trio has survived to this day on cereal boxes and in advertising, singing and dancing and crackling and popping for kids everywhere.

SNP-1

SNP-1. Paper Masks,
1933. Kellogg's copyright with unsigned Vernon Grant art. Each - **$30 $60 $90**

SNP-2

SNP-2. Booklet,
1933. Six pages of Vernon Grant art and combination picture game. - **$25 $50 $75**

SNP-3

SNP-4

SNP-3. Comic,
1933. Vernon Grant art on 8 pages plus 2 pages of premiums for Singing Lady. - **$15 $30 $50**

SNP-4. Blotter,
1930s. Vernon Grant art. - **$15 $25 $35**

SNP-5   SNP-6   SNP-7   SNP-8

SNP-5. "Snap/Pop" China Salt & Pepper Shakers,
1930s. - **$8 $15 $25**

SNP-6. "Pop" Face Ring,
1952. Brass bands holding soft rubber head that changes expressions by turning small knobs. - **$175 $450 $650**

SNP-7. "Snap" Face Ring,
1952. Brass bands holding soft rubber head that changes expressions by turning small knobs. - **$150 $375 $550**

SNP-8. "Crackle" Face Ring,
1952. Brass bands holding soft rubber head that changes expressions by turning small knobs. - **$75 $200 $300**

SNP-9

SNP-10

SNP-9. Cloth Pattern Doll,
1954. Uncut - **$20 $40 $60**
Mailer - **$10 $20 $40**

SNP-10. Cloth Pattern Doll,
1954. Uncut - **$20 $40 $60**
Mailer - **$10 $20 $40**

SNP-11

SNP-12

SNP-11. Cloth Pattern Doll,
1954. Uncut - **$20 $40 $60**
Mailer - **$10 $20 $40**

SNP-12. "Pop" Rice Krispies Hand Puppet,
1950s. Kellogg's copyright on neck. From set of three.
Each - **$15 $30 $45**

SNP-13

SNP-13. Friendly Folk Wood & Fabric Figure Set,
1972. Frosted Mini-Wheats. Accent by simulated hair or
fur. Each - **$3 $5 $8**

SNP-14

SNP-15

SNP-14. Vinyl Figure Set,
1975. Each - **$12 $20 $35**

SNP-15. Glow Plastic Figures,
c. 1980. Snap, Crackle, Pop, Tony, Tony Jr., Toucan Sam,
Dig 'Em, Tusk (elephant). Each - **$2 $3 $5**

SNOW WHITE & THE SEVEN DWARFS

Disney's first full-length animated feature, *Snow White
and the Seven Dwarfs* was both a cinematic master-
piece and a box office smash. The film, a retelling of
the Grimm brothers' 19th century fairy tale, premiered
in December 1937 and went on to break attendance
records in the U.S. and throughout the world.
Manufacturers rushed to jump on the bandwagon, producing a wealth of licensed items that elevated Dopey,
Grumpy, Doc, Bashful, Sleepy, Happy, and Sneezy, as

well as Snow White, to the level of Mickey and other
earlier Disney characters as merchandising phenomena. Toys, dolls, games, costumes, storybooks, comic
books, clothing, umbrellas, food and drink, watches
and clocks, lamps and radios, jewelry, furniture--the
list of Snow White items is virtually endless.

SNO-1

SNO-1. Board Game,
1937. Johnson & Johnson Tek Toothbrushes. Board edge
held perforated playing pieces.
Complete With Slip Case Wrapper - **$35 $75 $125**
Board Only - **$15 $30 $50**

SNO-2

SNO-3

SNO-2. Snow White Mask,
1937. Procter And Gamble. At least nine, including Dwarfs
and Witch issued by Procter And Gamble and others.
Each - **$15 $35 $50**

SNO-3. Grumpy Mask,
1937. Proctor and Gamble. From Snow White series. -
$15 $30 $50

SNO-4

SNO-4. Movie Herald,
1938. Various theaters. - **$10 $15 $30**

SNO-5

SNO-5. "Snow White's Spice Roll" Recipe Folder,
1938. Texas Electric Service Co. Four-page leaflet featuring her and Happy. - **$10 $20 $35**

SNO-6

SNO-7

SNO-6. Gum Wrapper,
1938. Dietz Gum Co. Also see item SNO-9. -
$30 $50 $80

SNO-7. Dairy Glasses,
1938. Various sponsors. Set of eight. Several sets with
small height differences. Each - **$10 $15 $25**

SNO-8

SNO-8. "Moving Picture Machine",
1938. Pepsodent toothpaste.
Assembled With All 56 Pictures - **$125 $250 $375**
Unpunched - **$150 $375 $550**

SNO-9

SNO-9. Dietz Gum Co. Box,
1938. Held 100 packages. Also see item SNO-6. -
$75 $175 $300

SNO-10

SNO-11

SNO-10. "Jingle Club" Membership Request Card,
1938. Various retailers. Offers Jingle Book and membership button. - **$20 $40 $75**

SNO-11. "Jingle Book" With Mailer Envelope,
1938. Various retailers. Album for bread company pictures.
Envelope - **$8 $15 $25**
Book - **$25 $50 $90**

SNO-12   SNO-13

**SNO-12. "Snow White Jingle Club Member" Cello.
Button,**
1938. 1-1/4" size, widely distributed by businesses sponsoring the club. - **$10 $20 $30**

**SNO-13. "Snow White Jingle Club" 3-1/2" Cello.
Button,**
1938. Large version for employee of store participating in
club advertising promotion. - **$175 $300 $700**

SNO-14

SNO-14. Milk Glass Cereal Bowl,
1938. Post's Huskies Whole Wheat Flakes. - **$20 $40 $70**

SNO-15   SNO-16

SNO-15. Sleepy Beanie,
1938. - **$30 $60 $90**

SNO-16. Grape-Nuts Cereal Sign,
1938. Scarce. - **$75 $150 $300**

SNO-17

SNO-17. Palmolive Cut-Out Sheets,
c. 1938. European issue, set of 12 sheets.
Uncut Set - **$100 $200 $300**

SNO-18

SNO-19

SNO-18. Post Toasties Box Back With Cut-Outs,
c. 1938. Back Panel - **$10 $20 $30**

SNO-19. "Dopey's Christmas Tree" Book,
c. 1938. Various department stores. - **$25 $50 $75**

SNO-20

SNO-21

SNO-20. Snow White Paddle,
1938. Rare. Kraft premium. - **$30 $60 $120**

SNO-21. Bracelet - Painted,
1938. Small figure charms of Snow White and the Seven
Dwarfs. Store bought. - **$35 $60 $100**

SNO-22

SNO-23

SNO-22. Boxed Cut-Outs By Whitman,
1938. Store item. Unused Near Mint - **$250**
Boxed and Cut - **$50 $100 $150**

SNO-23. Paper Doll Book,
1938. Rare. Little Orphan Annie radio premium. Large
red version was made to replace regular paper doll give-
away book. See LAN-64 and 67.
Unpunched Book - **$300 $750 $1000**

SNO-24

SNO-25

**SNO-24. Department Store 18x25" Paper Hanger
Sign,**
c. 1938. Various stores. Same image both sides for
Christmas toy departments. - **$75 $175 $300**

**SNO-25. "Guards Of The Magic Forest" 18x20" Paper
Mounting Chart For Bread Premium Pictures,**
c. 1938. Unidentified bread company. Holds 36 cut-out pictures completing forest scene. Unused - **$100 $200 $300**
Completed - **$150 $300 $450**

SNO-26

SNO-27

SNO-26. "All Star Parade" Glass,
1939. From a set of dairy product containers picturing various Disney characters. - **$10 $20 $40**

SNO-27. Dopey Studio Fan Card,
c. 1939. - **$20 $40 $75**

SNO-28

**SNO-28. "Snow White And Seven Dwarfs Crocus
Bulbs" With Folder And Mailer,**
1948. Bab-O Cleanser of B. T. Babbitt, Inc. Folder
describes proper measures for successful growth of actual
crocus flowers from enclosed bulbs.
Near Mint Complete - **$100**
Mailer - **$20 $30 $50**
Folder - **$10 $25 $40**

SNO-29

SNO-29. "Dopey Bubble Gum Club" Secret Code Folder,
1940s. Yankee Doodle Gum Co. - **$20 $40 $75**

SNO-30

SNO-30. Bendix Washing Machines Comic,
1952. - **$10 $30 $75**

SNO-31

SNO-32

SNO-33

SNO-31. "The Milky Way" Comic Booklet,
1955. American Dairy Association. - **$10 $30 $75**

SNO-32. "Dairy Recipes" Booklet,
1955. American Dairy Association. - **$10 $20 $35**

SNO-33. "Mystery Of The Missing Magic" Comic,
1958. Various advertisers. - **$10 $20 $40**

SNO-35

SNO-34

SNO-34. Bread Labels,
1950s. Eight designs shown from set of sixteen.
Each - **$2 $4 $6**

SNO-35. Bread Label Picture,
1950s. Various sponsors. Holds 16 label cut-outs.
Completed - **$30 $100 $150**
Blank - **$20 $50 $100**

SNO-36

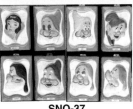

SNO-37

SNO-38

SNO-36. "Snow White" Paper Game,
1960s. Royal Gelatin. Complete - **$15 $30 $75**

SNO-37. Thin Plastic Wall Plaques,
1960s. Reynolds Wrap. Set. - **$10 $20 $40**

SNO-38. McDonald's Acrylic On Metal Pin,
1980s. - **$8 $15 $25**

SOUPY SALES

Born Milton "Soupbone" Hines in North Carolina in 1926, Soupy Sales grew up to become television's long-term clown and master of wacky pie-in-your-face humor. Wearing a battered top hat and giant polka-dot bow tie, his slapstick shows combined corny jokes, puns, zany conversations with animal puppets such as White Fang and Black Tooth, and the inevitable cream pies. After local television outings in Detroit in 1953, *The Soupy Sales Show* went national on ABC in 1955, again in 1959-1961, and in 1962 sponsored by Jell-O, and to syndication in 1965. *The New Soupy Sales Show* was syndicated in 1979-1980. Sales also hosted game shows and teen dance programs and made countless guest appearances on a number of variety programs. In the 1960s he created a popular dance called The Mouse. *The Official Soupy Sales Comic Book* was published in 1965. Items are usually copyrighted Soupy Sales--W.M.C. (Weston Merchandising Corp.)

SOU-1

SOU-2

SOU-3

SOU-1. "Soupy Sales Society" 3-1/2" Cello. Button,
1950s. - **$8 $15 $25**

SOU-2. "Soupy Sales Society Charter Member" 3-1/2" Cello. Button,
1965. - **$5 $10 $15**

SOU-3. "SSS" 3-1/2" Cello. Button,
c. 1965. - **$5 $10 $15**

SOU-4

(SOU-5 image)

SOU-5

SOU-4. "Soupy Sez" 3-1/2" Cello. Button,
c. 1965. - **$10 $20 $30**

SOU-5. "Soupy Sales" 3" Litho. Button,
1965. - **$20 $35 $60**

SOU-6

SOU-6. "Op-Yop" Toy Promotion Store Sign,
1968. Paper banner 11x34" for "Op-Yop Funtastic
Spinning Toy" by Kramer Designs. - **$35 $60 $100**

SOU-7

SOU-8

SOU-7. Miniature License Plate,
1960s. Marx Toys of Great Britain. 2-1/4x4" litho. tin possible prototype or probable limited issue example. -
$10 $20 $30

SOU-8. "Wallet-Size Photos" Display Box,
1960s. Topps Gum. Countertop box originally holding
gum/photo card packs. Empty Box - **$25 $50 $75**

SPACE MISC.

The mysteries of the stars have always fascinated
earth-bound humans, with poets and scientists alike
dreaming of soaring into space and exploring the planets. In the 20th century, even before Yuri Gagarin's
historic flight in 1961, there was Buck Rogers and
Flash Gordon and Captain Video. These and other
comic strip, film, and television heroes, along with toy
manufacturers, accounted for countless space-orient-
ed premiums and novelties--spaceships, rockets, exotic space guns, games, puzzles, and robots. In addition,
many items have been issued to commemorate events
in the ongoing official program of space exploration.

SMC-1

SMC-2

SMC-1. "Starr Of Space" Record,
c. 1953. Produced and recorded by Al Gannaway for Bill
Brody Company. 7x7" sleeve holds 78 rpm record featuring original cast of 1953-1954 radio series. - **$15 $30 $50**

SMC-2. "Space Guide" Mechanical Card,
1958. Swift's Premium franks and bacon. Diecut cardboard
with revolving disks to provide planetary information. -
$8 $15 $25

(SMC-3 image)

SMC-3

SMC-4

SMC-3. "Dan Dare" Cello. Button,
1950s. English issue for popular space hero of comics and
radio. - **$10 $20 $30**

SMC-4. "Dan Dare" Cello. Button,
1950s. English issue depicting him in space helmet. -
$10 $20 $30

SMC-5

SMC-5. Space Fantasy Scene Card,
1950s. Bond Bread. 3-1/2x6-1/4" ink blotter. - **$5 $10 $15**

SMC-6

SMC-7

**SMC-6. "Space Helmet And Rocket Ray Gun" Paper
Poster,**
1950s. General Electric refrigerators. Colorful 21x49"
poster offer for space toys to youngsters bringing parents
to "Roto-Cold" refrigerator demonstration. -
$100 $250 $400

SMC-7. "Speedy Spaceman" Toy With Cereal Box,
c. 1960. Nabisco Rice Honeys. Plastic figure activated by
loss of air from attached balloon following inflation.
Box - **$50 $75 $100**
Toy - **$10 $20 $30**

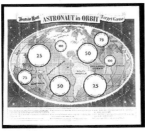

SMC-8

SMC-8. Astronaut In Orbit Target Game, Map And Parts,
1963. Tootsie Roll. Plastic launcher assembly parts and 17x20" paper target map in mailer box.
Near Mint Boxed Unassembled - **$100**
Assembled With Target - **$20 $40 $60**

SMC-9
SMC-10

SMC-9. Crater Critters,
1968. Kellogg's Apple Jacks. Pictured are five of the eight, vinyl figures, each about 3/4" to 1-1/4" tall.
Each - **$5 $10 $15**

SMC-10. Cereal Box Flat With Crater Critters Ad,
1968. Kellogg's Apple Jacks. - **$150 $300 $500**

SMC-11
SMC-12

SMC-11. "Captain Jet" Cello. Button,
1960s. "Channel 2" sponsorship includes CBS-TV logo. - **$12 $20 $30**

SMC-12. "Billy Blastoff" Toys Booklet,
1970s. Eldon Toys. Full color 16-page comic story booklet illustrating space, scuba and other toys in "Billy Blastoff" series. - **$5 $10 $15**

SPACE PATROL

High adventure in the wild, vast reaches of space! Missions of daring in the name of interplanetary justice! Led by Commander Buzz Corry, the crew of the spaceship Terra policed the galaxies for the United Planets of the 30th century, traveling through time and battling crazed scientists, space pirates, and weird creatures.

Space Patrol was first broadcast locally on KECA-TV in Los Angeles in March 1950. Six months later it went national on the ABC television and radio networks, where it aired until 1955. Corry, played by Ed Kemmer, was accompanied by young Cadet Happy (Smokin' rockets!), played by Lyn Osborne, and lovely Carol Karlyle, played by Virginia Hewitt, as they triumphed over such villains as Mr. Proteus, Captain Dagger, the Space Spider, and the evil Black Falcon, alias Prince Baccarratti.

The shows were sponsored by Ralston cereals (1951-1954) and Nestle foods (1954-1955), and dozens of program-related items were created for premium use and retail sales. Space suits, helmets, communicators, signal flashlights, a miniature spaceport, a rocket cockpit, Paralyzer Ray Gun, Cosmic Smoke Gun, trading cards, comic books and club membership material were among the available merchandise.

Many licensed items were sold by the May Stores on the west coast, but national distribution was limited. In 1952-1953, a wide variety of merchandise could be purchased through catalog flier order blanks from "Space Headquarters" Hollywood, California. In 1954 Ralston awarded a $30,000 replica of Buzz's spaceship to a young contest winner. Items are normally copyrighted Mike Moser Enterprises.

SPC-1

SPC-1. Plastic Dome Compass,
1951. Store item. Came with boxed wristwatch by US Time. - **$25 $50 $75**

SPC-2

SPC-2. "Space Patrol" Metal Buckle On "Jet-Glow" Belt,
1951. Decoder on back of buckle, belts usually no longer glow. Complete - **$75 $175 $250**
Buckle Only - **$40 $75 $125**

SPC-3

SPC-4

SPC-3. Membership Card,
1952. - **$15 $60 $100**

SPC-4. Official Catalogue,
1952. Shows 22 items priced for sale. - **$35 $75 $125**

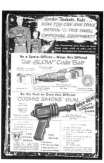

SPC-5

SPC-6

SPC-5. Wheat Chex Cereal Box - 12 oz.,
1952. "Jet Glow" code belt and cosmic smoke gun pictured on back. Membership kit offer. Shows badge. - **$75 $225 $375**

SPC-6. Ralston Club Membership Kit,
1952. Letter, handbook, photo, envelope.
Complete Near Mint - **$300**
Handbook - **$50 $75 $150**
Others, Each - **$10 $20 $35**

SPC-7

SPC-8

SPC-7. "TV Digest" With Cover Article,
1952. Weekly issue for October 11 with two-page article including photos. - **$15 $25 $50**

SPC-8. Space Patrol Premium Offer Sheet,
c. 1952. Ralston Cereals. Instruction for Cosmic Smoke Gun plus offer of member insignia and kit. - **$10 $20 $30**

SPC-9

SPC-9. "Chart Of The Universe" 8x11",
1952. - **$50 $100 $175**

SPC-10

SPC-10. "Space Patrol" Comic Book Vol. 1 #1,
1952. Back cover premium ad. - **$60 $200 $650**

SPC-11

SPC-12

SPC-11. "Space Patrol" Vol. 1 #2 Comic Book,
Oct.-Nov. 1952. Store item by Approved Comics. - **$50 $150 $465**

SPC-12. Cosmic Smoke Gun,
1952. Smaller 4-1/2" size in red plastic. - **$75 $125 $240**

SPC-19

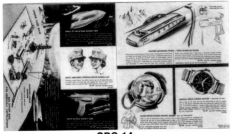

SPC-13

SPC-13. Space-O-Phone Set,
1952. Boxed - **$50 $75 $150**
Phones Only - **$25 $50 $75**

SPC-19. "Outer Space Plastic Helmet",
1952. Store item and also used as a contest prize.
Includes inflatable vinyl piece that fits around neck.
Near Mint Boxed - **$1000**
Helmet Only - **$150 $250 $400**

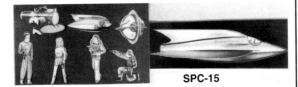

SPC-14

SPC-20

SPC-21

**SPC-14. "Lunar Fleet Base" Instruction
Sheet/Premium Catalogue,**
1952. - **$50 $125 $175**

**SPC-20. Rice Chex Cardboard Hanging Mobile Store
Display,**
1953. Scarce. Each part printed identically on both sides,
largest part is 27" wide. - **$300 $900 $1300**

**SPC-21. "Magic Space Pictures" Five-Part Diecut
Cardboard Store Ceiling Mobile,**
1953. Scarce. Ralston Wheat Chex. Hanger display with
20" wide upper title part. - **$300 $900 $1300**

SPC-15

SPC-15. Ralston "Lunar Fleet Base",
1952. Rare. Plastic parts shown, set also includes cardboard buildings, etc. Near Mint In Mailer - **$3000**
Complete Used - **$300 $1000 $1600**

SPC-23

SPC-16

SPC-17

SPC-18

SPC-22

SPC-22. Plastic Microscope,
1953. Came with plastic slides. Complete -
$60 $100 $160

SPC-16. Plastic Badge,
1952. Metallic red, blue, and silver finish. -
$75 $150 $300

SPC-17. Cosmic Glow Rocket Ring,
1952. Unmarked Space Patrol premium plastic holding
glow-in-dark powder in viewer. - **$400 $750 $1200**

SPC-23. Ralston Cardboard "Outer Space Helmet",
1953. Includes one-way viewing panel.
Near Mint With Mailer - **$200**
Complete Helmet - **$60 $80 $150**

SPC-18. "Space Patrol Blood Boosters" Litho. Tin Tab,
1952. - **$35 $70 $125**

SPC-25

SPC-24

SPC-26

SPC-24. Magic Space Picture,
1953. Set of 24. Each - **$12 $25 $30**

SPC-25. Binoculars,
1953. Green plastic premium issue, black plastic store
item. Each - **$50 $85 $150**

SPC-26. "Terra V" Rocket Film Projector,
1953. Also known as the Project-O-Scope. Four strips with
six frames each. Projector - **$75 $175 $300**
Film - **$35 $90 $125**
Instructions - **$30 $60 $90**

SPC-28

SPC-27

SPC-27. "Interplanetary Coin Album",
1953. Schwinn Bicycles, others. Slotted for 24-coin set
plus supplemental Schwinn coins. - **$60 $150 $200**

**SPC-28. "Interplanetary Space Patrol Credits" Plastic
Coin,**
1953. Four denominations each for Moon, Saturn, Terra in
gold, blue, black or silver (most common).
Silver - **$3 $8 $12**
Other Colors - **$5 $12 $20**

SPC-30

SPC-29

SPC-29. Wheat Chex Cereal Box - 12 oz.,
1953. Cadet Happy and magic space picture offer shown
on front. Microscope kit offer on side. -
$100 $250 $400

SPC-30. Christmas Catalogue Mailing Folder,
c. 1953. Shows 13 items priced for sale. - **$40 $90 $135**

SPC-31

SPC-31. "Ralston Rocket" Card,
c. 1953. - **$25 $80 $125**

SPC-33

SPC-32

SPC-32. Ralston "Buzz Corry Color Book",
c. 1953. Example picture shows both covers. -
$30 $70 $100

SPC-33. Smoke Gun,
c. 1953. 6" green metallic. Came on card with smoke packets "Good For 10,000 Safe Shots".
Gun Only - **$100 $250 $300**
On Card - **$200 $450 $600**

SPC-34

SPC-35

SPC-34. Man-From-Mars Totem Head,
1954. Includes silvered one-way plastic sheet for viewing.
In Envelope - **$40 $75 $150**
Assembled - **$25 $50 $75**

**SPC-35. Periscope Cardboard Assembly Kit In Mailer
Envelope,**
1954. Near Mint In Envelope - **$400**
Assembled - **$50 $175 $250**

SPC-36

SPC-37

SPC-36. Hydrogen Ray Gun Ring,
1954. - **$150 $240 $325**

SPC-37. Ralston Trading Card,
1950s. Wheat and Rice Chex. One card insert per box, set of 40. Star And Planets Series (13) - **$5 $10 $25**
Rockets, Jets And Weapons Series (14) - **$5 $10 $25**
Space Heroes Series (13) - **$5 $10 $25**
Except Buzz Corry-Cadet Happy Each - **$8 $20 $45**

SPC-39

SPC-38

SPC-38. Cast Photos Folder,
1950s. Dr. Ross dog & cat food. Front cover has photo, back cover facsimile signatures. - **$50 $80 $150**

SPC-39. Plastic Frame Character Charms,
1950s. Unsure if Ralston premium or vending machine issue. Each - **$10 $30 $40**

SPC-41

SPC-40

SPC-40. "Space Patrol" Title Printer Plastic Ring,
1950s. Top has "Space Patrol" printed backwards for correct stamped image after inking from included tiny ink pad.
Complete -**$350 $475 $600**
Missing Ink Pad - **$125 $175 $250**

SPC-41. Plastic Dart Gun,
1950s. Store item. Sold with two darts.
Complete - **$50 $75 $125**
Gun Only - **$30 $50 $75**

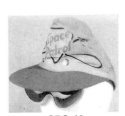

SPC-42

SPC-43

SPC-42. Fabric "Cosmic Cap",
1950s. Store item by Bailey of Hollywood. -
$75 $150 $250

SPC-43. Gun & Holster Set
1950s. Holster has rare silver Space Patrol Cadet badge on top of flap. Blue telescope gun is unmarked & has whistle on butt of gun.
Holster With Badge - **$100 $200 $300**
Blue Gun - **$15 $25 $40**

SPC-44

SPC-45

SPC-44. Plastic Rocketship Barrette,
1950s. Store item by Ben-Hur. On Card - **$40 $100 $150**

SPC-45. Plastic Gun Barrette,
1950s. Store item by Ben-Hur. On Card - **$40 $100 $150**

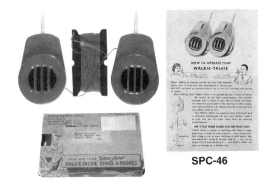

SPC-46

SPC-46. Walkie Talkies With Box & Instructions,
1950s. Scarce. Communication line with two plastic red walkie talkies. Rare Space Patrol premium box has Space graphics on back with Commander Cory on front.
Complete - **$150 $375 $525**

SPC-47

SPC-47. Plastic "Emergency Kit",
1950s. Store item by Regis Space Toys. Handle contains flashlight. Complete - **$300 $600 $1500**
Box and Yellow Insert - **$100 $200 $400**

SPC-48   **SPC-49**

SPC-48. "Commander" Vinyl Rain Hat With Cardboard Tag,
1950s. Store item by Marketon Co. with license of Space Patrol Enterprises. Hat - **$50 $100 $175**
Tag - **$20 $50 $75**

SPC-49. "Space Patrol Cadet" Silvered Metal Badge,
1950s. Made in Japan. Near Mint On Card - **$350**
Badge Only - **$75 $175 $275**

SPC-50

SPC-50. "United Planets Treasury Department Top Secret Diplomatic Pouch" Set,
early 1950s. 11-1/2x11-1/2" portfolio holding Space Patrol stationery, United Planets currency bills, full color United Planets stamps, 16-page color stamp album, United Planets plastic coins and coin album.
Complete - **$75 $125 $200**

SPEED GIBSON OF THE I.S.P.

Young Speed Gibson, at the age of 15, was an ace pilot and member of the International Secret Police in this radio adventure series that was syndicated briefly in 1937-1938. Speed, along with his uncle, top agent Clint Barlow, and pilot Barney Dunlap, circled the globe in their ship The Flying Clipper on the trail of the criminal Octopus gang. "Suffering whang-doodles, Speed."

SGB-1

SGB-1. Code Book Manual,
c. 1937. Dreikorn's Orange Wrap Bread. Includes membership card and oath to sign. - **$40 $100 $175**

SGB-2

SGB-2. Adventure Map With Promotion Record And Envelope,
c. 1937. Peter Pan Bakery and others.
Map - **$50 $150 $250**
Promotion Record - **$15 $40 $50**
Envelope - **$5 $20 $25**

SGB-3   **SGB-4**

SGB-3. "African Adventure And Clue Hunt" Map,
c. 1937. Brown's Bread Ltd. (Canada). - **$65 $250 $300**

SGB-4. "Wings" Newspaper #1,
c. 1937. Cote's Master Loaf Bread. - **$20 $75 $100**

SGB-5   **SGB-6**

SGB-5. I.S.P. Club Membership Application Postcard,
c. 1937. Offers free Code Book and Badge for submission of grocer's name. - **$10 $20 $30**

SGB-6. "Speed Gibson's Bread" Store Sign,
c. 1937. Paper poster 10x17" including club membership offer text plus local imprint for radio station. -
$50 $100 $150

SGB-7   **SGB-8**

SGB-7. "Rocket-Gyro X-3" Balsa/Cardboard Flying Toy With Mailer,
c. 1937. "Hikes" chocolate-coated wheat cereal.
Assembled toy flown by rubber band.
Near Mint With Mailer - **$160**
Without Mailer - **$25 $75 $110**

SGB-8. Stroehmann's Bread "Prize Winner" Cello. Badge,
c. 1937. Various sponsors.
With Stroehmann's Imprint - **$12 $20 $35**
Other Company Imprints - **$15 $30 $60**

SGB-9   SGB-10   SGB-11

SGB-9. "Secret Police I.S.P." Litho. Club Member Button,
c. 1937. - **$10 $25 $35**

SGB-10. Member's Small Blue/Silvered Brass Button,
c. 1937. Phil A. Halle. - **$12 $40 $50**

SGB-11. Gorman's Bread "Speed Gibson Flying Police" Enameled Brass Badge,
c. 1937. - **$20 $50 $75**

SGB-13

SGB-12

SGB-12. Badge,
1937. Dreikorn's Bread. Flying Police Badge, shaped like a shield. - **$25 $50 $75**

SGB-13. Badge,
1937. Dreikorn's Bread. Long Flying Police Badge, with two stars on it. - **$30 $60 $90**

SGB-14   SGB-15

SGB-14. "Speed Gibson Flying Corps I.S.P." Brass Badge,
c. 1937. Pictures him in aviator helmet above airplane. - **$50 $125 $175**

SGB-15. I.S.P. "Canadian Division" Club Card,
c. 1937. Back has code used during Speed Gibson African adventures. - **$25 $75 $100**

SGB-16

SGB-17

SGB-16. "Speed Gibson/Secret Police I.S.P." Canadian Cello. Button,
c. 1937. Made by Shaw Mfg. Co., Toronto. - **$20 $50 $90**

SGB-17. "Speed Gibson's Great Clue Hunt" Paper Sheet,
1938. Unidentified bread company. Pencil activity sheet for following radio broadcasts. Rare. - **$65 $250 $350**

SPEEDY ALKA-SELTZER

Alka-Seltzer, an antacid/analgesic combination tablet, was first marketed in 1931 by Miles Laboratories of Elkhart, Indiana. From 1951 to 1964 product promotion featured a perky little fellow with a prominent forelock and a tablet for a hat. Originally called Sparky, Speedy evolved into a popular spokesfigure in television commercials and in promotional items issued by the manufacturer. Speedy is translated as Pron-Tito in Spanish.

SAS-3

SAS-1

SAS-2

SAS-1. Bank 5-1/2" Rubber Figure,
1950s. Earliest version with word "Bank" below coin slot on top of hat, later version without word.
First Version - **$75 $300 $450**
Later Version - **$65 $250 $350**

SAS-2. Cardboard Store Display,
1950s. - **$75 $125 $150**

SAS-3. "Speedy Alka-Seltzer" Enameled Brass Figural Pin,
c. 1950s. Back has threaded post fastener for lapel or button hole. - **$20 $40 $60**

SAS-4

SAS-4. "Pron-Tito" Spanish Translation Sign,
1962. Cardboard 21x28" with full color art. -
$50 $85 $125

SAS-7

SAS-6

SAS-5

SAS-5. Store Display 8" Vinyl Figure,
1960s. - **$200 $500 $800**

SAS-6. "Pron-Tito" Spanish Litho. Tray,
1960s. - **$50 $100 $150**

SAS-7. Small Flicker Sheet,
1960s. About 1-1/2" square with "Pron Tito" name on his hat. He holds magician's wand and when tilted, a glass of the product appears. - **$15 $40 $60**

THE SPIDER

Created by pulp author R.T.M. Scott in the 1930s, the Spider was actually Richard Wentworth, a wealthy New York crime fighter who divided his time between battling master criminals and hiding his true identity from the police. In the 1933 tale *Spider Strikes* and in the pulps into the 1940s, Wentworth's symbol, the drawing of a red spider, marked the foreheads of his vanquished and deceased criminal opponents. The same symbol appears on the pulp magazine club ring.

SPD-1

SPD-2

SPD-1. Movie Theater Club Member Card,
1938. Columbia Pictures. Rare. For 15-episode serial "The Spider Web" based on "The Spider Magazine" stories. -
$50 $250 $300

SPD-2. Spider Enameled Metal Ring,
1939. Scarce. Spider Magazine and theater give-away. -
$1500 $4500 $9200

SPD-3

SPD-3. "The Spider Returns" Movie Serial 9x10-1/2" Handbill,
1941. Columbia Pictures. - **$20 $40 $60**

SPD-4

SPD-5

SPD-4. "The Spider Returns" Movie Serial 9x12" Handbill,
1941. Columbia Pictures for local theater imprint. -
$25 $50 $85

SPD-5. "The Spider Returns" Movie Pressbook,
1941. Columbia Pictures. Contents show ring, example of pulp cover, club card, mask. -
$100 $200 $350

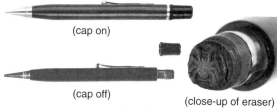

(cap on)

(cap off)

(close-up of eraser)

SPD-6

SPD-6. Cello. Mechanical Pencil With "The Spider" Eraser,
c. 1942. Rare. The Spider pulp magazine. End cap covers rubber eraser with image on top surface. Succeeded Spider ring as premium, produced in very limited quantity. - **$300 $1250 $2050**

SPIDER-MAN

Writer Stan Lee and artist Steve Ditko created *Spider-Man* for the Marvel Comics Group in the 1960s and the superhero has been battling for justice ever since. *Spider-Man* debuted in *Amazing Fantasy* #15 in August 1962. Six months later he appeared in his own comic book, the start of a series that continues to this day. (A syndicated newspaper strip started publication in 1979.) Teenage Peter Parker, who acquired his super-human powers after being bitten by a radioactive spider, takes on a variety of villains and criminals, all the while working as a photographer for the New York *Daily Bugle* and struggling with the problems of a typical 1962 adolescent. In recent years, Peter has taken on the added responsibility of marriage to his long-time girlfriend Mary Jane.

On television an animated *Spider-Man* series aired on ABC from 1967 to 1970, and *Spider-Man and His Amazing Friends* appeared on NBC in 1981. A 1977 live-action CBS special with Nicholas Hammond was followed by a brief prime-time series in 1978 and scattered repeats for a year. The character was also featured on *The Electric Company*, speaking only in word balloons visible on the screen. In 1995 Ralston Foods introduced Spider-Man sweetened rice cereal, complete with trading cards inside specially marked boxes. Fox television launched an animated version of the popular character in 1994 with Christopher Daniel Barnes voicing Peter Parker/Spider-Man. Like Fox's (now WB's) *Batman* series, the guest voices were supplied by a veritable who's who of Hollywood. Ed Asner played J. Jonah Jameson, Martin Landau voiced the Scorpion, Roscoe Lee Brown supplied the voice for the Kingpin, and Mark Hamill (*Batman*'s Joker) voiced Hobgoblin. *Spider-Man* ended its original run of episodes in February 1998. In the last few years, numerous Spider-toys have appeared, chiefly from Toy Biz. Merchandised items are usually copyrighted Marvel Comics.

SPM-1

SPM-2

SPM-3

SPM-1. "The Amazing Spider-Man" 3-1/2" Cello. Button,
1966. Store item. #6 from numbered series.
Near Mint Bagged - **$35**
Loose - **$10 $15 $25**

SPM-2. Litho. Metal Bicycle Attachment Plate,
1967. Store item by Marx Toys. - **$12 $25 $50**

SPM-3. "Hong Kong" Vending Machine Aluminum Ring,
1960s. - **$15 $25 $50**

SPM-4

SPM-5

SPM-4. Spider-Man Vitamins Ring,
1976. Hudson Pharmaceutical Co. - **$30 $45 $75**

SPM-5. Spidey Super Stories Record,
1977. Peter Pan Records and Children's Television Workshop. Features Electric Company cast in "Spider-Man is Born" and 7 other stories. Narrated by Morgan Freeman. - **$3 $5 $8**

SPM-6

SPM-7

SPM-8

SPM-6. Plastic Magnetic Compass,
1978. - **$5 $10 $15**

SPM-7. "Spider-Man" 2-1/4" Cello. Button,
1978. Store item by Rainbow Designs. - **$3 $8 $12**

SPM-8. "Make Mine Marvel" Cello. Button,
c. 1970s. Marvel Comics promotion featuring Spider-Man image. - **$5 $10 $15**

THE SPIRIT

The Spirit was created by Will Eisner in 1940 in the unusual form of a comic book insert to be included with the comic sections of Sunday newspapers. The feature, distributed by the Register and Tribune Syndicate, survived until 1952, accompanied by a daily strip from 1941 to 1944. *The Spirit*--actually Denny Colt, a Central City crime fighter in a meager eye mask--has become a strip classic. There have been numerous comic book reprints from the 1940s into the 1990s, and a TV series pilot was broadcast in 1987. A brand new comic book series, *The Spirit--The New Adventures*, debuted in 1998 from Kitchen Sink Press with creator Eisner supervising some of the most popular modern comic book professionals.

SPR-1

SPR-1. "Paper Mask",
c. 1942. Various newspapers for Sunday comic book supplement beginning June 1940. - **$75 $250 $400**

SPR-2   SPR-3

SPR-2. "Star Journal" Cello. Button,
c. 1942. Various newspapers. For Sunday comic book supplement. - **$40 $80 $150**

SPR-3. "Minneapolis Morning Tribune" Cello. Button,
c. 1942. Announcement for daily comic strip. -
$50 $100 $ 175

SPR-4

SPR-4. "The Spirit" Example Of Weekly Newspaper Comic Insert,
1940s. Various newspapers 1940-1952. Prices vary widely by issue date, artist, condition. Consult "Overstreet Comic Book Price Guide".

SPY SMASHER

Playboy Alan Armstrong took on the identity of *Spy Smasher* to battle America's domestic enemies for Fawcett Publications during World War II. The caped crusader made his debut in *Whiz Comics* #1 in 1940, had his own comic book from 1941 to 1943, made a brief appearance as *Crime Smasher* in 1948, and finally was allowed to expire in 1953. Republic Pictures released a 12-episode chapter play in 1942 starring Kane Richmond in a life-and-death struggle against Nazi agents. Like Captain Marvel, the Marvel Family and the rest of the Fawcett Characters, Spy Smasher is now the property of DC Comics. He recently resurfaced on the cover of *The Power of Shazam* #24 (1997).

SPY-1

SPY-2

SPY-3

SPY-1. Fawcett Picture,
c. 1941. Title inscription "Hero Of Whiz Comics And Spy Smasher Comics". - **$75 $150 $225**

SPY-2. "I Am A Spy Smasher" Litho. Button,
c. 1941. For comic book club member. - **$15 $25 $50**

SPY-3. "Spy Smasher" Argentine 27x41" Movie Serial Paper Poster,
1942. - **$50 $125 $200**

SPY-4

SPY-5

SPY-4. "Spy Smasher" 27x41" Movie Serial Poster,
1942. Republic Pictures. - **$200 $400 $750**

SPY-5. Movie Three-Sheet,
1942. Republic Pictures serial. - **$2000 $4000 $6000**

SPY-6

SPY-6. "Victory Batallion" Member Card,
c. 1942. Fawcett Publications. - **$50 $100 $200**

STAR TREK

The *Star Trek* phenomenon, originating in the futuristic Gene Roddenberry TV series that aired on NBC from 1966 to 1969, has grown over the years into an international community of devoted fans, generating four additional TV series, eight movies, dozens of books, comic books, an animated cartoon, countless Trekkie conventions, and millions of dollars in licensed merchandise.

On television *Star Trek* was followed by *Star Trek: The Animated Series* (1973), *Star Trek: The Next Generation* (1987), *Star Trek: Deep Space Nine* (1993), and *Star Trek: Voyager* (1995). The first movie--*Star Trek-The Motion Picture* (1979)--was followed by *Star Trek II: The Wrath of Khan* (1982), *Star Trek III: The Search for Spock* (1984), *Star Trek IV: The Voyage*

Home (1986), *Star Trek V: The Final Frontier* (1989), *Star Trek VI: The Undiscovered Country* (1991), *Star Trek: Generations* (1994), and *Star Trek: First Contact* (1996), with a ninth planned for November 1998. Captain Kirk (William Shatner) has been succeeded by Captain Picard (Patrick Stewart), Captain Sisko (Avery Brooks), and Captain Janeway (Kate Mulgrew). Spock (Leonard Nimoy) and the rest of the original crew may be gone, but the U.S.S. Enterprise and the U.S.S. Voyager continue to boldly cruise the galaxies, where no man has gone before, well into the future. Paramount Pictures holds the copyright.

STR-1

STR-1. Action Fleet Punch-Out Mobile,
1978. M&M/Mars Inc. Includes six punch-out sheets, instruction sheet, poster. In Envelope - **$20 $35 $50**

STR-2   STR-3

STR-2. "The Bridge" McDonald's Meal Box,
1979. Two versions: Reverse panel pictures Mr. Spock or Dr. McCoy. Unused/Flat - **$5 $12 $25**

STR-3. "Spacesuit" McDonald's Meal Box,
1979. Unused/Flat - **$5 $12 $25**

STR-4   STR-5

STR-4. "Klingons" McDonald's Meal Box,
1979. Unused/Flat - **$5 $12 $25**

STR-5. "Transporter" McDonald's Meal Box,
1979. Unused Flat - **$5 $12 $25**

STR-6   STR-7

STR-6. "United Federation Of Planets" McDonald's Meal Box,
1979. Unused/Flat - **$5 $12 $25**

STR-7. McDonald's Plastic Secret Compartment Ring,
1979. Set of four: Kirk, Spock, U.S.S. Enterprise, insignia. Each - **$20 $40 $60**

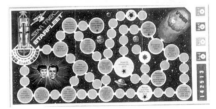

STR-8

STR-8. Star Fleet Game,
1979. McDonald's. - **$5 $8 $12**

STR-9

STR-9. Matches,
1979. Promo for *Star Trek-The Motion Picture*. Premium offer inside. - **$5 $10 $15**

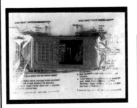

STR-10   STR-11

STR-10. "Star Trek Video Communicator" Packaged Toy,
1979. McDonald's Happy Meals. Unopened packet contains 4" plastic toy with full color picture strip from series of five. Each Sealed - **$3 $6 $10**
Each Loose - **$1 $3 $5**

STR-11. "Star Trek Navigation Bracelet" Toy,
1979. McDonald's Happy Meals. Unopened packet containing 9" plastic bracelet plus sheet with color portrait stickers, paper scene strip for bracelet viewer.
Sealed - **$3 $6 $10**
Loose - **$1 $3 $5**

STR-12

STR-12. Spoon Premium,
1970s. - **$30 $40 $60**

STR-13

STR-14

STR-13. Twentieth Anniversary 3" Plastic Badge,
1986. - **$5 $10 $15**

STR-14. Pocket Books 2-1/4" Tin Tab,
1986. - **$10 $15 $25**

STR-15

STR-15. Cheerios Box With First Promotion For Star Trek The Next Generation,
1987. Boxes contained six different sticker portraits to determine winners of 75,000 replicas of Enterprise (4" pale blue vinyl) by Galoob. Box - **$30 $75 $150**
Each Sticker - **$5 $10 $20**
Replica - **$75 $150 $250**

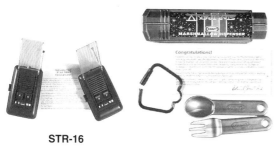

STR-16

STR-17

STR-16. Walkie-Talkie Communicators,
1989. P.J. McNerney & Associates. *Star Trek V* film tie-in offered by Procter & Gamble. Also came with instruction sheet. - **$25 $50 $75**

STR-17. Marshmallow Dispenser and Utensils,
1989. Kraft premium offered in conjunction with *Star Trek V*. Includes plastic dispenser, fork, spoon, and belt hook. Letter signed by "Admiral James T. Kirk" congratulates recipient. - **$10 $20 $35**

STR-18

STR-18. Sign,
1991. Space exploration stamp promo. Also promotes *Star Trek VI*. - **$25 $50 $75**

STAR WARS

George Lucas' movie trilogy--St*ar Wars* (1977), *The Empire Strikes Back* (1980), and *Return of the Jedi* (1983)--chronicles the battle between good and evil a long time ago in a galaxy far, far away. Luke Skywalker (Mark Hamill), Princess Leia (Carrie Fisher), and Han Solo (Harrison Ford), along with Chewbacca the Wookiee and the droids C-3PO and R2D2, lead the Rebel Alliance in their epic struggle against Darth Vader and the Imperial Forces of the Empire. The phenomenal success of the films has spawned a world of merchandised items--action figures, comic books, novels, video games, trading cards, etc. An audio adaptation was broadcast on National Public Radio in 1980. The movies were digitally remastered for home video in 1995, and enhanced versions of the films were re-released theatrically as "Special Editions" in 1997, with additional scenes and all-new special effects. These releases were the prelude to the first new Star Wars films in fifteen years--"Episode I" of the Star Wars saga will debut in the summer of 1999, with two sequels to follow (the original trilogy serve as Episodes IV-VI). The new trilogy will chronicle the rise and fall of Luke's father, Anakin, fated to transform into the evil Darth Vader. If the first trilogy is any indication, these prequels should spawn a whole new interest in the series, with plenty of new merchandise to collect and enjoy.

STW-1

STW-1. Lucky Charms Box,
1977. General Mills. Offers four "Character Stick-ons". -
$5 $10 $20

STW-2

STW-2. Cocoa Puffs Box,
1977. General Mills. Offers four "Robot" stick-ons. -
$5 $10 $20

STW-3

STW-3. Trix Box,
1977. General Mills. Offers four "Creature" stick-ons. -
$5 $10 $20

STW-4

STW-4. Cantina Adventure Set,
1977. Store item by Kenner. Sears Exclusive with blue
Snaggletooth figure. - **$100 $200 $300**

STW-5

STW-5. Boxed Ring Set,
1977. Store item. 20th Century Fox Film Corp. copyright
depicting R2-D2, Darth Vader, C-3PO.
Near Mint Boxed Set - **$15**
Each - **$2 $3 $4**

STW-6

STW-6. "Star Wars 16 Trading Cards" Signs,
1977. Wonder Bread. 12x16" poster sign and 5-1/2x18"
shelf sign for cards packaged in bread loaves.
Poster - **$30 $60 $100**
Shelf Card - **$10 $25 $50**

STW-7

**STW-7. Lucky Charms Cereal Box With Hang Gliders
Offer,**
1978. Boxes included four different punch-outs.
Box - **$50 $75 $150**
Punch-Outs Each - **$10 $20 $40**

STW-8   STW-9

STW-8. "Star Wars Weekly" Vol. 1 #1,
February 8, 1978. English edition by Marvel Comics
International. - **$5 $10 $15**

STW-9. Cello. Button,
1978. From 14-button set depicting the characters. Each -
$5 $12 $20

STW-10

STW-10. Procter & Gamble 19x20" Paper Posters,
1978. Set of three. Set - **$10 $20 $35**

STW-11

STW-12

STW-13

STW-11. "The Empire Strikes Back" Cards,
1980. Burger King. Set of 36. Set - **$10 $20 $30**

STW-12. Radio Promotion Cello. Button,
1981. National Public Radio/KBPS. Lucasfilms copyright. -
$10 $15 $30

STW-13. Cookie Box,
1983. Pepperidge Farms. Complete - **$10 $20 $35**

STW-14

STW-14. "Return of the Jedi" Poster,
1983. 17-1/2x22" premium promotional poster from Oral B
Star Wars Toothbrush. Shows set of six at bottom with
coupons. Poster With Coupons - **$10 $20 40**
Without Coupons - **$5 $10 20**

STEVE CANYON

Following his success with *Terry and the Pirates*,
Milton Caniff created his *Steve Canyon* comic strip for
distribution by Field Enterprises in 1947. Canyon, who
runs a small airline, finds adventure and exotic women
in all corners of the globe as he fights criminals and
international spies. As the Cold War progresses, he
sees service in Korea, Vietnam, and other hot spots,
frequently doing battle with dangerous women. Comic
books appeared in the late 1940s and 1950s, a radio
adaptation with Barry Sullivan was syndicated in 1948,
and a TV series with Dean Fredericks aired on NBC in
1958-1959 and was rerun on ABC in 1960. The newspaper strip ended publication in 1988. Items are copyrighted Field Enterprises Inc.

STV-1   STV-2

STV-1. "Steve Canyon" Newspaper Club Cello. Button,
c. 1947. New Journal Comic. - **$15 $35 $75**

**STV-2. "Copper Calhoon With Steve Canyon"
Newspaper Club Cello. Button,**
c. 1947. New Journal Comic. From same series as preceding item with "Calhoon" name as spelled. - **$15 $30 $65**

STV-3   STV-4

STV-3. "P.I." Cello. Button,
c. 1947. - **$40 $75 $125**

**STV-4. "Daily Record/Sunday Advertiser" Cello.
Button,**
c. 1950. Various newspapers. - **$50 $115 $175**

STV-5   STV-6

STV-5. "Steve Canyon's Airagers" Wings Litho. Tab,
1950s. - **$15 $25 $40**

STV-6. Space Goggles On Picture Card,
1950s. Store item by Rock Industries. Gold finish slitted
plastic goggles of similar nature to sunglasses.
Carded - **$15 $30 $50**

STV-7

STV-7. Chesterfield Cigarettes "Meet Steve Canyon-NBC TV" 21x22" Cardboard Store Poster,
1950s. - **$35 $60 $100**

STRAIGHT ARROW

Straight Arrow was a Western adventure radio series that was broadcast from 1948 to 1951, first on the Don Lee network on the west coast, and starting in 1949 on the Mutual network nationally. The series was created for the National Biscuit Company as a means of promoting Nabisco shredded wheat. Boxtop premiums, on-package items, and retail products were offered in impressive quantities, all related to his scripted adventures.

Straight Arrow was actually young Steve Adams, owner of the Broken Bow Ranch, until innocent people were threatened or evil-doers plotted against justice. Then Adams would ride to his secret cave, mount his golden palomino Fury, and gallop out of the darkness as Straight Arrow, a Comanche warrior ready to fight for law and order. Howard Culver played Adams, and Fred Howard was his sidekick Packy McCloud.

Among the *Straight Arrow* premiums were several rings, a Mystic Wrist Kit containing an arrowhead and cowrie shell, an arrowhead flashlight, Indian war drum, bandanna, patch, and feathered headband. Sets of Injun-Uity cards, originally packaged in the cereal boxes, were later reissued as bound volumes.

Straight Arrow comic books with sales reaching one million per month, were published from 1950 to 1956, many containing advertisements for the program's premiums and other merchandise. A daily newspaper strip distributed by the Bell Syndicate appeared from 1950 to 1952. "Kaneewah, Fury!"

STA-1

STA-1. Large 20x36" Diecut Cardboard Store Sign,
c. 1948. Promotes radio series on Mutual Network. - **$600 $1500 $2500**

STA-2. Two-Red Feathered Headband With Mailer,
1948. Includes two feathers. A second version has a 1949 copyright and says "Nabisco Shredded Wheat" under portrait. Near Mint In Mailer - **$175**
Headband Only - **$50 $80 $135**

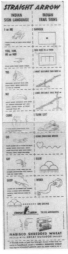

STA-3

STA-4

STA-3. "Indian Sign Language/Indian Trail Signs" Paper,
1948. Came with headband. - **$25 $50 $100**

STA-4. Standee,
1948. 5' 7" tall. Promotes Mutual Network Radio show. - **$800 $1700 $2800**

STA-2

STA-5

STA-6

STA-5. Radio Broadcast Reminder 12x15" Cardboard Store Sign,
1949. Diecut to extend feathers at top edge. - **$125 $250 $400**

STA-6. Store Display Framed Picture,
1949. Nabisco. Display promotion for set of 12 jigsaw puzzles of matching illustrations to the framed pictures. Example pictured is titled "Straight Arrow With Packy And Fury, To The Rescue." - **$40 $60 $125**

STA-8

STA-9

STA-7

STA-7. "Book One" Box Insert Cards,
1949. Set of 36. Each - **$1** **$2** **$3**

STA-8. Bandanna,
1949. - **$20** **$30** **$50**

STA-9. Bandanna Gold Plastic Slide,
1949. - **$25** **$38** **$50**

STA-10

STA-11

STA-10. Gold Luster Metal Spring Tie Clip,
1949. Scarce. Bar image of arrow. - **$75** **$200** **$300**

STA-11. War Drum,
1949. Complete Boxed - **$75** **$200** **$300**
Drum Only - **$50** **$100** **$200**

STA-12

STA-13

STA-14

STA-12. War Drum,
1949. 12" tall cardboard/thin rubber with beater stick.
Complete - **$65** **$125** **$200**

STA-13. Jigsaw Puzzle,
1949. Set of 12. Each In Envelope - **$15** **$25** **$40**
Loose - **$5** **$15** **$15**
Box For 10 Puzzles (Rare) - **$50** **$150** **$225**

STA-14. Nabisco Shredded Wheat 4x10" Cardboard Display Sign,
c. 1949. - **$150** **$250** **$400**

STA-15

STA-16

STA-15. Radio/Comic Strip Pressbook,
1950. Rare. Contains comic strips, list of premiums, sales information. - **$200** **$600** **$800**

STA-16. Straight Arrow Coloring Book,
1950. Premium and store item. - **$25** **$100** **$175**

STA-18

STA-17

STA-19

STA-17. Mystic Wrist Kit Instructions,
1950. Instructions on how to use kit also explains hidden secret word on bottom. - **$15** **$30** **$50**

STA-18. Mystic Wrist Kit,
1950. Gold plastic bracelet with container holding arrowhead and cowrie shell. Near Mint Boxed - **$200**
Bracelet and Parts - **$50** **$100** **$150**
Insert - **$10** **$20** **$30**

STA-19. Plastic Powder Horn With String Cord,
1950. - **$50** **$150** **$275**

STA-20

STA-21

STA-22

STA-26

STA-27

STA-20. Brass Portrait Ring,
1950. - **$20 $40 $60**

STA-21. Golden Nugget Picture Ring,
1950. Gold plastic with view lens holding picture scene within cave interior, also known as "Cave Ring". Shows Straight Arrow, his horse Fury and his assistant Packy McCloud. Some versions show black and white photo of child that ordered the ring. - **$75 $150 $250**

STA-22. "Book 2" Box Insert Cards,
1950. Set of 36. Each - **$1 $2 $3**

STA-26. "Injun-Uities" 21x27" Store Announcement Poster,
1951. Scarce. Pictures 12 "Injun-Uities" Nabisco cards from first series. - **$150 $500 $800**

STA-27. "Straight Arrow Injun-Uities Manual",
1951. Series 1 and 2 box inserts in book format. - **$15 $25 $40**

STA-23

STA-24

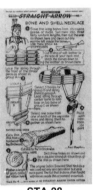

STA-28

STA-29

STA-30

STA-23. Tribal Shoulder Patch,
1950. - **$10 $20 $35**

STA-24. Patch Instructions,
1950. Rare. Tells about patch and how to become a big chief. - **$25 $50 $75**

STA-28. "Book Three" Box Insert Cards,
1951. Set of 36. Each - **$1 $2 $3**

STA-29. "Rite-A-Lite" Order Form,
1951. - **$10 $20 $30**

STA-30. Rite-A-Lite Arrowhead With Cap On Bottom,
1951. Scarce. Gold heavy plastic battery operated light. Discontinued because of use of material for Korean War. - **$150 $600 $1000**
Missing End Cap - **$60 $90 $150**

STA-25

STA-31

STA-32

STA-25. Target Game with Box,
1950. Store item. Metal target with bow-like launcher to fire "magnetic arrows." - **$75 $200 $350**

STA-31. Rite-A-Lite Arrowhead Cancellation Letter,
1951. Rare. - **$100 $175 $225**

STA-32. Glow-In-Dark Membership Card,
1951. - **$35 $150 $225**

STA-33   STA-34

STA-33. "Book Four" Box Insert Cards,
1952. Set of 36. Each - **$2 $3 $4**

STA-34. Props,
1952. Nabisco. Two pieces. For TV Puppet Theater. Goes with STA-35. Each - **$5 $10 $15**

STA-35

STA-35. Punch-Out Puppets Sheet,
c. 1952. Comes with instruction card and two play script cards. See STA-34. Unpunched - **$12 $20 $30**

STROMBECKER MODELS CLUB

A model kit maker (principally aviation) from the 1930s onward, Strombecker Co. sponsored a model building club with a code book and series of badges to denote club ranks based on model building expertise. A similar club was sponsored by competitor Megow Co.

SMC-2   SMC-3

SMC-1

SMC-1. Club Manual,
1930s. Includes secret code, photos of famous adult club members, photos of airplane and locomotive models. - **$15 $25 $40**

SMC-2. "Apprentice" Bronze Finish Badge,
1930s. - **$8 $15 $25**

SMC-3. "First Class" Bronze Finish Badge,
1930s. Awarded for building four models in four categories. - **$12 $20 $35**

SMC-4   SMC-5

SMC-4. "Airman 1st Class" Club Rank 3" Metal Wings Badge,
1930s. Silver finish with red shield, one star. - **$10 $20 $30**

SMC-5. "Wing Leader" Club Rank 3" Metal Wings Badge,
1930s. Gold finish, blue shield, two stars. - **$10 $20 $30**

SMC-6

SMC-7

SMC-6. "Captain" Club Rank Metal Wings Badge,
1930s. Brass finish, green shield, three stars for highest rank. - **$15 $25 $40**

SMC-7. Club Application Folder,
c. late 1940s. Features "Captain 'Jet'" and pictures "Air Man 1st Class" tin badge to be received.
Folder - **$5 $12 $25**
Badge - **$8 $15 $35**

SUNSET CARSON

Michael Harrison, born in 1922, took his cowboy name for a supporting role in the 1944 film *Call of the Rockies*. Carson starred in a number of action-packed "B" Westerns for Republic Pictures in the 1940s, but his cowboy skills were demonstrated to greater advantage as an international rodeo star and trick rider in the Tom Mix Circus. Several Sunset Carson comic books were published in 1951, and adaptations of his films appeared in a number of issues of *Cowboy Western Comics* in the early 1950s.

SUN-1

SUN-1. "Republic Pictures" Felt Pennant,
1940s. - **$10 $20 $30**

SUN-2

SUN-2. "Sunset Carson" Cello. Button,
1940s. - **$10 $20 $30**

SUN-3

SUN-3. Sunset Carson/Monte Hale Records Offer,
c. 1950. Illinois Merchandise Mart. Paper sheet offering recorded adventures "Sunset Carson And The Black Bandit" and "Monte Hale And The Flaming Arrow." - **$10 $20 $30**

SUPER CIRCUS

What started out as a kids' radio quiz program in Chicago became one of television's highest-rated children's shows. *Super Circus*, a weekly variety spectacular, aired on ABC-TV from 1949 to 1956. Claude Kirchner acted as ringmaster, Mary Hartline--with dazzling blonde hair and miniskirt--twirled her baton, and clowns Cliffy, Nicky, and Scampy took care of the slapstick. Among the sponsors were Weather Bird shoes, Canada Dry, Kellogg's cereals, Quaker Oats, Mars candy, and Sunkist. Also, Mary Hartline Enterprises marketed a line of dolls, toys, children's clothes, food products, records, and books. The show moved to New York in 1955, and Jerry Colonna and Sandy

Wirth replaced Kirchner and Hartline for the final season. *Super Circus* comic books appeared between 1951 and 1956.

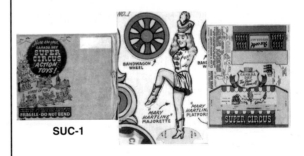

SUC-1

SUC-1. "Super Circus Action Toy" Punch-Out Kit With Envelope,
1950. Canada Dry. Set of 10 punch-out sheets. Unused In Mailer - **$40 $100 $175**

SUC-2

SUC-2. "Weather-Bird Shoes" Photos,
c. 1950. From a set. Each - **$5 $10 $12**

SUC-3

SUC-3. "Mary Hartline" Hand Puppet,
c. 1950. Three Musketeers. - **$15 $40 $50**

SUC-4

SUC-4. "Super Circus Side Show" Punch-Out Kit With Envelope,
c. 1950. Milky Way candy bars. Punch-out sheet opens to 11x34". Complete In Mailer - **$50 $125 $175**

SUC-5

SUC-6

SUC-5. "Super Circus Club" Member's Litho. Button,
1951. Canada Dry. - **$5 $20 $30**

SUC-6. Spiral-Bound Photo Book,
1951. - **$25 $75 $100**

SUC-8

SUC-7

SUC-7. Weather Bird Shoes Comic Book Vol. 1 #1,
1951. - **$10 $30 $60**

SUC-8. Iron-On Transfer Sheets,
1951. Weather-Bird shoes. Four tissue sheets in reverse image picturing Mary, Scampy, Nicky, Cliffy.
Each - **$3 $6 $10**

SUC-10

SUC-9

SUC-9. "Super Circus Snickers Shack" Punch-Out With Mailer,
c. 1951. Mars, Inc. Punch sheet opens to 11-1/2x17".
Complete In Mailer - **$50 $100 $150**

SUC-10. "TV Guide" With Cover Article,
1953. Weekly issue for August 21 with color photo cover of Mary Hartline and Claude Kirchner plus two-page article. - **$15 $25 $40**

SUC-11

SUC-12

SUC-11. Hard Plastic Doll,
1950s. Mars Candy and store item. Seen marked "Ideal" or "Lingerie Lou Doll." - **$35 $125 $200**
Picture Box - **$20 $40 $60**

SUC-12. Punch-Out Puppets With Envelope,
1950s. Snickers Candy Bars.
Unused In Mailer - **$30 $90 $150**

SUC-13

SUC-13. Postcard,
1950s. Premium from TV show, pictures 6 cast members - **$20 $35 $50**

SUPERMAN

Clark Kent's secret identity might just be the worst-kept secret ever. Consistently certified as one of the most recognized characters in the world, Superman is the very definition of a superhero (in fact, he's probably the reason for the word superhero). Not only was he dynamic and unlike anything anyone had seen before, but the marketing plan built around and executed for Superman was virtually a "how to" road map for future marketing executives.

When writer Jerry Siegel and artist Joe Shuster created Superman in 1933, they probably had no idea of the tremendous force they would unleash on an unsuspecting public. It wasn't until five years later, though, that *Action Comics* #1 (June 1938) launched Superman into comic books and captured the attention of children. The daily newspaper strip first appeared seven months later (January 1939) and adults began to take notice. A companion comic, *Superman*, followed that summer and included the first mention of Supermen of America, the official Superman fan club. The club's first contest began December 1, 1939 and ended January 28, 1940; the prize became one of the most sought-after Superman collectibles ever, the Supermen of America patch (see entry in this section). Two weeks later, February 12, 1940, Superman radio show took the airwaves for the first time and captured the imagination of entire families. Before long, characters Clark Kent and Lois Lane (and thanks to the radio show, several others) became fast friends with America's reading and listening public. The phenomenon had begun.

There have been thousands of Superman comic books, and daily and Sunday comic strips appeared from 1939 to 1967. On radio *The Adventures of Superman* aired from 1940 to 1951, on the Mutual network from 1940 to 1949, then on ABC. Bud Collyer starred as Superman from 1940 to 1949, and Kellogg's Pep sponsored from 1943 to 1947. The series moved successfully to prime-time television syndication (1953-1958), mainly on ABC outlets, with George Reeves in the lead and Kellogg's Sugar Frosted Flakes as sponsor.

The first Superman cartoons were 17 six-minute theatrical shorts made by the Fleischer Studios for Paramount Pictures in 1941-1943. Television cartoons, with Bud Collyer returning as the voice of Superman, aired on CBS in the late 1960s under various titles: *The New Adventures of Superman* (1966-1967), *The Superman/Aquaman Hour of Adventure* (1967-1968), and *The Batman/Superman Hour* (1968-1969). Superman was also part of the *Superfriends* animated series on ABC in the 1970s, and a musical show, *It's a Bird...It's a Plane...It's Superman*, had a brief run on Broadway in 1966 and was shown on ABC-TV in 1975. Superman returned to the cartoon airwaves in 1996 on the WB network and now airs as part of *The New Batman/Superman Adventures*.

Superman's movie career began with two 15-episode chapter plays from Columbia Pictures, *Superman* (1948) and *Atom Man vs. Superman* (1950), with Kirk Alyn in the lead roles. *Superman and the Mole Men*, with George Reeves starring, was released in 1951 and later served as a pilot for the TV series. *Superman - The Movie* (1978), with Christopher Reeve and Margot Kidder--a box office smash--was followed by *Superman II* (1981), *Superman III* (1983), and *Superman IV: The Quest for Peace* (1987). A new Superman motion picture, tentatively under the guidance of *Batman* and *Batman Returns* director Tim Burton, is presently scheduled to be released in 1999. *Lois and Clark: The New Adventures of Superman* ran on ABC-TV from 1993 to 1997 and presently airs in re-runs on the TNT cable network with Dean Cain as Clark/Superman and Teri Hatcher as Lois Lane.

Superman marked his 60th anniversary in June 1998. He is presently published in four monthly titles, *Action Comics*, *Adventures of Superman*, *Superman*, and *Superman: The Man of Steel*, as well as a quarterly, *Superman: The Man of Tomorrow*. A cartoon companion comic, *Superman Adventures*, is also published monthly, and the character appears from time to time in many other DC titles. Over the course of his career he's been transformed, transmogrified and even killed, but Superman keeps coming back in his never-ending battle for truth, justice and the American way. Items are typically copyrighted National Comics Publications, Inc., National Periodical Publications, Inc. or DC Comics.

SUP-1

SUP-2

SUP-1. "Action Comics" Flier,
1939. Sent to magazine wholesalers requesting they inform retailers Superman strip appears only in "Action Comics". -
$300 $750 $1200

SUP-2. "Action Comics" Cover Letter,
1939. Came with flier above. - **$250 $500 $750**

SUP-3

SUP-4

SUP-3. Action Comics "Superman" Litho. Button,
1939. Back inscription "Read Superman/Action Comics Magazine". - **$40 $75 $150**

SUP-4. Letter,
1939. N. Y. World's Fair. - **$100 $300 $500**

SUP-5

SUP-5. Superman Contest Prize Ring,
1940. Rare. 12 known. Inscribed "Supermen Of America, Member." Issued by DC Comics promoted in Superman and Action Comics. 1600 issued. Silver base, gold luster image, red accent on logo and around lettering. -
$7500 $30000 $100000 (price varies widely)

SUP-7

SUP-6

SUP-8

SUP-6. Letter,
1940. Came with Action Comics Patch. -
$200 $500 $1050

SUP-7. Patch,
1940. Scarce. Has "Action Comics" at bottom of front
side. - **$1500 $6000 $10000**

SUP-8. Patch,
1940. Rare. Prize same as the above Supermen of
America Patch except has word "Leader" at bottom. -
$2000 $8000 $15000

SUP-10

SUP-9

SUP-9. Candy Patch,
1940. - **$500 $2500 $5000**

SUP-10. Handkerchief,
1940. - **$500 $1200 $2100**

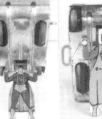

SUP-11

SUP-11. Marx Wind-Up Tin Tank
1940. Store item. - **$200 $400 $1000**

SUP-12

SUP-14

SUP-13

SUP-12. Large Candy Box,
1940. - **$250 $600 $1100**

SUP-13. Superman Cut-Out Book,
1940. Produced by Saalfield Publishing Company of
Akron, Ohio. There were two editions; one had a red cover
and the other was blue. Each - **$750 $1800 $2500**

**SUP-14. "Superman's Magic Flight" Cardboard
Mechanical Toy,**
1940. - **$250 $600 $1100**

(front)   SUP-15   (back)

**SUP-15. "Superman's Christmas Adventure" Comic
Book,**
1940. First superhero premium comic book. First issue,
various stores. - **$500 $1500 $4000**

SUP-16

SUP-17

SUP-18

SUP-16. Gum, Inc. "Superman" Enameled Brass Badge,
1940. Offered on wrappers holding Superman gum cards. - **$750 $2500 $4000**

SUP-17. Rectangular Fabric Patch,
1940. Scarce. - **$750 $3000 $5500**

SUP-18. "Macy's Superman Adventure" Gummed Sticker,
1940. Macy's department store, applied to purchased items. - **$30 $80 $100**

SUP-19

SUP-20

SUP-19. "Krypto-Raygun" With Box,
1940. Store item by Daisy Mfg. Co. Came with seven film-strips. Complete Boxed - **$300 $600 $1200**
Gun Only - **$100 $200 $300**
Filmstrip - **$5 $15 $25**

SUP-20. Wood And Composition Jointed Doll,
1940. Store item by Ideal Toys. Includes cloth cape. - **$300 $900 $1800**

SUP-21

SUP-21. Superman Die-Cut Ad,
1940. Promotes radio show on WHP radio station. About 4-1/2" high. Other ads feature different stations. - **$50 $100 $175**

SUP-22

SUP-22. Superman Bubble Gum Club Prizes Folder,
1940. Gum, Inc. Shows 15 items, most also available in stores, available for cash and Superman Gum labels or free of charge for securing new club members. The "Superman American" brass club badge was 10¢ and 5 wrappers or 10 new members. - **$150 $350 $750**

SUP-24

SUP-23

SUP-23. Bowman Bubble Gum Box,
1940. Sold for **$7500** in 1998. Probably unique.

SUP-24. "Democrat" Newspaper Cello. Button,
1940. Rare newspaper premium. - **$500 $1000 $1500**

SUP-25

SUP-26

SUP-25. Superman Wristwatch in Box,
1940. Made by New Haven Clock Co. and distributed by the Everbright Watch Company. Two different bands shown (brown band at bottom, black band at top). - **$750 $1500 $1750**
Box and Insert Only - **$350 $750 $900**

SUP-26. Candy & Surprise Cut-Out Panels,
1940. Set of 36. Candy company ring offered for 10 coupons and 10 cents or 75 coupons.
Cut Box Front With Coupon - **$20 $40 $60**
Cut Back With Card - **$20 $40 $60**

SUP-27   **SUP-28**

SUP-27. Superman Candy Secret Compartment Initial Brass Ring,
1940. Leader Novelty Candy Co. Recipient's inital on top cover. First version with red/white/blue image of Superman glued on inside surface of removable top. -
$2000 $7500 $22000 (price varies widely)

SUP-28. Superman Gum Secret Compartment Brass Ring,
1940. Rare. Pictures Superman, lightning bolt and letter "S". Top snaps off. No Superman image under top. -
$5000 $20000 $50000 (price varies widely)

SUP-29

SUP-31

SUP-30

SUP-29. Superman Christmas Adventure Ticket,
1940. Admission ticket to Macy's Christmas Adventure play. This ticket has sponsor radio station WOR on the front. Other sponsors include Superman, Inc., Leader Novelty, and American Journal. Each - **$100 $200 $300**

SUP-30. Superman Thanksgiving Day Parade Ad Card,
1940. Similar in size to a postcard, promoted Macy's effort at Thanksgiving Day Parade. The Superman display was the largest balloon featured in the 1940 parade. -
$150 $300 $400

SUP-31. Superman Letter From Macy's,
1940. Colorful letter which informed kids about Christmas Adventure play. - **$150 $350 $500**

SUP-32

SUP-33

SUP-34

SUP-32. Plaster "Carnival" Statue,
c. 1940. Various colors. - **$50 $150 $275**

SUP-33. "Superman/American" Brass Figural Badge,
1940. Gum Inc. for Superman Bubble Gum Club members - **$75 $125 $250**

SUP-34. Cartoon Movie 6' Standee,
1941. From Fleischer cartoon film. -
$8000 $20000 $27000

SUP-35   **SUP-36**

SUP-37

SUP-35. Syroco-Style 5-1/2" Figure,
1942. Wood composition in brown with red accents on logo and red cape. Promotional item from DC Comics for Superman comic books to distributors and retailers. - **$1000 $3000 $4000**

SUP-36. Syroco-Style 5-1/2" Painted Figure,
1942. Full color, made of cellulose nitrate. See previous item. - **$1000 $3000 $5000**

SUP-37. Superman Defense Club Badge,
1942. Same as SUP-33; 1940 badge offered again in conjunction with Defense Club milk program. Not to be confused with the Superman Junior Defense League bread program badge (see SUP-40). - **$75 $125 $250**

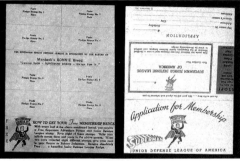

SUP-38

SUP-38. Superman Junior Defense League Membership Folder,
1942. Includes membership card and holder on back to paste membership pledge stamps. When the card was filled with eight stamps, it was redeemable at the local grocer for a Superman Junior Defense League pin.
Folder Complete - **$200 $400 $600**
Membership Card Only - **$100 $200 $300**
Superman Sticker Stamps Glued Each - **$10 $20 $30**

SUP-39

SUP-39. Superman Adventure Cards With Stamps,
1942. Rare. 24 adventure picture cards were issued in 1942 for the Superman bread campaign. The pledge stamps were detachable in order to paste them on the folder and receive the Junior Defense League pin. These cards are rare with the stamps still intact. Less than 25 exist. Each - **$175 $375 $450**

SUP-40

SUP-41

SUP-40. Superman Junior Defense League Bread Badge,
1942. Premium for complete folder with stickers glued to back. - **$60 $90 $160**

SUP-41. Bread Certificate,
1942. Used to promote Junior Defense League of America. - **$200 $400 $600**

SUP-42

SUP-43

SUP-42. "The Adventures Of Superman" Comic Booklet,
c. 1942. Py-Co-Pay tooth powder. Eight-page color booklet. - **$100 $250 $500**

SUP-43. Bread Loaf Paper,
c. 1942. Stroehmann's Bread. 4" tall diecut glossy paper, probably a loaf wrapper sticker listing call letters and broadcast times for "The Adventures Of Superman" radio program. - **$150 $300 $450**

SUP-44

SUP-45

SUP-44. "The Adventures Of Superman/Armed Services Edition" Book,
1942. Superman Inc. Paperback edition. - **$50 $125 $200**

SUP-45. DC Comics Portrait Sheet,
c. 1942. Reverse shows covers of "Superman" #14, "World's Finest" #5, "Action Comics" #47. - **$75 $200 $300**

SUP-46

SUP-47

SUP-48

SUP-46. Cardboard Shield Badge,
c. 1942. Rare. Superman Bread. - **$200 $500 $850**

SUP-47. "Superman-Tim Club" Litho. Button,
c. 1942. Back slogan "Member In Good Standing". - **$15 $25 $50**

SUP-48. "Superman-Tim Club" Litho. Button,
c. 1942. - **$15 $25 $50**

SUP-49

SUP-50

SUP-49. Superman Defense Club Milk Bottle Lids,
1942. Each cardboard lid contains a number and a pledge.
These lids were collected and redeemable with the milkman for a Superman American pin. These lids are rare; a
complete set does not exist. Each - **$75 $150 $250**

SUP-50. Superman Defense Club Membership Card,
1942. Roberts Milk sponsor. At the same time the
Superman Junior Defense League of America bread campaign was going on, Superman was also promoting milk
under this club name. Note the word "Junior" is deleted
and "League" is changed to "Defense."
With Green Tab Notice Intact - **$100 $225 $350**

SUP-51

SUP-52

SUP-51. Superman #18 With Pinback on Cover,
1942. Premium pinback was pinned to Superman #18 to
promote Action Comics, the other Superman title. See next
item.

SUP-52. Action Comics "Superman" Litho. Button,
1942. Back inscription "Read Superman Action Comics
Magazine". - **$35 $65 $115**

SUP-53

SUP-53. Decoder Folder,
1943. Scarce. Similar to one used in club kit. Pictures
comics on the reverse. Given away at theaters. -
$100 $250 $350

SUP-54

SUP-54. Kellogg's Pep Box Back,
1943. #3 from series from first year of Superman radio
sponsorship. - **$20 $60 $80**

SUP-55

SUP-55. Superman-Tim Birthday Postcards,
1943. Various designs. Each - **$20 $50 $75**

SUP-56

SUP-57

SUP-56. "Superman Transfers" Pack,
1944. Detective Comics. Store packet containing "A Whole
Flock Of Honest-To-Goodness" water transfer pictures. -
$100 $250 $400

**SUP-57. "Superman's Christmas Adventure" Comic
Book,**
1944. Various stores. Example photo shows cover and first
page. - **$100 $300 $850**

SUP-58

SUP-59

SUP-60

SUP-58. "Superman's Christmas Play Book" Comic Book,
1944. Various stores. Candy cane and Superman cover. - **$100 $250 $750**

SUP-59. "Sincerely, Superman" Charity Reply Postcard,
1944. Response card for March of Dimes contribution. - **$75 $150 $250**

SUP-60. "Superman-Tim Club" Felt Patch,
1945. Various stores. Six different known.
Each - **$200 $750 $1200**

SUP-61   SUP-62

SUP-61. Superman Glow-In-The-Dark Picture,
c. 1945. Probable store item, at least four different known. - **$75 $150 $250**

SUP-62. Metal Hood Ornament,
c. 1946. Store item by L. W. Lee Mfg. Co.
6-1/2" Chrome Finish - **$1300 $2600 $4000**
4-1/2" Chrome Or Gold Finish - **$1400 $3100 $4500**

SUP-63

SUP-63. "Superman-Tim Press Card",
c. 1946. Opens to 9" to hold 12 poster stamps.
No Stamps - **$50 $90 $150**
Each Stamp Add $10

SUP-64   SUP-65

SUP-64. Pep Calendar Sign,
1946. - **$100 $300 $500**

SUP-65. Grocer's Calendar Card,
1947. Kellogg's Pep. Very colorful 4-1/2x9-1/2" monthly card urging stock and display of cereal featuring Superman endorsement. Pictured example is for September. - **$500 $1000 $1500**

SUP-66

SUP-66. Magic Record Set,
1947. With color folder that holds records. - **$75 $150 $250**

SUP-67

SUP-68

SUP-69

SUP-67. Sterling Silver Full-Dimensional Charm,
1947. Del Weston. Only 1-1/8" tall with red enamel painted cape. - **$100 $200 $300**

SUP-68. "Superman-Tim Club Membership Card",
1947. Various clothing stores. - **$30 $75 $100**

SUP-69. "Superman-Tim" Gummed Album Stamp,
May 1947. Various participating stores. Issued monthly 1947-1950 to mount in club magazine.
Each - **$12 $40 $60**

SUP-70   SUP-71

SUP-70. DC Comics Picture,
1948. Back pictures comic book covers. - **$50 $125 $200**

SUP-71. "Radio Quiz Master Games With Model Microphone" With Mailer Envelope,
1948. National Comics. Superman name on envelope and game but no picture. Includes punch-out cardboard microphone. Mailer - **$10 $35 $60**
Game - **$30 $100 $180**

SUP-72

SUP-72. Membership Kit,
1948. DC Comics. Includes envelope, letter, certificate, code folder, cello. button.
Complete With Envelope - **$150 $225 $400**
Letter - **$20 $40 $60**
Certificate - **$60 $80 $120**
Code Folder - **$20 $30 $60**
Button - **$20 $35 $60**

SUP-73

SUP-73. "Gilbert Hall Of Science" Catalogue,
1948. A. C. Gilbert Co. - **$75 $150 $250**

SUP-74

SUP-74. "Superman-Tim Store" Birthday Postcard,
1948. - **$20 $35 $75**

SUP-75

SUP-75. "Superman Bubble Gum" Maker's Stationery With Envelope,
1949. Fo-Lee Gum Corp., Philadelphia. Stationery letterhead pictures Superman, bottom margin includes his name. Envelope - **$10 $25 $50**
Stationery - **$50 $100 $150**

SUP-76

SUP-76. "Superman" Enameled Brass Shield,
1949. Fo-Lee Gum Corp., Philadelphia. Reverse has two brass tabs to fold rather than bar pin. - **$1000 $2500 $5000**

SUP-77

SUP-77. "Kellogg's Pep Real Photos" 22x32" Poster,
1949. Folder that opens from 11x16" picturing movie and sports stars miniature photos offered individually as box inserts and in enlarged size as mail premiums. Superman image is pictured in two details. - **$200 $400 $600**

SUP-78

SUP-79

SUP-78. Sunny Boy Cereal Code Premium,
1940s. Scarce. Canadian issue. - **$100 $300 $500**

SUP-79. Superman-Tim Bracelet,
1940s. Scarce. - **$350 $650 $1000**

SUP-80

SUP-81

SUP-82

SUP-80. "Superman-Tim" Magazine,
1940s. One of two examples shown. Issued monthly
August 1942-May 1950. See next item for prices.

SUP-81. "Superman-Tim Magazine,
1940s. Issued monthly August 1942-May 1950.
First Issue - **$75 $225 $650**
Typical Other Issues - **$15 $50 $130**

SUP-82. War Savings Bond Poster,
1940s. 12-1/2"x19-1/2". **$3000 $7000 $10000**

SUP-83

SUP-83. Superman-Tim Club Card,
1940s. Red, white and blue with Secret Code chart on
reverse. - **$30 $55 $90**

SUP-84   SUP-85

SUP-84. Superman-Tim Celluloid Pin,
1940s. - **$500 $1000 $1500**

SUP-85. Superman-Tim "Press Card",
1940s. Reverse blocks for 12 code stamps.
Card - **$75 $125 $200**
Each Stamp Mounted - **$5 $8 $12**

SUP-86   SUP-87

SUP-86. Superman-Tim Silvered Brass Store Ring,
1940s. Depicts Superman flying above initials "S T". -
$1000 $4000 $9000 (price varies widely)

**SUP-87. Kellogg's "Superman Crusader" Silvered
Brass Ring,**
1940s. - **$75 $150 $250**

SUP-88

SUP-89

SUP-88. "Superman-Tim" Felt Pennant,
1940s. Scarce. Various clothing stores. Seen in yellow or
red. Each - **$150 $600 $800**

SUP-89. Superman-Tim "Redback" Currency Bills,
1940s. Each - **$5 $8 $15**

SUP-91

SUP-90

SUP-90. "Superman-Tim Club" Bat Toy,
1940s. Various participating stores imprinted on back.
Diecut masonite with litho. paper art from set that included
rubber darts to strike at. - **$50 $150 $200**

SUP-91. "Superman-Tim Club" Bat Toy,
1940s. Various participating department stores imprinted
on back. Diecut masonite with litho. paper design. -
$50 $150 $200

SUP-92

SUP-92. Superman Belt in Box,
1940s. Belt by Pioneer has metal circular buckle with
Superman on front and graphics on leather strap.
Boxed - **$100 $200 $300**
Belt and Buckle - **$75 $100 $200**
Buckle Only - **$35 $65 $100**

SUP-93   SUP-94

SUP-93. Superman Pep Box,
1940s. Promotes Pep comic character pinbacks. -
$150 $350 $450

SUP-94. Superman Valentine,
1940s. Valentine created by Quality Art Novelty Company
in February, 1940. Many different. Each - **$30 $65 $125**

SUP-95

SUP-96

SUP-97

SUP-95. "Supermen Of America" Color Variety Cello. Button,
1940s. DC Comics. Pictures him in white shirt with red/yellow chest symbol, rare variety from DC files, apparently for test purposes. - **$200 $500 $800**

SUP-96. "Supermen Of America" Club Cello. Button,
1940s. Scarce 7/8" size in full color. - **$150 $300 $500**

SUP-97. "Atom Man Vs. Superman" 6' Movie Standee,
1950. Columbia serial. - **$2000 $4000 $7500**

SUP-98

SUP-99

SUP-98. One-Sheet,
1950. Promotes Atom Man Vs. Superman serial. - **$1000 $1750 $2500**

SUP-99. Superman Certificate,
1951. - **$60 $80 $120**

SUP-100

SUP-101

SUP-100. Superman TV Guide,
September 25, 1953. Featured George Reeves on the cover as Clark Kent and Superman. Inside was a story about the popular TV show. - **$250 $500 $750**

SUP-101. "Superman Muscle Building Club" Litho. Button,
1954. Store item. Came with child's exercise set. - **$40 $125 $200**

SUP-102

SUP-103

SUP-102. Kellogg's Stereo-Pix Box Back,
1954. Sugar Frosted Flakes. #3 from series of 3-D assembly panels. Uncut Box Back - **$30 $60 $100**

SUP-103. "The Superman Time Capsule" Comic Book,
1955. Kellogg's Sugar Smacks. From set of three. - **$50 $140 $425**

SUP-104   SUP-105

SUP-104. "Duel In Space" Comic Book,
1955. Kellogg's Sugar Smacks. From set of three. - **$40 $125 $375**

SUP-105. "The Supershow Of Metropolis" Comic Booklet,
1955. Kellogg's Sugar Smacks. From set of three. - **$40 $125 $375**

SUP-106

SUP-106. Kellogg's "Flying Superman" Toy Offer Box,
1955. Complete Box - **$75 $300 $525**

SUP-107

SUP-107. Kellogg's "Flying Superman" Thin Plastic Toy With Instruction Leaflet,
1955. Fragile premium flown by rubber band.
Instructions - **$40 $75 $100**
Figure And Plastic Stick - **$100 $200 $300**

SUP-108

SUP-109

SUP-108. "Krypton Rocket" Plastic Set With Launcher,
1955. Kellogg's. Rockets in red, blue, or green plastic with Superman logo. Each Rocket - **$10 $40 $60**
Launcher - **$25 $75 $150**

SUP-109. Kellogg's Belt And Buckle,
1955. Aluminum buckle with plastic belt.
Buckle - **$40 $75 $150**
With Belt - **$75 $125 $200**

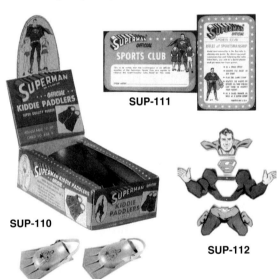

SUP-111

SUP-110

SUP-112

SUP-110. Superman Kiddie Paddlers in Box,
1955. The popularity of the TV program prompted Super Swim Inc. to feature Superman on the packaging of this product. The boxes represent some of the best graphics produced in the 1950s. Each box also contained a Safety Swim Club membership card.
Complete - **$70 $165 $255**
Box - **$50 $125 $175**
Kiddie Paddlers - **$20 $40 $80**

SUP-111. "Sports Club" Membership Card,
c. 1955. Store item. Came with swim fins or goggles. -
$10 $20 $35

SUP-112. Kellogg's Dangle-Dandy Box Back,
1955. Uncut Box Back - **$25 $50 $80**
Trimmed Out Figure - **$15 $30 $60**

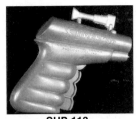

SUP-113

SUP-114

SUP-113. Kellogg's "Space Satellite Launcher Set",
1956. Came with two plastic spinners.
Complete With Spinners - **$200 $500 $750**
Box And Instructions - **$25 $50 $100**

SUP-114. Life-Size Cardboard Store Display,
1956. Kellogg's Corn Flakes. Top diecut to hold jumbo display cereal box. Promotes Superman TV series.
Display Without Box - **$300 $750 $1500**
Display Box Only - **$100 $200 $400**

SUP-115

SUP-115. "Kellogg's Fun Catalog",
1950s. - **$25 $50 $85**

SUP-116

SUP-116. "Superman Candy & Toy" Box,
1950s. Novel Package Corp. 1x2-1/2x4" long cardboard with "Play Card" back panel. - **$150 $300 $700**

SUP-117

SUP-117. Playsuit Mailing Folder,
1950s. Promotion to retailers from Funtime Playwear, Inc. - **$25 $60 $125**

SUP-118

SUP-118. Fan Club Card,
1950s. Probably came with playsuit by Funtime Playwear. - **$20 $35 $70**

SUP-119

SUP-120

SUP-119. George Reeves Fan Card,
1950s. DC Comics. - **$35 $75 $150**

SUP-120. Toy Watch,
1950s. Store item by Esco, West Germany. - **$50 $125 $200**

SUP-121

SUP-122

SUP-123

SUP-121. "Supermen Of America" Cello. Button,
1950s. DC Comics. - **$20 $40 $60**

SUP-122. "Supermen Of America" Color Variety Cello. Button,
1950s. DC Comics. Pictured in white shirt rather than blue with red/yellow chest symbol. Rare variety from DC files, apparently for test purposes. - **$200 $500 $800**

SUP-123. "Supermen Of America" Cello. Button,
1961. National Periodical Publications. Final version of series with 1961 copyright on rim edge. Same dated bottom was used for 1965 kit. - **$15 $25 $50**

SUP-124

SUP-125

SUP-124. "Initiative Award" Poster 11x14",
c. 1963. Independent News Co. Inc. given to comic book retailers. - **$40 $75 $100**

SUP-125. DC Publisher Response Letter To Fan Letter,
1964. National Periodical Publications Inc. Mentions upcoming Superboy television program and 80-page Giant DC Annuals. - **$15 $25 $40**

SUP-126

SUP-126. Superman Membership Certificate,
1965. Last year for the Club. May be the rarest of all varieties of Superman Certificates since their beginning in 1939. Lack of participation in the Club was probably due to the strong market for Marvel Heroes which diverted interest from the DC Heroes. - **$150 $250 $350**

SUP-127

SUP-128

SUP-127. Superman Litho. Button,
1966. N.P.P. Inc. Vending machine issue, set of eight. Each - **$5 $10 $15**

SUP-128. Superman Club 3-1/2" Cello. Button With Retail Box,
1966. Store item. Box originally held quantity of buttons.
Button - **$5 $10 $20**
Empty Box - **$25 $50 $75**

SUP-129

SUP-130

SUP-129. "Superman Golden Records" Boxed Set,
1966. N.P.P. Inc. Includes comic book, LP record, iron-on patch, membership card with secret code, Supermen Of America litho. button. Complete - **$20 $40 $75**

SUP-130. "New Adventures Of Superman" Gummed Paper Sticker,
1966. CBS-TV. For introduction of Saturday morning animated series beginning September 10.
Unused - **$10 $20 $35**

SUP-131   SUP-132

SUP-131. Superman Costume for Capt. Action,
1966, 1967. Complete costume with a plastic figure of Krypto the dog in the box. The 1967 version came with a flasher ring as a bonus. Boxed Costume - **$1300**
Loose, No Box - **$250**

SUP-132. Eating Set,
1966. Knife and fork, store bought.
On Card - **$50 $75 $150**
Each Utensil Loose - **$5 $10 $15**

SUP-133

SUP-133. Superman Plastic Identification Label,
1960s. These were logo ads attached to comic book racks in the early '60s. Each - **$50 $75 $125**

SUP-134   SUP-135

SUP-134. "All Star Dairy Foods" Plastic Truck Bank,
1960s. - **$35 $60 $100**

SUP-135. Vending Machine Header Card,
c. 1971. Includes Marvel and DC characters in form of magnet, sticker, rubber figures and Wonder Woman/Diana Prince flicker picture. - **$50 $100 $175**

SUP-136

SUP-136. Record,
1972. Coca-Cola premium. - **$15 $25 $50**

SUP-137

SUP-137. "Original Radio Broadcast" Vol. 1 Record Album,
1974. Kellogg's Corn Flakes. Issued as set of four.
Each - **$5 $30 $50**

SUP-138

SUP-138. Kellogg's Corn Flakes Cereal Box - 12 oz.,
1976. Offers record album. Superman appears on front and back of box - **$40 $85 $150**

SUP-139

SUP-139. Post Sugar Crisp Cereal Box - 12 oz.,
1975. Offers mini comic books. Superman appears on front; Superman, Batman, Robin, and Wonder Woman on back of box - **$40 $85 $150**

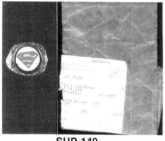

SUP-140

SUP-141

SUP-140. Nestle's Domed Ring With Mailer,
1976. Near Mint With Mailer - **$65**
Ring Only - **$20 $40 $60**

SUP-141. "I Saw Superman" 3-1/2" Cello. Button,
1976. Issued for Albright-Knox Art Gallery exhibit. -
$15 $30 $60

SUP-142

SUP-142. Drake's Trading Cards 23x32" Store Sign,
1978. - **$15 $30 $50**

SUP-143

SUP-143. "Super Heroes Fun Book And Check List",
1978. Various bread companies. Check list for sticker set. See next item. - **$15 $30 $50**

SUP-144

SUP-145

SUP-144. Super Hero Stickers,
1978. Various bread companies. Set of 30. See SUP-143. Each Unused - **$1 $2 $3**

SUP-145. "Superbank" 3-1/2" Cello. Button,
1970s. Garden State National Bank, probably others. -
$15 $25 $45

SUP-146

SUP-146. Post Honey-Comb Cereal Box,
1970s. Superman appears on front; offers Superman poster - setof 4 on back of box - **$50 $100 $150**

SUP-147

SUP-148

SUP-147. "Superman Peanut Butter" 7x11"
Paper Store Sign,
1981. Includes pad of t-shirt order forms. - **$25 $40 $60**

SUP-148. Clark Kent Super Powers Figure,
c. 1984. Kenner mail order premium.
Boxed - **$40 $60 $100**
Loose - **$25 $40 $75**

SUP-150

SUP-151

SUP-149

SUP-149. Super Powers Standee,
1984. 1st standee to promote Superboy. -
$100 $200 $300

SUP-150. Kryptonite Ring,
1990. Toy Biz. Came packaged with Superman action
figure. - **$10 $20 $30**

SUP-151. Syroco-Style Limited Edition Figure,
1995. 4" tall, 250 made. Mint - **$100**

SUP-152

SUP-152. Burger King Standee,
1997. Six foot tall standee promoting cartoon TV show. -
$50 $75 $100

SYROCO FIGURES

Adolph Holstein, a skilled European immigrant wood-carver, founded the Syracuse Ornamental Company in 1890, specializing in making hand-carved decorative components for the furniture industry. Demand for the company's intricate products soon exceeded production capacity, so Holstein developed a process to mass-produce replicas of the carvings by compressing a mixture of wood flour, waxes, and resins into molds. In the 1930s and 1940s the company changed its name to Syroco Inc. and manufactured a line of novelty items--cigarette boxes, pipe racks, plates, serving trays, and figurines of popular entertainers, comic strip characters and public personalities, for sale in roadside souvenir shops. Syroco Inc. continues in business to this day, but production of the figures was discontinued by about 1950.

Syroco products of greatest interest to premium collectors are the 1941 Great American Series of historic personalities (about 6" tall) and the 1944 series of King Features Syndicate comic strip characters (about 4-5" tall). There are 24 known characters. Pillsbury Mills, Inc. offered the following 12 as premiums in 1944 each for 25¢ and a Pillsbury Enriched Farina box top: Alexander, Annie Rooney, Archie, Barney Google, Blondie, Cookie, Dagwood, Jiggs, Little King, Popeye, Tim Tyler, Wimpy.

Similar wood composition figures are pictured in sections on Captain Marvel, Pinocchio and Superman. While these are also generically known as "syroco" figures, the 1945 Captain Marvel figure and the Pinocchio character figures are attributed to Multi Products, Chicago. This inscription appears on the Pinocchio figures.

SYR-1   **SYR-2**   **SYR-3**   **SYR-4**

SYR-1. Ben Franklin,
1941. Great American Series. - **$40 $80 $200**

SYR-2. George Washington,
1941. Great American Series. - **$40 $80 $200**

SYR-3. Will Rogers,
1941. Great American Series. - **$50 $120 $275**

SYR-4. Buffalo Bill,
1941. From Great Americans series. - **$75 $150 $300**

SYR-5   **SYR-6**   **SYR-7**   **SYR-8**

SYR-5. Alexander Syroco Figure,
1944. This and the following 23 figures comprise a set of 24 King Features Syndicate characters, all from 1944. -
$20 $40 $100

SYR-6. Annie Rooney,
1944. - **$30 $100 $150**

SYR-7. Archie In Uniform,
1944. - **$30 $100 $150**

SYR-8. Barney Google In Navy Uniform,
1944. - **$25 $75 $125**

SYR-9   **SYR-10**   **SYR-11**   **SYR-12**

SYR-9. Blondie,
1944. Scarce. - **$60** **$150** **$350**

SYR-10. Captain,
1944. - **$30** **$100** **$150**

SYR-11. Casper,
1944. - **$20** **$85** **$125**

SYR-12. Cookie,
1944. - **$20** **$40** **$100**

| SYR-13 | SYR-14 | SYR-15 | SYR-16 |

SYR-13. Dagwood,
1944. - **$30** **$100** **$150**

SYR-14. Flash Gordon,
1944. Scarce. - **$200** **$600** **$1000**

SYR-15. Fritz,
1944. - **$25** **$75** **$125**

SYR-16. Hans,
1944. - **$25** **$75** **$125**

| SYR-17 | SYR-18 | SYR-19 | SYR-20 |

SYR-17. Jiggs,
1944. - **$40** **$110** **$175**

SYR-18. Little King,
1944. - **$40** **$150** **$250**

SYR-19. Maggie,
1944. Scarce. - **$200** **$350** **$500**

SYR-20. Rosie,
1944. Rare. - **$200** **$400** **$500**

| SYR-21 | SYR-22 | SYR-23 | SYR-24 |

SYR-21. Olive Oyl,
1944. - **$200** **$300** **$400**

SYR-22. Phantom,
1944. Scarce. Brown Costume - **$300** **$900** **$1500**
Purple Costume - **$250** **$800** **$1250**

SYR-23. Popeye,
1944. - **$50** **$120** **$225**

SYR-24. Prince Valiant,
1944. - **$75** **$160** **$375**

| SYR-25 | SYR-26 | SYR-27 | SYR-28 |

SYR-25. Tillie In Uniform,
1944. Scarce. - **$200** **$350** **$500**

SYR-26. Tim Tyler In Navy Uniform,
1944. - **$20** **$75** **$125**

SYR-27. Toots,
1944. Scarce. - **$200** **$350** **$500**

SYR-28. Wimpy,
1944. - **$40** **$80** **$150**

SYR-29

SYR-29. Comic Character Statuettes Ad,
1945. Pillsbury Farina Cereal. Sunday comic section ad offering figures of Dagwood, Cookie, Alexander, Blondie, Popeye, Wimpy, Tim Tyler, Archie, Jiggs, Little King, Annie Rooney, Barney Google. - **$35** **$75** **$150**

TALES OF THE TEXAS RANGERS

With stories said to be based on the files of the Texas Rangers between the 1830s and the 1950s, this series aired on NBC radio from 1950 to 1952, with Joel McCrea as Ranger Jace Pearson. A television version was broadcast from 1955 to 1957 on CBS and from 1957 to 1959 on ABC, with Willard Parker and Harry Lauter as the leading lawmen. General Mills sponsored the radio series and Tootsie Rolls candy joined the cereal company in sponsoring the TV version. *Texas Ranger* and *Jace Pearson* comic books appeared in the 1950s. Items may be copyrighted Screen Gems Inc.

TXS-1

TXS-1. Membership Kit,
c. 1955. Curtiss Candy. Box Or Card - **$10 $25 $35**
Silvered Metal Badge - **$20 $45 $60**
Ring - **$20 $35 $60**

TXS-2

TXS-3

TXS-2. Candy Display Card,
c. 1955. Curtiss Candy Co. - **$25 $50 $75**

TXS-3. Jace Pearson Fan Photo,
c. 1955. - **$8 $12 $20**

TXS-4

TXS-4. "Baby Ruth" Candy Bar Box,
c. 1955. Curtiss Candy Company. Pictured and named are stars Jace Pearson and Clay Morgan. 8x9-1/2x2" deep originally holding 24 bars. - **$25 $60 $85**

TARZAN

Between 1911 and 1944 Edgar Rice Burroughs (1875-1950) wrote some 26 Tarzan novels, creating a world of adventure where justice and fair play triumph in the hands of an English orphan raised by apes in the African jungle. One of the most popular fictional characters of all time, Tarzan has thrilled readers and viewers throughout the world in print, in comics, in feature films and chapter plays, on radio, and on television. Tarzan's first appearance was in *All Story Magazine* in October, 1912.

The first Tarzan movie was the 1918 silent *Tarzan of the Apes*, starring Elmo Lincoln, but the best remembered apeman is undoubtedly Olympic hero Johnny Weissmuller, who originated the abiding victory cry and made a dozen Tarzan films between 1932 and 1948. Notable among the many other cinema Tarzans: Buster Crabbe (1933), Lex Barker (1949-1953), and Gordon Scott (1955-1966). Including the silents and chapter plays, there have been more than 40 Lord of the Jungle movies.

The *Tarzan* comic strip, distributed by Metropolitan Newspaper Service, debuted in 1929 and lasted until 1973. A Sunday version from United Feature Syndicate appeared in 1931. There have been numerous *Tarzan* comic books, with reprints of the strips starting in 1929 and original material starting in the late 1940s.

There have been two series of *Tarzan* radio programs, the first (1932-1936) syndicated by WOR in New York with the Signal Oil Company as a sponsor until 1934, the second (1952-1953) on CBS, sponsored by Post Toasties. Premiums from the 1930s series include membership material in a Tarzan Club and a number of items from such sponsors as Foulds macaroni, Kolynos toothpaste, Bursley coffee, Hormel foods, and the dairy industry.

A live-action TV adaptation starring Ron Ely was aired on NBC in 1966-1968 and rerun on CBS in 1969, and animated versions from Filmation studios were broadcast on CBS from 1976 to 1981. The University of Louisville in Kentucky maintains an extensive Burroughs Memorial Collection of printed material and memorabilia.

Dark Horse Comics published *Tarzan: The Lost Adventure*, a previously unreleased Burrough's manuscript completed by author Joe R. Lansdale, in both serialized and novel formats. They have also produced a comic book mini-series, *Tarzan vs. Predator at the Earth's Core*, as well as an ongoing *Tarzan* comic. Tarzan can also be seen in a weekly syndicated TV show, *Tarzan: The Epic Adventures*.

TRZ-1

TRZ-2

TRZ-7

TRZ-1. Movie Premium,
1918. Photo of Tarzan actor Elmo Lincoln. - **$25 $50 $75**

TRZ-2. "Elmo Lincoln In Adventures Of Tarzan" Movie Serial Paper Mask,
1921. Great Western Producing Co. 15-chapter serial imprinted on back for local theaters. - **$75 $250 $350**

TRZ-7. Plaster Statues,
1932. Fould's Products. The basic set of 12 includes Tarzan, Kala, Numa, three monkeys, Sheeta, Jane, D'Arnot Fr. Lt., pirate, cannibal, witch doctor. See next item. Set Painted - **$100 $250 $500**
Set Unpainted - **$150 $300 $600**

TRZ-3

TRZ-4

TRZ-8

TRZ-3. "The Tarzan Twins" Book,
1927. Store item. - **$60 $250 $400**

TRZ-4. Cardboard Bookmark,
c. 1920s. Grosset & Dunlap, publisher of Edgar Rice Burroughs novels. - **$15 $25 $50**

TRZ-8. Fould's Background For Plaster Statues,
1932. Scarce. - **$100 $250 $400**
Offer Blank - **$20 $40 $60**

TRZ-5

TRZ-6

TRZ-9

TRZ-5. Gift #1 And #2 Promo,
1932. Foulds Products. Radio premium printed on unstapled paper. - **$75 $125 $200**

TRZ-6. Promo
1932. Toddy Malted Drink. Premium gift sheet for statues. Printed on unstapled paper. - **$75 $125 $200**

TRZ-9. Plaster Statue Set Additions Order Coupons,
c. 1932. Foulds' Macaroni, Spaghetti or Egg Noodles. Box insert papers for "Leopard Of Opar" and "Princess La, High Priestess Of Opar", later and probably final additions to the earlier set of 12. Each Order Form - **$50 $125 $200**
Each Statue Painted - **$75 $125 $250**
Each Statue Unpainted - **$100 $200 $300**

TRZ-10

TRZ-10. "Signal Tarzan Club" Member Card,
1932. Signal gasoline. Qualifies recipient as "Charter Member Of The Tribe Of Tarzan". - **$100 $300 $400**

TRZ-11   **TRZ-12**

TRZ-11. "Signal Tarzan Club" Cello. Button,
1932. Signal Oil Co. - **$20 $50 $80**

TRZ-12. "Tarzan Of The Apes" Jigsaw Puzzle,
c. 1932. Screen Book Magazine.
In Envelope, Sealed - **$650**
Near Mint With Envelope - **$450**
Loose - **$25 $80 $175**

TRZ-13   **TRZ-14**

TRZ-13. "Tarzan The Fearless" 9x14" Cardboard Sign,
1933. Rare. - **$75 $150 $300**

TRZ-14. Northern Paper Mills Color Poster For Masks,
1933. - **$250 $600 $1100**

TRZ-15

TRZ-15. Paper Masks,
1933. Northern Paper Mills. Set of three picturing Tarzan, Numa the Lion, Akut the Ape. Tarzan - **$25 $60 $100**
Each Animal - **$15 $40 $75**

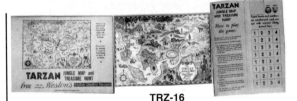

TRZ-16

TRZ-16. "Tarzan Jungle Map And Treasure Hunt" Game With Mailer Envelope,
1933. Rare. Canadian version has "W" above logo for Weston's English Quality Biscuits. U.S. version has "T" above logo. Australian version has sponsor name of Pepsodent Toothpaste. Playing pieces printed on envelope back, except Australian version, which has separate sheet with perforated pieces.
Canada Near Mint In Mailer - **$600**
Canada Map Only - **$100 $300 $450**
U.S. Near Mint In Mailer - **$700**
U.S. Map Only - **$125 $400 $600**
Australia Near Mint In Mailer - **$500**
Australia Map Only - **$115 $225 $400**
Australia Parts Sheet Only - **$25 $50 $75**

TRZ-17

TRZ-17. Paper Film,
1933. Scarce. Hormel Soups. - **$75 $250 $400**

TRZ-18   **TRZ-19**

TRZ-18. Tarzan Cup Magic Picture Cutouts,
1933. Rare. Complete Uncut - **$100 $300 $450**

TRZ-19. Johnny Weissmuller Picture,
1933. Rare. Wheaties premium for Jack Armstrong program. - **$40 $125 $200**

TRZ-20

TRZ-20. "Notebook Filler" Paper Wrapper Band,
c. 1933. Store item. Reverse pictures Mickey Mouse
Ingersoll watch offered for saved bands. - **$10 $25 $40**

TRZ-21

TRZ-21. "Tarzan 'Rescue'" Puzzle Game,
1934. Store item by Einson-Freeman Co. -
$150 $300 $600

TRZ-22

TRZ-22. "Drink More Milk" Bracelet,
1934. Rare. Radio premium. - **$800 $1750 $3000**

TRZ-23

TRZ-23. Tarzan of the Air Promo with Mailer,
1934. - **$60 $140 $200**

TRZ-24

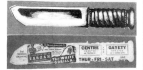

TRZ-25

TRZ-24. "Tarzan Of The Apes" Book,
1935. Various advertisers. - **$25 $60 $100**

**TRZ-25. "The New Adventures Of Tarzan" Cardboard
Knife Movie Give-Away,**
c. 1935. Various theaters. - **$20 $50 $80**

TRZ-26

TRZ-27

TRZ-26. "Tarzan And His Jungle Friends" Booklet #1,
1936. Tarzan Ice Cream Cup. First of listed series of 12. -
$60 $125 $225

TRZ-27. "Tarzan: Gift Picture No. 1 Of A Series",
1937. "Tarzan Appears Each Month In Tip Top Comics
Magazine Copyright 1937 By United Feature Syndicate
Inc." Art by Rex Maxon. - **$75 $200 $300**

TRZ-28

TRZ-29

TRZ-28. "Tarzan And A Daring Rescue" Booklet,
1938. Pan-Am gasoline and motor oils. Title page offers
bow and arrow set plus school bag premiums. -
$75 $150 $250

TRZ-29. "Tip Top Comics" 11x14" Store Sign,
c. 1938. - **$125 $200 $300**

TRZ-30

TRZ-31

TRZ-32

TRZ-30. Clans Manual,
1939. Tarzan Clans of America, Tarzana, California.
Complete procedures and rituals for organizing and running a clan. - **$150 $350 $600**

TRZ-31. Celluloid Pocketknife With Steel Blades,
1930s. Store item made by Imperial. - **$150 $400 $900**

TRZ-32. French Cello. Figure,
1930s. 2-1/2" tall marked "F Clairet". - **$250 $650 $1000**

TRZ-33

TRZ-33. "Myles Salt Cut-Outs" Boxes,
1930s. Panels picture Tarzan, Dan Dunn, Ella Cinders.
Tarzan Box Uncut - **$35 $75 $150**
Others Uncut Each - **$10 $25 $40**

TRZ-34

TRZ-34. Safety Club Cards,
1930s. Various radio sponsors. Two cards printed each
side, originally joined by perforation. One card to order
badge, one card of safety pledges. Pair - **$100 $350 $500**

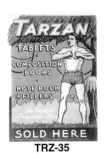

TRZ-35　　**TRZ-36**

TRZ-37

**TRZ-35. School Paper Supplies 10x14" Cardboard
Store Sign,**
1930s. Birmingham Paper Co. - **$100 $200 $300**

TRZ-36. "Tarzan Cups" 12x18" Paper Store Poster,
1930s. - **$100 $200 $300**

**TRZ-37. "Tarzan Ice Cream Cup" 10x20" Paper Store
Poster,**
1930s. - **$100 $200 $300**

TRZ-38

TRZ-39

TRZ-38. "Tarzan Cups" 6x19" Paper Store Poster,
1930s. Offers premiums for lids saved. - **$60 $125 $200**

**TRZ-39. "Tarzan And The Crystal Vault Of Isis" Card
#18,**
1930s. Schutter-Johnson Candies. Card title "The Electric
Menace" from numbered set of 50. Each - **$10 $20 $35**

TRZ-40　　　　**TRZ-41**

TRZ-40. "Tarzan Te Puro" Tea Canister With Lid,
1930s. Litho. tin Spanish issue from Uruguay. -
$35 $60 $90

TRZ-41. "Tarzan" Club Cello. Button Variety,
1930s. 1-1/4" size but no sponsor name and without words
"Safety Club." See TRZ-47 and 48. - **$125 $300 $550**

TRZ-42　　　　**TRZ-43**

**TRZ-42. "The Son Of Tarzan" Movie Serial Cardboard
Ad Blotter,**
1930s. Scarce. - **$30 $100 $150**

TRZ-43. "Tarzan The Tiger" Movie Serial Cello. Button,
1930s. Universal. Four known with this title, four known
with "Tarzan the Mighty" title. Each depicts animal or bird.
Each - **$20 $40 $75**

TRZ-44　　　　**TRZ-45**　　　　**TRZ-46**

**TRZ-44. "Tarzan Radio Club/Drink More Milk"
Enameled Brass Badge,**
1930s. Scarce. - **$150 $500 $850**

**TRZ-45. "Tarzan Radio Club/Bursley Coffees"
Enameled Brass Badge,**
1930s. Scarce. - **$150 $500 $850**

TRZ-46. "Vita Hearts" Litho. Club Button,
1930s. - **$125 $250 $400**

TRZ-47   **TRZ-48**   **TRZ-49**

TRZ-47. "Tarzan Safety Club" Cello. Button,
1930s. 7/8" version. See TRZ-41. - **$80 $200 $375**

TRZ-48. "Feldman's Tarzan Safety Club" Cello. Button,
1930s. 1-1/4" version of previous button with sponsor's
name. - **$100 $275 $525**

**TRZ-49. "The Nielen Tarzan Club" Member's Cello.
Button,**
1930s. - **$125 $275 $525**

TRZ-50   **TRZ-51**   **TRZ-52**

TRZ-50. Club Member Cello. Button,
1930s. Gano Downs Boys & Girls Shops. -
$125 $275 $525

TRZ-51. "Sons Of Tarzan Club" Cello. Button,
1930s. Facsimile Johnny Weissmuller signature. Theater
contest issue, match number to win prize. - **$50 $80 $125**

TRZ-52. "Tarzan's Grip" Australian Cello. Button,
1930s. - **$100 $200 $400**

TRZ-53   **TRZ-54**

TRZ-53. Advertising Flip Booklet,
c. 1940s. Thom McAn shoes. Pages flipped one direction
show Tarzan spearing an ape, reverse page sequence
shows grateful child getting Thom McAn shoes from dad. -
$50 $100 $150

TRZ-54. Dell Publishing Co. Pictures,
1950. One sheet consisting of five photos.
Near Mint In Mailer - **$125**
Loose - **$25 $50 $80**

TRZ-55

TRZ-55. Plastic Flicker Picture Rings,
1960s. Set of six. Gold plastic bases. Each - **$10 $15 $20**

TEENAGE MUTANT NINJA TURTLES

Donatello, Leonardo, Michaelangelo, and Raphael
burst upon the scene in 1984 in issue #1 of *Teenage
Mutant Ninja Turtles*. The pizza-loving sewer dwellers
and their ninja master thrived not only in comic books
but in a 1988 animated TV series, movies in 1990, 1991,
and 1993, millions of premiums from Burger King, a
concert tour sponsored by Pizza Hut, merchandising,
and licensing to promote hundreds of products. After
a waning of interest, a recent attempt to revitalize the
characters with the addition of a female Turtle has
proven moderately successful. "Cowabunga!"

TMT-1

TMT-1. Fan Club Kit Ad and Coupon,
1988. Playmates Toy Co. - **$10 $20 $30**

TMT-2

TMT-2. Fan Club Kit,
1988. Playmates Toy Co. Envelope with bandanna, letter,
story comic, sticker, charter member certificate with perforated membership card. Set - **$40 $65 $90**

TMT-3

TMT-4

TMT-3. Movie Promotion 2-1/8" Cello. Button,
1990. Mirage Studios. - **$3 $5 $10**

TMT-4. Nabisco Shreddies Canadian Cereal Box,
1990. Box offers first four of eight "Power Rings".
Complete Box - **$150**
Turtles Rings - **$5 $10 $15**
Other Character Rings - **$8 $12 $20**

TMT-5

TMT-5. Animated Television Cel,
c. 1990. Store item sold through retailers such as K-Mart in
a bag with header card or through galleries in other formats. Backgrounds are usually color laser copies.
Near Mint - **$25**
Higher Values May Apply Depending On Image And
Background

TMT-6

TMT-6. Nabisco Shreddies Canadian Cereal Box,
1991. Box offers last four of eight rings.
Complete Box - **$200**
Turtles Rings - **$5 $10 $15**
Other Character Rings - **$8 $12 $20**

TELEVISION MISC.

Television, only an experimental and isolated technical
dream through the 1930s, would likely have erupted
sooner if not for the World War II years. But erupt it did
in the late 1940s to present day norm of scarcely any
household in the United States without at least one TV
set. Early TV programming could be much more easily
sponsored by a single sponsor per show. It has been
estimated that an early sponsor could well finance an
entire season or more for the current cost, in equal
dollars, of a 30-second advertising spot during recent
Super Bowl telecasts. The basic cost of TV advertising, of course, is a prior consideration to the supplemental cost of premiums; thus the noticeable lack of
mail premium offers so prevalent in the radio and earliest TV eras. Premiums associated to TV characters or
shows are now most likely found as part of a retail
item if indeed offered at all. This book section depicts
a sampling of premium collectibles from a wide variety of shows.

TEL-1

TEL-2

TEL-1. Dumont "Small Fry Club" Cello. Button,
1947. Dumont television network, hosted by Big Brother
Bob Emory. - **$10 $15 $25**

TEL-2. Big Brother "Small Fry Marionette",
1948. Small Fry Club. "Small Fry Girl" in box. "Big Brother
Show" was on radio and converted over to TV. It was one
of the first marionette TV shows. Boxed - **$50 $100 $150**

TEL-3

TEL-4

TEL-3. Jackie Gleason Photo Card,
1940s. NBC TV premium. - **$20 $40 $50**

TEL-4. "Crosley's House Of Fun" Comic Booklet,
1950. Crosley Appliances. - **$5 $8 $12**

TEL-5

TEL-6

TEL-5. Early Version Beany Hand Puppet,
c. 1950. Sears store item. From era of KTLA-TV (Los Angeles) show "Time For Beany". - **$75 $200 $350**

TEL-6. "4 Norge TV Comic Masks" With Envelope,
1951. Norge Appliances. Paper masks of Ed Wynn, Jack Carson, Danny Thomas, Jimmy Durante. Unpunched In Envelope - **$30 $50 $80**

TEL-7   TEL-8

TEL-8. "TV Guide" 8x11" Vending Rack Insert Card,
c. 1952. Design based on Sgt. Joe Friday of Dragnet police TV series. - **$15 $30 $50**

TEL-8. Jack Webb "Dragnet" Sponsor Endorsement Sign,
c. 1952. Fatima Cigarettes. Diecut cardboard countertop sign 16x16" with easel back. - **$50 $125 $200**

TEL-9

TEL-9. "Jerry Lester 'Bean Bag' Club" Kit,
1953. Genesee Beer & Ale. Includes membership card, button, message card. Complete - **$10 $20 $30**

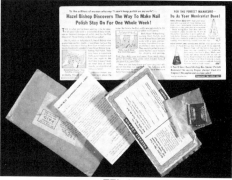

TEL-10

TEL-10. This is Your Life - Book Shaped Locket,
1953. With coupon and ad. Complete - **$50 $100 $175**
Locket Only - **$10 $20 $40**

TEL-11   TEL-12

TEL-11. "Rocket Ranger March" Record,
c. 1953. Store item. From 1953-1954 CBS-TV show "Rod Brown Of The Rocket Rangers" on Columbia label. - **$10 $20 $35**

TEL-12. "The Adventures Of Ozzie And Harriet" Fan Photo,
c. 1953. H. J. Heinz Co. Nelson family photo including sons David and Ricky for show newly sponsored by Heinz over ABC network. - **$8 $15 $25**

TEL-14

TEL-13

TEL-15

TEL-13. Sid Caesar "Your Show of Shows" Cardboard Sign,
1953. 10-1/2x13-1/2". - **$40 $80 $150**

TEL-14. "Groucho Marx" Fan Postcard,
1954. Back ad for "You Bet Your Life" NBC-TV show. - **$20 $40 $65**

TEL-15. "Father Knows Best" Cast Photo Postcard,
c. 1954. Oversized 5-1/2x7" card picturing Anderson family

TEL-16

TEL-17

TEL-16. "Jack Webb Fan Club" Membership Card,
1954. For star of Dragnet TV series. - **$8 $12 $20**

TEL-17. "Dragnet Code Chart" Cardboard Decoder,
1955. Sponsor unknown. - **$10 $20 $30**

TEL-18

TEL-19

TEL-18. "Dragnet 714 Club" Metal Badge, Card and Case,
1955. Store item. - **$15 $25 $35**

TEL-19. "Dragnet Whistle" 20x20" Cardboard Store Sign,
1955. Kellogg's Corn Flakes.
Sign - **$50 $100 $150**
Whistle - **$1 $3 $5**

TEL-20

TEL-21

TEL-20. Sgt. Bilko Cardboard Ad Fan,
c. 1955. Amana Refrigeration. - **$10 $20 $50**

TEL-21. "Chester A. Riley" Fan Postcard,
c. 1955. Cast photo of "Life Of Riley" series. - **$8 $15 $25**

TEL-22

TEL-23

TEL-22. Nelson Family Fan Photo,
c. 1956. Pictures Ozzie, Harriet, Ricky, David with facsimile signatures. - **$10 $25 $40**

TEL-23. "Win A Sgt. Bilko Money Tree" Contest Folder,
1957. Joy liquid dishwashing soap. Contest expired October 15. - **$8 $15 $30**

TEL-24

TEL-25

TEL-24. "The Adventures Of Ozzie & Harriet" Candy Box,
c. 1958. Almond Joy candy bars of Peter Paul Candies. TV sponsorship also indicated for "Maverick" series. - **$35 $60 $80**

TEL-25. Jack Paar 12" Cardboard Standee,
1950s. Schrafft's. - **$60 $90 $120**

TEL-26

TEL-27

TEL-26. Jack Paar Beech-Nut Gum Container,
1950s. Held small free sample boxes. - **$30 $60 $90**

TEL-27. TV Cameraman Plastic Pull Toy,
1950s. Kraft Foods. - **$40 $90 $150**

TEL-28

TEL-28. "RCA TV Coloring Book",
1950s. - **$8 $15 $30**

TEL-29

TEL-30

TEL-29. "Crusader Rabbit Club" Member's Cello. Button,
1950s. Celluloid 1-1/4" - **$20 $80 $100**
Litho. 1-1/8" - **$15 $30 $60**

TEL-30. Television Bread Loaf End Label,
1950s. Pictured example from set depicts "Television Demonstrated" in 1927. Each - **$8 $15 $30**

TEL-31

TEL-31. "Pinky Lee Party Pack",
1950s. Includes booklet, place mats, napkins, party hats, cardboard figures, "Pin The Hat On Pinky" poster with paper hats. Near Mint In Envelope - **$100**

TEL-32

TEL-32. Buffalo Bill, Jr. Belt Buckle and Plastic Belt With Instructions,
1950s. Milky Way. Near Mint Boxed - **$135**
Buckle Only - **$20 $30 $50**

TEL-33   TEL-34   TEL-35

TEL-33. Ding Dong School Bell,
1950s. - **$20 $40 $60**

TEL-34. "Hollywood Off-Beat" TV Show Starring Melvyn Douglas - Dixie Cup Promo,
1950s. - **$20 $40 $60**

TEL-35. Flying Turtle Club Beany TV,
1950s. - **$20 $40 $80**

TEL-36   TEL-37

TEL-36. I Led Three Lives Promo,
1950s. Small cardboard tag. - **$20 $40 $60**

TEL-37. "Winky Dink And You" TV Art Kit,
1950s. Includes erasable "magic" window, crayons and erasing cloth. - **$40 $60 $125**

TEL-39

TEL-38

TEL-38. Nabisco Major Adams TV Sign 13x13",
1950s. Promotes TV show, "Major Adams Trailmaster." Earlier TV program called Wagon Train. - **$50 $100 $175**

TEL-39. Dinah Shore Promo 2 1/2"x5",
1950s. Chevrolet TV premium. - **$10 $25 $40**

TEL-40

TEL-42

TEL-41

TEL-40. Beat The Clock Brochure,
1950s. Sylvania promo for TV program. 10x15". 12 pgs. of great graphics of stars. - **$25 $50 $75**

TEL-41. Captain Kangaroo Puzzle Postcard,
1950s. Kellogg's premium. 8 puzzle pieces. Prize for art drawing submitted to show. - **$25 $50 $75**

TEL-42. "Captain Kangaroo" Cup,
1950s. Colgate toothpaste. Figural plastic with inset flicker eyes. - **$8 $15 $25**

TEL-43   TEL-44

TEL-43. "TV Bank" Litho. Bank,
1950s. Various companies. - **$10 $20 $30**

TEL-44. "Farfel" Ceramic Mug,
1950s. - **$15 $25 $40**

TEL-53

TEL-45

TEL-52

TEL-47

TEL-54

TEL-46

TEL-45. "Gene London Club" 3" Cello. Button,
1950s. Channel 10, Philadelphia TV station. - **$5 $10 $15**

TEL-46. Robin Hood Hat,
1950s. Store bought. - **$20 $40 $80**

TEL-47. Arthur Godfrey Sponsor Ad Photo,
1950s. Snow Crop Frozen Foods. Pictured are Godfrey
and Teddy Snow Crop symbol character. - **$8 $15 $30**

TEL-52. "New! Beany & Cecil In '62!" Cello. Button,
1962. Mattel Toys with Bob Clampett copyright. Probably
from industry toy show. - **$30 $100 $200**

TEL-53. "The Munsters Theatre" Gum Card Box,
1964. Leaf Gum. - **$60 $100 $150**

TEL-54. "Chipmunks/Soaky" Cardboard Record,
1964. Colgate-Palmolive. - **$5 $8 $12**

TEL-48

TEL-49

TEL-50

TEL-48. "Jackie Gleason Fan Club" Cello. Button,
1950s. - **$30 $50 $90**

TEL-49. "Winky Dink" Litho. Button,
1950s. - **$10 $20 $35**

TEL-50. "The Ghost Rider" Cello. Button,
1950s. WCAU-TV (Philadelphia). - **$8 $15 $25**

TEL-56

TEL-55

TEL-55. "Mr. Ed March Of Comics" #260,
1964. Various sponsors. - **$8 $15 $30**

TEL-56. "Jimmy Nelson's Instant Ventriloquism"
Record Album,
1964. Album also pictures Danny O'Day and Farfel. -
$8 $12 $20

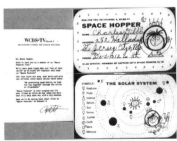

TEL-51

TEL-51. "Space Hopper" Club Letter And Card,
c. 1960. WCBS-TV, New York City. Items for "Captain Jet"
club. Letter - **$8 $15 $20**
Card - **$10 $15 $25**

TEL-57

TEL-57. Beverly Hillbillies Pipe With Mailer,
1965. TV premium. Corncob top pipe blows bubbles. -
$10 $25 $40

TEL-58-60

TEL-58. Man From U.N.C.L.E. Membership Kit Instructions,
1965. Premium, sponsor unknown. - **$10 $20 $30**

TEL-59. Man From U.N.C.L.E. Membership Kit Card,
1965. Premium, sponsor unknown. - **$15 $30 $50**

TEL-60. Man From U.N.C.L.E. Membership Kit Photo,
1965. Premium, sponsor unknown. - **$20 $40 $60**

TEL-61   **TEL-62**   **TEL-63**

TEL-61. Man From U.N.C.L.E. Plastic Badge,
1965 Store item that came with various sets by Ideal Toy Corp. - **$10 $20 $35**

TEL-62. "Napoleon Solo" 3-1/2" Cello. Button,
1965. Store item. From "The Man From U.N.C.L.E." - **$5 $12 $20**

TEL-63. "The Men From U.N.C.L.E." 6" Cello. Button,
1966. - **$20 $30 $50**

TEL-64   **TEL-65**

TEL-64. "Mrs. Beasley" Talking Doll,
1966. Store item by Mattel. Includes plastic glasses.
Talking - **$75 $150 $250**
Not Talking - **$40 $80 $150**

TEL-65. Munsters Flicker Picture Rings,
c. 1966. Vending machine issue. Set of four plastic rings in either silver or blue base.
Silver Base Each - **$35 $55 $75**
Blue Base Each - **$15 $32 $50**

TEL-66

TEL-66. Flipper "Magic Whistle" 5"x24" Paper Store Sign,
c. 1966. P.F. Flyers footwear of B.F. Goodrich. - **$15 $25 $50**

TEL-67

TEL-67. Dolphin "Magic Whistle" Plastic Assembly Parts On Card,
c. 1966. P.F. footwear of B.F. Goodrich. "Flipper" not named but card pictures dolphin, assembled whistle is to produce tone "That Sounds Like A Dolphin".
Unassembled With Card - **$15 $30 $50**
Assembled - **$8 $15 $25**

TEL-68

TEL-68. Vulture Squadron Set Of Soft Rubber Figures,
1969. Kellogg's Froot Loops. Typically about 1-1/2" tall.
Each - **$5 $12 $20**

TEL-69

TEL-69. "Dastardly And Muttley" Kite Safety Booklet,
1969. Color comic produced in association with Reddy Kilowatt with 16 pages of comics and activities involving electricity. - **$10 $25 $45**

TEL-70

TEL-71

TEL-72

TEL-78

TEL-70. Addams Family Plastic Ring Figures,
1960s. Store item. Set of four, originally on card also holding attachment ring. Near Mint Carded - **$300**
Each Ring With Base - **$2 $3**

TEL-71. "Maynard" G. Krebs Composition Bobbing Head,
1960s. Store item. - **$125 $300 $500**

TEL-72. "Dr. Ben Casey M.D." Composition Bobbing Head,
1960s. - **$50 $100 $175**

TEL-74

TEL-75

TEL-73

TEL-73. "Dr. Kildare" Composition Bobbing Head,
1960s. - **$75 $125 $250**

TEL-74. Gumby Flexible Plastic Ring,
1960s. - **$4 $6 $10**

TEL-75. Danny Thomas Flicker Small Sign,
1960s. Post Corn Flakes. - **$50 $100 $125**

TEL-76

TEL-77

TEL-76. "Flipper" Fan Postcard,
1975. - **$10 $20 $35**

TEL-77. "I Dream Of Jeannie" Doll,
1977. Store item by Remco. 6-1/2" tall version.
Boxed - **$75 $150 $250**
Loose - **$50 $125 $200**

TEL-78. "Battlestar Galactica Space Station Kit",
1978. General Mills. Includes manual, punch-out control center and headset, activator card, patch, 11 mission cards, poster, four iron-on transfers.
Near Mint In Mailer - **$100**

TENNESSEE JED

The frontier adventures of Jed Sloan aired on ABC radio from 1945 to 1947. Acting as an undercover agent for General Grant in the period just after the Civil War, Sloan was a deadly marksman who daily did away with cattle rustlers and other villains of the Western Plains. Tip-Top bread and cakes was the sponsor. A single issue of a giveaway comic book was published in 1945.

TEN-1

TEN-1. Exhibit Card And Cardboard Dexterity Puzzle With Envelope,
1945. Tip-Top Bread.
Near Mint In Mailer - **$85**
Card - **$5 $20 $30**
Puzzle - **$10 $30 $40**

TEN-2

TEN-3

TEN-2. Oversized Cardboard Ear For Radio Broadcasts,
1945. Tip-Top Bread. 3x5" with attachment tabs. -
$12 $35 $50

TEN-3. Tip-Top Bread Comic Book,
1945. Inside has adventure map keyed to radio broadcasts. - **$15 $45 $100**

TEN-4

TEN-4. Tip-Top "Horse Puzzle" Cards With Envelope,
c. 1945. Three-card picture placement puzzle with solution on envelope back. - **$20 $50 $75**

TEN-5

TEN-5. Pumpkin Mask,
1945. Tip-Top Bread. - **$30 $65 $100**

TEN-6   TEN-7

TEN-6. "Tennessee Jed Magic Tricks" Booklet,
1940s. Tip-Top Bread. Sixteen pages of illustrated tricks using household products. - **$10 $20 $30**

TEN-7. Picture Card,
1946. Tip-Top Bread. Radio premium. Jed kneeling on one knee. - **$10 $20 $30**

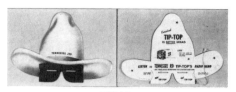

TEN-8

TEN-8. Paper Mask,
1946. - **$15 $40 $60**

TEN-9

TEN-10

TEN-9. "Atom Gun" Cardboard Clicker,
1946. Ward's Tip-Top Bread. - **$20 $75 $100**

TEN-10. Cardboard Ink Blotter,
c. 1946. - **$10 $25 $40**

TEN-11

TEN-12

TEN-11. Magnet Ring,
c. 1946. Brass base with diecut arrowhead designs holding top magnet. - **$125 $225 $450**

TEN-12. Look-Around Brass Ring,
c. 1946. - **$100 $325 $550**

TEN-13

TEN-13. "Catch The Ring" Toy,
1947. Cardboard with attached string and metal ring. - **$10 $30 $40**

TERRY AND THE PIRATES

Milton Caniff created his *Terry and the Pirates* adventure comic strip in 1934 for the Chicago Tribune-New York News Syndicate. The scene of the action was China, and young Terry Lee and his pal Pat Ryan were to come up against a variety of evil-doers and exotic women, notably the infamous Dragon Lady. During World War II Terry became an Air Force pilot and, along with Colonel Flip Corkin, battled the Axis. The strip ceased publication in 1973. A number of *Terry and the Pirates* comic books were published between 1939 and 1955, including giveaways from Sears & Roebuck, Buster Brown, Canada Dry, Libby Foods, Weather Bird shoes and others.

Radio adaptations aired on NBC from 1937 to 1939, sponsored by Dari-Rich chocolate drink, and on ABC from 1943 to 1948, sponsored by Quaker Oats, Puffed Wheat, and Puffed Rice. A 15-episode chapter play was released by Columbia Pictures in 1940 with William Tracy as Terry, and a syndicated television series aired in New York in 1952-1953 and had continued distribution through the 1950s.

TER-1

TER-2

TER-3

TER-1. "Terry And The Pirates Meet Again",
1936. Tarzan Ice Cream Cups. Booklet #10 from series of various character titles. - **$20 $45 $85**

TER-2. Quaker Puffed Wheat Comic Book,
1938. - **$1 $2 $5**

TER-3. "Adventures Of Terry And The Pirates" Booklet,
1938. From Whitman Penny Books series with inside ad for "Super-Comics" and "Crackajack Funnies" comic books. - **$15 $25 $35**

TER-4

TER-5

TER-4. "Treasure Hunter's Guide" Booklet,
1938. Dari-Rich Chocolate Drink. Contents basically about stamp collecting. - **$20 $40 $60**

TER-5. "Ruby Of Genghis Khan" Comic Activity Book,
1941. Rare. Libby's fruit and vegetable juices. Contents include pencil puzzles, games, coloring pages, magic tricks, cut-out dolls. - **$200 $500 $1500**

TER-6

(GAME PIECES SHOWN ATTACHED TO SCOPE AT BOTTOM LEFT)

TER-6. "Terryscope" Cardboard Assembly Kit,
1941. Rare. Libby, McNeill & Libby. Pictures six characters, one side features secret code. Game pieces came attached to side of unassembled Terryscope.
Near Mint Terryscope Unassembled - **$600**
Terryscope Assembled - **$100 $300 $480**
Game Pieces (Four Different) - **$80**
Mailer - **$30 $60 $100**

TER-7

TER-7. Libby's Display Sign,
1942. Sign is probably unique; shows Terry showing how to get plane spotter premium. Gold archives.
Sold for **$1365**

TER-9

TER-8

TER-8. "Victory Airplane Spotter" Cardboard Mechanical Disk With Envelope,
1942. Libby, McNeill & Libby. Pictures Terry, Pat, April, Burma, Connie plus identifies 16 warplane silhouettes. - **$75 $175 $325**

TER-9. Quaker Oats B-25 Mascot Plane Photo,
1943. - **$15 $30 $50**

TER-10

TER-11

TER-10. "Pilot's Mascot" Wooden Button,
1943. Wire loop reverse for wearing with a safety pin. Came with Quaker Cereals B-25 airplane picture. - **$10 $20 $35**

TER-11. Quaker Oats Pictures,
c. 1944. Set of six. Pat Ryan, Burma, Terry, Phil Corkin, Dragon Lady, Connie. Near Mint In Mailer - **$500**
Each - **$20 $60 $75**

TER-12

TER-12. Quaker "Wings Of Victory" Box,
c. 1945. Set of 12 warplane back pictures.
Each Complete Box - **$50 $150 $250**
Each Cut Picture Panel - **$5 $20 $25**

TER-13

TER-13. Quaker Cereals "Sparkies Jingle Contest" Postcard,
1946. - **$8 $20 $40**

TER-14

TER-15

TER-14. Pirate's Gold Ore Detector Ring,
1947. Quaker Cereals. Brass with aluminum/plastic tele-scope viewer holding tiny gold flakes. Documented by radio show episode titled "Quaker Puffed Wheat and Quaker Puffed Rice bring you Terry and the Pirates - the new and exciting adventure of Terry Lee and the Pirate Gold Detector Ring." The episode begins with Terry speaking about his long search for this ring. -
$50 $100 $150

TER-15. "Tattoo Transfers" Set In Envelope,
c. 1948. Coco-Wheats cereal. 22 water transfer pictures on two sheets, "Pack No. 9". - **$25 $50 $75**

TER-16

TER-17

TER-16. Artist George Wunder Personal Christmas Card,
c. 1948. - **$20 $40 $60**

TER-17. Character Stamps For Contest Entry,
1940s. Quaker Oats. Awarded to entrants in bicycle contest announced in part by radio broadcasts. - **$30 $60 $90**

TER-18

TER-19

TER-18. "Terry Jingle" Contest Postcard,
1940s. Quaker Puffed Wheat and Rice Sparkies. Acknowledgement card for entrant. - **$20 $35 $50**

TER-19. "Canada Dry" 13x17" Cardboard Ad Sign,
1953. (Has 1952 copyright.) Offered a comic book with purchase of every carton of soda. - **$100 $150 $250**

TER-20

TER-20. "Hot Shot Charlie Flies Again" No. 1 Comic Book,
1953. Canada Dry. From set of three. - **$15 $40 $95**

TER-21

TER-21. "Terry And The Pirates In Forced Landing" Comic Book #2,
1953. Canada Dry. Third book in set "Dragon Lady In Distress". Each - **$15 $40 $95**

TER-22

TER-23

TER-22. Canada Dry "Chop-Stick-Joe" Litho. Button,
1953. From set of five also including Terry, Burma, Dragon Lady, Hot Shot Charlie. Each - **$10 $20 $30**

TER-23. "See Terry On TV" 3" Flicker Button,
c. 1953. Canada Dry. - **$30 $50 $75**

TER-24

TER-24. Comic Book Ad,
1950s. Canada Dry. - **$10 $20 $30**

THREE LITTLE PIGS

Disney's *The Three Little Pigs*, based on a Grimm brothers fairy tale, premiered in New York in 1933 and went on to become one of the most successful animated cartoons ever produced. The story of the pigs-- Fifer, Fiddler, and Drummer--defending their homes and defying the wolf at the door, entranced children and adults alike. The merry theme, *Who's Afraid of the Big Bad Wolf*, became one of the most popular songs of the 1930s. Merchandising was extensive, and many Disney licensees added pig and wolf items to their product lines.

TLP-1

TLP-1. Three Little Pigs Paper Mask,
1933. Lord & Taylor (and others), publisher is Einson-Freeman Co. Each - **$15 $30 $50**

TLP-2

TLP-3

TLP-2. Walt Disney Studio Christmas Card,
1933. - **$200 $350 $750**

TLP-3. "Who's Afraid Of The Big Bad Wolf" Sheet Music,
1933. Store item. Words and music to song "From The Walt Disney Silly Symphony The Three Little Pigs." - **$15 $30 $50**

TLP-4

TLP-4. Ingersoll Animated Pocketwatch With Box,
1934. Store item. Wolf's eye winks, red color on dial often faded. Near Mint Boxed - **$1800**
Watch - **$300 $600 $1000**

TLP-5

TLP-6

TLP-5. "Who's Afraid Of The Big Bad Wolf" Cello. Button,
c. 1935. Pictured as give-away in Disney merchandise catalogues of the time. - **$50 $75 $150**

TLP-6. Three Little Pigs Ceramic Ashtray,
1930s. Store item. - **$40 $65 $90**

TLP-7

TLP-7. Three Little Pigs Enameled Brass Matchbox Holder,
1930s. Store item. - **$15 $25 $40**

TLP-8

TLP-8. Bab-O Folder With Three Pigs Picture,
1930s. - **$25 $50 $75**

TLP-9

TLP-9. China Compartment Dish,
1930s. Store item also used as premium. -
$50 $100 $150

TLP-10

TLP-11

TLP-10. "Who's Afraid Of The Big Bad Wolf"
Pocketknife,
1930s. Scarce. Store item by Geo. Schrade Co. Steel with
silvered brass and enamel paint grips. - $50 $100 $150

TLP-11. "Who's Afraid Of The Big Bad Wolf" Enameled
Brass Badge,
1930s. Pig at piano. - $40 $85 $150

TLP-12   TLP-13

TLP-14

TLP-12. "Three Little Pigs/Who's Afraid Of The Big Bad
Wolf" Enameled Brass Badge,
1930s. Version pictures Fiddler Pig. - $40 $85 $150

TLP-13. "Who's Afraid Of The Big Bad Wolf" Tin Toy
Watch With Moving Hands,
1930s. Store item. Finished in four colors. -
$75 $125 $200

TLP-14. Lil Bad Wolf Glass Tumbler,
1985. Fanta soda. For German distribution with inscriptions
mostly in German. - $8 $12 $20

THREE STOOGES

Slapstick and comic mayhem were the wacky hall-
marks of the Three Stooges in their two dozen feature
films and almost 200 two-reelers made between 1930
and 1965. The original trio--Moe Howard, his brother
Curly, and Larry Fine--went from success in vaudeville
to cult status in Hollywood and later to enduring popularity via television reruns in the late 1950s. (Another
brother, Shemp, took over when Curly died; Joe
Besser replaced Shemp on his death; and Joe DeRita
later replaced Besser.) Animated cartoon series produced by Hanna-Barbera were syndicated on televi-
sion--*The Three Stooges* in 1965 and *The Three
Robonic Stooges* in 1978. Comic books appeared from
the late 1940s to the 1970s. Will the Stooges' brand of
comedy continue into the future? "Soitenly!"

THR-1

THR-1. "Moving Picture Machine" Newspaper Ad,
1937. Pillsbury's Farina. - $25 $60 $100

THR-2

THR-2. "Moving Picture Machine" Cardboard
Punch-Out Kit,
1937. Pillsbury's Farina. Came with films #5 and #6 based
on actual movie "False Alarms," others available by purchasing more Farina. Scarce.
Unpunched - $350 $1000 $2000
Assembled - $150 $500 $800

THR-3

THR-4

THR-3. Photo With Ad Reverse,
c. 1937. Pillsbury's Farina. Back offer is tied to Columbia Pictures promotion. - **$50 $125 $200**

THR-4. "Three Stooges" 3-D Comic Vol. 1 #2,
1953. St. John Publishing Co. - **$40 $120 $300**

THR-5

THR-5. Vending Machine Display Paper For Picture Rings,
1959. - **$15 $25 $40**

THR-6

THR-6. "Fan Club Of America" Membership Kit,
1959. Includes envelope, cover letter, sheet of stamps, "fan club franchise" certificate, sheet of four membership cards and two 5"x7" black and white photos.
Complete - **$50 $100 $200**

THR-7

THR-9

THR-8

THR-7. "Three Stooges/I'm Curly" Ring,
1959. Gold plastic base with two flicker portraits. Also issued with Moe and Larry. Each - **$10 $17 $25**

THR-8. Movie/Fan Club Photo Card,
1964. Black and white picturing them from movie "The 3 Stooges Go Around The World In A Daze" with facsimile signatures. - **$10 $20 $30**
Each Real Autograph Add - **$25 $50 $75**

THR-9. Group Portrait 2-1/4" Cello. Button,
c. 1960s. No sponsor, made by St. Louis Badge Co. - **$15 $30 $50**

THR-10

THR-10. Triple Image Ceramic Bank,
c. 1960s. Store item. - **$150 $300 $600**

THR-11

THR-12

THR-11. Happy Birthday Record,
1960s. Possible premium, personalized to individual first name. - **$10 $20 $30**

THR-12. "Clark/Collector Cups" 3" Cello. Button,
1993. - **$5 $10 $18**

THURSTON, THE MAGICIAN

Howard Thurston (1869-1936) was a master magician who made a triumphant world tour in the early years of the 20th century, performing before royalty and notables. Thurston's exploits and adventures were dramatized in a short-lived radio series on the NBC Blue network in 1932-1933. The program, known as *Thurston, the Magician* or *Howard Thurston, the Magician*, was sponsored by Swift & Co.

THU-6 THU-7 THU-8

THU-6. "Thurston's Book Of Magic #1",
1932. Swift & Company. Shows illustrations and explains how to do different tricks. - **$15 $35 $50**

THU-7. "Thurston's Book Of Magic #2",
1932. Swift & Company. Shows illustrations and explains how to do different tricks. - **$15 $35 $50**

THU-8. "Thurston's Book Of Magic #3",
1932. Swift & Company. Shows illustrations and explains how to do different tricks. - **$15 $35 $50**

THU-1

THU-2

THU-1. "Good Luck/Thurston" Cello. Button,
c. 1920. - **$15 $35 $75**

THU-2. "Good Luck" Card,
c. 1920s. - **$5 $10 $15**

THU-3 THU-4

THU-3. Magician Coin,
1928. Good Luck Charm premium. Says "Thurston The Magician" on front. - **$20 $40 $60**

THU-4. Magician Coin,
1929. Rare. Says "Thurston The Magician" on front. - **$30 $60 $120**

THU-9 THU-10 THU-11

THU-9. "Thurston's Book Of Magic #4",
1932. Swift & Company. Shows illustrations and explains how to do different tricks. - **$15 $35 $50**

THU-10. "Thurston's Book Of Magic #5",
1932. Swift & Company. Shows illustrations and explains how to do different tricks. - **$15 $35 $50**

THU-11. Trick Packets,
c. 1932. Swift & Co. At least 11 in set. Each - **$3 $10 $20**

THU-5

THU-5. "Thurston's Dream Book",
c. 1920s. 32-page dream interpretation booklet sold for 25 cents through Thurston's Mystic Palace, Beechurst, Long Island, New York. - **$15 $25 $35**

TIM CLUB

This club, headed by "Tim," a cartoon image lad with no surname, existed as early as 1929. Membership loosely consisted of youngsters that patronized clothing stores electing to join the "Tim" endorsement theme. Premiums included code books, stamp albums and pin-backs related to "Pie Eater" activities. Tim's merchandising clout was revitalized beginning in the early 1940s by addition of a super partner, Superman to be exact. Tim carried on his tradition but became the second banana in the new "Superman-Tim Store" promotion. Premiums continued, apparently free, including a monthly mailer newsletter/clothing catalogue/activities manual imprinted by local store name.

Superman was prominently featured in each. Additional premiums were pin-back buttons, pennants, album stamps, Secret Code and other membership items. Superman-Tim currency was also available. The Club was still officially licensed to Tim Promotions, Inc. of New York City. Kay Kamen, who guided the club's successful marketing efforts, is the subject of a feature article in this edition.

TIM-1

TIM-1. Code Books,
c. 1930. Participating Tim stores. Pictured examples are for 1929, 1930, 1933. Each - **$8 $12 $20**

TIM-2   **TIM-3**

TIM-2. "The Knicker" Magazine,
1930. Monthly publication, pictured example is for October. Each contains 12 pages with local store imprint on back cover. Each Issue - **$4 $8 $12**

TIM-3. Tim Rancho Code Book,
1935. Pie Eater's Club premium. 16 pages. - **$4 $8 $12**

TIM-4   **TIM-5**

TIM-4. Pie-Eater Club Member Happy Birthday Letter,
1930s. Metropolitan (clothing) store. Invites recipient to pick up free pie. - **$10 $15 $25**

TIM-5. "Tim's Official Stamps",
1930s. Participating stores. For mounting in album supplied by store. Each - **$3 $10 $15**

TIM-6

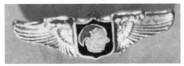

TIM-7

TIM-6. Cello. Club Button,
1930s. Red, white, blue and gold. - **$8 $15 $30**

TIM-7. Silvered Metal Portrait Ring,
1930s. Raised portrait with dog portrait on each band, possibly sterling. - **$100 $250 $500**

TIM-8

TIM-8. Tim Wings,
1930s. Scarce. Store premium. - **$30 $90 $150**

TIM-9   **TIM-10**

TIM-9. "Tim's Magazine",
1940. Participating stores. Issued monthly. Each - **$5 $10 $15**

TIM-10. Tim's "Redback" Currency,
1940s. Various stores. Various denominations. Each - **$2 $5 $8**

TIM-11   **TIM-12**   **TIM-13**

TIM-11. "Pie Eaters Club/Tim" Litho. Button,
c. 1940s. - **$3 $6 $10**

TIM-12. "Tim's Store For Boys" Cello. Button,
c. 1940s. - **$5 $10 $20**

TIM-13. "Tim's Official Pie Eaters Club" Cello. Button,
c. 1940s. - **$3 $10 $15**

TIM-14   TIM-15   TIM-16

TIM-14. "Pie Eaters Club/Tim" Cello. Button,
c. 1940s. - **$3 $10 $15**

TIM-15. "Tim's Lucky Coin",
c. 1940s. Front portrait, back inscription "From Tim's Official Store". Brass. - **$10 $20 $40**

TIM-16. "Tim's Club For Boys" Litho. Button,
1940s. - **$10 $25 $40**

TIM TYLER

Cartoonist Lyman Young created *Tim Tyler's Luck* for the King Features Syndicate as a daily strip in 1928 and as a Sunday page in 1931. Tim's adventures took him to Africa, where he joined the Ivory Patrol to help maintain law and order. A syndicated radio program aired in 1936-1937, a series of comic books appeared in the 1940s, and Universal Pictures released a 12-episode chapter play, also called *Tim Tyler's Luck*, in 1937, with Frankie Thomas as Tim.

TYL-1

TYL-1. "Tim Tyler In The Jungle" Pop-Up Book,
1935. Store item by Blue Ribbon Press, Pleasure Books Inc. Twenty pages including three double-page color pop-ups. - **$75 $150 $250**

TYL-2   TYL-3

TYL-2. "Tim Tyler's Luck/Ivory Patrol Club" Cello. Button,
1937. Universal Pictures. For 12-chapter movie serial. - **$30 $60 $100**

TYL-3. "Tim Tyler Ivory Patrol Club/Viva" Cello. Button,
c. 1937. - **$40 $75 $150**

TOM AND JERRY

The classic helter-skelter cat-and-mouse rivalry between Tom and Jerry was brought to life in 114 theatrical cartoons created by the Hanna-Barbera team for MGM between 1939 and 1957. The animated superstars, with Tom generally chasing Jerry and with hardly ever a word of dialogue, won seven Oscars between 1943 and 1952. MGM produced additional *Tom & Jerry* series in 1961-1962 and in 1963-1967. *Tom & Jerry: The Movie* ("They talk!") was released in 1993.

The cartoon stars debuted on television when the Hanna-Barbera shorts aired on CBS Saturday mornings from 1965 to 1972. A made-for-TV series under a variety of names appeared starting in 1975. *Tom & Jerry Kids* premiered on the Fox Children's Network in 1990. The mischievous duo continues to win fans to this day. Licensing and merchandising of the characters has been extensive.

TMJ-1

TMJ-1. Movie Flip Booklets,
1949. Grape-Nuts Flakes. Box inserts from series of 12 based on M-G-M or Walter Lantz cartoon characters. Each - **$5 $12 $20**

TMJ-2   TMJ-3

TMJ-4

TMJ-2. "Tom & Jerry Go For Stroehmann's Bread" Litho. Button,
1950s. - **$8 $12 $20**

TMJ-3. "ABC Minors/M.G.M.'s Tom And Jerry" Cello. Button,
c. 1960s. English Issue. - **$10 $15 $25**

TMJ-4. "March Of Comics" Booklet,
1970. Child Life Shoes. Issue #345 reprinting 1970 comic book story. - **$2 $5 $10**

TMJ-5

TMJ-5. Scooter Friction Drive Toy With Box,
1972. Store item by Marx Toys. Plastic toy in image of Tom as operator and Jerry as sidecar passenger.
Near Mint Boxed - **$90**
Loose - **$15 $30 $60**

TMJ-6

TMJ-7

TMJ-6. Boxed Vinyl Figure Banks,
1978. Store item authorized figures packaged individually in matching "Money Box" cartons.
Near Mint Each Boxed - **$40** Each Loose - **$8 $15 $25**

TMJ-7. Ceramic Pencil Holder,
1981. Store item made for Gorham Products. -
$10 $20 $40

TOM CORBETT, SPACE CADET

Set in the 24th century, this television space adventure followed the exploits of three young cadets as they trained in their spaceship Polaris to become officers of the Solar Guards. The series, based on Robert Heinlein's 1948 novel *Space Cadet* and scripted with the technical advice of rocket scientist Willy Ley, was distinguished by scientific accuracy and innovative camera effects. Corbett's unit at the Space Academy included Roger Manning (So what happens now, space heroes?) and Astro, a quick-tempered Venusian youth. Veteran actor Frankie Thomas played the part of Corbett.

Tom Corbett, Space Cadet was one of the few series to appear on all four commercial TV networks, and on two of them simultaneously. The show, which was broadcast live, debuted on CBS in 1950, moved to ABC in 1951-1952, appeared on NBC in the summer of 1951, on the Dumont network in 1953-1954, and again on NBC in 1954-1955. Sponsors were Kellogg's cereals (1950-1952), Red Goose shoes (1953-1954), and Kraft Foods (1954-1955). The series also ran on ABC radio for six months in 1952, featuring the same cast as sponsored by Kellogg, and as a simulcast on NBC in 1954-1955, sponsored by Kraft.

In print, a Corbett comic strip distributed by the Field Newspaper Syndicate appeared from 1951 to 1953, comic books between 1952 and 1955, and a series of Corbett novels from Grosset & Dunlap between 1952 and 1956.

Merchandising of Tom Corbett material was extensive, including toys, a watch, lunch boxes, space goggles, and helmets. Kellogg's promoted a Space Academy membership club that offered badges, rings, patches, a cardboard decoder, ID cards, and autographed photos. Items are normally copyrighted Rockhill Productions.

TCO-2

TCO-1

TCO-3

TCO-1. Membership Kit Cast Photo,
1951. - **$15 $40 $60**

TCO-2. "Space Cadet" 2-1/8" Cello. Button,
1951. Part of club membership kit. - **$50 $150 $200**

TCO-3. Fabric Patch,
1951. Part of member's kit. - **$20 $40 $75**

TCO-4

TCO-5

TCO-4. Certificate,
1951. Part of member's kit. - **$20 $45 $75**

TCO-5. Kellogg's Cardboard Decoder,
1951. Came with membership kit. - **$35 $90 $150**

TCO-6

TCO-6. "Tom Corbett Space Cadet News" Vol. 1 #1,
1951. Kellogg's. Part of member's kit. - **$35 $100 $150**

TCO-7

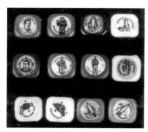

TCO-8

TCO-7. "Rocket Rings" Comic Book Page Ad,
1951. Kellogg's Pep cereal. - **$2 $4 $6**

TCO-8. Kellogg's Plastic Rings With Insert Pictures,
1951. Set of 12. Near Mint Set - **$300**
Each - **$10 $15 $20**

TCO-9

TCO-9. Cereal Box With "Tom Corbett Space Cadet Squadron" Back,
1951. Also pictures "Rocket Launching Plane Catapulting Aircraft Carrier". Complete Box - **$150 $300 $400**

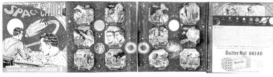

TCO-10

TCO-10. Butter-Nut Bread End Label Album #1,
1952. Various sponsor imprints. Complete with 24 bread labels. Album #2 was also issued with additional set of 24 labels. Near Mint Complete - **$500**
Album Only - **$30 $80 $125**
Each Label - **$5 $10 $15**

TCO-11

TCO-12

TCO-11. Fischer's Buttercup Bread End Label Album No. 2,
1952. Various sponsors. Holds labels #25-48.
Near Mint Complete - **$500**
Album Only - **$30 $80 $125**
Each Label - **$5 $10 $15**

TCO-12. "TV Digest" With Cover Article,
1952. Weekly issue for August 23 with two-page article including photos. Front cover also pictures songstress Patti Page. - **$15 $30 $50**

TCO-13

TCO-13. Kellogg's Pep Flat - 8 oz. Cereal Box,
1952. Astro "Space Cadet" pictured on back. Also promotes Tom Corbett TV show. - **$125 $250 $500**

TCO-14   **TCO-15**

TCO-16

TCO-14. "Tom Corbett/Space Cadet" Silvered Metal Ring,
c. 1952. - **$50 $75 $100**

TCO-15. Rocket Ring,
c. 1952. Silvered brass and white gold luster metal inscribed on underside "Space Cadet/Tom Corbett Unit". - **$175 $300 $550**

TCO-16. Metal Badge,
c. 1952. - **$15 $35 $75**

TCO-17

TCO-18

TCO-17. "Electronic Inter-Planet 2-Way Phone",
1953. Store item. Cardboard box holding pair of plastic phones and coil of wire. Boxed Set - **$100 $200 $300**
Each Phone - **$25 $50 $75**

TCO-18. View-Master Set,
1954. Store item. - **$15 $25 $35**

TCO-19

TCO-20

TCO-19. Die-cut Metal Pin,
1954. In Sears catalogue, came with purchase of Corbett flashlight. - **$20 $75 $125**
On Card - **$250**

TCO-20. Metallic Silver Fabric Cap with Sunglasses,
1950s. Scarce. Probable premium. - **$50 $75 $150**

TCO-22

TCO-21

TCO-21. Official Hat,
1950s. Scarce. Probable store item. Includes plastic badge on front. - **$75 $150 $300**

TCO-22. Fiberboard Helmet,
1950s. Scarce. Probable store item. Includes plastic badge on front. - **$75 $150 $200**

TCO-23

TCO-24

TCO-23. Litho. Clicker Gun,
1950s. Store item by Marx. - **$50 $125 $200**

TCO-24. "Two-Way Electronic Walkie-Talkie Phone" Set,
1950s. Store item by Remco. Phone Set - **$30 $60 $100**
Instructions - **$15 $30 $50**
Code Card - **$15 $30 $50**

TCO-25

TCO-26

TCO-25. Rocket-Lite Squadron Club Card,
1950s. Reverse instructions for Space Cadet pin-on rocket light. - **$10 $30 $40**

TCO-26. Kellogg's "Space Cadet Rocketship" Plastic Flicker Disk,
1950s. From series picturing various Tom Corbett (and other) scenes. - **$8 $12 $25**

TCO-28

TCO-27

TCO-27. Spaceship Balloon With Mailer,
1950s. Comes with unpunched cardboard base & two balloons. Probably store bought. - **$75 $125 $175**

TCO-28. Visor,
1950s. Cardboard cut-out from cereal box. - **$15 $25 $35**

TCO-29

TCO-29. Model Craft Set,
1950s. Box, powder, can, glue, paint set and 8 rubber molds. You could send off 10¢ for each extra mold. You could collect up to 350 different. Features molds for 7 Tom Corbett Space Cadet cast consisting of Tom, Roger, Astro, Captain Strong, Dr. Dale, and a Vesuvian as well as the logo for the TV show. - **$150 $350 $500**

TOM MIX

Tom Mix (1880-1940), the greatest Western film star of the silent era, was born and grew up in rural DuBois, Pennsylvania. He enlisted in the Army at the outbreak of the Spanish-American war in 1898 and achieved the rank of first sergeant. His overseas military adventures are part of the legend, not reality, as he never left the United States. After leaving the Army in 1902 he moved to Oklahoma and found work as a drum major, bartender, and part-time ranch hand. In 1904 he attended the St. Louis World's Fair as a member of the Oklahoma Cavalry Band. In 1905 he went to work as a "cowboy" for the Miller Brothers' 101 Real Wild West Ranch, barnstormed in other Wild West shows, and served as a deputy sheriff and night marshal.

Tom Mix's movie career began in 1909 for the Selig Polyscope Company, first as an advisor and troubleshooter, then doubling as a stunt man, and ultimately starring in, writing, and directing some 64 silent shorts. By 1917, when he was hired by William Fox Productions, he was a star, and by 1921 he was one of the country's 10 top box office attractions. Over a period of 10 years he made 78 silent features for Fox, most of them as an idealized Western hero, doing his own stunts and riding his chestnut steed, Tony the Wonder Horse, to fame and fortune. He made another six silent features in 1928-1929 for the Film Booking Office, then left Hollywood to tour and star in Sells Floto Circus from 1929 to 1931.

Returning to films, he and Tony Jr. made his first talkies, nine features for Universal Pictures in 1931-1932, and his last movie, *The Miracle Rider*, a 15-episode chapter play, for Mascot Pictures in 1935. That same year he bought a circus, and from 1935 to 1938 the Tom Mix Circus toured the country and performed for crowds of admirers. In 1940 he was killed in an automobile accident in Arizona.

The Tom Mix radio program aired from 1933 to 1950, on NBC until 1944, then on the Mutual network. Ralston cereal was the exclusive radio program sponsor. Various actors played Tom in what was billed as a Western detective program. Tom and the Ralston Straight Shooters operated out of the T-M Bar Ranch, solving mysteries, crusading for justice, finding water for the cattle, even fighting saboteurs during the war years. Helping out, along with Tony, were young Jimmy and Jane, the Old Wrangler, Sheriff Mike Shaw, Wash the cook, and Pecos Williams, a singing sidekick played by Joe "Curley" Bradley until he took over the role of Tom in 1940.

Ralston offered hundreds of Tom Mix premiums--rings, flashlights, magnifiers, whistles, sirens, spurs, telescopes, wooden guns, comic books, photo albums, badges, anything that could carry the familiar Ralston checkerboard design or the T-M Bar brand. Tom's first comic book appearance was in issue #1 of *The Comics* in 1937, and he had his own books in the 1940s and 1950s. Ralston briefly revived the Straight Shooters in 1982-1983 as a 50th anniversary tribute, offering a comic book, patch, cereal bowl and watch in exchange for box tops. The Tom Mix Museum in Dewey, Oklahoma, opened in 1968.

TMX-1   TMX-2

TMX-1. "Complete Novel Magazine" With Movie Story, 1928. Pulp issue #35 for March featuring Tom Mix novel based on William Fox Production silent film "Daredevil's Reward." - **$75 $150 $225**

TMX-2. Photo Cover - Fox Trot Song Book, 1929. Four pages. Store bought - **$25 $50 $100**

TMX-3   TMX-4   TMX-5

TMX-3. "Sells Floto Circus" Cello. Button, c. 1929. Word "Sells" is part of circus proper name. Mix toured with circus 1929-1931. - **$20 $40 $75**

TMX-4. "Tom Mix For Sheriff" Cello. Button, c. 1930. - **$200 $400 $800**

TMX-5. "Tom Mix With Tony/Universal Pictures" Cello. Button, 1932. From his 1932-1933 years at Universal. - **$65 $125 $200**

TMX-6   TMX-7

TMX-6. Chewing Gum Wrapper With Deputy Ring Offer, 1933. National Chicle Co. Product copyright is 1933. Ring offer expired June 30, 1935. - **$80 $100 $120**

TMX-7. "The Life Of Tom Mix" First Club Manual, 1933. - **$40 $80 $150**

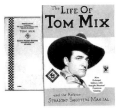

TMX-8

TMX-15

TMX-16

TMX-15. Revolver,
1933. Earliest gun, opens and cylinder revolves. -
$40 $80 $150

TMX-16. Cowboy Hat,
1933. Rare premium. Name is not on inside. -
$150 $400 $925

TMX-9

TMX-8. Club Manual "Enlarged Edition",
1933. Near Mint With Mailer - **$150**
Loose - **$40 $75 $125**

TMX-9. Premium Catalogue Sheet,
1933. - **$20 $40 $65**

TMX-17

TMX-18

TMX-17. Leather Wrist Cuffs,
1933. Shown at left, no Mix identification, depicts cowboy
with lariat. Set of Two - **$60 $125 $200**
With Mix Identification and Star (shown at right)
Set of Two - **$300**

TMX-18. Metal Spurs With Leather Straps,
1933. No Mix identification, horse head on top strap.
Rubber rowels each have two metal jangle weights. -
$100 $175 $250

TMX-10

TMX-11

TMX-10. Tom Mix & Tony Photo,
1933. - **$15 $25 $40**

TMX-11. Paper Lario With Tricks And Stunts Sheet,
1933. Tricks Sheet - **$35 $80 $125**
Lario - **$50 $125 $200**

TMX-19

TMX-20

TMX-21

TMX-19. Fabric Bandanna,
1933. - **$30 $60 $125**

TMX-20. "Straight Shooters" Fabric Patch,
1933. - **$15 $25 $50**

TMX-21. "Good Luck/TM" Spinner,
1933. - **$20 $40 $65**

TMX-12   **TMX-13**

TMX-14

TMX-12. Cigar Box Label,
1933. - **$20 $40 $80**

TMX-13. Cigar Box Label,
1933. - **$20 $40 $80**

TMX-14. Postcard,
1933. - **$10 $20 $40**

TMX-22

TMX-23

TMX-24

TMX-22. Horseshoe Nail Ring,
1933. Generic horseshoe nail with silver luster. No Tom
Mix markings. - **$20 $30 $40**

TMX-23. "TM" Spinner Ring,
1933. Rare. Possibly a circus souvenir. -
$800 $1600 $3000

TMX-24. "Lucky Pocket Piece" Brass Medalet,
c. 1933 "Exhibit Supply Company/Chicago" on reverse
inside with horseshoe design. - **$25 $50 $90**

TMX-25

TMX-26

TMX-25. Radio Program 15x24" Cardboard Sign,
c. 1933. Printed both sides. - **$100 $200 $400**

TMX-26. "Tom Mix" Bisque 5" Figurine,
c. 1933. Rare. Store item. Only figural Mix item known.
Made in Germany, marked #3509. - **$800 $2500 $5000**

TMX-27

TMX-28

TMX-27. Rodeorope And Full Color Box,
1934. Store item. - **$100 $300 $410**

TMX-28. National Chicle Co. Gum Booklet #2 Example,
1934. 48 numbered booklets. Each - **$10 $20 $35**

TMX-29

TMX-29. Press Book,
1934. Rare. Elaborate 12 page book which features Tom
Mix's first serial, "The Miracle Rider." Talks about Tom
Mix's radio audience reaching 25 million listeners, his product line, and how to get premiums. Shows all 15 chapter
lobby cards and posters. 16x 21" - **$300 $750 $900**

TMX-30

TMX-31

TMX-30. Premiums Catalogue Folder Sheet,
1934. Catalogue designated C 135 G. - **$20 $35 $50**

TMX-31. Ralston Radio Ad Cardboard Sign,
1934. Diecut cardboard 20x32" urging listenership over
NBC Red Network. - **$250 $400 $800**

TMX-32

TMX-33

**TMX-32. "Official Commission/Ranch Boss"
Certificate,**
1934. Promotion certification with facsimile signature of
Tom Mix and "The Old Wrangler" as witness. -
$100 $200 $300

TMX-33. Paper Mask,
1934. Scarce. - **$250 $500 $750**

TMX-34

TMX-34. Premiums Catalogue Folder Sheet,
1934. Catalogue designated C 135 O. - **$15 $30 $45**

TMX-35

TMX-35. "Series A" Photo Set,
1934. Set of five. Each Photo Or Mailer - **$10 $25 $50**

TMX-36

TMX-36. "Series B" Photo Set With Envelope,
1934. Set of five photos. Each Photo Or Mailer -
$10 $25 $50

TMX-38

TMX-37

TMX-37. Zyp Gun With Mailer Envelope,
1934. Scarce. Metal spring gun with rubber cup dart. Also
known as Tom Mix Target Gun.
Gun With Dart - **$150 $450 $650**
Mailer - **$15 $35 $50**

TMX-38. "Tom Mix Deputy" Gold And Silver Finish Brass Ring,
1935. National Chicle Gum. Required 75 certificates
clipped from gum wrappers. - **$1450 $3200 $6800**

TMX-39

TMX-39. Tom Mix Big Little Book Puzzles (Boxed),
1935. Store item. - **$100 $275 $425**

TMX-40

TMX-41

TMX-40. Paint Book,
1935. Store item. - **$100 $250 $400**

TMX-41. "Miracle Riders" Picture Folio,
1935. Holds 15 bw numbered photo pages apparently cor-
responding to 15 serial chapters. Distributed by theaters,
sponsored by Tootsie Rolls. Set - **$125 $275 $425**

TMX-43

TMX-42

TMX-42. "Miracle Rider" Serial Club Cello. Button,
1935. Mascot. - **$100 $300 $500**

TMX-43. "Shooting Gallery" Cardboard Target With Box,
1935. Store item by Parker Brothers. Includes rubber band
gun. - **$75 $250 $350**

TMX-44

TMX-45

TMX-44. Western Song Book,
1935. Sixty-eight page book shows photos of Tom Mix and
promotes his films. Includes letter from Tom Mix. -
$50 $100 $200

TMX-45. Theater Instructions,
1935. 7-step instruction sheet. - **$15 $25 $35**

TMX-46

TMX-47

TMX-46. Litho. Portrait Button,
1935. Canvas Products Co., St. Louis. Five buttons given
with purchase of Tom Mix tent. - **$35 $75 $150**

TMX-47. "The Trail Of The Terrible 6" Booklet,
1935. - **$15 $40 $85**

TMX-48

TMX-48. "Western Movie" Cardboard Mechanical Viewer,
1935. Film scenes from "The Miracle Rider" Mascot Pictures serial. - **$60 $135 $200**

TMX-49

TMX-50

TMX-51

TMX-49. "Western Movie" Cardboard Box Viewer,
1935. Film scenes from "Rustlers Roundup". -
$50 $175 $225

TMX-50. "Miracle Rider" Dixie Ice Cream Lid,
1935. - **$5 $12 $25**

TMX-51. Spinning Rope,
1935. Red, white and blue twine with Mix Ralston endorsement on wooden grip. - **$40 $80 $140**

(ENLARGED VIEW)

TMX-52

(ENLARGED VIEW)

TMX-53

TMX-52. Suede Leather Chaps,
1935. - **$50 $150 $250**

TMX-53. Suede Leather Cowgirl Skirt,
1935. - **$60 $150 $250**

TMX-54

TMX-55

TMX-54. Metal Spurs With Leather Straps,
1935. Straps have TM Bar Ranch symbol. -
$75 $140 $225

TMX-55. Leather Wrist Cuffs,
1935. - **$60 $150 $250**

TMX-58

TMX-56

TMX-57

TMX-56. Suede Vest,
1935. - **$60 $120 $175**

TMX-57. Brown Leather Holster,
1935. Cover panel has Tom Mix markings. -
$75 $175 $250

TMX-58. Leather Bracelet With Foil On Brass Title Plate,
1935. Tom Mix or Ralston markings on both front and back. Named in ads "Lucky Wrist Band".
Complete - **$25 $60 $100**
No Strap - **$15 $30 $60**

TMX-59

TMX-60

TMX-61

TMX-59. Straight Shooter Bracelet With Checkerboard Logo,
1935. Silvered brass. - **$150 $250 $400**

TMX-60. Sun Watch,
1935. - **$20 $40 $85**

TMX-61. Bar Brand Branding Iron With Ink Pad Tin,
1935. Brass stamper has TM initials and checkerboard design. Branding Iron - **$25 $50 $85**
Ink Tin - **$10 $20 $35**

TMX-62

TMX-63

TMX-64

TMX-62. Compass With Magnifier,
1935. Unmarked Ralston premium. Aluminum case with eyelet. - **$15 $25 $40**

TMX-63. Lucky Charm Sterling Silver Horseshoe,
1935. - **$90 $150 $250**

TMX-64. "TM" Ralston Logo Brass Ring,
1935. Named in ads "Tom Mix Lucky Ring". -
$60 $90 $125

TMX-65

TMX-65. Premium Catalogue Folder,
1936. - **$15 $30 $50**

TMX-66

TMX-67

TMX-66. Wood Gun With Cardboard Handles,
1936. Cylinder revolves but gun doesn't open. -
$60 $90 $150

TMX-67. Championship Cowboy Belt Buckle,
1936. Brass with foil paper insert, also came with belt.
Buckle Only - **$35 $75 $125**
Buckle And Belt - **$50 $100 $165**

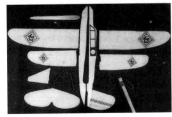

TMX-68

TMX-68. Flying Model Airplane Kit,
1936. Scarce. Balsa wood with Ralston logo decals. -
$150 $300 $500

TMX-70

TMX-69

TMX-71

TMX-69. "Rocket Parachute",
1936. Consists of balsa and cardboard launcher, wood stick with rubber band, metal figure string joined to paper parachute. Boxed - **$50 $100 $175**
Loose - **$35 $60 $100**

TMX-70. Fountain Pen With Mailer Envelope,
1936. Pen cap has Tom Mix ranch brand symbol decal.
Pen - **$40 $80 $150**
Mailer - **$8 $12 $20**

TMX-71. Girl's Brass Dangle Charm Bracelet,
1936. Scarce. Charms depict ranch symbol, Tom on Tony, steer head, six-shooter. Also called "Championship Cowgirl Bracelet". - **$200 $750 $1100**

TMX-72

TMX-73

TMX-74

TMX-72. Signet Ring Newspaper Advertisement,
1936. - **$10 $20 $30**

TMX-73. Lucky Signet Ring,
1936. Brass bands topped by raised personalized single initial designated by orderer. - **$100 $175 $275**

TMX-74. "Marlin Guns" Brass Target Ring,
1937. Marlin Firearms Co. For his endorsed Tom Mix Special .22 caliber rifle. - **$100 $175 $250**

TMX-75

TMX-75. Premium Catalogue Folder,
1937. Pictured premiums include Signet Ring. -
$60 $70 $80

TMX-76 **TMX-77**

TMX-76. "Ralston Straight Shooter News" Vol. 1 #1 Issue,
1937. - **$35 $60 $125**

TMX-77. "Ralston Straight Shooter News" #2,
1937. - **$20 $50 $80**

TMX-78

TMX-78. Baby Turtle Newspaper Advertisement,
1937. Premium was a real live baby turtle with Mix decal on its shell. - **$10 $15 $30**

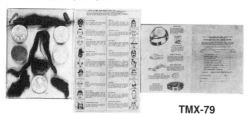

TMX-79

TMX-79. Movie Make-Up Kit With Paper,
1937. Five tins with TM brand and words Clown, Indian, Chink, Mexican, Negro. Complete - **$50 $75 $150**
Each Tin - **$3 $5 $8**

TMX-80

TMX-80. "Tom Mix Circus" 9x23" Felt Pennant,
1937. - **$150 $300 $500**

TMX-81 **TMX-82**

TMX-81. "Postal Telegraph Signal Set",
1937. Cardboard box with metal tapper key. - **$35 $75 $125**

TMX-82. Silver Frame Photo,
1937. Photo is personalized by recipient first name. - **$35 $50 $90**

TMX-83 **TMX-84** **TMX-85**

TMX-83. Straight Shooter Metal Badge With Foil Paper Insert,
1937. Silver luster. - **$25 $50 $100**

TMX-84. Straight Shooter Brass Badge,
1937. Foil paper symbol. - **$35 $75 $125**

TMX-85. Straight Shooter Badge Lead Proof,
c. 1937. Unique - **$750**

TMX-86 **TMX-87**

TMX-86. Prototype "Ranch Boss" Enameled Brass Badge,
c. 1937. Trial design for Ralston approval by Robbins Co., Massachusetts with enamel emblem rather than foil paper. Unique - **$4000**

TMX-87. Prototype "Tom Mix Ralston Straight Shooters" Star Brass Badge,
c. 1937. Trial design for Ralston approval by Robbins Co., Massachusetts. Unique - **$4000**

TMX-88

TMX-88. Premium Catalogue Sheet,
1938. - **$15 $25 $45**

TMX-90

TMX-89

TMX-89. Metal Telescope,
1938. Near Mint With Mailer - **$150**
Loose - **$35 $60 $100**

TMX-90. Secret Ink Writing Kit,
1938. Includes: manual, cardboard decoder, two glass vials of ink and developer. Manual - **$50 $150 $400**
Decoder - **$15 $50 $100**
Each Vial - **$10 $40 $60**

TMX-91

TMX-92

TMX-91. Telephone Set,
1938. Litho. tin transmitter and receiver units joined by string. - **$30 $60 $90**

TMX-92. Bullet Flashlight,
1938. 3" silvered brass tube with plastic end cap holding bulb. - **$50 $75 $125**

TMX-93

TMX-94

TMX-93. Wrangler Badge Folder,
1938. - **$40 $85 $150**

TMX-94. "Wrangler" Brass Badge,
1938. - **$40 $80 $160**

TMX-95

TMX-96

TMX-97

TMX-95. Wrangler Badge Lead Proof,
c. 1938. Unique - **$750**

TMX-96. "Wrangler" Metal Badge With Foil Paper Insert,
1938. Version pictures him frontally rather than partial profile. Issued in either silver or gold luster.
Either Version - **$50 $125 $250**

TMX-97. "Ranch Boss" Brass Rank Badge,
1938. Centered by foil paper emblem. - **$100 $300 $525**

TMX-99

TMX-98

TMX-98. Ranch Boss Badge Lead Proof,
c. 1938. Unique - **$2000**

TMX-99. Look-In Mystery Ring,
1938. Brass with tiny view hole for inside portrait photo of Tom with Tony. - **$150 $225 $400**

TMX-100

TMX-100. Premium Catalogue Folder Sheet,
1939. - **$20 $30 $45**

TMX-101

TMX-102

TMX-101. Wood Gun,
1939. No moving parts. - **$50 $85 $150**

TMX-102. Streamline Parachute Plane,
1939. Scarce. Balsa wood with designs in red and blue. Metal hinged wings. Came with parachutist and parachute, see next item. Plane Only - **$125 $275 $425**

TMX-104

TMX-103

TMX-105

TMX-103. Streamline Plane Parachutist And Parachute,
1939. Rare. Came with previous item. Metal figure smaller than 1936 Rocket Parachute and parachute is green. - **$25 $150 $225**

TMX-104. Cardboard Periscope,
1939. Blue Tube - **$25 $40 $75**
Black Tube - **$35 $60 $100**

TMX-105. Signal Flashlight,
1939. 3" metal tube with lens disk for red, green or clear light. Lens often missing and plastic end cap often cracked. Complete - **$30 $60 $125**

TMX-106   TMX-107   TMX-108

TMX-106. "Straight Shooters" Pocketknife,
1939. - **$30 $60 $90**

TMX-107. Brass Compass And Magnifier,
1939. Magnifying lens swings out. - **$20 $35 $75**

TMX-108. Pinback,
1930s. - **$60 $150 $250**

TMX-109   TMX-110

TMX-109. Ralston Diecut Accordion Fold Display Sign,
1930s. Rare. - **$400 $1000 $1600**

TMX-110. Cinema Star Card #7,
1930s. England. Wills Cigarettes premium. - **$10 $20 $30**

TMX-111   TMX-112

TMX-111. Dixie Cup Lid,
1930s. Promotes Miracle Rider movie. - **$20 $30 $50**

TMX-112. Hollywood Gum Card,
1930s. - **$20 $40 $60**

TMX-113   TMX-114   TMX-115

TMX-113. "Wild West Club" Member Cello. Button,
1930s. Rare. - **$250 $500 $1000**

TMX-114. "Toledo Paramount Theater" Movie Cello. Button,
1930s. Scarce issue from a single theater in Ohio. - **$125 $350 $550**

TMX-115. "Yankiboy Play Clothes" Cello. Button,
1930s. Yellow rim 1-3/4" size. - **$35 $60 $100**

TMX-116

TMX-116. "Rodeo Box" Cardboard Pencil Case,
1930s. Probably a store item or circus souvenir. Inscribed for "Tom Mix & Tony" with rodeo generic art. - **$35 $75 $125**

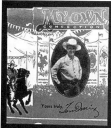

TMX-117   TMX-118   TMX-119

TMX-117. "My Own Confection" Candy Box,
1930s. Casey Concession Co. Cardboard box for "Rare Sunshine Vitamin D" Candy probably sold at Tom Mix live performances. - **$35 $75 $150**

TMX-118. Cello./Steel Pocketknife,
1930s. Store item by Imperial. - **$40 $75 $150**

TMX-119. "Yankiboy Play Clothes" 2" Cello. Button,
1930s. Orange rim. - **$25 $40 $75**

TMX-120

TMX-120. Pocketknife 6x24" Paper Store Sign,
1930s. Scarce. - **$150 $250 $400**

TMX-121

TMX-121. Rexall Toothpaste Puzzle,
1930s. In Envelope - **$35 $60 $100**
Loose - **$20 $40 $60**

TMX-123

TMX-122

TMX-122. "Capturing Outlaws In The Bad Lands",
1930s. Compliments Ralston Corn Flakes. Paper photo
with facsimile Mix inscription and signature. Reverse has
short story "As Told By The Old Wrangler". -
$50 $90 $150

TMX-123. Humming Lariat
1930s. Store item. - **$40 $100 $150**

TMX-124

TMX-125

TMX-124. Promo,
1930s. Hand-out to promote Tom Mix film "The Miracle
Rider." - **$10 $20 $30**

TMX-125. Book And Album,
1930s. Autograph book and birthday album. Theater premium, 20 pages. Has write-up on Tom Mix and promotes
film "The Best Bad Man." - **$30 $65 $100**

TMX-126

TMX-126. "Purina Bread" Handbill,
1930s. For various groceries. - **$35 $70 $100**

TMX-127   TMX-128

TMX-127. "Tom Mix Comics Book 1",
1940. Ralston premium sent via mail so rarely found in top
condition. Eleven additional issued between 1940-1942. -
$275 $800 $2700

TMX-128. "Tom Mix Comics Book 2",
1940. - **$90 $275 $800**

TMX-129   TMX-130

TMX-129. "Stars Of Our Radio Program" Fan Card,
1940. Back has form message for sending verses to contest song. - **$30 $75 $150**

TMX-130. Gold Ore Assayer's Certificate,
1940. Came folded with watch fob. - **$20 $45 $85**

TMX-131

TMX-132

TMX-133

TMX-131. Gold Ore Watch Fob,
1940. - **$20 $50 $75**

TMX-132. Tom Mix's Make-Up Kit,
1940. Greasepaint in tin canisters of red or black checkerboard design. Other contents are instruction sheet, eye patch, imitation glasses, false nose and false teeth, and two moustaches. Near Mint With Mailer - **$300**
Each Tin - **$8 $12 $20**
Nose or Teeth - **$15 $25 $50**
Other Pieces - **$5 $12 $20**

TMX-133. Indian Blow Gun Target Printer's Engraving Plate,
1940. Unique - **$1000**

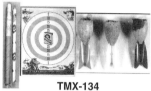 

TMX-134 **TMX-135**

TMX-134. Indian Blow Gun Set,
1940. Scarce. With paper target, four darts, mailer tube.
Near Mint With Mailer - **$540**
Target - **$50 $100 $150**
Blow Gun - **$50 $100 $150**
Each Dart - **$15 $30 $40**

TMX-135. Telegraph Set With Box Mailer,
1940. Cardboard with metal tapper key.
Telegraph - **$35 $60 $100**
Box - **$10 $20 $35**

TMX-136 **TMX-137** **TMX-138**

TMX-136. Straight Shooters Manual,
1941. - **$20 $35 $75**

TMX-137. "Tom Mix Comics" #3,
1941. - **$60 $175 $500**

TMX-138. "Tom Mix Comics" #4,
1941. - **$60 $175 $500**

TMX-139 **TMX-140** **TMX-141**

TMX-139. "Tom Mix Comics" #5,
1941. - **$60 $175 $500**

TMX-140. "Tom Mix Comics" #6,
1941. - **$60 $175 $500**

TMX-141. "Tom Mix Comics" #7,
1941. - **$60 $175 $500**

TMX-142 **TMX-143**

TMX-144

TMX-142. Six-Gun Brass Decoder Badge,
1941. Gun turns brass pointer on reverse to one of nine code words. - **$60 $175 $150**

TMX-143. "Captain" Silvered Brass Spur Badge,
1941. - **$60 $175 $250**

TMX-144. "Tom Mix Comics" #8,
1942. - **$60 $175 $500**

TMX-145 **TMX-146**

TMX-145. "Tom Mix Comics" #9,
1942. - **$60 $175 $500**

TMX-146. "Tom Mix Commandos Comics" Book 10,
1942. - **$40 $125 $400**

TMX-147 **TMX-148**

TMX-147. "Tom Mix Commandos" Comic Book #11,
1942. - **$40 $125 $400**

TMX-148. "Tom Mix Commandos" Comic Book #12,
1942. - **$40 $125 $400**

TMX-149

TMX-150

TMX-151

TMX-157

TMX-158

TMX-159

TMX-149. "Tom Mix" Signature Ring,
1942. Brass with sterling silver top plate. -
$100 $175 $275

TMX-150. "Secret Manual",
1944. - **$25 $60 $100**

TMX-151. Siren Ring,
1944. Brass with enclosed siren disk wheel for blowing. -
$25 $62 $100

TMX-157. Fabric Patch No Flocking,
1945. Scarce version also likely issued with 1945 club
manual. - **$40 $75 $150**

TMX-158. Tom Mix And Tony "Last Picture" Photo,
1946. Black and white photo card captioned "This is the
last picture taken of Tom and Tony together" prior to Mix
death in 1940. Ralston premium with publication date on
reverse of May, 1946. - **$30 $60 $90**

TMX-159. Curley Bradley Fan Photo Card,
1946. Radio portrayer of Tom Mix, back has Safety Code. -
$20 $50 $75

TMX-152

TMX-153

TMX-154

TMX-152 "Tom Mix Straight Shooters Album" Manual,
1945. Near Mint With Envelope - **$125**
Manual Only - **$25 $50 $75**

TMX-153. "One-Act Play" Offer Sheet,
1945. Offered script for play titled "The Straight Shooters
Secret," issued with 1945 manual. No copy of the script is
known. - **$15 $25 $40**

TMX-154. Cloth Patch,
1945. Issued with 1945 club manual. Red flocking on white
fabric. - **$20 $35 $60**

TMX-160

TMX-160. Glow Belt With Secret Compartment Buckle,
1946. Complete - **$50 $80 $150**
Buckle Only - **$25 $50 $75**

TMX-161

TMX-161. Decoder Buttons With Card,
1946. Set of five litho. buttons. Complete Near Mint - **$125**
Each Button - **$8 $12 $20**

TMX-155

TMX-156

**TMX-155. Straight Shooters Service Ribbon And
Medal,**
1945. Fabric over metal bar pin suspending glow-in-dark
plastic medal. - **$30 $100 $175**

**TMX-156. "Curley Bradley The Tom Mix Of Radio" 78
RPM Three-Record Al bum,**
c. 1945. Universal Recording Corp. - **$50 $100 $200**

TMX-162

TMX-163

TMX-162. "Luminous Compass-Magnifying Glass",
1946. Near Mint In Mailer - **$250**
Loose - **$20 $60 $100**

TMX-163. Dobie County Sheriff Siren Badge,
1946. - **$20 $50 $100**

TMX-165

TMX-164

TMX-164. Folder Mailed With Siren Badge,
1946. - **$15 $30 $65**

TMX-165. "Look-Around" Ring,
1946. Near Mint In Mailer - **$250**
Ring Only - **$75 $110 $150**

TMX-167

TMX-166

TMX-168

TMX-166. "Rocket Parachute" Version #2 Re-issue With Box,
1947. Similar to original 1936 item with portrait added on mailer box. Boxed - **$75 $125 $200**

TMX-167. "Tom Mix Bureau Of Identification File Card",
1947. Scarce as card was meant to be returned with member's fingerprints and ID bracelet number. - **$35 $60 $90**

TMX-168. Identification Bracelet,
1947. Personalized by single initial designated by orderer. - **$15 $25 $50**

TMX-169

TMX-170

TMX-169. Magnet Ring,
1947. Brass with silver finish magnet. - **$45 $70 $125**

TMX-170. "Magnet Ring" Paper Slip,
1947. - **$30 $35 $40**

TMX-171

TMX-171. "Super-Magnetic Compass Gun And Signal Whistle" Instruction Sheet,
1948. Reverse offers five other premiums. - **$10 $20 $30**

TMX-172

TMX-173

TMX-172. Super Magnetic Compass Gun And Whistle,
1948. Both gun and arrowhead whistle glow in dark. - **$50 $100 $175**

TMX-173. "Tom Mix Safety Story" Poster,
1948. Yankee Network Station. Opens to 17x22". - **$35 $75 $125**

TMX-174

TMX-158. Cowboy Spurs,
1949. Aluminum with glow in dark rowels. - **$40 $75 $125**

TMX-175

TMX-176

TMX-177

TMX-175. "Signal Arrowhead" Plastic Whistle/Siren/ Magnifier,
1949. - **$30 $75 $125**

TMX-176. Musical Ring,
1949. Aluminum slide whistle on brass base. - **$50 $75 $125**

TMX-177. Miniature Gold-Plated TV Viewer,
1949. Scarce. Only 200 made for executives. - **$75 $200 $325**

TMX-178   **TMX-179**

TMX-178. "RCA Victor" Miniature TV Film Viewer,
1949. Brass back includes Tom Mix name. - **$20 $30 $50**
Add $10 Per Mix Film Disk

TMX-179. Ray O Print Outfit,
1940s. With tin holder for negative and photo paper with
envelope. - **$50 $125 $175**

TMX-181

TMX-180

TMX-182

TMX-180. Marbles,
1940s. Ralston premium with 18 marbles in bag. -
$25 $50 $75

TMX-181. Premiums Catalogue Sheet,
1950. Came with 1950 model TV and Tiger-Eye Ring as
single package. - **$10 $20 $30**

TMX-182. "RCA Victor" Miniature TV Film Viewer,
1950. Version without Mix name on reverse. -
$20 $35 $50
Add $10 Per Mix Film Disk

TMX-183

TMX-184

TMX-183. "2 For 1" Ralston Premium Offer Ad,
1950. Comic book page picturing miniature RCA Victor
television set and Magic-Light Tiger-Eye Ring as joint mail
premiums. - **$1 $3 $5**

TMX-184. "Toy Television Set" Instruction Sheet,
1950. - **$15 $25 $40**

TMX-185

TMX-185. "Golden Plastic Bullet Telescope" Instruction Sheet,
1950. Reverse side offers five other premiums. -
$10 $20 $30

TMX-187

TMX-186

TMX-188

TMX-186. "Tom Mix Color Book",
1950. - **$10 $20 $35**

TMX-187. Magic-Light Tiger-Eye Ring,
1950. Plastic with glow in the dark top. - **$100 $200 $325**

TMX-188. Golden Plastic Bullet Telescope & Birdcall,
1950. Gold plastic holding inside bird call whistle.
Complete - **$25 $50 $75**
Without Whistle - **$10 $20 $40**

TMX-189

TMX-189. "Tom Mix Ralston Straight Shooters Club" Revival Membership Kit,
1982. 50-year membership card, fabric patch, comic book-
let, early years photo reprint, current premium photo sheet.
Each - **$3 $5 $10**

TMX-190

TMX-191

TMX-190. "Tom Mix Ralston Straight Shooters" Revival Cereal Bowl,
1982. - **$10** **$15** **$25**

TMX-191. Revival Wristwatch,
1982. - **$50** **$100** **$300**

TONY THE TIGER

The Kellogg Company adopted Tony the Tiger in 1952 to speak for the company's Sugar Frosted Flakes. Tony was originally created by Martin Provensen, a children's book illustrator. The robust, smiling cartoon tiger is anything but shy, constantly reminding us that his cereal is Gr-r-reat!

TNY-1 **TNY-2**

TNY-1. Vinyl Inflated Figure,
1953. - **$10** **$25** **$40**

TNY-2. Plastic Bank,
1967. - **$30** **$45** **$70**

TNY-3 **TNY-4**

TNY-3. Hard Plastic Cookie Jar With Box,
1968. Jar Only - **$25** **$50** **$80**
Boxed - **$40** **$75** **$100**

TNY-4. "Astronaut Breakfast Game" Litho. Button,
1960s. White or blue background. - **$3** **$8** **$12**

TNY-7

TNY-5 **TNY-6**

TNY-5. Plush And Cloth Doll,
1970. - **$15** **$25** **$40**

TNY-6. Vinyl Doll With Movable Head,
c. 1974. - **$20** **$35** **$60**

TNY-7. Noisemaker Attachment,
1970s. Hard plastic with attachment brackett for bicycle handlebar. Top disk wheel produces growling sound when turned. - **$15** **$35** **$75**

TNY-8 **TNY-9**

TNY-8. Plastic Radio,
1980. Battery operated. Boxed - **$30** **$40** **$60**
Loose - **$10** **$20** **$35**

TNY-9. Stainless Steel Cereal Spoon,
1983. - **$5** **$10** **$15**

TNY-10

TNY-10. Frosted Flakes Canadian Issue Box,
1990. Offers Spider-Man and Tony The Tiger comic in English/French. Box - **$25** **$40** **$85**
Comic - **$10** **$20** **$40**

TNY-11

TNY-11. Large Stuffed Doll With Tag,
1997. Sold at grocery stores. - **$5** **$15** **$25**

TOONERVILLE FOLKS

Fontaine Fox's comic cartoon panels apparently began appearing in newspapers in 1915. The following year the Toonerville Trolley was introduced, and in 1920 the Bell Syndicate began distributing Fox's Sunday page as *Toonerville Folks*. The ramshackle trolley and its Skipper, along with such Toonerville denizens as Mickey (Himself) McGuire, the Powerful Katrinka, and the Terrible-Tempered Mr. Bang, delighted millions of readers for 40 years. Several collections of reprints were published in the early years, a series of two-reel live-action film comedies were released in the 1920s, and Burt Gillett produced Toonerville animated shorts in 1936. The strip survived until 1955.

TOO-1

TOO-2

TOO-1. Cartoon Book,
1921. Store item published by Cupples & Leon Co. - **$40 $115 $265**

TOO-2. Coca-Cola Ad Folder,
1931. - **$20 $40 $65**

TOO-3

TOO-3. Cracker Box,
1931. Uneeda Crackers by Nabisco. - **$100 $200 $300**

TOO-4

TOO-4. Paper Masks,
1930s. Westinghouse Mazda Lamps. Examples from set. Also seen with "Super Shell" gasoline ad on reverse. Each - **$15 $25 $40**

TOO-5

TOO-5. Comic Gum Wrapper,
1930s. Our Gang gum wrapper from Canada. Art by Fontaine Fox. - **$20 $35 $65**

TOO-6

TOO-7

TOO-8

TOO-6. Mickey McGuire Bisque,
1930s. Store item, German made. - **$25 $75 $115**

TOO-7. "Mickey McGuire Club" Cello. Button,
1930s. Probably a newspaper issue. Pictured is traditional derby hat with frayed crown. - **$20 $40 $75**

TOO-8. "The Terrible Tempered Mr. Bang" Ad Poster,
1930s. Eveready Mazda automobile lamps. Paper 20x30". - **$75 $150 $250**

TOO-9

TOO-9. Vaseline Petroleum Jelly Cut-Out Sheet,
1930s. Uncut - **$40 $85 $150**

TRIX

General Mills introduced Trix fruit-flavored corn puffs around 1955, and the distinctive Trix-loving rabbit made his debut on the cereal boxes and in animated television comercials in 1959. The original rabbit was a hand puppet that appeared in the introduction to *Rocky and His Friends*, *Captain Kangaroo*, and other General Mills-sponsored programs. "Silly rabbit, Trix are for kids."

TRX-1

TRX-2

TRX-3

TRX-1. Tiddly Wink Miniature Plastic Game,
c. 1960s. Lidded container holding small dexterity game featuring disks picturing Trix Rabbit. - **$8 $15 $20**

TRX-2. Vinyl Squeaker Figure,
1978. - **$15 $25 $35**

TRX-3. Club Stickers,
c. 1970s. Set Of Five - **$5 $10 $25**

TRX-4

UDN-3

TRX-5

TRX-4. "Walky Squawky Talky" Cardboard Units In Envelope,
1970s. With Envelope - **$15 $25 $50**
Loose - **$10 $20 $30**

TRX-5. Plastic Ramp Toy,
1970s. Designed to walk on inclined surface. - **$15 $30 $50**

TRX-6   TRX-7

TRX-8

TRX-6. "Yes! Let The Rabbit Eat Trix!" 2-1/4" Litho. Button,
1970s. For affirmative voter in contest, back has metal clip. - **$5 $15 $25**

TRX-7. "No! Trix Are For Kids!" 2-1/4" Litho. Button,
1970s. For negative voter in contest, back has metal clip. - **$5 $15 $25**

TRX-8. Contest Vote Thank-You Letter,
1970s. Accompaniment letter to litho. buttons for entrant in contest to determine if Trix Rabbit should be allowed to eat Trix cereal. - **$5 $10 $20**

UNCLE DON

Between 1928 and 1949, broadcasting regionally from New York radio station WOR, Uncle Don Carney entertained kids with stories, poems, jokes, songs, birthday announcements, and advice on health and behavior. Carney, whose real name was Howard Rice, started in vaudeville as a trick pianist and turned his air time into a classic children's program. Along with nonsense syllables, pig latin, and made-up words, Uncle Don promoted a number of "clubs" related to the products of his many commercial sponsors. The show was aired on the Mutual network for one season (1939-1940), sponsored by Maltex cereal. Uncle Don also read the comics on the air on Sunday mornings, and narrated *The Adventures of Terry and Ted* on CBS radio in 1935-1936. The often-told tale that Carney, after signing off one night, said "I guess that'll hold the little bastards" with the microphone still on, apparently never happened.

UDN-1

UDN-2

UDN-1. Uncle Don Bank,
1920s. Two types. Each - **$10 $20 $40**

UDN-2. "Lionel Engineers Club" Cello. Button,
1930. - **$35 $75 $150**

UDN-3. Uncle Don's "Earnest Saver Club" Tin Bank,
c. 1938. Various banks. Wrapper design of character with "Bank Book" body. - **$10 $40 $60**

UDN-4

UDN-5   UDN-6

UDN-4. "Maltex 100% Breakfast Club" Litho. Button,
c. 1939. - **$3 $5 $10**

UDN-5. Uncle Don Letter and Mailer,
1930s. Savings Club. - **$20 $40 $60**

UDN-6. Uncle Don's "Terry And Ted And Major Campbell" 12x19" Map,
1930s. Bond Bread. Map follows route of trio in their "Land Cruiser" pictured at bottom. - **$40 $80 $160**

UDN-9

UDN-7   **UDN-8**

UDN-7. "Terry And Ted On The Trail Of The Secret Formula" Booklet,
1930s. Bond Bread. Story told by Uncle Don with color pictures. - **$5 $12 $20**

UDN-8. Autogiro Theme Photo,
1930s. Popsicle. Pictures Uncle Don as aviator with facsimile signature inscription for Popsicles. - **$5 $10 $15**

UDN-9. "Borden Health Club" Cello. Button,
1930s. - **$8 $12 $20**

UDN-10

UDN-12

UDN-11

UDN-10. "Ice Cream Club/Borden" Cello. Button,
1930s. - **$5 $8 $12**

UDN-11. "Borden's Health Club Honor Prize",
1930s. "Uncle Don" brass bar holding cloth ribbon suspending cello. pendant with reverse image of Borden milk bottle. - **$10 $20 $30**

UDN-12. "Bosco Club" Cello. Button,
1930s. Pictured holding jar of chocolate drink syrup product. - **$10 $15 $25**

UDN-13   **UDN-14**   **UDN-15**

UDN-13. "Good Humor/G.H.H.C." Cello. Button,
1930s. Pictured in Good Humor Ice Cream uniform. - **$12 $20 $35**

UDN-14. "I.V.C. Club" Cello. Button,
1930s. - **$3 $6 $10**

UDN-15. "Mutual Grocery Club" Cello. Button,
1930s. - **$5 $8 $12**

UDN-16   **UDN-17**   **UDN-18**

UDN-16. "Castles Ice Cream Club" Cello. Button,
1930s. - **$5 $12 $20**

UDN-17. "Remitypers" Cello. Button,
1930s. Remington Typewriters. - **$10 $15 $25**

UDN-18. "Taystee Bread Club" Cello. Button,
1930s. - **$8 $15 $25**

UNCLE WIGGILY

Uncle Wiggily Longears, an elderly rabbit in a tailcoat, was created by writer Howard R. Garis for a nationally syndicated newspaper column of bedtime stories that began appearing in 1910. Drawings were added for a Sunday page that ran from 1919 through the 1920s, and a daily comic strip appeared in the mid-1920s, illustrated by various artists. Wiggily comic books were published between 1942 and 1954, and there have been dozens of *Uncle Wiggily* story books. On radio, Albert Goris was Wiggily, telling bedtime stories to his young audience.

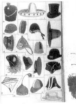

UWG-1

UWG-1. "Put A Hat On Uncle Wiggily" Party Game Kit,
1919. Store item by Milton Bradley. Game sheet is 22x27". Uncut In Envelope - **$40 $80 $125**

UWG-2

UWG-4

UWG-3

UWG-2. China Mug,
Copyright 1924. House named "Ovaltine House". Also
came without name. With Name - **$20 $80 $130**
No Name - **$35 $100 $175**

UWG-3. China Plate,
Copyright 1924. Scarce. Store item by Sebring Pottery Co.
Design matches mug. - **$50 $200 $275**

UWG-4. China Bowl With Silverplate Trim,
1924. Rare store item by Sebring Pottery Co. Design
matches mug and plate. - **$100 $250 $400**

UWG-5

UWG-6

**UWG-5. "Hollow Stump Bungalow" Pressed
Cardboard Toy With Figures,**
1920s. Store item by Androscoggin Pulp Co. 3-D resi-
dence and 10 diecut thin cardboard characters, each on
wooden base. Bungalow - **$75 $150 $250**
Each Figure - **$10 $20 $30**

UWG-6. "Hollow Stump Club" Cello. Button,
1946. WNJR Radio, Newark, New Jersey established by
Newark Evening News. After Howard Garis retired from
the newspaper, he read Uncle Wiggily stories over the air.
Club membership and button distribution reached about
9,000 boys and girls. - **$35 $75 $150**

UNCLE WIP

Philadelphia radio station WIP, owned and operated by
Gimbel's department store, started broadcasting in
March 1922. Uncle Wip's Kiddie Club was a late-afternoon children's program organized by the store in the
1930s, probably as early as 1936.

UWP-2

UWP-1

**UWP-1. "Uncle Wip And His Friends/Their Bed-Time
Stories" Book,**
1923. - **$10 $50 $75**

UWP-2. "Uncle Wip's Kiddie Club" Certificate,
1930s. Rare. - **$30 $75 $100**

UWP-3   UWP-4   UWP-5   UWP-6

UWP-3. "See Me At Gimbels" Cello. Button,
1930s. Gimbels department store, Philadelphia. -
$20 $40 $75

**UWP-4. "Uncle Wip's Kiddie Club At Gimbels" Cello.
Button,**
1930s. Gimbels department store, Philadelphia. -
$10 $20 $35

**UWP-5. "Uncle Wip's Kiddie Club/Listen In 6.45 P.M."
Cello. Button,**
1930s. Gimbels department store, Philadelphia. -
$10 $20 $30

UWP-6. "Kiddie Klub/Gimbels" Cello. Button,
1930s. Gimbels department store, Philadelphia. -
$3 $6 $10

UWP-7

UWP-8

UWP-7. "Uncle Wip's Radio Girls" Cello. Buttons,
1930s. - **$10 $20 $30**

UWP-8. "Uncle Wip's Toyland" Clerk Badge,
1930s. Gimbels department store. 1-3/4x2-3/4" cello. slotted in rear for insertion of clerk's name paper. -
$15 $35 $75

UNDERDOG

Loveable, humble canine Shoeshine Boy was in actu-
ality plucky superhero Underdog, whose magic cape
and energy pills gave him the power to overcome mad
scientists and villains, such as Simon Bar Sinister and
Riff Raff, and rescue Sweet Polly Purebred, ace TV
reporter. This animated series, with Wally Cox providing the voice of Underdog, aired on NBC from 1964 to
1966, moved to CBS from 1966 to 1968, then went back
to NBC from 1968 to 1973. *Underdog* comic books
appeared in the early 1970s. Items are normally copyrighted Leonardo Productions.

UND-1

UND-1. "Super Saturday Cavalcade" Cartoons Promotional Photo,
1966. CBS-TV. Pictures stars of new Saturday morning lineup of animated color cartoons including Underdog. - **$8 $15 $25**

UND-2   UND-3   UND-4

UND-2. Dakin Co. Vinyl Figure,
1960s. Store item. Comes with blue felt cape. - **$35 $100 $175**
Near Mint Boxed - **$250**

UND-3. Underdog Mug,
1960s. Rare. Parents Magazine premium. - **$50 $100 $200**

UND-4. Underdog Club Ring,
1970. Charlton Comics. Silvered plastic expansion band with black on red paper picture. - **$25 $50 $75**

UND-5

UND-6

UND-5. Fan Club Membership Card,
1970. Charlton Comics. Part of fan club kit. - **$5 $10 $15**

UND-6. T-Shirt,
1970. Charlton Comics. - **$35 $75 $125**

UND-7

UND-8

UND-7. Sweatshirt,
1970. Charlton Comics. - **$50 $100 $150**

UND-8. Color-Your-Own Giant Posters,
1970. Charlton Comics. Set of six black and white 17x22" posters sent folded. Offered as "3 Good Guys/3 Funny Bad Guys" with pairs consisting of Underdog/Simon, Cad; Dudley Do-Right/Snidely Whiplash; Bullwinkle, Rocky/Boris Badinov, Natasha. Each Uncolored - **$10 $25 $40**
Each Colored - **$5 $10 $15**

UND-9

UND-10

UND-9. Premium Offer Poster,
1974. Pacific Gas and Electric. 16x21". - **$20 $45 $75**

UND-10. "Kite Fun Book",
1974. Pacific Gas and Electric. - **$5 $12 $20**

UND-11

UND-12

UND-11. Simon Bar Sinister Plastic Ring,
1975. Vending machine. - **$50 $75 $125**

UND-12. "Saturday Cartoon Magnets",
1975. Breaker Confections, Division of Sunline Inc., St. Louis. Set of four including Rocky, Bullwinkle, Speedy Gonzales, Underdog. Order Folder - **$5 $12 $25**
Each Magnet - **$3 $8 $18**

UND-14

UND-13

UND-13. Pepsi Glass,
c. 1970s. One of 5 Leonardo TTV characters in 16 oz. size. This one comes with and without Pepsi logo. - **$5 $10 $20**

UND-14. Plastic Cup And Bowl,
1970s. Store item. Each - **$5 $10 $20**

UND-15

UND-16

UND-15. "Underdog" Plastic Ring,
1970s. Vending machine item. Image in slight raised relief. - **$100 $175 $270**

UND-16. Underdog Rings Vending Machine Card,
1970s. 5x7" insert display card diecut to hold six example plastic character image rings. - **$10 $15 $20**

UND-18

UND-17

UND-17. "March Of Comics" Issue,
1981. No sponsor imprint on pictured example. Issue #479 by Western Publishing Co. - **$2 $5 $10**

UND-18. "Macy's Thanksgiving Day Parade" Souvenir 3" Cello. Button,
1981. Pictures parade balloon figures of Underdog and Bullwinkle. - **$10 $20 $30**

U.S. JONES

Defender of democracy in the all-American way, U.S. Jones had a brief comic book life at the outset of World War II. Jones made his first appearance in issue #28 of *Wonderworld Comics* in August 1941, and two issues of his own book appeared in 1941 and 1942. U.S. Jones Cadets received a decoder, a pinback button, and other membership material.

USJ-2

USJ-1

USJ-1. Secret Code Card,
1941. Rare. Part of member's kit. Has instructions for use of 26 different code keys. - **$125 $400 $600**

USJ-2. Cadets Membership Card,
1941. Rare. Part of member's kit. - **$75 $225 $350**

USJ-4

USJ-3

USJ-3. Cadet Cover Letter And Cadet Civil Defense Sheet,
1941. Rare. Part of member's kit. Explains kit and duties with pledge text. Each - **$50 $100 $125**

USJ-4. "U.S. Jones Cadets" Comic Book Club Cello. Button,
1941. Rare. Part of member's kit. - **$600 $2500 $4500**

VIC AND SADE

Considered by many to be one of the greatest radio shows ever, *Vic and Sade* has been called a true original and the best American humor of its day. The series told of events in the daily lives of radio's home folks-- Victor Gook, his wife Sade, their son Rush, and Sade's Uncle Fletcher--who lived in the little house halfway up in the next block in the town of Crooper, Illinois. Written by Paul Rhyer, *Vic and Sade* aired on the NBC, CBS, and Mutual networks from 1932 to 1946. The program was supported by local advertisers the first two years until Crisco took over as longterm sponsor. Fitch's Cocoanut Shampoo sponsored in 1946.

VAS-1

VAS-1. Hometown Paper Map With Mailer Envelope,
c. 1942. Rare. Procter & Gamble. 14x16" map of "Crooper, Illinois/40 Miles From Peoria" with cast member pictures at lower corner. Also issued on cardboard.
Envelope - **$5 $20 $25**
Map - **$50 $150 $200**

WHEATIES MISC.

Wheaties, the Breakfast of Champions, was the result of a kitchen accident in 1921 when some gruel spilled on a hot stove and turned into crispy flakes. The Washburn Crosby Company in Minneapolis developed the cereal and began marketing it regionally in 1924. Advertising on radio, including the world's first singing commercial, proved successful and by 1928, when Washburn Crosby joined with other grain millers to form General Mills, Wheaties was an established product. Over the years sponsorship of such popular radio programs as *Jack Armstrong* and *Skippy*, as well as continuing promotion that linked the product to major figures in sports and the movies, has kept Wheaties an all-American favorite breakfast food. This section shows an assortment of their baseball and non-character premiums.

WHE-2

WHE-3

WHE-1. "Earl Averill" Box Back,
1937. From a series of baseball stars described by their 1936 season statistics. - **$15 $25 $40**
Complete Box - **$80 $160 $320**

WHE-2. Knothole Drilling Insect 2-1/2" Cello. Button,
c. 1930s. - **$15 $30 $50**

WHE-3. Auto Emblems,
no date. Ten different tin U.S. car emblems, mailer and instructions. Each - **$3 $6 $12**

WHE-4

WHE-5

WHE-6

WHE-4. "Champs" Of The U.S.A. Box Back #1 Stamp Set,
1930s. Shows 3 different cut-out stamps of Charles Ruffing, Lynn Patrick, and Leo Durocher. - **$10 $25 $35**

WHE-5. "Champs" Of The U.S.A. Box Back #2 Stamp Set,
1930s. Shows 3 different cut-out stamps of Joe Dimaggio, Mel Ott, and Ellsworth Vines. - **$25 $50 $75**

WHE-6. "Champs" Of The U.S.A. Box Back #3 Stamp Set,
1930s. Shows 3 different cut-out stamps of Jimmie Foxx, Bernie Bierman, and Bill Dickey. - **$15 $30 $50**

WHE-7

WHE-8

WHE-9

WHE-7. "Champs" Of The U.S.A. Box Back #5 Stamp Set,
1930s. Shows 3 different cut-out stamps of Joe Medwick, Madison "Matty" Bell, and Ab Jenkins. - **$5 $10 $20**

WHE-8. "Champs" Of The U.S.A. Box Back #6 Stamp Set,
1930s. Shows 3 different cut-out stamps of John Mize, Davey O'Brien, and Ralph Guldahl. - **$5 $10 $20**

WHE-9. "Champs" Of The U.S.A. Box Back #7 Stamp Set,
1930s. Shows 3 different cut-out stamps of Joe Cronin, Cecil Isbell, and Byron Nelson. - **$5 $15 $25**

WHE-10

WHE-11

WHE-12

WHE-10. "Champs" Of The U.S.A. Box Back #8 Stamp Set,
1930s. Shows 3 different cut-out stamps of Paul Derringer, Ernie Lombardi, and George I. Myers. - **$5 $15 $25**

WHE-11. "Champs" Of The U.S.A. Box Back #12 Stamp Set,
1930s. Shows 3 different cut-out stamps of Hugh McManus, Luke Appling, and Stanley Hack. - **$5 $15 $25**

WHE-12. Miniature Metal License Plates With Mailer,
1953. Offered in four sets of 12 plus bonus District of Columbia if all ordered at same time.
Each License - **$2 $7 $10**

WHE-13

WHE-13. "Funny Stuff" Comic,
1946. Books were taped to boxes.
Good - **$80**
Fine - **$250**

WHE-14

WHE-15

WHE-14. Box Flat - 1 oz.,
1953. Has rare George Mikan basketball card on back -
the key to the set. - **$125 $250 $500**

WHE-15. Wrapped Coins,
1955. 17 international coins pictured with Wheaties wrapper. Each wrapper explains coin and facts about each
country. Coin with wrapper was a premium given away in
each box of Wheaties. Each - **$3 $6 $10**

(OUTSIDE)

(INSIDE)
WHE-16

WHE-16. Coin Card,
1955. Holder for 15 coins. International set. - **$20 $40 $60**

WHE-17. "Champy's Theatre" With Hand Puppets,
1957. 17x44" theater assembly sheet offered as part of
mail purchase of Champy and Mr. Fox puppets based on
creation by Bill Baird for Mickey Mouse Club TV show.
Theater - **$15 $30 $50**
Each Puppet - **$10 $30 $50**

WHE-18

WHE-19

WHE-20

WHE-18. "Auto Emblems" Box,
1950s. Shows all 31 emblems offered.
Complete - **$25 $100 $150**

WHE-19. British Auto Metal Emblems,
1950s. Set of 10, Bentley and MG not shown.
Each - **$3 $10 $15**

WHE-20. Continental Auto Metal Emblems,
1950s. Set of 10. Volkswagen, Citroen, Bugati not shown.
Each - **$3 $10 $15**

WHE-21

WHE-22

WHE-21. Hike-O-Meter,
1950s. Pedometer with aluminum rim. - **$10 $18 $30**

WHE-22. Red Records,
1950s. Cereal premiums. Various popular folk, sea & traditional songs on labels. Each - **$12 $25 $40**

WHE-17

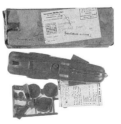

WHE-23

WHE-24

WHE-23. Land And Water Rover,
1950s. General Mills. Red plastic car with propeller. Runs on land and water. Complete - **$35 $75 $125**

WHE-24. Rare Rock Card,
1950s. With 11 different rocks in descriptive mailers.
Display Card with Mailer - **$10 $35 $50**
Rocks in Mailer each - **$10**

WHE-26

WHE-25

WHE-25. Flying Air Car,
1960. Rare. General Mills. Large, wide, Cobra Mark II battery powered car.
With Instructions and Mailer. - **$50 $100 $150**

WHE-26. Miniature Reflective Paper License Plates With Mailer,
1963. Wheaties Bran With Raisin Flakes. Probable set of 25 for scattered states in reflective flocked surface with peel-off back. Each License - **$2 $4 $6**

WILD BILL HICKOK

James Butler "Wild Bill" Hickok (1837-1876) was a U.S. Marshal in Kansas after the Civil War with a reputation as a marksman and a deadly lawman. Hollywood produced a number of fictionalized versions of the Hickok legend as portrayed by such stars as William S. Hart, Bill Elliott, Roy Rogers, Bruce Cabot, and Gary Cooper. In 1951, with Guy Madison as Hickok and Andy Devine as his sidekick Jingles, *The Adventures of Wild Bill Hickok* came to television and radio. The television series, sponsored by Kellogg's Sugar Corn Pops, aired until 1958, first in syndication, then on CBS (1955-1958), and on ABC (1957-1958). The radio version lasted until 1956, with Kellogg also sponsoring until 1954. Hickok comic books appeared from the late 1940s to the late 1950s. "Hey, Wild Bill, wait for me!"

WLD-1

WLD-1. "Secret Treasure Guide" And Treasure Map 25x36",
1952. Kellogg's Sugar Corn Pops.
Near Mint In Mailer - **$125**
Treasure Guide Booklet - **$10 $20 $35**
Treasure Map - **$20 $40 $75**

WLD-3

WLD-2

WLD-2. Kellogg's Breakfast Game Score Card,
c. 1952. One side printed by game chart for entering daily breakfast diet over one-month period to be certified by school teacher and then presented to parents. -
$10 $20 $30

WLD-3. Cereal Mini-Box,
c. 1952. 4" tall "Kel-Bowl-Pac" one ounce individual serving box of Sugar Corn Pops with front panel art. -
$65 $140 $200

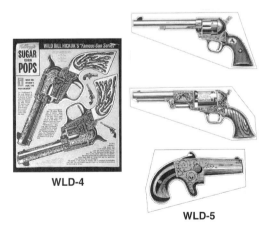

WLD-4

WLD-5

WLD-4. Kellogg's Sugar Pops Cereal Box With Cut-Outs,
1952. Features Jingles and promotes "Famous Gun Series Cut-Outs." Back shows Wild Bill's gun "The Peacemaker."
Each Box - **$75 $150 $200**
Box Back Only - **$50**

WLD-5. Original Art For "Famous Gun Series" Cut-Outs,
1952. 3 different shown. Each - **$100**

WLD-6

WLD-7

WLD-6. Kellogg's "Old-Time Gun Series,"
1954. Kellogg's Sugar Corn Pops. Plastic old time gun series. Derringer, 41 cal.brown handle. With instructions and mailer. - **$25 $60 $100**

WLD-7. Kellogg's "Old-Time Gun Series,"
1954. Kellogg's Sugar Corn Pops. Plastic old time guns. Flintlock Militia Pistol was originally offered for 50¢ and 1 box top. Fifty cents was a lot of money in those days and the guns are all rare. With instructions and mailer. - **$25 $60 $100**

WLD-8

WLD-8. Kellogg's Sugar Pops Cereal Box,
1950s. The "Famous Guns of History" series is featured. Small plastic guns in each package. Box back was used for mounting guns. Eight guns pictured on back of box. Jingles pictured on front. Also offered generically in Pep cereal. Complete Box - **$75 $175 $250**
Box Back Only - **$60**

WLD-9

WLD-9. Kellogg's "Famous Guns of History" Series,
1950s. Kellogg's Sugar Corn Pops. Four packages shown. Each Package (Two Guns) - **$10 $20 $40**

(front)

(back)

WLD-10

WLD-10. Kellogg's Sugar Pops Cereal Box Flat - 5 oz.,
1954. Jingles and his horse Joker pictured on front. Stereo-pix cut-out of the West on back. #1 of series. - **$75 $160 $225**

WLD-11

WLD-12

WLD-13

WLD-11. Cereal Display Box,
c. 1952. Kellogg Co. of Canada. - **$50 $250 $450**

WLD-12. Hickok/Guy Madison Fan Postcard,
1954. - **$5 $12 $18**

WLD-13. "Jingles" Cello. Button With Attachment,
c. 1954. Fabric ribbon holds miniature metal six-shooter. - **$10 $15 $25**

WLD-14

WLD-15

WLD-14. Deputy Marshal Certificate,
1955. Probably a Kellogg's Sugar Corn Pops premium. - **$15 $40 $60**

WLD-15. Deputy Marshal Certificate,
1955. Wild Bill & Jingles pictured. - **$20 $50 $80**

WLD-16

WLD-17

WLD-18

WLD-16. "Special Deputy" Copper Luster Tin Star Badge,
1956. Kellogg's. Set of six. Others without Hickok/Jingles name are: Deputy Sheriff, Junior Ranger, Sheriff.
Each - **$5 $10 $20**

WLD-17. Kellogg's "Wild Bill Hickok/Deputy Marshal" 2-1/4" Silvered Tin Star Badge,
1956. Set of six, see previous and following item. -
$8 $12 $25

WLD-18. Kellogg's "Jingles/Deputy" 2-1/4" Gold Luster Tin Badge,
1956. Set of six, see previous items. - **$8 $12 $25**

WLD-19 **WLD-20**

WLD-19. Rifle Series,
1956. Sugar Corn Pops premium. Buffalo Sharps rifle in original package promoted by Jingles. Six different miniature rifles offered. Each - **$10 $25 $40**

WLD-20. Hickok/Jingles Waxed Cardboard Milk Carton,
1950s. Various dairies. - **$20 $40 $75**

WLD-21
WLD-22

WLD-21. "Drink Milk" Vinyl Tumbler,
1950s. Various sponsors. -**$20 $50 $75**

WLD-22. Promo Press Kit & 10 Photos,
1950s. Rare. - **$30 $100 $150**

WLD-24
WLD-23

WLD-23. "Kellogg's Sugar Corn Pops" Cereal Box,
1950s. 16 "Famous Indian" drawings on back panels.
Complete Box - **$50 $150 $225**

WLD-24. Color Photo Litho. Button,
1950s. - **$15 $40 $60**

WLD-25 **WLD-26** **WLD-27**

WLD-25. Hickok & Jingles "We're Pardners" Litho. Button,
1950s. - **$12 $20 $35**

WLD-26. "Wild Bill Hickok/Marshal" 2-1/4" Silvered Brass Badge,
1950s. With insert paper photo, came with wallet and club member card. Badge Only - **$15 $35 $70**
Three Piece Set - **$50 $100 $175**

WLD-27. "Marshal Wild Bill Hickok" Silvered Brass Badge On Metal Clip,
1950s. Came with related wallet. - **$15 $30 $50**

WILLIE WIREDHAND

The National Rural Electric Cooperative Association was formed in 1942 as a support group for public power and rural electrification. In 1951 the association created the figure of Willie Wiredhand to personify and characterize its aims. The smiling little fellow with an electric plug and cord for a torso has appeared on mugs, towels, Christmas ornaments, water bottles, magnets, pinback buttons, etc., and is still doing his job after almost 50 years.

WWH-1
WWH-2
WWH-3

WWH-1. Willie Wiredhand Cello. Button,
1950s. For "Member" of Rural Electrification program. -
$10 $15 $20

WWH-2. Willie Wiredhand Cello. Button,
1950s. Designated for "Director" of Rural Electrification
program. - **$20 $40 $60**

WWH-3. Willie Wiredhand Oval Cello. Button,
1950s. - **$20 $40 $60**

WWH-4   WWH-5

WWH-4. Willy Wiredhand Night Light,
1960s. National Rural Electric Cooperative Association.
Plastic replica bulb with flat plane back pronged for insertion in household receptacle. Inscribed for local cooperative with initials copyright "NRECA." - **$15 $30 $50**

WWH-5. Glass Ashtray,
c. 1960s. Dark translucent glass centered by figure image
surrounded by other images of his household benefits.
Imprinted for a local sponsoring company. - **$35 $75 $125**

WINNIE THE POOH

A.A. Milne (1882-1956) published his classic children's
stories *Winnie-the-Pooh* in 1926 and *The House at
Pooh Corner* in 1928. A short-lived radio adaptation
aired on NBC in 1935, but the Disney Studios gave new
life to the beloved characters in a series of 30-minute
animated films. *Winnie the Pooh and the Honey Tree*
(1965), *Winnie the Pooh and the Blustery Day* (1968),
and *Winnie the Pooh and Tigger Too* (1974) were produced for theatrical release and later telecast as prime-
time specials on NBC, sponsored by Sears, Roebuck &
Company. A fourth short, *Winnie the Pooh and a Day
for Eeyore*, was broadcast on the Disney Channel in
1986. The cartoons were true to the Milne originals,
with Pooh, Eeyore, Kanga and Baby Roo, Wol the Owl,
Tigger, Piglet, and the other characters joining
Christopher Robin in a variety of woodland adventures. Disney also released a number of Pooh comic
books between 1977 and 1984.

WIN-2

WIN-1

**WIN-1. "Puppets Wheat Puffs Cereal" Plastic
Container,**
1966. Nabisco. Metal lid bottom. With Lid - **$20 $40 $60**

WIN-2. Spoon Sitter Vinyl Figures,
1966. Nabisco. Seven in set, Christopher Robin not shown.
Each - **$3 $8 $12**

WIN-3

WIN-4

WIN-3. "Now We Are Fifty" Cello. Button,
c. 1976. Publisher is Eagle Regalia Co., New York City, for
apparent anniversary of character creation by A. A. Milne
although picturing Piglet and Pooh in unauthorized but
Disney image. - **$10 $20 $30**

**WIN-4. "Winnie-The-Pooh And Friends" Glass
Tumbler,**
1970s. Sears, Roebuck & Co. Set of three.
Each - **$3 $6 $10**

WIN-6

WIN-5

**WIN-5. "Wardrobe Gets My Vote!" 3x4" Cello.
Rectangle Button,**
1980. - **$10 $20 $40**

WIN-6. "Grad Nite '81" 3-1/2" Cello. Button,
1981. From Disneyland graduation series of early 1980s
picturing various characters. - **$3 $5 $8**

THE WIZARD OF OZ

L. Frank Baum (1856-1919) wrote 14 Oz books, but it
was the first, *The Wonderful Wizard of Oz*, published in
1900, that served as the basis of MGM's 1939
Technicolor spectacular, *The Wizard of Oz*. (A musical
theatrical adaptation ran on Broadway in 1903, a silent
film was made in 1925, and a radio version sponsored
by Jell-O aired on NBC in 1933-1934.) The 1939 film,
with an all-star cast headed by Judy Garland, has
proved to be an enduring classic, repeated annually on
television for millions of viewers since the 1950s.
There have also been Oz theme parks and resorts, an

exhibit at the Smithsonian, appearances in Macy's Thanksgiving Day parade, comic books, and extensive licensing in dozens of categories.

WIZ-1   **WIZ-2**   **WIZ-3**

WIZ-1. "What Did The Woggle Bug Say?" Cello. Button,
1904. Book advertising button. - **$20 $60 $140**

WIZ-2. Woggle Bug Cello. Button,
1904. Book advertising button. Colors on coat vary from yellow to green. - **$20 $60 $140**

WIZ-3. "The Woggle-Bug Book," 1905. Store item. 11x15" 48-page storybook by L. Frank Baum illustrated by Ike Morgan, published by Reilly & Britton Co., Chicago. - **$250 $500 $750**

WIZ-5

WIZ-4

WIZ-6

WIZ-4. Magazine Story Poster 13x22",
1905. For issue of St. Nicholas magazine with art by F. Richardson for Baum serial story "Queen Zixi Of Ix". - **$150 $250 $400**

WIZ-5. "Read The New Baum Book/The Scarecrow Of Oz" Cello. Button,
1915. Early and rare book advertising release. - **$500 $1200 $2500**

WIZ-6. "Wonderland Of Oz" Map 16x22",
1932. Philadelphia Evening Bulletin newspaper. - **$150 $600 $850**

WIZ-7   (FRONT)   **WIZ-8**   (BACK)

WIZ-7. Jackpumpkinhead And The Sawhorse,
1933. Jell-O softbound book. - **$40 $100 $150**

WIZ-8. Ozma And The Little Wizard,
1933. Jell-O softbound book. - **$40 $100 $150**

WIZ-9   (FRONT)   **WIZ-10**   (BACK)

WIZ-9. Tik Tok And The Nome King,
1933. Jell-O softbound book. - **$40 $100 $150**

WIZ-10. The Scarecrow And The Tin Woodman,
1933. Jell-O softbound book. - **$40 $100 $150**

WIZ-11   **WIZ-12**   **WIZ-13**

WIZ-11. Movie Advertising Cello. Button,
1939. Scarce. Seen with "Loew's" (theater) and "Hecht's" (Baltimore department store) imprints. - **$200 $400 $750**

WIZ-12. Dorothy Mask,
1939. Distributed by department stores and others. - **$15 $30 $50**

WIZ-13. Scarecrow Mask,
1939. Distributed by department stores and others. - **$15 $30 $50**

WIZ-14   **WIZ-15**   **WIZ-16**

WIZ-14. Cowardly Lion Mask,
1939. Distributed by department stores and others. -
$15 $30 $50

WIZ-15. Tin Woodman Mask,
1939. Distributed by department stores and others. -
$15 $30 $50

WIZ-16. Wizard Mask,
1939. Distributed by department stores and others. -
$15 $30 $50

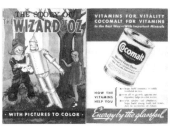 

WIZ-17   WIZ-18

WIZ-17. "The Story Of The Wizard Of Oz" Coloring Book,
1939. Cocomalt. Premium Version - **$15 $30 $60**
Store Version Without Cocomalt Ad - **$12 $25 $50**

WIZ-18. Dorothy Glass,
1939. Sealtest Cottage Cheese. Seven known: Dorothy, Toto, Scarecrow, Tin Woodman, The Cowardly Lion, The Good Witch, The Bad Witch. The Wizard is unknown.
Each - **$50 $80 $125**

WIZ-19   WIZ-20   WIZ-21

WIZ-19. Movie 3" Cello. Button,
1939. M-G-M Studio. - **$50 $150 $300**

WIZ-20. "Frank Morgan" Movie Contest Cello. Button,
1939. M-G-M Studios. 1-1/4" size, set of five also includes Judy Garland, Ray Bolger, Jack Haley, Bert Lahr. This size has serial number to match for winning prize.
Each - **$100 $200 $400**

WIZ-21. "Jack Haley" Cello. Button,
1939. From 7/8" series of five characters with Oz film title in Spanish. Each - **$50 $125 $250**

WIZ-22

WIZ-22. Pictorial Fabric Scarf,
1939. Store item. Two different designs with numerous color variations. - **$75 $150 $300**

WIZ-23   WIZ-24

WIZ-25

WIZ-23. Scarecrow Valentine,
1940 Store item. From set of 12 picturing various characters by American Colortype Co. Each - **$20 $50 $75**

WIZ-24. "Magic Sand" Packet Envelope,
c. 1940. Various theaters. Contains sand "From Along The Yellow Brick Road.." - **$100 $250 $500**

WIZ-25. "S & Co." Glass Tumblers,
1953. Swift Peanut Butter. Six designs with wavy, plain or fluted bases. Characters depicted are Dorothy, Toto, Scarecrow, Cowardly Lion, Tinman, and the Wizard.
Each - **$5 $10 $15**

WIZ-26

WIZ-26. Vinyl Hand Puppets,
1965. Procter & Gamble. Eight in set. Cardboard theater also issued. Each Puppet - **$5 $12 $25**
Theater - **$20 $45 $75**

WIZ-27

WIZ-27. Set Of 12 Litho. Buttons,
1967. Samson Products. Vending machine distribution.
Each - **$3 $6 $10**

WIZ-28

WIZ-28. "Magic Kit",
1967. Store item by Fun Inc. - **$25 $40 $75**

WONDER WOMAN

Wonder Woman was created by psychologist/writer William Moulton Marston (pen name: Charles Moulton). The comics' first major female superhero debuted in issue #8 of *All Star Comics* in December 1941 and had her own comic book by the next summer. Wonder Woman came from mysterious Paradise Island (no men allowed) to America as Diana Prince to help fight World War II. Over the years she has also battled aliens and terrorists, lost her flag-like costume and superpowers, regained them, dabbled in I Ching, and fallen in and out of love. A comic strip appearance in 1944 had a short life, and a hardback anthology was published in 1972. There have been two TV movies-- *Wonder Woman* (1974) with Cathy Lee Crosby, and *The New, Original Wonder Woman* (1975) with Lynda Carter--and a TV series, also starring Carter, that aired on ABC (1976-1977) and CBS (1977-1979). The character was also featured in the *Superfriends* cartoon that aired on ABC in the 1970s. A new live-action TV series is now in development. Items are usually copyrighted DC Comics or Warner Bros. TV.

WON-1

WON-2

WON-1. "Sensation Comics" Litho. Button,
1942. Rare. Offered in May issue of Sensation Comics. - **$500 $2500 $3500**

WON-2. WWII Infantile Paralysis Comic Book Postcard Premium,
1940s. Rare. - **$100 $400 $600**

WON-3

WON-4

WON-3. Valentine Card,
1940s. Store item. Diecut stiff paper folder with inner message "For You, Valentine, I'd Move Heaven And Earth!" - **$25 $50 $75**

WON-4. "Wonder Woman" 3-1/2" Cello. Button,
1966. Store item. #14 from series.
Near Mint Bagged - **$40**
Loose - **$12 $20 $30**

WON-5

WON-6

WON-5. Boxed Board Game,
1967. Store item by Hasbro. Also features other Justice League of America characters. - **$25 $75 $150**

WON-6. Proof Ingot,
1974. Used as incentive to promote other DC Comics character ingots. Only 300 made. Near Mint - **$200**

WON-7

WON-9

WON-8

WON-7. "Wonder Woman" 2-1/4" Cello. Button,
1975. Store item by Rainbow Designs. DC Comics copyright. - **$3 $8 $12**

WON-8. Metal Ring With Cello. Portrait,
1976. N.P.P. Inc. Brass finish with copyright on underside. - **$50 $75 $100**

WON-9. Watch,
1977. Store item by Dabs.
Near Mint Boxed - **$175**
Loose - **$35 $75 $125**

WON-10

WON-11

WON-10. Pepsi Glass,
1978. - **$5 $10 $15**

WON-11. "See The Superheroes At Sea World" Photo,
1970s. Sea World appearance souvenir. Batman and Wonder Woman pictured with facsimile signatures. - **$10 $20 $30**

WOODY WOODPECKER

Between 1940 and 1972 Walter Lantz created more than 200 animated shorts featuring the hyperactive woodpecker with the raucous laugh (supplied by Lantz's wife). Over the years Woody evolved from a multicolored lunatic into an appealing red-haired imp. His musical theme, *The Woody Woodpecker Song,* was nominated for an Academy Award in 1948. *The Woody Woodpecker Show* aired on the Mutual radio network in 1952-1954 and came to ABC television for the 1957-1958 season, then to NBC in 1971-1972 and 1976-1977. Woody made a number of comic book appearances starting in 1942. Items are normally copyrighted Walter Lantz Productions.

WDY-1

WDY-1. Promo,
1951. Scarce. 6 pages (4 pages of comics). - **$100 $225 $325**

WDY-2

WDY-2. Cards With Folder,
1953. Carnation Corn Flakes. Eighteen Walter Lantz cards. Set - **$75 $125 $180**

WDY-3

WDY-4

WDY-5

WDY-3. "Hi Pal!" Cello. Button,
1957. Came on store bought doll. - **$8 $15 $30**

WDY-4. Premium Booklet,
1958. Kellogg's Rice Krispies. 4 pages of recipes and a 1958 quarter. - **$25 $50 $75**

WDY-5. Premium Comic Chevrolet,
1950s. - **$15 $45 $120**

WDY-6

WDY-7

WDY-8

WDY-6. Spoon,
1950s. Cereal premium. - **$10 $20 $30**

WDY-7. Comic,
1950s. Scotch Tape sponsor. - **$15 $45 $120**

WDY-8. Movie Label,
1950s. - **$10 $20 $30**

WDY-10

WDY-9

(FRONT)　**WDY-14**　(BACK)

WDY-9. Swimming Figure,
1962. Kellogg's Cereals. Plastic jointed toy propelled by rubber band. Near Mint Boxed - **$125**
Unboxed - **$30 $65 $90**

WDY-14. Stars Cereal Swimmer Offer,
1967. Cereal box flat. - **$40 $80 $120**

WDY-10. Parking Pass,
c. 1963. Lantz Studios. - **$30 $60 $90**

WDY-17

WDY-15

WDY-16

WDY-11

WDY-11. Kellogg's Plastic Mug And Cereal Bowl,
1965. Bowl image of log trough. Set - **$25 $40 $70**

WDY-15. Gum Box Display Card,
1968. Fleer Gum. - **$8 $12 $25**

WDY-16. Figural Harmonica,
c. 1960s. Possible Kellogg's premium. Plastic full figure with harmonica reed formed in tail. - **$15 $30 $50**

WDY-17. Plastic Portrait Ring,
c. 1970s. Vending machine issue. - **$5 $8 $12**

WDY-12

WDY-18

WDY-12. Kellogg's Plastic Door Knocker Assembly Kit,
1966. Canadian issue. Boxed - **$20 $40 $60**
Built - **$15 $25 $40**

WDY-18. Spoon,
1970s. Store bought. - **$10 $25 $35**

(FRONT)　**WDY-13**　(BACK)

WDY-13. Rice Krispies Stuffed Toy Offer,
1966. Cereal box flat. - **$40 $80 $120**

WORLD'S FAIRS

International expositions blossomed into creative and technical spectacles in the 19th century, first in Europe and then in the United States, providing a mix of fine arts, industrial progress, and nationalist emotions. In addition to promoting international understanding, world's fairs produced an abundance of collectible souvenirs. Major American fairs include the Centennial Exposition (Philadelphia, 1876), World's Columbian Exposition (Chicago, 1893), Cotton Centennial (New Orleans, 1894), Pan-American (Buffalo, 1901), Louisiana Purchase (St. Louis, 1904), Panama-Pacific (San Francisco, 1915), Sesquicentennial (Philadelphia, 1926) Century of Progress (Chicago, 1933-1934), California Pacific International (San Diego, 1935-1936), Great Lakes (Cleveland, 1936-1937), Golden Gate International (San Francisco, 1939-1940),

Francisco, 1939-1940), World of Tomorrow (New York, 1939-1940), and New York World's Fair (1964-1965).

WFA-1

WFA-2

WFA-3

WFA-7

WFA-8

WFA-9

WFA-1. U.S. Centennial Pennant,
1876. 18x24" vertical swallow-tail linen fabric including border design of 38 stars representing states admitted to the Union as of celebration year. - **$75 $125 $200**

WFA-2. Spoon ,
1893. World's Fair spoon shows picture of Columbus and Administration Building. Sold at Fair. - **$25 $50 $75**

WFA-3. Ticket - Chicago 1893,
1893. Unused 1893 child's ticket for World's Fair in Chicago. Children dreamed of the chance of attending the World's Columbian Exhibition in 1893. It is very rare to find an unused ticket that was bought at the Fair. Complete - **$25 $65 $100**

WFA-7. Sky Ride Promo ,
1933. Chicago World's Fair premium came with Frank Buck Club material. - **$25 $50 $75**

WFA-8. Puzzle - Boxed ,
1933. Chicago World's Fair 11x16" puzzle sold at Fair. - **$15 $30 $60**

WFA-9. Salt And Pepper Shakers ,
1934. Chicago World's Fair - Hall of Science pictured on each shaker. Sold at Fair. - **$20 $40 $60**

WFA-4

WFA-5

WFA-6

WFA-10

WFA-11

WFA-4. Pan-American Exposition "Swift & Company" Cello. Button,
1901. Caricature art for meat products. - **$15 $25 $50**

WFA-5. Pan-American Exposition Cello. Button,
1901. Pictured is establishment and proprietor of "Cheyenne Joe's Rocky Mountain Tavern." - **$20 $40 $60**

WFA-6. St. Louis World's Fair Cello. Button,
1904. Pictured is Thomas Jefferson under alternate title of the fair "Universal Exposition." - **$10 $20 $30**

WFA-10. "Sears, Roebuck & Co." Chicago World's Fair Key Holder,
1933. Cello. and brass 3" key case dated for opening year of the fair. - **$25 $50 $75**

WFA-11. New York World's Fair Enameled Brass Star Badge,
1939. Souvenir issue for youthful "Safety Monitor." - **$60 $140 $200**

WFA-12

WFA-13

WFA-14

WFA-12. New York World's Fair "Westinghouse" Robot Pin,
1939. Diecut thin brass figural pin of Robot Elektro giant mechanical man of Westinghouse Exhibit. - **$5 $10 $15**

WFA-13. New York World's Fair "Westinghouse" Robot Cello. Button,
1939. Images of robot and robot dog "Elektro And Sparko." - **$30 $60 $100**

WFA-14. New York World's Fair "Abbott & Costello" Cello. Button,
1939. Nomination of Costello for mayor and Abbott for "Commissioner Of Laffs" of "World's Fair Midway." - **$25 $50 $80**

WFA-15

WFA-15. "Wonder Bread" New York World's Fair Sticker Signs, 1939. 11x18" and 9" diameter full color signs gummed on front for store window application. Both include image of "Wonder Bakery" exhibit building. Each - **$10 $25 $40**

WFA-16

WFA-16. Penny Bracelet 1939,
1939. Boxed. 14 KT gold plated. Sold at the World's Fair. - **$25 $50 $75**

WDY-17

WFA-17. "Today At The Fair" New York World's Fair Schedule Newspaper, 1939. Daily edition #118 for Monday, August 28 with eight pages of either daily or continuous events. Back page includes photo of "Elektro," the seven-foot tall robot of Westinghouse exhibit. - **$25 $50 $75**

WFA-18   WFA-19

WFA-18. Bike Product New York World's Fair Ad Poster,
1939. New Departure Coaster Brake. Photo endorsement by Grover Whalen, fair director, on 16x25" poster. - **$25 $50 $75**

WFA-19. "108 World's Fair Recipes" Booklet,
1939. Souvenir of Borden Exhibit of New York World's Fair with 32 pages of recipes and Elsie illustrations. - **$10 $20 $35**

WFA-20

WFA-21

WFA-20. "Either World's Fair" Contest Paper Poster,
1939. 16x25" by unidentifed sponsor offering prize of free trips f or boys and girls to either Golden Gate Exposition of San Francisco or New York World's Fair. - **$75 $150 $250**

WFA-21. New York World's Fair Clown Doll,
1939. 15" tall wood and composition doll in orange and blue fabric outfit. - **$100 $200 $300**

WFA-23

WFA-22

WFA-22. New York World's Fair Closing Day Pennant,
1940. 4x9" felt fabric inscribed for visit on final day October 27th. - **$10 $25 $40**

WFA-23. New York World's Fair Flicker Ring,
1964. Silvered plastic base topped by alternating image of Unisphere and souvenir text. - **$8 $12 $20**

WFA-24

WFA-24. "World's Fair Twins" Kissing Bobbing Head Set,
1965. Pair of composition symbolic twins with spring-mounted heads and inner magnet behind pursed lips.
Boxed - **$50 $100 $150**
Loose - **$35 $70 $100**

WORLD WAR II

American involvement in World War II was intense on the home front as well as the war zones. With millions of young men and women in uniform and far from home between early 1942 and 1945, family members and loved ones wanted to follow events as they occurred in Europe and in the Pacific. A number of advertisers answered the call by offering war maps and atlases and other print material that brought home details of the military movements and battles.

WWII-1

WWII-1. Reading Kit - Boxed,
1942. Says "Hours of entertainment for service men", included 5 different pulp magazines. - **$100 $200 $300**

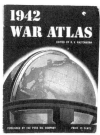
WWII-2

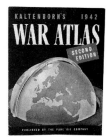
WWII-3

WWII-2. Atlas Map,
1942. Pure Oil premium. 16 pages. Edited by H. V. Kaltenborn. - **$20 $30 $45**

WWII-3. Atlas Map - 2nd Edition,
1942. Pure Oil premium. 16 pages. - **$20 $30 $45**

WWII-6

WWII-4   WWII-5

WWII-4. H. V. Kaltenborn Photo,
1942. Radio premium with Kaltenborn in uniform with "C" on sleeve for news correspondent. - **$10 $20 $30**

WWII-5. "Eat To Beat The Devil" Booklet,
1942. Servel refrigerators. 32-page listing of health and nutrition tips with front cover caricature art of Hitler as the devil. - **$10 $20 $30**

WWII-6. Anti-Mussolini Plaster Ashtray With Sticker Label,
1943. - **$60 $100 $150**

WWII-7

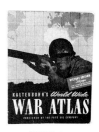
WWII-8

WWII-7. "Radio At War Picture Book",
c. 1943. Various sponsors. Depicts programs and stars of "Blue Network." - **$15** **$25** **$45**

WWII-8. Atlas Map - Victory Edition,
1943. Pure Oil premium. 20 pages. - **$25** **$35** **$50**

WWII-9

WWII-9. "Capt. Ben Dix" Comic Book,
1943. Bendix Aviation Corp. - **$10** **$20** **$40**

WWII-10

WWII-11

WWII-10. Anti-Hitler Plaster Toothpick Holder,
c. 1943. - **$85** **$150** **$300**

WWII-11. Hitler Plaster Pin Cushion,
c. 1943. Large Size - **$75** **$150** **$250**
Smaller "Hotzi Notzi" Size - **$50** **$80** **$125**

WWII-13

WWII-12

WWII-12. "Target Tokyo" Cardboard Wheel Game,
1944. Tip-Top Bread. - **$15** **$25** **$50**

WWII-13. "Sky Heroes" Stamp Album,
c. 1944. Sinclair Oil Corp. Twenty stamps in set.
Complete - **$25** **$50** **$100**

WWII-14

WWII-14. Anti-Hitler Composition Pig Bank,
c. 1944. Squeaking mechanism rarely works.
Not Working - **$75** **$125** **$200**

WWII-15

WWII-16

WWII-15. Christmas Card,
1944. Christmas card from the United States Army in Italy. - **$5** **$10** **$20**

WWII-16. Pacific Map,
1944. Pure Oil premium. Folds out to show battle areas in Pacific. - **$25** **$35** **$50**

WWII-18

WWII-17

WWII-19

WWII-17. Victory Map Set,
1944. Pure Oil Co. Two sections fold out into huge wall map. - **$30** **$60** **$90**

WWII-18. Hitler Skunk,
c. 1944. Ceramic composition. - **$50** **$100** **$150**

WWII-19. "Victory Star Tumblers" Glasses Set,
c. 1944. Pillsbury's Flour. Set - **$25** **$60** **$80**

WWII-20

WWII-20. "Exide Batteries At War" Book,
1946. Illustrations similar to Dixie Ice Cream series. - **$20** **$50** **$90**

WWII-21

WWII-21. Esso War Maps,
1940s. Periodic revisions in war years. Each - **$5 $12 $20**

WWII-22   WWII-23   WWII-24

WWII-22. Lowell Thomas NBC War Map 16x20",
1940s. Radio premium. Two sided colorful map of the World. - **$30 $65 $100**

WWII-23. Kaltenborn Campaign Book,
1940s. Pure Oil premium. News editor for Roosevelt vs. Willkie election. - **$15 $30 $40**

WWII-24. Photo,
1940s. H. V. Kaltenborn . Edits the news. No uniform. - **$5 $10 $20**

WWII-26

WWII-25

WWII-27

WWII-25. Radio Sign,
1940s. Features Uncle Sam telling people to listen to updates on the War. - **$25 $50 $75**

WWII-26. Cartoon Slogan Matchbook,
1940s. Topps Gum. Cover includes security slogan illustrated by cartoonist O. Soglow, creator of The Little King comic strip. Complete - **$15 $30 $50**

WWII-27. Bill Henry's Presidential Election Map,
1940s. - **$25 $35 $50**

WYATT EARP

Legendary gunfighter and lawman Wyatt Earp (1848-1929) has been portrayed in at least two dozen Hollywood Westerns by such stars as George O'Brien, Randolph Scott, Richard Dix, Henry Fonda, Joel McCrea, Burt Lancaster and Kevin Costner. On television *The Life and Legend of Wyatt Earp* starred Hugh O'Brian in a serial drama that aired on ABC from 1955 to 1961. The series followed the romanticized adventures of Earp as a frontier marshal in Ellsworth and Dodge City, Kansas, and Tombstone, Arizona. Comic books appeared from 1955 on. Most licensed items came from the TV series and are copyrighted Wyatt Earp Ent. Inc.

(FRONT)   WYT-2   (BACK)

WYT-1

WYT-1. "Buntline Special" Gun On Card,
c. 1955. Store item. 6x20" card holds 18" long plastic clicker replica gun popularized on TV series.
Carded - **$75 $125 $200**
Uncarded Gun - **$35 $60 $100**

WYT-2. Cheerios Box,
1955. Back panel has cut-out parts for "Peacemaker" gun on 10-1/2 oz. box; "Paterson" gun on 7 oz. box.
Each Complete Box - **$75 $200 $275**

WYT-3

WYT-4

WYT-3. "Marshal Wyatt Earp" Sterling Silver Initial Ring,
1958. Cheerios. Engraved personal initial, TV show copyright. - **$40 $60 $80**

WYT-4. "Marshal Wyatt Earp" Metal Badge On Card,
c. 1958. Store item. On Card - **$15 $25 $40**
Loose - **$8 $10 $20**

X-MEN

Stan Lee and Jack Kirby created the X-Men, a band of superpower teenage mutant fighters crusading for justice and the acceptance of mutants in an increasingly prejudiced society. Introduced in issue #1 of *X-Men* in 1963, Cyclops, The Angel, The Beast, and Marvel Girl joined with Professor X to foil the evil schemes of arch-enemy Magneto. The book was suspended briefly in 1970, then revived with reprints and, starting in 1975, new adventures and new characters were introduced, sparking a run that has proliferated into numerous other titles and a huge surge in popularity. Including Specials and Annuals, Marvel has published well over 300 *X-Men* comic books. An animated version debuted on the Fox Children's Network in 1992, and a live-action feature film is currently in development.

XMN-3

XMN-2

XMN-1

XMN-1. X-Men #1,
Sept. 1963. Marvel Comics. Origin and first appearance of the X-Men. - **$350 $1100 $5500**

XMN-2. Plastic Badge With Reverse Needle Post/Clutch,
1988. Marvel. - **$2 $4 $6**

XMN-3. Gold Ring,
1993. Diamond Comics Distribution seminar giveaway. 25 made. - **$750**

XMN-4 (TOP) XMN-5 (SIDE)

XMN-4. Silver Ring,
1993. Diamond Comics Distribution seminar giveaway. - **$125**

XMN-5. Xavier Institute Class Ring,
1994. 10k gold. - **$400**
Sterling Silver Version - **$75**
Bronze Finished Pewter Version - **$20**

THE YELLOW KID

Richard F. Outcault's *Yellow Kid* is generally considered to be the first true comic strip. After appearances as a minor character in the *Hogan's Alley* gag panels in the *New York World* in 1895, the bald, jug-eared kid in a nightshirt grew in popularity and, by the beginning of 1896, his nightshirt was yellow. Outcault never gave him a name, so readers referred to him as the yellow kid. William Randolph Hearst hired Outcault for his *New York Journal* later that year and titled his panels *The Yellow Kid*. Outcault dropped the strip in 1898 and went on to other work, but the Kid made licensing history in promoting a wide range of products such as chewing gum, candy, cookies, games, puzzles, cigarettes, soap, bicycles, highchairs, and whiskey.

YLW-1

YLW-2

YLW-1. Yellow Kid And Lady 18x24" Paper Announcement Poster For New York Journal's Colored Sunday Supplement,
1896. Scarce. Also reads "Wait For It-It Is Coming" including artists' names Archie Gunn and R. F. Outcault. - **$1000 $2000 $3500**

YLW-2. Wooden Cigar Box,
1896. - **$200 $400 $750**

YLW-3 YLW-4

YLW-3. Advertising Card,
1896. Sweet Wheat Chewing Gum. - **$75 $150 $250**

YLW-4. Gum Card #11 Example,
1896. Adams' Yellow Kid Chewing Gum. Set of 25, two styles: small number or large number (see next item). Small Numbers Each - **$10 $15 $40**

YLW-6

YLW-5

YLW-5. Gum Cards #6 and #21,
1896. Adams' Yellow Kid Chewing Gum. Examples from set of 25 with large numbers. Each - **$10 $15 $40**

YLW-6. Yellow Kid First Button In Set,
1896. High Admiral cigarettes. The first 35 buttons in the set are the most frequently found. Each - **$10 $25 $40**

YLW-7 YLW-8 YLW-9

YLW-7. Cello. Button #35,
1896. Buttons #35-94 become scarcer as the button number becomes higher. #90-94 are the scarcest. #95-100 were never issued. - **$25 $40 $65**

YLW-8. Yellow Kid With Various Flags Cello. Button,
1896. High Admiral Cigarette. Buttons numbered 101-160 depict him holding some type of flag, usually with the name of a country. Each - **$20 $40 $65**

YLW-9. Theatrical Production Cello. Button,
1896. - **$10 $20 $40**

YLW-10 YLW-11

YLW-10. Yellow Kid For President McKinley Enameled Brass Lapel Stud,
1896. Small figure inscribed "Hogan's Alley Is Out Fer McKinley". - **$125 $400 $750**

YLW-11. "The Latest And The Greatest" Sheet Music Clipping From Newspaper,
c. 1896. Rare. - **$75 $250 $400**

YLW-12 YLW-13 YLW-14

YLW-12. "The Original Yell-er Kid" Cello. Button,
c. 1896. - **$75 $150 $250**

YLW-13. Miniature Painted White Metal Figure Stickpin,
c. 1896. - **$20 $40 $75**

YLW-14. Pewter Candy Mold,
c. 1896. - **$50 $100 $175**

YLW-15

YLW-16

YLW-17

YLW-15. Trade Card,
c. 1896. Various advertisers. - **$30 $60 $125**

YLW-16. Chocolate Ad Paper Bookmark,
c. 1896. Hawley & Hoops Breakfast Cocoa. Pictured are penny chocolate pieces in figural images including Yellow Kid. - **$20 $60 $125**

YLW-17. Soap Figure,
c. 1896. Store item by D. S. Brown & Co.
Near Mint Boxed - **$500**
Loose - **$100 $200 $300**

YLW-18

YLW-18. Toy Sand Pail,
1896. 3-1/2" tall by 4-1/2" diameter full color litho tin including four perimeter cartoon images copyright by R. F. Outcault. - **$500 $1000 $1800**

YLW-19

YLW-20

YLW-19. Calendar Postcard,
January 1914. Various advertisers. Series of monthly calendar cards with 1911 Outcault copyright.
Each - **$25 $50 $75**

YLW-20. Ink Blotter,
Early 1900s. Rare. - **$75 $200 $300**

YLW-21

YLW-21. Ad Dies in Box,
1920s. Box with four dies & four ad flyers. -
$100 $200 $400
Box - **$20 $30 $40**
Each Die - **$25 $50 $70**
Each Ad - **$5 $10 $20**

YLW-22

(ENLARGED VIEW)

YLW-23

YLW-22. "Big Bubble Chewing Gum" Cello. Button,
c. 1930. Full inscription "There Is Only One Yellow Kid Big Bubble Chewing Gum". - **$15 $30 $60**

YLW-23. Pulver Gum Co. With Yellow Kid Logo,
1930. 8-1/2x13" stationery sheet with typewritten message dated July 1 to Pulver salesmen offering prizes for sale of gum machines. Yellow Kid symbol is upper left. -
$15 $30 $50

YOGI BEAR

Hanna-Barbera's Yogi Bear, a TV cartoon and merchandising superstar, was introduced in 1959 on *The Huckleberry Hound Show* and two years later was starring in his own series. The genial bear in a pork-pie hat, trailed by his diminutive pal Boo Boo, spent his time panhandling and swiping picnic baskets from visitors to Jellystone Park. Yogi's love interest was Cindy Bear (Ah do declare!). *The Yogi Bear Show* was syndicated from 1961 to 1963, sponsored by Kellogg cereals; *Yogi's Gang* with Yogi leaving the Park to crusade for the environment, was broadcast on ABC from 1973

to 1975; and *Yogi's Space Race* appeared on NBC from 1978 to 1979. Yogi has also appeared teamed with other Hanna-Barbera characters and in several TV specials. Yogi comic books began publication in 1959. His popularity continues to this day. Items are normally copyrighted Hanna-Barbera Productions.

YOG-3

YOG-1

YOG-2

YOG-1. Vinyl And Plush Doll,
1960. Store item and Kellogg's premium. 19" tall. -
$20 $50 $75

YOG-2. Ceramic Figurine,
c. 1960. Store item. - **$20 $40 $75**

YOG-3. "Hey There, It's Yogi Bear" Litho. Button,
c. 1960. - **$10 $20 $35**

YOG-5

YOG-4

YOG-4. Plastic Bank,
c. 1960. Store item by Knickerbocker. - **$20 $30 $50**

YOG-5. Yogi Bear Game Cloth,
1962. Kellogg's Corn Flakes. 35x45" vinyl sheet; markers of Yogi, Huck, Quick Draw, Mr. Jinks; spinner; instructions; 24 red or black checkers picturing Yogi or Huck.
Near Mint In Mailer - **$50**
Complete/Loose - **$10 $20 $35**

YOG-6

YOG-7

YOG-8

YOG-6. "Yogi Bear For President" Litho. Button,
1964. Hanna-Barbera copyright. Comes in 2-1/4" or 3-1/2" size. Small - **$20 $30 $60**
Large - **$15 $30 $50**

YOG-7. "Yogi Bear For President" 3" Litho. Button, 1964. - **$15 $30 $60**

YOG-8. Purex Bottle Bank With Wrapper, 1967. Near Mint With Wrapper - **$75**
Bottle Only - **$15 $30 $55**

YOG-9

YOG-10

YOG-9. Stamped Image Plastic Ring, 1960s. Unknown sponsor. Hanna-Barbera copyright. - **$15 $40 $75**

YOG-10. Newspaper Strip Promotion Cello. Button, 1960s. Sunday Tribune, possibly Chicago. - **$15 $30 $50**

YOG-11

YOG-11. Yogi Bear Hat, 1960s. Kellogg's premium. - **$20 $30 $40**

YOG-13

YOG-12

YOG-12. Yogi Bear Cereal Box, 1960s. - **$100 $250 $350**

YOG-13. "Procter & Gamble Dividend Day '85" 2-1/4" Cello. Button, 1985. Used by employees at amusement park outing. - **$5 $10 $20**

Colgate's Ribbon Dental Cream sponsored this radio serial in the early 1930s, relating adventures in the California Gold Rush of 1849. Premiums included a map of the gold territory and punch-out versions of an Indian encampment and a wagon train. The program was apparently broadcast only regionally.

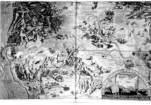

YFN-1

YFN-1. United States Adventure Map With Envelope, c. 1932. Colgate-Palmolive-Peet. Map opens to 20x31".
Envelope - **$10 $25 $30**
Map - **$40 $100 $150**

YFN-2

YFN-2. Capt. Sam's Wagon Cardboard Punch-Out Folder, c. 1932. Rare. Colgate-Palmolive-Peet. Sheet opens to 19x37". Unpunched - **$40 $100 $175**

YFN-3

YFN-3. Indian Village, c. 1932. Rare. Colgate-Palmolive-Peet. Sheet opens to 19"x37". Unpunched - **$60 $150 $225**

Don Diego de la Vega, alter ego of Zorro, the fox, was created by author Johnston McCulley in serialized magazine stories around 1919. In the tradition of *The Scarlet Pimpernel*, Don Diego posed as an effete dandy until it was time to defend the oppressed; then out came the black cape, mask, and sword. Zorro has a long film history, ranging from the 1920 silent *The Mark of Zorro*, starring Douglas Fairbanks Sr., to the 1981 spoof *Zorro, the Gay Blade,* with George Hamilton (and George Hamilton). On television Guy Williams played the flashy 19th century fencer in the popular Disney series that aired on ABC from 1957 to 1959. Some 24 years later Disney produced a comic version, *Zorro and Son,* that lasted less than two months on CBS in 1983. Zorro comic books appeared from 1949 to 1961, 1966 to 1968, and 1990-1991. The

original TV series generated a wide variety of related merchandise, copyrighted by Walt Disney Productions. The new 1998 feature film, *The Mask of Zorro*, stars Antonio Banderas as the masked avenger, with Anthony Hopkins as his swash-buckling predecessor.

ZOR-1   ZOR-2   ZOR-3

ZOR-1. "Don Q/Son Of Zorro" Cello. Button,
1925. Pictures movie title star Douglas Fairbanks, Sr. - **$60 $140 $225**

ZOR-2. 7up Litho. Ad Button,
1957. 1-3/8" size. The 1-1/8" litho. variety appeared about 1990. Unsure if reproduction or quantity find-it is extremely common.
1-3/8" Size - **$8 $15 $30**
1-1/8" Size - **$1 $2 $3**

ZOR-3. 7up Litho. Tin Advertising Tab,
1957. Also marked "ABC/TV". - **$12 $20 $40**

ZOR-4   ZOR-5   ZOR-6

ZOR-4. Fan Postcard,
c. 1958. - **$10 $15 $25**

ZOR-5. Plastic Boot Mug,
c. 1958. Store item. - **$20 $40 $60**

ZOR-6. TV Station Litho. Tin Tab,
c. 1950s. - **$15 $25 $60**

ZOR-7   ZOR-8   ZOR-9

ZOR-7. "Zorro Candy" Display Box,
1950s. Super Novelty Candy Co. Held multiple packages. - **$20 $60 $125**

ZOR-8. Paper 23x36" Dry Cleaning Bag Cut-Out Costume,
1950s. Various sponsors. - **$20 $30 $50**

ZOR-9. "Official Ring" Ad Paper,
1950s. - **$20 $30 $40**

ZOR-10   ZOR-11   ZOR-12

ZOR-10. Plastic Ring,
1950s. Silver band with black top and name in gold. - **$30 $45 $60**

ZOR-11. Plastic Ring,
1950s. Entirely black except name in gold. - **$30 $45 $60**

ZOR-12. English Plastic Lapel Stud,
1950s. Quaker Puffed Wheat. - **$20 $40 $60**

ZOR-13

ZOR-13. Hat with Mask,
1960s. Store item. - **$30 $60 $80**

ZOR-14   ZOR-15

ZOR-14. Zorro #0 Premium Comic
1993. Indicia says November. Topps Comics. Special preview edition polybagged with all Topps Comics distributed that month. A comic shop/newsstand edition was produced with a card stock cover, a cover price of $1.00 U.S./$1.25 Canada, and the words "Special Deluxe Collectors Edition" in place of "Special Collectors Edition" on this version. - **$1**

ZOR-15. Zorro #1 Preview Edition
1993. Indicia says October. Topps Comics. Special preview edition was produced in two versions, each an 8-page, self-covered excerpt from the full Zorro #1. A newsprint version was distributed to comic book specialty shops with distributor catalogs. The second version, on a glossy stock, was polybagged with Topps Comics' other titles. - **$1**

Bordman, Gerald. *American Musical Theatre*. New York: Oxford University Press, 1978.

Brooks, Tim & Marsh, Earle. *The Complete Directory to Prime Time Network TV Shows*. 3rd ed. NY: Ballantine Books, 1985.

Brown, Hy. *Comic Character Timepieces: Seven Decades of Memories*. West Chester, PA: Schiffer Publishing, Ltd. 1992.

Bruce, Scott. *Cereal Box Bonanza: The 1950s*. Paducah, KY: Collector Books, 1995.

Bruce, Scott & Crawford, Bill. *Cerealizing America*. Boston: Faber & Faber, 1995.

Bruce, Scott. *Flake: The Breakfast Nostalgia Magazine*. Cambridge, MA: 1990-1995.

Claggett, Tom, ed. *The Premium Exchange*. St. Clair Shores, MI: December 1976-January 1978.

Davis, Stephen. *Say Kids! What Time Is It? Notes From The Peanut Gallery*. Boston: Little, Brown and Company, 1987.

Dinan, John A. *The Pulp Western*. San Bernardino, CA: Borgo Press, 1983.

Douglas, George H. *The Early Days of Radio Broadcasting*. Jefferson, NC: McFarland & Co., 1987.

Dunning, John. *Tune in Yesterday*. Englewood Cliffs, NJ: Prentice-Hall, 1976.

Erickson, Hal. *Television Cartoon Shows: An Illustrated Encyclopedia 1949 Through 1993*. Jefferson, NC: McFarland & Co., 1995.

Fenin, George N. & Everson, William K. *The Western*. New York: Orion Press, 1962.

Fischer, Stuart. *Kids' TV: The First 25 Years*. New York: Facts on File, 1983.

Geissman, Grant. *Collectibly Mad: The Mad And EC Collectibles Guide*. Northhampton, MA: Kitchen Sink Press, 1995.

Goulart, Ron. *Cheap Thrills*. New Rochelle, NY: Arlington House, 1972.

Goulart, Ron, ed. *Encyclopedia of American Comics*. New York: Facts on File, 1990.

Goulart, Ron. *Great History of Comic Books*. Chicago: Contemporary Books, 1986.

Grossman, Gary H. *Saturday Morning TV*. New York: Dell, 1981.

Hake, Ted. *Hake's Americana & Collectibles Auction Catalogues Nos. 17-133*. York, PA: 1971-1995.

Hake, Ted. *Hake's Guide to Advertising Collectibles*. Radnor, PA: Wallace-Homestead, 1992.

Hake, Ted. *Hake's Guide to Comic Character Collectibles*. Radnor, PA: Wallace-Homestead, 1993.

Hake, Ted. *Hake's Guide to Cowboy Character Collectibles*. Radnor, PA: Wallace-Homestead, 1994.

Hake, Ted. *Hake's Guide to TV Collectibles*. Radnor, PA: Wallace-Homestead, 1990.

Hake, Ted & King, Russell. *Collectible Pin-Back Buttons 1896-1986*. Radnor PA: Wallace-Homestead, 1991.

Halliwell, Leslie. *Halliwell's Film Guide*. 7th ed. New York: Harper & Row, 1990.

Heide, Robert & Gilman, John. *Cartoon Collectibles*, Garden City, NY: Doubleday, 1983.

Hickerson, Jay *The Ultimate History of Network Radio Programming and Guide to All Circulating Shows*. 2nd ed. Hamden, CT: Presto Print II, 1992.

Hirschhorn, Clive. *The Warner Bros. Story*. New York: Crown, 1979.

Horn, Maurice, ed. *The World Encyclopedia of Comics*. New York: Avon Books, 1977.

Inman, David. *The TV Encyclopedia*. New York: Putnam, 1991.

Keaton, Russell. *The Aviation Art of Russell Keaton*. Northampton, MA: Kitchen Sink Press, 1995.

Lenburg, Jeff. *The Encyclopedia of Animated Cartoon Series*. Westport, CT: Arlington House, 1981.

Levin, Marshall N. and Hake, Theodore L. *Buttons In Sets 1896-1972*. York PA: Hake's Americana & Collectibles Press, 1984.

Maltin, Leonard. *Of Mice and Magic*. New York: McGraw-Hill, 1980.

Maltin, Leonard. *TV Movies and Video Guide*. 1991 ed. New York: Penguin, 1990.

Mandelowitz, Hy. *The Premium Guide*. New York: November 1977-August 1979.

Matetsky, Amanda Murrah. *The Adventures Of Superman Collecting*. West Plains, MO: Russ Cochran, Ltd., 1988.

Melcher, Jack, ed. *Radio Premium Collectors Newsletter*. Waukegan, IL: January 1973-September 1975.

Mix, Paul E. *The Life and Legend of Tom Mix*. South Brunswick & NY: A.S. Barnes, 1972.

Morgan, Hal. *Symbols of America*. New York: Viking Penguin, 1986.

Moskowitz, Milton, Levering, Robert & Katz, Michael. *Everybody's Business*. New York: Doubleday, 1990.

Norris, M.G. "Bud." *The Tom Mix Book*. Waynesville, NC: The World Of Yesterday, 1989.

Olson, Richard D., ed. *Little Orphan Annie Reader*. New Orleans, LA: 1979-1980.

Olson, Richard D., ed. *The R.F. Outcault Reader: The Official Newsletter Of The R.F. Outcault Society*. Slidell, LA:1993.

Overstreet, Robert M. *The Overstreet Comic Book Price Guide. 25th ed.* New York: Avon, 1995.

Overstreet, Robert M. *Overstreet Premium Ring Price Guide*. Timonium, MD: Gemstone Publishing, Inc. 1994.

Paquin, Mike. *"Put on a 'Funny Face,'" Collecting Figures*, pp. 74-75, June, 1995.

Penzler, Otto, Steinbrunner, Chris & Lachman, Marvin, eds. *Detectionary*. Woodstock, N.: Overlook Press, 1977.

Rinker, Harry L. *Hopalong Cassidy King Of The Cowboy Merchandisers*. Atglen, PA: Schiffer Publishing, Ltd., 1995.

Santelmo, Vincent. *The Official 30th Anniversary Salute To GI Joe 1964-1994*. Iola, WI: Krause Publications, 1994.

Sarno, Joe, ed. *Space Academy Newsletter*. Chicago: July 1978-October, 1981.

Scarfone, Jay and Stillman, William. *The Wizard of Oz Collector's Treasury*. West Chester, PA: Schiffer Publishing, Ltd. 1992.

Selitzer, Ralph. *The Dairy Industry in America*. New York: Magazines for Industry, 1976.

Smilgis, Joel, ed. *Box Top Bonanza*. Moline, IL: December 1983-No. 49, 1991.

Stedman, Raymond William. *The Serials. 2nd ed.* Norman, OK: University of Oklahoma Press, 1977.

Swartz, Jon D. & Reinehr, Robert C. *Handbook of Old-Time Radio*. Metuchen, NJ: Scarecrow Press, 1993.

Terrace, Vincent. *Radio's Golden Years*. San Diego, CA: A.S. Barnes, 1981.

Thompson, Steve. *The Walt Kelly Collector's Guide: A Bibliography and Price Guide*. Richfield, MN: Spring Hollow Books.

Tumbusch, Tom. *Tomart's Price Guide to Radio Premium and Cereal Box Collectibles*. Dayton, OH: Tomart Publications, 1991.

Weiss, Ken & Goodgold, ed. *To Be Continued....* New York: Bonanza Books, 1972.

Woolery, George W. *Animated TV Specials*. Metuchen, NJ: Scarecrow Press, 1989.

Woolery, George W. Children's *Television: The First Thirty-Five Years, 1946-1981*. Part I. Metuchen, NJ: Scarecrow Press, 1983.

Woolery, George W. Children's *Television: The First Thirty-Five Years, 1946-1981*. Part II. Metuchen, NJ: Scarecrow Press, 1985.

INDEX

This index covers the subject histories and listed items in all 350 category sections. Actual people are entered alphabetically by last name. All other entries are alphabetical by the first word, disregarding articles A, An, and The.

PRESIDENT'S NOTE

I trust you've enjoyed this new edition of **Hake's Price Guide To Character Toys**. As impressive as the first edition was, I'm even more proud of this new volume.

Ted Hake's years of dedicated research and investigation continue to pay off for our fellow collectors, and I think you'll agree that he's done an amazing job of expanding on the information brought to light in the previous book.

Bob Overstreet, with his own detective work and his network of advisors, contributed a wealth of background information and pricing. Ted and Bob have each authored many books, but by working together on this guide I believe they have raised the bar for all future price guides.

Both of them were ably assisted by our staff at Gemstone Publishing. In executing the editorial and design plans for this book, they have taken the lessons learned in production of the first edition and further developed the presentation of this remarkable material.

Reviewers have praised **Hake's Price Guide** as a model of what a price guide should be, but I hope you'll write and let us know your thoughts on the subject. Only sustained, serious interaction with our fellow collectors will continue to propel future editions of Hake's Price Guide to new levels.

I would like to extend a particular welcome to our new readers. You have picked a superb time to join us. This new edition arrives as character collectibles are enjoying an unprecedented boom in attention. As you've probably read elsewhere in this book, there are many factors driving the increased cultural awareness of the nostalgic impulse. To meet the needs of this growing multitude of collectors, new programs are popping up on television and radio; the newsstands are stocked with a vast array of periodicals; and the show circuits are packed weekend after weekend. This is a great time to become involved with this exciting hobby. You might even say the future of the past is incredibly bright!

As with the first edition of **Hake's Price Guide To Character Toys**, there's one more section to go following this note–more than fifty pages of full-color, representing a wide selection of highly sought after items, awaits you!

Gemstone Publishing hopes you enjoy this guide, and we all look forward to your comments.

Sincerely,

Stephen A. Geppi

Stephen A. Geppi
President and
Chief Executive Officer

J & P Coats Promo Calendar (1888)

Wheatlet Cereal Standee
(1900)

J & P Coats Promo Card (1880s)

J & P Coats Promo
Card (1880s)

Promo Card (1900)

Star Soap Nursery Rhymes Book
(1901)

Early advertisers began their exploration into the use of characters with children and animals. These pieces date from the
1880s to 1901 and are representative of the period.

CHAS. CHAPLIN

CHARLIE CHAPLIN

Clockwise from top left: **(A) Painted Plaster Figurine** (1915); **(B) Comic Capers** reprints 16 pages of the daily comic strip (1917); **(C) Movie Promotional Mask** for The Gold Rush (1924); **(D) Puppet, Mailer and Instructions** (1920s); **(E) Charlie Chaplin in the Movies** also reprints 16 pages from the daily comic strip; in the center is a **(F) Handbill from 1920's** *The Kid* which co-starred Jackie Coogan (in his first role), who went on to become Uncle Fester on *The Addams Family*.

**Captain, Hans & Fritz
Syroco Figures (1944)**

Mama & Kids Figurine
Hollow bisque group
figure (c.1920)

Character Buttons (1946)
From the PEP Cereal series of 86 buttons

Heat Image Post Card (1906)
From **American Journal Examiner**, hidden
image appears when heat is applied

**"Hingees" Punch-Out
Figures Kit (1945)**

A series of six **Happy Hooligan Postcards** dating from 1904-1906 representing Fred Opper's comic strip which first appeared in 1900.

(Above) One of the most detailed and colorful premium maps ever produced was from the **Black Flame** radio show (1938), sponsored by Hi-Speed Gas. Close-ups below are the show's cast of characters (left) and one of the detailed stamps surrounding the map's border (right). The map came without stamps, which were obtained on subsequent visits to Hi-Speed Gas service stations.

The first American comic strip hero to blast into the wide-open realm of science fiction, Buck Rogers' adventures carried him into the 25th century for the first time in 1929. These **Three Puzzles** and their box date from 1945 and are exceptionally colorful examples of the danger and excitement of the future which the novel, the comic strip, and the subsequent radio, film and television adaptations portrayed.

The **Heinz 57 Premium Map** (above) is one of the great collectibles honoring aviation pioneer Charles Lindbergh. The **Flight Celebration Cap** (1927, below) had room on the back for a sponsor's imprint. The **Flexible Flyer Button** (c. 1928) and the **"Our National Hero - Col. Lindbergh" Ashtray** (1927) also celebrated Lindy's accomplishment - the first solo, non-stop transatlantic flight.

When Pan American World Airways (Pan Am) initiated their "China Clipper" service from the U.S. to Asia, they also continued the development of the public's interest in aviation. The incredible **Promotional Poster** for Kraft Malted Milk (above) measures in at 32" x 42" and offered free China Clipper gliders to the first 50 children attending a matinee. The **Standee** (right) measures 10" x 14" and advertises the same premium, but with the Kraft product visible. Gold Archives.

U.S. Centennial Pennant (1876)

1940 Closing Day Pennant (1940)

Frank Buck's Jungleland Pennant (1939)

Unused Child's Ticket (1893) A spectacular find!

Recipes Book from Borden (1939)

World's Fair Twins Kissing Bobbing Head Dolls Set (1965)

Some of Dick Tracy's 1938 premiums were very confusing. On the **Two-Sided Sign** (right), a source of many Tracy premiums, some of the items offered did not indicate that they had anything to do with Dick Tracy. The **Chinese Checkers Set** (below right) is a perfect indication of this. Look, however, at the Mailer (lower right with checker pieces). Dick Tracy is featured on the return label (close-up). In the case of several items, the mailer is the only way to track its origin. On the other hand, the walkie talkies on the **Two-Sided Sign (Side A)** didn't carry any Tracy markings on the sign, but the actual premiums did. **The Dick Tracy Jr. Detective Kit Sign** (below left) offered customers a free kit with the purchase of a Dick Tracy hat.

Side A

Side B

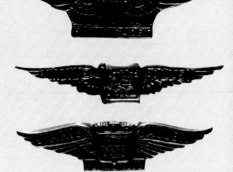

The Air Adventures of Jimmie Allen soared out of radios across America from 1933 to 1943, and premiums were an integral part of the program from the start. Pictured above are the **(A) Flight Lesson #4 Manual**, **(B) Flying Membership Card**, **(C)** a **Membership Certificate**, **(D) Skelly Oil Map** of Kansas and **(E)** a **Seasons Greetings Card** from the characters. In the right column, an impressive series of premium wings badges.

Little Women Jewel Box Ad (1930s)

Big Boy Hamburger Menu (1949)

**Terry & The Pirates
Ad for Canada Dry** (1953)

**Jack Dempsey Ad for
Rippled Wheat**
(1930s)

**Comics Parade
Ad for Force Cereal**
(1940s)

Buck Rogers Rocket Pistol Ad (1930s)
Back cover of **The Open Road for Boys** magazine

A

B

F

E

C

One of the most popular and enduring western characters since 1933 has been the Lone Ranger. There are a significant number of Lone Ranger collectibles available including (clockwise, from left) **(A)** The Lone Ranger **Safety Pledge Certificate** (1938), the **(B) Coca Cola Premium Record** (1972), **(C) The Lone Ranger Round-up Vol. 1 #3** (1939), the **(D) Victory Corps Club Promo** (1942), the complete **(E) Lone Ranger Club Kit** from Merita bread, and **(F) "Hi-Yo, Silver,"** the Lone Ranger's song.

D

A popular pastime from the '20s to the early '50s was collecting movie star cards. Products looking to encourage repeat business would frequently package the **Movie Star Cards** with their products and offer **Albums** to store them in as a premium. Two examples from the 1930s: Churchman's (above) and John Player & Sons (below) were both British cigarette manufacturers.

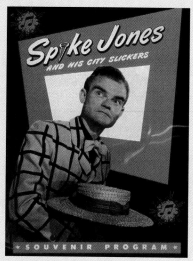

Spike Jones Souvenir
Program

"I Want A Divorce" Game (1936)

Stars of Radio Book

"Meet The Missus" Game (1940)
sponsored by Automatic Soap Flakes

Punch-Out
Card from
Kellogg's The
Singing Lady

Blue Coal was the long-time sponsor of *The Shadow* radio show. These three **Blotters** date from the 1930s. The top and bottom blotters measure 8" wide, and the middle one measures 5". All three promoted the Sunday radio broadcasts of the cloaked man who knew what evil lurked in the hearts of men.

A two-fold prize! Not only does **Snow White and the Seven Dwarfs Paper Dolls** (1937) represent Walt Disney's first feature-length animated film (1937), but it was a **Little Orphan Annie** radio premium! This rare large red version was made to replace the regular, smaller paper doll give-away book when its inventory was depleted. This particular find included the mailer and cancellation notice for the previous edition.

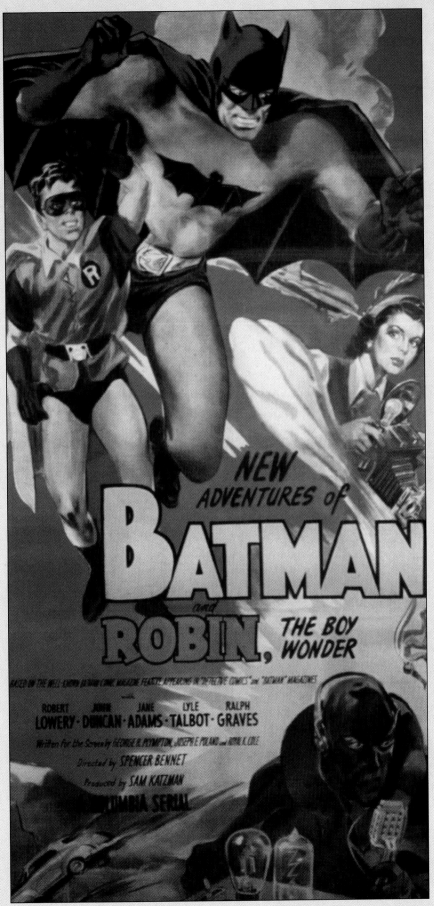

After a year (1997) in which *Batman & Robin* proved to be such a disappointment, it might seem cruel to show this spectacular piece. *The New Adventures of Batman and Robin* is an imposing **Three-Sheet** which promoted the 1949 Columbia Pictures serial.

CAPTAIN MARVEL

The Adventures of Captain Marvel - Chapter 1. This 1941 **One-Sheet** is one of the most sought-after prizes in Captain Marvel collecting. The stunning color and solid visuals (with Captain Marvel showing off his muscles, cape and logo at the same time!) make this piece highly collectible. Less than 10 **Chapter 1** One-Sheets are known to exist!

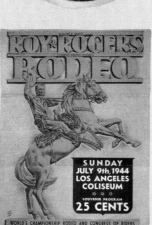

He might have been born Leonard Slye, but Americans have known him as Roy Rogers, "King of the Cowboys," since 1938's *Under Western Stars*. Perhaps the first Hollywood star to fully understand the power of marketing, Roy appeared on radio and television, in films, magazines and comic books, at rodeos and in many special events. **Dixie Ice Cream Pictures (A & B)** show him and wife Dale Evans in the 1940s. Pictured at center is **(C)** the combination **Pocket Watch and Stop Watch**. Also pictured are the **(D) Official Cowboy Outfit**, and the **(E) Program** from the 1944 **Roy Rogers Rodeo** in Los Angeles.

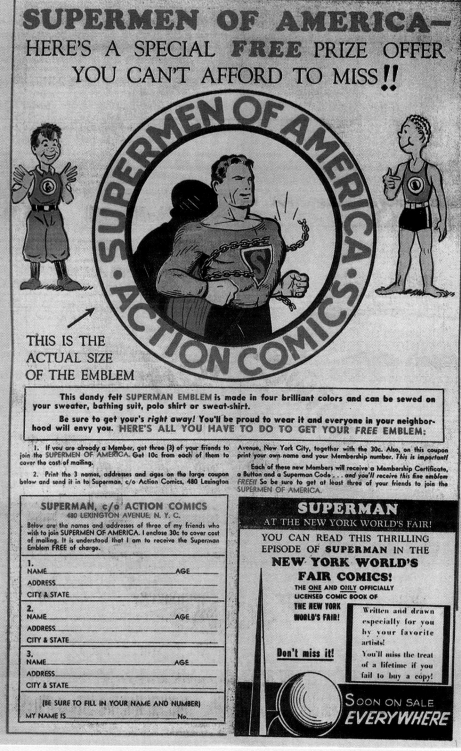

Supermen of America Recruiting Flyer (1939). Coinciding with **Superman** #2, this 10 1/2" x 15" flyer was mailed to members of the Supermen of America club, who were urged to recruit three new members (at 10¢ each). For doing so, the recruiting member received the Supermen of America patch, now prized as one of the most highly collectible Superman items known. A special mailer was also printed for this flyer.

In 1949 the Fo-Lee Gum Corp. offered this spectacular **Enameled Brass Shield** as a premium.

A beautifully colored **Superman Promotional Poster** for Kellogg's PEP cereal (1940s).

This **Carnival Statue** (1940s) is scarce!

The **1940 Bowman Box** came packed with "Super Bubble Gum and Adventure Story Cards," which sold for 1¢ a pack. Probably unique. The gum wrappers contained the coupon for the rare Superman Gum Ring.

A spectacular find for any Superman collector, an **Unused Ticket** for Macy's "**Superman Adventure**," November 1940.

Bold, strong colors and the imposing figure of Captain Midnight highlight this scarce, great **Captain Midnight Three-Sheet** from the 1940s serial.

Eskimo (1970s)
Eskimo Pie Premium

Ben Franklin (1970s)
Franklin Life Insurance Premium

Ceresota Mill Worker (c.1910)
Ceresota Flour Premium

Tastykake Chef (1970s)
Tastykake Bakeries Premium

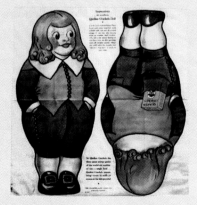

Quaker Crackles Cereal Doll (1930)
Rare, uncut Quaker Oats Premium

Johnny Bear (1925)
Uncut Kellogg's Corn Flakes premium from
Goldilocks & The Three Bears

CLOTH DOLLS

War Bond with Cardboard Stand-Up
Frame (1944)

Dell Comic Book Promo (1940)

Donald Duck
Peanut Butter Bank (1940s)

3D Wiggle Display (1950s)
features Donald
and Cheerios Kid

Donald Duck Jackets Button
(c.1935)

Post's Cereal Bettleware Bowl (1930s)
features Donald in center of bowl

"Wanna Fight" Contest Button
(1930s)

Just as heroes come in all shapes and sizes, so do their premiums and other trinkets. Here's an assortment: **(A) Captain Marvel Blotter** (top left), **(B) Green Hornet Button** (top right), **(C) Green Lama Code Letter** (center right), **(D) Thor Pennant** (center left), **(E) Captain America Club Card** (bottom right) and the **(F) Tarzan Radio Club "Drink More Milk" Bracelet** (bottom of the page).

The classic **Die-Cut Sign** for the Kellogg's Aeroplane above promoted Kellogg's Corn Flakes and the free planes offer. This particular **Premium Plane** itself measured 13 1/2" x 20"; both rare items are from the 1930s. Gold Archives.

Display for
Post Toasties
(1930s) featuring
Mickey Cut-Outs

Mickey Mouse Globetrotters Sign (1937)

Mickey Mouse
Club/Disneyland
Badge (1963)

Mickey Mouse Bread
Poster (1930s)

Mickey Mouse
Globetrotters
Door Hanger
(1930s)

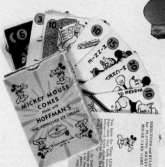

Mickey Mouse
Card Game (1934)
Ice Cream Premium

MICKEY MOUSE

This 1' x 4" **Philip Morris standee** from the 1940s harkens back to a day when the familiar page boy, Johnny, regularly called out, "Call for Phillip Morris!"

PHILIP MORRIS

AMERICA'S FINEST CIGARETTE

"Call for PHILIP MORRIS"

Clarabell Face/Hat
(1950s)

**Capt. Video Flying
Saucer (1951)**

**Space Patrol Cosmic
Glow (1950s)**

**Green Hornet
Secret Compartment (1947)**

Joe Penner Face Puzzle
(1940s)

Tom Corbett Rocket
(1950s)

RINGS

**Tom Mix Straight Shooter
Variant (1936)**

Quake Friendship Figural
(1960s)

Quisp Ray Gun
(1965)

Knights of Columbus (1940s)
with Green Hornet base

**Smokey Stover Canada
Dry (1964)**

Columbian World's Fair
(1893)

735

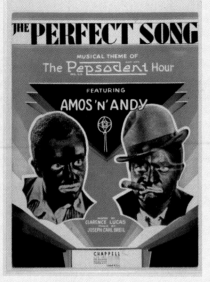

Amos 'n' Andy
"The Perfect Song"

"Archie" of Duffy's Tavern
"Leave Us Face It
(We're In Love)"

Tom Mix
"Tom Mix Western Songs"

Jimmie Durante
"Inka Dinka Doo"

Popeye
"I'm Popeye
The Sailor Man"

George Washington

Benjamin Franklin

Buffalo Bill

Will Rogers

SYROCO FIGURES

Milton Caniff's Terry of **Terry and the Pirates** advertised **Terry's Official Victory Airplane Spotter**, a 1942 Libby's promotional sign. Probably unique. Gold Archives.

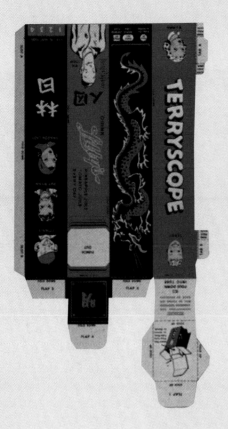
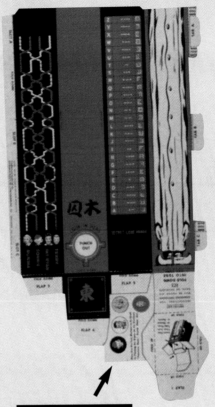

Game Pieces

The perfect double-combination prize from the archives of Gordon Gold! The **Terryscope** and its **Mailer** worked as two prizes in one. The mailer carried instructions for assembling and using the Terryscope on **Side A** and featured games on **Side B**. The **Game Pieces** came attached to one of the two sheets from which the Terryscope was formed. This premium is almost never found with the game pieces still attached.

Side A

Side B

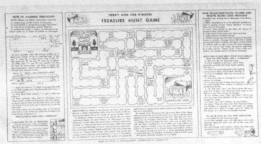

TERRY & THE PIRATES

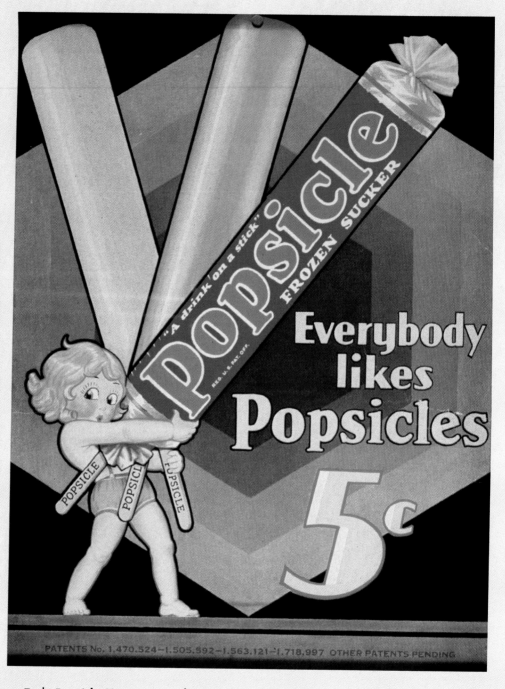

Early **Popsicle Sign**. Very early promotional piece for Popsicles when they were 5¢ each prior to being marketed in the still-familiar twin pack. The twin pack (two Popsicles for the same 5¢ price) started during the Great Depression. The young girl was eventually replaced by Popsicle Pete.

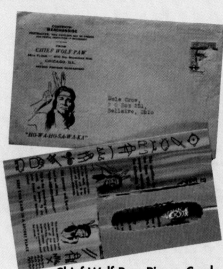

Chief Wolf Paw Pin on Card,
with Mailer (1930s)

The Great
Gildersleeve
Promotional
Record (1930s)

Prudential
Family Hour Ad
(1940s)

Rudy Vallee
Promo Photo
(1930s)

Buck Rogers Dixie
Ice Cream Photo (1930s)

Chief Wolf Paw's Farewell Booklet & Mailer
with gum still intact (1930s)

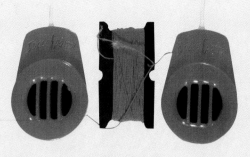

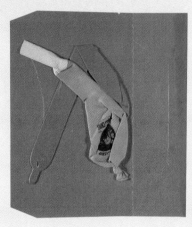

Purists debate the term "Sci-Fi," but can there be any doubt it fits the early science fiction TV shows like **Tom Corbett, Space Cadet, Space Patrol,** or **Captain Video**? Tom Corbett is represented by the **Spaceship Balloon** (center). The **Space Patrol Walkie Talkies** and its mailing box are on the top row. The **Captain Video Radio Scillograph** set is below.

"The Breakfast of Champions" is a champion source of premiums. Top left and right, respectively, are **The Offensive Game** (1945) and **The Defensive Game** (1946), two baseball instruction premium books. Center are 10 different U.S. **Auto Emblems** and their mailer (1950s). Bottom left is a 1953 **Wheaties Box** with a rare George Mikan basketball card on the back. Bottom right is a 1973 premium record featuring **Jack Armstrong, The All American Boy**, who was also no slouch in the premiums department.

A popular collectible from any generation...masks! **Franken Berry** (1980s) above is plastic. **Dick Tracy** (below right) from the 1930s is die-cut paper, and the **Batman Beanie** (below left) from 1966 is felt and cardboard. **Grumpy** from *Snow White* (bottom right) from 1937 is also die-cut paper. The **Hopalong Cassidy Mask**, a prototype from the Gold Archives (bottom left), was from the 1950s. Premium **Tarzan Masks** were advertised on the color poster (center).

Born in 1860, Annie Oakley joined the Buffalo Bill Wild West Show in 1885 as a skilled marksman. She continued to set and break records until as late as 1920. She has been the subject of numerous films, TV shows and other storytelling media. The **Annie Oakley Movie Hanger** (above) stems from the 1935 RKO film starring Barbara Stanwyck. The surrounding **Cardboard Badge, Cardboard Flip Badge** and **Celluloid Button** (left, top to bottom) feature TV Annie Gail Davis (1955). The Annie Oakley **Hat** also celebrated the character. Gail Davis appeared at the "Big D" Dallas 1996 convention and spent hours signing autographs for her fans and talking with them while suffering from advanced cancer. She died shortly thereafter. This page is dedicated to her memory.

Trick or Treat Store Sign
(1960s)

**Boy Scouts
of America
Recruiting
Promotion
Button**
(1975)

Casper Mugs (1970s)

Boston Market Premium Decoder (1997)
Open (above) and **Closed** (below)

Sliding Puzzle (1961)

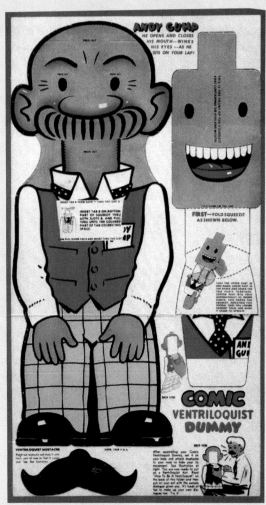

The Gumps, one of the most popular comic strips in the first half of the 20th century, began in 1917 and ran through 1959. The **Display** above advertises the **Dummy** at right as a premium for Malt-O-Meal. This item is probably unique! Gold Archives.

GUMPS

In 1943, Kellogg's offered this **Military Insignia Buttons Banner** in support of PEP cereal. Note the Beanie Cap which was also offered in conjunction with this promotion.

In 1949, *The Cisco Kid* offered **The Cisco Kid's Range War Game** with punch-out game pieces. Rare!

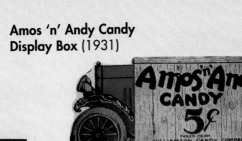

Amos 'n' Andy Candy Display Box (1931)

Captain Tim Healy Dixie Ice Cream Picture (c. 1939)

Radio Broadcasts Guide Sign featuring *Chandu, The Magician* (1930s)

Twinkie The Kid 4' Anniversary Standee (1990)

Dick Tracy Picture Card (1930s). Retailer incentive candy premium.

MISCELLANEOUS

Dudley Do-Right Patch (1970s)

Dick Tracy Patch (1930s)

Junior Justice Society of America
Club Fabric Patch (1942)

ID4 (Independence Day)
Area 51 Patch (1996)

Hop Harrigan "Keep 'Em Flying"
Club Fabric Patch (c.1942)

Pep Boys Premium Patch (1930s)

This large (20" x 36") **Straight Arrow Standee** promoted both the show, its sponsor Nabisco, and their product, Shredded Wheat.

Sky King *TV Eye* Cover (1956)

John Wayne Wallet
(1950s)

Buffalo Bill Circus
Premium Photo
(1920s)

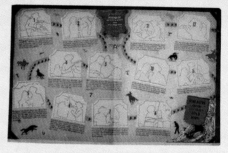

Gene Autry's Western Story Round-Up & Picture Album
(1950s, front and interior)

Matt Dillon and Miss Kitty
Cigarette Sign (1954)

Gabby Hayes Dixie Ice Cream
Picture (1947)

Buzza Cardozo Greeting Cards Sign
(c.1950) Die-cut sign for Hoppy's
line of cards

Crayon Set in Box (1950s)

**Bill Boyd Dixie Ice
Cream Picture** (c.1938)

Christmas Card with Celluloid Button
(c.1950)

Born in 1895, William Boyd became one of the most memorable western stars of all time as Hopalong Cassidy. First in film and on radio, and then later on television, "Hoppy" was adored by generations of children.

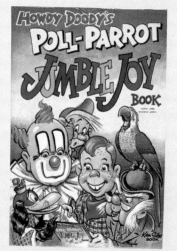

As one of the most popular characters in collecting, Howdy Doody is represented in many different areas. This package of **Kellogg's Rice Krispies** (top left) featured a cut-out **Howdy Doody Mask** on the back of the package (top right). The **Mobile Pictures** (center) included Howdy, Clarabell, Tom Corbett and Gabby Hayes. Poll-Parrot shoes offered the **Jumble-Joy Book** (left) as a premium.

Photo Doody (circa 1949) was actually the Doody everyone saw on magazine covers and in press photos. Virtually identical to Howdy, Photo had none of the strings and was thus much more photogenic. He recently sold at auction for $113,431, making him the first comic character advertising piece to sell for more than $100,000.

S P O K E S M E N

Every so often a character almost transcends the nature of his goal and becomes widely recognized by people who might not even be certain of what the character is supposed to represent. Two of our three ad spokesmen -- **Mr. ZIP** (who was created in 1963 to promote awareness of the then-new Zip Code system) and **Reddy Kilowatt** (who was created in 1926 to promote the electric power industry) -- probably fit that description. Sprout, the assistant of sorts to the Green Giant, only came on the scene in the 1970s, so he probably has a while to go yet. Pictured clockwise from top left, **Mr. ZIP Poster**, **Mr. ZIP Bank**, **Sprout Radio**, and **Reddy Kilowatt Glow-in-the-Dark Plastic Figure**.

HOW TO USE–GET THE MOST FUN
quake
explorer's 1

GEOLOGIST HAMMER
Use METAL TIPPED end to test ore
content of the ROCKS and other metal
specimens. Cover on bottom of HAN-
DLE comes off, to carry. MAPS in

From their beginnings in 1965, the psuedo-epic battles between miner **Quake** and alien **Quisp** were a brilliant marketing stratagem since the two almost identical cereals were produced by the same company (Quaker Oats, hence two cereals beginning with "Qu"). The victors in the feud were those of us on the sidelines. Great premiums included the **Quake Plastic Miner's Helmet** with working battery-powered light (right), and the **Quake Explorer's Kit** (above). The **Quisp Cloth Doll** (above right) is another great find.

QUISP & QUAKE

DOCTOR WHO

Who would have thought from such humble beginnings would have arisen an international hit program with a devoted fan following the world over? His most popular (with the viewers, that is) enemies were the Daleks, represented above with the **Sevans Dalek Model Kit**. Center is the original artwork for the cover of the **Amazing World of Doctor Who Ty-Phoo Tea Book**. Below left and right, respectively, are a UK box of **Kellogg's Sugar Smacks** featuring The Doctor and the **Sugar Smacks Badges**.

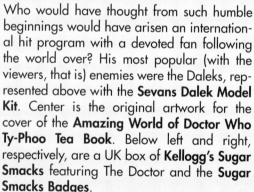

758

(A) The Muppet Show Lunch Box (top left, with accompanying plastic bottle), like other lunch boxes from the '60s, '70s and early '80s, has proved to be a popular item. If you've got one, you can tell your friends about it when you call them on your **(B) Kermit The Frog Telephone** (top right). Also shown are the **(C& D) Kermit The Frog and Miss Piggy Ceramic Mugs** (center left and center right, respectively), the **(E) Kermit The Frog Figural Container** (lower left), a **Cello Button** advertising **(F) Miss Piggy's Calendar of Calendars** (lower center) and the **(G) Miss Piggy Ceramic Figural Bank** (lower right).

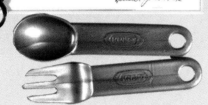

(Above left) *Star Trek V* **Marshmallow Dispenser and Utensils** (1989 Kraft premium), (Above right) **Star Trek Die-Cut Promotional Sign** for U.S. Post Office and *Star Trek VI* (1991). (Below) **Star Trek Navigation Bracelet** from *Star Trek - The Motion Picture* (1979 McDonald's Happy Meal premium), and (Bottom) **Star Trek Walkie-Talkie Communicators** (1989 Procter & Gamble premium), another *Star Trek V* promotion.

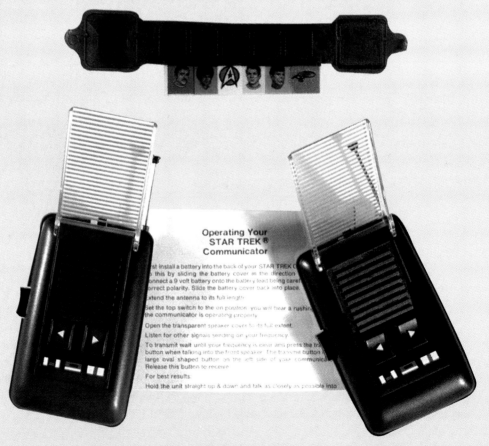

The impressive **Superman Standee** from Burger King's 1997 promotion
for the WB cartoon show and Burger King's Superman premiums.

❖ The New Duck Times ❖

Volume 2 Issue 2   **Special Edition**

The Uncle $crooge Money Mobile

© DISNEY

PROTOTYPE

The Uncle Scrooge Money Mobile is the second in a series of highly collectible Uncle $crooge memorabilia produced by Pride Lines. Pride Lines is a long time licensee of the Walt Disney Company, and for the past 18 years has produced some of the nicest Disneyana collectibles ever seen.

Hand-crafted in the United States of America, the quality of these highly detailed $crooge collectibles is unmatched. Are you a collector who feels they don't make them like they used to? That may be true, but not with Pride Lines. Pride Lines produces hand-crafted pieces of history.

This is not a collectible for everyone. This is a collectible for the Disneyana collector that is serious about his/her collection. This piece is a must for any $crooge collector. In addition to its finely detailed design, each $crooge holds in his hand his most prized possession, his number one dime. This dime is an actual United States silver dime from the early 1900s. Not only is this a rare collectible, but part of U.S. history.

For more information about this or other $crooge collectibles,
please call our sales staff at The New Duck Times.

1-800-726-6708

RUSS COCHRAN'S COMIC ART AUCTION

Russ Cochran's Comic Art Auction, which has been published regularly since 1973, specializes in the finest comic strip art, comic book art, and illustrations by artists such as Frank Frazetta and Carl Barks.

If you collect (or would like to start a collection of) classic strips such as **Krazy Kat**, **Tarzan**, **Flash Gordon**, **Prince Valiant**, **Dick Tracy**, **Terry and the** **Pirates**, **Gasoline Alley**, **Li'l Abner**, **Pogo**, **Mickey Mouse**, **Donald Duck**, or comic book art from **EC Comics**, then you need to subscribe to this auction!

To subscribe to **Russ Cochran's Comic Art Auction**, send $20.00 (Canada $25.00; other international orders, $30.00) for a four-issue subscription. These fully illustrated catalogs will be sent to you by first class mail prior to each auction. If you're still not sure about subscribing and would like a sample issue from a past auction, send $1.00 to **Gemstone Publishing, P.O. Box 469, West Plains, MO 65775**, or call **Toll Free (800) 322-7978**.

MD residents must ad 5% sales tales; MO residents add 6.225% sales tax; CA residents add 7.25% sales tax (San Diego County residents 7.75%).